HANDBOOK OF
TEACHING
AND
POLICY

Longman
New York & London

HANDBOOK OF TEACHING AND POLICY

EDITED BY **LEE S. SHULMAN**
Stanford University

GARY SYKES
National Institute of Education

To the Institute for Research on Teaching

Handbook of Teaching and Policy

Longman Inc., 1560 Broadway, New York, N.Y. 10036
Associated companies, branches, and representatives throughout the world.

Developmental Editor: Lane Akers
Editorial and Design Supervisor: Joan Matthews
Production Supervisor: Ferne Y. Kawahara
Manufacturing Supervisor: Marion Hess

Table 5.3 is reprinted from D. Christensen, "Accreditation in Teacher Education: A Brief Overview," *Journal of Physical Education and Recreation*, February 1980, Vol. 5, No. 2, p. 43, by permission of the American Alliance for Health, Physical Education, Recreation, and Dance.

Table 13.1 is reprinted from John C. Flanagan et al., *Five Years after High School*, Project Talent, Five-Year Follow-Up, American Institutes for Research and Pittsburgh University, p. 2-7, by permission of the American Institutes for Research.

Library of Congress Cataloging in Publication Data

Main entry under title:

Handbook of teaching and policy.

   Includes index.
    1. Teaching—Addresses, essays, lectures.
2. Education and state—United States—Addresses, essays, lectures. I. Shulman, Lee S. II. Sykes, Gary.
LB1025.2.H295   1983   371.1′02   82-17182
ISBN 0-582-28375-2

MANUFACTURED IN THE UNITED STATES OF AMERICA

Contents

Preface

In a delightful and telling simile, Gerald Grant compares school systems to various fruits and vegetables. At the century's turn the American high school was an avocado: a solid core of adult authority, a meaty, homogeneous middle layer of students, and a thin skin of external policies. By 1950 the high school had evolved into a canteloupe with a thicker skin of external policies particularly in the more progressive states, but still a firm core of local authority and a relatively uniform but greatly expanded student body. By 1983, however, the school has become a watermelon with a thick rind of external policies, a large and diverse student body, and adult authority scattered throughout like watermelon seeds. Efforts by actors outside of schools to influence what goes on within have accelerated and intensified in recent years more rapidly than easy accommodation allows. Systematic inquiry too has not caught up with the cumulative developments affecting the schools so that the heat-to-light ratio in discourse about educational policy is unusually high.

The present volume grew out of a concern at the National Institute of Education for these developments. Under the auspices of NIE's Teaching-Policy Studies Team, a series of papers was commissioned to examine the teaching-policy connection from a variety of perspectives. We sought as writers classroom teachers, policymakers, policy analysts, and researchers. We selected topics of current and enduring interest: What makes an effective school? How do teachers learn to teach? What is the relationship between educational equity and quality? How has collective bargaining affected teaching? We asked each author to reflect on the policy implications of their analysis. We brought the chapter authors together first to present and discuss their initial ideas, then to critique draft chapters. In this way each chapter benefited from review by a broad range of others.

The term "handbook" typically has two denotations. It may refer to a compendium of practical, authoritative advice on some topic; or regarding scholarly matters, to a definitive, comprehensive, up-to-date review of knowledge on a (usually) well-bounded subject. This handbook neatly fits neither description, but shares a family resemblance with the latter. The relationship between teaching and policy is not a domain of knowledge nor even a particularly well-bounded subject. Rather it represents the confluence of two streams of intellectual activity—research on teaching and policy analysis—which have proceeded largely independent of one another. The turn in recent decades to policy as a means of influencing events in schools and classrooms provides the raison d'être for joining these streams. Furthermore, most writing about teaching excludes the teacher's point of view; the teacher's voice is rarely heard in learned councils on the state of teaching or in policymaking circles. To the perspectives of the researcher and policy analyst, then, this volume adds that of the teacher, a practice we hope future efforts of this sort will follow.

Selecting topics for inclusion here was difficult, given the unbounded nature of the territory. We opted to sample from the research on teaching, to include a number of issues currently engaging policy analysts, to tap a number of perennial questions, and to represent some ongoing research projects of special interest. The result covers considerable ground within the overall architecture for the volume, justifying the "handbook" appellation, although the list of chapters could doubtless be expanded. The audience for the volume includes policy analysts and policymakers at federal, state, and local levels; researchers and others interested in teaching; representatives of professional associations; and informed citizens.

Several officials at the National Institute of Education were most helpful in stimulating and supporting this project and we wish to extend our thanks and appreciation to them. These include Michael Timpane, former Director of NIE; Marc Tucker, former Associate Director of the Program on Educational Policy and Organization (EPO); and Saul Yanofsky, Acting Associate Director for EPO.

For one of the editors (LSS), the preparation of this volume was nurtured by two unusual organizations. During the 1979–80 academic year, a fellowship at the Center for Advanced Study in the Behavioral Sciences at Stanford provided unparalleled opportunity for study, reflection, and dialogue. During that year, the plan for this book was developed. I am grateful to the Center for the solitude and stimulation of that experience, and to the financial support for that fellowship provided by the Spencer Foundation and the National Institute of Mental Health (National Research Service Award 2 T32 MH 14581–04).

The Institute for Research on Teaching at Michigan State University, with which I have been associated since its conception, has provided a unique interdisciplinary and interpersonal locus for my efforts since 1975. The women and men of that organization have been colleagues and mentors, friends and role models. In appreciation for their patience and skill in educating me over the years, and in anticipation of the significant contributions they will continue to make to the understanding of teaching and policy, we dedicate this volume to the Institute for Research on Teaching.

Lee S. Shulman
Stanford, California

Gary Sykes
Washington, D.C.

List of Contributors

Marianne Amarel is a visiting lecturer at the School of Education, Stanford University. For the previous seventeen years she was a senior research associate at the Educational Testing Service. She did undergraduate work at Columbia University and pursued graduate study in social psychology at Rutgers. Her research has included the evaluation of educational programs, study of teachers' conceptions of curriculum and instruction, and investigations of how children learn to read. Her writings include *Beyond Surface Curriculum* (1976) and the forthcoming *Inquiry into Meaning* (both with Bussis and Chittenden).

Rebecca Barr is a research associate in the Department of Education, University of Chicago, and a professor of education, National College of Education, Evanston, Illinois. She was a second-grade teacher in Chicago and taught high school drop-outs in Kalamazoo, Michigan, before receiving the Ph.D. in reading and educational psychology from the University of Chicago. As member of the Chicago faculty, she served as director of the Reading Clinic. Her research interests are in the study of classroom instruction and in reading disabilities.

Gabriella Belli is a doctoral candidate in educational statistics and a research intern at the Institute for Research on Teaching, Michigan State University. She has taught mathematics for several years at the junior and senior high school levels.

Katherine Boles is a member of the Boston Women's Teachers' Group, a support group for teachers which conducts research and sponsors workshops. Currently she is a fourth grade teacher with the Brookline, MA public school system. She received her B.A. from Hofstra and an M.A. in French literature from New York University.

William Clune is a professor, University of Wisconsin Law School, and faculty associate, Wisconsin Center for Education Research. He received a Ll.D. from Northwestern Law School and has pursued graduate work in sociology. His major interests are constitutional law and law and education. Publications include *Private Wealth and Public Education* (1970) with John Coons and Stephen Sugarman and numerous articles in law reviews, the most recent of which is, "What 'Implementation' Isn't: Toward a General Framework for Implementation Research" (*Wisconsin Law Review*, 1981).

Joseph M. Cronin is president of the Massachusetts Higher Education Assistance Corporation. From 1975 to 1980 he was the Illinois State Superintendent of Education, prior to which he served as the state secretary of educational affairs in Massachusetts. He received an Ed.D from Stanford University, has published more than fifty articles and reviews, and is author of *The Control of Urban Systems* (1973), and *Organizing an Urban School System for Diversity* (1973). His current interests include the financing of higher education, urban education, and educational policy issues generally.

Patrick L. Daly is a teacher of social studies at Edsel Ford High School in Dearborn, Michigan, where he has taught for twenty-five years. Daly has been a leader in the American Federation of Teachers and is currently one of the national vice-presidents of the AFT. He did both undergraduate and graduate work at the University of Michigan. He has been a member of the Directorate of the Institute for Research on Teaching, the Advisory Board of Pittsburgh's Learning Research and Development Center, and the National Institute of Education's panel for review of regional educational laboratories and centers.

Robert Dreeben is a professor of the sociology of education, University of Chicago, where he has been since 1968. He received the M.A.T. at Columbia and taught seventh-grade English for several years before returning to Harvard to complete a Ph.D. in the Department of Social Relations. His research has focused on the realities of schooling from the perspectives of its participants. His publications include *On What Is Learned in School* (1968), *The Nature of Teaching* (1970), and the forthcoming *How Schools Work* (with Rebecca Barr).

Richard F. Elmore is an associate professor in the Graduate School of Public Affairs, University of Washington. He received an Ed.D. in educational policy from Harvard University. His publications include *Reform and Retrenchment* (1981) with Milbrey McLaughlin, and "Organizational Models of Social Program Implementation" (*Social Policy*, 1978). Currently he is completing a study of the local implementation of youth unemployment policy. His major area of interest is the effects of federal-state policies on local organization and functioning.

Gary D. Fenstermacher is a professor of foundations of education, Virginia Polytechnic Institute. He previously taught philosophy of education at UCLA, where he directed the Teacher Education Laboratory and served as the higher education representative on the California Commission for Teacher Preparation and Licensing. He received his Ph.D. in philosophy from Cornell University and has written widely on issues in the study of teaching and the conduct of teacher education.

Robert Floden is an associate professor of teacher education and a senior researcher at the Institute for Research on Teaching, Michigan State University. He received the B.A. from Princeton in philosophy, taught high school mathematics, and then continued for the Ph.D. from Stanford University in the philosophy of education. His research interests are in teacher education and teacher development, philosophical analyses of educational and social science research, and the determinants of teachers' content decisions.

Sara Freedman is a member of the Boston Women's Teachers' Group, a support group for teachers which conducts research and sponsors workshops. She received her B.A. from Brandeis University and has taught in the Boston area for some years. With colleagues she has recently completed an interview study of teachers and is now making research results available to teachers.

Donald Freeman is a professor of teacher education and a senior researcher at the Institute for Research on Teaching, Michigan State University. After undergraduate work at Grinnell College, he received the Ph.D. in educational psychology at Michigan State University. He was a member of the faculty at Miami University of Ohio. His research interests are in the evaluation of teacher education programs and the influence of texts and tests on teachers' content decisions.

Thomas Good is a professor of education and a senior scientist at the Center for Research in Social Behavior, University of Missouri, Columbia. After undergraduate work at the University of Illinois, he received the Ph.D. from the University of Indiana and joined the faculty of the University of Texas School of Education and its Research and Development Center for the Study of Teacher Education. His research has included the study of teaching effectiveness, teacher expectations and teacher education. He is the editor of the *Elementary School Journal*. Among his writings are *Teacher-Student Relationships* (1974) and *Looking in Classrooms* (1978), both with Jere Brophy.

Thomas F. Green is the Margaret Slocum professor of education, Syracuse University. He received his Ph.D. in philosophy from Cornell and taught at the South Dakota School of Mines and Michigan State University before moving to Syracuse in 1964. His interests encompass a wide range of topics in the philosophy of education and in the study of educational systems. He is a member of the National Academy of Education. His writings include *The Activities of Teaching* (1971) and *Predicting the Behavior of the Educational System* (1980).

J. David Greenstone is a professor in the Department of Political Science and the College, University of Chicago. He received his Ph.D. in political science from the University of Chicago and cites as present research interests American political thought and culture. His publications include *Race and Authority in Urban Politics* (1973; 1975) with Paul Peterson, and *Public Values and Private Power in American Democracy* (1982).

Jane Jackson is a member of the Boston Women's Teachers' Group, a support group for teachers which conducts research and sponsors workshops. She received her B.A. from Radcliffe and an M.A. in literature from the University of London. She has taught in Boston area schools for some years.

Linda A. Jacobsen is a research associate at the Center for Demography and Ecology, University of Wisconsin-Madison, where she is a doctoral candidate in sociology. Her major interests, and the subject of her doctoral dissertation, concern the patterns, determinants, and returns of women's education, training, and work experience. She has recently completed a monograph on changing family and household structures in the United States.

Charles T. Kerchner is associate professor of education and public policy, Claremont Graduate School. Following a career as journalist with the Times Publishing Company in Florida, he received a Ph.D. in education from Northwestern. Author with Anthony Cresswell and Michael Murphy of *Teachers, Unions, and Collective Bargaining in Public Education* (1980) as well as several recent journal articles on collective bargaining, he cites the organizational and political implications of labor relations in education as his chief interest.

Donna H. Kerr serves as the director's special assistant for research and corporate affairs at the Institute for Advanced Study, Princeton, New Jersey. She is on leave from the University of Washington, where she is associate dean for graduate studies and research in the College of Education. She received a Ph.D. in philosophy and education from Columbia University, and cites her current interests as the epistemology and politics of knowledge utilization and the role of metaphor in learning and inquiry. She is the author of *Education Policy: Analysis, Structure, and Justification* (1976) and articles in various journals of philosophy.

Michael Kirst is a professor of education, Stanford University, and immediate past president of the California State Board of Education. He received his Ph.D. in political economy from Harvard University. He is the author of numerous publications; his latest book with Frederick Wirt is *Schools in Conflict* (1982). Politics and the financing of public education is his basic area of interest.

Lucy Knappen is an elementary school teacher in the Lansing, Michigan, public schools and a doctoral candidate in teacher education, Michigan State University. She has been a teacher collaborator at the Institute for Research on Teaching for several years.

Therese Kuhs is an assistant professor of mathematics education, University of South Carolina. She was an elementary school teacher and supervisor of mathematics curriculum in the Pittsburgh area before coming to Michigan State University as a research intern at the Institute for Research on Teaching. She has a Ph.D. in mathematics education from Michigan State University. Her research interests are in the teaching of mathematics and mathematics curriculum, with special reference to teachers' conceptions of mathematics.

Sara Lawrence Lightfoot is a professor of education, Harvard Graduate School of Education. After undergraduate study at Swarthmore, she completed her Ph.D. at Harvard in the sociology of education. Her research has focused on the ecology of classrooms and schools, the relationships between families and schools, and most recently, on making sense of contemporary schooling through developing portraits of American secondary schools. Her writings include *Beyond Bias* (with Carew, 1979) and *Worlds Apart* (1979).

Douglas E. Mitchell is an associate professor of education at the University of California-Riverside, and a member of the California State Educational Management and Evaluation Commission. He received his Ph.D. in political science from the Claremont Graduate School. His most recent book is *Shaping Legislative Decisions: Educational Policy and the Social Sciences* (1980). His major interests on which he has written in a variety of journals include collective bargaining, local decision-making, and teacher work structures, the subject of his most recent study.

Sharon Feiman Nemser is an associate professor of teacher education and a senior researcher at the Institute for Research on Teaching, Michigan State University. She received her M.A. from the University of Chicago, and she taught English at the Laboratory School and in New York City high schools for several years before completing doctoral work at Teachers College, Columbia University, in curriculum and instruction. She was the director of the elementary teacher education program, University of Chicago. Her research centers around questions in the development of teachers—the role of ideas in teaching, teacher education, and teacher centers.

Paul E. Peterson is a professor in the Departments of Political Science and Education and chairman of the Committee on Public Policy Studies at the University of Chicago. He received his Ph.D. in political science from the University of Chicago, where his interests include urban politics, educational policymaking, and the structure of American federalism. His publications include *School Politics-Chicago Style* (1976), *City Limits* (1981), and the forthcoming *Federal Policy and American Education*.

Andrew Porter is a professor of educational psychology, associate dean, and co-director of the Institute for Research on Teaching, Michigan State University. After completing doctoral work at the University of Wisconsin in psychometrics, he joined the Michigan State faculty in educational statistics. He has been head of the program on measurement and methodology at the National Institute of Education and associate director of that agency. His interests are in the design and analysis of educational experiments, program evaluation, and the influences on teachers' content decisions.

Michael Rutter is a professor of child psychiatry in the Institute of Psychiatry, University of London. He received his medical education at the University of Birmingham and the bulk of his psychiatric training at the Maudsley Hospital in London and Albert Einstein School of Medicine in New York. His research has encompassed a wide range of topics involving the environmental antecedents of mental health and school performance, including maternal deprivation, concepts and treatment of autism, effects of poverty on development and the cumulative effects of schools on their pupils. Among his writings are *Fifteen Thousand Hours* (with Maughan, Mortimore, and Ouston, 1979) and *Cycles of Disadvantage* (with Madge, 1976).

William Schmidt is a professor of educational psychology, the chairman of the Department of Counseling, Educational Psychology and Special Education, and a senior researcher at the Institute for Research on Teaching, College of Education, Michigan State University. He received his Ph.D. in educational statistics from the University of Chicago. His research interests are the development and application of multivariate statistical methods, the study of integration and meaningfulness in the teaching of language arts, the effects of actual school/curricular experiences on the achievement of secondary-school students, and the determinants of teachers' content decisions.

John Schwille is a professor of teacher education and a senior researcher at the Institute for Research on Teaching, Michigan State University. He received the Ph.D. from the University of Chicago in comparative education. He has been a member of the research staff of the International Education Association's comparative studies of educational achievement in Stockholm and head of the program on measurement and methodology at the National Institute of Education. His research interests are in the politics and sociology of education, comparative studies of educational systems, and the external influences on teachers' content decisions.

Albert Shanker has been president of the American Federation of Teachers since 1974. He is also a vice president of the AFL–CIO and a member of their Executive Council, and is president of the UFT, New York City's teacher organization. He has done graduate work at Columbia University, contributes frequently to national magazines and scholarly journals, and writes the "Where We Stand" column appearing in the *New York Times* each Sunday. He is active in a variety of local, national, and international labor and education organizations as well.

Lee S. Shulman is a professor of education and an affiliated professor of psychology, Stanford University. He did undergraduate and graduate work at the University of Chicago, where he received a Ph.D. in educational psychology. From 1963 to 1982 he was a member of the faculty at Michigan State University, serving as a professor of educational psychology and medical education and as co-director of Institute for Research on Teaching. His research interests are in the study of teaching, professional education in both teaching and medicine, and the psychology of instruction. He is a member of the National Academy of Education. His writings include *Medical Problem Solving* (with Elstein and Sprafka, 1978).

James A. Sweet is a professor of sociology, University of Wisconsin-Madison, where he also serves on the staff of the Institute for Research on Poverty. He received his Ph.D. in sociology from the University of Michigan and has interests in demography and family sociology, including fertility, the labor force, and the family. His publications include *Women in the Labor Force* (1973) and *Post-War Fertility Trends and Differentials in the U.S.* (1977).

Gary Sykes is a research associate at the National Institute of Education, where he heads the Teaching-Policy Studies Team in the Program on Educational Policy and Organization. He received graduate training from Stanford University in the field of curriculum instruction. With Jon Schaffarzick he co-edited *Value Conflicts and Curriculum Issues* (1979). His current areas of interest include the study of teaching and of educational policy as it affects teaching.

Emily S. Trumbull is a sixth-grade teacher at Riddle Elementary School in Lansing, Michigan. Riddle was established as an innovative fifth/sixth grade center after several years of collaborative planning by teams of teachers. She has eighteen years of experience in elementary school teaching in Lansing and in elementary schools in New York and Massachusetts. She did her undergraduate work at Syracuse University and pursued graduate study at Boston University and Michigan State University in special education and in counseling.

Annette B. Weinshank is a teacher of reading at Otto Middle School in Lansing, Michigan. She has also been a teacher collaborator with a half-time research appointment at the Institute for Research on Teaching since 1976. A teacher with more than twenty years of classroom experience, she completed her Ph.D. in educational psychology at Michigan State University and conducts research on the diagnosis and remediation of reading difficulties.

HANDBOOK OF
TEACHING
AND
POLICY

PART I

Complexities of Schools and Classrooms

Policy, as Thomas Green notes in his chapter, always deals with what is good in general, on the whole, and for the most part. Policy, of necessity, abstracts and simplifies. To make sound policy, however, requires among other things a grasp of the complexities with which policy deals. In the case of education these complexities have to do with schools and classrooms. Part I of this handbook offers three chapters which provide insights on the working of schools. Research in recent years has begun to carefully explore the relationship between what goes on in schools and the outcomes of schooling for students. The question animating such research has not been *whether* certain levels and kinds of resources make a difference, but *how* they make a difference. That is, what processes within schools transform physical and human resources into outcomes, and, more to the point, what resource mixes and instructional and organizational strategies optimize desired outcomes.

The three chapters in this part exemplify this research while illustrating just how complex is the working of schools. Michael Rutter provides a detailed, critical review of the literature on school effectiveness. Research on this subject has developed a number of traditions distinguished according to the meanings employed for "effects," the outcomes examined, the methods used, and other factors. Rutter searches this wide and varied literature for the answers to a number of crucial questions: Are the multiple desirable outcomes of schooling highly associated with one another, or do they trade off? Are school effects practically significant, do they generalize to children's out-of-school lives, and do they persist? What qualities of schools matter most in producing desirable outcomes, and with what confidence can we claim a causal relationship between school processes and resources and school effects? While these questions and their answers indicate the difficulties with any easy generalizations about schools, Rutter concludes that school effects over and above classroom effects are significant and that while this research cannot serve as conclusive ground for policy or practice, it is beginning to provide helpful leads.

The second chapter, by Thomas Good, provides a classroom-level complement to Rutter's school-level analysis. Surveying a large, burgeoning field of research on teaching, Good chooses to concentrate on two key topics: the effects of teacher expectations and the work on teacher effectiveness. Work on his first topic has progressed substantially, documenting the subtle but marked variations in teacher behavior toward students, specifying the relationship between teacher expectations and student achievement, and proposing explanations for teachers' differential treatment of students. Research on teacher effectiveness, Good argues, has begun to converge on teacher behaviors associated with student learning. He particularly cites the research

1

which resulted in the concept of "active teaching" for elementary-level basic skills, then he goes on to cautions about the limitations of this research and suggestions for further inquiry. Other topics—classroom management, time allocation, and cooperative learning—have also proven fruitful, and Good concludes optimistically that research on teaching in the 1970s has demonstrated that teachers make a difference and that useful, practical knowledge is beginning to accumulate.

Robert Dreeben and Rebecca Barr's chapter provides a connecting link between the chapters by Rutter and Good. Their chapter sets forth a framework for productive processes within schools, revealing the relationships among levels of the organizations. Their analysis seeks to link the operation of school, classroom, and within-classroom processes to the use of resources such as time, materials, and the distribution of student aptitudes. This latter resource they regard as most essential—the "hand" a teacher is "dealt"—which deeply influences instructional strategy. In the second section of their chapter, Dreeben and Barr apply their framework to two instances of educational policy—desegregation and mainstreaming—to illuminate the relationship between policymaking and the working of schools. Altering the racial composition of schools, they note, will not necessarily result in instructional adaptations, while solutions to the problem of mainstreaming may reside at higher levels of the school organization than the classroom. How to link the productive apparatus of schools to policy implementation is an extremely difficult problem, they argue, for which there is yet but a slender knowledge base.

CHAPTER 1

School Effects on Pupil Progress
Research Findings and Policy Implications

Michael Rutter

Over the last fifteen years there has been a vigorous controversy on the questions of whether schooling "matters" and of whether schools have "effects" on the behavior and attainments of the children who attend them (Averch, Carroll, Donaldson, Kiesling, and Pincus, 1972). On the one hand, during the late 1960s and early 1970s there came to be a widespread acceptance among academics that schools "made little difference." In large part, this view stemmed from James Coleman's (Coleman et al., 1966) report on "Equality of Educational Opportunity" and from Christopher Jencks' (Jencks, Smith, Acland, Bane, Cohen, Gintis, Heyns, and Michelson, 1972) reanalysis of those and other data. Jencks' conclusions that "equalizing the quality of high schools would reduce cognitive inequality by one per cent or less" and that "additional school expenditures are unlikely to increase achievements, and redistributing resources will not reduce test score inequality" were both widely quoted and interpreted as meaning that schooling had such minor marginal effects that the educational process was scarcely worth the relatively large resources poured into it. Many people also came to believe that school social systems were a fruitless area of research (Hauser, Sewell, and Alwin, 1976). These pessimistic views were reinforced by Jensen's (1969) claim that "compensatory education has been tried and it apparently has failed"; by Bowles' (1971) assertion that "educational inequalities are rooted in the basic institutions of our economy"; and by Bernstein's (1970) urging that "education cannot compensate for society."

On the other hand, at the same time as teachers felt that they were being given the message that their work was largely a waste of time, other critics were blaming them for much of the ills of society (see Lightfoot, 1978, and Thornbury, 1978, for a summary of some of these commentaries on schools and Husen, 1979, for a most thoughtful discussion of the criticisms of the school as an institution and of the challenges and issues involved in school reform). Even the titles of books on the subject carried an emotive message of condemnation (e.g., *The Underachieving School, Death at an Early Age*, and *Pedagogy of the Oppressed*—see Rutter, 1980a). Recently, under the title of *The Literacy Hoax*, Paul Copperman (1978) concluded that "with skills down, assignments down, standards down, and grades up, the American educational system perpetrates a hoax on its students and on their parents."

Yet, against this background of gloom, despondency, and hostile attacks, other writers have recently claimed that "schools can make a difference" (Brookover, Beady, Flood, Schweitzer, and Wisenbaker, 1979); that "schools can do much to foster good behavior and attainments, and that even in a disadvantaged area, schools can be a force for the good" (Rutter, Maughan, Mortimore, Ouston, with Smith, 1979); that there are "unusually effective schools" (Klitgaard and Hall, 1975); that "what goes on in schools is highly relevant to students" (Madaus, Kellaghan, Rakow, and King, 1979); and that the type of school attended is "enormously consequential," especially for less able children (Halsey, Heath, and Ridge, 1980).

At first sight, these claims and counterclaims seem hopelessly at odds with one another. It is not surprising, therefore, that some academic critics have scathingly attacked the recent empirical studies on the quite mistaken assumption that they are claiming that all is well with educational standards (Eigerman, 1980) or that improved schooling would remove inequalities in society (Acton, 1980). In actuality, neither claim has been made (see Rutter, Maughan, Mortimore, Ouston, and Smith, 1980a; Rutter, Maughan, Mortimore, and Ouston, 1980b) and at least some of the dispute stems from confusion as to what is meant by "effects".

ASPECTS OF SCHOOLING NOT REVIEWED

As the overall question of school effectiveness could be considered in relation to numerous different aspects of schooling, before considering the different meanings of school "effects," it is necessary to indicate which aspects of schooling will *not* be discussed in this review. In developing countries where school facilities may not be available to the whole of the population, it is appropriate to ask if children's cognitive development is influenced by whether or not they attend school. Such evidence as is available suggests that it is (Sharp, Cole, and Lave, 1979; Stevenson, Parker, Wilkinson, Bonnevaux, and Gonzales, 1978). The evidence on the effects of school closure in Western societies, either as a result of war (De Groot, 1951) or of attempts to avoid racial integration (Jencks et al., 1972) are in keeping with that conclusion—as are the findings on the benefits of continued schooling during late adolescence (Harnqvist, 1968; Husen, 1951). However, as the issue has few (if any) policy implications for countries such as the UK or the USA, where education is compulsory and freely available, it will not be considered further here.

There is an extensive literature on the effects of compensatory education programs during the preschool years. The findings suggest that these programs are associated with immediate IQ gains, but also that these gains are not maintained after the first few years of regular schooling (Bronfenbrenner, 1974; Horowitz and Paden, 1973; Rutter and Madge, 1976). On the other hand, more recent evidence suggests that, although the IQ gains do not persist, there may be other educational benefits that do endure (Darlington, Royce, Snipper, Murray, and Lazar, 1980; Schweinhart and Weikart, 1980). The findings have important theoretical and policy implications, but they are outside the scope of this paper—as is very early education generally.

In recent years there has been an increasing interest in what have come to be called "alternative schools" (Deal and Nolan, 1978; Duke, 1978). These take a variety of forms but, in general, they have emerged as a "do your own thing" reaction to the traditional educational model. Many emphasize a wide range of student needs, with as much focus on affective characteristics as scholastic achievements, and often there is an emphasis on opportunities for parents, students, and teachers to actively influence the goals and functioning of the school. Little is known on how their effects compare with those of traditional schools and this educational movement will not be considered further here.

The development of quantified measures of the classroom environment constitutes one of the major developments in the field of school effectiveness research. The research of Moos (1979) and his colleagues has been particularly influential in iden-tifying typologies of classroom settings based on features such as teacher-pupil and student-student relationships, task orientation, emphasis on competition, degree of structure and teacher control, and student participation and innovation. Brief reference is made to work of this kind in considering the extent to which school variables show consistent associations with measures of pupil progress, but throughout this review emphasis is placed on teacher or school *actions*, rather than on attitudinal measures of atmosphere or climate. The point is that, although it is clear that the climate of a school is most important (see Moos, 1979), it is necessary to consider what staff must do to create the desired school atmosphere. That issue constitutes the focus of the discussion in this paper of the qualities of schools that do and do not matter.

THE DIFFERENT MEANINGS OF SCHOOL "EFFECTS"

A detailed comparison of the conflicting claims on "effects" clearly shows that the term has been given several entirely different meanings by different writers.

Effects in Terms of the Proportion of Variance Accounted For

Perhaps the most frequent (and most traditional) way of looking at "effects" has been in terms of the amount of population variance in scholastic attainment accounted for by schooling (or any other variable). Thus, Jencks et al. (1972) concluded that school variables accounted for a mere 2 to 3 percent of the variance, a figure far below the estimated 50 percent attributable to family background. Other studies have varied somewhat in the precise figures derived from their statistical analyses, but with one exception (Madaus et al., 1979, discussed below), all have agreed in finding that far more of the variance in pupils' attainment is attributable to family variables than to school variables. Accordingly, we must accept that this general conclusion is both valid and amply confirmed. At first sight, it would seem to mean that families con-stitute a much more important influence on scholastic attainment than do schools. However, although this is an apparently obvious inference from the statistics, for several rather different reasons it is not a justifiable one.

Put in its simplest form, the estimates are based on the correlations (or degree of association) between the differences in some predictor variable (in this case schools) and the differences between individuals in some outcome variable (in this case scholas-tic attainment). It follows that the figures obtained will be influenced by at least three main factors: the choice and measurement of the outcome variable, the choice and measurement of the predictor variable, and the extent of variation (i.e., differences) on the predictor variable. All have been found to be most important in practice as well as in theory.

Until recently, most studies have relied on tests of verbal ability as the measure of attainment. However, schools do not have the teaching of verbal skills as their main objective. Accordingly, the estimates of school effects have been based on measures that bear very little relationship to anything most schools would aim to teach. As Madaus et al. (1979) put it, "Conclusions about the direct instructional effects of schools should not have to rely on evidence relating to skills taught incidently." Rather, the criterion should consist of direct measures of specific attainments related to the schools' curriculum. Several recent studies (Postlethwaite, 1975; Brimer,

Madaus, Chapman, Kellaghan, and Wood, 1978; Madaus et al., 1979) have shown that school variables account for a greater proportion of the variance on pupils' achievement in public examinations on specific curriculum-based subjects than on norm-referenced tests of general attainment. Even so, school variables still account for only a minority of the variance.

The measurement of the predictor variable also makes a difference. Most surveys have not only considered a very narrow range of school variables but also usually have focused only on one or other aspect of resources. As Jencks et al. (1972) pointed out, such measures fail to take into account anything about the internal life of the school; its attitudes, values, and mores; or its qualities as a social organization. But recent studies which have examined a much wider range of school characteristics (see Brookover, Beady, Flood, Schweitzer, and Wisenbaker, 1979; Rutter et al., 1979) have found that it is just these social, rather than financial, variables which *do* account for much of the variation between schools.

A further technical point in this connection is that if some measure of the school as a whole is utilized, all children at the same school have to be given the same school "score" (see Rutter et al., 1979). This involves the quite misleading assumption that all children at any one school receive the same school experiences; the consequence is that the results based on such statistical analyses are bound to underestimate the size of school effects.

But, the last consideration—namely the extent of variation on the predictor—is the most crucial of all. Other things being equal, a predictor with a wide range will always account for a higher proportion of the variance than a predictor with a narrow range. Because it is likely that schools tend to be more homogeneous than are families and because the difference between the "best" and the "worst" schools is likely to be far less than that between the "best" and the "worst" homes, it necessarily means that (as assessed in terms of the proportion of population variance accounted for) family variables will usually have a greater "effect" than school variables.[1] But this does not necessarily mean that schools have a lesser influence than families on achievement. The point is made most easily by means of an extreme hypothetical example. Suppose that the "outcome" variable consists of pupils' achievement on Sanskrit, that the books on Sanskrit are available only to the teachers at school, and that all schools are equally good at teaching Sanskrit. Because Sanskrit can be learned only at school, schools are necessarily the only direct causal influence on Sanskrit achievement. But, because of variations in pupils' ability to learn (as a result of both genetic and environmental influences), some children would achieve much higher levels of attainment on Sanskrit than other children. However, because all schools teach Sanskrit equally well, schooling would account for *none* of this individual variation. In short, in these terms, schools would show a *zero* "effect" on Sanskrit achievement in spite of the fact that *all* Sanskrit was necessarily learned only as a result of schooling!

It is clear that the proportion of variance explained by schooling is a very poor guide to the real influence of schools in helping children gain good levels of scholastic achievement. It also follows from these (and other) considerations that the estimates of school "effects" obtained in this way have no clear policy implications.

School Effects in Terms of Reducing Inequality

A second approach to school effects concerns an analysis of their importance in increasing or decreasing inequality—the method adopted by Jencks and his colleagues

(1972). The argument here is based on the general assumption that inequalities are in themselves undesirable and therefore that schools should in some way operate to reduce inequalities in scholastic attainment, in employment opportunities and status, and in income and wealth. As already noted, Jencks et al. (1972) concluded that "equalizing educational opportunity would do very little to make adults more equal" and that even if there was substantial positive discrimination with schools giving most help to the most disadvantaged children, still this would not result in people ending up appreciably more equal as a result. A more recent report by Jencks (1979) has shown a rather greater effect of education on occupational status, with the main advantage coming from the role of a college education in helping people enter higher-status occupations. Nevertheless, the overall findings support the earlier conclusion that education at an elementary or high school level has a rather marginal role as an agency for reducing inequality.

Statistically speaking, although expressed in a different form, these conclusions are based on the same figures as those that give rise to estimates of school effects in terms of proportion of population variance accounted for. Consequently, they suffer from the same limitations. If the analyses could be repeated using rather better measures of schooling and more appropriate measures of scholastic attainment, schools would be found to have a slightly greater effect as a force for increasing or decreasing inequality. But, it is clear that even with perfect measures all round, the conclusion that changes in education could do little to reduce inequalities would still remain.

There are several rather different reasons why this is the case. To begin with, so far as employment, social status, and incomes are concerned the inequalities are influenced by many broader political, economic, and social factors that have little to do with schools as such. No changes in schools are likely to produce more jobs, or diminish inequalities in income, or redistribute inherited wealth, and it is ridiculous to suppose that they could have that effect. But, even if attention is confined to the very much narrower issue of scholastic attainment, it is unlikely that changes in schooling could do much to reduce the extent of individual differences.

This is so because: (a) there is a rather weak association between disadvantaged children and disadvantaged schools; many disadvantaged children do not attend disadvantaged schools, and even within disadvantaged schools many children are not disadvantaged (Barnes and Lucas, 1974); (b) elementary schools that boost achievement are not especially likely to be in the same district as secondary schools that boost achievement (Jencks et al., 1972), so that a child attending a less good elementary school may well go on to a superior high school, and vice versa; (c) the variations in scholastic achievement within any one school, and always much greater than the variations between schools, because genetic, family, and other influences all lead to heterogeneity in ways that are independent of schooling (Jencks et al., 1972; Rutter and Madge, 1976); and (d) one of the main ways in which individual differences operate is in terms of an ability to take advantage of opportunities, and this is so whether the differences reflect genetic variations or are the result of the family environment. The only way to have a substantial effect in reducing individual differences in scholastic attainment is to severely restrict and impair the schooling of the most advantaged pupils. If homogenization is the goal, that is often most easily accomplished by *reducing* the quality of the experiences available to children. It is probably no accident that in the London study of secondary schools, the variations in attainment between pupils were least (i.e., there was the greatest reduction of inequality) in the schools with the *poorest* overall levels of outcome (Rutter et al., 1980b).

However, that conclusion serves to emphasize that the issues of social inequality and individual differences are far from synonymous. It is neither possible nor desirable that everyone should be made equal to everyone else in every respect (Jencks et al., 1972). Nevertheless, in all societies large and troubling inequalities of opportunity and of living standards generally remain (Black, 1980; Rutter and Madge, 1976; Townsend, 1979), and it is desirable that these be remedied. The policy implication from this type of analysis of school effects is that raising the quality of schooling is unlikely to make a major impact on this problem. On the other hand, it does not necessarily follow that improvements in the educational system would not reduce some forms of undesirable unequal opportunity even if this would have little effect on the extent of individual differences. This possibility is most appropriately considered by examining the third approach to school effects, that of groups effects in terms of raising standards.

School Effects in Terms of Raising Standards

The essential feature of this approach that differentiates it from the others that have been considered is that the *school* rather than the individual child constitutes the unit of analysis. The effect in this case relates to the question of whether raising the quality of schooling could have an impact in raising overall standards of attainment; that is, an effect on *levels* rather than on *variance*. Basically that question is tackled by comparing schools rather than children and by asking whether some schools consistently produce better than average educational outcomes. If they do (and if it can be shown that the schools have indeed produced or *caused* the superior outcomes, so that the good results are not simply a function of their having an intake of above average pupils from more favored family backgrounds), then clearly there is the potential for all schools to do the same and for standards to be raised thereby. As Klitgaard and Hall (1975) and Edmonds (1979) both make clear, the existence of such unusually effective schools would have very important implications for educational policy even if they were very rare. The point is that if they are rare, they may make little impact on overall standards *now*, but if all schools could achieve the same quality, then the potential impact in the *future* could be very great indeed. Also, it needs to be emphasized that this effect on *level* may have no effect on *variance*. The distinction is well brought out by Jack Tizard (1975) in his discussion of secular changes in the height of British school children. During the last half-century the average height of London school children aged seven to twelve years has risen 9 centimeters, probably as a result of better nutrition. But this very great improvement in the physique and health of children has been associated with no alteration in the extent of individual variations in height.

As this type of school effect is the one with the greatest potential implications for educational policy, the empirical research findings warrant more detailed discussion. But before the "effects" are considered, we need to turn our attention to the prior question of outcome variables, that is, the issue of school effects on *what*?

VARIETY OF OUTCOME VARIABLES

As already noted, many of the large-scale earlier studies utilized verbal ability measures as the outcome variable. While clearly this is not a particularly suitable criterion measure for school effectiveness, it is not self-evident what should replace it, and different studies have followed different approaches. Hence, we need to ask what behaviors *should* schools be aiming to effect?

Scholastic Attainment

It is generally agreed that the outcome variables must include some measure of scholastic attainment, as the teaching of skills in specific school subjects such as English, mathematics, or the sciences constitutes one of the central objectives of all schools. But what sort of attainment measure is most appropriate? Madaus et al. (1979) have argued against the use of standardized norm-referenced tests on the grounds that they are designed to maximize individual differences and that they are insensitive to particular curricula. The former objection was not borne out by their own data in that the standardized tests of English and mathematics showed *less* within-school class variation and *greater* between-class variation than most of the public examinations. The latter objection is relevant to some school subjects but surely not to subjects such as reading or English where the educational objectives and curricula are broadly comparable across schools. A more pertinent concern is that the achievement tests should tap skills largely taught in the schools whose effectiveness is being assessed. This consideration *does* reduce the suitability of norm-referenced standardized tests for *secondary* schools, but for a somewhat different reason from that given by Madaus et al. (1979). By their nature, such tests are designed to assess skills across the whole range. This is a disadvantage in the case of secondary schools just because it is likely that all the basic skills will have been acquired in *primary* school before entering secondary school. In contrast, public examinations can be, and generally are, designed to assess pupils' mastery of the contents of particular curricula (and hence may focus on the higher-level skills, taking the elementary skills largely for granted). On the other hand, the norm-referenced standardized tests may well be those most appropriate for the evaluation of the effectiveness of elementary schools (as in Brookover et al., 1979).

In Britain, it is possible to use public examination results at age 16 years as the criterion of scholastic attainment because the pupils at virtually all schools take similar examinations. Accordingly, this has been the most widely employed criterion in secondary schools (Brimer et al., 1978; Madaus et al., 1979; Reynolds, Jones, and St. Leger, 1976; Rutter et al., 1979). These examinations have all the advantages of being explicitly tied to the curricula followed in the schools and so are directly relevant to school objectives. However, they are by no means free of problems because the exams are not designed to be suitable for the least able pupils, because there are two sets of exams (one for the brighter pupils and one for those in the middle of the ability range), and because there is not exact comparability across school subjects. Nevertheless, in spite of these limitations there is no doubt that they constitute the best criterion of scholastic achievement available for older secondary school pupils. Unfortunately, there is no adequate equivalent in the United States.

Classroom Behavior

Although there is continuing debate within the educational world on the pros and cons of the so-called "traditional" and "progressive" approaches and on the degree of structure or formality in the classroom that is appropriate, nevertheless most people accept that it is desirable that pupils be attentive, interested, and engaged in their work and that disruptive behavior should be discouraged. Accordingly, various measures of classroom behavior have been employed as indicators of school effectiveness. Teacher ratings of pupil behavior have been found to be useful (Rutter, Yule, Quinton, Rowlands, Yule, and Berger, 1975), but, probably, they are the least satisfactory in view of the uncertainty on how far teachers in different schools utilize the same standards. Pupil self-reports are likely to be rather more valid, and at least so far as objective, easily quantifiable behaviors (such as skipping classes or writing graffiti) are concerned, they should be reasonably comparable across schools. Self-reports have been used successfully both in elementary (Heal, 1978) and secondary schools (Rutter et al., 1979). Almost certainly, the most satisfactory measure of all is systematic, minute-by-minute recording of classroom behavior by external observers. For example, Rutter el al. (1979) used this method to assess the proportion of 10-second observation periods in which pupils were engaged in off-task activities or in which there was shouting across the room or openly disruptive behavior. Much earlier, Revans (1965) used films of school classes to produce rather similar measures. More judgmental ratings by participant observers have also been employed (Reynolds, Jones, St. Leger, and Murgatroyd, 1980). However, the big disadvantage of all observational techniques is that they are enormously time-consuming both in undertaking the observations and in data processing.[2]

Absenteeism

If pupils are to learn from classroom teaching, it is necessary that they attend school regularly; thus, a high level of attendance is generally recognized as a necessary goal for all schools, as well as an indicator that schools are doing their job well (Jones, 1980; Reynolds et al., 1980). The daily registers employed by schools to record the attendance of all pupils have proved to be a most convenient, and generally satisfactory, source of data for assessing schools' average levels of attendance. Marked variations between secondary schools in attendance levels have been found in several studies (Rutter et al., 1979; Reynolds et al., 1980). However, in that it is known that attendance levels vary markedly with age (with absenteeism at its height in the last year of compulsory schooling—see Rutter, 1979), it is essential to utilize identical age groups when making comparisons between schools.

Attitudes to Learning

In considering the assessment of scholastic achievement, the focus was on the acquisition of specific skills (as in reading or mathematics), on the gaining of specified factual knowledge, and on the understanding of its meaning. Obviously, this is a necessary educational objective but, equally obviously, it is not a sufficient one (Rutter, 1979). Young people must acquire the basic skills but also they must know how to *apply* the skills in their everyday life. The fundamental issue is not whether people can read, spell, and do sums in an exam but rather whether they can *use* those skills to read for pleasure, to acquire new knowledge, and to cope with the demands of new technologies in the factory and in the home. Most of all—as we live in a rapidly changing world with changing demands—education must fit us to deal with these altering conditions. Clearly, one of the main educational objectives must be learning *how to learn*, how to acquire new knowledge, and how to evaluate new claims and new discoveries. This involves the acquisition of particular skills but also it requires an attitude of mind. While this would be generally agreed by educators, the systematic measurement of an interest in learning and of self-motivated education after leaving school has proved difficult to undertake in practice.

Nevertheless, researchers have attempted to obtain some indicators of these "hard-to-measure" aspects of school effectiveness. For example, Pedersen, Faucher, and Eaton (1978) used teacher ratings of pupil "effort," "leadership," and "initiative." Interestingly, they found persistent differences in these proxy measures of positive self-concept according to which teacher the child had in his first grade of elementary school. Brookover et al. (1979) used self-rating scale of the pupils' self-concepts of academic ability and of a self-reliance. Similarly, Reynolds et al. (1980) obtained data on children's self-concepts and levels of self-esteem, and Marjoribanks (1978) used self-ratings to assess children's enthusiasm for school. It is clear that these measures tap only a few of the relevant aspects of attitudes to learning, but equally they indicate that it should be possible to develop more penetrating measures of this type.

Continuation in Education

Of course, one reflection of pupils' attitude to learning is whether or not they continue in some form of education after reaching the end of compulsory schooling. This has been used as a school outcome measure in several studies of school effectiveness on the grounds that, in part, it is likely to reflect both commitment to the educational process and also the likelihood of greater scholastic achievement (Reynolds et al., 1976; Rutter et al., 1979). In Britain, compulsory schooling ends at 16 years in the fifth form, with staying on into the sixth form for 2 or 3 additional years purely voluntary. Interestingly, even for pupils of comparable intellectual ability, there are major variations between secondary schools in the proportion staying on.

In both Britain and the United States, the proportion of pupils going on to college or to some other form of further education provides another alternative with the same two advantages. Again, it has been employed by several different investigators as one criterion of school effectiveness (see Jencks et al., 1972; Reynolds et al., 1980).

Employment

Education is generally viewed as having as one of its objectives the preparation of young people to cope better with their jobs on leaving school and to gain the skills required to provide the entry to training schemes which make the most of their work talents. Insofar as this is so, various aspects of employment have also been used as indicators of school effectiveness. Reynolds et al. (1976) used the proportion of school leavers still unemployed 4 months after leaving school as one measure; Gray, Smith, Rutter (1980) used time taken to get the first job, whether unemployed one year after school-leaving, dismissal during the first year of work, job satisfaction, job skill level, and whether the job involved further training; and Pedersen et al. (1978) used a rather complex overall measure of adult status which took into account housing and personal appearance as well as occupational prestige.

Social Functioning

Schools vary in the extent to which they regard other aspects of personal functioning as included in their educational objectives. However, quite apart from their role in giving children scholastic skills, schools serve as a setting for socialization experiences which, presumably, may act for the better or the worse. Hence, it would seem reasonable to include measures of social skills or quality of interpersonal relationships among possible indicators of school effectiveness. Thus, for example, Hallinan (1979) studied the effects of classroom organization on children's patterns of friendship choice and clique formation; various studies of "open classrooms" have assessed cooperative behavior, creativity, and curiosity (see Horwitz, 1979); Smith and Connolly (1976) examined the effects of variations in the amount of space and in the availability of play materials on the play characteristics and social interactions of nursery school children; Moos (1979) related measures of the classroom environment to high school students' sense of well-being and satisfaction with learning; and numerous studies have investigated the effects of desegregation on cross-racial social interactions and attitudes (St. John, 1975; Stephan, 1978). In recent years, too, there has been discussion of the possible role of schools in preparing young people to become better parents (Department of Health and Social Security, 1974; Harman and Brim, 1980).

As a proxy for the negative side of one feature of social behavior, delinquency rates have also been included in several studies—all of which have shown substantial variations between schools in this measure, although they differed somewhat in the extent to which this appeared to be a function of school intake characteristics (Finlayson and Loughran, 1976; Gath, Cooper, Gattoni, and Rockett, 1977; National Institute of Education, 1978; Power, Alderson, Phillipson, Schoenberg, and Morris, 1967; Reynolds and Murgatroyd, 1977; Reynolds et al., 1976; Rutter et al., 1979; West and Farrington, 1973).

Associations Between Different Measures of Outcome

The indicators discussed cover a rather wide range of outcomes which have no necessary connection with one another, and it is important to consider how far they are intercorrelated. The question here, of course, is *not* whether measures of scholastic achievement, attendance, and delinquency are associated with each other at an individual *child* level but rather whether those *schools* with generally superior levels of scholastic achievement are also those with better than average attendance and with below average delinquency. There are only a few studies which have used multiple indicators but, with one exception, they are agreed in showing moderate intercorrelations. Thus, Reynolds et al. (1980) found rank correlations of 0.52 between attendance and delinquency and 0.55 between attendance and academic attainment; Rutter et al. (1979) found rank correlations of 0.77 between delinquency and attendance, 0.68 between delinquency and academic outcome, and 0.72 between delinquency and behavior; Gath et al. (1977) found a rank correlation of 0.31 between child guidance clinic referral rates and probation rates; and Rutter et al. (1975) found that the school characteristics associated with high rates of reading difficulties were generally similar to those associated with behavioral deviance.

The one exception to this pattern of moderate consistency in outcome is the study of 68 Michigan elementary schools by Brookover et al. (1979). There was a weakly positive association between the two pupil report measures of self-concept and self-reliance (circa 0.2 to 0.3) but a somewhat lower association between self-reliance and measured achievement (about 0.2) and a near zero correlation between self-concept and achievement. It seems that pupil attitudes may not necessarily reflect objective measures of pupil achievement. The implications of these differences for later functioning remain to be determined. However, although attitudes and behavior do not seem to be highly associated, the various objective measures of different facets of outcome (such as attendance, classroom behavior, and scholastic achievement) have been found to show substantial intercorrelations.

Nevertheless, although most studies show *moderate* levels of agreement between different indicators, the correlations fall well short of unity. There are a few schools with superior outcomes on some measures but inferior outcomes on others. For example, in the Rutter et al. (1979) study of 12 secondary schools in inner London, there was one school which ranked second in terms of good behavior but *last* on attendance and next to last on exam success. The implication is that, even though schools that are effective in one respect tend also to be effective in others, the factors that lead to each type of successful outcome may not be quite the same. So far, little if any progress has been made in identifying these differences. But the question remains, and it is important that future investigations seek to differentiate the school processes which specifically predispose to good behavior in the classroom from those which specifically predispose to superior scholastic achievement. The clear implication is that, so far as possible, *multiple* indicators of school effectiveness should always be employed.

Another aspect of the same broad question regarding consistency in outcomes is whether or not schools effective for one group of pupils are also effective for other different groups. Thus, one might ask whether the school features that facilitate good outcomes for the intellectually most able children are the same as those that lead to success for the least able; or whether the schools that are effective for socially favored white children are also those most effective for socially disadvantaged black children; or whether the school policies that help older children are the same as those helpful to younger children; or whether the practices that "work best" with boys are similarly effective with girls. So far, these questions have been little investigated and, indeed, were not considered at all in most of the studies. Rutter et al. (1979) found that, on the whole, schools effective for one group of pupils tended to be similarly effective for others. However, it would be foolhardy to suppose that this will always be the case, and the matter needs to be examined in greater detail.

DETERMINATION OF SCHOOL EFFECTS IN RAISING STANDARDS

With these considerations in mind we need to turn now to an assessment of the empirical evidence on the extent to which schools may be effective in raising standards of pupil attendance, behavior, or achievement. Several rather different methodological problems have to be faced in looking at this evidence.

Do Schools Differ in Pupil Outcome?

The first basic question is whether or not schools do in fact differ "significantly" on any of the relevant measures of pupil success. All investigations have agreed in showing *huge* differences between schools. For example, Reynolds et al. (1976) in a study of South Wales schools found that in one school half the pupils went on to college whereas in another less than 1 in 11 did so; Power et al. (1967) in a study of secondary schools serving one London borough found that average annual delinquency rates varied from 1 percent to 19 percent; and Rutter et al. (1979) in another inner London study found that secondary school rates of very poor attendance varied from 6 percent to 26 percent. Clearly, there are vast differences between schools in pupil outcome, but what do the differences mean and to what are they due?

Are the Differences Merely a Consequence of Variations in Intake?

The first major issue, here, is whether the interschool differences are just a reflection of the fact that whereas some schools admit a high proportion of behaviorally difficult, educationally backward children, other schools have intakes of predominantly well behaved children with above average scholastic skills. The latter group of schools is likely to have better outcomes simply because they deal with a more favored school population; their greater success reflects their intake and in no way provides a measure of their effectiveness as educational institutions. It is obvious that school outcomes can be compared only after taking into account the characteristics and family backgrounds of the pupils they admit. A number of different approaches to this methodological problem have been followed.

The method followed by Power (Power et al., 1967; Power, Benn, and Morris, 1972), in one of the first studies to claim major school effects, was to equate the schools in terms of the catchment area they served. However, this is a weak and unsatisfactory means of control in view of the large differences between children and families within the same catchment area. Gath et al. (1977) slightly improved on this by a more detailed statistical analysis of the association between electoral ward (i.e., geographical area) rates and school rates, but the analysis is flawed both by the fact that catchment areas and electoral wards are not coterminous and by the failure to take into account individual differences within areas.

An alternative approach has been to compare schools with similar intakes. This method was used by Finlayson and Loughran (1976), who showed that pairs of schools that were closely comparable on the social characteristics of their catchment areas differed sharply in delinquency rates. Similarly, Reynolds (Reynolds and Murgatroyd, 1977; Reynolds et al., 1976) found that schools with markedly differing rates of attendance, delinquency, and college entrance had intakes that were similar in terms of the measured intelligence of their pupils. However, as in all methods that attempt to control for intake, the particular intake measures used are crucial. This was evident in a later report of the Reynolds et al. (1980) study which showed that the secondary schools comparable on IQ were *not* comparable in terms of the reading and arithmetical skills of their pupils at the time of entry to the schools. Moreover, it was found that, to a substantial extent, the school variations in outcome were accounted for by the variations in intake.

An extension of this same approach has been to compare schools which differ markedly in pupil success but which are *matched* on intake variables. Brookover et al. (1979) used this procedure in comparing high- and low-achieving elementary schools matched on socioeconomic status, racial composition, and type of community served. Yet another variant is to identify schools with high levels of scholastic attainment in spite of having intakes usually associated with low achievement. Weber (1971) did this in his study of four inner-city elementary schools with a preponderance of children from low-income ethnic minority families but yet with levels of reading as good as or better than national norms. The finding on both these last two studies of schools with superior outcomes in spite of having markedly disadvantaged intakes argues that the schools have been effective in obtaining good achievement when low attainment was to be expected ordinarily.

Another way of dealing with the impact of intake differences is to use some form of statistical analysis to examine the extent to which schools vary in outcome, after having taken intake variations into account. Brookover et al. (1979) did this by means of multiple regression analyses in which the social and racial composition of the student body served as the intake measure. The results showed that major differences between schools remained even after intake characteristics had been taken into account statistically. However, this method suffers from the limitation that input was measured on the basis of a school average rather than on an individual-by-individual basis. On the other hand, several other studies have been able to utilize intake measures which were obtained on an individual basis for each of the pupils in each of the schools. Brimer et al. (1978) examined public examination grades in a sample of British secondary schools, after taking into account the children's family background characteristics (parental education and social class) and (for a small subsample) verbal reasoning scores. Madaus et al. (1979) used a comparable approach with examination results for children at Irish secondary schools. Both studies showed significant school effects even after intake features had been allowed for statistically.

A variant of this same approach is to use the results of this type of statistical analysis based on *individual* predictors of outcome to predict *school* outcomes (in which these are determined according to their intake characteristics). Klitgaard and Hall (1975) did this with three sets of American data in order to identify "statistical outliers"; in other words, schools with levels of achievement consistently better than predicted from intake features. Rutter et al. (1979) did much the same[3] with secondary schools in inner London. Lezotte and Passalacqua (1978) used the child's own level of achievement on the same scholastic measure to predict *changes* in scholastic attainment over the following year. They showed that children's progress on reading and mathematics at elementary schools was significantly associated with *which* school they attended, even after taking into account their prior level of attainment.

All statistical analyses of the type which attempts to "control for" or "take account of" differences between schools in intake characteristics rely on several assumptions, three of which are often not met. Firstly, the predictors may not function in the same way within all schools. For example, Rutter et al. (1979) found that the associations between intellectual ability and attendance differed significantly between schools. Secondly, the intercorrelations between variables may differ between schools. Thus, Brookover et al. (1979) found that students in majority-black schools had significantly higher mean self-concepts of academic ability than those in white schools, even though their mean level of achievement was lower. Thirdly, there may be so little overlap between schools in some of the predictor variables that statistical adjustments are unwarranted. For example, Maughan et al. (Note 3) found that the intakes to academically selective and to nonselective schools scarcely overlapped with respect to the proportions of behaviorally deviant pupils in the intake (almost none in the selective schools) and of black pupils (very few in the nonselective schools). In all these instances it is necessary to restrict analyses to subgroups of schools or to subgroups of pupils within schools which *are* directly comparable. This was done in all three studies cited, and having done so, large statistically significant school differences were still apparent.

Although the many studies to which reference has been made in this section have followed somewhat varied statistical approaches and have differed in the range and quality of intake predictors available, they have agreed in showing that the differences between schools in pupil outcome are *not* merely a function of variations in intake.

Choice of Intake Predictor Variables

Of course, one's confidence in the validity of that conclusion is heavily dependent on whether or not the investigators have chosen the most appropriate predictors. This is the point most strongly emphasized by those critics who remain sceptical about the existence of any sizeable school effect (see Heath and Clifford, 1980, for one of the more thoughtful critiques). The pertinence of this criticism is clearly illustrated by the already-mentioned Reynolds study, which had to somewhat modify its conclusions when better intake predictor variables became available (Reynolds et al., 1980). Also, it is evident that the most appropriate predictor for one type of pupil outcome may not be the most appropriate for other different outcomes. Thus, Rutter et al. (1979) found that behavior in primary school was a good predictor for later delinquency in girls but a rather poor predictor in boys. But, in that study, as in most others, the combination of parental occupation and verbal reasoning score proved to be the most generally satisfactory intake variable for predictive purposes. Heath and Clifford (1980) argued that parental occupation is an inadequate proxy for all the many family variables which may influence children's school progress and also that the secondary school effects may have been a consequence of prior experiences in primary school. However, Maughan, Mortimore, Ouston, and Rutter (1980) have pointed out that the evidence from other studies (e.g., Hutchinson, Prosser, and Wedge, 1979) suggests that the addition of other family variables would make very little difference to predictive power; moreover, a further analysis of the Rutter et al. (1979) study showed that primary school measures were not associated with secondary school outcomes apart from attendance.

Of course, it is never possible to be entirely sure that some unmeasured intake variable was not responsible for the school outcome differences in any particular study. On the other hand, this does not seem at all likely in view of the similar findings from the many studies, of quite different school populations, that vary a good deal in the measures used and in the statistical analyses employed. It is also important that the larger-scale studies of many schools are supported by the smaller-scale investigations of individual schools that have strikingly good outcomes in spite of markedly disadvantaged intakes. As Klitgaard and Hall (1975) emphasize, the finding of *any* outlier schools of that type provides a strong argument that schools *can* be effective in raising standards.

Do the School Differences Persist over Time?

On the other hand, that argument carries with it another danger, as explicitly recognized by Klitgaard and Hall. In any sample, there are likely to be a few outliers that arise by chance alone. If their occurrence is to carry any meaning, it is necessary to go on to show that it is the *same* schools that continue to perform above expectation year after year. That has indeed been found in all the studies which have examined the question. For example, Reynolds et al. (1976) found a concordance coefficient of 0.85 for school attendance rates over 7 years and of 0.56 for academic attainment over the same period of time. These rates were not adjusted for variations between schools in intakes, but this was done in the Rutter et al. (1979) study which showed similar stability in intake-adjusted outcomes over 3 or 4 years.

Do School Variables Predict Outcome?

The findings discussed thus far indicate that there are sizeable temporally stable differences between schools in pupil outcomes which are not attributable to the characteristics of the pupils at the time they entered the school. The inference is that the school differences must be due to "something else." It does not necessarily follow that the "something else" concerns the characteristics of the schools themselves. In order to conclude that there is a true school "effect," we need to show *both* that the school differences are *not* attributable to nonschool factors *and* that the differences *are* due to measurable features of the schools themselves.

This second issue has been studied by a number of different investigators in both Britain and the United States during the last decade, all of which have found significant associations between various measures of school climate, ethos, or social organization and pupil outcomes. Brookover et al. (1979) used student, teacher, and principal questionnaires to obtain measures of the school "climate" and found that these were significantly associated with academic outcome differences between schools even after school composition had been taken into account. Rutter et al. (1979) used a combination of detailed time and event-sampled observations in the classroom, pupil questionnaires, and teacher questionnaires to evaluate school "process" and found that it was strongly associated with the children's behavior and academic achievements even after the school outcomes had been adjusted for individual intake characteristics and after the composition of the school as a whole had been taken into account. Other statistical studies (Brimer et al., 1978; Madaus et al., 1979; Reynolds et al., 1980), as well as more qualitative case studies of schools (Brookover et al., 1979; Clegg and Megson, 1968; Weber, 1971), have concurred in showing that differences in outcome between schools *are* systematically associated with identifiable features of the schools as social organizations. This consistent finding provides strong support for the suggestion that there are important school effects on pupil behavior and attainments.

A Causal Association?

Before discussing in greater detail the school features associated with more successful outcomes, we need to ask how we can tell whether the associations represent truly *causal* effects. In short, have the schools, through their policies and practices, *caused* the children to have higher (or lower) levels of achievement, attendance, and good behavior? Or is it just that school features reflect a more complex set of causal processes which are not a direct function of any actions of the school staff themselves? This last possibility demands serious consideration in that all studies have shown a very substantial overlap between the composition of the student body and the school climate or ethos measures (Ainsworth and Batten, 1974; Brimer et al., 1978; Brookover et al., 1979; Madaus et al., 1979; Rutter et al., 1979; Reynolds et al., 1980). Perhaps, the school climate is itself *created* by the students that go there (together with the family and community influences that accompany them), so that it is only incidentally (and noncausally) associated with pupil outcome.

Certainly, it is highly likely that factors outside the school, as well as pupil peer group influences within it, help shape any school. No school is an island. Nevertheless, several separate strands of evidence suggest that it is most unlikely that this is the whole story; rather, the findings point to the probability of a causal effect. The relevant data include: (a) the findings from case studies of matched pairs that schools with *similar* intakes but *different* outcomes differ on school climate variables in a predictable manner (Brookover et al., 1979); (b) the findings from larger-scale statistical studies that school climate or ethos variables still correlate significantly and uniquely with pupil outcome even after the overlap with school composition has been taken into account statistically (Brimer et al., 1978; Brookover et al., 1979; Madaus et al., 1979; Rutter et al., 1979); and (c) the relative positions of schools on the relevant measures of behavior and attainment at the beginning and end of schooling, which show that the measures of school process correlate more highly with pupil characteristics when they leave the school than when they entered it (Maughan et al., 1980). This last point utilizes the presence of an *increased* correlation between school measures and pupil measures at outcome compared with those at intake to infer the direction of the causal process. If the pupil characteristics shaped teacher behavior and the overall school climate, rather than the other way round, the strongest association would be expected to be with the intake measures (i.e., the opposite of those found empirically). Thus, Maughan et al. (1980) found that the school process measures correlated 0.44 with academic attainment at intake but 0.76 with academic attainment at the end of secondary schooling and 0.39 with children's behavior at intake but 0.92 with their behavior later in their secondary schooling.

All three of these rather different types of findings provide strong circumstantial evidence of a causal effect. The observation that similar conclusions follow from different research designs and strategies on disparate school populations adds particular strength to the causal inference. However, firm and unambiguous evidence on causation can come only from experimental studies in which school practices are deliberately changed. If the effect is truly causal, the change should be followed by the predicted alterations in pupil outcomes. Such studies have yet to be undertaken[4] and, in any case, would be difficult to evaluate. Firstly, in real life situations (as distinct from the laboratory), the planned changes may not take place quite as intended and may also be accompanied by unplanned modifications. Changing school populations as a result of rising or falling birthrates or population movement, national or regional economic crises, or political decisions on school policy may all interfere with the research strategy. Secondly, some of the pupil outcomes (such as public examination results at the time of school-leaving) are based on years of school experience so that there is an inevitable long time lapse between the educational change and the outcome to be tested. In addition, during those years it is possible that many other unplanned changes will have also taken place. For both reasons, such research will need to focus on more immediate short-term goals as well as trying to trace the links to the more distant educational objectives. Nevertheless, in spite of these (and other) difficulties, investigations of planned change in schools would be most informative and are much needed. The fact that such action studies have been found to be possible in hospitals (Revans, 1972; Wieland, 1981), which constitute different but equally complex social organizations, offers hope that the same should be possible in schools.

EXTENT OF SCHOOL EFFECTS

Size of School Effects

We have concluded that there are important school effects and that the effects probably represent causal influences. But how great are these effects? That is to say, how much difference does it make to an individual child's scholastic progress which school he attends? An idea of the size of effect is probably best obtained by considering some of the results from the few investigations which have given findings in this form. Thus, Rutter et al. (1979) found that, *after adjusting for intake characteristics*, children at the most successful secondary school got four times as many exam passes on average as children at the least successful school. Or expressed another way, children in the *bottom* 25 percent of verbal ability in the most successful school on average obtained as many exam passes as children in the *top* 25 percent of verbal ability at the least successful school. Brookover et al. (1979) found that children in the most successful white elementary school obtained academic achievement scores on average about one standard deviation (equivalent to some 15 IQ points) above those in the unsuccessful white elementary school matched for intake. The difference between the successful and unsuccessful black schools was even greater.

Even from these few findings it is clear that school effects can be very substantial indeed. Nevertheless, it is important to appreciate that the differences concern *averages* and that within *all* schools there are children with both superior and inferior achievement. Also, it should be emphasized that the differences concern schools at the very extremes of the range. Many schools differ very little in their effects and the findings cannot be taken as reflecting the *overall* importance of school effects. Rather they give some impression of what might be achieved by raising the standards of the worst schools to the level of the best.

But that impression must be accepted as very approximate indeed. Firstly, it assumes that the whole of the difference between the schools is due to school effects. Clearly that is unlikely to be the case. There are certain to be unmeasured qualities of the children, their family, or their out-of-school environment that were not taken into account but yet which influenced their academic performance to some extent. Secondly, some of the school effects themselves are likely to stem from historical and ecological factors outside the schools' control. Both of these considerations imply that the figures given constitute an *over*estimate of how much could be done to improve children's achievement through bringing the quality of the worst schools up to that of the best. However, there is a third consideration which suggests that they constitute an *under*estimate. That is, the "best" schools in the two studies cited refer simply to the "best" on just one particular measure within a relatively small sample of schools. They do not constitute the "best" in a wider sense; not only is it highly likely that still better schools exist elsewhere but also it would be unduly pessimistic to suppose that we could not improve on present functioning in even the better schools. For all these reasons, it would be quite unwarranted to treat the figures as providing anything more than a very rough and ready guide. Nevertheless, the results do show that the effects of improving the quality of the worst schools are likely to be great enough to be of considerable practical importance.

Generalization of Effects

Insofar as school effects need to be seen in terms of children's attitudes and behavior as well as their exam performance, we need to ask how far the effects generalize to the children's activities outside school. Not much empirical evidence is available on this question. Undoubtedly, the effects are most strongly evident in the here-and-now situation of the school classroom. Nevertheless, the findings show effects which extend somewhat more widely than that. For example, several studies have shown that there are school effects on delinquency rates, although most delinquency takes place outside school hours and off school premises (e.g., Reynolds et al., 1976; Rutter et al., 1979). Also, school effects have been shown for self-concepts and self-reliance (Brookover et al., 1979).

No adequate guide to the degree of generalization of effects is possible from existing evidence. However, there is extensive evidence from other research that most forms of children's behavior show considerable situation-specificity (Mischel, 1979; Rutter, 1979). Hence, it must be expected that this will apply also to school effects, which are likely to have only a rather limited generalization of situations outside school.

Persistence of Effects

That might seem to suggest that there would be little persistence of school effects beyond the time of school-leaving. However, that involves a false parallel between generaliz-ation and persistence. Effects may persist because individuals have been set onto dif-ferent life paths rather than through the persistence of behavioral patterns as such. For example, in the London study of secondary schools (Rutter et al., 1979), pupils were followed up to the end of their first year after leaving school (Gray et al., 1980). The findings showed that there *were* school effects on employment insofar as schooling in-fluenced attendance, school dropout, examination success, and continuation of schooling into the sixth year. But there were no consistent school effects on employ-ment which did not operate through these mechanisms. In other words, school effects continued after pupils left school not because they permanently changed children's personality or characteristic mode of functioning, but rather because the immediate effects (in terms of school dropout or educational qualifications) either opened up or closed down further opportunities. Schooling had long-lasting effects because its im-mediate results set in motion a train of events which then in turn resulted in persistent sequelae.

Pedersen et al.'s (1978) study of the remarkable persistence of the effects of being taught by one particular first grade teacher gave rise to similar conclusions. They found that children taught by this teacher had better grades throughout the rest of elementary school and, even more surprisingly, showed superior status when followed up into adult life. Path analysis showed that this teacher had a major effect on chil-dren's academic achievement and their work effort and initiative in both the first and second grades but that her *direct* effects after that were negligible. On the other hand, her *indirect* effects were considerable because the initial effects led on to further de-velopments yielding a cumulative benefit in later stages of life.

Too few follow-up studies have been undertaken for any firm conclusions on per-sistence of school effects to be drawn. However, substantial persistence in some indi-viduals is likely simply because schooling has an effect on educational qualifications and college entry and both of these constitute "entry permits" to certain types of occupations. In addition, it is possible that there may be some continuing effects as a result of changes in habits of work or attitudes to learning or self-concepts, but there is no evidence on how far this is the case.

THE QUALITIES OF SCHOOLS THAT DO AND DO NOT MATTER

Having shown that there is strong circumstantial evidence that schools can and do have important effects on the behavior and attainments of their pupils, we need next to consider the findings on the further question of *which* school features seem to be associated with beneficial effects. The evidence on this point is limited to the few studies which have systematic data relevant to comparisons of the features of schools performing better than expected and those performing at levels below expectation. A number of investigations have noted that successful schools tend to differ in the expressed attitudes of their staff and pupils and hence in their overall climate or atmosphere (Brimer et al., 1978; Brookover et al., 1979; Finlayson and Loughran, 1976; McDill and Rigsby, 1973). The same has been observed in more qualitative case studies. Weber (1971) commented on "the order, sense of purpose, relative quiet and pleasure in learning" (p. 26) in the four successful inner-city schools he studied; and Brookover et al. (1979) observed that "the majority of the staff members in the higher achieving schools within each pair studied seemed to demonstrate attitudes and behaviors that were conducive to higher achievement, and the majority of the staff in the lower achieving schools did not" (p. 133). The question, however, is what *actions* must be taken to bring about this positive and beneficial atmosphere? To answer that question we are restricted to the relatively few studies with systematic quantified data on school policies and staff behavior (Heal, 1978; Reynolds et al., 1980; Rutter et al., 1979), together with the more qualitative case studies which have assessed similar variables (Brookover et al., 1979; Clegg and Megson, 1968; Goldman, 1961; Pablant and Baxter, 1975; Shoemaker and Fraser, 1981; Weber, 1971; Wynne, 1980). However, in addition, where relevant, reference is made to findings comparing successful and unsuccessful classrooms or teachers—as well as those concerned with schools as a whole. The findings are most conveniently reviewed by considering in turn different types of school features which possibly might be important (see Rutter, 1980a).

Resources and Physical Plant

The large-scale studies which gave rise to the view that schools "made little difference" were agreed in showing that variations between schools in the general resources available to them did *not* account for differences in pupil outcome (see, e.g., Kemp, 1955; Plowden, 1967; Coleman et al., 1966; Jencks et al., 1972). That is, factors such as the overall expenditure per pupil, number of books in the school library, teacher-pupil ratio, and teacher qualifications did not show any systematic relationship with pupils' levels of attainment. As already noted, these early studies were severely limited by their reliance on tests of verbal ability as measures of pupils' scholastic attainment. Nevertheless, more recent investigations with both more wide-ranging and more appropriate measures of outcome have produced broadly comparable results. Thus, Brookover et al. (1979), in their study of Michigan elementary schools, found that "personnel inputs" (such as teachers' salary, teacher experience, and percentage of teachers with graduate degrees) showed little association with pupil outcome once the association with student-body composition had been taken into account. On the other hand, these variables were related to achievement in the predominantly black schools. Rutter et al. (1979), in their study of inner London secondary schools, found that the age of the school buildings and the amount of space available were not associated with outcome. Even some of the nonsignificant trends went in a direction the reverse of what might have been expected; for example, the overcrowded schools tended to have somewhat better outcomes.[5] Similarly, Reynolds et al. (1980), in their study of South Wales secondary schools, found little association between the quality of the physical plant of the school and pupil outcome. Weber (1971), in his case study of four successful inner-city elementary schools in the United States, also commented that none had particularly good physical facilities.

It is clear that neither the level of financial resources nor the quality of the buildings constitute features which are essential for effective schooling. Of course, this conclusion is necessarily limited to the range studied. Although the schools investigated included some in pretty unsatisfactory buildings, most had a fairly adequate level of financial resources. It would be foolish to suppose that resources are of no importance; clearly, a basic minimum is essential. Moreover, the findings do not necessarily mean that a severe *cut* in resources would have no ill effects. To the contrary, it might have quite serious effects in terms of the damage done to staff and pupil morale by the need to stop or curtail successful programs. As noted below, if cuts led to inadequate maintenance of the buildings, this, too, might well impair school effectiveness. Nevertheless, within the general range of resources usually available to schools, the precise level seems to be of limited importance with respect to pupil outcomes. We may conclude that an increase in resources is *not* likely to be an effective means of improving standards. Of course, the ways in which resources are employed may well be important.

Size of School and Size of Class

Two particular aspects of resources—namely, size of school and size of class—warrant specific mention. The findings on school size show that generally this does *not* seem to constitute a variable which is strongly associated with outcome (e.g., Brookover et al., 1979; Galloway, 1976; Rutter et al., 1979), although a few studies have shown a minor advantage in outcome for pupils in smaller schools (e.g., Reynolds et al., 1980). Of course, it is likely that the size of the school will have some effect on its character and style (although not necessarily in the direction of small being better), and it may have an effect on pupil activities (Gump, 1980). Thus, Barker and Gump (1964) found that pupils in large schools were less likely to be involved in after-school activities than those attending small schools. Ross, Bunton, Evison, and Robertson (1972) found much the same, but as the large schools tended to be in urban areas, this may have been a reflection of the location of the school rather than its size. Heal (1978) found misbehavior more common in large primary schools, but it seemed that this may have been because the larger schools had had to use temporary accommodation in order to cope with rising rolls. The consequences of size for the life of the school warrant further study. In such studies it will be important to examine the possibilities that there may be a threshold effect for size and that school size may be more important for certain subgroups of students (see Garbarino, 1980). It is possible that, other things being equal,[6] there may be marginal advantages in having somewhat smaller schools, but it is clear that very large schools can be highly successful and that, in itself, a reduction in the average size of schools would not be likely to do anything to raise standards.

The average class size or the overall pupil-teacher ratio also has been found to have no consistent association with pupil success or outcome (Educational Research Service, 1978). Indeed, several studies have found that children in large classes or in schools with a low ratio of teachers to children make better than average progress (Little, Mabey, and Russell, 1971; Davie, Butler, and Goldstein, 1972; Rutter et al.,

1975). At first sight, that seems a most surprising finding in that common sense suggests that it ought to be easier to teach well in a smaller class. Moreover, two recent reports (Glass and Smith, 1978; Smith and Glass, 1979) have argued that, contrary to the conclusions of previous reviews, reduced class size *does* lead to increased academic achievement. We need, therefore, to consider the nature of the evidence and of the issues involved.

There are a variety of reasons why caution is needed before taking any of the findings at their face value. In the first place, popular schools are likely to have larger classes just because they are oversubscribed and schools with a high proportion of disadvantaged children may be allotted extra teachers just because of the low levels of attainment. Both tendencies are likely to create results with a quite misleading bias in favor of large classes. Greater weight needs to be attached to studies with random allocation of pupils, or at least with something approaching that. A further consideration is that it makes little sense to examine class size without paying attention to the style of teaching. On the face of it, it would seem implausible that class size would make much difference to the effectiveness of lecturing, which involves a minimum of active participation by pupils. On the other hand, teaching by means of individual tutoring or in which individual participation is crucial (such as by pupils reading out aloud) could well be affected by class size if only because the sheer amount of teaching time per child will necessarily be less in large classes. Another related consideration is the ability of the pupils. One study suggested that the least able students may have a particular need for small classes (Summers and Wolfe, 1977), and certainly it is probable that class size will be more critical for children whose handicaps impair their ability to profit from group methods of instruction.

With these issues in mind, the research findings may be examined. Most reviews (see, e.g., Educational Research Service, 1978) have concluded that within the mid-range of about 25 to 34 pupils, class size had little if any decisive impact on the academic achievement of the general run of pupils above the primary grades; on the other hand, small classes appear to facilitate the learning of reading and mathematics in the first few years of schooling and also may aid the academic progress of handicapped or disadvantaged pupils. The Glass and Smith (1978; Smith and Glass, 1979) studies, which claimed a much stronger and more general beneficial effect of small classes, used a method of "meta-analysis" to pool the results of different studies using different measures. There are many methodological problems in the ways in which this was done (see Educational Research Service, 1980). Even so, an examination of their data clearly shows that, in keeping with previous reviews, class size makes little difference to achievement within the wide range of 20 to 40 pupils. The advantage of small size, again in keeping with previous conclusions, was largely confined to differences in class size below 20 and particularly to the effects of size on pupils' achievement in tutoring groups.

Undoubtedly, there are further educational issues in relation to the effects of class size which require further study. Nevertheless, in spite of all caveats, it seems reasonably clear that it is possible to run a very well functioning school with fairly large classes and, moreover, that with the general run of pupils there seems to be very little to gain from any *overall* cutting of class sizes by just a few pupils, from say 30 to 25. On the other hand, it is probable that there are educational advantages in having smaller groups when utilizing tutoring or other methods which rely on active individual participation.

The findings have three important policy implications. Firstly, any relatively small, across-the-board increase or decrease in class size is unlikely to make much difference to overall levels of academic achievement. Hence, if extra funds become available for schooling, it would be unwise to use them to provide extra teachers to be evenly distributed across the schools as a whole. Secondly, because class size may be most important for tutorial groups or for teaching handicapped children or for teaching reading and arithmetic in the first few grades, the *distribution* of teachers is an important matter. For example, even without any change in the number of teaching staff, it might be profitable to increase the size of all regular classes by a child or two in order to have a really effective cut in the size of remedial classes. If these were reduced from, say, 15 children to 5 children, that would certainly allow a more individual approach to the teaching of the small proportion of pupils with severe learning disabilities, a shift which might have sizeable educational benefits. Alternatively, or in addition, the extra staff provided by a marginal increase in the average size of regular classes could be used to free junior teachers to observe other classes and to receive in-service training in classroom management (a great need—see below). Thirdly, if extra resources or a redistribution of staff allow a reduction in the size of some classes, it is important to see that it is done in a way which ensures that teachers take the opportunity to modify their teaching approaches accordingly.

Organizational Structure

There has been much debate in schools on the most advantageous systems of academic and counseling organization, but the available evidence suggests that no one system has overriding advantages. Particular passion has been aroused over the pros and cons of mixed-ability teaching versus tracking. In general, the evidence suggests that the average academic performance of children in schools using a tracking system is broadly comparable to that of children in schools with mixed-ability classes (Passow, Goldberg, and Tannenbaum, 1967; Lunn, 1970; Jencks et al., 1972; Rutter et al., 1979). In Weber's (1971) group of four particular successful elementary schools, one placed a strong emphasis on mixed-ability teaching and three used some form of homogeneous grouping. On the other hand, Acland (Note 1) and Lunn (1970) showed that in British primary schools there was some scholastic advantage to being in the top stream, even after initial differences in achievement and social background had been taken into account. Hargreaves' (1967) participant observation study in a British secondary school suggested that pupil subcultures and teacher attitudes tend to become polarized along the lines of tracking arrangements so that lower-tracked children may become labelled as failures and perceive themselves as such. Similarly, Kelly (1975) found that low-track position was associated with low self-esteem (although the data were not such as to differentiate the effects of tracking from the effects of low cognitive skills). Perhaps for these reasons, the results of some (but not all) empirical studies suggest that, at least for the early years of secondary schooling, mixed-ability teaching may have some advantages for less able children without any appreciable lowering of standards for the more able (Lacey, 1970 and 1974; Postlethwaite and Denton, 1978).

No completely unambiguous policy implications stem from these research findings, which are somewhat inconsistent and inconclusive. However, the fact that there are no decisive advantages for either mixed-ability teaching or tracking indicates that no great gains could be expected from a firm commitment to either system and hence that probably it would be unwise to specify that either system should be followed exclusively. On balance, it seems that there may be some advantages to mixed-ability teaching with younger children. However, higher up the school there may be greater difficulties in teaching subjects (such as mathematics or science or languages) that rely on the mastery of certain basic skills before more advanced aspects of the subjects can be taught. To the extent that that is so, some tracking according to pupil skills in particular subjects may well be desirable and advantageous overall. Probably, rather than decide on the overall adoption of one system or the other, it is better to take individual decisions according to particular subjects and age groups. What is important, then, is to take steps to ensure that, when tracking is employed, it does not carry with it the disadvantages that often follow but which do not necessarily accompany it.

Three steps may be tentatively put forward in terms of both the factors observed in less successful schools using tracking methods and what is known about possible effects more generally. Firstly, the tracking should be strictly in terms of the pupils' demonstrated ability in particular subjects. This means that subjects should be taught initially on a mixed-ability basis until it is clear that differential rates of progress make a more homogeneous grouping desirable. For the same reason, tracking for any particular class should be in terms of performance on that particular subject, rather than on IQ or any other general measure. Similarly, individual tracking by subject is to be preferred to across-the-board tracking for all subjects. It also follows that, if tracking is to be by demonstrated performance, mobility between tracks should be freely available according to pupils' progress or lack of progress. Thus, Brookover et al. (1979) commented that in successful schools students were grouped on their tested performance on specific subjects rather than on teacher perceptions, the curriculum was arranged so that there was easy movement from one track to another, and many (rather than few) tracks were used so that there were relatively small differences between tracks, a feature which also facilitated movement between groups. Secondly, the choice of track should not be accompanied by any differences in the quality of teaching. Many of the disadvantages sometimes associated with being in the bottom track come from the fact that the bottom-track classes are allocated to the weakest or the least experienced teachers. To be in that class is then a mark of failure for the teacher as well as the pupil. Thirdly, it has often been the case that bottom-track children lose out on nonacademic, as well as academic, aspects of schooling—being less often picked for positions of responsibility or to represent the school in sports, music, or drama. If being in the bottom track is not to lead to negative labelling and loss of self-esteem, it is necessary that pupils in all tracks get ample and equivalent opportunities for encouragement, reward, responsibility, and participation in the life of the school.

Different systems of providing counseling (that is, care with respect to the nonacademic aspects of pupils' emotional, social, and behavioral development) have been less studied. The London study (Rutter et al., 1979) found no differences in outcome according to whether schools were organized on a year-based or house-based system. It was important that some form of pastoral care was readily available, but the particular administrative organization for providing it seemed less crucial. Indeed, it appeared that informal sources may be particularly important. Pupil outcomes tended to be better in schools where ordinary teachers were available to see children about problems at any time (not just at fixed periods) and where pupils reported that, if they needed to, they would talk to a member of staff about a personal problem. On the whole, children were more willing to consult *ordinary* teachers about personal difficulties in schools with a counsellor or a teacher with special pastoral responsibilities. The suggestion is that schools that make formal provision for pastoral care are also likely to have ordinary teachers who are seen by the pupils as more approachable and who actually do talk to more children about problems. However, this need not be the case. Reynolds et al. (1980) found that in some schools the expectations that particular senior staff would have a special responsibility for dealing with truancy meant that ordinary teachers took less of a role in ensuring good attendance. It appeared from their findings that this was associated with greater truancy problems—although whether this was a cause or an effect could not be determined. The empirical findings are much too slender for any firm policy implications but, perhaps, it may be important when setting up formal arrangements through counselling or other services to ensure that this does not detract from the informal, more everyday pastoral concerns of all teachers.

Another aspect of organization concerns sex composition. In Britain, the state educational system includes both single-sex and coeducational schools. Opinions differ on the merits and demerits of each, but the limited available empirical evidence suggests that neither has any marked overall advantage in terms of scholastic achievement (Dale, 1974; Douglas, Ross, and Simpson, 1968; Rutter et al., 1979). However, the London study showed a slight trend, which fell short of statistical significance, for boys' behavior (both in and out of school) to be better when attending coeducational schools. It is not known whether these nonsignificant trends represent real, albeit small, effects. But, whether or not they do, the effects do not seem to be large enough for there to be any clear-cut policy indications.

Balance of Intake and Composition of Student Body

Most studies have shown that pupil outcomes tend to be somewhat less good, an average, in schools with a heavy preponderance of ethnic minority, socially disadvantaged, or intellectually less able children (e.g., Brimer et al., 1978; Brookover et al., 1979; Coleman et al., 1966; Jencks et al., 1972; Kratcoski and Kratcoski, 1977; Reynolds et al., 1980; Rutter et al., 1979). The size of the effect has varied somewhat from study to study, with differences only evident at the extremes in some British studies (Barnes and Lucas, 1974; Mabey, 1974), but with few exceptions the effect has always been present. However, the interpretation of the finding has been complicated by the fact that in most instances schools with a relative excess of socially disadvantaged children have also been different in a host of other ways. Moreover, the meaning of the associations may be influenced by which aspect of the balance of intake it is that matters—ethnic distribution, social distribution, or intellectual mix. Sometimes it is wrongly assumed that these amount to the same thing because, *on average*, black children are more likely than white children to be socially disadvantaged and because social disadvantage tends to be associated with somewhat lower levels of cognitive performance. Of course, that is so, but the findings refer to group differences of only moderate size to which there are many individual exceptions.

The inner London secondary school study (Rutter et al., 1979) looked at the separate effects of different types of balance of intake with respect to four different measures of pupil outcome. Firstly pupil behavior showed *no* association with any of the balance measures. Secondly, ethnic balance and behavioral balance (i.e., proportion of children already showing behavioral difficulties at the time of admission) each correlated significantly with only one of the four outcomes. Thirdly, *academic* balance (i.e., the proportion of intellectually able and less able children) showed the strongest and most consistent association with outcome, correlating significantly with all but pupil behavior; occupational balance correlated with scholastic achievement but not with the other outcome measures.

The relative lack of importance of ethnic balance in this study stands out and raises questions as to whether the achievement of an even ethnic distribution across all schools would do anything to effect educational standards. Of course, the finding refers to London rather than to the United States, where the cultural situation, as well as educational circumstances, is quite different. Thus, in London, black teenagers have a better school attendance record and are more likely to stay on at school than their white counterparts, in spite of their, on average, lower levels of scholastic attainment (Gray, Note 2). Nevertheless, a review of the effects in the United States of desegregation and busing has shown no marked or consistent effects on scholastic achievement for either the black children placed in predominantly white schools or on the white children in schools to which black children have been added (St. John, 1975). Of course, there are many reasons why desegregation should occur, but it does not appear that, *in itself*, the ethnic balance in a school has any marked effects on pupil outcome.

Occupational balance seemed of some importance, but the strongest effect was seen with respect to academic balance. This is interesting in that, of course, intellectual level is the one characteristic reflected in the balance measures which is most directly related to the educational process. The finding means that, quite apart from the *individual* benefits of above average intellectual ability, a child of *any* level of ability is likely to make better progress if taught in a school with a relatively high concentration of pupils with good cognitive performance. In other words, there is some kind of *group* effect such that the school performance as a whole is influenced by the composition of the student body.

The crucial question with respect to policy implications is *how* this effect arises and by *which* mechanisms it operates its influence on pupil outcome (if indeed the statistical association does truly reflect a causal influence). Three main findings are relevant in this connection. Firstly, although an important factor in relation to pupil outcome, the balance of intake is far from an overriding influence. This is shown by the statistical analyses in the London study of 12 secondary schools (Rutter et al., 1979) which demonstrated that *other* school factors were significantly associated with pupil success even after the composition of the student body had been taken into account and by the similar findings from the study of Michigan elementary schools by Brookover et al. (1979). It is also demonstrated by Weber's (1971) finding of effective inner-city schools with a preponderant intake of socially disadvantaged ethnic minority children and by Brookover et al.'s (1979) comparison of pairs of successful and unsuccessful schools in which both had closely similar intakes.

Secondly, the London study (Rutter et al., 1979) showed that the balance of a school's intake was not significantly associated with other measures of school process. This indicates that, at least in the schools studied, the influence of academic mix did *not* operate primarily through its effects on teacher attitudes or behavior or through its effects on overall school functioning. Of course, teachers are likely to be influenced to some extent by the characteristics of the children they teach (and the positive but nonsignificant associations between balance and school process measures are consistent with that happening). On the other hand, the implication is that the main mechanism is of some other kind—probably related to some aspects of the peer group itself.

Only speculations are possible on just how this occurs, but it is likely that the explanation lies in the achievements open to pupils. At present, exam success and college entry are the most public indications of success, but intellectually less able pupils are unlikely to perform well on exams and are unlikely to gain entry to college. When a preponderance of pupils in schools are likely to fail in these terms, it is probable that many of them will not identify with school goals and aims. In this way, peer groups with cultures contrary to educational objectives may develop and exercise an influence on other pupils.

The third finding is that the effects of balance of intake seem to operate over a wide range. Thus, in the London study in which all the schools were relatively disadvantaged, those with more favored intakes tended to have better outcomes (Rutter et al., 1979). But, it was also found that the academically selective schools (i.e., those which took only the more able children) had even better outcomes still (Maughan, Ouston, and Rutter, Note 3). The latter study did not include other measures of school functioning so that it was not possible to determine whether the better results were a function of the balance *per se*, but it seems likely that it was a factor.

Several policy implications stem from these research findings. As already noted, the presence of a heavily disadvantaged intake need *not* prevent a school from being effective. Also, it appears more important that schools have a reasonable balance of intellectually able and less able children than that children are distributed evenly in social or ethnic terms. Nevertheless, the implication is that there are considerable disadvantages in an educational system that allows such as uneven distribution of children that some schools have intakes with a heavy preponderance of the intellectually less able. There can be no dodging the need to ensure a reasonable balance of intakes between schools, but it is not obvious what is the best way of doing this (Rutter, 1979). The findings point to the major drawbacks of either a community school system (if the presence of ghettos means that some communities include a very high proportion of disadvantaged children) or an open market system (if a combination of parental choice and school acceptance of applications can result in a severe imbalance between the intakes of different schools). Forced busing to schools outside the district has not proved a particularly good solution either, in view, among other things, of the resentments it can arouse, of the long periods spent in travel to and from school, and of the difficulties in linking school friendships with out-of-school activities. In the long term it is likely to be best to ensure that communities are sufficiently socially mixed so that community schools would fairly automatically get a reasonable balance of intakes (Rutter, 1979). In the shorter term, however, there is no satisfactory alternative to local authorities maintaining a degree of control over admissions to ensure a fair parity between intakes. Obviously, it is desirable for this to be done in a way which is in keeping with parental and child choice. This cannot happen so long as some schools are markedly inferior to others. Accordingly, the most urgent requirement is to improve the quality of schooling generally and especially to upgrade the worst schools.

It should be added that the findings on balance of intake may also have implications for the nature of school goals and aims. The maintenance of academic standards is important (see below), but if it is true that the explanation of the effects of balance lies in the achievements open to pupils (and this has yet to be established), then it is necessary to ask what goals there should be for the intellectually less able pupils. What are the educational objectives in their staying on at school into the middle and late teens? If schools are unclear, what they are expecting less able older pupils to accomplish, it is not surprising that many pupils decide that there is no point in staying on and so drop out. The implication is that goals and aims for this group of students may need to be thought through carefully.

Academic Emphasis

During recent years a variety of well-conducted studies of teaching and of classrooms have shown not only that teaching "matters" but also that the crucial components of effective teaching include a clear focus on academic goals, an appropriate degree of structure, an emphasis on active instruction, a task-focused approach, and high achievement expectations (see Bennett, 1978; Brophy, 1979a and b; Good, 1979; and Rosenshine, 1979, for reviews of the evidence). Moreover, these conclusions, initially based on correlational data, have now received some support from experimental studies in which the ideas have been put into practice for the teaching of mathematics (Ebmeier and Good, 1979; Good and Grouws, 1979) and of reading (Anderson, Evertson, and Brophy, 1979; Stallings, Needels, and Stayrook, 1979).

These findings apply to studies that compared teachers or classrooms *within* schools, but similar conclusions have stemmed from studies making comparisons *between* schools. Effective schools have tended to be characterized by the regular setting and marking of homework, an appropriately high level of academic expectations, a high proportion of time devoted to active teaching, group planning of the curriculum, and checks of some kind to ensure that teachers did in fact follow the intended practices (Brookover et al., 1979; Rutter et al., 1979; Weber, 1971). Successful schools seem to vary in *how* they express academic concerns,[7] but they are differentiated from unsuccessful schools by their consistent and appropriate emphasis on academic matters and by the fact that this attitude is accompanied by specific actions designed to translate expectations into practice. Of course, it might be thought that the observed association between high teacher expectations and high pupil achievement simply means that teachers are good judges of children's abilities. However, the findings make clear that this cannot be the whole explanation because there are schools with relatively able children that nevertheless have low expectations of them; because, conversely, schools with disadvantaged children may yet have high expectations; and because at any given ability level, children's scholastic achievement tends to be higher in schools (or classes) with a strong academic emphasis and high expectations.

Classroom Management

But it is not enough for there to be a general academic emphasis in the school; this must also be accompanied by appropriate classroom management designed to bring the best out of the children. Some of the features associated with school effectiveness include a high proportion of lesson time spent on the subject matter of the lesson (as distinct from setting up equipment, handing out papers, dealing with disciplinary problems, etc.); a high proportion of teacher time spent interacting with the class as a whole, rather than with individuals; a minimum of disciplinary interventions; lessons beginning and ending on time; clear and unambiguous feedback to pupils on both their performance and what was expected of them; and ample use of praise for good performance (Brookover et al., 1979; Rutter et al., 1979). Once again, the features which have been found to differentiate effective schools closely parallel those found to characterize effective teaching in the studies of individual classrooms (Brophy, 1979a and b; Brophy and Putnam, 1979; Good, 1979; Rosenshine, 1979); because of this there can be reasonable confidence that the findings are valid and meaningful.

The variables probably reflect the requirements for two different, although closely interrelated, processes: (a) the gaining of the pupils' attention together with the maintenance of an orderly environment conducive to good teaching and learning and (b) the most effective means of instruction. So far as the first is concerned, it is important for teachers to be actively engaged in teaching primarily because this is necessary to keep good order rather than because of the extra minutes of instruction time available. When teachers spend a lot of time distributing resources or organizing things *after* the lesson should have begun, they are likely to lose the attention of the class with the attendant risk of increasing the likelihood of disruptive behavior. Much the same applies to the use of frequent disciplinary interventions in the classroom; a disciplinary style which involves constant checking and reprimands both disrupts the attention and interest of the rest of the class and tends to create a negative atmosphere. That this is the appropriate explanation is suggested by Rutter et al.'s (1979) finding that these variables were more strongly associated with pupil behavior than with scholastic achievement as such.

The value of a class-based style of instruction is important for the same reason (an excessive focus on the individual in the teaching of whole class groups tends to mean that the teacher loses contact and involvement with the rest of the class) but also because it maximizes the instruction time for *all* pupils and hence constitutes a more effective form of pedagogy. It is not, of course, that large group teaching is generally better than individualized teaching (to the contrary, tutorial teaching is more effective than lecturing for many purposes) but rather that, if the class is organized for class-based teaching, it is important to use a teaching style which keeps the *whole* group involved.[8]

Two further empirical findings are important in drawing implications for policy. Firstly, Rutter et al. (1979) found that in all schools (successful and less successful) inexperienced teachers tended to use inefficient techniques of classroom management. Secondly, the experimental studies have shown that teachers can be helped to improve their classroom management skills. We may infer that colleges do not adequately prepare trainee teachers in what Marland (1975) aptly calls "The Craft of the Classroom" and that the main difference between schools in this matter lies in their success (or lack of it) in helping young teachers acquire these skills on the job. The policy implications, then, concern both the need to improve this aspect of teacher training and also the need to provide in-service training in classroom management. Perhaps, too, the findings suggest the need for external advisors. Currently, advice tends to be more readily available on the skills involved in teaching specific subjects such as reading, mathematics, or languages; but there is a need for similarly skilled advice on classroom management issues. For this to be fully effective it will also be necessary for advisors to have the opportunity of freely observing everyday school functioning (Rutter, 1979).

Discipline and Pupil Conditions

Traditionally, discipline has tended to be regarded as more or less synonymous with punishment. However, all the studies of schools show that this is highly misleading. The findings indicate that good discipline (meaning keeping good order and maintaining appropriate rule enforcement) is essential in any well-run school but that *frequent* punishment is not only an ineffective means of achieving good discipline but also, in some circumstances, it may make that goal more difficult to achieve. Rutter et al.

(1979) found that group-based discipline standards were helpful in ensuring that both staff and pupils knew what was expected of them; both Reynolds et al. (1980) and Rutter et al. (1979) found that rule enforcement was more effective when primarily left to ordinary teachers to undertake on the spot rather than relying on frequent interventions by senior staff; and, as already indicated, classroom discipline has been found to work best when teachers are aware of what is going on in all parts of the classroom and deal with disruptive behavior firmly with the minimum of interference with the lesson but without constant nagging and checking on minor issues (e.g., Kounin, 1970; Brophy and Evertson, 1976; Rutter et al., 1979).

In the inner London study of secondary schools (Rutter et al., 1979), the use of *unofficial* physical sanctions (slapping and cuffing pupils) was associated with worse pupil behavior, but the association for *official* corporal punishment, although in the same direction, fell just short of statistical significance. On the other hand, Clegg and Megson (1968) and Reynolds and Murgatroyd (1977) found that high rates of corporal punishment were associated with more delinquency and poorer attendance. Heal (1978) found that misbehavior was worse in primary schools with formal punishment systems. Similarly, Reynolds et al. (1980) found that schools which attempted to enforce control over many minor aspects of pupil behavior tended to have more truancy.

It appears, then, that efficient methods of discipline are important but that excessive use of punishment may aggravate disruptive behavior and poor attendance by creating a tense, negative atmosphere. Some use of sanctions and punishment is necessary, but in the long run good discipline is achieved by the majority of pupils *wanting* to participate in the educational process rather than doing so merely through fear of retribution.

Several other findings also point to the probable importance of this feature. Rutter et al. (1979) found that schools with better pupil outcomes were characterized by greater use of praise for good work during lessons and more frequent public praise for individual children in assemblies or other meetings. Brookover et al. (1979) found the same but also noted the more *discriminating* use of praise and disapproval in successful schools. Rutter et al.'s (1979) findings also indicated that a pleasant and comfortable school environment was associated with better outcomes. Several issues appear relevant here. Praise and encouragement are necessary, first of all, as a means of feedback to pupils on what is and is not acceptable behavior and achievement. But also, they are important in setting the emotional tone of the school and hence in influencing pupil morale. Many studies have shown that people with a positive view of their own worth tend to be more achieving and that people's self-esteem is much influenced by the manner in which they are treated by others (Helmreich, 1972). Moreover, studies of institutions other than schools indicate that people work and behave better when they are well looked after and feel that those in charge understand and respond to their personal needs (Kahn and Katz, 1960; Sinclair, 1971).

Perhaps, care of the school buildings warrants special mention in this connection. When financial resources are limited, there is often a feeling that it is better to give up the repair, maintenance, and decoration of the buildings rather than sacrifice any other aspect of education. However, the empirical findings suggest that this may be unwise. Rutter et al. (1979) found that pupil outcomes were better in schools which were kept in good order and in good decorative condition, with broken furniture rapidly repaired and graffiti quickly removed. Pablant and Baxter (1975) found much the same. Two mechanisms seem operative here. Firstly, intervention research in hospitals and other institutions (see, e.g., Holahan and Saegert, 1973) has shown that people's morale and behavior generally tend to improve when the environment is upgraded. Secondly, several studies have shown that neglected buildings are particularly prone to vandalism (see Rutter, 1979).

In addition, it may be that there is a modelling effect such that pupils are more likely to respect school property if, through good maintenance, it is shown that the staff do too. Certainly, it is clear from Clegg and Megson's (1968) case study and Rutter et al's (1979) quantitative investigation that better time keeping by *staff* is associated with better attendance by *pupils*. The finding that pupil behavior is worse in schools where teachers respond (illegally) to provocation and disruption by hitting students or pushing them around (Rutter et al., 1979) may also reflect the effect of adverse models of behavior provided by teachers.

Pupil Participation and Responsibility

The point was made above that in the long run good pupil outcomes were likely to be dependent on pupils *wanting* to participate in the educational process. It was suggested that this could be encouraged by providing good working conditions, a pleasant and positive atmosphere, an expectation that the children could and would succeed, and by effective and interesting teaching. Another aspect of school life which may be important in this connection is the extent of children's opportunities to take responsibility and to participate in the running of their school lives (as by holding posts of prefect or class officer or by taking an active role involving responsibility in other school activities). Several studies have shown that outcomes tend to be better when such opportunities are widespread throughout the school such that the majority of pupils can participate in some way (Ainsworth and Batten, 1974; Reynolds and Murgatroyd, 1977; Rutter et al., 1979). The findings from the Rutter et al. (1979) study also suggested that shared out-of-school activities between staff and pupils may be helpful. As in other organizations (see Lieberman, 1956; Kuhn, 1964), the more that pupils can achieve satisfaction in taking roles of responsibility within the educational system, the more they are likely to identify with that system's objectives.

Of course, it would be naive to suppose that the views of teachers and of pupils could ever be identical (any more than the attitudes of factory workers and managers can be the same—Dubin, 1962; Vroom, 1969). Some conflict is intrinsic in the situation itself. Nevertheless, the range of conflict issues can be reduced and their management undertaken in a more harmonious atmosphere by the steps mentioned.

It might also be supposed that good relationships between staff and parents should be helpful in this connection. Unfortunately, few data on this point are available. Reynolds et al. (1980) found that pupil attendance was better in schools in which a high proportion of parents visited the school regularly; but Brookover et al. (1979) found that high parental involvement was associated with poor achievement in white schools, although it correlated with good achievement in black schools. Neither study examined the *quality* of parent-staff relationships (which may not be reflected in the *frequency* of parent visits to the school). Until the findings are clarified, there can be no clear policy implications.

Staff Organization

The school process variables considered so far have been concerned with features of school practice that are associated with better pupil outcomes. However, given that we have a notion of some of the factors which make for effective schooling, there is the further question of what types of staff organizations are most likely to facilitate the implementation of appropriate change (when that is needed) or the maintenance of good practice (when that is the case). Few empirical data on this point are available. Rutter et al. (1979) found that pupil outcomes were better when both the curriculum and approaches to discipline were agreed upon and supported by the staff acting together—suggesting the importance of some kind of schoolwide set of values and norms of behavior. This was also reflected in the finding that in the more successful schools, teachers reported that their senior colleagues checked on their maintenance of agreed-upon policies. It was also implicit in the finding that pupil success was greater in schools with leadership and decision making at a senior level combined with a decision-making process in which all teachers felt that their views were represented and seriously considered.

However, these variables provide a most inadequate picture of the elements needed for effective leadership. Presumably, there must be some kind of long-term strategy together with a knowledge of *how* to bring the changes about and how to choose the most appropriate order and sequence of actions needed to make the implementations of change a success. Presumably, too, there are managerial approaches which serve to facilitate changes and which make it more likely that the staff will work together successfully and harmoniously to undertake the tasks needed. However, so far, studies of school effectiveness have not provided evidence on these matters (the broader literature on managerial styles is beyond the scope of this review).

School or Classroom Effect

Throughout this paper, effects have been discussed in terms of "schools," with the implication that a whole school constitutes a meaningful entity. Of course, this is not to suggest that this is the only, or even the most important, unit of analysis. To the contrary, there is evidence that individual teachers and particular classes (Bennett, 1978; Brophy, 1979a and b; Good, 1979; Pedersen et al., 1978) can have important effects which differentiate them from other teachers and classes operating within the same school. Moreover, it is apparent in the research findings discussed above that some of the school effects act through what is done by individual teachers in terms of classroom management or pupil discipline. To that extent, school effects may be thought of as just the sum of separate teacher or classroom effects.

However, there are several findings which make it clear that that constitutes an inadequate concept. Thus, as discussed above, several studies have found large and significant differences between schools in pupil success, differences which existed above and beyond variations *within* schools. This implies that there were schoolwide influences which served to make it more (or less) likely that individual teachers would conduct their classes in an effective manner or which operated outside the classroom. In fact, the evidence indicates that both occur. The former is suggested by the observation that some schools have a much higher proportion of classrooms where effective management techniques are being employed. The overall institutional effect which extends beyond the classroom and beyond direct teacher-pupil interactions is suggested by three different observations in the Rutter et al. (1979) study. Firstly, most of the school variables had only an indirect connection with the outcome measures with which they were statistically associated. For example, of the list of school features that correlated with attendance, most did not involve any kind of teacher or school response to absconding or truanting as such. Secondly, it seemed that the *same* teacher actions sometimes led to quite *different* results in different schools. For example, if children were left alone in lessons to get on with their own work, in some schools they did just that. In others any direct relaxation of control led to an increase in disruptive behavior. It appeared that there was something about the ways in which the children were dealt with in general which influenced their behavior even when there was no direct supervision by staff. Thirdly, many school variables which correlated with pupil success did not refer to actions which bore directly on individual children. For example, some were concerned with the maintenance and decor of school buildings, and others were concerned with staff punctuality. In addition, some variables, although they affected individuals, did so in ways which extended well beyond the classroom. This applied, for instance, to the extent to which pupils were given positions of responsibility in the school or were expected to care for their own resources. It is also relevant that measures of teacher attitudes and style in other studies show some consistency across schools—suggesting that the classroom ethos is influenced by school norms as well as by teacher characteristics (Revans, 1965, 1982).

This evidence, plus the rich observations stemming from the case studies of individual schools (e.g., Brookover et al., 1979; Weber, 1971), strongly suggests that it is meaningful to speak of the ethos of the school as a whole (while still recognizing marked variations between teachers and between classrooms within any single school). As Goodlad (1975) put it, schools are social systems with responsibility and capability for their own self-improvement. Insofar as that is the case, there is a need to focus on schoolwide measures which may facilitate more effective teaching and learning and on the qualities which make for a successful social organization.

Ethos and Pedagogy

In that connection, this paper has largely focused on measures and variables which refer to the management of social groups—either in terms of the classroom or the school as a whole. The empirical research findings discussed above clearly indicate that these variables are indeed associated with the likelihood of pupils achieving success in the various different aspects of schooling and in particular with levels of scholastic achievement. In part, this seems to be because the overall functioning of the school as a social organization affects pupil attendance, behavior, and attitudes to learning and to the educational process as a whole. If children are to learn from their teachers, they need to attend school regularly and to pay attention in class. However, it is obvious that good attendance and behavior are not sufficient in themselves. The measures outlined in this paper have been concerned with school features which serve to make it easier for staff to teach well and for pupils to profit from that teaching. But what and how much is actually learned will depend on both the curriculum and the pedagogic skills employed by the teacher. These topics are beyond the scope of this review, but it is clear that they constitute the essential elements in successful schooling, which are allowed to have their optimal impact through the school ethos variables considered here.

NOTES

1. The Madaus et al. (1979) study is interesting in this connection in that it constitutes the sole study to show greater school effects than family effects. The authors suggest that this unex-

pected result was a consequence of sample attrition (over 40% loss) resulting in a sample of pupils from rather homogeneous family backgrounds.

2. There is also the possibility that the presence of the observer may alter the patterns of classroom behavior. But this is not usually a major problem in comparisons between schools in that the effects of the observer tend to be rather similar in all schools.

3. But using analyses of variance and log linear analyses in preference to multiple regression analyses. An earlier report (Rutter, 1977) had also employed standardization techniques. All the different statistical techniques for taking into account intake characteristics in this, and in other studies, have been consistent in showing major variations between schools in outcome.

4. Although there has been an informative anecdotal account of the changes in one school following the appointment of a new principal (Clegg and Megson, 1968) and a useful description of a group of schools working together to improve their levels of functioning (Culver and Hoban, 1973; Goodlad, 1975).

5. Studies of nursery school classrooms, too, indicate that, within reasonable limits, spatial density has only a modest effect on children's behavior, although competition for scarce play materials has a greater impact (Gump, 1980).

6. Usually, other things are not equal when considering size. Thus, it is easier in larger schools to ensure that there is an adequate range of courses to provide for the needs of both the educationally handicapped and the scholastically advanced.

7. Of course, academic emphasis should not be regarded as synonymous with structure and direct instructions. Other evidence suggests that highly structured direct teaching is most effective in the transmission of factual information but that more flexible, exploratory approaches involving pupil participation may be more effective in helping children develop ideas, concepts, and modes of self-expression (see, e.g., Brophy, 1979 a and b; Good, 1979; Miller and Dyer, 1975; Stallings, 1975). The debates on whether "open classrooms" are better than traditional approaches (see Horwitz, 1979) or on whether "formal" methods are preferable to "informal" methods (Aitken, Bennett, and Hasketh, 1981; Bennett, 1976; Gray and Satterley, 1981) are probably misplaced. Neither system has an overall superiority but both include elements of good practice. The ways in which academic emphasis is translated into particular pedagogic practice will necessarily depend on many variables including the subject being taught, the specific educational goals, and probably the age of the pupils.

8. This observation may well have implications for how the mainstreaming of handicapped pupils is carried out. Many handicapped pupils cope perfectly well with large group teaching and they provide no problem in integration. Similarly, others with more severe or more complex multiple handicaps can be integrated into regular schools by their being placed in tutorial groups that allow individualized teaching. However, what could be damaging to both the handicapped child and to other normal children in the class is to place a child needing individualized teaching in a large group where class-based approaches are being employed.

REFERENCES

Acland, H. Social determinants of educational achievement: An evaluation and criticism of research. Ph. D. Thesis, University of Oxford, 1973.

Acton, T. A. Educational criteria of success: Some problems in the work of Rutter, Maughan, Mortimore, and Ouston. *Educational Research*, 1980, 22, 163–169.

Ainsworth, M. E. and Batten, E. J. *The effects of environmental factors on secondary educational attainment in Manchester: A Plowden follow-up.* London: Macmillan, 1974.

Aitken, M., Bennett, S. N. and Hasketh, J. Teaching styles and pupil progress: A re-analysis. *British Journal of Educational Psychology*, 1981, 51, 170–186.

Anderson, L., Evertson, C. and Brophy, J. An experimental study of effective teaching in first grade reading groups. *Elementary School Journal*, 1979, 79, 193–233.

Averch, H. A., Carroll, S. J., Donaldson, T. S., Kiesling, H. J. and Pincus, J. *How effective is schooling? A critical review and synthesis of research findings*. Santa Monica, Calif.: Rand Corporation, 1972.

Barker, R. G. and Gump, P. V. *Big school, small school*. Stanford, California: Stanford University Press, 1964.

Barnes, J. H. and Lucas, H. Positive discrimination in education: Individuals, groups and institutions. In T. Leggatt (ed.), *Sociological theory and survey research*. London: Sage, 1974.

Bennett, S. N. *Teaching styles and pupil progress*. London: Open Books, 1976.

Bennett, S. N. Recent research on teaching: A dream, a belief and a model. *British Journal of Educational Psychology*, 1978, *48*, 127–147.

Bernstein, B. Education cannot compensate for society. *New Society*, 1970, *387*, 344–347.

Black, Sir D. (Chairman). *Inequalities in health*. London: Department of Health and Social Security, 1980.

Bowles, S. Unequal education and the reproduction of the social division of labor. *Review of Radical Political Economics*, 1971, *3*. Reprinted in Karabel, J. and Halsey, A. H. (eds.), *Power and ideology in education*. New York: Oxford University Press, 1977.

Brimer, A., Madaus, G. F., Chapman, B., Kellaghan, T. and Wood, R. *Source of differences in school achievement*. Slough, Bucks.: NFER, 1978.

Bronfenbrenner, U. *Is early intervention effective? A report on the longitudinal evaluations of pre-school programmes*. Washington, D.C.: Office of Child Development, U.S. Department of Health, Education, and Welfare, 1974.

Brookover, W., Beady, C., Flood, P., Schweitzer, J. and Wisenbaker, J. *School social systems and student achievement: Schools can make a difference*. New York: Praeger, 1979.

Brophy, J. Teacher behavior and its effects. *Journal of Educational Psychology*, 1979a, *71*, 733–750.

Brophy, J. E. *Advances in teacher effectiveness research*. Institute for Research on Teaching Occasional Paper No. 18. East Lansing, Mich.: Michigan State University, 1979b.

Brophy, J. and Evertson, C. M. *Learning from teaching*. Boston: Allyn & Bacon, 1976.

Brophy, J. and Putnam, J. Classroom management in the elementary grades. In D. Duke (ed.), *Classroom management*. The 78th Yearbook of the National Society for the Study of Education, Part II. Chicago: University of Chicago Press, 1979.

Clegg, A. and Megson, B. *Children in distress*. Harmondsworth, Middx.: Penguin Books, 1968.

Coleman, J. S. et al. *Equality of educational opportunity*. Washington, D.C.: U.S. Government Printing Office, 1966.

Copperman, P. *The literacy hoax: The decline of reading, writing and learning in the public schools and what we can do about it*. New York: Wm Morrow, 1978.

Culver, C. M. and Hoban, G. J. (eds.). *The power to change: Issues for the innovative educator*. New York: McGraw-Hill, 1973.

Dale, R. R. *Mixed or single-sex school? Vol. III: Attainment, attitudes and overview*. New York: Humanities Press; London: Routledge and Kegan Paul, 1974.

Darlington, R. B., Royce, J. M., Snipper, A. S., Murray, H. W. and Lazar, I. Preschool program and later school competence of children from low income families. *Science*, 1980, *208*, 202–204.

Davie, R., Butler, N. and Goldstein, H. *From birth to seven: A report of the National Child Development Study*. London: Longman, 1972.

Deal, T. E. and Nolan, R. R. *Alternative schools: Ideologies, realities, guidelines*. Chicago: Nelson-Hall, 1978.

De Groot, A. D. War and the intelligence of youth. *Journal of Abnormal & Social Psychology*, 1951, *46*, 596–597.

Department of Health and Social Security. *The family in society: Preparation for parenthood*. London: Her Majesty's Stationery Office, 1974.

Douglas, J. W. B., Ross, J. M. and Simpson, H. R. *All our future: A longitudinal study of secondary education*. London: Peter Davies, 1968.

Dubin, R. Industrial workers' worlds: A study of the "central life interests" of industrial work-ers. In A. M. Rose (ed.), *Human behaviour and Social processes: An interactionist approach.* London: Routledge and Kegan Paul, 1962.

Duke, D. L. *The retransformation of the school: The emergence of contemporary alternative schools in the United States.* Chicago: Nelson-Hall, 1978.

Ebmeier, H. and Good, T. The effects of instructing teachers about good teaching on the mathematics achievement of fourth-grade students. *American Educational Research Jour-nal,* 1979, *16,* 1–16.

Edmonds, R. Some schools work and more can. *Social Policy,* 1979, *9,* 28–32.

Educational Research Service. *Class size: A summary of research.* Arlington, Va.: Educational Research Service, 1978.

Educational Research Service. *Class size research: A critique of recent meta-analyses.* Arlington, Va.: Educational Research Service, 1980.

Eigerman, H. School education and social equality. *Review of Education,* 1980, *6,* 187–201.

Finlayson, D. F. and Loughran, J. L. Pupils' perceptions in high and low delinquency schools. *Educational Research,* 1976, *18,* 138–145.

Galloway, D. Size of school, socio-economic hardship, suspension rates and persistent unjus-tified absence from school. *British Journal of Educational Psychology,* 1976, *46,* 40–47.

Garbarino, J. Some thoughts on school size and its effects on adolescent development. *Journal of Youth and Adolescence,* 1980, *9,* 19–31.

Gath, D., Cooper, B., Gattoni, F. and Rockett, D. *Child guidance and delinquency in a Lon-don borough.* Maudsley Monographs No. 24. London: Oxford University Press, 1977.

Glass, G. V and Smith, M. L. *Meta-analysis of research on the relationship of class size and achievement.* San Francisco, Calif.: Far West Laboratory for Educational Research and Development, 1978.

Goldman, N. A socio-psychological study of school vandalism. *Crime and Delinquency,* 1961, *7,* 221–230.

Good, T. Teacher effectiveness in the elementary school: What do we know about it now? *Jour-nal of Teacher Education,* 1979, *30,* 52–64.

Good, T. and Grouws, D. The Missouri mathematics effectiveness project: An experimental study in fourth grade classrooms. *Journal of Educational Psychology,* 1979, *71,* 355–362.

Goodlad, J. I. *The dynamics of educational change: Towards responsive schools.* New York: McGraw-Hill, 1975.

Gray, G. Paper in preparation. 1982.

Gray, G., Smith, A. and Rutter, M. School attendance and the first year of employment. In L. Hersov and I. Berg (eds.), *Out of school: Modern perspectives in truancy and school refusal.* Chichester: Wiley, 1980, p. 343–370.

Gray, J. and Satterly, D. Formal or informal? A reassessment of the British evidence. *British Journal of Educational Psychology,* 1981, *51,* 187–196.

Gump, P. V. The school as a social situation. *Annual Review of Psychology,* 1980, *31,* 553–582.

Hallinan, M. T. Structural effects on children's friendships and cliques. *Social Psychology Quarterly,* 1979, *42,* 43–54.

Halsey, A. H., Heath, A. F. and Ridge, J. M. *Origins and destinations: Family, class and education in modern Britain.* Oxford: Clarendon Press, 1980.

Hargreaves, D. N. *Social relations in a secondary school.* London: Routledge and Kegan Paul, 1967.

Harman, D. and Brim, O. G. *Learning to be parents: Principles, programs and methods.* Beverly Hills: Sage Publications, 1980.

Harnqvist, K. Relative changes in intelligence from 13 to 18. *Scandinavian Journal of Psy-chology,* 1968, *9,* 50–82.

Hauser, R., Sewell, W. and Alwin, D. High school effects on achievement. In W. Sewell, R. Hauser, and D. Featherman (eds.), *School and academic achievement in American society.* New York: Academic Press, 1976.

Heal, K. H. Misbehaviour among school children. The role of the school in strategies for prevention. *Policy and Politics*, 1978, *6*, 321–333.

Heath, A. and Clifford, P. The seventy thousand hours that Rutter left out. *Oxford Review of Education*, 1980, *6*, 3–19.

Helmreich, R. Stress, self-esteem and attitudes. In B. T. King and E. McGinnies (eds.), *Attitudes, conflict and social change*. London: Academic Press, 1972.

Holahan, C. J. and Saegert, S. Behavioral and attitudinal effects of large scale variation in the physical environment of psychiatric wards. *Journal of Abnormal Psychology*, 1973, *82*, 454–462.

Horowitz, F. D. and Paden, L. Y. The effectiveness of environmental intervention programs. In B. M. Caldwell and H. N. Ricciuti (eds.), *Review of child development research, Vol. 3*. Chicago: University of Chicago Press, 1973.

Horwitz, R. A. Psychological effects of the "open classroom." *Review of Educational Research*, 1979, *49*, 71–86.

Husen, T. The influence of schooling upon IQ. *Theoria*, 1951, *17*, 61–68.

Husen, T. *The school in question: A comparative study of the school and its future in western societies*. London: Oxford University Press, 1979.

Hutchinson, D., Prosser, H. and Wedge, P. The prediction of educational failure. *Educational Studies*, 1979, *5*, 73–82.

Jencks, C. *Who gets ahead?* New York: Basic Books, 1979.

Jencks, C., Smith, M., Acland, H., Bane, M. J., Cohen, D., Gintis, H., Heyns, B. and Michelson, S. *Inequality: A reassessment of the effect of family and schooling in America*. New York: Basic Books, 1972.

Jensen, A.R. How much can we boost IQ and scholastic achievement? *Harvard Educational Review*, 1969, *39*, 1–123.

Jones, A. The school's view of persistent non-attendance. In L. A. Hersov and I. Berg (eds.), *Out of school: Modern perspectives in truancy and school refusal*. Chichester: Wiley, 1980.

Kahn, R. L. and Katz, D. Leadership practices in relation to productivity and morale. In D. Cartwright and A. Zander (eds.), *Group dynamics: Research and theory, Vol. 2.* New York: Harper & Row, 1960.

Kelly, D. H. Tracking and its impact upon self-esteem: A neglected dimension *Education*, 1975, *96*, 2–9.

Kemp, L. C. D. Environmental and other characteristics determining attainments in primary schools. *British Journal of Educational Psychology*, 1955, *25*, 67–77.

Klitgaard, R. E. and Hall, G. R. Are there unusually effective schools? *Journal of Human Resources*, 1975, *10*, 90–106.

Kounin, J. S. *Discipline and group management in classrooms*. New York: Holt, Rinehart and Winston, 1970.

Kratcoski, P. C. and Kratcoski, J. E. The balance of social status groupings within schools as an influencing variable on the frequency and character of delinquent behavior. In P. C. Friday and V. L. Steward (eds.), *Juvenile justice: international perspectives*. New York: Praeger, 1977.

Kuhn, M. H. Major trends in symbolic interacting theory in the past twenty-five years. *Sociological Quarterly*, 1964, *5*, 61–84.

Lacey, C. *Hightown Grammar: The school as a social system*. Manchester: Manchester University Press, 1970.

Lacey, C. Destreaming in a "pressured" academic environment. In J. Eggleston (ed.), *Contemporary research in the sociology of education*. London: Methuen, 1974.

Lezotte, L. W. and Passalacqua, J. *Individual school buildings* do *account for differences in measured pupil performance*. Institute for Research on Teaching Occasional Paper No. 6. East Lansing, Mich.: Michigan State University, 1978.

Lieberman, S. The effects of changes in roles on the attitudes of role occupants. *Human Relations*, 1956, *9*, 385–402.

Lightfoot, A. *Urban education in social perspective.* Chicago: Rand McNally, 1978.

Little, A., Mabey, C. and Russell, J. Do small classes help a pupil? *New Society,* 1971, *18,* 769–771.

Lunn, J. C. B. *Streaming in the primary school.* Slough, Bucks.: NFER, 1970.

McDill, E. L. and Rigsby, L. C. *Structure and process in secondary schools.* Baltimore: Johns Hopkins University Press, 1973.

Mabey, C. *Social and ethnic mix in schools and the relationship with attainment of children aged 8 and 11.* London: Centre for Environmental Studies Research Paper No. 9, 1974.

Madaus, G. F., Kellaghan, T., Rakow, E. A. and King, D. J. The sensitivity of measures of school effectiveness. *Harvard Educational Review,* 1979, *49,* 207–230.

Marjoribanks, K. Family and school environmental correlates of school related affective characteristics: An Australian study. *Journal of Social Psychology,* 1978, *106,* 181–189.

Marland, M. *The craft of the classroom: A survival guide.* London: Heinemann Educational, 1975.

Maughan, B., Mortimore, P., Ouston, J. and Rutter, M. Fifteen thousand hours: A reply to Heath and Clifford. *Oxford Review of Education,* 1980, *6,* 289–303.

Maughan, B., Ouston, J. and Rutter, M. Paper in preparation, 1982.

Miller, L. B. and Dyer, J. L. Four preschool programs: Their dimensions and effects. *Monographs of the Society for Research in Child Development,* 1975, *40,* Serial No. 162.

Mischel, W. On the interface of cognition and personality: Beyond the person-situation debate. *American Psychologist,* 1979, *34,* 740–754.

Moos, R. H. *Evaluating educational environments.* San Francisco: Jossey-Bass, 1979.

National Institute of Education. *Violent schools, safe schools. The safe school study report to the Congress.* Washington, D.C.: U.S. Department of Health, Education, and Welfare, 1978.

Pablant, P. and Baxter, J. C. Environmental correlates of school vandalism. *Journal of the American Institute of Planners,* 1975, *241,* 270–379.

Passow, A. H., Goldberg, M. and Tannenbaum, A. J. (eds.), *Education of the disadvantaged: A book of readings.* New York: Holt, Rinehart and Winston, 1967.

Pedersen, E., Faucher, T. A. and Eaton, W. W. A new perspective on the effects of first grade teachers on children's subsequent adult status. *Harvard Educational Review,* 1978, *48,* 1–31.

Plowden Report (The). *Children and their primary schools.* Central Advisory Council for Education (England). London: Her Majesty's Stationery Office, 1967.

Postlethwaite, K. and Denton, C. *Streams for the future: The long-term effects of early streaming and non-streaming. The Final Report of the Banbury Enquiry.* Banbury: Pubansco Publications, 1978.

Postlethwaite, T. H. The surveys of the International Association for the Evaluation of Educational Achievement (IEA): Implications of the IEA surveys of achievement. In A. C. Purvis and D. V. Levine (eds.), *Educational policy and international assessment.* Berkeley, Calif.: McCutchen, 1975.

Power, M. J., Alderson, M. R., Phillipson, C. M., Schoenberg, E. and Morris, J. N. Delinquent schools? *New Society,* 1967, *10,* 542–543.

Power, M. J., Benn, R. T. and Morris, J. N. Neighbourhood, school and juveniles before the courts. *British Journal of Criminology,* 1972, *12,* 111–132.

Revans, R. W. Involvement in school. *New Society,* 1965, 26 August, 9–12.

Revans, R. W. *Hospitals: Communication, choice and change.* London: Tavistock, 1972.

Revans, R. W. An assessment of adolescent attitudes. In *The origins and growth of action learning.* Collected papers. London: Chartwell Bratt, 1982, in press.

Reynolds, D., Jones, D. and St. Leger, S. Schools do make a difference. *New Society,* 1976, *37,* 223–225.

Reynolds, D., Jones, D., St. Leger, S. and Murgatroyd, S. Schools factors and truancy. In L. Hersov and I. Berg (eds.), *Out of School: Modern perspectives in truancy and school refusal.* Chichester: Wiley, 1980.

Reynolds, D. and Murgatroyd, S. The sociology of schooling and the absent pupil: The school as a factor in the generation of truancy. In H. C. M. Carroll (ed.), *Absenteeism in South Wales: Studies of pupils, their homes and their secondary schools.* Swansea: Faculty of Education, University of Swansea, 1977.

Rosenshine, B. Content, time and direct instruction. In P. Peterson and H. Walberg (eds.), *Research on teaching: Concepts, findings and implications.* Berkeley, Calif.: McCutchon, 1979.

Ross, J., Bunton, W. J., Evison, P. and Robertson, T. S. *A critical appraisal of comprehensive schooling: A research report.* Slough, Bucks.: NFER, 1972.

Rutter, M. Prospective studies to investigate behavioral change. In J. S. Strauss, H. M. Babigian and M. Roff (eds.), *The origins and course of psychopathology.* New York: Plenum, 1977.

Rutter, M. *Changing youth in a changing society.* London: Nuffield Provincial Hospitals Press, 1979; Cambridge, Mass.: Harvard University Press, 1980.

Rutter, M. Secondary school practice and pupil success. In M. Marland (ed.), *Education for the inner city.* London: Heinemann Educational, 1980.

Rutter, M. and Madge, N. *Cycles of disadvantage.* London: Heinemann Educational, 1976.

Rutter, M., Maughan, B., Mortimore, P., Ouston, J. with Smith, A. *Fifteen thousand hours: Secondary schools and their effects on children.* London: Open Books, 1979; Cambridge, Mass.: Harvard University Press, 1979.

Rutter, M., Maughan, B., Mortimore, P., Ouston, J. and Smith, A. School education and social equality: A reply to Hyman Eigerman, *Review of Education*, 1980a, *6*, 231–233.

Rutter, M., Maughan, B., Mortimore, P. and Ouston, J. Educational criteria of success: A reply to Acton. *Educational Research*, 1980b, *22*, 170–174.

Rutter, M., Yule, B., Quinton, D., Rowlands, O., Yule, W. and Berger, M. Attainment and adjustment in two geographical areas. III. Some factors accounting for area differences. *British Journal of Psychiatry*, 1975, *126*, 520–533.

St. John, N. H. *School desegregation: Outcomes for children.* New York: Wiley, 1975.

Schweinhart, L. J. and Weikart, D. P. *Young children grow up: The effects of the preschool program on youths through age 15.* Monographs of the High/Scope Educational Research Foundation No. 7, Ypsilanti, Mich.: The High/Scope Press, 1980.

Sharp, D., Cole, M. and Lave, C. Education and cognitive development: The evidence from experimental research. *Monographs of the Society for Research in Child Development*, 1979, No. 178.

Shoemaker, J. and Fraser, H. W. What principals can do: Some implications from studies of effective schooling. *Phi Delta Kappan*, 1981, *61*, 178–182.

Sinclair, I. A. C. *Hostels for probationers.* London: Her Majesty's Stationery Office, 1971.

Smith, M. L. and Glass, G. V. *Relationship of class size to classroom processes, teacher satisfaction and pupil affect: A meta-analysis.* San Francisco, Calif.: Far West Laboratory for Educational Research and Development, 1979.

Smith, P. K. and Connolly, K. J. *The ecology of preschool behaviour.* Cambridge: Cambridge University Press, 1981.

Stallings, J. Implementation and child effects of teaching practices in follow through classrooms. *Monographs of the Society for Research in Child Development*, 1975, *40*, Serial No. 163.

Stallings, J., Needels, M. and Stayrook, N. *How to change the process of teaching basic reading skills in secondary schools: Phase II and Phase III.* Palo Alto, Calif.: S.R.I. International, 1979.

Stephan, W. G. School desegregation: An evaluation of predictions made in Brown v. Board of Education. *Psychological Bulletin*, 1978, *85*, 217–238.

Stevenson, H. W., Parker, T., Wilkinson, A., Bonnevaux, B. and Gonzales, M. Schooling, environment and cognitive development: A cross-cultural study. *Monographs of the Society for Research in Child Development*, 1978, No. 175.

Summers, A. A. and Wolfe, B. L. Do schools make a difference? *American Economic Review*, 1977, *64*, 639–652.

Thornbury, R. *The changing urban school*. London: Methuen, 1978.

Tizard, J. Race and IQ: the limits of probability. *New Behaviour*, 1975, *1*, 6–9.

Townsend, P. *Poverty in the United Kingdom: A survey of household resources and standards of living*. Harmondsworth, Middx.: Penguin Books, 1979.

Vroom, V. H. Industrial social psychology. In G. Lindzey and E. Aronson (eds.), *The handbook of social psychology (second edition)*, *Vol. 5, Applied social psychology*. London: Addison-Wesley, 1969.

Weber, G. *Inner city children can be taught to read: Four successful schools*. Council for Basic Education Occasional Paper No. 18. Washington, D.C.: Council for Basic Education, 1971.

West, D. J. and Farrington, D. *Who becomes delinquent?* London: Heinemann Educational, 1973.

Wieland, G. F. (ed.), *Improving health care management: Organization development and organization change*. Ann Arbor, Mich.: Health Administration Press, 1981.

Wynne, E. A. *Looking at schools: Good, bad and indifferent*. Lexington, Mass.: D. C. Heath & Co., 1980.

CHAPTER 2

Research on Classroom Teaching

Thomas Good

INTRODUCTION

We know considerably more about classroom teaching than we did a decade ago. In 1970 the accumulated knowledge about the effects of classroom processes on student achievement was weak and contradictory. In some curriculum areas at the elementary school level, we now have more information. Within less than a decade, the literature on *basic skills* instruction in reading and mathematics in elementary school has moved from a state of confusion to a point where experimental studies can be designed upon a data base. Although classroom teaching and learning is, and is likely to remain, a problematic activity, the field has developed some important concepts that have rich application value.

Classroom research was an active and productive area in the 1970's. It is imposs-ible to do justice to this research in a few pages; hence, in writing this chapter I was encouraged by the editors to discuss a few topics comprehensively rather than to pro-vide a summary of all relevant research areas. I have chosen to emphasize teacher ex-pectation and teacher effectiveness research, because these were among the most active research areas in 1970's and both topics appear to be related to student performance. Three general goals of this chapter are: (1) to describe the teacher expectation and teacher effectiveness research performed in the 1970's and to suggest why research took the form that it did; (2) to discuss some of the problems associated with this re-search and to present some recent attempts to improve upon it; and (3) to discuss possible policy implications that are suggested by these inquiries.

Three substantive conclusions based upon the research review will be discussed in this chapter. The first is that teachers can make a measurable difference in students' learning of basic skills. Data collected in the 1970's provide convincing proof that teachers can and do make important differences in student learning. Second, low achievers can benefit from appropriate instruction, and there are now ample data to support this contention. The third conclusion is that we have gained some insight into teaching strategies and teacher beliefs which make a difference in certain instructional settings. In particular, it seems that positive but appropriate teacher expectations for student learning, good management techniques, and active teaching (teaching that pro-vides conceptual and procedural direction, frequent feedback, and opportunities for student success) are key features of instruction that promote students' mastery of basic skills. Despite some progress, much more knowledge is needed about classroom phenomena before more optimal learning environments can be designed for students across a variety of learning outcomes. Any advocacy of uniform teaching practices thus seems both premature and doomed to failure.

Social Context for Research in the 1970's

Research does not take place in a vacuum, and researchers study issues that are perceived to be important at a particular time and for which funding is available. Researchers help to define what is important, but they are also affected by definitions which others hold. Hence, it is useful to briefly characterize the social context of the 1960's that in part affected research in the 1970's.

In the early 1960's public investment and confidence in education were at an all-time high. Public enthusiasm was eroded in the mid-1960's in part because of the *initial* results of Head Start programs that appeared to present evidence that massive funding of preschool programs was not paying off in rich educational dividends. In part, this disappointment was created by the unrealistically high expectations which some social scientists had generated for these programs and also because of a lack of understanding about the complexity of the change process. Ironically, just when some insight into structuring and designing preschool programs was beginning to be achieved, research funding was substantially reduced. (For an example of recent data supporting the value of preschool programs, see Schweinhart and Weikart, 1980; Becker and Gersten, 1982).

The apparent failure of Head Start programs was soon reinforced by findings of Coleman et al. (1966). Their results led many persons to erroneously conclude that education did not affect many students' educational progress. Unfortunately, early evaluations of Head Start programs and Coleman et al.'s results did not include *observations* of individual learning settings. Thus the possibility that some programs and some teachers were making an important difference was masked by the way in which the data had been analyzed. In addition to these disappointing research results, the voices of many other educational critics were soon heard. Many books appeared in the late 1960's contending that schools did little to help students learn, particularly minority children (e.g., Jonathan Kozol's *Death at an Early Age*).

As Good, Biddle, and Brophy (1975) pointed out, it had become almost national sport in the late 1960's to criticize teachers and schooling, and there appeared to be a growing uneasiness about supporting educational endeavors with public funds. This uneasiness about adverse public reaction toward education led to much educational innovation in the late 1960's, and early 1970's. There was growing concern, and increased efforts were made to "individualize" instruction and to make schools more "humane" than they presumably had been. Ironically, most of the prescriptive plans and activities occurred in the absence of any rigorous analytic effort to describe what took place in American schooling. Schwab was writing accurately in 1969 that we had little notion about what took place in the average American classroom.

Critics were not categorically wrong about American schooling. There was (and is) much that could be improved in American classrooms. However, the call for *immediate solutions* without an adequate understanding of the problem was inappropriate, and similar forms of premature advocacy have occurred frequently at other crisis points in American education (for example, the advocation of curriculum reform following Russia's successful launching of Sputnik).

A Need for Observational Data

Although the response of many educators in the late 1960's to growing public disillusionment was to attempt major reform, many social scientists maintained a growing interest in trying to *understand* and to *describe* classrooms. This interest in *observing* classroom life was increased when Rosenthal and Jacobson published their 1968 study, *Pygmalion in the Classroom*. Although the basic design of their study and the veracity of their findings have been questioned by a number of educational critics, Rosenthal and Jacobson did much to create interest in studying teaching behavior as a possible determinant of student performance.

Impetus for studying classrooms more broadly (not simply counting the number of teacher and student behaviors that occurred in the classroom) and trying to understand the viewpoints and motivation of classroom participants, as well as their behavior, also began in the late 1960's. In particular, the books *Life in Classrooms* by Jackson and *The Complexities of an Urban Classroom* by Smith and Geoffrey did much to convince some educational researchers that detailed studies of classroom events were needed prior to the development of meaningful intervention strategies.

TEACHER EXPECTATIONS, TEACHER BEHAVIOR, AND STUDENT INFLUENCE

It is beyond the purpose of this paper to review extensively the existing literature on teacher expectation effects. There are several comprehensive reviews, and the interested reader can consult these sources (Brophy, 1982; Braun, 1976; Brophy and Good, 1974; Cooper, 1979; Cooper and Good, in press; Dusek, 1975; Rosenthal, 1974). A good portion of the research conducted in the 1970's was classroom observational research aimed at determining what teachers *do* in their interactions with high- and low-achieving students. Much of this research was organized around the model produced by Brophy and Good (1970). Their conceptual model for examining potential teacher expectation effects included the following steps: (1) the teacher expects specific behavior and achievement from particular students; (2) because of these varied expectations, the teacher behaves differently toward different students; (3) this treatment communicates to the students what behavior and achievement the teacher expects from them and affects their self-concepts, achievement motivation, and levels of aspiration; and (4) if this treatment is consistent over time and if the students do not resist or change it in some way, it will shape their achievement and behavior. High-expectation students will be led to achieve at higher levels, whereas the achievement of low-expectation students will decline; (5) with time, students' achievement and behavior will conform more and more closely to the behavior originally expected of them.

One of the major findings of this extensive literature on how teachers treat high- and low-achieving students in the classroom has been the fact that teachers *vary* greatly in their classroom behavior. There is ample research evidence to show that there are differences in teacher behavior *between* classrooms (for example, some teachers praise a great deal and other teachers praise comparatively little) and *within* classrooms (some students in a particular classroom receive more praise than do other students). The extent to which teachers differentiate in their behavior toward high- and low-achieving students has been found to represent an individual difference variable. Differences toward high and low achievers have been found in both quantitative studies (Brophy and Good, 1970; Cooper and Baron, 1977; Good, Cooper, and Blakey, 1980) and in qualitative studies (Levine and Mann, 1981; McDermott, 1976).

It is not clear whether teachers who differentiate sharply in their behavior toward highs and lows do so because of personality variables (defensiveness, rigidity), school or classroom organizational variables, or characteristics that individual pupils and groups of students bring to the classroom. Although the causes of differential interaction are not definitely established, Brophy and Good (1974) estimated that about ⅓ of the classroom teachers who have been observed in related research have shown patterns of highly differentiated behavior toward high and low achievers. Carew and Lightfoot (1979) reported that teachers who teach at the same grade level in the same school vary more on many instructional dimensions than teachers who teach in different schools. It would thus seem that at least some of the variation in teacher behavior toward high- and low-achieving students can be explained by teachers' personalities and their beliefs about instructional behavior.

Differences in Teacher Behavior Toward High- and Low-Achieving Students

Teachers have been found to differentiate their behavior toward students perceived by teachers as high achievers (highs) or low achievers (lows) in a variety of ways. Some of the replicated findings are listed below.

1. Seating slow students farther from the teacher and/or seating lows in a group.
2. Paying less attention to lows in academic situations.
3. Calling on lows less often to answer classroom questions or to make public demonstrations.
4. Waiting less time for lows to answer questions.
5. Not staying with lows in failure situations (providing clues, asking follow-up questions).
6. Criticizing lows more frequently than highs for incorrect public responses.
7. Praising lows less frequently than highs after successful public responses.
8. Praising lows more frequently than highs for marginal or inadequate public responses.
9. Providing low-achieving students with less accurate and less detailed feedback than highs.
10. Failing to provide lows with feedback about their responses more frequently than highs.
11. Demanding less work and effort from lows than from highs.
12. Interrupting the performance of low achievers more frequently than that of high achievers.

The behaviors listed above simply indicate some of the ways in which *some* teachers differentiate in their behavior toward high- and low-achieving students. They do not necessarily represent inappropriate behavior. For example, a teacher who does not call on low students frequently during public participation may still be effective if that teacher is working with low achievers privately and attempting to develop their responding skills so that they can become more active participants later in the year. A single process measure thus *cannot* be used as a sign of effective or ineffective communication. The desirability of a particular teaching behavior depends in part upon the teacher's total instructional plan, the content being taught, and the characteristics of individual students.

Although it is important not to overinterpret differences in teacher behavior that highs and lows receive in the classroom, it is important to question the need for differential treatment when it is identified. Allington (in press) argues that students in low-reading groups often learn less because teachers believe these students have unique needs. He argues that if students in the low group were taught more like students in the high group, they would perform more appropriately. Allington raises a number of questions about the needs of students in high- and low-reading groups, and an examination of his work should challenge teachers and policymakers to consider more fully the assumptions they hold about *how* to instruct students in high- and low-reading groups.

Teacher Expectations and Student Achievement

Most of the research on teacher expectations conducted in the 1970's was correlational in nature and simply examined differences in teacher interaction patterns with high- and low-achieving students. There is thus no firm basis for arguing that certain patterns of teacher behavior *cause* higher (or lower) student performance. Because these studies are correlational, it could be argued that teachers held higher expectations in some instances because students were achieving at higher levels (West and Anderson, 1976). Still, there are consistent data to illustrate that positive teacher expectations are associated with student achievement gains.

McDonald and Elias (1976), in a large study of teacher effectiveness, found a positive relationship between teacher expectations and student achievement. Similarly, Brophy and Evertson (1976) found that teachers who were obtaining the highest achievement from students were teachers who perceived students as capable of learning schoolwork and who viewed themselves as competent in teaching the curriculum. Studies of school effects have found that teachers in high-achievement schools, in contrast to those in less effective schools, appear to believe that students can and will learn (Brookover et al., 1978; Edmonds, 1979; Rutter et al., 1979).

Other research has also demonstrated the *plausibility* of teacher expectation effects. Mary Martin and Sam Kerman sensitized teachers who taught in inner-city schools in Los Angeles to potential ways in which low expectations might be communicated by using the dyadic classroom observation system and related research presented in the book *Looking in Classrooms* (Good and Brophy, 1973). They also helped teachers to develop communication skills for interacting with low-achieving students in effective ways. Their results showed that after training, experimental teachers were able to elicit better student achievement and more favorable attitudes than were control teachers (Martin, 1973). In addition to the expectation training, teachers also had the opportunity to observe other teachers and to be observed themselves by other teachers. The achievement and attitude growth of students in the experimental classes was thus probably due to an increased repertoire of teaching skills as well as to higher expectations. Still, it seems plausible that teachers' increased confidence in their ability to work with low achievers was at least a partial determinant of pupil achievement. Although the data base is not complete, in all naturalistic studies attempting to relate teacher expectations with student achievement, positive correlations have been obtained.

Teaching Dilemma

Clearly, teachers can expect *too much* or *too little* in their instructional interactions with students. This dilemma also has to be addressed by curriculum specialists who write textbooks and by policymakers. There is research evidence that teachers can and do err in making assignments too easy or too difficult. However, in general, existing evidence suggests that teachers are more likely to expect too little from students that they perceive as having limited ability. Inappropriately low performance expectations are often associated with good teacher intentions, but such expectations still have harmful effects. As a case in point, in an analysis of social studies materials, Bob Germain (personal communication) has found instances of too much structure and direction. He found that textbooks were giving cues to poor readers about where they could find the answers to questions that appeared at the end of the chapter. The cues embedded in the text materials were probably provided to help slow readers (in order not to overwhelm them). However, the practical effect appeared to encourage less reading and less thinking.

I recently observed a similar attempt by a reading teacher to provide appropriate structure (which turned out to be inappropriate) and help for students in a low-reading group. The teacher made an out-of-class assignment for all students. The high-reading group was to read a book and then to prepare a 10- to 15-minute oral report for class presentation. In contrast, low achievers were asked to prepare a bulletin board illustration for material that they had already read in class. High achievers were asked to read an extra book and were provided with practice in oral communication. Students in the low-reading group were simply doing a mechanical task on a story that they had already read. Although the assignment appeared to be made so as not to overwhelm low readers, it actually provided even fewer opportunities for low-achieving students to practice reading skills.

Explanations for Differential Teacher Behavior

Why is it that some teachers differentiate in their behavior toward high- and low-achieving students in ways that seem inappropriate? One basic reason is that classrooms are very busy and complex environments and it is difficult for teachers to maintain an accurate assessment of the frequency and quality of their interactions with individual students. Philip Jackson (1968) has suggested that elementary school teachers have over 1000 interpersonal exchanges a day. Thus, teachers may interact more or less frequently with certain students because of the speed and complexity with which classroom life unfolds.

A second explanation involves the fact that much classroom behavior has to be *interpreted* before it has meaning. Teachers have to react quickly to student behavior in ongoing classroom settings. When a teacher asks a question and a student raises an eyebrow and makes no response, the teacher has to interpret the student's lack of response and raised eyebrow. Does the raised eyebrow mean that the student is thinking about the response (and hence, the teacher should allow the student more time to respond), or does it mean that the student is hopelessly lost? Some research (for example, a recent ethnographic study by Kathryn Anderson-Levitt, 1981) suggests that teachers may systematically interpret cues in ways that are consistent with their initial expectations. Once a teacher develops an expectation that a student is not capable of learning, the teacher interprets subsequent ambiguous classroom events (and many classroom behaviors are ambiguous) in a way consistent with that original expectation (Good, 1980).

A third reason why teachers show more or less variation in their behavior toward high- and low-achieving students involves the issue of *causality*. Some teachers believe that they can and will influence student learning (for example, see Brophy and Evertson, 1976). Such teachers may interpret student failure as the need for more instruction, more clarification, and eventually, increased opportunity to learn. Other teachers, because they assign blame rather than assume partial responsibility for student failure, may interpret failure as the need to provide less challenge and less opportunity to learn.

Another explanation for differential teacher behavior is student behavior. Students present themselves in different ways to teachers and these self-presentation styles may influence teacher responses. Dee Spencer-Hall (1981) has noted that some students are able to *time* their misbehavior in such a way as to escape teacher attention, whereas other students who misbehave at comparable rates are reprimanded considerably more frequently because the timing of their misbehavior is inappropriate. Similarly, Carrasco (1979) suggests that students may demonstrate competence in a style that escapes teacher attention.

Metz (1978) provides another illustration of how students may influence teacher behavior. She reports that students in low-track junior high classrooms like to do seatwork and dislike public interaction and classroom lecture. In part, low achievers prefer seatwork (and encourage teachers to assign more seatwork) because it presents less *risk* to them. Finally, McDermott (1976) found that in one classroom low achievers received less reading practice because they were interrupted frequently by other students during reading instruction. The interruptions were partly due to the fact that the low achievers' behavior during reading group allowed other students to interrupt them. Hence, students appear to be an active part of the expectancy cycle. The overt behavior of some students encourages and reinforces teaching effort, whereas the overt behavior of other students discourages teaching.

I have discussed several reasons why teachers may behave differently toward high- and low-acheiving students: the *complexity* of the classroom; the *ambiguous* nature of student performance; teachers' beliefs about *causality* (their ability to cause or to influence student performance); and *students' behavior*. Obviously, these are dynamic influences and they often occur in combination. For example, in ongoing work, Confrey and Good have noted that in one class students were placed into either a high- or low-mathematics group on the basis of their teachers' *interpretation* of the students' performance during the first weeks of mathematics class. The assignment of students to the high group was based in part upon the *speed* with which they were performing mathematics tasks.

Ironically, during a week of observation, students in the low group often watched what the teacher was doing in the high group and in interview sessions they indicated that they observed the highs because they wanted to get a step ahead and learn what the high group was learning. Unfortunately, because the teacher was interested in speed of performance and because lows spent *time* watching the other group rather than doing their own seatwork, their incomplete seatwork assignments reinforced the teacher's original expectations and supported the belief that the assignment into high and low groups was correct. Students' interpretations of their classroom roles and their behavior influenced teacher behavior.

This discussion is in no way intended to criticize teachers. The author feels that most teachers are sincere professionals trying to do the best they can under difficult circumstances. Indeed, in contrast to the literature of the 1950's and 1960's which often depicted teachers in pejorative ways, most classroom research in the 1970's—having utilized an *observational* framework (whether from an ethnographic or quantitative perspective)—has consistently produced basically positive views of classroom teachers as they deal with the complex tasks that confront them (Good, Biddle, and Brophy, 1975; Mehan, 1979; Metz, 1978). The hypothetical model presented above simply suggests that classrooms are complex environments and that motivated teachers need ways to help them deal with the complexities of teaching. Available data suggest that teachers are willing and interested in learning more about their classroom behavior and will attempt to change and improve it when they are presented with plausible, understandable information about their behavior (see, for example, Carrasco, 1979; Good and Brophy, 1974; Good and Brophy, 1978).

Variability in Teacher Behavior Toward "Low" Students

As noted above, teachers show individual differences in the ways they interact with low-achieving students, and these differences are sometimes very dramatic. Some teachers criticize low achievers more frequently than highs per incorrect answer and praise lows less per correct answer. However, in other classrooms teachers praise marginal or incorrect answers given by low achievers. Good and Brophy (1980) contend that these findings reflect two different types of teachers. Teachers who reward marginal answers are unnecessarily protective of lows. Teachers who criticize lows for incorrect responses seem to be basically intolerant of these pupils and unwilling to deal with failure (and perhaps unwilling to examine their role in the failure process). Both types of teacher behavior will convey to students the idea that effort and class performances are not related. However, such differences in teacher behavior may create *interpretation* difficulties for low achievers and make it difficult for them to understand what is expected of them in their student role (Good, 1981). Consider the implications of variable teacher behavior for a third grade low-achieving student who is called upon frequently and finds teacher acceptance for virtually any verbalization. Upon moving to the fourth grade, however, the student finds that he/she is seldom called upon, seldom praised, and is criticized more frequently than other students. Such discontinuities in teacher expectations and behavior may reduce student effort and, in time, contribute to a *passive* learning style (What is expected of me?). It seems unfortunate that students who have *least adaptive capacity* may be asked to make the *greatest adjustment* as they move from classroom to classroom. It seems probable that low-achieving students receive more varied behavior because teachers agree less about how to respond to students *who do not learn* than about how to react to successful learning experiences (i.e., some teachers react to a poor performance by ignoring it, others by criticizing it, and yet others react to poor performance with gratuitous praise).

It has also been argued (Good, 1981) that within a school year low achievers may be asked to adjust to more varied behavior than high-achieving students. This suggestion is based upon the fact that many low achievers have different teachers in addition to their regular classroom teacher, for example, remedial math, reading, or speech teachers. Although there are no detailed reports on how remedial teachers differ in their instructional behavior from regular classroom teachers (if indeed they do), multiple teachers increase the chances for students to encounter different expectations and different instructional behaviors.

Unfortunately, we have little research evidence directly examining the behavior that a student receives as he/she moves into a different grade or the consistency between the behavior of regular classroom teachers and remedial teachers. However, indirect evidence suggests that for some students great discontinuities in behavioral performance expectations exist as they move from classroom to classroom or from school to school. These differences in role expectations may make it difficult for students to understand what is expected of them and, indeed, may lead to student uncertainty about the value of a particular subject matter, because teachers have different beliefs about the importance of that same subject or the way in which the subject should be taught. Some of the potential transitional problems that face students as they move from the elementary school to intermediate schools are being addressed by Betty Ward, Bill Tikunoff, John Mergendoller, Alexis Mitman, and others in ongoing work at the Far West Lab (see, e.g., Mitman 1981).

Problems Related to Research on Teacher Expectations

Most of the existing research on teacher expectations has concerned teacher verbal behavior directed toward high- and low-achieving students. Many other aspects of teacher and student behavior could be profitably examined. Existing research has focused primarily upon teachers' performance expectations (beliefs) for individual students. It would be instructive and important to broaden subsequent research efforts to examine teachers' *preferences* and *norms* in addition to their *beliefs* about the capability of individual students (Biddle, 1979). Presumably, teachers' preferences (the extent to which they feel attachment or rejection toward individual students) and teachers' norms about how they should interact with low-achieving students may also be influential determinants of classroom behavior. However, these areas have been largely neglected (for exceptions, see Brophy, Evertson, Anderson, Baum, and Crawford, 1981; Carew and Lightfoot, 1979; Good and Brophy, 1972; Jackson et al., 1969; Levine and Mann, 1981). Comprehensive attempts to understand how teachers vary their instructional behaviors toward individual students are also. scarce. Although there is a vast literature on teacher behavior toward high- and low-achieving students, this research has largely examined teacher behavior toward high and low students generally, without looking for possible idiosyncratic influences of particular students (for an exception, see the work of Carew and Lightfoot, 1979; Levine and Mann, 1981).

Classroom Composition and Student Effects

More studies of the effects of the *composition of students* in a particular classroom need to be done. Certain combinations of students may make it more ot less difficult for teachers to interact with individual low achievers (Beckerman and Good, in press; Thelen, 1960). Teachers commonly report that some classes are much more difficult and/or enjoyable to teach than others, yet we have comparatively little information about characteristics of classes that lead teachers to respond in different ways and about how teachers' expectations for an entire class subsequently influence classroom behavior or expectations for individual students. More research emphasis needs to be placed upon how different distributions of students influence teacher behavior and whether different types of students within a classroom influence teacher expectations and beliefs about classroom instruction.

Existing research on student expectations has conceptualized teachers as the dominant source of influence and students as reactive to teachers. Some investigators have argued that the direction of causality might very well be reversed (e.g., West and

Anderson, 1976). Researchers need to study more actively the ways in which students influence teachers. Several examples of student influences upon teachers were presented earlier in this paper (McDermott, 1976; Metz, 1978; Spencer-Hall, 1981). There are other examples of how students may influence teacher behavior. Copeland (1979) has reported that when student teachers were placed in certain classrooms, they were unable to use skills that they had learned *unless* the cooperating teacher had been using the skills previously. Doyle (1980) has noted that students may attempt to control teacher behaviors that represent risk to themselves. An empirical illustration of Doyle's argument is reflected in the work by Copeland (1979) and in the work of Metz (1978) (low-achieving students pressured the teacher for more seatwork assignments).

Although student effects are real, it should be emphasized that some teachers may be effective in mediating those influences if they are aware of them and if they desire to do so. I recently observed the same teacher teaching the same subject to two different classes. The instructor had told me that his reaction to each class was completely different. He perceived one class as an easy but boring class to teach and saw the other class as an easy but enjoyable class to instruct. Students in the "enjoyable" class raised considerably more substantive questions than did the boring class. In several visits, I consistently saw students in the enjoyable class pursue their own agenda and observed many content discussions taking place in that classroom that did not occur in the other class. Despite the differences in student initiation and participation styles in the two classrooms, this particular instructor was able to reduce these differences to some extent when he *chose* to do so because he was *aware* of the student influence. Still, there were consistent pressures presented by the two classrooms which had an impact not only in terms of classroom interaction but also affected the actual curriculum content that students were exposed to. Recent studies have illustrated that student influences upon teachers are real, but we still have few conceptual systems for *describing* those effects and few explanatory mechanisms for *understanding* those influences.

Outcomes

One problem in research on teacher expectation effects has been the infrequent measurement of student progress of outcomes (changes in achievement or attitude over time). What measurement of achievement has taken place has tended to occur at the end of the year and there have been few attempts to relate specific outcomes (what students learn during a particular week) to detailed observation of a learning experience (that is, observation during the week in which learning is being measured). Typically, differential teacher behavior collected at one point in time (perhaps collected in October) has been related to student achievement scores at some distant point in time (e.g., in April). If we are to understand *how* teacher expectations and behaviors influence students and how student behavior and expectations influence teachers, we need to examine more immediate outcomes of instruction (Cooper and Good, in press).

We know very little about the effects of expectations and behavior upon immediate classroom events. Fortunately, there is a growing interest in examining this question. More careful attention to immediate classroom outcomes should lead to increased understanding of the relationship between beliefs, behavior, and achievement. Linda Anderson and her colleagues, in ongoing research at Michigan State University (Anderson, 1981), have found that many students, especially low achievers, are often left without adequate information for doing assigned seatwork.

Similar conclusions concerning the lack of attention by teachers to immediate student outcomes have been reached by Confrey and Good (in progress). They observed a secondary English class while the instructor was teaching a unit on paragraph composition. Three times the instructor emphasized that students should use personality descriptors, not physical descriptors, in writing a composition paragraph. During the lesson the instructor wrote a sample paragraph with the students on the board. In part because of the *rapid* nature of the interaction that took place during the writing of the paragraph on the board, the instructor included some physical descriptors in the paragraph. Students then had to decide whether to follow the original instructions (don't use physical descriptors) or to follow the model paragraph on the board. Unfortunately, the instructor did not monitor the work of the students, nor did he talk to individual students once they had started to write their paragraphs. A good opportunity for correcting misunderstandings was thus lost. Much could probably be learned about the influence or expectations on the instructional process if more attempts were made to understand short-term instructional outcomes.

Curriculum Research

Although there has been extensive examination of how some teachers vary their behavior toward high- and low-acheiving students, few investigations have examined the possibility that students receive different curriculum assignments. There is a great deal of anecdotal evidence to suggest that high and low achievers in the same classroom receive different curriculum assignments, yet little formal, systematic study of the possibility has taken place (for a discussion of related issues, see Keddie, 1971). Nor has the possibility that a subject area might create expectations which influence teacher and/or student behavior been studied. There is some reason to believe that this will be a fruitful and important line of inquiry. For example, Soltz (1976) has found that teaching behavior is different across curriculum areas. Individual elementary school teachers instruct differently when presenting various subject areas. Jorgenson (1978) has reported that in some classes 85% of the students were required to learn from material that was beyond their reading ability. These potential mismatches between student ability and content would appear to represent an important area of inquiry (and the Jorgenson results suggest that teachers can err on the side of expecting *too much* from students as well as too little). Future research needs to emphasize curriculum variables; however, it should be clear that I am not advocating curriculum research like that which took place in the 1950's, when the behavior and beliefs of teachers and students were ignored. Curriculum variables need to be integrated in the ongoing study of classroom process and into research that concomitantly pays attention to student and teacher beliefs.

Grouping

In the past, tracking and other forms of ability grouping have received considerable research attention. Unfortunately, during the 1970's, when investigators began to examine classroom *process*, little attention was paid to what takes place during high- and low-group instruction. Although there are some exceptions (e.g., McDermott, 1976; Weinstein, 1976; Eder, 1981), there have been few studies concerning how teachers' expectations vary toward students who have been placed in different groups. There were also few studies concerning the expectations that students hold for their own learning potential as a function of being placed into high and low groups. We need to know much more about how grouping variables affect both teacher and student beliefs and behavior. There is sufficient evidence to indicate that grouping has powerful effects upon student achievement (Webb, 1980, 1977; Weinstein, 1976), but we know little about why these effects take place (Weinstein, 1976). Recently there has been growing interest in placing students into groups and allowing them to teach one another (e.g., Johnson, 1981; Slavin, 1980; Wilkinson and Calculator, 1982). Furthermore, researchers are trying to assess how the composition of students placed into the learning group affects process (student interactions) and outcomes (learning of material). Several interesting studies have been conducted but their findings yield no firm conclusions about optimal assignment patterns (e.g., Peterson, Janicki, and Swing, 1980; Webb, 1977). If we are to promote more thoughtful and successful teaching behavior (whether teachers or students act as instructors), we need to understand much more thoroughly the consequences of placing students into groups (in particular how placement affects expectations and performance).

Comprehensive Research

For some time individual aspects of the instructional process have been studied. Some research has examined how teachers interact with high- and low-achieving students. Other research has been concerned with how teachers teach various subjects differently. Unfortunately, there has been no comprehensive research which includes teacher, content, and student variables in the same research design. The benefits of such comprehensive research will be enhanced if researchers attempt to understand the motivation which underlies the behavior of individual teachers and students. As Fenstermacher (1980a) argues, the study of what occurs in classrooms will not lead to increased understanding of classroom events *per se*.

If we are to develop more adequate understandings of strategies for dealing with low-achieving students in the classroom, we need to have increased insight concerning how teachers and students approach their learning tasks and how tasks (Doyle, 1980) and classroom structures (Bossert, 1979) influence teachers' and students' tasks.

Longitudinal Research

Most educational research focuses upon particular students and teachers at a certain time. However, both teachers and students bring a history of classroom experience to any particular instructional setting. To interpret ongoing instructional activities accurately, it seems that more attention needs to be paid to past experiences of teachers and students. It would seem that certain forms of discontinuity would be helpful and other forms of discontinuity in teacher expectations and behavior would lead to difficulty for students. Such basic information would be helpful in understanding why certain students may develop erroneous beliefs about their own ability to affect instructional outcomes and in explaining some of the misconceptions that students develop about subject matter (Confrey and Lanier, 1980; Erlwanger, 1975). That is, some students may develop the belief that a subject such as mathematics is arbitrary because their teachers utilize completely different approaches to the subject from year to year.

Similarly, more careful study of teachers' past classroom experiences may lead to more sensitive and helpful interpretations of their ongoing classroom behavior. A previous example described high-achieving students who were asked to read a book and to make an oral classroom report. Low achievers in the same class were asked to write a bulletin board description of a book that they had already read. Perhaps the differential assignment for high- and low-achieving students was based upon *past failures* that the teacher had in making appropriate and useful assignments for low achievers (they didn't read a book on their own outside of class). If educators are to encourage active teaching of low-achieving students, they need to know much more about possible failures and successes that teachers and students have experienced in the past.

POLICY IMPLICATIONS OF TEACHER EXPECTATION RESEARCH

It has been argued that teacher expectations are related to classroom performance and to student achievement. It has also been argued that we need much more research before articulate recommendations can be made. However, it would appear that its present body of knowledge does contain implications for educational policy.

Focus upon Decision-Making Skills

Observational studies of classrooms have revealed that classroom life is complex and that particular forms of interaction vary from setting to setting. Importantly, observational data suggest that the *problem* varies from classroom to classroom. Some teachers assign lows material that is too ambiguous and too difficult, but other teachers assign lows content that is too easy (this appears to be the more common problem). Some teachers spend too little time with low achievers, but other teachers appear to find appropriate time and ways of relating to students perceived as low ability. Hence, rules such as "increase the number of times 'lows' are called on and the frequency of their 'praise'" will do more harm than good (i.e., some teachers are already doing these behaviors appropriately and an increase in their behavior would have dysfunctional effects).

The variables that affect teaching and learning are numerous, complex, and interrelated. *Knowledge* related to teacher expectation effects is therefore best imparted to teachers along with judgmental and *decision-making* skills about its appropriate use rather than presenting teachers with a list of behaviors they need to perform. An important policy step would be the transformation of existing knowledge about teacher and student expectation effects into an organized curriculum (readings, *videotapes*) that begins to sensitize teachers to issues involved in forming and communicating low expectations. This curriculum would also enable teachers to develop skills for applying such knowledge in various contexts and problem situations. Such development efforts (e.g., preparing videotapes illustrating subtle expectation effects) should be carefully researched to see if training efforts do in fact provide teachers with enhanced skills for understanding and communicating effectively with students in real classrooms. Fortunately, some work encouraging teachers' use of decision-making skills generally (Amarel, 1981) and specifically in the area of teaching expectations (Good and Brophy, 1978) has been completed.

Increased Opportunity for Observation

In in-service settings, the chance for teachers to observe more frequently in other classrooms, particularly in classrooms of teachers who are teaching similar students under somewhat similar circumstances, will provide an excellent opportunity for teachers to identify more profitable ways for interacting with high- and low-achieving students. That teachers can benefit from observation has at least been partially verified by the work in the Los Angeles County School Project (Martin, 1973). In terms of creating an interest in modifying behavior, the opportunity to observe a successful classroom is quite compelling. Once teachers have the opportunity to see students responding in a manner that they heretofore felt unlikely, the more likely it is that teachers will attempt to find strategies that work for them in their own classrooms, in order to obtain similar student responses.

Efforts should also be made to improve principals' observational skills and interest in establishing peer review procedures that are for instructional development and stimulation (i.e., not evaluation). Unfortunately, despite the commonly asserted belief that one of the principal's main duties is to provide instructional leadership, most principals and many curriculum supervisors do not have the skills necessary for this task. Most principals take only limited course work in curriculum and instructional areas and have little expertise or appreciation for helping teachers to become more skillful in controlling their expectations about students or subject matter. More course work in these areas for administrators *would seem essential* if the advantages of classroom observation are to be realized.

Teacher Education

Information about ways in which teachers sometimes differ in their behavior toward high- and low-achieving students should be part of instruction in all teacher education programs. The extent to which this information is presently contained in such curricula is unknown. However, informal contact with teachers suggests that many teachers do not have formal ways for thinking about, or ways for monitoring, their interactions with different types of students. In short, they do not have a model for considering or explaining why low expectations might be communicated in the classroom.

Available evidence indirectly indicates that lows receive more varied classroom teaching behaviors than do highs. It seems plausible that part of the variation is due to the lack of teacher agreement about how to respond to student failure. Teacher education programs could play a valuable role by helping prospective teachers to understand that a degree of failure will be present in any teaching situation (learning occurs in stages and reteaching is often necessary). Programs should develop teachers' skills to allow them to interpret student failure as a challenge and should provide teachers with better-conceptualized strategies for responding to student failure.

In particular, teacher education programs need to create role definitions which specify that the teacher is there primarily to actively teach and that failure calls for reteaching rather than rationalization. Methods classes should stress *diagnosis* and remediation following failure. Teacher education programs need more emphasis upon adapting instruction after initial teaching. Too much of the orientation tends to be that learning is nonproblematic if certain methods are faithfully applied. If anything, observation of teaching shows that learning is very problematic (e.g., students interpret the same teacher behavior in different ways) and that teachers need greater tolerance and understanding in dealing with students when success is not immediate.

Instruction that encourages prospective teachers to think about the need to coordinate their beliefs (e.g., reactions to failure) and behavior (criteria for evaluating student work) is also needed. Variation in teacher beliefs and behavior may often have desirable effects on some students, especially when teachers explain the reasons for change (. . . last year different criteria were used for grading your composition papers; this year emphasis is placed upon X because . . .). However, unexplained discrepancies that exist between classrooms would appear to negatively affect in some cases students' motivation (especially low achievers). Pre-service and in-service activities should encourage teachers to develop a coordinated curriculum but should not undermine the initiative of individual classroom teachers. Serious and successful instruction involves not only the purposeful teaching of students in a given class but also building *meaningful* continuity and variety across consecutive grade levels.

Another area that remains uninvestigated is the beliefs and expectations that teachers have when they begin college and when they graduate from teacher education programs. Because the literature on teacher effectiveness was so dismal in the late 1960's, it is possible that many training programs erode teacher motivation by stressing the difficulties associated with teaching. In other institutions, graduating teachers may suffer from a different problem; they may enter classrooms with unrealistically high beliefs about their ability to motivate students.

Teaching seems to be a very tough, demanding, but doable job (Good and Brophy, 1980). Unrealistically high and unrealistically low expectations about the task of teaching and teachers' ability to influence low achievers, in particular, may have subtle effects upon teachers' subsequent classroom behavior. However, at present virtually no information exists about the expectations of beginning and graduating teachers, particularly about the expectations they hold for teaching and for improving the performance of low-achieving students. We need to more seriously assess the effects of teacher training upon prospective teachers' beliefs and expectations about their role as teachers.

Support for New Research

I believe there is sufficient data available to make teachers aware of various aspects of classroom communication that often inhibit the performance of certain students and that application of such knowledge (if done well and with a decision-making focus) could provide more interesting and efficient learning experiences for more students than is presently the case. However, I believe that we have just begun to understand the relationship between expectation and performance.

More integrative and comprehensive research is needed if we are to understand the dynamic and reciprocal effects of students, teachers, and situations. It may appear "odd" to see "more research" as a policy suggestion, because recent research suggests that teaching is an interactive process that requires teachers to react differentially to the needs and responses of individual students and that data are not sufficient for helping teachers to fully understand or to intellectually fulfill this role.

TEACHER EFFECTIVENESS RESEARCH

Concern with what teachers actually *do* in the classroom led many researchers to focus on how teachers interacted with high- and low-achieving students. An *incidental outcome* of this research was the demonstration that teachers vary greatly *across* classrooms in their behavior, as well as in how they distribute their time and resources *within* classrooms. Teachers have been found to vary widely in the type and quantity of classroom questions that they ask, in the time that they spend in presenting new material versus review, in the amount of time they spend in general recitation settings versus seatwork settings, and in how they organize classrooms for instruction (whole class, individualized, small groups). The discovery of such variations in structure and behavior led many investigators to become interested in their impact upon student achievement and behavior.

Other pressures and opportunities also directed increased attention to the effect of teaching variables upon students' subject matter mastery. The National Institute of Education's interest and systematic funding of research to study basic skill acquisition in elementary schools created an opportunity for intensive observational work. Because many educational researchers, sociologists, anthropologists, and psychologists were interested in observing and understanding classroom phenomena, support for inquiry to basic skill areas in elementary schools resulted in much research attention to this particular question. As a result of such research, it is now possible to make some statements about the effects of teacher behavior upon students' subject matter acquisition in the elementary school setting. Descriptions of substantive findings and methodological issues associated with teacher effectiveness research can be found elsewhere (Berliner, 1977; Brophy, 1979; Doyle, 1977, 1979; Good, 1979, 1982; Medley, 1979; Rosenshine, 1979; Peterson and Walberg, 1979).

Context for Teacher Effectiveness Studies

Teacher effectiveness research in the 1970's was motivated by dissatisfaction with previous research which had been conducted in laboratory settings and with field studies of teaching that included only limited observation of what actually transpired in classrooms. There was also a growing dissatisfaction with prescriptive solutions which were not based upon an understanding of existing classroom practices and constraints.

Research on teacher effectiveness proceeded without a theoretical focus, in part because researchers wanted to understand teaching as it actually took place. Although the motivation of individual researchers varied considerably, it is my belief that the atheoretical structure of recent effectiveness research took the form that it did not because researchers had no interest in theory, but because existing theory and conceptualization were quite narrow, and because of the belief that prescriptive action without more rigorous understanding of classroom phenomena would continue to be self-defeating. In general, then, most effectiveness research was motivated by two unanswered questions: (1) How could one characterize teacher and student interactions in American classrooms? and (2) Do certain forms of teacher behavior have a more positive influence on student achievement than other patterns of teacher behavior?

A Case Study

One way to illustrate the potential as well as the problems of effectiveness research is to consider in depth one specific program of research, a program on mathematics learning which Doug Grouws and I coordinated at the University of Missouri. Because it is research that I have helped to conduct, I am both very familiar with it and in some respects I am in a good position to criticize it.

Our initial research on this problem began with a sample of over 100 third- and fourth-grade teachers who taught in a middle-class, urban school district and used the same textbook. To make comparisons across teachers, it was necessary to develop an operational definition of effectiveness. In our research we used student performance on a standardized achievement test in mathematics as a way of estimating instructional progress. We realized that a standardized achievement score was not a perfect measure of classroom learning and that in some cases the test content did not overlap with the content that classroom teachers actually taught (as a case in point, see Porter et al., 1978).

We nevertheless felt that there was a reasonable consensus among teachers and standardized test developers as to what constituted the mathematics curriculum in the elementary school. However, it is important to realize that initially this was an *assumption* that we made and that by using standardized achievement results as a criterion for effectiveness, we restricted our claims for effectiveness to only those aspects of the teaching role related to producing gains on such tests. Other important teaching behaviors and student outcomes are not covered in our research (and in most other effectiveness research).

Looking at test scores over a 3-year period, we found that teachers varied considerably in their impact on students' learning, despite the fact that they were using the same textbook and in most cases were teaching comparable students (that is, the mean class achievement scores were very similar in the fall). Our initial data were a demonstration of an apparent *teacher effect*. Some teachers produced much more mathematics learning than did other teachers teaching in comparable settings.

Our focus was on observing *stable* teachers because we wanted to identify mathematics teaching strategies which appeared to make a difference in student mastery of basic skill areas. We felt that teachers who had a stable and relatively high or low level of effectiveness would be an excellent basis for estimating the relative effectiveness of different teaching behaviors. Hence, our observational research focused upon teachers who were consistently high and low across several consecutive years in their ability to produce student performance on standardized achievement tests. Interestingly, teachers who had extreme effects on achievement (very high and very low) used a large-group teaching format. Hence, format did not predict achievement. Since we were interested in observing high and low teachers, our study became an examination of large-group teaching as teachers who used individualized or small-group techniques tended (as a group) to have average effects on student achievement.

We found that stable, high and low large-group teachers differed in their classroom behavior. That is, more and less effective teachers taught in different ways, and some of these differences in teaching behavior were consistent across the two groups of teachers.

Within the constraints of our operational definition, more effective teachers, in contrast to less effective teachers, were found to (1) present information more actively and clearly in the development stage of the lesson (that part of the lesson in which teachers stress the meaning of the material); (2) be task-focused (most of the period was spent on mathematics, not socialization); (3) allow students to initiate more academic questions; (4) be basically nonevaluative and create a relatively relaxed learning environment with comparatively little praise or criticism; (5) express higher achievement expectations (more homework, somewhat faster pace, more alerting); and (6) have fewer behavioral problems.

Although we were pleased with the naturalistic findings in that they provided some clear contrasts between relatively high and low gain classrooms, we were aware of the fact that these were only correlational results and that they did not necessarily imply that these teacher behaviors *caused* student achievement. It could be that behaviors not studied in our observational research were more directly related to achievement (e.g., more effective teachers plan more thoroughly and because of this, they are more task-focused and assign more homework). We felt that it was important to determine whether a more direct association could be established between the behaviors that were identified in our observational, naturalistic study and student achievement.

In particular, we wanted to see if we could instruct teachers to behave in ways consistent with the behavior of "effective" teachers and to determine what, if any, impact such behavior would have on student achievement. Because of the expense involved in field testing the program, we wanted it to be as comprehensive as possible. Thus, in addition to including the contrasts obtained in our earlier naturalistic studies, we tested some of the promising findings from other teacher effectiveness studies, as well as results from previous experimental mathematics studies. Writing the training program resulted in a 45-page manual for teachers. The program, as pointed out elsewhere (Good and Grouws, 1979), is a system of instruction: (1) instructional activity is initiated and reviewed in the context of *meaning*; (2) students are prepared for each lesson stage to enhance involvement and to minimize errors; (3) the principles of

TABLE 2.1.   Summary of Key Instructional Behaviors*

Daily Review (First 8 minutes except Mondays)
    a. Review the concepts and skills associated with the homework.
    b. Collect and deal with homework assignments.
    c. Ask several mental computation exercises.

Development (About 20 minutes)
    a. Briefly focus on prerequisite skills and concepts.
    b. Focus on meaning and promoting student understanding by using lively explanations, demonstrations, process explanations, illustrations, etc.
    c. Assess student comprehension.
        1. Use process/product questions (active interaction).
        2. Use controlled practice.
    d. Repeat and elaborate on the meaning portion as necessary.

Seatwork (About 15 minutes)
    a. Provide uninterrupted successful practice.
    b. Maintain momentum—keep the ball rolling—get everyone involved, then sustain involvement.
    c. Use alerting—let students know their work will be checked at the end of the period.
    d. Provide accountability—check the students' work.

Homework Assignment
    a. Assign homework on a regular basis at the end of each math class except Fridays.
    b. Homework should involve about 15 minutes of work to be done at home.
    c. Homework should include one or two review problems.

Special Reviews
    a. Weekly Review/Maintenance
        1. Conduct during the first 20 minutes each Monday.
        2. Focus on skills and concepts covered during the previous week.
    b. Monthly Review/Maintenance
        1. Conduct every fourth Monday.
        2. Focus on skills and concepts covered since the last monthly review.

---

* Definitions of all terms and detailed descriptions of teaching requests are presented in Good, T., Grouws D., and Ebmeier, H., *Active mathematics teaching: Empirical Research in Elementary and Secondary Classrooms.* New York: Longman, Inc., in press.

distributed and successful practice are built into the program; (4) active teaching is demanded, especially in the developmental portion of the lesson (when the teacher explains the concept being studied, its importance, etc.). An overview of the program is presented in Table 2.1.

We tested the program in 40 classrooms: about half of the classrooms were assigned to experimental conditions, and the other half to control conditions. Experimental teachers read the manual and were given approximately 2½ hours of training. Several procedures were employed to ensure that the control group was motivated to pursue achievement gains in mathematics, and we feel that a strong control for Hawthorne[1] effects was built into the project (for details, see Good and Grouws, 1979).

One major question was whether teachers would be willing to implement the program. On the basis of observers' records, it was found that the experimental teachers implemented the program very well (with the exception of certain recommendations concerning how to handle the development portion of the lesson). Because experimental teachers did use the program, it was possible to determine how the experimental training and subsequent teaching activity influenced student achievement and attitudes.

Pre- and post-testing with the standardized achievement test indicated that after 2½ months of the program, the performance of students in experimental classrooms was considerably higher than those in control classrooms. It was also found that the experimental students' performance increase continued for at least some time following the treatment. Regular end-of-year testing by the public school system indicated that approximately 3 months after the program had ended, the experimental students were still performing better than the control students. We also constructed a content test that more closely matched the material which teachers were presenting than did the standardized test. The results on this test also showed an advantage for experimental classes, although differences between control and experimental classrooms were not as large as they were on the standardized achievement test (see Good and Grouws, 1979, for additional details and explanations).

We were also interested in knowing if the achievement gains came at the expense of student attitudes toward mathematics. Results of pre- and post-testing on a 10-item attitude scale revealed that experimental students reported significantly more favorable attitudes at the end of the experiment than did control students. Thus, the achievement gains did not appear to come at the expense of students' interest in mathematics. Finally, it is important to note that anonymous feedback from teachers in the project indicated that they felt the program was practical and that they planned to continue using it in the future. Obviously, if teachers are to continue using the program, they must feel comfortable with it.

Research elsewhere has indicated that teachers have a favorable reaction to the program even when it is presented and discussed without the involvement of the developers (Andros and Freeman, 1981; Keziah, 1980). Also, in research at the junior high level it appears that secondary teachers have implemented the program with positive impact on students' verbal problem-solving ability (Good and Grouws, 1981). Finally, it is important to note that our basic findings have been replicated by others (See Good, Grouws, and Ebmeier, in press).

Our research on mathematics instruction, especially at the elementary school level, has convinced us that teachers do make a *difference* in student learning and that in-service teachers can be trained in such a way that student performance can be increased. The system of instruction that we see as important can be broadly characterized as *active teaching*. It is instructive to note that in our experimental work active teaching was an important difference between teachers who were getting good achievement gains and those who were getting lower-than-expected gains. Teachers whose students made higher gains were much more active in presenting concepts, explaining the meanings of those concepts, providing appropriate practice activities, and monitoring those activities prior to assigning seatwork. The fact that these teachers appeared to look for ways to confirm or disconfirm that their presentations had been comprehended by students was particularly important. They assumed partial responsibility for student learning and appeared to be ready to reteach when necessary.

This difference in active teaching *across* classrooms is comparable to differences found *within* classrooms in teacher expectation research. That is, in the teacher expectation literature, there is evidence that in some classrooms low-achieving students receive less active and less meaningful teaching than high-achieving students. In our effectiveness research in mathematics we have found that some teachers are less active in teaching the *entire* classroom. Active instructional efforts seem to be an important aspect of teaching that is related to achievement gain, at least in basic skill areas.

Several other research efforts were directed at identifying teachers who were consistent in their effects, and this observational research attempted to pinpoint the ways in which more and less effective teachers differed in their classroom behavior. These results have been reviewed by several researchers. For example, Jere Brophy (1979) summarized observational studies of teacher effectiveness in the following way: "In summary, learning gains are most impressive in classrooms in which students receive a great deal of instruction from, and have a great deal of interaction with, the teacher, especially in public lessons and recitations that are briskly paced but conducted at a difficulty level that allows consistent success" (p. 747). Barak Rosenshine (1979) has argued that the following teaching acts are critical aspects of successful instruction in basic skill areas: (1) a clear focus is kept on academic goals; (2) an effort is made to promote extensive content coverage and high levels of student involvement in classroom tasks; (3) teachers set clear instructional goals and actively monitor student progress toward those goals; (4) learning activities are structured and feedback is immediate and academically oriented; and (5) environments are created that are task-oriented but relaxed.

In addition to the several naturalistic studies of more and less effective teachers, there also have been a few attempts to experimentally intervene in the teaching process to determine whether teacher behavior changes and student achievement could be increased. An especially good review of four of these field experiments has been provided by Gage and Giaconia (1980). Gage and Giaconia note that there is solid evidence which indicates that it is possible to change teaching behaviors in desired directions through relatively inexpensive in-service teacher education programs. They note that changes in teacher behavior have occurred in experiments with random assignment of schools and/or teachers to training conditions and that the results show consistent improvement in student achievement. The reviewers have also noted that these four experiments differ considerably from previous educational experiments. In particular, they were conducted in regular classrooms; the instructional treatment has operated for an extended period of time; the experiments used practicing teachers (not student teachers); and the teaching behaviors manipulated in these experiments were realistic in the sense that other teachers already had been observed exhibiting these behaviors. The experiments thus had ecological validity because they were advocating that teachers perform behaviors which other teachers had been able to exhibit in the ongoing realities of the classroom environment (Good, 1979).

Problems Associated with Teacher Effectiveness Research

Many of the problems associated with teacher effectiveness research parallel those reported earlier in the description of teacher expectation research. It would be possible to repeat most of those criticisms here, emphasizing that much more information is needed about the beliefs that teachers and students have in experimental and control classrooms. These and other criticisms of effectiveness research have been discussed elsewhere (e.g., Doyle, 1979). To illustrate some of the problems associated with this type of research, it will be useful to raise questions about the interpretability of the findings from the Missouri Mathematics Effectiveness Program.

One important consideration is that in a variety of studies using the Missouri Mathematics Program, experimental groups have done better than related control groups. However, the magnitude and importance of the differences are more evident for some teacher and student combinations than others. It is clear that certain combinations of students and teachers together tend to do better using the treatment than do other combinations of students and teachers (Ebmeier and Good, 1979). The effects of the program on some teacher-student combinations have been replicated by Janicki and Peterson (1981). It also seems that the classroom organizational structure interacts with the effects of the instructional treatment (Ebmeier, Good, and Grouws, 1980).

It should be evident that there is *no* single system for presenting mathematics concepts effectively. For example, some of the control teachers in our studies have obtained high levels of student achievement using instructional systems that differ from those presented in the program we have developed. More information about the classroom contexts and particular combinations of teachers and students that make the program more or less effective is needed.

It is satisfying to see that the instructional program we have developed seems to be a viable system which teachers are willing to implement and that it has positive influences upon student achievement. We now need to know much more about *why* some teachers employ the system more fully than do others and the types of local school features (including child characteristics and classroom structure) that lead to greater levels of implementation. In particular, it would seem necessary to study mathematics teachers who use individualized and small-group practices more successfully than do other teachers. Researchers need to study the conditions that lead to success in various organizational settings and to determine which types of students and teachers benefit from these patterns of instruction.

Longitudinal Studies

A related question is whether alternate approaches to mathematics would be more successful after students have been exposed to 2 or 3 years of instruction in our program. Different approaches to mathematics could be important (and needed) at different stages in students' development. Unfortunately, there has been no attempt to evaluate the cumulative impact of programs over time and to study the possibility that as students develop certain skills and abilities, they might benefit from different approaches to instruction. For example, one of the reasons that sustained *active teaching* (focus on meaning of content, teacher modeling) may have generally positive effects is because many teachers have become instructional managers. In time as more teachers become more active instructors, it would seem that students would have greater potential for successful peer and self-directed learning and that teaching would have to be adjusted accordingly.

Management versus Instruction

Most recent naturalistic and experimental research in elementary school settings has yielded concepts which relate to successful learning and which can be taught to classroom teachers. However, an examination of these concepts reveals that in general they provide suggestions about how to organize and manage learning systems rather than information about how to vary instruction. We have found in our own research that teachers' implementation problems occur more in the development stage of the lesson than they do in other areas (Good, Grouws, and Ebmeier, in press). Clearly, from an instructional point of view, development is the core of teaching mathematics. More data are needed about variations in teacher behavior within the development portion of the lesson and about how different approaches to this phase of the lesson affect student comprehension. Although the general instructional structure that we have tested in our program appears to relate consistently to student gains, it may very well be that different mathematics topics (fractions vs. estimation skills) are better taught with different instructional procedures. Instructional variables (and content) should more often be the focus of teacher effectiveness studies.

Limitations of Existing Practice

The model that has been used to identify successful teachers in the teacher effectiveness literature has been employed in other areas as well. For example, Krutetskii (1976) has studied how superior students learn mathematics. These and other efforts to study successful teachers and learners share at least two common problems. First, it may be that the average teacher or student cannot use those skills that are used by successful teachers and students. We do not know whether the inability of some teachers to implement the development stage of our program was due to training procedures or to some teacher characteristic (energy, clarity, beliefs about teaching practice, etc.) or student characteristics. The second problem is the obvious limitation of basing change models only on what successful teachers (or students) have been found to do. To advocate this in any rigorous fashion would be the equivalent of telling the American automobile industry to build cars only on the basis of the most successful performance characteristics available today. Some cynics might note that the American car industry has already been responding to this assumption, given its unwillingness to embrace the four-cylinder engine until recently.

Programs based upon a synthesis of what successful practitioners *do* are currently popular and have yielded important statements which have helped to develop a concrete data bank to describe normative practice in American schools. Many previous attempts to bring about innovations in American schools have suffered from a lack of knowledge about the constraints, beliefs, and realities of classroom practice. Because we are becoming somewhat more knowledgeable about what takes place in American classrooms, it may be possible to build better models of alternative instructional systems that go beyond existing practice but at the same time are informed by the limitations of conditions under which teachers must necessarily teach.

Theory

Given the paucity of information about classroom practice that existed in the late 1960's, the attempt to gain normative information about classroom practice using atheoretical approaches was probably useful. The search for dimensions of teaching that might relate to student performance was probably somewhat broader than it would have been had narrow but carefully articulated dimensions of teaching been pursued. However, I personally feel that we have now reached the point in classroom research where attempts to develop better theories and better models of instructional process are acutely needed.

As a case in point, we have evidence that the Missouri Mathematics Program in general had a positive impact upon the *mean* performance of students in experimental classrooms, but we have no data to explain why the program worked. I suspect that the program had an impact because many elementary school teachers simply do not emphasize the meaning of the mathematical concepts they present to students and they do not actively teach these concepts. Too much mathematics work in elementary schools involves a brief teacher presentation and a long period of seatwork. Such brief explanations for seatwork do not allow for meaningful and successful practice of concepts that have been *taught*, and the conditions necessary for students to discover or use principles on their own are also lacking.

It seems plausible that the emphasis in our program upon the development stage of the lesson leads teachers to think more deeply about the concepts that they are presenting and to search more actively for better ways of presenting those concepts to students. Furthermore, because of the way in which the development stage of the lesson is conducted, the program of instruction should allow teachers to see students' errors before they have a chance to practice those mistakes for a long period of time. This feature of the program seems to be especially desirable because some research has suggested that it is very difficult for students to tell teachers that they do not understand instruction. The clear development lesson would help students to understand more fully the concepts that they must master and how those concepts are related to other concepts that they have learned. The development phase of the lesson thus helps both teachers and students to develop a better rationale for learning activities and to develop a sense of continuity.

The controlled practice portion of the lesson aids both teachers and students in understanding whether the basic concepts and mechanics are being understood. This is especially the case if teachers have developed the expectation that initial teaching often is associated with less than adequate student comprehension and that student mistakes call for reteaching, not rationalization. Such information can allow teachers to correct and to reteach aspects of the lesson so that students develop appropriate conceptual understandings and skills prior to sustained practice. Also, it is hypothesized that students would be much more active thinkers during the development and controlled practice portions of the lesson. This is because students know that seatwork and their homework are intimately related to these activities. Hence, successful understanding during controlled practice leads to successful seatwork and successful homework. The checking of seatwork allows teachers one final opportunity to correct misunderstandings prior to the assignment of homework.

Following successful practice, brief homework assignments should offer students positive learning experiences that provide for both better integration of material and also the development of more appropriate student attitudes about mathematics and their ability to learn it. In particular, students will probably conclude that increased personal effort during mathematics instruction leads to positive learning experiences. Students would thus be presenting more positive feedback to teachers about mathematics instruction (e.g., handing in completed homework and exhibiting positive verbal and nonverbal behaviors during mathematics instruction, which in turn increase teachers' expectations that they can present mathematics effectively, leading to renewed efforts on their part to carefully plan and teach the mathematics lesson).

The preceding statements are only a few of the beliefs and hypotheses that we hold about *why* the mathematics program was working. It is important to note that these hypotheses need to be tested if a more adequate understanding of the antecedent conditions necessary for successful mathematics learning is to be developed. For example, research is needed to determine if in fact experimental teachers identify more student errors and can more readily understand those mistakes during the development stage than do control teachers who use different teaching techniques. It would be equally important to determine whether students in experimental classrooms are more active thinkers during the developmental portion of the lesson than are students in control classrooms (perhaps by asking students to do problems immediately after the development portion of the lesson). Similarly, more research is needed concerning the conditions under which student errors are developmentally helpful and lead to increased student effort to integrate material, rather than debilitating and convincing students that they do not understand mathematics. When teaching effectiveness researchers begin to examine their embedded assumptions by stating and testing the specific ways in which student learning is influenced, the conditions under which certain teaching and learning strategies are useful will become clearer than they are at present.

POLICY IMPLICATIONS OF TEACHER EFFECTIVENESS RESEARCH

Study of Successful Practitioners

The attempt to describe how successful teachers (within the operational definition of standardized achievement tests) influence student achievement in basic skill areas has yielded some important information which practitioners can consider in evaluating their educational goals and classroom process. The research produced to date does not provide a basis for prescriptive action, but it does provide some useful information about what classroom teachers do and some of the differences in student achievement associated with various forms of teacher classroom behavior. Such information would seem to be important content for any teacher education program.

Policy action designed to stimulate additional research on teacher effectiveness could profitably take three forms. First, to build upon the existing data base, it is important to begin testing explanatory theories, to help us to understand why recent field experiments have proved successful. Such testing may yield broader models of teaching that will further improve teaching practice.

Research needs to be designed to examine the successful practice of individualized teaching and small-group instruction. We know that some teachers obtain good results using small-group instruction, but we know virtually nothing about how teachers who obtain those gains differ from other teachers who use small instructional groups in mathematics but who do not obtain high levels of student achievement. Particular characteristics of those teachers who use those individualized techniques effectively, and the types of concepts which are most amenable to those instructional formats, need to be specified.

Policy action should also encourage research that studies practitioners who have been identified for intensive study on some basis other than their ability to produce gains on standardized achievement tests. It strikes me as curious (given the present emphasis upon problem-solving behavior) that nowhere in the literature can I find statements describing what takes place when teachers attempt to teach problem solving during mathematics instruction. How do classroom teachers define problem solving and how do they attempt to teach it? As a starting point, if one wanted to improve mathematical problem solving, it would be reasonable to determine what teachers do in this instructional area and to study those teachers who teach problem solving more effectively than other teachers.

A model which attempts to find master teachers who operate effectively in the constraints of the real world is worth examination. In many cases, it may be impossible to find teachers who consistently obtain a particular, desirable student outcome. If schools or teachers cannot affect a criterion measure, it is fruitless to attempt to find outstanding schools and individuals. Hence, the model suggested here would *not* apply to all potential outcomes of schooling.

Active Teaching

The concept of active teaching is an important aspect of effective teaching that has evolved from recent naturalistic and experimental research in the area of teacher effectiveness. Teachers who are more active in presenting information, pay attention to the meaning and conceptual development of content look for signs of student comprehension and/or confusion, and provide successful practice opportunities appear to have more achievement gains than do teachers who are less active and who rely more upon seatwork and other classroom activities. Most of this research has been focused on elementary classrooms; however, in the area of secondary mathematics there are reasonably consistent data as well (e.g., Evertson, Anderson, Anderson, and Brophy, 1980; Weber, 1978).

I use the concept of active teaching rather than the term direct instruction (which has been used to describe the pattern of behavior of teachers who obtain higher-than-expected achievement from students) because it represents a broader concept of teaching than does the existing research base. In active teaching, the initial style can be *inductive* or *deductive*, and student learning can be *self-initiated* or *teacher-initiated* (especially if thorough critique and synthesis activities follow student learning attempts). Active teaching also connotes a broader philosophical base (active teaching can occur in classrooms using a variety of classroom organizational structures), and active teaching should become somewhat less direct as students become more mature and instructional goals become concerned with affective and process outcomes (Good, 1979). Others prefer the term direct instruction because it relates more to actual research evidence. However, to reiterate, I prefer the term active teaching because it is a concept rather than a set of findings and thus appears more comprehensive. The concept of active teaching can be applied in both teacher-led instruction as well as in student-team learning/instruction (e.g., Peterson, Janicki, and Swing, 1980; Slavin, 1981; Webb, 1977).

Active teaching provides an important instructional construct for characterizing the teaching role. With the apparent growing pressure for teachers to function as classroom managers rather than as instructors, more emphasis should be placed in teacher education programs upon helping teachers to understand the concept of active teaching. As was emphasized in the section on teacher expectation policy issues, the dissemination of this knowledge should be in a *decision-making* context that helps teachers to adapt the concept to particular types of content and students. The development of videotapes that illustrate the concept of active teaching during ongoing, interactive scenes from real classrooms would be particularly important. Clearly, the effects of such simulation activities upon teachers' judicious use of the concept in real classrooms should be assessed.

OTHER RESEARCH TOPICS IN THE 1970's

Two major research areas (teacher expectations and teacher effectiveness) have been discussed to illustrate the descriptive and observational nature of classroom research in the 1970's and its potential use in helping to understand classroom behavior. Although many school critics in the late 1960's and early 1970's argued that a "sameness" permeated American classrooms, research in the 1970's has convincingly demonstrated that large variations in teacher behavior, goals, and curricula exist in American schools. Often classrooms look the same but place very different learning demands on students (Doyle, 1979). Other classrooms seem different on the surface but present task structures (Doyle, 1979), organizational structures, and/or activity structures (Bossert, 1979) which are quite similar. Although more remains to be known about the antecedent conditions that lead to varied classroom behaviors and the effects of those variations in classroom processes upon student outcomes, it is clear that there are no simple solutions for improving classroom learning. I would be remiss if I did not at least briefly mention other important research that took place in the 1970's, research which further enables us to describe and to understand classroom behavior.

In addition to illustrating that there is variation in teacher behavior between classrooms, research in the 1970's also demonstrated that there is variance between teacher behaviors that are believed to be advocated in teacher education programs and behaviors occurring in actual teaching practice. Brophy (1981) has noted that the frequency of teacher praise in classrooms is considerably lower than the frequency advocated in many teacher education programs. He indicated that this is probably fortunate, because teacher praise as it is commonly used in classrooms does not always have the desirable effects upon student achievement that many advocates of frequent praise have maintained.

Recent research has also questioned the "rational" model of curriculum planning that is often emphasized in teacher education programs (Clark and Yinger, 1980; Peterson and Clark, 1978; Peterson, Marx, and Clark, 1978). Some studies indicate that teachers can plan too much, as well as too little, and that instead of emphasizing objectives followed by the identification of activities which might be useful in accomplishing those objectives, teachers in their actual planning time emphasize content and activities which will be presented. More studies of what *teaching* methods teacher education programs advocate and the extent to which teachers utilize this advice in their actual teaching are needed. In particular, it will be important to assess whether the way in which teacher planning is conceptualized in some institutions has more positive impact upon teachers' willingness to act as proactive decision makers (e.g., Borko et al., 1979; Shavelson, 1981) than the way it is dealt with in other teacher education training programs.

Many studies of classrooms have noted that teachers vary from one another in their behavior, and in many cases such variation has been associated with student outcomes (typically achievement). One area of active research interest has been classroom management, and several important studies have indicated that teachers manage classes in a variety of ways and that some teachers are more successful managers than others. Many studies and reviews have highlighted the differences between more and less successful managers (e.g., Brophy and Putnam, 1979; Kounin, 1970). In particular, systematic, naturalistic, and experimental research by Carolyn Evertson, Edmund Emmer, and others at the University of Texas Research and Development Center for Teacher Education has provided a set of important statements about classroom management. Research on classroom management has yielded some useful guidelines, but no simple behavioral solutions for all teaching contexts. Some teachers overmanage classrooms and some teachers undermanage classrooms; hence, advocacy for more management is a simple and self-defeating strategy.

Time allocation research has consistently verified the fact that teachers vary greatly in how they allocate instructional time across different subject matters and in the extent to which they actively involve students during allocated instructional time. Teachers vary greatly in the time they allocate to particular subjects and to topics within subject areas (Bennett, in press; Berliner, 1979; Fisher et al., 1978). Furthermore, there are both correlational and experimental data which indicate that time allocation relates to student achievement (Denham and Lieberman, 1980; Rosenshine, 1980; Stallings, 1980). The problems associated with translating these results into policy actions have been argued by a number of individuals (Confrey, 1981; Fenstermacher, 1980b; Griffin, 1981; Karweit and Slavin, 1980a, 1980b; Kepler, 1980; Webb, 1981). Information on time allocation may be useful if it is applied in ways that facilitate teacher decision-making skills and if such information is not applied in a prescriptive and simple fashion (e.g., lengthen the time for math and increased achievement will follow). The quality and appropriateness of time utilization is much more important than time per se. Indeed, in our first naturalistic study of more and less effective mathematics teachers we found that both groups of teachers spent about the same amount of time on mathematics but varied considerably in *how* they used time.

Important research concerning how teachers organize classrooms for learning (Bossert, 1979) and how the learning tasks that teachers present influence classroom interaction (Doyle, 1979) has also been conducted. Although such research has not systematically linked organization and task structure variables to student achievement, these approaches have provided new and alternate ways of looking at classroom behavior. They should have considerable potential for explaining classroom behavior, and the potential impact of these research efforts for educational policy is very high.

Other recent research in the 1970's has tried to alter the structure of "traditional" teaching patterns. In contrast to other studies reported in this chapter, which have examined what teachers do in the classroom, these researchers have constructed new forms of classroom behaviors. Much of this research has focused upon open classrooms. Unfortunately, what constitutes an "open classroom" has not been clarified and investigators use a variety of definitions for this term (Harrison, Strauss, and Glaubman, in press). Furthermore, in many studies open classrooms have not been observed, so that it is not clear how teachers in open classrooms and these classroom environments differ (if they do) from more "traditional" teaching. Still, there are some reasons to believe that some students benefit from placement in classes that allow more autonomy (Peterson, 1979).

Some very interesting recent research has been conducted in classrooms where students work in groups and teach one another (Peterson, Janicki, and Swing, 1980; Webb, 1970, 1980; Wilkinson and Calculator, 1982). This research has illustrated ways in which this approach can work effectively and the conditions that have to be met if student group learning is to be effective; however, much remains to be learned. There has also been a growing interest in cooperative learning, stimulated by laboratory research in social psychology (Aronson et al., 1978; DeVries and Slavin, 1978; Johnson and Johnson, 1975; Sharan and Sharan, 1976; Slavin, 1980, in press). Much more information is needed about how students behave in these settings, but preliminary outcome data are interesting and suggest that cooperative learning strategies may facilitate achievement, at least in certain situations.

GENERAL POLICY IMPLICATIONS

In this chapter several potential policy implications have been suggested, especially following the teacher expectation and teacher effectiveness sections. These policy suggestions will not be repeated in detail here, but it is useful to describe some of the major implications that have resulted from classroom research conducted in the last decade.

Low-Achieving Students Can Learn

Perceptions of low achievers' learning potential are often too low; there is evidence that lows can and do benefit from active teaching. Data collected in the teacher expectation, teacher effectiveness, and students-as-teachers paradigms demonstrate that low-achieving students can benefit from systematic instruction. It is evident that teachers can also err by having too high expectations and by constructing too demanding environments; however, in general low achievers are more likely to suffer from understimulation and underteaching, especially when lows are isolated from other students and taught as a group. Information about the learning potential of lows needs to be disseminated, and active attempts need to be made to develop more constructive ways for teaching these students.

Teachers Make a Difference

Naturalistic studies have found that teachers vary greatly in terms of their active teaching capacity, their classroom managerial abilities, their time allocation decisions, and their use of students as teachers. There are also experimental field studies which show that improvement in these areas can lead to increased student achievement, at least in basic skill subject areas. Such research does not yield rules or guidelines for successful teaching, but it does provide important constructs for the study and potential improvement of instruction, if teachers can adapt this information to the conditions under which they teach. Research results need to be disseminated, but in ways which encourage teachers to creatively adapt the information to their own instructional situations (Good and Brophy, 1978). More qualitative research which intensively studies classroom process and helps to clarify student and teacher behaviors in specified contexts is also needed. In particular, future classroom process research should more intensively examine the motivation and belief systems of teachers and students and the actual content that students and teachers respond to, while continuing the study of what teachers and students do in the classroom.[2] Much research indicates that on occasion the study of only what teachers and students *do* can be misleading. Ultimately, I hope that more comprehensive studies will lead to contextual theories of instruction that help us to understand why certain patterns of instruction appear to be more successful than others under defined circumstances.

Research Funding for Holistic Studies

Research that helps practitioners and researchers to understand and to deal with classrooms in a holistic sense is important. Most research historically has tended to deal with a single aspect of classroom life. Although these studies occasionally provide rich and meaningful concepts, they do not consider the classroom as a complete unit. Holistic research is needed because teachers and students are affected by many classroom variables simultaneously. Recent studies have become much more comprehensive (e.g., Carew and Lightfoot, 1979), but research must become even broader and more ambitious if a more extensive understanding of the holistic nature of classrooms is to emerge. In particular, new studies need to capture the "social" as well as academic aspects of schooling (e.g., see Eder, 1982; Florio, 1979). Such studies will not occur without *systematic funding* that encourages comprehensive, longitudinal inquiry by multidisciplinary teams.

Recent data collected using both quantitative and qualitative methods have demonstrated that classrooms are more complex than many educators thought. Extant literature contains many arguments that quantitative techniques alone are insufficient for understanding classroom life (e.g., Stubbs and Delamont, 1976), as well as illustrations of the weaknesses of the qualitative approach (e.g., McNamara, 1980). If new insights and understandings are to be achieved, I believe they will come through the creative synthesis of both of these general strategies of inquiry. As Power (1977) and Koehler (1978) have contended, both research methods are legitimate and necessary. However, the deployment of these strategies in completely independent ways seems to be an inefficient approach.

Teacher Education

Little is known about the content, beliefs, and skills that teacher education programs communicate to preservice teachers. In particular, information about how teacher education programs help teachers in training to develop translation skills for interpreting research and for adapting what is known about instruction to the contexts in which they will teach is missing. It would appear that many teacher education programs could add important experiences to their curricula in order to improve the observational skills of teachers and their ability to use information gained through observation to adapt instruction to individual students (Amarel, 1981; Good and Brophy,

1978). Recent research evidence has helped to substantiate what classroom teachers have always known—to do an *effective* job in the classroom teachers must possess ability, skills, and work very hard. Given the demands of teaching, teacher education programs should be much more careful in selecting and graduating students than they have in the past. In particular teacher education programs should place more attention on demonstrating that teachers can successfully use principles and concepts in actual classroom situations.

In-Service Teachers

The careful study of multiple ways to involve practitioners in their own self-study and improvement is an important area of inquiry. Teachers seldom have a chance to see other teachers teach and to share ideas about how to improve instruction. Teachers need more opportunities for classroom observation and more skills for taking advantage of those opportunities. It will be increasingly important to develop models which encourage teacher inquiry and bring recent research findings and concepts to teachers' attention.

Theorists and researchers should develop communication models which disseminate information and also help teachers to develop translation skills for adapting new information to their own contexts. Likewise, teachers need to make researchers more aware of the particular constraints under which they teach. Much more information is needed about how (and when) to involve practitioners in conducting and applying research. This question has been addressed by some researchers (Far West Laboratory, San Francisco; Institute for Research on Teaching, Michigan State University), and some useful conceptualization has occurred (e.g., Connelly and Ben-Peretz, 1980). However, at present we are just beginning to learn how researchers and teachers can work collectively and profitably together (Good and Grouws, 1981; Tikunoff, Ward, and Griffin, 1979). If their collaborative roles are to be understood, systematic funding to encourage research in this area must be forthcoming. Such funding would be an important investment in gaining knowledge useful for the formation of social policy.

SOME FINAL THOUGHTS

To describe and/or to understand classroom learning is an enormously complex task. The realization of the complexity of classrooms should cause us to be suspicious of simple models of teaching that offer universal solutions and should encourage us to take divergent approaches to the study of teaching. We know considerably *more* about classrooms now than we did a decade ago. With sufficient funding, the research community can work in close contact with teachers and school administrators in the 1980's to produce useful insights and concepts that can improve our understanding of classroom learning in important ways. Research in the past 10 years has yielded important dividends and more research that is carefully conceived and programmatic in nature will also be an important investment of social funds.

I emphasize continued research as a policy issue partly because I believe we need much more basic knowledge about what takes place in classrooms and why. I also advocate continued study and the application of research results in a decision-making format because I believe that the general public, including policymakers, tend to over-react to research results (either by ignoring them or interpreting them too literally) and to consider such findings too narrowly. Others have made similar points. Dr. Lois Ellen Datta, an official at the National Institute of Education, was quoted as making a similar point in the *Report on Education Research Newsletter* (April 29, 1981): "The problem is that research findings command a lot of public attention. They generate headlines, often misleading ones: 'Bilingual Education Fails,' 'Private Schools Better,' 'Head Start Works,' 'Girls Can't Learn Math.'" She argues that such headlines influence public beliefs, and beliefs influence action (including the acceptance of only certain forms of educational activity as legitimate and the willingness to fund certain programs). As a response to this problem, Datta has encouraged the funding of research on opposing views and advocated that historians be used more to keep things in perspective (many solutions that are offered for current problems have been applied in the past and found to have a set of problems associated with their implementation and effects).

I agree with her emphasis, but I would also encourage a broader understanding of what research can and cannot do. In particular, policymakers need to realize that it takes time to develop a reasonable response to issues inherent in public education and that research clarifies issues, raises new questions, and suggests ways of responding to problems; it does *not* solve problems. Decisions are made by local school districts and individual schools and teachers. Hopefully, these decision makers can use research evidence to examine their problems.

Concepts that are derived from classroom research provide guidelines or frames of reference that allow teachers to think about, and attempt to alter, their teaching situations. Classroom theories or concepts can be of value in extending the number of dimensions that a teacher, supervisor, or researcher uses to study the classroom, in increasing the number (and range) of hypotheses (alternative strategies) considered, and in increasing awareness of possible consequences of selected actions by all participants (Good and Power, 1976).

Much of the problem and inefficiency of educational reform is due to the frequent acceptance of one fact as a cure-all, only to discard this solution for a new one a few years later. Artley (1981) has reviewed the major methods used to improve reading instruction in the 1900's. He notes that while all the reform programs (different approaches to individualized reading) have had some desirable features, they have not solved the problems of all students. He writes, "In other words, an over-emphasis on certain aspects of a program almost invariably results in neglect of others, and thus change comes about as a reaction to existing programs." I feel that educators, especially classroom teachers, have to carefully adapt research findings to their own situations. However, I am not advocating a laissez faire decision-making approach. I have argued elsewhere that teachers need to "prove" the validity of their teaching practices by examining the impact of changes in instructional programs on themselves and students (Good and Brophy, 1978; Good and Brophy, 1980).

Other educators have a different orientation toward the value of research. For example, Phillips (1980) writes, "The bottom line is that social scientists have not been able to discover generalizations that are reliable enough, and about which there is enough professional consensus, to form the basis for social policy . . . so the wise educational practitioner ought not to hold his or her breath waiting for new, reliable, far-reaching breakthroughs by researchers. A skeptical, if not cynical, attitude toward research seems to be justified."

I think that Phillips is fundamentally wrong, although I agree that social scientists have not been able to produce classroom generalizations that are reliable enough and about which there is enough professional consensus to form a basis for educational policy that mandates specific teaching behaviors. However, I contend that the purpose of educational research is not to produce *the* answer for educational practitioners. Human learning, particularly in complex social settings, is affected by so many factors that simple blueprints will never apply to all the diverse situations that practitioners confront. At best, educational research may help practitioners to analyze their own teaching settings and to become more adept at seeing, understanding, and reacting to the conditions which they face (Good and Power, 1976).

However, I do feel that some researchers have oversold the value of their research in terms of its potential for immediate and specific policy implication. I agree with Prawat and Floden (in press) and Confrey (1981) that we need to develop more appropriate expectations for the type of contribution that research can play in policy formation.

To reiterate, classrooms are complex environments and it is not easy to describe, to understand, or to improve them. Kepler (1977) and Shulman (1978) have cautioned educators about an overreliance upon the scientific paradigm for the production of simple answers. Research findings do not translate themselves. In order to make research applicable, findings need to be related to the particular characteristics of individual classrooms (Schwab, 1969).

The relationship between social research and social policy is complex and there is a need for researchers and policymakers to be explicit about their assumptions and expectations. I find myself in substantial agreement with the position taken by Lindblom and Cohen (1979) that research does not directly translate into policy and with Shulman (1981), who has argued that research is a disciplined form of inquiry and represents an important mechanism for rising above personal experience, which by necessity is always selective and incomplete.

Considering the variety of teacher and student behaviors that have been identified in various classrooms through observational research in the 1970's, it seems that most views of "classroom success" (whether held by teacher educators, teachers, or researchers) have been too simple, and increased ways of understanding classroom diversity and ways for responding to it are needed (others have reached similar conclusions; see, for example, Zahorik, 1981). Research is only one mechanism for responding to this need, but in my viewpoint it is an important and necessary component of social policy.

There is no one "problem" in American education and thus there is no one area in which to search for universal "prescriptions." It now seems evident that students' learning can be undermined by classroom treatment that is too *different* from what other students receive as well as by educational opportunities that are too *similar* (Good and Stipek, in press). Research in education is now yielding new concepts that can be used to identify and analyze classroom issues more comprehensively than was previously possible. It is my belief that continued research that illuminates classroom problems and alternatives more fully will enable motivated teachers to teach more thoughtfully and effectively.

NOTES

1. Hawthorne effect implies that the positive results produced by an experiment are due to increased motivation because subjects realize they are part of an experiment and *not* because

of the value of the program. Interestingly, in this project a Hawthorne effect was observed in that control teachers' classrooms exhibited higher achievement than would be expected. However, achievement in experimental classes still far exceeded that in control classrooms. Thus, the mathematics program was found to have an effect that transcended motivational effects.

2. It would be possible, of course, to study students' and teachers' lives outside of school-rooms as there is reason to believe that what teachers (e.g., Spencer Hall, in press) and students (Medrich et al., 1982) do outside of school influences what occurs inside of school (and vice versa).

REFERENCES

Allington, R. Reading instruction provided readers of differing abilities. *Elementary School Journal*, in press.

Amarel, M. *Literacy: The personal dimension*. A paper presented at the annual meeting of the American Educational Research Association, Los Angeles, April 1981.

Anderson, L. *Student responses to seatwork: Implications for the study of students' cognitive processing*. A paper presented at the annual meeting of the American Educational Research Association, Los Angeles, April 1981.

Anderson, L., Evertson, C., and Brophy, J. An experimental study of effective teaching in first-grade reading groups. *Elementary School Journal*, 1979, *79*(4), 193–233.

Anderson-Levitt, K. *Memory and talk in teachers' interpretations of student behavior*. A paper presented at the annual meeting of the American Educational Research Association, Los Angeles, April 1981.

Andros, K., and Freeman, D. *The effects of three kinds of feedback on math teaching perform-ance*. A paper presented at the annual meeting of the American Educational Research Asso-ciation, Los Angeles, April 1981.

Aronson, E., Blaney, N., Stephan, C., Sikes, J., and Snapp, M. *The jigsaw classroom*. Beverly Hills, Calif.: Sage Publications, 1978.

Artley, A. Individual differences and reading instruction. *Elementary School Journal*, in press.

Becker, W., and Gersten, R. A follow-up of follow through: The later effects of the direct in-struction model on children in fifth and sixth grades. *American Educational Research Jour-nal*, 1982, *19*, 75–92.

Beckerman, T., and Good, T. The classroom ratio of high- and low-aptitude students and its effect on achievement. *American Educational Research Journal*, in press.

Bennett, N. Time and space: Curriculum allocation and pupil involvement in British open schools. *Elementary School Journal*, in press.

Berliner, D. Impediments to measuring teacher effectiveness. In G. Borich and K. Fenton (eds.), *The appraisal of teaching: Concepts and process*. Reading, Mass.: Addison-Wesley, 1977.

Berliner, D. Tempus educare. In P. Peterson and H. Walberg (eds.), *Research on teaching: Concepts, findings, and implications*. Berkeley, Calif.: McCutchan Publishing Corporation, 1979.

Biddle, B. *Role theory: Expectations, identities and behaviors*. New York: Academic Press, 1979.

Borko, H., Cone, R., Russo, N., and Shavelson, R. Teachers' decision making. In P. Peterson and H. Walberg (eds.), *Research on teaching: Concepts, findings, and implications*. Ber-keley, Calif.: McCutchan Publishing Corporation, 1979.

Bossert, S. Task and social relationships in classrooms: A study of classroom organization and its consequences. American Sociological Association, *Arnold and Caroline Rose Mono-graph Series*. New York: Cambridge University Press, 1979.

Braun, C. Teacher expectation: Socio-psychological dynamics. *Review of Educational Research*, 1976, *46*, 185–213.

Brookover, W., Schweitzer. J., Schneider, J., Beady, C., Flood, P., and Wisenbaker, J. Elementary school social climate and school achievement. *American Educational Research Journal*, 1978, *15*, 301–318.

Brophy, J. Teacher behavior and its effects. *Journal of Educational Psychology*, 1979, *71*, 733–750.

Brophy, J. On praising effectively. *Elementary School Journal*, 1981, *81*, 269–278.

Brophy, J. *Research on the self-fulfilling prophecy and teacher expectations.* A paper presented at the annual meeting of the American Educational Research Association, New York City, 1982.

Brophy, J., and Evertson, C. *Learning from teaching: A developmental perspective.* Boston: Allyn & Bacon, 1976.

Brophy, J., Evertson, C., Anderson, L., Baum, M., and Crawford, J. *Student characteristics and teaching.* New York: Longman, Inc., 1981.

Brophy, J., and Good, T. Teachers' communication of differential expectations for children's classroom performance: Some behavioral data. *Journal of Educational Psychology*, 1970, *61*, 365–374.

Brophy, J., and Good, T. *Teacher-student relationships: Causes and consequences.* New York: Holt, Rinehart and Winston, 1974.

Brophy, J., and Putnam, J. Classroom management in the elementary grades: A literature review. In D. Duke (ed.), *Classroom management. The 78th yearbook of the National Society for the Study of Education* (Part II). Chicago: University of Chicago Press, 1979.

Carew, J., and Lightfoot, S. *Beyond Bias.* Cambridge: Harvard University Press, 1979.

Carrasco, R. *Expanded awareness of student performance: A case study in applied ethnographic monitoring in a bilingual classroom* (Social Linguistic Working Paper No. 60), Austin, Tex.: Southwest Educational Development Laboratory, April 1979.

Clark, C., and Yinger, R. *The hidden world of teaching: Implications of research on teacher planning.* Paper presented at the annual meeting of the American Educational Research Association, Boston, April 1980.

Coleman, J., Campbell, E., Hobson, C., McPartland, J., Mood, A., Weinfield, F., and York, R. *Equality of educational opportunity.* Washington, D.C.: Superintendent of Documents, U.S. Government Printing Office, 1966.

Confrey, J. Time to learn: A review from the subject matter perspective. *Elementary School Journal*, in press.

Confrey, J., and Good, T. A view from the back of the classroom: Integrating student and teacher perspectives of content with observational and clinical interviews, in progress.

Confrey, J., and Lanier, P. Students' mathematics abilities: Improving the teaching of general mathematics. *School Science and Mathematics*, 1980, *80*, 549–556.

Connelly, F., and Ben-Peretz, M. Teachers' roles in the using and doing of research in curriculum and development. *Journal of Curriculum Studies*, 1980, *12*, 95–107.

Cooper, H. Pygmalion grows up: A model for teacher expectation communication and performance influence. *Review of Educational Research*, 1979, *49*, 389–410.

Cooper, H., and Baron, R. Academic expectations and attributed responsibility as predictors of professional teachers' reinforcement behavior. *Journal of Educational Psychology*, 1977, *69*(4), 409–418.

Cooper, H., and Good, T. *Pygmalion grows up: Studies in the expectation communication process.* New York: Longman, in progress.

Copeland, W. Student teachers and cooperating teachers: An ecological relationship. *Theory Into Practice*, 1979, *3*, 194–199.

Denham, C., and Lieberman, A. (eds.). *Time to learn.* Washington, D.C.: U.S. Department of Education, 1980.

DeVries, D., and Slavin, R. Teams-games-tournaments (TGT): Review of ten classroom experiments. *Journal of Research and Development in Education*, 1978, *12*, 28–38.

Doyle, W. Learning the classroom environment: An ecological analysis. *Journal of Teacher Education*, 1977, *28*, 51–55.

Doyle, W. Classroom tasks and students' abilities. In P. Peterson and H. Walberg (eds.), *Research on teaching: Concepts, findings, and implications*. Berkeley, Calif.: McCutchan Publishing Corporation, 1979.

Doyle, W. *Student mediating responses in teaching effectiveness* (NIE-G-76-0099 Final Report). Denton: North Texas State University, 1980.

Dusek, J. Do teachers bias children's learning? *Review of Educational Research*, 1975, *45*, 661–684.

Ebmeier, H., and Good, T. The effects of instructing teachers about good teaching on the mathematics achievement of fourth grade students. *American Educational Research Journal*, 1979, *16*, 1–16.

Ebmeier, H., Good, T., and Grouws, D. *Comparison of ATI findings across two large-scale experimental studies in elementary education*. A paper presented at the American Educational Research Association Annual Conference, Boston, April 1980.

Eder, D. Ability grouping as a self-fulfilling prophecy: A micro-analysis of teacher-student interaction. *Sociology of Education*, 1981, *54*, 151–173.

Edmonds, R. Effective schools for the urban poor. *Educational Leadership*, 1979, *37*, 15–18.

Erickson, F. What makes school ethnography "ethnographic"? *Council on Anthropology and Educational Quarterly*, 1977, *8*(2).

Erlwanger, S. Case studies of children's conceptions of mathematics—Part I. *Journal of Children's Mathematical Behavior*, 1975, *1*, 157–283.

Evertson, C. Differences in instructional activities in average- and low-achieving junior high English and math classes. *Elementary School Journal*, in press.

Evertson, C., Anderson, C., Anderson, L., and Brophy, J. Relationships between classroom behaviors and student outcomes in junior high mathematics and English classes. *American Educational Research Journal*, 1980, *17*, 43–60.

Fenstermacher, G. Learning from teaching from teachers. *Journal of Teacher Education*, 1980a, *31*(5), 63.

Fenstermacher, G. On learning to teach effectively from research on teacher effectiveness. In D. DeVries and A. Lieberman (eds.), *Time to learn*. Washington, D.C.: U.S. Department of Education, 1980b.

Fisher, C., Filby, N., Marliave, R., Cahen, L., Dishaw, M., Moore, J., and Berliner, D. *Teaching behaviors, academic learning time and student achievement* (Final Report of Phase III-B, Beginning Teacher Evaluation Study). San Francisco: Far West Laboratory, 1978.

Florio, S. The problem of dead letters: Social perspectives on the teaching of writing. *Elementary School Journal*, 1979, *80*(1), 1–7.

Gage, N., and Giaconia, R. *The causal connection between teaching practices and student achievement: Recent experiments based on correlational findings* (Tech. Rep.). Stanford, Calif.: Stanford University, Center for Educational Research at Stanford, 1980.

Good, T. Teacher effectiveness in the elementary school: What we know about it now. *Journal of Teacher Education*, 1979, *30*, 52–64.

Good, T. Classroom expectations: Teacher-pupil interactions. In J. McMillan (ed.), *The social psychology of school learning*. New York: Academic Press, 1980.

Good, T. A decade of research on teacher expectations. *Journal of Educational Leadership*, 1981, *38*, 415–423.

Good, T. *Classroom research: What we know and what we need to know* (Tech. Rep. No. 9118). Austin: University of Texas, The Research and Development Center for Teacher Education, February 1982.

Good, T., Biddle, B., and Brophy, J. *Teachers make a difference*. New York: Holt, Rinehart and Winston, 1975.

Good, T., and Brophy, J. Behavioral expression of teacher attitudes. *Journal of Educational Psychology*, 1972, *63*, 617–624.

Good, T., and Brophy, J. *Looking in classrooms* (1st ed.). New York: Harper and Row, 1973.

Good, T., and Brophy, J. Changing teacher and student behavior: An empirical investigation. *Journal of Educational Psychology*, 1974, *66*, 390–405.

Good, T., and Brophy, J. *Looking in classrooms* (2nd ed.). New York: Harper and Row, 1978.

Good, T., and Brophy, J. *Educational psychology: A realistic approach* (2nd ed.). New York: Holt, Rinehart and Winston, 1980.

Good, T., Cooper, H., and Blakey, S. Classroom interaction as a function of teacher expectations, student sex, and time of year. *Journal of Teacher Education*, 1978, *29*, 85–90.

Good, T., and Grouws, D. The Missouri mathematics effectiveness project: An experimental study in fourth grade classrooms. *Journal of Educational Psychology*, 1979, *71*, 355–362.

Good, T., and Grouws, D. *Experimental research in secondary mathematics classrooms: Working with teachers* (NIE-G-79-0103 Final Report), May, 1981.

Good, T., Grouws, D., and Ebmeier, H. *Active mathematics teaching: Empirical research in elementary and secondary classrooms.* New York: Longman, in press.

Good, T., and Power, C. Designing successful classroom environments for different types of students. *Journal of Curriculum Studies*, 1976, *8*, 45–60.

Good, T., and Stipek, D. Individual differences in the classroom: A psychological perspective. In G. Fenstermacher and J. Goodlad, (Eds.), *1983 NSSE yearbook*, forthcoming.

Griffin, G. Time-on-task: A review. *Elementary School Journal*, in press.

Harrison, J., Strauss, H., and Glaubman, R. The impact of open and traditional classrooms on achievement and creativity: The Israeli case. *Elementary School Journal*, in press.

Jackson, P. *Life in classrooms.* New York: Holt, Rinehart and Winston, 1968.

Jackson, P., Silberman, M., and Wolfson, B. Signs of personal involvement in teachers' descriptions of their students. *Journal of Educational Psychology*, 1969, *60*, 22–27.

Janicki, C., and Peterson, P. Aptitude-treatment interaction effects of variations in direct instruction. *American Educational Research Journal*, 1981, *18*, 63–82.

Johnson, D. Student-student interaction: The neglected variable in education. *Educational Researcher*, 1981, *10*, 5–10.

Johnson, D., and Johnson, R. *Learning together alone.* Englewood Cliffs, N.J.: Prentice-Hall, Inc., 1975.

Jorgenson, G. *Student ability—material difficulty matching: Relationship to classroom behavior.* A paper presented at the meeting of the American Educational Research Association, Toronto, March 1978.

Karweit, N., and Slavin, R. *Time-on-task: Issues of timing, sampling and definition* (Tech. Rep.). Baltimore: The John Hopkins University, Center for Social Organization of Schools, October 1980a.

Karweit, N., and Slavin, R. Time-on-task: Issues of timing, sampling and definition (Tech. (Tech. Rep.). Baltimore: The John Hopkins University, Center for Social Organization of Schools, 1980b.

Keddie, N. Classroom knowledge. In M. Young (ed.), *Knowledge and control: New directions for the sociology of education.* London: Collier-MacMillan, 1971.

Kepler, K. *Descriptive feedback: Increasing teacher awareness, adopting research techniques.* A paper presented at the annual meeting of the American Educational Research Association, New York, April 1977.

Kepler, K. BTES: Implications for preservice education of teachers. In C. Denham and A. Lieberman (eds.), *Time to learn.* Washington, D.C.: U.S. Department of Education, 1980.

Keziah, R. Implementing instructional behaviors that make a difference. *Centroid* (North Carolina Council of Teachers of Mathematics), 1980, *6*, 2–4.

Koehler, V. Classroom process research: Present and future. *Journal of Classroom Interaction*, 1978, *13*, 3–11.

Kounin, J. *Discipline and group management in classrooms.* New York: Holt, Rinehart and Winston, 1970.

Kozol, J. *Death at an early age.* Boston: Houghton Mifflin, 1967.

Krutetskii, V. *The psychology of mathematical abilities in school children.* Chicago: University of Chicago Press, 1976.

Levine, H., and Mann, K. *The "negotiation" of classroom lessons and its relevance for teachers' decision-making.* Paper read at the annual meeting of the American Educational Research Association, Los Angeles, April 1981.

Lindblom, C., and Cohen, D. *Usable knowledge: Social science and social problem-solving.* New Haven, Conn.: Yale University Press, 1979.

Martin, M. *Equal opportunity in the classroom* (ESEA, Title III: Session A Report). Los Angeles: County Superintendent of Schools, Division of Compensatory and Intergroup Programs, 1973.

McDermott, R. *Kids made sense: An ethnographic account of the interactional management of success and failure in one first-grade classroom.* Unpublished doctoral dissertation, Stanford University, 1976.

McDonald, F., and Elias, P. *The effects of teaching performance on pupil learning* (Final Report, Vol. 1, Beginning Teacher Evaluation Study, Phase II, 1974–1976). Princeton, N.J.: Educational Testing Service, 1976.

McNamara, B. The outsider's arrogance: The failure of participant observers to understand classroom events. *British Educational Research Journal,* 1980, 6(2).

Medley, D. The effectiveness of teachers. In P. Peterson and H. Walberg (eds.), *Research on teaching: Concepts, findings, and implications.* Berkeley, Calif.: McCutchan Publishing Corporation, 1979.

Medrich, E., Roizen, J., Rubin, V., and Buckley, S. *The serious business of growing up: A study of children's lives outside school.* Berkeley: University of California Press, 1982.

Mehan, H. *Learning lessons: Social organization in the classroom.* Cambridge, Mass.: Harvard University Press, 1979.

Metz, M. *Classrooms and corridors: The crisis of authority in desegregated secondary schools.* Berkeley: University of California Press, 1978.

Mitman, A. et al. *The junior high transition study: Students' perceptions of transition and school* (mimeo). San Francisco: Far West Laboratory for Education Research and Development, 1981.

Peterson, P., and Clark, C. Teachers' reports of their cognitive processes during teaching. *American Educational Research Journal,* 1978, *15*, 555–565.

Peterson, P., Janicki, T., and Swing, S. *Individual characteristics and children's learning in large-group and small-group approaches: Study.II* (Tech. Rep. No. 561). Madison, Wis.: University of Wisconsin, Wisconsin Research and Development Center for Individualized Schooling, October 1980.

Peterson, P., Marx, R., and Clark, C. Teacher planning, teacher behavior, and student achievement. *American Educational Research Journal* 1978, *15*, 417–432.

Peterson, P., and Walberg, H. (eds.), *Research on teaching: Concepts, findings, and implications.* Berkeley. Calif.: McCutchan Publishing Corporation, 1979.

Phillips, D. What do the research and the practitioners have to offer each other? *Educational Researcher,* 1980, *9*, 17–24.

Porter, A., Schmidt, W., Floden, R., and Freeman, D. *Impact on what? The importance of content covered* (Research Series No. 2). East Lansing: Michigan State University, Institute for Research on Teaching, 1978.

Power, C. A critical review of science classroom interaction studies. *Studies in Science Education,* 1977, *4*, 1–30.

Prawat, R., and Floden, R. A review of research in education. *Elementary School Journal,* in press.

Rosenshine, B. Content, time, and direct instruction. In P. Peterson and H. Walberg (eds.), *Research on teaching: Concepts, findings, and implications.* Berkeley, Calif.: McCutchan Publishing Corporation, 1979.

Rosenshine, B. How time is spent in elementary classrooms. In C. Denham and A. Lieberman (eds.), *Time to learn*. Washington, D.C.: U.S. Department of Education, 1980.

Rosenthal, R. *On the social psychology of the self-fulfilling prophecy: Further evidence for Pygmalion effects and their mediating mechanisms*. New York: MSS Modular Publications, 1974.

Rosenthal, R., and Jacobson, L. *Pygmalion in the classroom: Teacher expectations and pupils' intellectual development*. New York: Holt, Rinehart and Winston, 1968.

Rutter, M., Maughan, B., Mortimore, P., Ouston, J., and Smith, A. *Fifteen thousand hours: Secondary schools and their effects on children*. Cambridge: Harvard, 1979.

Schwab, J. The practical: A language for curriculum. *School Review*, November 1969, 1–23.

Schweinhart, L., and Weikart, D. Young children grow up: The effects of the Perry preschool program on use through age 15. *Monographs of the High/Scope Educational Research Foundation*, No. 7, Ypsilanti, Mich.: High/Scope Press, 1980.

Sharan, S., and Sharan, Y. *Small-group teaching*. Englewood Cliffs, N.J.: Educational Technology Publications, 1976.

Shavelson, R. *Review of research on teachers' decision making*. A paper presented at the annual meeting of the American Educational Research Association, Los Angeles, April 1981.

Shulman, L. *Investigations of mathematics teaching: A perspective and critique* (mimeo report). East Lansing: Michigan State University, Institute for Research on Teaching, June 1978.

Shulman, L. Disciplines of inquiry in education: An overview. *Educational Researcher*, 1981, *10*, 5–12; 23.

Slavin, R. Cooperative learning. *Review of Educational Research*, 1980, *50*, 315–342.

Slavin, R. A case study of psychological research affecting classroom practice: Student team learning. *Elementary School Journal*, in press.

Smith, L., and Geoffrey, W. *The complexities of an urban classroom: An analysis toward a general theory of teaching*. New York: Holt, Rinehart and Winston, 1968.

Soltz, D. *The various teacher: Subject matter, style, and strategy in the primary classroom*. A paper presented at the annual meeting of the American Educational Research Association, San Francisco, April 1976.

Spencer Hall, D. Looking behind the teacher's back. *Elementary School Journal*, 1981, *81*, 281–289.

Spencer Hall, D. The personal lives of teachers. *Elementary School Journal*, in press.

Stallings, J. Allocated academic learning time revisited, or beyond time on task. *Educational Researcher*, 1980, *9*(11), 11–16.

Stallings, J., Needels, M., and Stayrook, N. *How to change the process of teaching basic reading skills in secondary schools: Phase II and Phase III, Final Report*. Menlo Park, Calif.: SRI International, 1979.

Stanford Program on teacher effectiveness: An experiment in teacher effectiveness and parent-assisted instruction in the third grade. Set of five papers presented at the annual meeting of the American Educational Research Association, Toronto, March 1978.

Stubbs, M., and Delamont, S. (eds.), *Explorations in classroom observation*. London: Wiley, 1976.

Thelen, H. *Education and the human quest*. New York: Harper and Bros., 1960.

Tikunoff, W., Ward, B., and Griffin, G. *Interactive research and development on teaching study* (JR & DT-79-11 Final Report). San Francisco: Far West Laboratory for Education Research and Development, 1979.

Webb, N. *Learning in individual and small-group settings* (Tech. Rep. No. 7). Stanford, Calif.: Stanford University, School of Education, Aptitude Research Project, 1977.

Webb, N. (Mimeo). Los Angeles: University of California, College of Education, 1980.

Webb, N. Review from the perspective of instructional processes. *Elementary School Journal*, in press.

Weber, E. The effect of learning environment on learner involvement and achievement. *Journal of Teacher Education*, 1978, *29*, 81–85.

Weinstein, R. Reading group membership in first grade: Teacher behaviors and pupil experience over time. *Journal of Educational Psychology*, 1976, *68*, 103–116.

Weinstein, R., Middlestadt, S., Brattesani, K., and Marshall, H. *Student perceptions of differential teacher treatment*. A paper presented at the annual meeting of the American Educational Research Association, Boston, April 1980.

West, C., and Anderson, T. The questions of preponderant causation in teacher expectancy research. *Review of Educational Research*, 1976, *46*, 185–213.

Wilkinson, L., and Calculator, S. Requests and responses in peer-directed reading groups. *American Educational Research Journal*, 1982, *19*, 107–120.

Zahorik, J. Using insights in education. *Journal of Teacher Education*, 1981, *32*, 10–13.

CHAPTER 3

Educational Policy and the Working of Schools

Robert Dreeben and Rebecca Barr

This paper treats the connection between public educational policymaking and the organization and workings of public schools. Both legislative and judicial policies in education have been directed over the past several decades toward guaranteeing the rights of individual children. Court decisions on school desegregation, starting with Brown, and the more recent legislation on the rights of the handicapped are two cases in point, and both are subjects of this discussion.

It is relatively easy to understand what individual rights mean in the context of individual transactions at arm's length: the right to buy a house in a particular neighborhood, to use a swimming pool, to ride a bus, or to eat in a restaurant. And while it may be difficult to implement policies that guarantee such rights, one can readily envision what a condition of partial or full implementation would look like. We know what individuals previously denied their rights should henceforth be able to do.

Much as our usual habits of speech and conventional ways of thinking construe education as an individualized enterprise—it should respect individual differences, adapt to individual needs, provide individualized instruction—the fact remains that schools deal with students in batches. Whatever individual outcomes are achieved, whatever individualized transactions occur, they happen in collective settings. Despite the individualistic tendencies in our educational language, schools as organizational realities are collective arrangements. Perhaps that is why we use an individualistic rhetoric to talk about them; for if they worked on an individual tutorial basis, there would be no reason to do so. We need only add here that public policies in the areas of desegregation and mainstreaming, consistent with the language of schooling, are designed to guarantee the rights of individuals, and because of that they do not explicitly recognize the collective character of schools.

While it might seem too obvious to mention, one way that school systems work is to divide up the school-age population of a district according to categorical distinctions: residential location determines access to particular schools, age determines membership in a grade, and ability may influence assignment to a class in the grade or to a group in a class. Schools operate on the principle that for their main purposes, students from the same neighborhood, of the same age, and of similar ability can be treated alike *despite* their individual differences within residential, age, and ability categories. In fact, some of the most critical aspects of school operation pertain precisely to the treatment of differences within these categories, instruction being primary among them. Because it is not possible to supply each student with an instructor, the school must fashion means for providing instruction suited to groupings of certain kinds, such as homogeneous or heterogeneous classes and groups within classes. We will argue the case that the groupings formed are responsive to the distribution of students, particularly to the distribution of their abilities, which serves as a guideline to the organization of instruction.

As public educational policies, both desegregation and mainstreaming attempt to guarantee individual rights by altering a prevailing distribution of students: in the first case by changing the racial composition of segregated schools and in the second by including handicapped students in classes composed of those without handicap.

We will argue that our understanding of these policies will be enhanced if we think about the integration of race and handicap distributions with the prevailing distributions of student characteristics (residence, age, and ability) upon which public school organization is conventionally premised. The first step in that argument, then, is to consider certain aspects of how schools are organized and how they operate. We will then discuss the two spheres of public policymaking in the light of how schools work. In each case, we will show the disjunction between policies formulated on the basis of individual rights and school organization based upon categories of individuals.

ORGANIZATION AND WORKINGS OF SCHOOLS

Over the past five years, we (Barr and Dreeben, 1981) have been investigating the operation and social organization of schools: the means, activities, resources, decisions, and mechanisms by which they work to bring about educational outcomes such as learning. Our work has moved in the direction of formulating how schools work. The ensuing discussion draws upon that formulation to identify its implications for the implementation of public policy.

Levels of Organization

It is obvious that labor in educational organizations such as school systems is divided; it is differentiated by task into different organizational levels in a hierarchical arrangement. While it is customary to think about hierarchies in the context of relationships of authority and rank, they are not simply manifestations of ranking and status distinction. They also represent organizational differentiation, a manifestation of labor and other resources having been divided, of the elements of production having been both separated and tied together in some workable arrangement. We are concerned here with hierarchy in this latter sense.

In an educational division of labor, school systems are comprised of several levels of administrative and staff officers as well as of "production" workers (teachers) occupying positions having district, school, and classroom jurisdictions. But in addition school systems are differentiated according to the resources they use: in particular, those of time and of the physical objects such as books that constitute instructional materials. School systems also contain one additional element: students who are both the clients of the organization, the intended beneficiaries of its services, and, because schools are engaged in effecting change in children, productive resources in their own right because they participate directly and actively in their own learning.

When organizations are differentiated structurally, it is because their parts make distinct contributions to the overall enterprise. This means that people located hierarchically at different places perform different kinds of activities; it also means that resources come into play in different ways depending upon where they are utilized.

More specifically, school systems characteristically contain a managerial component responsible for centralized financial, personnel, procurement, plant maintenance, and supervisory functions applicable to all their constituent elements. This component is also engaged in direct dealings with agencies of the federal and state governments as well as with locally based interest groups and units of municipal government. Activities occurring at this managerial level have nothing directly to do with running schools or teaching students but rather with the acquisition of resources, general supervision, and the maintenance of relationships with the surrounding community including supplies of labor. We refer to this as the *district* level of organization; its jurisdiction includes all schools in the district.

Even though districts are divided into levels (elementary and secondary) related to the ages of students, and some are also divided into geographical areas as well as into functional subdivisions, we are primarily concerned—at the next-lower organization level—with *schools.* Contrary to conventional belief, schools are not organizational units of instruction. They are structures akin to switching yards where children within a given age range and from a designated geographical area are assigned to teachers who bring them into contact with approved learning materials, specified as being roughly appropriate to age, during certain allotted periods of time. Schools deal in potentialities; they assemble a supply of teachers, of students, and of resources over a given period of time. Their central activities are the assignment of children to specific teachers, the allocation of learning materials to classrooms, and the arrangement of a schedule so that all children in the school can be allotted an appropriate amount of time to subjects in the curriculum.

These activities are the primary responsibility of school principals; they represent core functions peculiar to the school level of organization. This is so because decisions affecting the fate of all classrooms in a school are not likely to be left to individuals (teachers) who have classroom interests rather than whole-school interests primarily in mind and whose self interest puts them in a poor position to settle disputes among equals. Nor is it likely to be left to districtwide administrators whose locations and jurisdictions are too remote to make informed school-level decisions.

While these decisions constitute the core activities of school administrators, they do not exhaust their responsibilities. These frequently include planning curriculum, establishing disciplinary standards, and making school policies for homework, decorum in public places, and the like. But while these areas of concern are frequently characteristic of school administration, they are not peculiar to it because districtwide administrators and teachers may also participate at the school level in fulfilling responsibilities within their own respective jurisdictions.

While instruction is not the business of the school, it is the business of *classrooms* and of teachers responsible for the direct engagement of students in learning activities. Aggregations of children are assigned to specific teachers, who in turn direct their activities and bring them into immediate contact with various learning materials. These activities are more than potentialities because children's active engagement working with teachers and materials is what makes it possible for them to learn.

Because classes contain diverse aggregations of children, it is not automatic that the instruction appropriate for one member of that aggregation will be appropriate for another. Hence, teachers in the lower grades characteristically create an additional level of suborganization to manage activities not easily handled in a grouping as large as a class. For example, in primary grade reading, there are suborganizations called *instructional groups* which represent still another level of organizational differentiation.

Finally, there are *individual students*. It is only individuals who work on tasks, and it is only they who learn; so that while work tasks might be set for all students in the class or in a group, the individual members vary in how much work they do and in how much they learn.

We argue here not only that school systems can be described by their constituent organizational levels but that the events, activities, and organizational forms found at each level should be seen as representing distinct as well as partially overlapping agendas. Districts, schools, classes, and instructional groups are structurally different from each other; and what is more, they make different contributions to the overall operation of the school district.

Our recent work has been concerned with the lowest elementary school grades. We recognize, however, that not all schools have precisely the same organizational pattern. In the upper elementary grades, for example, formalized instructional groups characteristically used for reading tend to drop out; and in secondary schools, which lack self-contained classrooms, a departmental level of organization often appears as does formal tracking which distinguishes students largely on the basis of ability within schools but not within classes. Despite these variations, the general principle of differentiated structures and agendas holds.

Linkages Between Levels

If organizational levels are as distinct as this analysis suggests, how is it possible to think about a coherent school district organization? In other words, how should the connections between levels be formulated? Our basic contention is that each level of school system organization has its own core agenda even though certain activities are performed at more than one level. That is, events of differing character occur at each level to effect outcomes which are themselves characteristic of each level. For example, a school-level outcome becomes a productive condition at the class level yielding in turn a class-level outcome; and a class outcome in turn becomes a productive element at the instructional-group level yielding a group outcome; and so on. We have, then, a set of nested organizational layers, each having a conditional and contributory relationship to events and outcomes occurring at adjacent layers.

One way to study the linkages between organizational levels is to examine how resources manifest themselves and get transformed at each level. In this connection, the problem is to identify those locations where the distribution of resources remains roughly the same from level to level and those where the distribution changes. The changing distribution of resources provides indications of what parts of the organization simply transmit resources from one level to another and what parts change the composition of the resources: these latter changes, we believe, indicate that productive events are actually occurring, events that represent the direct application of the school's resources so that learning can occur. We are concerned here with distinguishing between how the school simply makes resources available and how it actually uses them. In order to show how this form of analysis might proceed, we will consider the case of the aptitude distribution of students.

School districts have at their command all sorts of resources: books and materials, time, the talents and preferences of teachers. But because schools depend in their operation upon the efforts and capacities of students, the abilities of students represent organizational resources in their own right; they are contributions to the overall workings of the school and to its outcomes. It is possible to examine the distribution of all resources at each level of school system organization. For example, one can think of the total pool of teachers in a district characterized by the distribution of experience. Perhaps one district assigns a random distribution of teachers so characterized to each school, while another assigns the more experienced teachers to one set of schools and the less experienced to another. And within schools, of course, the principal makes further assignments to classes, so that down the levels of the district, the distribution of a resource might stay the same or vary. And so it is with students aptitudes: we can trace their distribution from level to level. In our view, the most basic condition for the establishment of an instructional program is the distribution of students' aptitudes in a class. We take this position in the belief that teachers find ways to adapt their talents, time, and material resources to what children can do and to changes in what they can do. If they do not, instruction is not viable. (We note, however, that aptitude is not the only characteristic of children that figures into the design of an instructional program.)

Over the short run, school districts take the characteristics of children in a community population as given. And given the supply of children, the central administration assigns them to schools according to one or more well-known criteria: residential location, special need or talent, age, gerrymander, school racial composition.

The school itself can be regarded as a distribution of students' aptitudes, grade by grade, differentiated by age. One of the most fundamental administrative decisions is how a principal distributes each grade's student population into classes. Will they be random samples of the whole grade, will some be assigned disproportionate numbers of abler or less able students, will some be highly dispersed in their distributions while others are tightly clustered, will some have bimodal distributions while others have rectangular ones?

Whatever the reasons for composing different kinds of classes, the fact remains that each class distribution represents the "hand" that each teacher is "dealt." It then becomes the teacher's job to fashion the particular group of students into some kind of classroom organization that will permit instruction to take place more or less effectively. It must be recognized, moreover, that the schoolwide aptitude distribution constrains the variety of class distributions that can be composed. If, for example, the total spread of each grade is very narrow, whether it clusters around the bottom, middle, or top of the district range, there will be difficulty creating classes that have wide internal variation. Furthermore, if the school population is heavily weighted with low-ability students, there will be few very able ones either to divide up equally or to segregate into a single class. Class distributions, in short, are not cut out of whole cloth.

The teacher's task is to "play" the "hand"; that is, to devise an instructional program that takes account of the variety of student aptitudes represented in the class and to provide learning experiences for the different number of weakly, moderately, and highly talented students. As noted earlier, we do not maintain that aptitude is the only consideration that teachers take into account in organizing classes for instruction. They surely look at how mature their students are, how long they can keep working at a task, how well they get on with others—all considerations that influence not simply how well they can do academically but how much supervision and change of activity they require so that the classroom remains a liveable and workable place.

Our empirical evidence from fifteen first grade classes supports our contention that the class distribution of aptitude influences how teachers establish alternative group arrangements for carrying on reading instruction. We found, for example, that small classes (of about 20) with very few low-aptitude children were organized, at least for a while, in whole-class instruction and then reorganized in more or less close approximations of heterogeneous grouping. Larger classes (with 30 or more members) differed both in their initial grouping arrangements and in the subsequent modifications of them according to the number of low-aptitude children they contained. Teachers who had to deal with only the relatively small instructional burden of few such children were less constrained in the number of alternative grouping arrangements they employed. Those with many low-aptitude children invariably had to create a large low group as part of a classroom configuration consisting of three equal-sized groups.

The most important aspect of group formation turned out to be the mean aptitude level of each group. This group property was the major influence on the critical instructional decision of how much material to cover over a given period of time—the pace of instruction—which in turn was a major determinant of individual learning. Accordingly, through a set of intervening steps, the aptitude distribution of a grade (a school-level property) and, subsequently, the aptitude distribution of each class become constraining influences on how teachers organize classes for instruction with its consequent impact on individual learning.

What our formulation does is very simple. It locates the workings of schools at all organizational levels. It carries us some way in thinking about how the effectiveness of schools should be related to their workings. For example, it shows that classroom events have classroom outcomes, for when teachers transform a distribution of students according to ability to create instructional groups, they create class grouping arrangements which indeed are class outcomes. Group events likewise have group outcomes, for when teachers adapt instruction to the ability level of a group, they influence how much material the students in the group will cover. Coverage is a group outcome. Finally, the instruction of students in groups, influenced by their own characteristics, affects how much they learn. Learning is an individual outcome of schooling.

To a great extent, the effectiveness of outcomes from any particular level becomes known as they impinge on the workings of the next-lower level. For example, a principal's decisions about time available for activity within classes may be defective in that time blocks are too short to allow for the sustained instructional activities preferred by teachers. In a similar fashion, educational policies established in the federal and state legislatures and judiciaries which pertain to the allocation and use of school resources filter from level to level down through educational organizations. However well-conceived a policy may be as a matter of political or legal decision making, a well-intended policy will make little impact unless formulated in a way that takes into account the nature of a school's internal workings entailed in the production of its outcomes.

Although our work puts us in no position to identify all or even most of the organizational properties of schools that are relevant to the processes of educational policy making and implementation, we have made a beginning toward identifying elements of the workings of educational organizations. The concepts of multilevel productive processes within schools and the linkages of organizational levels through their outcomes are central to the formulation. So too is the idea that the events and activities comprising educational production are tied to the distributional properties of school system organization.

POLICY QUESTIONS

We turn now to the connection between our analysis of how schools work and matters of educational policy. We have no intention of treating educational policy making and implementation generally, but rather will consider two areas of national policy for which an understanding of school system and school operation is important. They are school desegregation and mainstreaming. In both cases we will try to show how paying attention to the distributional properties and levels of organization helps us to understand the connection between school production and educational policymaking.

School Desegregation

The Brown decision of 1954 contained two lines of argument whose implications do not necessarily lead to parallel implementations of policy. These are the notions of racial separation as inherent inequality and of separation as causing ill effects among individuals. It is not that these two lines of argument are inconsistent, but rather that the evidence required to show successful implementation is different in each case.

The inherent-inequality notion pertains most directly to constitutional rights; that rights of citizenship shall include equal access to public facilities, which means irrespective of race in this case. Segregation represents a denial of rights to a class of persons as a result of which there is a sense of social degradation that attends the arbitrary exclusion of a group of people from facilities to which access is guaranteed to others.

The second notion is that segregation creates bad effects because of the failure of segregated schools to provide equal educational results among individuals. It pertains to the technological adequacy of schools to produce equal educational results and gives rise to the kind of research represented by the Coleman Report, which among other things examined variations in school resources and their impact on individual achievement. While social degradation and poor learning are both ill effects, they are so in different ways. In the first instance, they pertain to the social position of a class of people; in the second, they pertain to the life circumstances of individuals.

While school desegregation (by whatever means) may well serve as a proper legal remedy for restoring constitutional rights—similar to the desegregation of restaurants, housing, swimming pools, public transportation, and state universities—through the guarantee of equal access to public facilities, desegregation does not necessarily guarantee that schools will operate differently to provide, in a technological and productive sense, better learning. The remedies for the technological inadequacies of the schools are not necessarily effected by the equalization of rights, any more than equal access to lunch counters is a guarantee of a good meal. This remedy simply guarantees the availability of meals of all qualities once there is no discrimination at the door.

With respect to both the constitutional and the technological considerations, the predominant social remedy over the past quarter-century of school desegregation has been to change the racial composition of the schools by redrawing catchment-area boundaries within school districts, altering feeder patterns, school pairing, and busing—voluntary and involuntary. In short, desegregation policy has entailed the reassignment of students, within the constraints imposed by demographic and housing patterns and by the boundaries separating municipalities, to change the racial composition of school populations.

Changing the racial composition of schools has been the subject of two distinct lines of research, typified by Gary Orfield's (1978) work on busing and Nancy St. John's (1975) on the impact of desegregation on educational outcomes—the academic and the noncognitive achievements of individuals. These works also represent attempts to assess progress in school desegregation on the constitutional rights side, to determine whether blacks have made progress in achieving their rights as citizens and whether successful law enforcement has taken place, and on the school effects side, whether desegregation has resulted in benefits to individuals—better learning—following the racial recomposition of schools and classes. Orfield in assessing busing treats it as a problem in effective law enforcement. St. John, by contrast, looks at the effects of the racial composition of schools and classrooms on individual learning and sentiment.

We will argue here that the legal remedies applied to the constitutional side of the desegregation question do not necessarily make schools work better. Changing the racial composition of schools or classrooms does not necessarily make them more productive or more likely to equalize the learning outcomes of black and white children. A successful desegregation plan may assure equal access of all children to comparable school resources and create schools that have similar racial compositions and thus assure equal rights of access. But that same plan does not necessarily alter the way schools operate beyond changing their racial composition. Only if racial composition can be shown to constitute an important element influencing instruction and achievement would we be able to say that equalizing rights of access can improve the working of the schools and, as a result, student performance.

Our evidence indicates, for example, that the distribution of students' aptitudes in schools represents a constraint upon the formation of classes and the resulting distribution of aptitudes within them. The aptitude distribution of classes, moreover, represents an important constraining influence upon the formation of subsequent instructional organization, particularly with respect to the establishment of reading groups which in turn have powerful effects on learning.

The school and class distributions of race are not the same thing as school and class distributions of aptitudes, however, because there is great variation in aptitude *within* racial categories. While our empirical study was not primarily concerned with racial differences, we did have predominantly white and predominantly black schools in our sample. Most interesting was the wide range of aptitude variation *within* both the black and the white classes—they resembled each other in range—and the extent of class-by-class variation in instructional arrangements and in learning found in both black and white schools. We take these findings as evidence for race not being a direct determinant of either how class instruction is organized or the amount of learning associated with instruction. We found racial composition and instructional organization, in short, to be independent. Of course, if one ignores the internal variation in classes, an association between race and learning can be found.

To the extent that our empirical findings hold more generally, then with respect to individual learning the distribution of school and class populations by race is rather beside the point. Teachers evidently respond to the distribution of students' aptitudes, which is a primary condition influencing the design of instructional arrangements. Busing and other constitutional remedies simply do not pertain to conditions shaping instructional organization. Admittedly, one could find schools in which the preponderance of low-aptitude children had a racial or ethnic identification. Under these conditions, race and aptitude would be confounded, and we would argue that our findings would then apply to race, but not necessarily for racial reasons.

On the surface, it might appear that school desegregation, seen from the perspective of individual benefits—better learning—is yet another example of a governmental policy gone wrong: a case where a policy enunciated at the apex of a governmental (judicial) hierarchy founders in its implementation at the local level. This conclusion seems unwarranted.

If we take first the constitutional rights side of the desegregation rulings, there is evidence that to the extent schools have been successfully desegregated—an extent that varies among communities—constitutional rights have been established or restored. But as we argued earlier, the law enforcement nature of the inherent-inequality doctrine does not necessarily have anything to do with individual benefits such as improved learning.

Second, from the individual benefits side, what is concluded about the effects of desegregation depends a great deal on how we conceptualize policymaking and policy implementing and on what we think about how far centralized policymaking can and should penetrate into the affairs of local organizations, such as schools.

There is much to be said for Burlingame's (1978) observation that "policies are usually add-ons to the existing interests of the system" (p. 240). They are attempts to effect change in already-existing systems which work according to standard (and not so standard) operating procedures, in response to prevailing conditions and their vicissitudes, and in ways that reflect the more or less successful resolution of conflicting interests. All of these forces have their own momentum in the steady or rocky workings of organizations.

Policy considerations affect the operation of local schools by representing another condition (or set of them) to which administrators and teachers orient themselves and respond as they deal with ordinary, prevailing realities on a continuing basis. And if this is the case, it is important to attend to this total constellation of conditions, including policies and attempts to comply with them, and not to think about school operation largely as a response to policy or as measured against considerations whose importance is specified by policy.

From the perspective of individual benefits in learning, a successful school desegregation policy does no more than change the racial composition of the schools. That in itself, for reasons we have already adduced, has no necessary bearing on the welfare of students as far as their learning from instruction is concerned. Their legal rights of individual citizenship, defined as equal access to public facilities, may have been restored. Instructional design appears to be shaped by how teachers modify the distribution of student characteristics in the classroom and in groups. And the establishment of groups is governed by considerations of what makes classes teachable, and they in turn are influenced by students' aptitudes and no doubt by other characteristics as well.

Only with the greatest difficulty do policies in the form of court decisions change the racial distributions of schools within districts. For a variety of political, social, and demographic reasons the racial characteristics of districts change over time and often frustrate the designs of policymakers. Influencing events that occur within schools, a fortiori, is an even more difficult procedure. The diversity of such events is virtually unreachable by attempts to implement the general expectations embodied in legislative and judicial policies. And surely, it is not possible to establish some arbitrary guideline indicating that such policies will penetrate thus far and no farther into the inner workings of school districts and schools in the interest of achieving equality of experience, however lofty the moral principle. But that is not the point. Rather, organizations do not roll over before such policies. They incorporate them insofar as their working personnel treat them as one among a number of conditions and contingencies, more or less recalcitrant in nature, that they must bear in mind as they go about their work of keeping the educational organization productive, or perhaps just operating.

In a sense, policy analysis represents a view from the top even when it seriously considers, as it often does, the problems at the bottom (see Elmore, 1979–80; Lipsky, 1980; Wilson, 1973). Its point of reference is usually some benefit in general policy terms and what happens to that benefit as members of the organization try to effect the policy. Operating organizations, however, are not *primarily* concerned with the general benefit but rather with the mission of the organization and the activities that keep it viable. Both of these—mission and operation—must come to terms with general policies, such as school desegregation, but are unlikely to be shaped in a major way by them simply because school systems have other jobs to do than to desegregate themselves, not to mention the fact that they may be called upon to respond to several policies, not all of them related or consistent. Accordingly, while the policy analysis perspective absorbs and subordinates organizational operation to a conception of the policymaking process, an organizational production perspective absorbs and sub-ordinates policy considerations to a conception of organizational operation and productivity.

From the perspective of policy analysis, our work on the productive activities of schools can help explain why the implementation of school desegregation policies will not markedly or consistently affect such intended individual benefits as learning. Neither instructional experiences nor learning outcomes are likely to be equalized by changing the racial composition of *schools*. The reason is that schools are organized for instruction at classroom and subclassroom levels on the basis of student characteristics—primarily aptitude but not excluding other characteristics—that to a considerable extent cut across race. This conclusion and its explanation, then, are no different in type from those emerging from many investigations that show how generally formulated policies founder when attempts are made to implement them at the street level, on the shop floor, or whatever the appropriate metaphor.

From an organizational point of view, we can envision the situation of a school principal faced each year with the problem of assigning students and teachers to classes and, in the process, determining explicitly or implicitly the aptitude composition of each class and perforce setting the conditions by which teachers establish their instructional programs. A desegregation policy that changes the school's racial composition may or may not change its composition by aptitude (or by social maturity, for example) and accordingly may or may not influence the way the principal composes classes. There remains, however, the outstanding question of whether a desegregated school population necessarily entails desegregated classrooms within the school. The new question before the principal, then, is in what way if at all will race be taken as an *additional* consideration—resulting from desegregation policy applying to schools— in the composition of classes. The issue of policy implementation thus appears as a new contingency attached to a set of ongoing considerations that the principal takes into account.

Mainstreaming

We now turn to the other case—mainstreaming—which we will treat in far less detail but which will alert us to other types of policy implications related to our work. Recent mainstreaming legislation requires that school systems develop plans to assure that all handicapped children receive an education within the least restrictive setting appropriate to their individual needs. Developing individual educational plans, annual case reviews, and due process procedures constitute the mechanisms through which mainstreaming is to be achieved. Note particularly the strong emphasis in this legislation on both the needs and the legal rights of individual children.

The difficulties of educating handicapped students and the appropriate remedies are defined to a substantial degree by certain numerical properties of the handicapped school-age population. According to the National Center for Educational Statistics (1980), the handicapped (those served by PL 94–142 and PL 89–313) constitute about eight percent of the school-age population—a small minority. Moreover, that group, far from being homogeneous in composition, is further differentiated by type of disability and again by the age of the children. Number, type, and age are all categories that pertain directly to the nature of classificatory arrangements prevailing in schools and to certain premises underlying them: in particular that classes are graded by age and that they have a more or less conventional size. Associated with these arrangements are assumptions that class members can benefit from instruction in such a collective setting and that age provides a workable estimate of the social and psychological maturity required to work more or less independently and peaceably.

Even before the passage of recent mainstreaming legislation, districts have had to find ways of coming to terms organizationally with the handicapped student population. The most fundamental difficulties are most obvious. On administrative, though not necessarily on educational, grounds a case can be made for providing separate facilities for the handicapped. But that case would have to differ for each type of handicap. Emotionally disturbed and acting out students, whether or not they are intellectually talented, are disruptive. The partially sighted and hard of hearing require special instructional techniques that burden the teacher instructing otherwise normal students. They also require different teaching techniques from each other. Orthopedically handicapped students may have no sensory or intellectual deficits but cannot move physically with the class. Mentally retarded students will not be sufficiently responsive to ordinary classroom instruction. For the same reasons that handicapped students may be difficult to teach in regular classrooms, they cannot be readily grouped together in a class for all handicapped, even though they may be in some schools.

School districts are chronically faced with the problem of finding enough students of similar age and with the same handicap for whom to mount appropriate programs. In this situation, it is not surprising that some districts have joined together in interdistrict consortia in order to pool numbers and resources to provide some stability to an otherwise numerically unstable population. This makes it possible, for example, for one school in a particular district to provide a class for the partially sighted and another school in a different district to provide a class for the mentally retarded, both drawing from a cross-district catchment area. An individual solution would require the expensive remedy of providing a tutor for each student; a classroom solution would place excessive instructional burdens on teachers; a school-level solution would provide one or more classes for all handicapped students irrespective of type and age.

All these solutions are either prohibitively expensive, instructionally undesirable, or assume—unrealistically—large, stable, age-specific numbers of particular types of handicapped students.

It is important to recognize, moreover, that organizational solutions do not by themselves solve the problems of how to provide appropriate instruction for children with each of the different kinds of handicap; and there is nothing in our work that sheds much light on such instructional procedures. Nevertheless, districtwide and cross-district organizational arrangements can establish conditions that are more or less conducive to mounting appropriate instruction.

Policy decisions for coping with the handicapped, as manifest in the mainstreaming legislation, deal with the problem from a legal perspective, stressing the guarantee of individual rights, and from a family perspective, stressing the wishes of parents who want the most appropriate education available for their children. But contrary to conventional wisdom and rhetoric, schools are unable as organizational entities to provide services adapted to the individuality of each child. In the nature of the case they deal with categories of children and within that constraint provide more or less well for the needs of each individual. In fact, there is no organization that can ignore its collective well-being in order to serve every individual uniquely. (Nor, we might add, is it obvious that treating each individual or the smallest possible aggregation as instructional units is the soundest procedure—but that is another topic.)

We have argued here that the size and distributional properties of the handicapped school population are such that they need to engage districtwide (and even cross-district) interests even if in some cases actual modes of dealing with the handicapped do not transcend the class or school levels. While the strong individual focus of mainstreaming legislation is understandable in light of the ideological climate and political pressures prevailing at the time of passage, it is nevertheless out of joint as a matter of policy, given the organizational realities that school districts must confront. We suspect that the impact of this legislation, with its mandates to design individual educational plans to engage the participation of parents, teachers, and specialists and to guarantee due process, will be to preempt substantial amounts of time in planning, monitoring, and enforcement that will not be devoted to instructional activities. We also suspect that this legislation will not contribute much to the exploration of new, workable organizational arrangements and that the latter will remain much as they have been. Finally, we suspect that the legislation will provide a favorable atmosphere that will make teachers and administrators more receptive to ways of including some handicapped students in ordinary classrooms who would not ordinarily be assigned to them. The mainstreaming of some students will now have legitimacy that it lacked before because of the legislation. In effect, the implementation of the present legislation is likely to consist of the adaptation of a new policy to ongoing ways of doing business, with marginal benefits taking the form of a more receptive climate than in the past. The underlying organizational problems, we believe, will go largely unresolved, perhaps because they are not resolvable, perhaps because the policy in its legislative form does not address the underlying organizational problems: how to respond to the numbers, ages, and types of handicapped children.

SUMMARY

Rather than dealing primarily with the nature of policymaking, this paper speaks most directly to the nature of the conditions and the activities fashioned to deal with them that comprise the social organization of schools. It draws attention to their inner workings across levels of organization and to a particularly crucial set of considerations involving the distributional composition of resources—in particular, the characteristics of students—that shapes the character of their productive activities. As we indicated earlier, we make no claim that these elements exhaust all that is important about the workings of schools; only that among other things, they are very important.

In the context of this volume about educational policy, we see this effort as providing useful knowledge about how schools work to produce what they do. In the cases of desegregation and mainstreaming, we see the distributional properties of school districts and their various levels of suborganization, particularly as they pertain to the characteristics of students, to be critical to understanding the implementation of broad educational policies. Both desegregation and mainstreaming policies put primary emphasis on the rights of individuals. At the same time, they do not take account of patterns of school organization that in the last analysis will influence whether those rights will actually be achieved. Desegregation policy is premised on the assumption that if the racial distribution at the school level is of the right composition and appropriate to guarantee the constitutional rights of individuals, then the inner workings of schools will be sufficient to bring about the individual learning benefits that the policy envisions. Our work on school production indicates that the second clause of that proposition may not be true; it also indicates why.

Mainstreaming policy is premised on the assumption that both the rights and the welfare of handicapped students are best guaranteed if maximum attention is directed to the particulars of each case. It is less cognizant of the fact that the aggregate of handicapped children in a given district is a peculiarly constructed distribution of a small proportion of students that for many reasons is exceedingly difficult to integrate into an organization designed to meet the needs of the nonhandicapped. To the extent that the remedies for the situation are in the first instance organizational, mainstreaming policy and the distributional realities of the situation fail to join. More generally, as far as policy formation and implementation are concerned, it does not follow that remedies designed to benefit individuals are most appropriately defined at the individual level. Benefits to individuals are perhaps more likely to ensue if policies are designed more around the workings of organizations and what they are competent and incompetent to do for individuals. That sort of thing, however, requires knowledge about how organizations work. Of course, if organizations turn out to be incompetent to achieve certain ends, given the prevailing states of knowledge and the art, then no amount of policy making and implementation can compensate.

What is really at issue in both the desegregation and the mainstreaming cases is how the productive apparatus of schools can be organized to provide acceptable learning levels for as many students as possible and to cope with the extraordinary demands that a minority of handicapped students present. These issues cannot simply be addressed by legislative and judicial policies; they must also be addressed with knowledge and expertise. Perhaps one reason that many broad legislative and judicial policies fail is that general policy solutions are invoked to solve problems for which we lack this knowledge and expertise. Policy, then, becomes a substitute for them. The provision of human services of a social character—we seem to do better in the medical area perhaps because more attention is devoted to the base of knowledge and expertise—has long been hobbled by the absence of workable knowledge. Policies, then, that enjoin people to achieve ends that they are capable of achieving are one thing; those that erroneously assume such capabilities to be in place when they are not or that fail to come to grips with the way things actually work are something else. But even when the formulation and implementation of public policies appear to be workable ways to effect social change, we must keep in mind that policies do not remake operating organizations into neutral means for their implementation. Policies at the lower organizational levels become one among several prevailing conditions and contingencies that constitute the organization's working environment.

REFERENCES

Barr, R. and Dreeben, R. *How schools work*. Unpublished manuscript, University of Chicago, 1981.

Burlingame, M. Impact of policy decisions on schools. In L. S. Shulman (ed.), *Review of research in education 5*. Itasca, Ill.: Peacock, 1978.

Elmore, R. F. Backward mapping: Implementation of research and policy decisions. *Political Science Quarterly*, 1979–80, *94*, 601–616.

Lipsky, M. *Street-level bureaucracy*. New York: Russell Sage, 1980.

National Center for Educational Statistics. *The condition of education*, (1980 Edition). Washington D.C.: U.S. Department of Education, 1980.

Orfield, G. *Must we bus?* Washington D.C.: Brookings, 1978.

St. John, N. H. *School desegregation outcomes for children*. New York: Wiley, 1975.

Wilson, J. Q. *Varieties of police behavior*. Cambridge: Harvard, 1978.

PART II

Teaching as Work and Profession

In the first part of the handbook the authors summarized the research on the characteristics of effective classroom teaching and effective schools. The papers in this part discuss the character of teaching as work. Who become teachers and how are they educated? What are the controversies over proper means for attracting and holding teachers in the profession? How do teachers learn to teach both from formal and informal sources? What roles are played by state and national agencies, unions, and other institutions in the quality and character of the teaching force? To the extent that neither effective teaching nor effective schools can be deployed in the absence of teachers, understanding the composition, quality, attractions, and problems of the teaching profession becomes central to any policymaker's attentions.

In the opening chapter of this section, Gary Sykes addresses the questions of teacher quality, its past traditions, its present state, and those policies he views as most promising for the future. From his perspective at the National Institute of Education, where he directs the program on teaching and policy, he examines the attempts to exert quality control over teaching through the vehicle of state laws that set standards for new entrants into the field, either via mandatory tests, higher preparation standards, or a combination of both. Sykes points out that we need both screens and magnets, both methods of filtering less competent individuals out of teaching and of attracting the truly talented into the field. After reviewing a number of studies documenting why both these processes are replete with difficulty, he entertains a number of ways in which policies can be drawn to improve the rewards of teaching.

Donna Kerr is also concerned with the quality of teaching in the United States. She is also concerned with the quality of those attracted to teaching and reviews in great detail the literature on the changing characteristics of candidates for teaching certificates. Her focus then rests on preparation for teaching, as she asks, "How bad is teacher education?" Kerr brings together a large number of studies summarizing the state of teacher education in America, drawing comparisons to other forms of undergraduate professional education. After examining questions of quality control and education beyond initial certification, she proposes a radical set of policies for the improvement of teacher quality.

Sharon Feiman Nemser is particularly concerned with "how" people learn to teach. Whereas Sykes and Kerr devote most of their attention to the characteristics of present and future teachers, the quality of those who remain in the profession and those who leave it, and the standards of teacher education programs, Nemser asks what is learned in learning to teach. Does it mean mastering the content to be taught? developing a personal style? acquiring the skills of classroom management? learning to explain, conduct discussions, group children, and test for achievement? Where are these learned? In what settings can such capabilities be enhanced during the course of a teaching career? How much impact do the varieties of pre-service and in-service teacher education have on the development of teachers? Most important, Nemser argues, schools must be understood as institutions in which teachers must continue to learn and develop along with their pupils. If the classroom serves as a central locus for continuing teacher education, then educational policies must reflect that understanding.

Cronin focuses on the ways in which the quality of teacher education is monitored and regulated at the state level. Two processes are involved: the accreditation of teacher preparation programs and the certification of individual candidates. Cronin reviews the variety of ways in which states deal with those processes and examines a variety of policies that have been proposed to improve the current conditions.

Sweet and Jacobsen then address the questions of the teacher work force from the perspective of supply and demand. Examining the problem demographically, they analyze the population and economic characteristics that produced the abundance of teachers we now call a surplus. They also review the general population characteristics that have created the decreased demand for teachers currently. Their analysis also focuses on changes in the patterns of employment, marriage, and fertility of the women who comprise the bulk of the teacher work force.

Among the most significant influences on the conditions of teaching today are the teacher unions. Collective bargaining agreements, strikes, platforms for negotiation have become central to defining the teacher role. Mitchell and Kerchner examine how labor relations have come to influence teaching. They give special attention to the manner in which particular patterns of job definition and administrative supervision serve to define the nature of a job as predominantly profession, craft, labor, or art. Each of these definitions carries important implications for the way teaching is pursued. They argue that collective bargaining and teacher organizations have encouraged the laboring conception of teaching work, while much of the rhetoric of teaching has pursued the concept of teaching as a profession. How one conceives of teaching work is clearly of great importance to educational policy. They conclude with a discussion of those implications.

CHAPTER 4

Public Policy and the Problem of Teacher Quality

The Need for Screens and Magnets

Gary Sykes

Teacher quality has emerged today as one of the major problems facing our educational system. To say this is not to denigrate America's teachers but to question how we attract, educate, and sustain them in this occupation. In a time of deep concern about the quality of education in this country indications are that we will require more of teachers intellectually and that teaching is decreasingly capable of attracting highly qualified college graduates. Stimulated by media accounts with such leads as "Help! Teacher Can't Teach," the public suspects a decline in teaching quality, and parents tend to compare their children's teachers unfavorably with their own. Deans in schools of education report that the quality of students entering the field has dropped, and they worry about teacher education's continuing negative stereotype on college and university campuses. Educational leaders make speeches about the problem and surveys of school board members, citizens, and school superintendents turn up teacher quality as a major concern.

This issue has risen as well to the attention of policymakers, who in the current climate of legislative and administrative activism are easily persuaded to sally forth against most any problem. Teacher quality, however, presents a series of knotty difficulties for public policy. On one hand, the availability and distribution of teachers in our society is determined by the invisible hand of many regional and subregional labor markets. Teacher supply and demand vary considerably from state to state, even district to district, in response to a wide range of social and economic trends. It is by no means clear that governments can efficiently intervene in a variety of local labor markets (Carroll, 1978). On the other hand, teachers are public employees and so the legitimate object of public policy. Furthermore, education is a central function in any society, touching most citizens directly, and teachers are critical to education, so the public has a strong interest in the quality of the teacher work force.

Confronted with mounting public concern about this issue, policymakers especially at the state level have responded via a variety of regulatory forays, seeking to set entry standards and to define the nature and extent of teacher preparation. The approach is time-honored and relatively common—state governments regulate some 800 occupations in the United States—but, this essay argues, will not by itself alleviate problems of teacher quality. Policymakers at state and local levels must complement

---

Opinions expressed are the author's. Endorsement by the National Institute of Education should not be inferred.

a regulatory approach to the issue of teacher quality with attention to the rewards of teaching. In the future our society will require more of teachers than ever before, yet this profession appears decreasingly able to attract, sustain, and hold talented people. We must devise policies and practices which make teaching more attractive and satisfying. Or, to use the organizing metaphor for this essay, public policy must create magnets to draw the talented in, as well as screens to keep the unqualified out.

What follows has four sections: first, a brief historical background followed by an assessment of likely future demands on teaching; next, a description and critique of state policy; then, a discussion of the rewards of teaching; and finally, recommendations for incentive-based policies.

THE EMERGENCE OF TEACHER QUALITY AS A POLICY ISSUE

Public concern about teacher quality is but the latest in a long history of suspicions about who teaches in America. Our social history reveals attitudes persistently equivocal toward teachers and a set of decidedly mixed messages about the status and value of this occupation.

In part the ambivalence about teachers manifests a more general strain in our culture which historian Richard Hofstadter identified in the title of his Pulitzer-prize-winning study, *Anti-Intellectualism in American Life*. Scholars, academics, artists, and others associated with the intellect have always been the object of suspicion and the butt of jokes as well as the source of awe and pride. The figure of the schoolteacher, Hofstadter (1963) notes, especially suffers this confused cultural legacy. As "... the first more or less full-time, professional representative of the life of the mind who enters into the experience of most children" (p. 309), the schoolteacher is entrusted with a vital mission, particularly in a nation whose greatest social invention, the very underpinning of its unique form of government, has been a universal, free, public education. Surely with such a noble charge, schoolteachers must enjoy the respect if not the reverence of the community? Not so. From the earliest days of the Republic teachers have as often been the source of ridicule, condescension, or pity as of respect. Furthermore, history suggests that the decision to teach has often been on a deficit basis, with the classroom a temporary stop on the way to something grander and more worthy and the job a sinecure for the timid and unaspiring or a grudging refuge for those passed over in marriage and the competition for more highly prized positions.

This overstates the case to be sure, and teaching has enjoyed a measure of public esteem and gratitude through the years. For many Americans teaching has been an attractive occupation, often a source of upward mobility and a means for realizing ideals of service to one's fellow man. For years, too, teachers were among the best-educated members of many local communities and so received respect as persons of learning and refinement. Teaching as well has been the premier occupation for college-educated women, affording one of the few professional, distaff careers available. And American letters contain more than a few endearing portraits of the schoolteacher. Yet despite this positive side, there is a long-standing taint associated with teaching and corresponding doubts about those who chose this occupation.

Historical evidence suggests that teaching has never attracted the best and brightest, which is not surprising given the status anomalies which surround it. Until recently, however, the public expressed little concern about this. On the whole, the bargain struck between society and its schoolteachers seemed a good one from society's point of view. Although committed in principle from the days of Horace Mann to universal, public education, in practice the school system served the populace quite selectively. Only a fraction of the entering student population completed high school (25 percent *still* drop out before graduation), while the immigrant poor and the minority student dropped out earlier in disproportionate numbers. The system then tended to deal with the lower levels of the ability distribution through a de facto policy of exclusion and indifference and was expected to serve the middle-American mainstream in a minimal way. Reading, writing, and 'rithmetic with a touch of citizenship filled the bill, and the system did not require intellectual giants to serve this agenda.

However, the evolution of rising educational attainment coupled with a concerted commitment to educational equity gradually intensified demands on the schools. The growth of the system alone created serious strains. The public-private, K–12 teacher work force now numbers some 2.1 million and so absorbs a major fraction of the college labor force. Unlike the medical profession, which in the wake of the Flexner report raised standards, shut down many medical schools, and restricted entry (Floden, 1980), the education professions have expanded rapidly to meet national need. To maintain, much less raise, quality in the face of rapid, massive growth by itself constituted a major problem, but our determination to hold more children longer in the schools, to supply a wider array of services to them (Tyack, 1979), and to establish academic achievement as an entitlement rather than an accomplishment has added immeasurable challenges to the job of teaching. The responsibility to produce learning has subtly shifted from student to teacher (Tomlinson, 1981; Travers, 1981) and today covers a broader array of students and a broader array of outcomes than at any previous time.

A New Consensus about Schooling

Today as well there are portents of a new consensus about the principal shortcoming of schooling. Beginning in the late sixties the cry, "Back to Basics!" captured the public mood and set the direction for change. The slogan made educationists uncomfortable, smacking of some primitive, simpleminded notion foisted on the experts, who had loftier, more interesting, more complicated things in mind for the schools, but there was no denying it tapped a powerful current of public opinion. Today, though, glimmers of a new consensus are appearing, a reaction to the orthodoxies of basics. Christopher Jencks (1978) first sounded the new note with an article in the *Washington Post* titled "The Wrong Answer for Schools Is: (b) Back to Basics." There he argued that students are not doing badly on basic skills achievement but do fail to acquire more complex cognitive skills. The problem is not with decoding skills in reading but with that complex bundle of cognitive processes known as comprehension; in mathematics, not with computation but mathematical reasoning and problem solving; and in writing not with grammar and mechanics but with the ability to produce coherent, literate paragraphs. These problems chiefly emerge at the secondary level, where tests indicate graduates also have less information. They are ignorant of literature, history, contemporary society, or scientific subjects and are unskilled at using reference works to acquire information.

Recent test results, especially from the National Assessment of Educational Progress (NAEP), bear this out. In a variety of subject areas including reading, writing, mathematics, and science, achievement among nine-year-olds has improved over the last decade. However, achievement gaps develop between the sexes and among the races as children continue through school, and seventeen-year-old students of all kinds reveal little ability to think clearly and to express themselves cogently. A study from the 1979–80 National Assessment of Reading and Literature concluded:

> American schools have been successful at teaching students to formulate quick and short interpretations, but have not yet developed in students the skills they need to explain and defend the judgments they make. The end result is an emphasis on shallow and superficial opinions at the expense of reasoned and disciplined thought (NAEP, 1981, p. 4).

At the middle and secondary levels, then, when students are expected to develop complex skills and to deepen mastery of subject matter, serious achievement problems clearly emerge. Yet the problem is in part rooted in elementary-level teaching. Prolonged, intense emphasis on drill-skill approaches to reading in the elementary grades drives out attention to comprehension, to the critical process of making meaning from the written word. One recent observational study of elementary reading, social studies, and science lessons concluded, "Practically no comprehension instruction was seen" (Durkin, 1979, p. 520). Estimates of time spent on comprehension in particular classrooms ranged from one to eleven percent of total classroom time. Without moving too far into debates over reading methods, it is fair to say that our system of teaching reading heavily emphasizes decoding at the expense of comprehension.

Inseparable from the emerging emphasis on higher-order cognitive skills such as problem solving, learning how to direct one's own learning, and comprehension is a concern that students engage and master more complex subject matter. Recent evidence, however, indicates that the secondary curriculum lacks intellectual rigor for many students (Coleman, Hoffer, and Kilgore, 1981; Jackson, 1981; Schmidt, Note 1). Although demanding and advanced-level subjects are available, only a minority of students choose them, while for many an incoherent collection of trivial electives and vocationally oriented courses compose the bulk of their program. A recent ethnographic study of two urban high schools portrayed the curriculum as the negotiated outcome of myriad entrepreneurial exchanges among teachers and students, with each group following their own interests, tastes, and concerns (Cusick, 1981). A social studies teacher created two economics courses based on his interest in the stock market; an English teacher offered "Music as Expression," featuring Bach, the Beatles, and the Beach Boys; and a business math teacher introduced computer programming, holding candy sales between classes to earn money for purchase of the computers. A fragmented, highly diversified curriculum with no center provides continuity of intellectual experience in only the most haphazard way; yet this is what many secondary schools purvey today.

In his famous essay on the aims of education, Alfred North Whitehead (1967) expressed two fears: the degradation of culture to scraps of information and the sterile transmission of inert ideas ". . . merely received into the mind without being utilized, or tested, or thrown into fresh combinations" (p. 1). His 1929 indictment of education accurately describes our current state of affairs. "The result of teaching small parts of a large number of subjects," he maintained, "is the passive reception of disconnected ideas, not illumined with any spark of vitality" (p. 2). That the school curriculum today hardly encourages the pursuit of intellectual excellence is surely a complicated matter but one thing is clear. To bend schools to this mission will require teachers deeply committed to intellectual excellence who exemplify this passion. The anti-intellectualism which Hofstadter perceived as a strain in our culture may be giving way to a call for a more truly educated citizen. As our society grows increasingly complex, the idea dawns on more Americans that both individual and collective survival depends on providing and acquiring a more sophisticated education and that the rhetoric of compensation, remediation, minimums, and basics obscures the real task for schools today.

Problems with the Teacher Work Force

If indeed a new consensus is emerging based on academic excellence and greater emphasis on complex cognitive skills, then demands will intensify for teachers capable of providing such an education. Such teachers must be masters of the disciplines they are to impart, and of a pedagogy that aspires to more than drill and memorization of facts. The evidence, however, on who is entering teaching is extremely disturbing, and the academic ability of education majors has become a major concern. Compared even to the overall national decline, SAT scores for education majors plummeted throughout the seventies, with similar declines appearing on such other tests as the National Teacher Exam and the Graduate Record Exam (Weaver, 1981). When college majors are ranked according to both a variety of standardized test scores and cumulative grade point average, education comes out near the bottom. That teaching attracts the least academically able *and* is decreasingly attractive appears incontrovertible.

In addition to this problem of quality, the supply of teachers is falling off. In the face of declining student enrollments and an oversupply of new teachers, enrollments in teacher education programs dropped nearly fifty percent between 1972 and 1980 (National Education Association, 1981, p. 5). Such a loss of students has jeopardized many teacher education programs with two results. Some universities have phased out teacher education, while others have lowered their standards to maintain enrollments. In the first case, the danger is that quality institutions are leaving the field, while the danger in the second is obvious. The lack of selectivity at the college level not only allows the ill-qualified to enter teaching but perpetuates the negative stereotype of teachers and teacher education majors long a commonplace on university campuses.

Projections indicate a rise in student enrollments by the late 1980s at the elementary level, and somewhat later at the secondary level, likely to touch off a new round of teacher shortages (National Center for Education Statistics, 1981, pp. 87f). Many communities (e.g., in the sunbelt states) are already searching for teachers in the face of climbing enrollments, and throughout the country shortages of mathematics, science, bilingual, and certain special education teachers are acute. In the past teacher shortages developed as a result of the rapid expansion of the educational system, especially as the "baby boom" generation reached school age. Then, as this generation went to college, they supplied a large number of new teachers. Future prospects, however, are not encouraging. Although college enrollments as a whole have not fallen off, the number of full-time students entering four-year colleges from secondary school will decline simply as the 18-to-24-year-old age group shrinks after 1982. This is the primary pool from which future teachers will likely be drawn. Even more discouraging is the drop in education enrollments. While undoubtedly a response to the depressed labor market for teachers this also reflects the declining attractiveness of teaching as a career for young people. The teacher shortages of the future are likely to result for the first time from teaching's dwindling power to draw young people into its ranks. This historically unprecedented development is deeply disturbing and means that we can no longer count on simple demographics to bail out the system.

Recruitment is not the only problem facing teaching today. Evidence on who is leaving the profession is equally worrisome. For example, one recent study using national data found attrition from teaching consistently related to measures of academic ability (Vance and Schlechty, Note 2): the more academically able the teacher, the more likely to leave teaching within the first few years. In fact, it appears that at each point of choice including initial and final selection of a college major, the choice of an occupation, and the continuing option to stay or move on, the decision goes against teaching among the most intellectually capable.

This finding, of course, does not bear pushing too far. People who leave teaching may simply find themselves ill-suited to this occupation, so their departure may benefit teaching. The most ambitious may also move out of the classroom soonest, on their way into educational administration or other lines of work. Again, ambition is not a sign of excellence in teaching and such upward mobility could be a boon to teaching by freeing those discontented (therefore ineffective) with a longer tenure in the classroom. Information about who enters and stays in teaching paves no royal road to firm judgments about the quality of teaching, but all things equal we would prefer that teachers be more rather than less academically capable. The tendency, however, appears to the contrary.

Concern over such aggregate statistics as the test scores of education majors and teacher-leavers conceals another problem more intractable still: the equitable distribution of teachers among school districts and within districts among schools. Districts offering the least pleasing living and working conditions naturally have the greatest difficulty attracting and holding teachers. Rurally isolated areas and inner cities in particular share this problem and have been unable to offset their competitive disadvantages with higher salaries or other benefits. Teacher turnover in both areas is reportedly quite high, with the classic mobility pattern of teachers featuring a move from inner city to suburban schools. (This pattern was somewhat disrupted in the seventies when declining enrollments forced seniority-based layoffs and the reassignment of teachers according to contract provisions and personnel policies [Murnane, 1981].) Longstanding problems of distribution complicate the issue of teacher supply considerably. The rich get richer and disadvantages tend to accumulate and cluster. Poor districts serving variously disadvantaged student populations confront the most acute manpower problems as well.

SCREENS WITHOUT MAGNETS: TRENDS IN POLICY TOWARD TEACHING

Policymakers especially at the state level have not been shy about addressing these teacher work force problems. In fact, efforts to keep up with new laws, regulations, and programs fall constantly behind the action. Nevertheless, certain trends are clear and a movement of sorts is discernible. In state after state the approach has taken its cue from the student competency testing movement. In addition to competency tests for teachers, state regulation has taken a variety of forms including standards for entry to teacher education programs, requirements for internships and other extensions of preservice education, behavioral assessments of new teachers' classroom practice by state agents, and provision for ongoing education up to and beyond the tenure decision. Depending on who is counting and how recently they have checked, over thirty states in the past three to four years have significantly revised their teacher licensing and certification requirements (Sandefur, 1981), a most rapid and explosive growth in educational policy.

Leading the charge have been the Southern states, most notably Georgia, Florida, Louisiana, South Carolina, and Oklahoma. The Southern Regional Education Board has also drawn attention to issues of teacher quality through a series of reports and task forces (Southern Regional Education Board, 1980, 1981). The regional origin of the so-called "competency assessment" movement reflects some of the difficulties Southern schools have traditionally faced in attracting qualified teachers given the South's lower-than-average salaries and expenditures on education. However, Arizona, Colorado, California, and Virginia have also recently mandated tests for certification and there has been considerable legislative and state board ferment in a variety of other states too.

This new body of school law varies somewhat from state to state but shares underlying assumptions about how to upgrade the occupation of teaching. A look at developments in a few states will illustrate the pattern. In Georgia, the state department of education took the lead in developing a new approach to assessment for certification. Their requirements include two paper-and-pencil tests: the first in basic skills, which all students must take for admission to their major area of study; the second, a criterion-referenced test for education majors in their teaching field upon completion of their undergraduate program. Finally, the most unusual aspect of Georgia's plan involves six in-class assessments of teachers during their first three years on the job by state observers. Beginning in the early seventies the state supported several research projects aimed at identifying and validating a set of generic competencies. This work resulted in an observer rating instrument which state inspectors use for their classroom visits. Teachers must receive acceptable performance ratings to qualify for a renewable certificate.

South Carolina's General Assembly recently passed the Educator Improvement Act, which establishes a variety of new certification and training requirements. Beginning college students must pass a basic skills exam to gain admission to a teacher education program; student teachers must complete a full semester of practice teaching and be observed at least three times by a university faculty member; provisional and annual contract teachers must also be observed a minimum number of times and receive feedback on these evaluations; finally, veteran teachers too must be observed and must earn credits for recertification in courses related to their subject areas. Connected to these testing and observation requirements are admonitions that the resulting information be fed back both to individuals and institutions who are then to remedy any deficiencies.

Oklahoma's new Bill 1706 is a similarly comprehensive effort. Provisions of this law increase admission standards into programs of education, require more clinical fieldwork in the preparation process, mandate competency examinations in subject areas before graduation, add an entry-year internship before certification, and include regular monitoring of first-year teachers by a committee composed of a principal, a consulting teacher, and a teacher educator. The heart of this legislation is this last provision, the Entry-Year Assistance Program. The state has appropriated funds to grant each consulting teacher a stipend of $500 per year, and each committee must recommend full certification or another year of supervision. At the end of the second year the committee makes a final decision on certification.

Themes in the New Legislation

These three examples are perhaps the most far-reaching of the recent state policy efforts to regulate teaching and illustrate the direction which policy is taking. There is first a palpable concern to prevent the unqualified from entering teaching and an underlying suspicion that people of *very* limited ability, i.e., functional illiterates, have in the past been able to become teachers. The traditionally shadowed status of teaching is certainly visible today in such suspicions. Tests to measure basic skills, mastery of subject matter, and even teaching-readiness are increasingly commonplace. The tests and cutoff scores are not particularly rigorous but do serve to screen out those who have failed to acquire minimal knowledge and skills.

This emerging body of state law also raises issues about control over standard-setting, with the ambivalent responses of educators suggesting underlying tensions. Teaching's public image might well benefit from the unequivocal commitment of teacher and teacher training organizations to high standards and to their enforcement as a matter of professional association policy. However, educators have been neither unanimous nor strong-willed in taking such a stand. Consequently state policymakers are increasingly inclined to step in and assert themselves, in effect chiding the education establishment for not doing a proper job of standard-setting. In principle the institutions which train teachers could be the guardians at the gate, allowing only those most qualified to enter. In practice, however, they survive and prosper by enrolling students, not by serving as the conscience of the profession. Over the past decade as enrollments have dropped, education programs have struggled to balance their own survival with the maintenance of entry standards. The outcome has not always been happy for the quality of the profession and so the states have become involved. This has meant though that standard-setting is a function decreasingly controlled by the teaching profession itself, a development which at least some educators decry.

Georgia's scheme extends the concern for standard-setting beyond paper-and-pencil instruments to behavioral assessments of a teacher's merit. The forerunner of this approach is competency-based teacher education, an effort begun in the sixties to organize a professional curriculum around a set of research-derived "teaching competencies" validated via correlation with student outcomes. Although this approach seems plausible, it has not widely taken hold and the validity of Georgia's fourteen competencies has been recently challenged by the very researchers who helped develop the program (Coker, Medley, and Soar, 1980).

In addition to the gatekeeping functions just outlined, a minor theme in some of the new legislation stresses continuing education for teachers and corrective feedback for training programs. The Louisiana legislature, for example, recently passed the Professional Improvement Program which provides salary incentives to teachers in exchange for participating in classes and workshops. To be eligible, teachers must submit a plan to a school-district committee made up of other teachers which justifies the particular courses and workshops they will take over a five-year period. Each committee will also have that teacher's most recent evaluation and may suggest modifications to the plan based on weaknesses set forth there. This same spirit animates provisions of the South Carolina and Oklahoma legislation. Programs as well as individuals are to benefit from evaluative information. The South Carolina act stipulates that colleges and universities are to receive results of the basic skills and teaching-area examinations ". . . in a form that will assist them in identifying strengths and weaknesses of their teacher training programs" (McDaniel, 1981, p. 118). The Alabama Board of Education has even considered linking certification of teacher education programs to their students' performances on the state's recently developed teacher certification tests (Education Week, 1981, p. 5).

Finally, arguments advanced by educators to extend preservice preparation (Denemark and Nutter, 1980; Smith, 1980) have proven influential in a number of states. While other professions such as law, medicine, and engineering have gradually increased the amount of special training necessary for licensing, teacher education has remained a fraction of the undergraduate program. To add more college and university coursework, however, would increase the initial costs of becoming a teacher beyond what the market might bear and fails to answer students' demands for more practical experience. The solution, as in the Oklahoma case, has been an intern year where the beginning teacher is supervised and evaluated on the job prior to receiving a full certificate. Rather than a sink-or-swim experience, the first year of teaching becomes an extension of the training program and establishes a further check point in the selection process. Costs may be spread among a university or college, a school district, and individual teachers so the burden on any one is not onerous. Such a scheme tilts preservice education toward an apprenticeship model emphasizing practical experience with professional support in the teacher's classroom without eroding the time devoted to academic preparation.

Tightening entry requirements, mandating evaluative feedback, and extending preservice training have a number of obvious benefits from the policymaker's perspective. In an era of rising public concern about the quality of teachers but declining prospects for greater expenditures on education, this accountability-oriented approach is doubly attractive. It allows keepers of the public purse to adopt a stern posture without much drawing on those purse strings. The new screens are a visible sign of concern about teacher quality, an expression of intent that only the qualified shall enter the public service in education (California now requires a basic skills test for would-be administrators as well as teachers). At the same time, the new screens are not expensive. To construct and administer tests, monitor results, and require more training involves relatively minor costs which can be distributed across individuals and institutions. Furthermore, in the face of an oversupply of teachers, screens make good sense. In prior decades a shortage of teachers made raising entry standards a somewhat futile symbolic gesture. Simply to have enough adults staffing the nation's classrooms required mass waivers of state and local requirements. Now, however, the time appears ripe for a new assertion of standards which can be enforced. Political support for such policies is strong, opposition weak and easily labeled as merely self-interested, and the costs minor. Little wonder that enthusiasm for standard-setting is enjoying a renascence.

Will the New Policies Improve Teacher Quality?

What is not yet clear, however, is whether these policies will substantially improve the quality of new teachers. The likelihood appears low for two reasons. First, implementation problems will burden such efforts. Second, this body of policy represents a lopsided approach to the problem. If teaching is decreasingly attractive to young people, then raising standards and restricting entry misses the point. In addition to setting standards public policy must provide incentives to make teaching more competitive as an occupation for the college-educated. This second point will take up the remainder of this essay, but a few words on the first point are necessary.

As noted, colleges and universities which prepare teachers must keep enrollments up to survive. This powerful motive is largely independent of the state of the teacher labor market and of the widely expressed concern for professional standards in teaching. State legislatures which on one hand allocate funds to teacher training programs on the basis of enrollments and on the other raise entry standards to such programs are sending a clear message to cut back. This ultimately means eliminating jobs, a painful proposition for any organization. Caught in this squeeze colleges and universities will adopt two courses of action: modest program reduction primarily through attrition and pro forma compliance with standards designed to maintain enrollments, hence budgets, hence faculty positions. So, for example, if grades are the criterion, then grade inflation is likely. If test scores are the criterion, then teaching to the test is likely. To prepare students for a test is not a bad thing in itself, but the resulting scores hardly certify that students possess the requisite skills and knowledge, especially when the tests are not very demanding to begin with and when students may take them several times. At best, then, the tests and other entrance requirements are likely to screen out only the abjectly deficient. Increased reliance on tests will raise the floor somewhat, but we should harbor no illusions that such a step will markedly improve the overall quality of the teacher work force.

Tougher tests and higher cutoff scores would meet this objection but raise other problems. One is the likelihood of teacher shortages within a decade or so which may once again require relaxation of standards simply to man classrooms. A more serious objection, however, is that minority candidates already fail the tests in disproportionate numbers. It would be unfortunate indeed if a policy aimed at improving the quality of teachers systematically excluded Black, Hispanic, and other minority candidates from this occupation. The Educational Testing Service has recently revised the National Teacher Examination (NTE) to counter charges of cultural bias, and the results may well make the test more difficult by emphasizing comprehension, analysis, and application of information rather than factual recall. The revised NTE will be a good test for the claim of a culture-free exam, but the collision between testing and affirmative action will continue to generate controversy. In the final analysis, however, none of these objections seriously undercuts the case for raising entry standards, and well-constructed tests are undoubtedly the fairest and most valid means for assessing certain prerequisites for teaching. At the same time, however, it appears likely that mandating higher entry standards will at best marginally affect the quality of students entering this field.

Requirements to increase in-class monitoring of teachers will likely be modest but innocuous reforms. In a sense they are hardly reforms at all. Most school districts already require administrators to routinely evaluate teachers based on classroom observations, checklists, and other devices. Whether such evaluations serve to improve teaching rests mainly on administrative discretion. Some principals and department heads take their responsibilities as instructional leaders quite seriously and work hard at staff development. Others rarely venture from their offices and conduct only the most pro forma assessments. Reforms which seek to improve the technical quality of behavioral assessments or to mandate more evaluations miss the point that this is primarily a human interactive process in which rewards are mutually exchanged, alliances formed, prejudices played out. The culture of most schools militates strongly against genuinely evaluative interchanges between administrators and teachers or among teachers. Evaluation consequently becomes a ceremony, a tacit agreement among school staff not to disrupt the "logic of confidence" which binds them all together (Meyer and Rowan, 1977). The chances that external mandates which set up oversight committees, introduce state agents as evaluators, or require more rigorous administrator assessment will alter this persistent feature of school culture are slim at best.

Finally, extending teacher preparation is a plausible notion in light of the miniscule amount of time currently devoted to this enterprise, but it raises suspicions about the payoff in terms of improved teaching. California, for example, requires for a permanent teaching credential a fifth year of study beyond the bachelor's degree to obtain a teaching certificate. Other states such as New York require a Master's degree to convert a five-year provisional certificate to a permanent one. In practice such requirements have merely impelled teachers to take the most convenient courses at the local community college to obtain their certificate. The upshot has not been to strengthen preservice education to any significant degree, as a hodgepodge of too often trivial courses strung out over several years hardly improves the quality of instruction.

The latest wrinkle shifts the emphasis from more coursework at the local college to an internship arrangement during the first year on the job. This appears a promising approach but much depends on the amount and quality of supervision actually provided to novice teachers. At present neither university faculty nor experienced teachers have the incentives, the resources, or the expertise to effectively supervise beginning teachers. College professors devote their energies to research, to their courses, and to university affairs. They are often far removed from the daily travails of life in classrooms. Experienced teachers are unaccustomed to working in a master-apprentice relationship with other adults, have few incentives to take time away from their own classes, and may not be familiar with the latest research on teaching. Again, these are not insuperable obstacles and over time with sufficient resources school districts and universities could develop the capacity to provide effective supervision. There is at present, however, no precedent for strong, effective supervision, and as argued below it will take a restructuring of the profession to make an intern year a truly valuable step on the road to becoming a master teacher.

Before turning to a discussion of the rewards of teaching, it may be helpful to recap the argument so far. Teaching in America developed as a special but shadowed occupation plagued by a number of status anomalies. In the post-Civil War years as the school system burgeoned, many communities turned to young women as a source of cheap but reasonably well-educated labor. Teacher salaries were set low and largely remained so. The profession filled with women, whose inexpensive labor for years constituted a hidden subsidy. The latter decades of the twentieth century, however, are witnessing the withdrawal of this subsidy as other professional careers open up for women. Teaching is unable to attract the academically capable to its ranks. In particular, aspiring college graduates with a grounding in mathematics and science can today earn double what a teacher makes, raising the specter of prolonged, intense shortages in these crucial subject areas. Finally, those schools most in need of excellent teachers are least likely to attract and hold them; turnover is high in urban and rural schools, seriously undercutting the quality of education provided there.

As we enter the twenty-first century the need for intellectually able teachers is likely to increase. Our school system today enrolls and retains more children for more years than ever before. Standards of literacy have subtly risen over the decades (Resnick and Resnick, 1977; Seitz, 1981), and the popular emphasis on basic skills may soon give way to concern for complex skills and for a deeper engagement with important subject matter. As intellectual excellence emerges as the new standard, the needed human resources may not be available to meet this challenge. Policymakers have not been oblivious to this problem, voting new policies which raise entry standards to teaching, increase assessment, and extend teacher education. These are worthwhile, necessary, but insufficient measures. They are likely to weed out the obviously unqualified and perhaps marginally improve the quality of first-year instruction. But in addition to screens, this profession needs magnets to draw in and hold the bright, able, and energetic college graduate. How to make teaching a more attractive occupation in a period of fiscal austerity is the critical policy issue for the near-term future.

THE REWARDS OF TEACHING

Occupations compete with one another for each generation's workers, a competition in constant flux due to shifting demographics, economic conditions, technological advances, cultural changes, and other macro-level factors. Each occupation has certain resources which make it attractive and ensure within broad limits its perpetuation. Before considering how to make teaching more appealing to young people, a look at its traditional attractions will be helpful. How has teaching been able to draw in young people? What is its appeal and how durable is it in light of current conditions? To anticipate, teaching possesses a number of enduring attractions so that fears about survival are clearly misplaced. However, a decline in the rewards of teaching and, equally important, a broad perception of this decline increasingly handicap this occupation in the competition for talented young people.

Writing about the occupation of teaching today means amending or updating Dan Lortie's thorough and insightful sociological portrait, *Schoolteacher*. Lortie treats the rewards of teaching in two chapters, one on recruitment, the other on career and work rewards. What follows draws primarily on Lortie's work, arguing, however, that developments subsequent to his study have undercut the classic attractions of teaching.

Teaching's Enduring Attractions

Lortie's analysis of teaching's enduring attractions reveals no surprises. When asked, teachers say they chose this profession because they enjoy working with other people. In a variety of surveys given over the years, this item consistently ranks first among teachers' reasons for joining. Closely coupled with this motive is a desire to serve, to perform a special mission. Teaching allows one to live out an ideal of service to one's fellow man and to engage in an intrinsically worthwhile vocation. The interpersonal and service themes are each powerful recruitment resources for teaching and are likely to appeal to some young people in every generation.

Material rewards—salary, vacations, fringe benefits, pension plans—Lortie lists as an inducement which he notes most teachers downplay in self-reports. He suspects, however, that material benefits, the job security offered by teaching, and the opportunity for upward mobility into white-collar work are potent attractions but that the ideology of teaching favors a service theme emphasizing dedication, sacrifice, and a strong sense of mission in the face of low salary and prestige. Recent findings from the work of economists tend to confirm Lortie's hunch that material rewards matter to teachers. Rather than draw on teacher surveys, economists examine teachers' responsiveness to wage differentials. Evidence indicates that teacher mobility both out of the profession and between districts is influenced by salary considerations (Baugh and Stone, Note 3). That teachers tend to leave the profession and move from one district to another in search of better salaries is not really surprising but contradicts the popular myth that teachers are service-oriented to the exclusion of material considerations. However, the material inducements of teaching likely affect men and women differently. Lortie argues that it is subjectively more costly for men to enter teaching as they must forego greater income opportunities than women and that the relative deprivation felt by male teachers explains the systematic tendency for teaching to attract more women than men.

Time compatibility is a third major attraction of teaching. Teacher working schedules have always been special, allowing extended holidays and a long break in the summer. Teaching allows women to integrate their work lives with family responsibilities because their work schedules coincide with their children's schooling. Teaching provides men more time for household responsibilities, too, as well as opportunities to undertake further study, pursue second jobs, and engage in recreational activities. Few other occupations offer such flexibility and this feature of teaching is likely a powerful attraction.

Accompanying these attractions of teaching are several social mechanisms encouraging entry. One is teaching's "subjective warrant," the sense that the job requires no special talents or extraordinary sacrifices. Entry is perceived as relatively easy. Coupled with this permissive warrant is the advantage that entry does not rule out pursuit of other occupations later on. College graduates may choose teaching as a temporizing measure while they consider what to do next and may easily reenter the profession after a time-out for family responsibilities or other work. Lortie also judges from his interviews that a variety of special circumstances encourage many young people to take up teaching. For example, some cite the influence of a favorite teacher of theirs while for others teaching is a family tradition. For minority children, the teacher may stand for mastery in the majority culture in which the student is marginal and insecure. Such an early identification may psychologically underpin the attractiveness of teaching for second-generation immigrants. Finally, blocked aspirations may benefit teaching, as this is a reasonably attractive second career for the college educated who cannot pursue their top choice. In this regard Lortie (1975) concludes that teaching functions ". . . as a stratification safety net which allows people to land without severe damage to their status aspirations" (p. 50).

Schoolteacher provides a portrait of teaching as easy to enter, an occupation possessing an unusual number of inducements relative to many other lines of work. Coupled with informal social mechanisms encouraging entry and a variety of other potent attractions has been the public subsidization of state teachers' colleges and the provision of easy college loans, notably the G.I. Bill in the postwar years. Lortie argues that preparation for teaching is one of the most widely accessible forms of vocational training offered by colleges and that "State governments played an important part in facilitating entry to teaching by creating low-cost, dispersed, and nonelitist training institutions" (p. 18). By this account at least, we should not worry about the attractiveness of teaching. Public support and informal inducements are plentiful, and teaching's recruitment prospects appear assured.

Uncertain Rewards in a Careerless Profession

There are complications, however, to this rosy picture. If eased access distinguishes teaching, so do the lack of rewards for persistence and commitment. Teaching is careerless, notes Lortie. There are no stages of advancement and few possibilities for progression. The twenty-year veteran is indistinguishable from the neophyte and the typical salary schedule features a gently rising income slope, with the top-scale salary no more than double that at entry level. To advance, men move into administration or leave the profession altogether. Career mobility for women has been conspicuously absent. The number of women elementary principals, for example, dropped from a high of over 50% in 1928 to the current level of 18%, with declines at the secondary level too (between 1965 and 1977, for example, women secondary principals dropped from 10% to 7% of the total) (Haven, Adkinson, and Bagley, 1980). Men consequently tend to enter teaching with little intention of staying. Women favor an in-out-in pattern, an accommodation to the birth of children and the demands of motherhood.

Career stages and differential rewards encourage workers to defer gratification and to maintain effort. An unstaged career which provides a uniform reward schedule based on seniority cannot command continued commitment. Teaching's incentive system is largely insensitive to variations in talent and effort. The dedicated exemplar receives the same salary, vacations, and other benefits as the drone who has retired on the job. Informal rewards controlled by the principal do exist, including, for example, selection for attendance at conferences; assignments to better classes with better schedules; coaching positions which enhance income; access to "soft" money; and selection for training programs (Wheatley, 1981, p. 262). These rewards, however, are relatively scarce. The consequence is an imbalance between job satisfaction and involvement. Those teachers who report working the longest hours do not express the highest level of satisfaction with work. Although the size of the imbalance is modest, this highlights the most glaring problem with teaching's incentive structure: the lack of advancement opportunities coupled with the scarcity of rewards for excellence and effort.

The primary rewards of teaching are intrinsic, however, and depend not on salary, advancement, or professional recognition, but on relationships with students and mastery of classroom processes. Such rewards fluctuate and *are* responsive to teacher efforts. "Reaching" youngsters and provoking their interest, having a good day or a good lesson, receiving thanks from students and former students, obtaining work from pupils, establishing and maintaining a well-disciplined, efficient classroom, these are some of the day-to-day gratifications of teaching. Yet teachers also testify to the difficulties of teaching, claiming that daily rewards are not plentiful. The knowledge of a job well done is surely satisfying, but on relatively few occasions do teachers receive direct rewards from students, parents, or administrators. Most often they face a perpetually daunting task—reaching each student day in and day out in a diverse class (or classes) of twenty-five or thirty on a broad range of outcomes.

A persistent theme in the interviews Lortie conducted with teachers was their deep uncertainty about how well they were doing. "The teacher's craft," he sums up, "is marked by the absence of concrete models for emulation, unclear lines of influence, multiple and controversial criteria, ambiguity about assessment timing, and instability in the product" (p. 136). Expectations placed on teachers are great, while their capacity to control the conditions of learning is limited. As a result, teachers must often settle for less than their occupational ideals call for. This discrepancy contributes to teachers' anxieties about their efficacy and with the infrequency of occasions for pride makes teaching a somewhat stingy occupation in terms of rewards.

Diminished Rewards in the Future

Lortie's portrayal reveals a trade-off between eased access and modest career and work rewards. What, though, of the future? No sea changes are likely but the relative attractions of teaching may well be diminishing. The problem, however, concerns quality not quantity, a distinction not addressed in Lortie's work. The question is not whether teaching can attract enough people, but whether it can attract and retain capable people. Increasingly it appears that teaching is losing the competition among professional occupations for the best college graduates.

The reasons are both obvious and subtle. The teacher labor market has been saturated for some time, meaning more competition for jobs and reduced interdistrict mobility as a way of obtaining better wages and working conditions. By the early seventies, entry to teaching was no longer as easy as Lortie's analysis suggests. The "baby boom" cohort hit the job market as the school-age population dropped, and teaching jobs in many communities disappeared. Teacher salaries rose significantly through the sixties but beginning in 1972 began to lose ground to inflation. And in many school systems extreme turbulence and uncertainty begotten of student desegregation, involuntary teacher transfers, and dismissal of teachers to accommodate declining enrollments threatened teaching's traditional job security. Over the last decade, then, the material benefits of teaching have seriously eroded.

By themselves, however, these changes are not telling. The entire college labor market has suffered of late, prompting a debate over whether Americans are "over-educated," as growth in the economic returns to higher education slowed (Freeman, 1976; Rumberger, 1981). Teaching salaries have lost ground to the Consumer Price Index, but so have most wages; teaching's position relative to comparable occupations is unchanged. And the teacher labor market is likely to rebound within the decade, renewing employment prospects first at the elementary, later at the secondary level. Likewise, the loss of security may also be a temporary phenomenon unlikely to persist much beyond the eighties. According to this view, we have pretty much weathered the storm and can expect a return to stability.

To explain the decline in teaching's drawing power, we must look further. One clue lies in public attitudes toward teaching. Is this profession still esteemed by parents concerned about their children's careers? Does teaching still appeal as a calling, a noble vocation offering the chance to serve? Apparently not. In response to the question, "Would you like to have a child of yours take up teaching in the public schools as a career?" the Gallup Poll reported 75% answering "Yes" in 1969, 67% in 1972, and 48% in 1980. Our society today probably produces as many young people seeking personal service careers as ever,* but teaching is no longer as attractive an option

---

* Although a number of commentators (Lasch, 1979; Yankelovich, 1981) portray youth today as self-centered and materialistic, the evidence is by no means clear. In a series of *Washington Post* articles titled "Coming of Age in the Eighties" Dan Morgan counters the common view of self-absorbed youth. For example, he notes that in 1977, 250,000 people between the ages of 14 and 18 applied for 40,000 positions in the Young Adult Conservation Corps. And, when George Gallup polled 18- to 29-year-olds in the "barometer county" of Dayton, Ohio, he discovered that one out of three young people desired a social services career of some sort. Gallup concluded, "The problem we face in America today is not a lack of willingness to serve or to help others, but to find the appropriate outlet for this." See Dan Morgan, "Growing Up Bored: 'There's Nothing to Do, so You Get High,'" *Washington Post*, Tuesday, December 29, 1981, A1–A6.

for them. Economic fears in the face of persistent inflation, periodic recessions, and a stagnant GNP contend with aspirations to serve and to work with people. Ironically, the one development—unionization and collective bargaining—which has enhanced the material benefits of teaching has also undercut public esteem for the profession and dispelled nobler illusions about teaching as a special calling. Faced with striking teachers, protracted contract negotiations, the NEA's heavy political activity at state and national levels, and the AFT's close affiliation with the AFL-CIO, the public sees little distinction between teachers, garbagemen, policemen, firemen, or other newly militant public employees. Teaching has significantly lost its innocence in the struggle for better pay and working conditions and so some of its appeal to the service ideals of youth.

In other respects, too, our society no longer supports a service ideal as it once did. The contrast between our two most recent decades is revealing. John Kennedy's ringing inaugural challenge. "Ask not what your country can do for you, but what you can do for your country," touched off an unprecedented era of public service. The sixties saw the birth of the Peace Corps, Vista, and Teacher Corps. Students received draft deferments to teach, and elite universities such as Harvard, Stanford, and Duke offered Master of Teaching programs under Ford Foundation auspices. A generation of college students eagerly sought ways to serve, and teaching was one such honorable vocation. Rather than feeling slightly embarrassed and considerably disadvantaged in relation to classmates heading to business, law, or medical school, students took pride in their idealism and their mission to serve.

The curtain rang down rather quickly on this drama of youthful idealism in the face of a bitter, divisive war, a spate of shocking assassinations, and a steadily worsening economy. In the seventies, the psychological and economic costs of vocational idealism escalated rapidly. Hard-eyed realists emerged from colleges, replacing the visionaries and rebels of the Camelot generation, and calculations of self-interest and the lure of careers offering good pay, prestige, and opportunities for advancement replaced the desire to serve and to forge a better society. Teaching's brief appeal to the college elite vanished almost as quickly as it had appeared.

The troubled relationship between adolescents and adults may also cause prospective teachers to shy away or to leave teaching early. Anecdotal and survey evidence indicates that secondary students find their work experiences and their peer subculture in school more compelling and enjoyable than their relations with parents and teachers or their engagement with school subjects (Benham, Giesen, and Oakes, 1980; Cusick, 1973; Steinberg et al., Note 4). Although enthusiastic high school teachers continue to spark students' interests, conditions today increasingly work against the junior high and high school teacher. The statistics on violence in schools and assaults on teachers grab the headlines, but the more widespread concern is with student apathy toward what teachers have to offer. The erosion of adult authority in home, school, and community has received considerable comment. In secondary schools this takes the form not so much of disruption and insolence (although these are often present), but of a denial that teacher intentions for students are worthwhile.

If Lortie is correct in stressing the primacy of teaching's psychic rewards won through engagement with students, there is good reason to believe such rewards are more difficult to come by. The effects on recruitment are twofold: some young teachers leave early in discouragement and prolonged exposure to teaching is no longer a potent recruitment resource. Rather than revere their teachers, many adolescents feel indifference toward them and perhaps wonder why anyone would take such a job. This trend primarily affects teaching at the junior high and secondary levels and is by no means universal nor inevitable. The literature on effective schools contributed by social scientists and journalists makes clear that in urban, suburban, and rural communities, in schools serving the affluent and the impoverished alike, positive, exciting things occur between teachers and students. Nevertheless, in many schools of all kinds a muted but marked conflict of generations has frustrated the best efforts of teachers and darkened perceptions of the joys of teaching.

Of all the reasons for the decline in teaching's relative attractiveness, however, the changing role of women in our society has had the most momentous impact. Despite fluctuations over time in the actual proportion of women in the teacher work force, this profession was institutionalized as women's work from the early days of the common school. Society served as chief beneficiary of this social fact, gaining a pliable, inexpensive work force for a burgeoning school system. However, women's under-valued labor constituted a hidden subsidy to education. The women's movement and the drive for equal rights coupled with economic pressures on women to work are changing all this. Professional careers formerly closed to women now beckon with results already apparent. For example, a recent Census Bureau report shows that among college-going women between 1966 and 1977, education majors dropped from 760,000 to 601,000 while business majors swelled from 204,000 to 819,000 (Adkison, 1981, p. 338). Corporations, law offices, and engineering firms accommodate women's family responsibilities, and day care is more available and socially acceptable. College-educated women have higher aspirations and seek personal fulfillment through professional careers as well as through marriage and motherhood.

Teaching continues to offer its particular appeals to women, but they are relatively less potent. Women can now make more money elsewhere, can integrate their work and family lives in professions other than teaching, and can pursue careers instead of merely taking jobs. No longer is teaching the zenith to which most college-educated women can aspire. Indeed, in the eyes of her more liberated peers, the contemporary schoolmarm appears out of it, an anachronism regarded askance by her confreres at cocktail parties and in the line at the supermarket. In the future, the best and the brightest women are likely to join their male counterparts in such fields as business, law, medicine, research, and government with teaching a significant loser in the competition for talent.

In addition to the probable loss of capable women, at least one recent development has also pulled talented male secondary teachers out of the schools. "Between 1960 and 1969," writes J. Myron Atkin (1981), "more than twice as many institutions of higher education were established than in any other ten-year period in American history: 700 new institutions, 80 percent of which were public, and about 70 percent of those two-year colleges — all needing teachers" (p. 92). The phenomenal growth of community colleges has provided a handsome alternative to secondary teachers whose first love is their subject matter, and a prime talent pool for these new institutions has been the secondary school. In the future, college graduates may move after advanced training directly into college teaching, or engage in it part-time, but in either case the expanded set of post-secondary institutions will continue to compete with secondary schools for talented teachers imbued with a love of their special subject.

Is Teaching an Imperilled Profession?

Such an array of reasons may convince that teaching is on its last legs, but the situation is not quite so dire. Over the near term, for example, we will continue to have an oversupply of teachers in most subject areas and in most regions of the country, supplemented by a reserve pool recently estimated at some 660,000 (NEA, 1981). Compared to prior decades such as the fifties when there were serious shortages, the system today looks positively flush. Districts can afford to be selective in hiring, to take only the best from a sizable pool of applicants. Enrollments in teacher education programs are dropping, but this indicates only the efficient operation of the teacher labor market: supply is adjusting downward to meet decreased demand. Although lags exist in these supply-demand adjustments, they are no more severe than in most labor markets and so little cause for alarm. School districts may need to take unprecedented steps in the future to attract teachers to areas of chronic shortage such as mathematics, but these are limited and relatively controllable problems.

It is likewise easy to exaggerate the alarums about teacher quality. Evidence from the 1920s onward suggests that teachers have never scored well on tests of academic ability or achievement (Chauncey, 1952; Learned and Wood, 1938; Wolfle, 1954). Yet generations of teachers have served America's youth tolerably well. Perhaps teachers' academic achievement is not preeminently important to student achievement. The 1965 Coleman report did locate a modest relationship between teacher verbal ability and student achievement which subsequent analyses confirmed, but such evidence offers slender support for an overweening concern about teacher test scores. Nearly half a century's worth of research failed to locate strong relationships between teacher characteristics of any sort and student outcomes (Getzels and Jackson, 1963), prompting the more recent attention to teaching behavior rather than teacher traits. As most parents know and any teacher will tell you, good teaching comes in a variety of flavors and styles and has as much to do with such qualities as enthusiasm, curiosity, caring, patience, optimism, tenacity, moral convictions — in short, with strength of character —as with intellect alone or grasp of subject matter. To rely on test scores as a proxy for teacher quality is surely a grievous mistake.

Are we wrong, then, to worry about who shall teach? In an overheated climate of rising expectations and media blitzes on the schools, have we overdramatized the concern for teacher quality based on misleading numbers and gloomy scenarios which fail to recognize the self-correcting tendencies in the ebb and flow of young people into occupations? On balance, although the evidence is imperfect and freely mixed with speculation about the future, the concern does not seem misplaced. Granted academic ability is not a proxy for good teaching, it surely is a desirable characteristic and perhaps even a necessary condition. At minimum teachers must have a sound grasp of the subject matter they are to impart. But as well we would wish that they have a love of learning and a commitment to intellectual excellence, to the life of the mind. Excellent teachers are also students of children's learning, who continually discover through classroom experience how best to guide the course of human development. It is not so farfetched to imagine that teachers who score well on tests measuring academic ability and achievement are most likely to have such qualities of mind and volition. The recent evidence on declining scores of prospective teachers is disturbing in part because the scores were low to begin with. As our society grows more complex, it seems likely that demands on education will increase, requiring more of teachers than new technologies, curricular materials, or administrative arrangements alone will provide. It is not amiss, then, to argue that the present holds the key to the future of teaching.

If teaching is not yet an imperilled profession, its prospects are not promising. Many of the traditional inducements to teach seem weaker today, while competing opportunities are more tempting. Teaching became a beleaguered profession in the seventies, and the toll exacted on teachers has been steep. A recent NEA survey (1982) reports that of teachers sampled in 1981, 24% probably would not and 12% certainly would not enter teaching if they could start over again (p. 74). By comparison, Lortie cites a 1967 NEA survey which reported comparable figures of 7.1% and 2% respectively (p. 91). This trend is marked and serious. Four of every ten teachers today are dissatisfied with their lot, while the news about recruitment and retention is equally discouraging. Policymakers and educators must improve the rewards of teaching as a necessary step toward the improvement of education.

SCREENS AND MAGNETS: IMPROVING THE REWARDS OF TEACHING

Public policy is a blunt instrument indeed for influencing so complex, so variable and varied, so human an activity as teaching. If carrots and sticks often fail to move donkeys, human responses to policies formulated at a far remove in place and time are all the more perverse (from the policymaker's viewpoint!) and unpredictable. That the problems for which policies are a solution often change character or even disappear before the solutions take effect has bedevilled more than one good intention, and that each policy solution likely generates new problems is by now common wisdom. Humility then always befits the making of recommendations, notwithstanding that clarion calls and hyperbole are frequently required to effect change. The joy of teaching is not a matter largely determined by public policy; it has more to do with the unique cultures of individual schools, with relations between a principal and a faculty, with the images, intentions, and behavioral repertoires teachers bring to their dealings with students, and with students' responses to their teachers and schools.

Nevertheless, policy can influence indirectly at least the quality of teacher work life and the occupational choices of future generations. Inducements which attract talented, capable people to teaching are as durable an investment as policymakers are likely to find. To date, however, the states' response to the issue of teacher quality has been primarily regulatory and insufficiently incentives-oriented. A comprehensive policy framework would include both approaches to ensure not only minimum standards of competence but the pursuit of excellence in this profession. Past policies provided access to training but eased entry without reference to quality. New policies must supply incentives selectively, discriminating on the basis of quality.

There is an approach broader still to the problem of teacher/teaching quality and it may be helpful to set the recommendations which follow in this context. Wise men of various stripes often imagine an ideal or perfect state of affairs as a device for evaluating actual departures from such a pristine condition. So economists find the notion of a perfect market useful, philosophers suppose pure embodiments of such virtues as truth, beauty, and justice, and sociologists postulate "ideal types" in their analyses of society. What might an ideal system for the regulation of the teacher work force consist of? To begin, such a system would well serve and optimally balance the twin values of excellence and equity. That is, the interplay of public policy, local administrative practice, and the dynamics of the teacher labor market would ensure (1) that the teaching ranks are filled and continuously renewed with talented, capable people and (2) that our society provides equitable access to this occupation at all points of choice. The proper balance of excellence and equity would result from the interaction of eight processes which together determine the composition and disposition of the teacher work force. These processes are:

Recruitment. Teaching must initially attract competent people, discouraging no one who might have potential to become a capable teacher.

Training. Teachers most likely are both born *and* made. Certain people are by nature suited to teaching, but much can be learned about this craft. There must be a system for preparing teachers, for imparting the skills and knowledge useful to effective teaching. Such training should be continuous, providing initial skills, on-the-job feedback in the early years, and ongoing education throughout a career.

Selection. Procedures for identifying the most promising candidates and for weeding out the unqualified must be both efficient and fair. They must ensure that only the competent are allowed to teach, without denying opportunities to those with potential to become good teachers.

Retention. Teaching should be sufficiently rewarding to hold capable teachers over the course of a career. As teachers mature and become increasingly expert in their practice, working conditions and career rewards should encourage their continuation in the profession.

Participation. Conditions of teaching must encourage daily exertion. Participation here refers to more than merely adequate, routinized behavior. It means commitment to excellence, to continuing development as a professional, to a search for sources of renewal, and to steady investment of energy in one's work.

Evaluation. The system must include means for appraising the work of teachers, both to supply corrective feedback and to provide the basis for termination decisions.

Termination. There must be efficient, fair procedures for terminating teachers who have proven themselves incapable of performing to minimum levels of competence or to observing minimum standards of comportment.

Distribution. Teaching talent should be efficiently and equitably distributed among school districts and within districts among schools. Each school should receive its fair share of capable teachers.

Needless to say, none of these processes operates ideally to ensure the twin goals of excellence and equity, nor has our society resolved how to pursue these sometimes conflicting values simultaneously. A thoroughgoing reform agenda would attend to each of these processes and much could be written about any one of them. (Note they are not logically all of a kind. Some are formal procedures, others informal processes; some refer to individual, others to collective behavior. Nevertheless, the list is useful as a frame for analysis). The focus here though is primarily on recruitment, retention, and to some extent on participation and distribution. The leading assumption behind this approach is that attracting talent to teaching is the first order of business today, taking precedence over other initiatives. That is, the quality of people entering and staying in teaching is a major constraint on what can be accomplished through teacher education or district personnel policies and practices. Nevertheless, it is useful to keep in mind prospects for reform in these other areas.

Recruitment Incentives and Rewards for Excellence

To make teaching more attractive to capable college graduates, policymakers must provide selective recruitment incentives. For example, federal and/or state agents might establish scholarship or fellowship programs for undergraduate study in education. Admission to such programs would be on a competitive basis with awards deferring a substantial portion of college tuition. In conjunction with such a scholarship series, colleges and universities might offer special programs of study involving accelerated work with the finest professors in the major disciplines. In this way, financial incentives coupled with high prestige and the promise of an unusually fine liberal arts education would provide a powerful inducement to enter the field of education. In return, students might be required to major in education, assuming they would go on to teach. A more stringent requirement would exchange several years of teaching for a scholarship, much as R.O.T.C. programs have operated for years.

Recruitment incentives alone, however, cannot ensure that young people will find teaching rewarding and so stay on. In fact, a likely response to a teaching fellowship program might be to minimize or avoid time spent in the classroom. To lure academically capable people into the field via fellowship money then coerce a grudging period of service is not likely to yield excellent teaching. (Also, how can it be ensured that participants serve the required time in the classroom? The school system after all is not the military, and the effort to track graduates might be quite cumbersome). Policymakers must initiate a series of other changes to make teaching rewarding for the new recruits. A necessary step is the introduction of differential rewards and incentives to serve several purposes. One is to recognize excellence and to encourage professionalism. Another is to attract qualified persons to subject areas of chronic shortage. A third is to attract teachers to locations where living and working conditions adversely affect recruitment and retention.

Schools and communities must find ways to reward and honor outstanding teachers. Formalized systems of merit pay tend to founder on the issue of objective criteria for teacher effectiveness and the burdens of information gathering and record keeping (Doremus, 1982). Short of merit pay plans, however, school boards could establish regular awards for outstanding teaching which might involve cash bonuses, award ceremonies, and coverage by the local media. A school committee composed of teachers and administrators could establish the award criteria and the nominating and selection procedures and make the award decisions. A program of awards for excellence would serve not only to recognize distinguished teaching but to draw attention to and celebrate outstanding achievement in education. The public relations benefits of such a program would be another selling point to superintendents and school boards. Ideally, the cash awards would be sizable and plentiful but selection discriminating. Even a few modest awards, however, could have tremendous symbolic value, standing as an assertion of excellence in teaching, a tangible reminder that every school in the nation has its unsung heroes. Such an affirmation is especially important in times when expressions of pessimism outnumber those of buoyancy and faith in education.

Incentives for Professional Growth

In addition to rewards for excellence, there should be incentives for professional growth available to all teachers. One example is a mini-grant program which makes awards to teachers on a competitive basis to develop new courses, materials, and the like. ESEA Title III (later Title IV-C) is an example of this approach at the federal level, but states and localities as well could set up such programs, as a number of teacher centers around the country have already done (NEA, Note 5). While the original rhetoric of ESEA Title III emphasized the replication and spread of local innovations (later carried on by the National Diffusion Network), the purpose here is primarily to encourage teacher engagement in professional matters. Modest evidence indicates that such grants can be successful in stimulating school change as well as professional development among teachers (Mann, 1982; McDonnell and McLaughlin, 1980, p. 100; Mosher, Note 6).

Another example of this sort which teachers find particularly valuable is sabbatical leave. Few districts today offer sabbaticals, and even in those that do, only a few teachers are eligible (Moore and Hyde, Note 7, pp. 83–84). Districts fear that year-long sabbaticals may serve no other purpose than to help teachers exit the profession, so changes are necessary. A complete program might involve sabbaticals of varying duration, from several months or a semester to a full year with requirements that teachers use the time off for professional development. Mini-grants and sabbaticals are but two examples of incentives for professionalism and many others are imaginable. Administrators typically control access to other professional activities such as attendance at conferences and participation on planning committees with release time. Such resources, however, are relatively rare and touch few teachers consistently; improving both their availability and intensity while tying them firmly to professional development should be a policy priority.

A note of caution, however, is worth sounding about extra pay for professional development. At first glance this appears a sensible, deserved incentive, especially in light of teachers' modest salaries. In fact, many districts have incorporated this principle in their salary schedules, providing salary increments for course taking toward advanced degrees. Other districts rely on stipends for staff development activities. But as such pay gets defined as part of the total benefits package and as teachers come to insist on the distinction between "regular" and "extra" work, this trend can both undercut professionalism and weaken the effects of extra pay. For example, Moore and Hyde (Note 7) found that in one district salary increments did not attract teachers to university coursework (p. 91). They further concluded that teacher expectations for extra pay tended to discourage school-initiated staff development (p. 80), confirming a similar finding in the RAND "Change Agent" Study (Berman and McLaughlin, 1978, p. 27; McLaughlin and Marsh, 1978, p. 75). The RAND authors found that extra pay for training either was not related or was negatively associated with program implementation, teacher change, student improvement, and program continuation. Staff development activities, then, must draw on the intrinsic motives of teachers to improve their practice and to work in a collegial manner toward the solution of commonly identified problems. Pay alone cannot induce such behavior but can and should be part of a district's approach to professional development.

Pay Differentials for Teachers

As well as salary supplements to reward excellence and encourage professional growth, pay differentials by subject area are necessary today. A controversial proposal, this, one which teacher organizations have vehemently opposed in the past. However, the number of students seeking careers in science and mathematics education has slowed to a trickle, with resultant shortages in most states. In a nation whose future is dependent on technological preeminence we cannot fail to provide students with a strong grounding in science and mathematics, and the gravest threat to such education is the growing lack of qualified teachers. The most direct, obvious, if politically unfeasible solution to this problem is a salary increase for teachers in shortage areas, creating a market adjustment to the problem of low supply. Such market-determined salary differentials have long been the norm at the postsecondary level; the time has come to introduce this principle at the secondary level as well.

Because this proposal is a radical one, two alternatives are worth considering. One is to encourage part-time teaching. Some school systems are already experimenting with volunteers from business, industry, and the retirement community, professionals who can offer courses in such subjects as calculus, chemistry, physics, advanced biology, and the like. To the extent that state licensing and certification laws prevent such practices, policymakers can establish waivers to allow more adults into the schools and set aside funds to pay individuals who wish to teach part-time. In some communities, too, the solution may be to let secondary students take courses at local colleges and universities, but this speaks only to the preparation of advanced students, not to the issue of general scientific literacy in our society. A second alternative relies on training as the most expedient response. If mathematics and science teachers have weak backgrounds in their subject areas, then staff development becomes a remedial activity devoted in effect to preparing teachers for what they are already doing (inadequately). Likewise, districts can negotiate with local universities to retrain and recertify experienced teachers in shortage subjects.

None of these approaches is free of objections. Pay differentials are bound to stir up rancor among teachers, who would ask with good reason why math and science are any more valuable than English or social studies. Nor is it clear what would constitute a "chronic" shortage in a "critical" area, triggering more pay. Likewise, part-time help seems a piecemeal solution not likely to provide the necessary manpower on a large and continuing scale. The private sector is unlikely to respond eagerly to this potential drain on its personnel, and while volunteers can certainly help out in many schools, they cannot carry the load. Finally, given the meager resources most school districts have for staff development and their generally poor record in managing this activity, there is little reason to believe they can provide quality education in academic disciplines even with the cooperation of local universities.

Because no approach unequivocally recommends itself, mixed strategies tailored to conditions in particular locales seem advisable. For example, the Houston Independent School District has been experimenting since the 1979–80 school year with a comprehensive plan of teacher pay incentives. The "Second Mile Plan" provides additional pay for outstanding attendance; participation in teacher training; service in schools with high concentrations of disadvantaged students; teaching in the shortage areas of mathematics, science, bilingual, and special education; and for student achievement beyond expectations (as determined by school average scores). Texas state law precludes teacher collective bargaining, so Houston has not faced strong opposition to this plan from teacher organizations. Other districts may be unable to adopt this approach because of political opposition, budget limitations (Houston's economy is booming), and the like. Such local factors determine the maneuvering room for reform, but trailblazing schemes such as Houston's give promise that change is possible and that political deadlocks can be broken.

The Houston plan illustrates another type of pay differential that is sorely needed. The distribution of teachers has long been as serious a problem as their overall supply and quality. Inner-city and rurally isolated districts offer living and working conditions which many prospective teachers find undesirable. Schools in such communities tend to have special difficulty in gaining and holding teachers. Staff turnover is frequently high with tenured teachers transferring to more affluent suburban schools if possible. How to make teaching rewarding in many of our urban and rural schools is a major problem, perhaps unsolvable on a large scale.

Pay incentives can alleviate such special recruitment problems but most likely need to be sizeable. In Britain, which has a national pay scale, a series of reforms beginning in the sixties established a "School of Exceptional Difficulty" allowance and an entry-level bonus for teaching in London. Recent research, however, found that the additional pay (ranging from 5% to 10% above the base) was not successful in attracting and holding teachers (Zabalza, Turnbull, and Williams, 1979, pp. 116–143). Two policy implications from Britain's experiences seem warranted. First, the size of the bonus or allowance must be substantial for real effects to obtain. Second, policy-makers may need to reshape the salary scale, building in steeper pay increases for teaching in locations with chronic high turnover and inadequate supply. Additional pay might both encourage teachers to stay on, thereby reducing turnover, and lure experienced teachers via transfers into disadvantaged schools. However, many inner-city school districts already offer higher pay than their suburban neighbors and yet fare poorly in the local job market. Furthermore, collective bargaining negotiations typically shape pay scales, not designs unilaterally imposed by management. So, absent massive pay increases, the effects of special allowances and modest alterations to the pay scale will be marginal at best.

Primarily in urban school districts and at the elementary level the chief response to problems of teacher quality has been the standardization of instruction. If school systems year after year face high turnover and an inability to attract qualified new teachers, salvation may appear to the superintendent and school board in the form of an instructional management system. Such schemes typically feature a sequence of highly specified objectives, a series of criterion-referenced tests, individual pacing of instruction, and an extensive system of records for tracking each student's progress toward mastery. Administrative control over instruction augments (if not replaces) the professional judgment of teachers, and the quality of instruction depends on the uniform, exact implementation of the system, rather than on the quality of individual teachers.

The invention of a method of teaching that does not rely on teachers is an age-old and beguiling prospect which has never materialized. In recent decades, for example, teaching machines and "teacher-proof" curricula failed notably to obviate the need for qualified teachers. Technical limitations of instructional management systems restrict their scope to basic skills instruction in the early grades and in remedial courses later on. More fundamentally, however, they undercut teachers' flexibility in responding to students. The best reading teachers, for example, utilize a variety of materials and approaches, tailoring instruction to individual differences in student learning styles and rates (Bussis, Chittenden, Amarel, and Klausner, Note 8). Administratively mandated systems of instruction not only hinder teachers' responsiveness to students but over time discourage teachers from learning to be responsive, from developing sensitivity to individual differences, and from broadening their repertoire of approaches. Ultimately such systems become self-fulfilling prophecies: routinized instruction, and the attendant loss of autonomy, makes teaching unpalatable for bright, independent-minded college graduates and fails to stimulate the pursuit of excellence among those who do enter. Over the long run, then, the routinization of instruction tends to de-professionalize teaching and to further discourage capable people from entering the field.

If, as just argued, instructional management systems are likely to be miseducative for teachers and students alike, emphasizing only lower-order cognitive skills while driving out time for a richer engagement with subject matter, and if modest increases in pay will not much improve the desirability of teaching in rural and inner-city schools, what is to be done? The simple, correct, but formless answer is, improve the quality of life in those schools. Young people must anticipate and discover that work in urban and rural schools is deeply rewarding and can be joyful rather than stressful, frightening, or numbing. Concern about the quality of teaching then naturally and inevitably broadens to a concern about the quality of life in schools and the reform of education writ large. Many teachers in inner-city and rural schools clearly enjoy satisfying work lives, and excellent schools serve all kinds of communities including those most impoverished. But charismatic principals, unusually dedicated teachers, and supportive parents are often in short supply, especially in concert with one another, and policy has not proven potent in affecting these ingredients for success. We press here against the limits of policy and the boundary of this essay. Strategies for school improvement may ultimately be the best hope for attracting and holding teachers in certain schools, but that is the subject for another paper.

Creating a Teaching Career

A final recommendation aims at the teaching career with implications for teacher training. The absence of opportunities for career advancement within teaching simply devastates prospects for holding all but the most dedicated of talented teachers. To expect capable, ambitious people to engage in the same activity year after year with no expansion of responsibilities or variety of work experience is unrealistic in the extreme. Attrition from teaching in the first five years is quite high (Charters, 1970; Mark and Anderson, 1978; Pavalko, 1970; Schlechty and Vance, 1981). But for those who stay on, such unvarying prospects often lead to a predictable response: routinization of instruction and the progressive disengagement from work and career in favor of second jobs, recreation, family responsibilities, or professional activity peripheral to classroom teaching (e.g. union activism) (Cusick, 1981, pp. 124–125; Lortie, 1975, p. 95). While an informal status hierarchy in many schools honors veteran teachers, according them special respect and influence, this feature of school culture is meager recompense for years of service in the classroom. The profession of teaching must be reconfigured to provide career rewards.

Specifically, state and local policymakers should consider creating one or more new teaching positions and roles. Britain, for example, has institutionalized the positions of master teacher and head teacher, with the latter mostly an administrative role. A master teacher would continue to teach part-time but would as well be responsible for assisting younger teachers and for such professional duties as curriculum development, test construction and evaluation, and so on. Primarily, though, master teachers would work closely with beginning teachers, providing them feedback, assistance, and support. Additionally, they would be responsible for school-based staff development, working with the principal and central office staff. Master teachers would serve schools and school districts as experts on teaching, responsible for keeping abreast of the latest research and for bringing research knowledge to practice. Consequently, their training and professional networks would overlap the research community; they could serve as that bridge between research and practice so glaringly absent today.

To develop and legitimate a cadre of master teachers would require a corresponding set of significant changes and accommodations. In exchange for relinquishing some control over teacher training, colleges and universities gain responsibility for training and supporting master teachers. School principals would share certain of their functions with master teachers, taking some pressure off that overburdened role, but perhaps weakening administrative control. Genuinely empowering master teachers in each of a district's schools would also require decentralization of such activities as staff development and curriculum assessment, with some continued coordination of these functions at the district level. To establish such a scheme on even a pilot basis, however, will require strong political leadership because this reform lacks a constituency but comes with powerful opposition. Teacher educators, teacher unions, and administrators are all likely to find aspects of this proposal threatening to their interests. However, the lack of a career is so major an impediment to the appeal of teaching that efforts to remedy this feature deserve serious consideration.

CONCLUSION: MODEST PROPOSALS IN SEARCH OF SUPPORT

Through its political processes our society allocates scarce resources to the alleviation of problems in proportion to their perceived severity and immediacy. Teacher quality is increasingly perceived as an issue requiring attention but the depth of the concern is not apparent. Regulatory and symbolic measures are the least costly forms of attention but by themselves are unlikely to be very effective. Those most concerned about this problem either out of economic self-interest or public-spiritedness are likely to call for one of two responses: a significant increase in educational expenditures to raise teacher salaries and reduce class sizes and/or a thoroughgoing reform of the educational system, ridding it of various evils plaguing educators and their clients. Both impulses are tempting as positions on the issue but the first is unfeasible while the second is too diffuse. This essay proposes a middle ground between inexpensive but ineffective gestures and sweeping reforms. The point of departure has been the rewards of teaching and the leading assumption that if such rewards are not enhanced, then our school system will not have the teachers required to successfully carry out its mission.

To make teaching rewarding ultimately requires that we make schools humane and productive places. Policy has a limited but important role to play in this task. Through effects on the structure and system of teaching rewards state and local policy can influence who enters and stays, how much care and energy teachers devote to their work, and how they pursue their own education as educators. The recommendations set forth here are modest both in terms of the dollars needed to carry them out and the extent of change entailed. For the most part the ideas are not new and have been debated in educational circles for years. Likewise, the problematic nature of teaching rewards has not gone unremarked. That teacher preparation is inadequate, that incentives for excellence in teaching are absent, and that teaching has no career are widely noted facts deeply rooted in the history of this profession. What is new, though, is the decline in teaching's relative attractiveness as an occupation. Furthermore, as a new consensus emerges about what constitutes an adequate education in our society, we will require high-caliber teachers to realize a higher standard and conception of education. Policymakers must attend to the problem of teacher quality, creating magnets as well as screens to promote excellence in teaching.

NOTES

1. Schmidt, W. H. *The High School Curriculum: It Does Make a Difference*. Unpublished manuscript, East Lansing, MI: Institute for Research on Teaching, 1981.
2. Vance, V. S. and Schlechty, P. C. The Structure of the Teaching Occupation and the Characteristics of Teachers: A Sociological Interpretation. Unpublished paper submitted to the National Institute of Education under Contract No. NIE-P-81-0100. Washington, D.C.: National Institute of Education, 1982.
3. Baugh, W. H. and Stone, J. A. Mobility and Wage Equilibration in the Educator Labor Market. Unpublished manuscript, Eugene, OR: Center for Educational Policy and Management, 1980.
4. Steinberg, L., Greenberger, E., Garduque, L., and McAuliffe, S. High School Students in the Labor Force: Some Costs and Benefits to Schooling and Learning. Manuscript submitted for publication, 1980.
5. National Education Association. Teacher Centers and Mini-Awards. Washington, D.C.: National Education Association, 1981.
6. Mosher, W. G. *Individual and Systemic Changes Mediated by a Small Educational Grant Program*. Unpublished manuscript, December, 1981. (Available from G. Wayne Mosher, St. Louis Metropolitan Teacher Center, 9137 Old Bonhomme Road, St. Louis, MO 63132).
7. Moore, D. R. and Hyde, A. A. Making Sense of Staff Development: An Analysis of Staff Development Programs and Their Costs in Three Urban School Districts. Unpublished manuscript, April, 1981. (Available from D. R. Moore and A. A. Hyde, Designs for Change, 220 South State Street, Chicago, Illinois 60604).
8. Bussis, A. M., Chittenden, E. A., Amarel, M., and Klausner, E. *Inquiry into Meaning*. Draft Final Report to the National Institute of Education on the ETS Collaborative Research Project on Reading, (Grant #NIE-G-79-0026). Princeton, NJ: Educational Testing Service, 1982.

REFERENCES

Adkison, J. A. Women in School Administration: A Review of the Research. *Review of Educational Research*, Fall, 1981, Vol. 51, No. 3, 311–43.

Atkin, J. M. Who Will Teach in High School? *Daedalus*, Summer, 1981, Vol. 110, No. 3, 91–103.

Benham, B. J., Giesen, P., and Oakes, J. A Study of Schooling: Students' Experiences in Schools. *Phi Delta Kappan*, January, 1980, Vol. 61, No. 5, 337–40.

Berman, P. and McLaughlin, M. W. Federal Programs Supporting Educational Change, Vol. VIII: Implementing and Sustaining Innovations. Santa Monica, CA: RAND Corporation, R-1589/8-Hew, May, 1978.

Carroll, S. J. The Federal Influence on the Production and Employment of Teachers. In M. Timpane (ed.), *The Federal Interest in Financing Schooling*. Cambridge, MA: Ballinger, 1978.

Charters, W. W. Some Factors Affecting Teacher Survival in School Districts. *American Educational Research Journal*, January, 1970, Vol. 7, No. 1, 1–27.

Chauncey, H. The Use of the Selective Service College Qualification Test in the Deferment of College Students. *Science*, July 25, 1952, Vol. 116, 73–79.

Coker, H., Medley, D., and Soar, R. How Valid are Expert Opinions about Effective Teaching? *Phi Delta Kappan*, October, 1980, Vol. 62, No. 2, 131–134; 149.

Coleman, J., Hoffer, T., and Kilgore, S. *Public and Private Schools*. Chicago: National Opinion Research Center, March, 1981.

Cusick, P. A. *Inside High School.* New York: Holt, Rinehart and Winston, 1973.

Cusick, P. A. A Study of Networks among Professional Staffs in Secondary Schools. *Educational Administration Quarterly*, Summer, 1981, Vol. 17, No. 3, 114–138.

Denemark, G. and Nutter, N. The Case for Extended Programs of Initial Teacher Preparation. Washington, D.C.: ERIC Clearinghouse on Teacher Education, 1980.

Doremus, R. R. What Ever Happened to . . . Kalamazoo's Merit Pay Plan? *Phi Delta Kappan*, February, 1982, Vol. 63, No. 6, 409–10.

Durkin, D. What Classroom Observations Reveal about Reading Comprehension Instruction. *Reading Research Quarterly*, 1978–79, Vol. XIV, No. 4, 482–528.

Education Week. Alabama May Link Certification with Teacher Test Results. *Education Week*, November 2, 1981, Vol. I, No. 9, 5.

Floden, R. Flexner, Accreditation, and Evaluation. *Educational Evaluation and Policy Analysis*, March–April, 1980, Vol. 2, No. 2, 35–46.

Freeman, R. B. *The Overeducated American.* New York: Academic Press, 1976.

Getzels, J. W. and Jackson, P. W. The Teacher's Personality and Characteristics. In N. L. Gage (ed.), *Handbook of Research on Teaching*. Chicago: Rand McNally & Co., 1963.

Haven, E. W., Adkinson, P. D., and Bagley, M. Women in Educational Administration: The Principalship. Washington, D.C.: National Institute of Education, 1980.

Hofstadter, R. *Anti-Intellectualism in American Life.* New York: Vintage Books, 1963.

Jackson, P. W. Comprehending a Well-Run Comprehensive: A Report on a Visit to a Large Suburban High School. *Daedalus*, Fall, 1981, Vol. 110, No. 4, 81–95.

Jencks, C. The Wrong Answer for Schools Is: (b) Back to Basics. *Washington Post*, February 19, 1978.

Lasch, C. *The Culture of Narcissism.* New York: W. W. Norton & Co., 1979.

Learned, W. S. and Wood, B. The Student and His Knowledge: A Report to the Carnegie Foundation on the Results of High School and College Examinations of 1928, 1930, and 1932, Bulletin No. 29. New York: The Carnegie Foundation for the Advancement of Teaching, 1938.

Lortie, D. *Schoolteacher: A Sociological Study.* Chicago: University of Chicago Press, 1975.

Mann, D. The Impact of IMPACT II. *Phi Delta Kappan*, May, 1982, Vol. 63, No. 9, 612–14.

Mark, J. H. and Anderson, B. D. Teacher Survival Rates—A Current Look. *American Educational Research Journal*, Summer, 1978, Vol. 15, No. 3, 379–82.

McDaniel, T. R. South Carolina's Educator Improvement Act: Portent of the Super School Board? *Phi Delta Kappan*, October, 1981, Vol. 63, No. 2, 117–119.

McDonnell, L. M. and McLaughlin, M. W. *Program Consolidation and the State Role in ESEA Title IV*. Santa Monica, CA: RAND Corporation, R-2531-HEW, April, 1980.

McLaughlin, M. W. and Marsh, D. D. Staff Development and School Change. *Teachers College Record*, September, 1978, Vol. 80, No. 1, 69–94.

Meyer, J. W. and Rowan, B. Institutionalized Organizations: Formal Structure as Myth and Ceremony. *American Journal of Sociology*, 1977, Vol. 83, No. 2, 340–63.

Murnane, R. Teacher Mobility Revisited. *Journal of Human Resources*, 1981, Vol. 16, No. 1, 3–19.

National Assessment of Educational Progress. *Reading, Thinking, and Writing: Results from the 1979–80 National Assessment of Reading and Literature*. Boulder, CO: Education Commission of the States, October, 1981.

National Center for Education Statistics. *Projections of Education Statistics to 1988–89.* Washington, D.C.: National Center for Education Statistics, 1981.

National Education Association. *Status of the American Public School Teacher, 1980–81.* Washington, D.C.: National Education Association, 1982.

National Education Association. *Teacher Supply and Demand in the Public Schools 1980–81.* Washington, D.C.: National Education Association, 1981.

Pavalko, R. Recruitment to Teaching: Patterns of Selection and Retention. *Sociology of Education*, Summer, 1970, Vol. 43, 340–53.

Resnick, D. P. and Resnick, L. B. The Nature of Literacy: An Historical Exploration. *Harvard Education Review*, August, 1977, Vol. 47, No. 3, 370–85.

Rumberger, R. *Overeducation in the U.S. Labor Market*. New York: Praeger Publishers, 1981.

Sandefur, J. T. State Reactions to Competency Assessment in Teacher Education. *Competency Assessment in Teacher Education*. Washington, D.C.: American Association of Colleges for Teacher Education, August, 1981.

Schlechty, P. and Vance, V. Do Academically Able Teachers Leave Education? The North Carolina Case. *Phi Delta Kappan*, October, 1981, Vol. 63, No. 2, 106–112.

Seitz, V. Literacy and the School Child: Some Perspectives from an Educated Country. *Edutional Evaluation and Policy Analysis*, November–December, 1981, Vol. 3, No. 6, 15–23.

Smith, B. O. A Design for a School of Pedagogy. Washington, D.C.: U.S. Department of Education, 1980.

Southern Regional Education Board. *The Changing Labor Market for Teachers in the South*. Atlanta, GA: Southern Regional Education Board, 1980.

Southern Regional Education Board. *The Need for Quality*. Atlanta, GA: Southern Regional Education Board, June, 1981.

Tomlinson, T. The Troubled Years: An Interpretive Analysis of Public Schooling since 1950. *Phi Delta Kappan*, January, 1981, Vol. 62, No. 5, 373–76.

Travers, R. M. W. Criteria of Good Teaching. In J. Millman (ed.), *Handbook of Teacher Evaluation*. Beverly Hills: Sage Publications, 1981.

Tyack D. The High School as a Social Service Agency: Historical Perspectives on Current Policy Issues. *Educational Evaluation and Policy Analysis*, September–October, 1979, Vol. 1, No. 5, 45–58.

Weaver, T. Demography, Quality, and Decline: The Challenge for Education in the Eighties. *Policy for the Education of Educators: Issues and Implications*. Washington, D.C.: American Association of Colleges for Teacher Education, 1981.

Wheatley, M. The Impact of Organizational Structures on Issues of Sex Equity. In P. A. Schmuck, W. W. Charters, and R. O. Carlson, *Educational Policy and Management: Sex Differentials*. New York: Academic Press, 1981.

Whitehead, A. N. *The Aims of Education and Other Essays*. New York: The Free Press, 1967.

Wolfle, D. *America's Resources of Specialized Talent*. New York: Harper and Brothers, 1954.

Yankelovich, D. *New Rules*. New York: Random House, 1981.

Zabalza, A., Turnbull, P., and Williams, G. *The Economics of Teacher Supply*. Cambridge: Cambridge University Press, 1979.

CHAPTER 5

Teaching Competence and Teacher Education in the United States

Donna H. Kerr

The sheer number of characters, the substantial measure of fate, and the intricacy and entanglement of plots could fund a 19th-century Russian novel. Legislatures, university administrations, schools and colleges of education, all manner of professional organizations, state education agencies, local education agencies, accrediting associations, and testing agencies by design and by default, directly and indirectly through interaction with one another, affect the level of teaching competence that is to be found in our schools and the related quality of teacher education. The general story line is this: the quality of teaching competence and teacher education fall well short of what they could and should be. Yet, deliberate policy decisions—decisions that might prompt improvements—abhor complexity, especially uninterpreted complexity. As is typical of society's larger problems, those surrounding teaching seem to escape any agency's ability to take single-handed ameliorative action. Witness the scores of ill-fated efforts to reform teaching and teacher education.

The point of this paper is twofold: (1) to offer a rough sketch, an overview, of the state of teaching competence and teacher education in the United States and (2) to recommend changes in policy and practice that, if made in concert, could create the conditions for a gradual upgrading of teaching competence and occasion a considerable qualitative improvement in teacher education. It is my hope that as an overview intended to distill and interpret information already collected by others, this paper will provide the degree of simplicity that policymakers who must answer to constituencies require. More particularly, it is my wish that such a brief overview suggest points on which the various characters must alter their current positions and practices if their larger interests are to be served—that is, if teaching competence and teacher education are to be improved significantly.

My thanks to economist Fritz Machlup, who persuaded me of the need for this paper and who funded it with grants from the Earhart Foundation and the National Institute of Education (NIE-G-80-105-8) as part of the background work for the forthcoming volume on education in his nine-volume series on *Knowledge: Its creation, distribution, and economic significance* (Princeton: Princeton University Press). Also, I wish to thank Katherine A. Carlson, James I. Doi, Clifford Foster, Alice Goldberg, Michael Hamlin, Sarah Jarvis, Harry Judge, Deborah Kent, Stephen T. Kerr, Rosemary Sheffield, Lee Shulman, and Richard Wilson for sharing with me their perspectives and insights. A version of this chapter is in press in the *Teachers College Record, 84,* 3, Spring, 1983, where it will appear with reactions written by educators from the United States and the United Kingdom.

JUST HOW INCOMPETENT ARE OUR TEACHERS?

Assessing the relative competence or incompetence of teachers calls for proxy measures. Let the first such measure be required degrees and certificates. In 1946 only 20 of our present states enforced a minimum requirement of a bachelor's degree for an elementary teaching certificate. By contrast, since the early 1970s, all states have required the bachelor's degree for the elementary certificate. While in 1946 approximately 40 states enforced the minimum standard of a bachelor's degree for secondary teaching certificates, all states have required a bachelor's degree since 1963 (Stinnett, 1974). Today's teachers appear yet more competent than the post-World War II cohort if we recall the issuance of emergency certificates as a way of providing at least some adult supervision in classrooms during that period of acute shortage of teachers. In 1946 one out of every seven teachers was allowed to enter the classroom with substandard credentials—thousands with little or no college credit; by comparison, in 1973 the ratio had diminished to about one in seventy; today less than one percent have no degree.[1] Thus, in the measure that credentials indicate competence, our teachers are considerably more competent (or at least notably less incompetent) than 30–35 years ago.

If, in comparison to an earlier era, today's teachers fare well, they earn astonishingly poor ratings when ranked with others who use a college degree as part of their professional preparation. As Weaver (1978) notes, the SAT, ACT, GRE, and NAEP scores of high school seniors and college students who plan to become teachers both have declined substantially in recent years and rank poorly with scores of students who plan to enter other fields. For example, in an examination of eight colleges, Weaver found that the decline in SAT scores of freshman elementary education majors clearly exceeded the national rate. Specifically, while in 1970–71 education students' average SAT verbal score (472) topped the national mean (455) and their average math score (506) also surpassed the national mean (488), in 1975–76 the scores of education students (417 verbal and 455 math) fell below the respective national means of 431 and 472. For the same year (1975–76) the American College Testing Program reported an enrolled freshman profile for 1,128 colleges and universities that indicates relative standings of students majoring in 19 fields of study. Education majors tied for 17th place on the math test and 14th place on the English test. During the same six-year period, education majors' GRE verbal scores declined 23 points, thus placing those preparing to teach significantly lower than students in eight of ten other fields (nursing, biological sciences, chemistry, aeronautical engineering, physical sciences, sociology, political science, and public administration) and significantly higher than only students in mechanical and chemical engineering. While the aspirant teachers' GRE quantitative scores fare better in the comparison group ranking between 1970 and 1975, they dropped from 39 to 51 points below the national average.

Statistically, far more can be and has been said about the decline in test scores of those who are entering teaching. But the point here is to illustrate rather than to present a detailed, encumbered account. As far as test scores count as proxy measures for competence, it must be said that those who are entering teaching are relatively incompetent. That is, this society's brightest and best are not entering teaching. Though it is true that teachers are now college graduates, they generally come from below the college average.

On the basis of the general increase in credentials of teachers since the post-World

War II teacher shortage and the more recent decline in test scores relative to those entering other fields, a Rip Van Winkle would reasonably surmise that we have been experiencing another teacher shortage—a shortage that has required the schools once again to accept the less-than-qualified. How else, according to simple economic sense, could teaching have lost such ground? As is well known, the problem has not been a teacher shortage, but a pupil shortage. A decline in the school-age population that began in 1969 set the stage for a marked surplus of teachers. Again, simple free-market economic sense might suggest that with a surplus, competition would allow only the most competent to remain in the classroom. To the contrary, Weaver (1978, p. 566) has persuasively demonstrated in the case of the teacher surplus that "as market demand for new graduates in a given field declines, the quality of the applicant pool prepared to enter that field will also decline." In short, the smart go elsewhere.

To understand this fairly newly acquired relative incompetence of teachers, it is essential to attend to the broader context. First, teachers' salaries have lost ground in the job market. While in 1970–71 teachers earned 27% above the average full-time employee, already in 1974 the teacher's salary was only 12% above the average (Freeman, 1976). Throughout the 1970s teachers continued to lose ground, dropping to an average annual salary of $16,000 in 1978–79 from over $17,000 in 1972–73 (adjusted to 1978–79 dollars) (Plisko, 1980, p. 50). To be sure, part of this loss in economic status can be attributed to a continuing general decline in the market power of college degrees. In 1958 only 5% of all college graduates were employed in nonprofessional or nonmanagerial jobs; in 1972, 30% of male graduates and 25% of female graduates were so employed (Weaver, 1978, p. 564). Part, but not all. Relative to education and social science-based employment, engineering, the health "industry," and business have been gaining ground. Economically it would be irrational for the more able student to choose teaching.

A second aspect of the broader context cannot escape notice: changes in job opportunities for women. Given that until only very recently teaching was one of the very few socially acceptable nondomestic careers for a woman, by far the greatest number of the brightest and best women who graduated from college and chose to work outside the home became teachers. But now women of that same description have career options that are socially, politically, and financially more attractive—enormously more attractive. In a study in North Carolina, scores on the National Teachers Examination tell the story. Between 1973 and 1980, the portion of relatively high scoring white females declined markedly, but the proportion of relatively high scoring males did not change (Schlechty and Vance, 1981, p. 108). The intellectually most able women are headed in new directions. Clearly, the merits of a beginning salary of $40,000 with a law firm far surpass what teaching might offer a bright, well-educated woman.

In brief, the pool of available teachers is becoming less competent because teaching itself is losing ground. With shifts in the political and economic climate that favor the health fields, engineering, and business and with a "brain drain" created by exceptionally able women's choosing other careers, teaching has become a less competently staffed profession. The talent pool from which new teachers can be drawn has diminished. Unfortunately, the dismal tale does not end with the intellectual diminution of the cohort of available new teachers. A couplet of additional insults add to the injury: the best of available new teachers are not being hired and the best of experienced teachers are leaving the schools.

To appreciate the seriousness of these last two indications of decline in teaching competency in the United States, one must see the connection between teachers' verbal abilities and what students learn. Some would assume such a link on the basis of years of learning and observing others learning. But there are others who, thinking of teaching as coaching, would call for a "proof." After all, so this line of reasoning goes, Coach Wooden did not himself have to be able to do the "sky hook" to teach Kareem Abdul-Jabbar to master it. Fortunately empirical evidence wrought by several studies confirms the connection. The oft-cited Coleman study (1966) showed that teachers' verbal ability correlated significantly with the verbal learning of students on all levels, though more strongly on the highest levels, where the teachers' verbal ability accounted for over 7% of the variance. Both Bowles and Levin (1968) and Hanuchek (1970) on reanalyzing Coleman's data agreed with and broadened Coleman's claim. For example, Bowles and Levin established a significant relationship between teachers' verbal ability and the general, not just verbal, achievement of students. Thus, there is scientifically garnered support for what to some had all along seemed evident from ordinary experience: teachers who are verbally more able and aware can more effectively offer the descriptions and explanations that are central to teaching.

Let, then, the story continue. By comparing the National Longitudinal Study sample of education majors in the class of 1976 who were selected for teaching jobs with those who were not, Weaver (1979, p. 30) found that those who were *not* hired to teach had higher scores on four of five measures of competence in reading, vocabulary, and math with the exception occurring in math. While it was clear from Weaver's findings that school administrators were not hiring the best new teachers, whether the best even sought teaching positions was unknown. To assess hiring practices in particular, Perry (1981) focused on the education graduates who actually sought positions. The findings are troublesome: while 36% of the applicants failed the Wesman Personnel Classifications Test of basic skills, 55% of those who were *hired* failed it. That is, while about one-third of the applicants were clearly not among the best, administrators managed to hire a group of teachers, over half of whom were indisputably not among "the best."

We have viewed two of the three pieces of the problem of incompetence in teaching. The intellectually most competent simply never enter the classroom for either of two reasons: (1) many of our best college students are lured away from the possibility of entering teacher education by the far brighter prospects of other careers; (2) of those who earn teaching certificates, many of the best are not hired to teach. We must proceed yet another step to complete the outlines of the full picture. Of those who do take teaching positions, the best leave the classroom. First, it is important to note that there is evidence that during the period of 1973 to 1980 teaching's holding power not only did not decrease but may even have increased slightly (Plisko, 1980; Schlechty and Vance, 1981). The percentages remain fairly constant: about 15% of first-year teachers leave; 10% depart in the second year; another 10% in the third; an additional 5–7% in each of the fourth, fifth, and sixth years (Schlechty and Vance, p. 110). Hence, sometime between the fifth and seventh year, only about half of those who were initially employed to teach remain in the schools. (Charters [1970] set the five-year departure figure at 62%.) In their study of retention rates for 1973–80, Schlechty and Vance (1981, p. 110) found that "there is a strong negative relationship between measured academic ability and retention in teaching." This relationship holds for both blacks and whites, though it is stronger among white teachers. (Because of complications in assessing the meaning of ability measures for black teachers, Schlechty and Vance focus on the data for white teachers.) As an illustration, consider two sets of figures. First, of all white females in the study who entered teaching in North Carolina in 1973, 52.93% remained in 1980; of those in the top 10% on the National Teachers Examination (NTE), 37.30% remained; of those ranked in the bottom 10% on the NTE, 62.50% remained. Second, each year after entry, those teachers in the higher ability ranges "leave teaching in greater proportionate numbers than do those in the lower ability ranges" (Schlechty and Vance, p. 111). For example, of the white females who had scored in the top decile and who still remained until 1979, 11.48% left the classroom, while the mean annual departure rate for the cohort was 5.69%. Likewise, of the top 10% of white males who began teaching in 1974, 13.16% departed in 1979, in contrast to a rate of 6.48% for their peers.

One wonders just what is going wrong. Why do the best teachers not stay in the classroom? Or why, more generally, is there such a high attrition rate for teachers?

According to popular and dated "wisdom" the explanation for the high attrition rate is simple. Women, who constitute a large proportion of the teaching corps (68%), drop out to have babies. Though a widely held belief, it does not accord with recent figures. For example, in Schlechty and Vance's study, 52.93% of white females and 64.35% of black females remained at the end of the 1973–80 period, while 57.76% of white males and 52.74% of black males had stayed. That about 5% fewer of the white females stayed than white males could at least in part be accounted for by the increasing job options for women. That about 12% more black women than black men remain clearly does not corroborate the popular belief. But even as the figures stand, neither white nor black women can reasonably be assigned responsibility for the high rate of teacher attrition any more than could male teachers.

Especially because attrition rates remain fairly constant, the causes are more likely to be found in the very nature and rewards of teaching as work in its present structure. The most obvious explanatory candidates would be the income profile of teachers and the lack of opportunity for professional advancement. As Lortie (1975, p. 84) observed, teachers' incomes are both unstaged and "front-loaded." That is, individuals who remain in teaching positions experience decreasing salary gains, for each pay increase represents a smaller percentage of the salary base than the preceding increment. Moreover, teachers' earnings begin at a level that constitutes a relatively high percentage of what they can ultimately hope to earn. In that teaching financially goes nowhere, it is little wonder that within every five to seven years half the teachers drop out.

But even if teachers were immune to economic desire and persuasion, the nature of teaching as structured in the schools would still tend to drive them away. The schools build boredom and stagnation into teaching. As Lipka and Goulet (1979, p. 20) note, teaching is one of the very few professions that "[do] not impose, or allow for, changes in the type of work activities as a function of experience." Or, as Lortie (1975, p. 84) puts it, "teaching is relatively 'career-less.'" That is, because teaching as presently structured does not allow for changes in the nature of activities, it offers no opportunities for upward mobility, an essential feature of careers in the strict sense. If teachers move up, they move out. To become a school administrator is to stop teaching. Without career stages that produce "cycles of effort, attainment, and renewed ambition," teaching can offer little to give the individuals stakes in their futures as teachers (Lortie, 1975, p. 85).

If the very nature of teaching truncates teaching careers, one would expect to find that teachers are relatively dissatisfied with their jobs. Indeed that seems to be the case. In a review of the literature, Fountain (1975, as cited in Sarason, 1978–79, p. 5) found that teachers are notably less satisfied with their jobs than other professional groups. In Fountain's own study, 50% of the teachers interviewed said that they "would rather be doing something else!" According to a 1980 survey by the National Education Association, 41% would not become teachers if they could turn the calendar back and begin college again (NEA Survey, 1980, p. 49). Interestingly, Fountain also found that those who entered teaching as a career change expressed greater satisfaction with teaching than did those who had worked only as teachers. Fountain hypothesizes that the higher level of satisfaction for "switch-ins" might be attributable to their relatively greater dissatisfaction with their previous work than with teaching. One could also hypothesize that the "switch-ins" in Fountain's study had simply not yet been in the classroom long enough to sense the weight of sameness in a teaching future. It is not at all difficult to understand how especially the brightest might choose to leave the classroom in favor of other employment.

In summary, to understand just how incompetent our teachers are, we cannot merely look at those who are employed in classrooms and inquire about how well those individuals are doing their jobs. Further, no pointing the finger at teachers who likely are doing as well as they have the ability to do will help them teach more competently. Neither will any form of remediation make them the brightest and the best that this country has to offer. A society's political and economic forces determine in what pursuits intellectual virtuosity will be rewarded. Neither with status nor with prestige nor with money do we reward teaching. We should not expect that we shall teach our young as competently as we could were our priorities otherwise—if we treasured highly the education of our young people.

For those bright and able persons who, against the social and economic grain, would choose to teach, we have failed to structure the work of teaching in a minimally acceptable way. With undifferentiated staffing and unchanging tasks, even the most patient of our best teachers could hardly be expected to endure, to teach for a career. We can reasonably expect only the numb and the dull to linger in teaching careers. That some exceptionally able teachers appear and remain in the classroom reflects the heroic commitment and extraordinary sacrifice of those rare individuals and not the wisdom of our institutional arrangements and expressed values.

On balance, it must be said that our teaching corps is unacceptably incompetent. But at the same time, it also must be said that this clearly warranted judgment reflects a kind of collective dishonesty. There is a disturbing duplicity in a society that itself fails to create the conditions that would foster teaching competence and then complains of incompetent teachers. Our teaching corps can be no more competent than we make it.

HOW BAD IS TEACHER EDUCATION?

Some observers attempt to assess the incompetence of teaching without taking into account factors exogenous to what goes on between teachers and students—factors such as the political and economic priorities of the society and the nature of the classroom and the school as a workplace. Typically the question of teaching incompetence arises when anything related to education or schooling goes wrong. Numerous problems ranging from the decline in SAT scores of high school students to the "general alienation of many students" call forth the complaint of teacher incompetence.[2] Without reference to the broader context, this perception of incompetence occasions the question of who is to blame. Obviously, so it is claimed, colleges of education are responsible for preparing teachers to teach; clearly they must not be doing their job. The narrowness of understanding that leads to this conclusion both miscasts the problem and misplaces the blame. The fundamental problem with teaching is that as a society we fail to give it our brightest and best; the blame is ours collectively. Yet, the question of just what constitutes teacher education is pertinent to an assessment of teaching competence or incompetence, for it is the programs of teacher education that define the minimums of professional preparation for those who find their ways into the classroom. Moreover, even if we were to provide the structures and conditions to entice our intellectually most able into the schools, there would remain the question of what should constitute professional education for teachers. Thus, it is appropriate to sketch the state of teacher education today.

The Undergraduate Environment

In the United States, teacher education takes place in nearly 1,400 colleges and universities, which is about 80% of all institutions of higher education. The figure is somewhat misleading, for 40% of those institutions, being small private colleges with total enrollments of under a thousand students, prepare relatively few teachers. Most who become certified to teach graduate from the other 60%, about 800 institutions, which include both public and private colleges and universities of every description (Smith, 1980, p. 87). The annual numbers of graduates from teacher education have decreased with the downward trend of the school populations and represent a delayed reaction to the decline in teaching positions. In 1964, 264,000 new college graduates were certified to teach. The number peaked in 1972 with 317,000 and then dropped to 190,000 by 1978. Because the yearly numbers certified to teach far exceed available positions, only a fraction of those who go through teacher education programs eventually teach. For example, in 1975–76, of the 227,000 graduates who were certified to teach, 178,000 sought teaching jobs; of those who looked, 93,000 succeeded in finding full-time teaching jobs (NCES, cited in Weaver, 1978, p. 558).

In a quantitative sense, teacher education has recently lost considerable ground in the universities and colleges. Yet, students continue to graduate with teaching credentials at a higher rate than the availability of teaching positions would seem to warrant or their declared intentions would predict. While the percentage of college freshmen intending to pursue a teaching career dropped from 23.5% in 1968 to 6.5% in 1975 (American Council of Education, *The American Freshman National Norms*, Washington, Annual, as cited in Carroll, 1977, p. 17), the pattern continues of far more students actually preparing to teach than initial intentions would have predicted. Here is where the figures astonish. In 1972–73, for example, almost two of every five undergraduates (38%!) in the United States were enrolled in teacher education programs (Clark and Marker, 1975, p. 60). Though the percentage had nearly halved by 1978 (21%) (Plisko, 1980, p. 48), teacher education continues to enroll about one in every five undergraduates.

Thus, in examining teacher education, one is looking at a major piece of all undergraduate education. The converse is true, as well. One cannot assess the quality of the curriculum of those preparing to teach without considering the quality of offerings in the arts and sciences. Roughly three-quarters of a prospective teacher's program of study is in the arts and sciences (Carnegie Commission, 1973, p. 90). That is, as presently structured, the whole of teacher education takes place in both colleges of arts and sciences and colleges of education and *not*, as popular belief would have it, solely in schools and colleges of education. So then, in whatever ways the arts and sciences are weak, teacher education is bound to suffer.

If, however, one were to conduct a survey of arts and sciences faculties of universities that have teacher education programs, one would find that attitudes toward the education faculties would belie this strong connection between teacher education and colleges of arts and sciences. Though hard data have yet to be collected, most anyone who has been a part of a university could attest both to the low regard in which schools and colleges of education are held and to the great effect this negative attitude has on teacher education. No other fact about teacher education is so telling. From that attitude have followed actions that serve to undermine whatever the quality of teacher education.

That a number of the best universities and colleges (for example, Bryn Mawr, Dartmouth, Mount Holyoke, Swarthmore, Oberlin, Wellesley, and Yale) have cut or are now considering terminating their teacher education programs expresses the attitude that teacher preparation is unworthy of a place in excellent universities and colleges (Travers, 1980, p. 127). (According to the Gourman ratings and college ratio ratings, over 60% of teacher candidates attend universities and colleges of low quality [Howsam, 1976, p. 128].) That colleges of education are commonly at the top of lists of academic units to be terminated when the state universities face budget cuts indicates the relative unimportance that universities assign teacher preparation. And that faculties in the arts and sciences have been known to object to attempts by education faculties to raise entrance requirements to teacher education programs reflects the belief that if teacher education has any role in a university, it is to serve as a dumping ground for the weakest students in the arts and sciences. Indeed, the negative attitude is so strong that those faculty members in the arts and sciences who contribute to teacher education by offering, for example, courses on science teaching or methods of teaching a foreign language jeopardize their own status in their home departments. However teacher education ails, such an attitude would seem to impute even a contagious condition.

In short, to be understood, the content, standards, and control of teacher education must be placed within the inhospitable (sometimes hostile) environment of undergraduate education.

The Content

With few exceptions, the nature of the content of teacher education has changed amazingly little over the last 50 years (Drummond and Andrews, 1980, p. 97). Moreover, teacher education programs are so much the same from institution to institution that a Trollope would surely mistakenly believe that a national curriculum had been imposed (Silberman, 1970, pp. 439ff.). To prepare to teach in a secondary school, students take four types of courses: some sort of introduction to education, educational or sometimes adolescent psychology, a general teaching methods course, and a subject-specific methods course in the student's specialty. For elementary teachers, students additionally take about six or seven methods courses for reading, social studies, mathematics, science, and art and music. Also, students on both levels usually do roughly six weeks of "student teaching" in the schools (Clark and Marker, 1975, p. 57).

This uniformity of programs over time and among institutions held through the

1970s, notwithstanding the talk of and, to a limited extent, the implementation of "competency-based teacher education" (CBTE). The less flattering characterizations of CBTE liken it to task analysis through time-and-motion studies of factory workers made famous by Taylor early in this century. This characterization complains about the narrowness of view that CBTE promotes: "Competency-based programs ignore or deemphasize the social, interactional, and hierarchical aspects of work in a school and school system" (Sarason, 1978–79, p. 3). More generous accounts cast CBTE as a way of (1) being clear about just what teachers ought to understand and know how to do and (2) designing their programs of study around that set of understandings and know-how (i.e., the "competencies"). While in this more sympathetic rendering CBTE strikes one as eminently sensible, it is unclear just how CBTE enthusiasts would distinguish a CBTE program from any other program of teacher preparation that is operating under the same constraints and that might be deemed reasonably relevant to teaching. Quite unsurprisingly, then, the elements of CBTE programs fit the long-standing pattern of teacher education. However distinctive the expectations for CBTE, as a movement it appears to have faded somewhat and stabilized with actual full-scale CBTE programs in about 13% of the 1,200 institutions that are affiliated with the American Association of Colleges for Teacher Education (Sandefur and Niklas, 1981, p. 3).

There are two contending explanations for why the content of teacher education has remained fundamentally the same for so long. First, one might reason that its endurance is a function of its soundness. Although institutions might from time to time experiment with a different pattern, eventually they return to the "tried and true." While initially plausible, this explanation must, I think, give ground to the second: the constraints on teacher education, remaining constant, have impeded the development of more sophisticated forms of teacher education. The two most constraining factors have been the undergraduate context and the remarkable underfunding of the professional education of teachers.

In that colleges of education generally conduct teacher education as part of students' undergraduate studies, the quality of teacher preparation cannot be enhanced if doing so would mean quantitatively increasing professional studies. Augmenting the professional component of prospective teachers' undergraduate studies would diminish the opportunities for studies of general culture and special scholarship that provide the substantive understandings upon which pedagogical studies rely. To allow professional studies to encroach yet further upon the general undergraduate curriculum would constitute a reversion to the 19th-century normal-school pattern that, as James Earl Russell articulated in 1900, would devastate prospects for the proper preparation for teaching (Report to the Trustees of Teachers College for 1900, as cited in Cremin [1978, pp. 9–10]).

There are two ways in which other career fields have developed their professional curricula to provide the sophistication warranted by expanding knowledge bases and additional responsibilities of those professions. Some, such as pharmacy and engineering, which have remained within the undergraduate context, have sacrificed general for professional studies and, in some cases, lengthened the time required for the bachelor's degree. Others, such as law and medicine, have extended the course of study to the graduate level. Save for the recommendation of particular emphases in undergraduate studies, these career fields have moved their professional studies in their entirety to the graduate level. With only isolated exceptions, teaching has taken neither course. A study of programs at one state university exemplifies the point by

TABLE 5.1.   A Comparison of Credit Hours of Professional Studies and Post-Secondary Time Required for Entrance into the Career Fields of Education, Law, Pharmacy, and Engineering[a]

	19—	Teaching '29	'39	'49	'79	Law '29	'49	'79	Pharmacy '29	'49	'79	Engineering '29	'49	'79
Credit Hours of Professional Studies	2[b]	50	30	41	43	128	128	128	93	102	114	98	120	112
	1[c]	—	90	59	70									
Percentage of Total Program	2	25	16	21	23	57	49	40	46	50	48	45	54	55
	1	—	48	32	36									
Post Secondary Years Required for Degree	2	4	4	4	4	5	6	7	4	4	5	4	4(5)	4(5)
	1	—	4	4	4									
Total Credits Required	2	198	185	187	188	230	263	312	204	206	207	218	224	220
	1	—	186	186	192									

[a] Condensed from tables prepared by Smith and Street (1980).
[b] Secondary School, English.
[c] Primary School.

comparing credit hours in professional studies and the overall post-secondary time needed for the degrees that the respective career fields require.

As can be seen on the chart in Table 5.1, professional pedagogic studies have actually decreased by 2% since 1929 on the secondary level and by 12% in the curriculum for prospective elementary teachers. By keeping teacher education within the four-year undergraduate program, universities have severely limited the possibilities for developing professional studies to underwrite a more highly research-based and extensive professional preparation.

To see the second way in which the undergraduate context of teacher education has impeded the development of more sophisticated forms of professional education, one must consider universities' use of discriminant funding of academic units. For economy of description here, let us regard only what is known as the Texas formula, which is used by 38 states to determine allocations to the various academic units on three levels: undergraduate, masters, and post-masters. The formula assigns a "complexity index" to each field of study. The lowest level, used in undergraduate education, is 1.00. Table 5.2 shows representative indices of career fields (Peseau and Orr, 1980, p. 100).

In a study of 20 universities in 1978, Peseau and Orr found that most states do in practice use the Texas formula. So when viewed as part of undergraduate studies, teacher education is treated budgetarily as a strictly academic program. A comparison with expenditures in the schools shows the result of the teacher education index. During the 1977–78 academic year, for example, the public schools spent an average of 1,400 dollars on each student; 927 dollars was spent on the education of teacher

TABLE 5.2.   Allocation Indices for Career Fields

Undergraduate	Masters	Post-Masters
1.00 (base)	1.75 law	8.79 education
1.04 teacher education	2.30 education	13.45 business
1.51 agriculture	3.27 business	16.52 agriculture
2.07 engineering	5.36 science	17.60 nursing & engineering
2.74 nursing	5.77 veterinary medicine	17.71 fine arts

candidates (Peseau and Orr, 1980, p. 100). The cat is left chasing its tail. Without a substantially higher allocation index, pedagogical faculties cannot possibly develop the complex and sophisticated clinical studies that teacher education sorely lacks; without highly developed and demonstrably successful clinical programs in place, universities would most likely be unwilling to adjust the index. Most certainly the index could not be increased sufficiently if it is bound to undergraduate norms. If declining SAT scores of high school students are in some measure a reflection of weakness in teacher education, then the universities (perhaps especially the best universities, the ones who set the standards)—not the schools and colleges of education—must admit a large share of the responsibility.

Standards of Professional Control

Being bound to undergraduate education may well have stifled the development of excellence in teacher education, but it has not hampered the imposition of standards by professional organizations. Generally one would rightly interpret a profession's insistence upon minimal standards for education of its new members as a positive step toward strengthening the quality of both professional education and practice. However, in the case of teacher education, the standards have evolved in a way that has both reinforced the entrenchment of professional teacher education on the undergraduate level and served to legitimize many of the weak programs (thus reinforcing, one suspects, the universities' low esteem for their pedagogic studies).

To know just how the profession's standards for teacher education have come to reduce rather than to enhance the prospects for substantial advances in the quality of teacher education, we shall need to review briefly the evolution of the chief accrediting agency, the National Council for Accreditation of Teacher Education (NCATE).

In the United States, the accreditation of programs of teacher education is done not by governmental agencies as in other countries, but by a nongovernmental association whose membership is drawn from organizations that purportedly represent the interests of school personnel, colleges of education, school boards, and the states. It is, then, from the fact that NCATE's member institutions prepare 87% of school personnel (Gubser, 1979, p. 4) and not from any official governmental sanction that NCATE gains the power to accredit programs of teacher education. NCATE has, then, no authority to require an institution to submit itself to an accreditation review, but it does have the authority to deny accreditation to those institutions that it has reviewed on request.

Before proceeding to sketch the history of NCATE and its standards, a distinction will avert misunderstanding. While NCATE is in the business of accrediting programs of teacher education, the states certify graduates of teacher education programs

TABLE 5.3.   NCATE Membership History[a]

	1954	1957	1965	1974
AACTE	6	7	10	8
NEA	6	6	6	8
CCSSO	3	1	1	1
NASDTEC	3	1	1	1
NSBA	3	1	1	1
Learned Societies	—	3	3	—
Other	—	—	—	5[b]

[a] From Christensen, 1980, p. 43.
[b] Council for Exceptional Children, National Association of School Psychologists, National Council of Teachers of Mathematics, American Association of School Administrators, Student National Education Association.

to teach. Some states grant an initial or provisional certificate to anyone who holds a bachelor's degree and has accumulated a specified number of credit hours in various subjects and student teaching. Other states require that the certificate applicant have completed a teacher education program consisting specifically of a state-approved curriculum. Though the details differ somewhat, the 50 states' requirements for certification are notably uniform and consonant with NCATE standards.[3] Given that most states participate in reciprocal teacher certification and that both the Council of Chief State School Officers (CCSSO) and the National Association of State Directors of Teacher Education and Certification (NASDTEC) are voting members of NCATE, this standardization of certification requirements is to be expected.

Accreditation of teacher education programs began in 1927 at the initiation of the American Association of Teachers Colleges (AATC), the precursor of the American Association of Colleges for Teacher Education (AACTE), whose members currently number about 900. Between 1927 and 1954 the AACTE developed standards and procedures for accrediting teacher education programs. In 1954, the AACTE, the National Education Association (NEA), the CCSSO, and the NASDTEC invited the National School Boards Association (NSBA) to join them in forming NCATE, a new agency to assume responsibility for the accreditation of programs of teacher education (Christensen, 1980, p. 42). Table 5.3 reflects the power plays of both the AACTE (along with the Learned Societies), as a representative of higher education, and the NEA, as a representative of rank-and-file teachers, to gain control.

The balance that was struck in 1974 reconstituted NCATE in its present form—a restructuring that allows for the regulated change of members and that broadens participation by adding four nonvoting associate members: the American Personnel and Guidance Association (APGA), the Association for Educational Communications and Technology (AECT), the Association of Teacher Educators (ATE), and the National Council for Social Studies (NCSS). The Coordinating Board includes 24 members (per Table 5.3) plus the four associate members and two representatives of the general public (Olsen, 1979, p. 2).

While NCATE was formed in 1954, not until 1974 did AACTE relinquish its sole power to evaluate, develop, and revise standards. The first standards to be set by NCATE as a whole were not implemented until 1979 (Christensen, 1980, p. 43). Those standards cover six areas: governance; curricula; faculty; students; physical resources; evaluation, program review, and long-term planning. To be eligible for NCATE review, a teacher education program must already have state approval and the university or college of which the program is a part must be accredited by the general regional accrediting association (e.g., the Western Association of Schools and Colleges).

In an estimation of the effect of NCATE's program of accreditation on the quality of teacher education, three points need to be made. First, NCATE and its standards can hardly help but function as a vehicle for special interest groups to register officially their concerns and to institutionalize their claims. NCATE has, after all, evolved as a compromise of special interests. Moreover, NCATE standards build in a requirement that the special interests not represented on the council itself be given their due as an institution shapes its teacher education programs: "In planning and developing curricula for teacher education, the institution studies the recommendations of national professional associations and learned societies and adopts a rationale for the selection and implementation of pertinent sets of recommendations for each teacher education program" (Standard 2.4). Thus, teacher education programs designed to satisfy NCATE standards can hardly help but emerge as patchwork rather than as integral wholes from anyone's point of view, especially the student's.

Second, rather than promoting a vision of what teacher education could and should be, the standards reinforce the current institutional arrangements. For example, Standard 2.1 (Design of Curricula) states: "Teacher education curricula are based on explicit objectives that reflect the institution's conception of the teacher's role. There is a direct and obvious relationship between these objectives and the components of the curriculum." If an institution regards the teacher as a glorified babysitter (as many do, in effect), so be it. As a second illustration of ways in which NCATE contributes, doubtless unwittingly, to current institutional constraints on teacher education, consider Standard 2.2 (The General Studies Component), which calls for "... a planned general studies component requiring that at least one-third of each curriculum for prospective teachers consist of studies in the symbolics of information, natural and behavioral sciences, and humanities." Clearly, NCATE does not attempt to extirpate teacher education from undergraduate studies; instead, it builds into its own standards a general program of undergraduate studies. As noted earlier, the understandings and perspectives that a liberal curriculum provides are essential for teaching well. But by designing such studies into the standards for a teacher education program rather than requiring them for admission to a teacher education program, NCATE has bought into and fortified the current arrangement.

Third, whatever NCATE's strengths and foibles, it applies its standards on a pass/ fail basis, rather than venturing judgments of quality. There is, of course, no requirement that an accrediting agency take the lead in assessing quality or in creating a vision of a far more sophisticated form of professional education. And, to be sure, a sense of what constitutes minimums is important to any profession. Yet, being accredited or reaccredited by NCATE is such an ordeal—requiring hundreds (sometimes thousands) of pages of "self-study"—that it tends to occasion celebration rather than the shrug that passing minimal muster warrants. As any faculty that has endured an NCATE review can attest, considerable energy is thus diverted into demonstrating the meeting of minimums.[4] Financially, as well, an NCATE review demands a substantial institutional investment: up to $100,000 by some estimates (Arnold, 1977, p. 62). Here I point not at NCATE by itself, but at NCATE in context. No agency comes around asking to see what the institution has done to get teacher education out of its present deservedly low-status rut.

On the whole, with its standards and representatives of status quo interests,

NCATE serves well to help schools and colleges of education perpetuate the present form of teacher education and (especially in light of a recent willingness to deny accreditation[5]) to encourage schools and colleges of education to do the best that can be done under the current constraints. Unfortunately, the best that can be done under present circumstances is to meet minimums. What is lacking is a political voice to alter the institutional constraints. Professional organizations of teachers, which have focused their actual efforts on collective bargaining have not significantly affected the quality of education even in classrooms, much less the quality of education of the profession (McDonnel and Pascal, 1979, p. 80). Yet, from where can the political pressure come to alter the current constraints of professional education if not from those who represent the profession?

Teacher education can only be as good as its placement on the undergraduate level allows, and that is not very good.

Teacher Education Beyond the Baccalaureate

To this point we have addressed teacher education up to the initial or provisional certification to teach. An increasing number of states are requiring additional college credits for the regular or standard certificate, which must be acquired within three to ten years (depending on the state) after the initial certificate for the teacher to continue to maintain legitimacy. In 1974, eight states required a fifth year of study and four more called for a master's degree (Stinnett, 1974, pp. 12–14). By 1982, 28 states had instituted a fifth-year requirement or expected some graduate credit (Kashdan, 1982). Though only a few states require a master's degree, presently (as noted earlier) 49% of all classroom teachers hold advanced degrees.

One might wonder if perhaps such a surge of post-baccalaureate work removes, at least in part, teacher education from the constraints that impede teacher education in the undergraduate context. There are, unfortunately, indications that post-baccalaureate teacher education has evolved as an extension of undergraduate teacher education, rather than as a more sophisticated form of professional education. One such indication comes from the fact that NCATE accredits post-baccalaureate as well as undergraduate programs. While it would of course be possible for the post-baccalaureate standards to differ in kind from the undergraduate standards, they do not. The NCATE post-baccalaureate program calls for courses, seminars, readings, and some sort of clinical ("direct and simulated") experience, just as does the undergraduate program. And as on the undergraduate level, the advanced NCATE standards set no expectations for clinical studies sophisticated by clinical professorships and highly qualified "teaching schools." That is, the standards nod to practice without displaying a clear understanding of how, specifically, practice might be actually bound to research and professional knowledge.

A second indication that post-baccalaureate teacher education does not differ appreciably from undergraduate teacher education can be seen in the fact that the increase in granted master's degrees in education corresponds with the decrease in the numbers graduating from teacher education programs. While about five years before the severe decline in the demand for teachers (1964–65), education accounted for 34.4% of all graduate degrees, by 1974–75 the figure had risen to 38.9% (Weaver, 1978, p. 561). One strongly suspects that being short of undergraduates, colleges of education did not hire new and different professors to undertake a different kind of education on the graduate level. Instead, they shifted staff from undergraduate programs to graduate programs. Both their conception of teacher education and their essentially nonclinical backgrounds and orientation went with them.

Third, most teachers do most of their post-baccalaureate work in programs funded on undergraduate norms. Fifth-year studies, being generally treated as an extension of the baccalaureate years, simply are not indexed to underwrite a qualitatively better program of professional education.

If graduate degrees for teachers have developed as extensions of the initial programs of teacher education, one might still hold out hope for a relatively new movement called "inservice" teacher education. In late 1975, seventeen states (i.e., representatives of state offices of education) formed the National Council of States on Inservice Education (NCSIE). By 1980 its membership had grown to 43 states and eight organizations, most of which carry over from the NCATE list: The American Association of School Administrators (AASA), the Association of Teacher Educators (ATE), the National Education Association (NEA), the American Federation of Teachers (AFT), the Teacher Corps Networks, Teacher Centers, the American Association of Colleges for Teacher Education (AACTE), and the National Association of State Directors of Teacher Education and Certification (NASDTEC). Sponsored originally by the U.S. Office of Education, NCSIE does not regulate or accredit programs, but serves more as a forum for giving information about and encouraging the development of inservice programs in the various states. While inservice teacher education programs vary from state to state, a general pattern is emerging: state boards of education or even state legislatures issue general guidelines or mandate specific requirements for the local education agencies to arrange for the "development" of teachers through mini-courses offered by institutions of higher education (read: colleges of education), but in the schools rather than on university and college campuses (NCSIE, 1980).

Given the top-down, bureaucratic direction of inservice education thus initiated, given the current press for "accountability" to state legislatures, and given the current economic distress of the states, there is considerable reason to expect that inservice education will generally come to little more than the states' making proclamations (without funding for programs) that teachers ought to know more than they do. Colleges of education will once again be chided for not taking a stronger, albeit under- or unfunded role in inservice education. And teachers will continue to be beleaguered by expectations of increasing competencies, now through inservice education, without the attendant changes in schools as workplaces that would allow for advancement. Too fragmented, too little, too late, and too underfunded, inservice education in its present state-bureaucratic cast does not offer a means for a fundamental change in the nature of teacher education.[6]

Thus, teacher education as it has evolved beyond the baccalaureate level has failed to escape either the constraints of undergraduate teacher education or the clutches of the special-interest groups that have kept teacher education where it is and what it is. Turning to teacher education in its present form (whether undergraduate or post-baccalaureate or inservice) for more highly competent teachers faces us in the wrong direction.

WHAT SHOULD BE DONE?

While there has been no shortage of suggestions about what should be done to improve teaching, three proposals have dominated discussion since the late 1960s. The first, "accountability," derived from the following reasoning: the schooling reforms of the late 1960s did not deliver increases in student learning; the taxpayers are not getting their money's worth; by instituting a program of testing to assess student learning, it can be determined just which teachers or schools are and are not doing their jobs effectively; teachers can, thereby, be held accountable for teaching well. Basically the idea was to develop a system for generating information on the basis of which managers could make personnel decisions. To that end, the U.S. Office of Education and two foundations supported the National Assessment of Educational Progress. By the mid-1970s, at least 30 states had adopted some form of accountability. As the Michigan experience with accountability illustrates (Murphy and Cohen, 1974), the task of improving the quality of teaching is far more complex than collecting scores and punishing those who fail to "get results." Even with tests that focus on achievement minimums, it is hard to know where to place the blame for low scores. Moreover, when scores are low, there remains the question of what can be done about them. Clearly, accountability measures could not even in theory elevate the general level of teaching competence; it could only weed out the worst. In short, for the effort expended very little has come of accountability programs, other than the generation of some data. Certainly teaching competence did not improve.

The second and more recent effort to improve teaching, "legislated competence," mandates changes in programs of teacher education. For example, the Oklahoma legislature enacted H.B. 1706 (effective January 31, 1982) to do such things as raise standards for admission to colleges of education, require competency examinations in subject areas before graduation, mandate an entry-year internship prior to certification, monitor the performance of beginning teachers, and require continuing education for teachers and teacher educators (Kleine and Wisniewski, 1981, p. 115). In a similar spirit, South Carolina's "Educator Improvement Act" (effective beginning with the 1981–82 academic year) establishes an entrance-to-exit system for the training, employment, and evaluation of public educators (McDaniel, 1981). Both pieces of legislation are predicated on teacher education's remaining essentially in its same form and on the schools' not changing in nature as workplaces. By implication, the legislators of the two states expect teaching competence to improve through the institution of a series of tests, checkpoints, required observations, and required participation in various activities within teacher education and teaching as they are structured under present constraints. Given the simplistic view of the constituents of teaching competence that leads to "legislated competence," in neither case would one be warranted in awaiting more than what the legislation requires: considerable quantities of paperwork and a more tightly bureaucratic, rationalized system—a system that in effect will further reduce the prospects for an overall improvement of teaching competence by serving to reinforce the present constraints on teaching and teacher education.

The third "solution" takes an equally narrow view in proposing a judicial approach. While the proposal has its variants, its general form is this: first, develop national minimum competency tests for teaching, such as the one that Florida began requiring in 1980; and second, declare teaching to be legally a profession, so that teachers will have to assume the legal responsibilities of professionals, including the defense of malpractice suits (Pabian, 1979, p. 14). This approach assumes that the key problem with teaching is that teachers are, without goading, unwilling to assume their responsibilities as teachers. The narrowness of this view is astonishingly naive. One cringes at the effect such a move would, at least at this point, have on the level of teaching competence. Not only would the smart continue to select other career options; the rational and frightened would leave as well.

But even if we regard proposals for reform that in the broader context make good sense, there is no single change in policy or practice that can effect a higher general level of teaching competence in the society. Rather, there is a set of measures that, if taken as a set and simultaneously, promises to change the nature of teacher education and to enhance the quality of teaching. Moreover, no one agency or kind of organization is in a position to make all the necessary changes. Every actor would have to assume at least part of the responsibility.

Recommendation 1

Major research universities (and only major research universities) should develop a three-year professional doctoral program in teaching. In most cases, I would recommend that the existing school or college of education be given five years to develop this new professional doctorate grounded in theory and empirical studies and supported by a research-wise clinical component—a doctorate to be indexed on the same level as nursing and engineering post-masters work. If the result of that effort does not pass a university review, then the university should call on its other resources to develop the program which could, then, be based perhaps in the psychology department or in a new interdisciplinary institute. The departmental affiliation matters not so much as does the ability to appreciate both the highly complex nature of professional knowledge in use and the ways in which professional studies and practice can be grounded in research.

Not just any university has the leadership and resources to develop a teaching doctorate of truly high quality. My guess would be that there are about 40 research universities that possess the faculty resources to develop such a program of professional studies, but only about 15–20 of those have the necessary administrative leadership and organizational flexibility. My point is this. It would be better to maintain the status quo than to counsel the proliferation of low-quality teaching doctorates. Any university should attempt to establish a professional doctorate program in teaching only by assembling a first-rate team of scholars and researchers who understand and respect the complexity of professional knowledge. That is, the pioneer universities must be willing to give the problem over to their brightest and best. The remaining 20–25 research universities could follow suit if they had the models to imitate.

In particular, major research universities should assume responsibility for developing this new doctoral program for three reasons. First, the professional teacher organizations have neither the political support nor the resources to mount such an effort. Second, many of the major research universities do possess the resources necessary to conceiving of and developing a program of clinical studies that would utilize the extant and growing stock of theoretical perspectives and empirical studies that illuminate human learning. And third, the universities, above all other institutions, should assume the lead in assuring that the society's highest levels of teaching competence reflect the best that can be, given the knowledge base. To give less is to fail to assume one of the university's central responsibilities and to leave the quality of the incoming freshmen to fate. Stanford President Donald Kennedy recently urged "the great research universities [to] return education to the list of primary outlets for applied social sciences."[7] I would argue that far more is at issue than finding new uses for the foundering social sciences. Teacher education is a matter of the university's social and cultural responsibility.

Recommendation 2

I am not arguing, as do some (Clark and Marker; Cogan; Cremin, for example) that all teachers ought to complete such a sophisticated professional doctoral program. The society simply could not afford the expense of over two million such degrees. Anyhow, such staffing would be unnecessary. A doctor of teaching for every 20–30 regular teachers in a school would be both affordable and efficient. The regular teachers could employ the most sophisticated diagnostic measures, instructional techniques, and assessment instruments with the guidance, supervision, and counsel of the head teachers. I am, to put the matter otherwise, recommending that schools be restructured to accommodate differentiated staffing. Indeed, the added expertise that the head teachers with teaching doctorates could bring to the schools would be affordable only with differentiated staffing. Only if there were the prospect of competitive salaries could some of the best and the brightest be attracted to the teaching doctoral programs; only if a school could structure its staff in a way that would allow the head teacher to improve the working competence of all of its teachers could school systems and states justify the added expense.

To date, both the NEA and the AFT have objected, sometimes vehemently, to proposals for differentiated staffing. This is one case in which the actors shall need to understand that while the recommendation may not appear to be in their previously declared, immediate interest, it would promote their more general interests. Any measure that would substantially increase the technical expertise of the profession could be used to advance the status of the entire profession. While technical competence alone does not ensure an increase in status (Nilson, 1979, p. 572), a certain level of competence—a level that teaching has yet to achieve—is necessary for teaching to become professionally competitive.

Recommendation 3

Both state and local education agencies should engage sociologists of work and social psychologists to redesign school as a workplace. As Sarason has cogently argued, "When criteria for competency do not reflect a concern for job satisfaction—when concern for job analysis is isolated from concerns about job satisfaction—we are, unwittingly to be sure, looking at [the human being] as machine" (1978–79, p. 4). There shall be little practical point in raising the level of a school's teaching competence by injecting highly sophisticated personnel into the system if the structure of teaching as an occupation continues to drive experienced teachers away. If Saab and Volvo could make what would appear to be inherently tedious work, the assemblage of automobiles, engaging at all and especially engaging over time, then surely we should be able to restructure teaching in a way that would build in new challenges and give teachers a sense of career direction and gain. Indeed, teaching would appear to be a case of an inherently interesting activity that schools have, in effect, reduced to a numbing repetition.

One suspects that a couple of social psychologists working experimentally with several schools just about anywhere could develop models that could be imitated successfully. What is required initially is perhaps a chief state school officer with some funds for experimentation, an empathetic district superintendent, several building principals who have the imagination to conceive of alternatives or who have the sophistication to understand what the social psychologists suggest plus a measure of courage, and a number of teachers who are interested in breaking away from the tedium. Specifically, I recommend that the chief state school officers undertake to develop at least one such alternative model within the next three to five years.

Recommendation 4

In an attempt to attract some of the best and brightest college students into teaching, states should establish testing alternatives to the present teacher education programs. A state might, for example, certify graduates to teach who score in the top 10% on the National Teacher Examination and who subsequently have, through a state arrangement, done an internship in the schools. Thus, the brightest who might consider teaching were it not for the requirement of taking education courses could circumvent that obstacle. Moreover, this arrangement would provide the much needed competition for schools of education.

Recommendation 5

Testing agencies (e.g., the Educational Testing Service) should begin immediately to develop licensure examinations for head teachers with teaching doctorates. To do so, they should engage the services of those who are developing the teaching doctorates at half a dozen of the major research universities. In addition to a pencil-and-paper portion, one would expect substantial clinical sections. Such a test could serve additionally as a way to check the relative strength of teaching doctoral programs.

Recommendation 6

State and private agencies that accredit and approve schools should begin to develop standards that will encourage the introduction of head teachers with teaching doctorates into school faculties. For the first ten to twenty years after the teaching doctoral programs open admissions, head teachers would be in very short supply and could be attracted only by the premier schools, both public and private. If, for example, 20 research universities were to develop programs and if each program were to grant 50 doctorates yearly, it would take roughly 40 years to provide one qualified head teacher for every 45 regular teachers. (Clearly, staffing the schools with as many teaching doctorates as could economically elevate the schools' level of teaching competence is a long-term project.) Accrediting agencies should give special recognition to those schools that hire those with teaching doctorates.

Recommendation 7

Schools and colleges of education should monitor increases in the drawing power of the teaching profession, as the work of teaching is restructured in the schools, as staffs are differentiated, and as the teaching doctorate is developed. When more of the best and the brightest are attracted into earning a teaching certificate, the schools and colleges should raise their admission standards, in particular the level of verbal ability required for admission.

Recommendation 8

Schools of education in universities and colleges that have graduate programs should quietly, as Oxford's Harry Judge (1980, p. 348) recommends, extricate regular teacher education from undergraduate studies. That is, they should begin to require a bachelor's degree for admission to teacher education programs and, where politically feasible, have the regular teacher education program (as distinct from the teaching doctoral program) reindexed on the master's level. Where a school or college of education is unable to develop an acceptably rigorous master's-level professional program, the university should choose either to terminate its teacher education program or to adopt the project as a universitywide task, so that the needed resources may be tapped.

Concluding Note

The point of these recommendations is to urge discussion on the prospects for recreating teacher education and teaching in ways that will enhance the level of teaching competence in the schools. The point is *not* to attempt to remake teaching on the medical model. With a delivery system fragmented by specialism, medicine has encountered its own difficulties in providing effective care. Different specialized physicians attending to different aspects of the body is simply not turning out to be a sound way to treat patients whose experience of self is as a whole. As Stephen Kerr (1979, p. 91) has noted, educators' interest in the medical analogy comes at a time when physicians themselves are finding fault with their 70-year history of specialism. My recommendations do not, then, propose that teaching competence be heightened by having teachers specialize in different aspects of learning. Rather, they suggest raising the level of teaching competence by creating highly sophisticated generalist teaching doctorates and by upgrading the corps of regular teachers. Given that we know the social and human costs of medical specialism, to repeat those errors would be unconscionable.

As proposals for action, these recommendations are interrelated and grand, some would say unrealistic. If it is unrealistic to expect the various actors to do what is necessary to increase this society's teaching competence, then I can see no future for teaching done other than as an amateur activity. That future, which would ramify socially, culturally, and politically, should give pause. In several ways we can ill afford to continue to countenance the society's teaching incompetence.

Why specifically should teaching competence matter? What is wrong with resting content with teaching done as an essentially amateur activity? Why should it matter that this society fails to define and reward teaching in a way that attracts and retains the best and the brightest? Why should we be concerned about this country's downward spiral in teaching competence and the attendant decline in student achievement?

The obvious, fundamentally unilluminating answer is that we should care, lest we undermine our educational system. The less obvious, but more instructive response displays what is at issue in a broader context. By design and by default, this society has chosen to promote pathology-based medicine, to encourage litigious forms of conflict resolution, and to engineer technologies for an ever-increasing military capability. The relatively lucrative, upward-bound professional careers in medicine, law, and engineering clearly reflect these values. That is, by design and by default this country has chosen to turn disease, disputes, and war into profitable career fields. At the same time, it has made most unattractive the activity of educating our young. The question is not whether resources should be dedicated to the maintenance of health, domestic tranquility, and international peace. Rather, the question is whether any society can afford to make their opposites profitable and to do so at the expense of education.

And why should education matter? There are those who are not content with education's value to individuals; they seek, instead, an indication of education's social utility. Highly optimistic in its projections when compared with other such reports, the *Global 2000 Report to the President* (1981, p. 3) states that "the problems of preserving the carrying capacity of the earth and sustaining the possibility of a decent life for the human beings that inhabit it are enormous and close upon us." Hardly a product of fanatical doomsayers, this report's sobering conclusions continue:

> Vigorous, determined new initiatives are needed if worsening poverty and human suffering, environmental degradation, and international tension and conflicts are to be prevented. There are no quick fixes. The only solution to the problems of population, resources and environment are complex and long-term. These problems are inextricably linked to some of the most perplexing and persistent problems in the world—poverty, injustice, and social conflict. New and imaginative ideas—and a willingness to act on them—are essential (p. 4).

In the face of such enormous, intertwined problems, we will have a warrant for hope only if we can attract at least some of our ablest (a group that is already not as bright as its predecessors) into teaching as a career. Especially no purported liberal democracy can counsel an ever-dwindling pool of talent. Not with problems so menacing and overwhelmingly complex.

We can afford to brook the imbalance no longer. Health and tranquility depend at least as much upon education of the general populace as upon expertise in medicine, law, and engineering. The task is to attract a reasonable portion of our brightest, most capable young people into teaching careers. That requires changing the conditions and substance of teaching and giving higher priority to the professional preparation of teachers.

NOTES

1. As Stinnett (1974) notes, many of those who today count as having substandard credentials would in the immediately post-World War II years have been considered fully qualified.
2. For one well-articulated example of such accounts that do not appeal to broader contextual factors, see Frye (1979).
3. For tables that economically give a comparative overview of the individual states' requirements for certification, see Stinnett (1974, pp. 12–14).
4. Some argue that NCATE standards should not be used even to judge whether teacher education meets minimal expectations, for the validity and reliability of the standards have not been established. See, for example, Larsen (1979, pp. 11–19).
5. While earlier NCATE was notably hesitant to deny accreditation even to the weakest of institutions, in 1979–80 it turned down 30% of reviewed teacher education programs (Tom, 1980, p. 25).
6. For one teacher's objections to the present top-down bureaucratic mode of in-service education, see Sharma (1982).
7. These are Kennedy's remarks as reported in the *Chronicle's* coverage of the colloquium on

"Higher Learning and the Nation's Future," sponsored by the Carnegie Foundation for the Advancement of Teaching. See "Stanford U. Plans Revitalization of the Education School," *Chronicle of Higher Education*, 2 December 1981, *23*(14), 6.

REFERENCES

Arnold, D. S., et al. *Quality control in teacher education: Some policy issues*. Washington, D.C.: AACTE, 1977. (ERIC Document Reproduction Service No. SP 010 745.)

Bowles, S., and Levin, H. The determinants of scholastic achievement: An appraisal of some recent findings. *Journal of Human Resources*, Winter 1968, *3*, 3–24.

Carnegie Commission on Higher Education (The). *Continuity and discontinuity: Higher education and the schools*. New York: McGraw-Hill, 1973.

Carroll, S. T. *Past and likely future trends in the labor market for teachers*, March 1977. (ERIC Document Reproduction Service No. SP 011 994).

Charters, W. W., Jr. Some factors affecting teacher survival in school districts. *American Educational Research Journal*, 1970, *7*, 1–27.

Christensen, D. Accreditation in teacher education: A brief overview. *Journal of Physical Education and Recreation*, February 1980, *51*(2), 42–44, 83.

Clark, D. L., and Marker, G. The institutionalization of teacher education. In K. Ryan (ed.), *Teacher education*, Seventy-fourth Yearbook of the National Society for the Study of Education, Part II. Chicago: University of Chicago Press, 1975, pp. 53–86.

Cogan, M. L. Current issues in the education of teachers. In K. Ryan (ed.), *Teacher education*, Seventy-fourth Yearbook of the National Society for the Study of Education, Part II. Chicago: University of Chicago Press, 1975, pp. 204–29.

Coleman, J., et al. *Equality of educational opportunity*. Washington, D.C.: U.S. Government Printing Office, 1966.

Cremin, L. A. *The education of the educating professions*. Nineteenth annual Charles W. Hunt Lecture presented at the Annual Meeting, American Association of Colleges for Teacher Education, Chicago, Illinois, February 1978. (ERIC Document Reproduction Service No. ED 148 829.)

Drummond, W. H., and Andrews, T. E. The influence of federal and state governments on teacher education. *Phi Delta Kappan*, October 1980, *62*(2), 97–100.

Estimated number of classroom teachers in instructional staff in the United States, Fall 1980 and Fall 1981. *Teacher Education Reports*, *3*(18), 5–6.

Freeman, R. B. *The labor market for college-trained manpower*. Cambridge, Mass.: Harvard University Press, 1971.

Frye, C. M. Who runs the schools? *Newsweek*, 5 September 1979, p. 13.

Global 2000 report to the President (The): Entering the twenty-first century. (Vol. 1). Washington, D.C.: U.S. Government Printing Office, 1981.

Gubser, L. Directors column. *NCATE Update*, January 1979, p. 4.

Hanuschek, E. The production of education, teacher quality, and efficiency. In *Do teachers make a difference?*, DHEW OE-58042. Washington, D.C.: U.S. Government Printing Office, 1970.

Howsam, R. B., et al. *Educating a profession*. Washington, D.C.: AACTE, 1976.

Judge, H. Teaching and professionalization: An essay in ambiguity. In E. Hoyle and J. Mcquarry (eds.), *World yearbook of education 1980: Professional development of teachers*. London: Kogan Page, 1980, pp. 340–49.

Kashdan, B. *What's new in governance, program, and licensure in teaching?* Washington, D.C.: NEA, 1982 (forthcoming).

Kerr, S. T. *Specialization among educators: Efficiency, power, and the medical analogy*. Final report on work supported by the National Institute of Education, Grant No. NIE-G-78-1066, December 1979.

Kleine, P. F., and Wisniewski, R. Bill 1706: A forward step for Oklahoma. *Phi Delta Kappan*, October 1981, *63*(2), 115–117.

Larsen, R. W. Examining standards: An important task for those involved in accreditation. *Action in Teacher Education*, Spring 1979, 1(3–4), 11–19.

Lipka, R. P., and Goulet, L. R. Aging—and experience-related changes in teacher attitudes toward the profession. *Educational Research Quarterly*, Summer 1979, *4*(2), 19–28.

Lortie, D. C. *Schoolteacher: A sociological study.* Chicago: University of Chicago Press, 1975.

McDaniel, T. R. South Carolina's Educator Improvement Act: Portent of the super school board. *Phi Delta Kappan*, October 1981, *63*(2), 117–119.

McDonnell, L., and Pascal, A. *Organized teachers in American schools.* A study prepared for the National Institute of Education, Grant R-2407-NIE. Santa Monica, Calif.: The Rand Corporation, 1979.

Murphy, J., and Cohen, D. K. Accountability in education—The Michigan experience. *Public Interest*, Summer 1974, *36*, 53–81.

National Council for Accreditation of Teacher Education. *Standards for accreditation of teacher education.* Washington, D.C.: NCATE, 1977.

National Council of States on Inservice Education (NCSIE). The state of inservice in brief. *Inservice*, February 1980, p. 4–21.

National Education Association. NEA survey investigates teacher attitudes, practices. *Phi Delta Kappan*, September 1980, *62*(1), 49–50.

Nilson, L. B. An application of the occupational "uncertainty principle" to the professions. *Social Problems*, June 1979, *26*(5), 570–581.

Olsen, H. C. Accreditation of teacher education is alive and kicking. *Action in Teacher Education*, Spring/Summer 1979, *1*(3–4), 1–9.

Pabian, J. M. Educational malpractice and minimal competency testing: Is there a legal remedy at last? *New England Law Review*, 1979, *15*(1), 101–127.

Peaseau, B., and Orr, P. The outrageous underfunding of teacher education. *Phi Delta Kappan*, October 1980, *62*(2), 100–102.

Perry, N. C. New teachers: Do the best get hired? *Phi Delta Kappan*, October 1981, *63*(2), 113–114.

Plisko, V. W. Staffing trends and the status of teachers. *The condition of education*, 1980 Edition. Statistical report of the National Center for Education Statistics. Washington, D.C.: U.S. Department of Education, 1980, pp. 47–49.

Sandefur, W. S., and Nicklas, W. L. *Involvement of AACTE institutions in competence based teacher education: A quest for quality in teacher preparation.* A paper presented at the annual meeting of the American Association of Colleges for Teacher Education in Detroit, Michigan, February 1981. (ERIC Document Reproduction Service No. ED 200 537.)

Sarason, S. B. Again, the preparation of teachers: Competency and job satisfaction. *Interchange*, 1978–79, *10*(1), 1–11.

Schlechty, P. C., and Vance, V. S. Do academically able teachers leave education? The North Carolina case. *Phi Delta Kappan*, October 1981, *63*(2), 106–112.

Sharma, T. Inservicing the teacher: A pastoral tale with a moral. *Phi Delta Kappan*, February 1982, *63*(6), 403.

Silberman, C. E. *Crisis in the classroom: The remaking of American education.* New York: Random House, 1971.

Smith, B. O. Pedagogical education: How about reform? *Phi Delta Kappan*, October 1980, *62*(2), 87–91.

Smith, D. C., and Street, S. The professional component in selected professions. *Phi Delta Kappan*, October 1980, *62*(2), 103–107.

Stinnett, T. M. *A manual of standards affecting school personnel in the United States*, 1974. (ERIC Document Reproduction Service No. ED 097 335.)

Tom, A. R. Chopping NCATE standards down to size. *Journal of Teacher Education.* Nov. – Dec. 1980, *31*(6), 25–30.

Travers, E. F. The case for teacher education at selective liberal arts colleges. *Phi Delta Kappan*, October 1980, *62*(2), 127–133.

Weaver, W. T. Educators in supply and demand: Effects on quality. *School Review*, August 1978, *86*(4), 522–593.

Weaver, W. T. In search of quality: The need for talent in teaching. *Phi Delta Kappan*, September 1979, *61*(1), 29–32, 46.

CHAPTER 6

Learning to Teach

Sharon Feiman Nemser

In an essay on what it means to teach, David Hawkins (1973) tells of an exchange between a veteran teacher of thirty-five years and a student teacher. The veteran commented that what held her to teaching after all these years was that there was still so much to be learned. The student teacher responded in amazement that she thought it could all be learned in two or three years. Hawkins observes: "It may be possible to learn in two or three years the kind of practice which then leads to another twenty years of learning. Whether many of our colleges get many of their students on to that fascinating track or whether the schools are geared to a thoughtful support of such learning by their teachers is another matter" (p. 7).

The two teachers in Hawkins' story represent competing views of teaching and learning to teach. The student teacher believes that learning to teach is the special province of the beginner. Once a certain level of mastery is achieved, the necessity for further learning on the teacher's part is basically over. Since teaching can be mastered in a relatively short time (two or three years), it must be rather predictable and routine work. By contrast, the veteran teacher believes that the work of teaching cannot be based entirely on past knowledge and experience. It must be informed by knowledge derived from studying the particular students and classroom situation. Moreover, this teacher recognizes that the classroom is not only a place to teach children, but a place to learn more about teaching and learning. For her, learning is part of the job of teaching.

Hawkins clearly admires the veteran teacher who, after thirty-five years, continues to learn from teaching. Perhaps she is one of those exceptional persons whose zest for learning and dedication to teaching keep them going year after year. And yet, Hawkins does not focus on this teacher's individual qualities, qualities that no doubt characterized her before she became a teacher. Rather, he directs our attention to the institutional settings where teachers study and work. He asks whether the colleges that prepare teachers and schools that employ them cultivate and support their capacity to learn from their teaching and to grow in their work. His observation implies that becoming a *learning* teacher is not only a matter of individual disposition, it also depends on how teachers are prepared and the conditions under which they carry out their work.

Hawkins' story introduces the main argument of this chapter which looks at how teachers learn to teach in relation to how they are taught. The argument has three premises: (1) that formal arrangements for teaching teachers and helping them to improve do not fit with what we know about how teachers learn to teach and get better at teaching over time; (2) that informal influences are far more salient in learning to teach, but have often miseducative effects; (3) that creating appropriate arrangements to support teachers' learning involves changing not only what we *do*, but also how we *think* about learning to teach throughout the teacher's career.

Formal and Informal Influence on Learning to Teach

Teacher educators are fond of talking about the preservice-inservice continuum as a way of expressing their view that professional education should be a continuous process, starting with preservice preparation, moving on to induction and continuing through the teacher's years of service. In fact, formal teacher education is quite discontinuous. There are no structural or conceptual links between preservice preparation and inservice education and training.

Nor is learning to teach synonymous with teacher education. In fact, when teachers talk about their professional learning they rarely mention formal preservice or inservice courses. Instead, they talk about the experience of teaching itself, and the chance to observe and talk with other teachers. A comprehensive look at learning to teach must take into account what we know about both formal and informal sources.

The State of the Art of Learning to Teach

In order to find out what is known about learning to teach, one must first decide what the phrase stands for. Does "learning to teach" mean developing a personal style or mastering the content to be taught or completing a certification program? All these interpretations have been linked with the notion of learning to teach and each points to a different body of research.

There are studies of teacher socialization and teacher development. There is research on teacher education and teacher training at both the preservice and inservice levels. There is a body of literature on staff development and school improvement. There are autobiographies and descriptive accounts by teachers about their teaching experiences over time. From all these sources together, one can begin to construct a general picture of how someone learns to teach and improves at teaching over time. Rarely is this topic addressed directly, however, and what we know is far from adequate. The following conclusion about the research on student teaching, the most highly valued and widely studied aspect of preservice preparation, also describes the state of the art in these other areas:

> A review of the research leaves one with a great feeling of urgency to expedite the study of student teaching; given its ascribed importance in teacher education, it is alarming to find so little systematic research related to it. Discussions and descriptive reports are plentiful but comprehensive basic study of the processes involved is lacking. (Davies & Amershek, 1969, p. 1384)

With few exceptions, the existing research tells us very little about the actual conduct of teacher preparation and inservice training. Nor does it say much about on the job learning.

This chapter offers a more comprehensive way of putting together a data base on learning to teach. It is organized chronologically around the four phases of a learning-to-teach. The first section focuses on the pretraining phase before prospective teachers even realize that they are learning things that will shape their future teaching. The second section looks at the preservice phase when future teachers undertake their formal preparation. The third section examines the induction phase which coincides with the first year of teaching, while the fourth section examines the inservice phase which covers the rest of the teacher's career. In each phase we are particularly concerned with the relative contributions of formal and informal influences on the teacher's capacity for continued learning.

This broad perspective has important implications for all who view the quality of teaching as a key to the quality of schooling. Effective schools have been defined as places where students learn. It is time to include in our definition a requirement about teachers' learning as well.

THE PRETRAINING PHASE: EARLY INFLUENCES ON LEARNING TO TEACH

Before teachers start their formal pedagogical work, they have already had considerable informal preparation for teaching. From infancy onward, they have been taught many things by other people, most prominently their parents and teachers. They have also been exposed to patterns and ideas of teaching and schooling that pervade the culture. Teacher educators tend to underestimate the pervasive effects of these formative experiences. There is little empirical research on the role of early experiences on learning to teach. Still, some researchers have argued that formal teacher preparation is not powerful enough to overcome the impact of early experiences. At least three different explanations have been offered.

An Evolutionary Account

Stephens (1969) proposes an "evolutionary" theory to account for basic pedagogical tendencies in teachers. Human beings have survived because of their deeply ingrained habits of correcting one another, telling each other what they know, pointing out the moral, supplying the answer. These tendencies have been acquired over the centuries and are lived out in families and classrooms. Thus children not only learn what they are told by parents and teachers, they also learn to be teachers. Just listen to the imitative play of young children and you will hear them instruct one another as their parents and teachers do. Prospective teachers have their share of these spontaneous pedagogical tendencies, but they also have a sense of mission. According to Stephens, this combination is far more powerful than our current teacher training efforts.

A Psychoanalytic Account

Wright and Tuska (1968) look to psychoanalytic theory for an explanation of how childhood makes a teacher. Their research focuses on the influence of important adults (mother, father, teacher) on the decision to teach and on subsequent teaching. Becoming a teacher is viewed as a way of becoming like the significant others in a person's childhood, some elementary teachers may unconsciously become like the example, female elementary teachers may unconsciously become like the interfering teachers who once frightened them, with the consequence that their pupils, in turn, become the victims they once were. Wright (1959) has also collected anecdotes, written by teachers, which illustrate that, for many, a conscious identification with a teacher during childhood is important. The following is a typical example:

> One of the nicest parts of the day was when my teacher told a story. I watched very carefully how she looked, and listened to the way her voice sounded as she

talked. At home, I would play school and talk to my imaginary children in exactly the same way that she had talked, retelling exactly the same stories . . . It all happened a long time ago, but it is still easy to remember how much this teacher meant to me. (p. 362)

A Socialization Account

Lortie (1966, 1975) emphasizes the powerful role that being a student plays in becoming a teacher. "Teachers start their professional preparation early in life, their entire school experience contributes to their work socialization" (1966, p. 56). From more than 10,000 hours of exposure to teachers, prospective teachers have stored up countless impressions of life in classrooms. Since "psyching out the teacher" may be crucial to a student's survival, it is often undertaken with considerable intensity. From this "apprenticeship of observation," students internalize models of teaching which are activated when they become teachers.

Lortie supports this theory of teacher socialization with interview data in which teachers acknowledge the influence of former teachers and the tangential role of their former training. While some teachers recognize this influence of the past, Lortie suggests that many are probably influenced in ways they do not perceive. In the press of classroom interaction, teachers end up imitating internalized models of past practice, e.g., doing what their second grade teacher did when the children got restless.

The tendency of teachers to maintain their early preconceptions supports the argument that formal preparation does not challenge early informal influences. When teachers describe former teachers, for example, they rarely alter the assessments they made when they were younger. Their favorite teacher still represents good teaching. Formal training does not mark a separation between the perceptions of naive laypersons and the informed judgments of professionals.

It is clear that students remember their teachers, but there is little basis for assuming that they can place teachers' actions within a pedagogical framework. As Lortie writes (1975), "What students learn about teaching is intuitive and imitative, rather than explicit and analytical; it is based on individual personalities rather than 'pedagogical principles'" (p. 62).

The Influence of Biography on Learning to Teach

Clearly biography is a powerful influence on learning to teach. Wright and Lortie stress the need for teachers to be freed from the "hand of the past," the influence of parents, teachers, and the culture at large. What Wright has in mind sounds closer to psychotherapy than education. What Lortie recommends is that future teachers be helped to examine their past, to see how it shapes their beliefs about the way schools ought to be. Unless future teachers get some cognitive control over prior school experience, it may influence their teaching unconsciously and contribute to the perpetuation of conservative school practices. On the other hand, Stephens has more faith in the adaptive pedagogical tendencies that have evolved over time and that make people capable of undertaking at least some aspects of teaching.

It is fruitful to look at these claims about the influence of the past in relation to significant qualities that future teachers believe they bring to their professional preparation, and to their hopes and expectations about what they will learn. Typically elementary education students cite warmth, patience, and empathy as qualities that they possess that will make them effective teachers. Rarely do they mention intellectual strengths or subject matter knowledge. What they most hope to learn through their professional studies are instructional techniques, ways of diagnosing learning problems, methods of classroom control (O'Shea, 1981).

Many judge the adequacy of their formal preparation by the extent to which it gives them technical knowledge. Unless formal training can modify pre-existent images of teachers and teaching, future teachers will practice what their teachers did. Skills have a place, but they cannot replace ideas. The likelihood that professional study will affect what powerful early experiences have inscribed on the mind and emotions will depend on its power to cultivate images of the possible and desirable and to forge commitments to make those images a reality.

THE PRESERVICE PHASE OF LEARNING TO TEACH

Most people think that when students enter college with the intention of becoming teachers, they spend most of their four years preparing for that role. Actually, as Howey, Yarger, and Joyce (1978) point out, "the majority of degree requirements met by teacher education students are not related to learning about teaching, learning how to teach or demonstrating the ability to teach" (p. 25). Elementary education students spend 25% of their academic career in education courses and another 13% in some form of supervised practice. Secondary education majors spend less.

Still, many teacher educators and students attach considerable hope to what professional education ought to and can achieve. Actually education courses and field experience offer distinct occasions for learning to teach. They represent commitments to ways of knowing and coming to know—formal knowledge and first hand experience—that are typically not articulated and often compete with each other.

Formal Knowledge and Learning to Teach

Education courses are the most formal and systematic part of learning to teach. They offer an opportunity to expose future teachers to the knowledge base of the profession. What this knowledge base consists of is unclear. Some are confident about its value and promise; others point out the limitations of theory and research as a basis for educational practice.

The prevailing view, modeled after the natural sciences, is that general principles about good teaching can be derived from social science theory and research and applied in the classroom. This view is institutionalized in the structure of the standard preservice curriculum—separate courses in educational foundations (psychology, philosophy, sociology) and methods of teaching followed by practice teaching.

Increasingly field experiences are being attached to education courses. This may be an attempt to help students "see" the relevance of formal coursework to classroom problems and make connections they might not otherwise make. On the other hand, it may reflect a stronger faith in the experiential side of learning to teach. There is some evidence for this interpretation. In a survey of 270 institutions preparing teachers, 99% indicated that they offered early (pre-student teaching) field experiences such as observation, tutoring, working with small groups, assisting with non-instructional tasks. Significantly, a quarter reported that they had no stated objectives for the experience (Webb, 1981).

The list of courses that education students take gives some indication of the knowledge presumed to be relevant to teaching. Unfortunately, we know very little about what these courses are like and how future teachers make sense of them. There is a general impression that teachers think their education courses are too theoretical and not sufficiently practical. Lortie (1975) interprets this to mean that the courses hold out unrealistic goals and high expectations without providing the practical know-how to make things happen.

Lortie's interpretation may be persuasive; it is also problematic. It implies that teacher educators could give teachers the practical know-how to realize their ideals. It ignores the power of ideals to challenge the taken-for-granted in prior experience and current models and to hold out high standards of effective practice. For example, without a view of more equitable and responsive classrooms, future teachers are more susceptible to what Katz (1974) calls "excessive realism," accepting the kind of teaching they observe as the upper and outer limits of the possible.

How future teachers encounter formal knowledge may influence what they think about the contributions of theory and research to teaching. If education courses nourish the belief that theory and research can give teachers rules to follow, they undermine the teacher's own problem-solving capacity and convey a false security about the authority of science. Formal knowledge can provide ways of thinking and alternative solutions, but the teacher must decide what the specific situation requires. Most preservice students want recipes. They rarely see a place for foundational knowledge except perhaps psychology. Even here they may often assume that psychology can provide prescriptions for classroom practice. William James' (1904/1958) message to teachers bears repeating not only in relation to educational psychology, but also in relation to research on teaching, a relatively new source of content for education courses:

> You make a great, a very great mistake if you think that psychology, being the science of the mind's laws, is something from which you can deduce definite programmes and schemes and methods of instruction for immediate classroom use. Psychology is a science, and teaching is an art; and sciences never generate arts directly out of themselves. An intermediary inventive mind must make the application by using its originality. (p. 23–24)

There is a prevailing myth that the university has a liberalizing influence on future teachers which is dissipated by the conservative influence of the schools during field experiences. Recent research on student teaching challenges this myth by showing how university seminars and supervisory conferences also encourage acquiescence and conformity to existing school practice (Tabachnick, Popkewitz and Zeichner, 1980). Education courses socialize future teachers too, but we know less about their message and its impact.

Student Teaching: Learning by Doing

Student teaching is generally viewed as a necessary and useful part of teacher preparation. Teachers typically regard it as the most valuable part of their preservice work. Even a critic like James Conant (1963) called it "the one indisputably essential element in professional education."

Student teaching is also the most widely studied aspect of learning to teach at the preservice level. Most of the empirical research focuses on changes in the attitudes and behavior of student teachers as a result of their student teaching experience and demonstrates Becker's (1964) assertion that people take on the characteristics required by the situations in which they participate. Some studies show how students become like their cooperating teachers, the professionals whom student teachers encounter most directly (Friebus, 1970). Some studies show that student teachers take on the attitudes and beliefs associated with the school bureaucracy. For example, a series of studies by Hoy (1967, 1968, 1969) and Hoy and Rees (1977) finds student teachers becoming more bureaucratic (e.g., more conforming and impersonal) and more custodial in their orientation by the end of their student teaching.

These findings are confirmed by a handful of field studies which describe how student teaching contributes to a utilitarian perspective that conflicts with the expressed purposes of teacher education programs (Iannaccone, 1963; Fox, Grant, Popkewitz, Romberg, Tabachnick and Wehlage, 1976; Tabachnick, Popkewitz and Zeichner, 1979–80). A summary of findings from one of these studies illustrates the dominant patterns (Tabachnick, Popkewitz and Zeichner, 1978):

1. Student teaching involved a very limited range of activities and interactions. When teaching occurred, it was typically concerned with short-term skills or routine testing and management procedures.
2. Student teachers had little control over their classroom activities. Why something taught was taken for granted and not questioned.
3. The student teachers defined the most significant problem of teaching as discipline. Keeping children busy and doing things that would insure that children moved through the lesson on time and in a quiet and orderly fashion became ends in themselves rather than means toward some specified educational purpose.
4. The student teachers seemed to develop a high degree of technical proficiency; however, they applied criteria of pupil success which were almost entirely utilitarian, separating their everyday activities from their ideas by maintaining a distance between theory and practice.

This research challenges the widespread belief that practical school experience necessarily helps people become good teachers. Long ago Dewey (1904/1965) warned against an early and exclusive focus on technique in field experiences because the prospective teacher would adjust his methods of teaching "not to the principles he is acquiring but to what he sees succeed and fail in an empirical way from moment to moment; to what he sees other teachers doing who are more experienced and successful in keeping order than he is; and to the injunctions and directions given him by others (p. 14)." While it may give future teachers a taste of reality, student teaching can also foster bad habits and narrow vision. What helps to solve an immediate problem may not be good teaching. A deceptive sense of success, equated with keeping order and discipline, is liable to close off avenues for further learning.

The Impact of Formal Preparation

It is impossible to understand the impact of preservice preparation without knowing more about what it is like. Sarason (1962) characterized the preparation of teachers as "an unstudied problem" and called for "detailed descriptions of how teachers are actually trained." We begin to know more, though, about student teaching. Research suggests that student teaching leaves future teachers with a utilitarian perspective in which getting through the day, keeping children busy, maintaining order are the main priorities. When preservice training gives students technical knowledge, they feel prepared for teaching and satisfied with their program. Good teaching appears to be a matter of using the right technique; learning to teach requires being there.

Schools alone are not responsible for bringing about these changes; despite a rhetoric of reflection and experimentation, universities also contribute to them. Or are they changes?

Some researchers found that student teachers did not change their perspectives during student teaching. Rather, student teachers became more articulate about stating and more skillful about implementing the perspectives they came with (Tabachnick, Zeichner, Densmore, Adler and Egan, 1982). This confirms the powerful influences of early models and preconceptions that remains unchallenged by preservice preparation. Changes are continuous, not discontinuous. This research supports Lortie's thesis about the continuity of influence from generation to generation in teaching.

Many people, including future teachers, expect that preservice training is a preparation for teaching. That seems unrealistic on several counts. Informal influences are too strong, the time is short, and preparing for teaching inevitably continues on the job. It would be far more realistic to think about preparing people to begin a new phase of learning to teach. That would orient formal preparation more toward developing *beginning* competence and laying a foundation for learning and teaching.

THE INDUCTION PHASE OF LEARNING TO TEACH

Under the best of circumstances, preservice teacher education can only provide a beginning. Whatever beginning teachers bring to their first teaching situation, that situation will have a powerful effect on them, shaping them to fit the requirements of the role and the place. Waller (1935) framed the issue almost fifty years ago when he wrote that those who enter the ranks of teachers

> do not know how to teach, although they may know everything that is in the innumerable books telling them how to teach. They will not know how to teach until they have got the knack of certain personal adjustments which adapt them to their profession, and the period of learning may be long or short. These recruits that face teaching as a life work are ready to learn to teach, and they are ready, though they know it not, to be formed by teaching. (p. 380)

At the same time, the first encounter with "real" (as opposed to student) teaching enables beginners to start seeking answers to their own questions. As Herbert Kohl (1976) puts it, "the essentials of learning to teach begin when one has the responsibility for a class or group of young people. At that point, it begins to be possible to know what resources are needed, what questions need to be answered by more experienced teachers, and what skills one needs" (p. 11). Thus the workplace is a setting for adaptation *and* inquiry during the first year of teaching.

Various labels (induction phase or transition phase) have been used to signal the fact that the first year of teaching has a character of its own, that it is different from what has gone before and likely to influence what is to come. Some go so far as to argue that what happens during the first year of teaching determines not only whether someone remains in teaching but also what kind of teacher they become. This assumes that the first year is *the* critical year in learning to teach. A recent request for proposals from the National Institute of Education (1978) asserted this position:

> The conditions under which a person carries out the first year of teaching have a strong influence on the level of effectiveness which that teacher is able to achieve and sustain over the years; on the attitudes which govern teacher behavior over even a forty year career; and indeed, on the decision whether or not to continue in the teaching profession. (p. 3)

We have no longitudinal data to test these assumptions about the relationship between the induction period and the teacher's long term development. Much of what we know about the first year of teaching comes from the firsthand accounts by beginning teachers who recall the year as an intense and stressful period of learning. Understandably, these accounts are subject to some limitations of perspective and colored by affect.

The Shock of Reality and Learning to Teach

Often beginning teachers approach their first assignments with idealistic and unrealistic expectations. After watching teachers for many years and participating in the routines and rituals of school life, beginning teachers may think they know what they are getting into. When they actually move to the other side of the teacher's desk, however, the once familiar scene looks strangely unfamiliar. In a chapter entitled "X is for the Unknown" in a book appropriately titled *Don't Smile Until Christmas*, Gail Richardson (1970) describes the combinations of hopes and fears that she brought to her first job as a high school math teacher:

> I was going to be a good teacher—interesting and fair and encountering my students as people...I would regard each student as an individual, having dignity and worth. I would create a class atmosphere that was friendly and encouraging, in which a person could make a mistake without being made to feel he was an idiot. I would communicate enthusiasm for my subject.
>
> These imprecise, flattering notions of myself as teacher were the thoughts that brought me to Belden High School. I knew little of the school, other than it was in a changing neighborhood. . . .
>
> Despite my optimistic self-concept, my expectations for the year did not reflect complete confidence for I was uncertain of grading, discipline and parental contact. . . . I also had preconceived notions of classroom mechanics. I anticipated three classes with no more than thirty-five students each. I hoped to receive copies of my text before school began so that I could begin planning. I was worried about what I would do on the first day. *From that first day, all my optimistic visions were gradually but steadily eclipsed by the reality which confronted me.* (p. 61; emphasis added)

Sometimes the first day of school proceeds smoothly as teachers and students size each other up, but the "honeymoon period" quickly ends and a sense of panic develops as beginning teachers realize how ill prepared they are for their teaching responsibilities. These responsibilities do not differ in any way from the responsibilities which an experienced teacher must handle (Lortie, 1975). Like everyone else, the beginning teacher must ready the room, organize the curriculum for the year, plan activities for the opening day.

The need to act, the pressure to respond, launches the beginning teacher on a period of trial and error learning. Lortie (1967) compares the beginner's entrance into the profession to Robinson Crusoe's struggle for survival.

> As for Defoe's hero, the beginning teacher may find that prior excellence supplied him with some alternatives for action, but his crucial learning comes from his personal errors; he fits together solutions and specific problems into some kind of whole and at times finds leeway for the expression of personal tastes. Working largely alone, he cannot make the specifics of his working knowledge base explicit, nor need he, as his victories are private. (p. 59)

Basically, beginners work things out on their own. This leaves room for self expression. But it also narrows the range of alternatives that will be tried and increases the likelihood that the novice will misinterpret successes and failures; this may help in the short run, but may not be educative in the long run. Nor need "what works" build and sustain a teacher's capacity to learn from teaching and to keep asking questions.

Beginning teachers may come to believe that good teaching is something you figure out on your own by trying out one technique after another. Differences among teachers appear to be simply matters of personal style. Such beliefs work against a commitment to keep on learning and to hold high standards of effective practice that make such learning possible.

Beginners' Problems and Where They Come From

A recurrent theme in accounts by beginning teachers is their attempt to establish a level of classroom control that allows them to teach (Fuchs, 1969; Ryan, 1970). Many first year teachers are reluctant to assume the role of classroom leader. They are unsure about what to teach and how. They have little feel for students and insufficient experience to predict student response. They are also unclear about how to evaluate students and communicate with parents.

These problems are often linked with inadequate preparation at the preservice level; however, as McDonald (1982) hypothesizes, contextual and personality factors also play a part:

> Certainly some of the beginning teachers' floundering . . . is due to lack of adequate preparation in the fundamentals of instruction. Some of it is due to a lack of proper organization so that beginning teachers are prepared for the subjects they are to teach. Some is due to a lack of adequate support at the time that they are teaching—support in the form of prescriptive advice about how to cope with certain kinds of problems. An unknown portion derives from the characteristics of the life and personality of the individuals who are beginning teachers. (p. 203)

These four claims deserve some attention since they have implications for what might be done to prevent or ameliorate at least some of the problems of beginning teachers. In regard to the first claim, it is not clear whether a grounding in (assumed) generic principles of teaching would help beginning teachers cope with the specific problems they may face. In fact, the extent to which a preservice program can do something about most of the problems of beginning teachers is altogether unclear.

The second claim is more straightforward. If proper organization means getting textbooks to beginning teachers before school opens and assigning them to teach subjects for which they have some preparation, then there is no reason why new teachers should have to cope with such problems. There are institutional solutions for some of the problems of the beginning teacher.

What constitutes, thirdly, adequate support and appropriate advice for a beginning teacher is tricky. Newberry (1977) found, for example, that beginning teachers were quite selective about whom to turn to. They relied almost entirely on teachers at their grade level whose "teaching ideologies" seemed compatible with their own and who "taught the way they wanted to."

Asking for help in order to get advice sets us a pattern for collegial interaction which depends on someone having a difficulty. Given this pattern, questions about teaching unrelated to problems will seem out of place (Little, 1981). Under such circumstances it is hard to separate judgments of competence from discussions of practice.

Finally the claim that some of the problems beginning teachers experience stem from their own personalities or life situation implies that some of their problems are not amenable to solution. If preservice programs are not selective, then the first year of teaching will become a point where some selection occurs. Not every problem of the beginning teacher can or should be resolved.

Should Support Be Provided?

Since the publication of the Conant Report (1963), which contained several specific recommendations about the support of beginning teachers, there have been repeated calls for the development of programs to assist beginning teachers (Ryan, 1970; Howey and Bents, 1979). Some experimental programs have been implemented with federal or foundation support, but most beginning teachers receive little help over and above what is available to all teachers (Grant and Zeichner, 1981). Two approaches to induction highlight some of the issues regarding support for beginning teachers.

The British have experimented with inductive programs for beginning teachers for the past five years. Although there is some variation among the pilot programs, most share the following characteristics (Bolam 1973, 1979):

1. Beginning teachers have a teaching load reduced by up to 25%.
2. An experienced teacher is appointed to help a group of not more than ten beginning teachers and is given released time to do so.
3. Special college courses are offered during the school year. These vary in length and do not carry credit or a tuition charge.

Whereas the British induction schemes are outside the assessment process, the state of Georgia has tied induction to the evaluation and permanent certification of beginning teachers. Each beginning teacher is regularly evaluated during the first year on the basis of fourteen competencies which were identified through an extensive program of research and development funded by the state. Beginning teachers are also evaluated by their school administrators and by a master teacher certified in the same area. All three determine when competence is achieved and what remediation is necessary (e.g., work with a master teacher or formal course work).

The assumption that beginning teachers should be "competent" or else get remediation ignores the fact that important aspects of learning to teach are associated with teaching experience over time. It also reinforces the view that teaching is relatively easy to master in a brief period of time. Furthermore, connecting induction with formal evaluation may legitimize a tendency already strong among beginners: to value technique that gets results over understanding that grows slowly.

Survival and Development

While survival may be the paramount goal of beginning teachers, how they survive will have consequences for the kind of teacher they will become. McDonald (1980) argues that the strategies a teacher uses to cope with first-year problems become the basis for a style that endures.

> The beginning teacher focuses on what is necessary to 'get the job done'—manage the class, prepare lessons, grade papers, teach each lesson. Effectiveness means doing these things reasonably well, without getting into trouble; it means being accepted, even liked by the students. The teaching practices which seem to produce these ends merge into a style, which—whatever its other merits—works for the beginner. This is his style, and he will rationalize it and ignore its limitations. (p. 44)

Future professional growth can be limited by teachers' reluctance to give up the very practices which helped them get through.

Of course, it is possible that the exhilaration of surviving the first year of teaching provides the necessary confidence to continue searching for better ways of teaching. It is unlikely that teachers with one year of experience will feel completely satisfied with their performance.

This interpretation highlights the tension between efforts to eliminate the problems of beginning teachers and efforts to support and sustain them in on-the-job learning. The view that problems should be prevented or eliminated overshadows the fact that problems often alert one to things that need work. If one has solutions in hand, why go on searching? Unnecessary trauma during the first year of teaching should certainly be avoided. But it is useful to subsume some of the problems of the beginning teacher under a perspective that looks at learning to teach in general and at learning from teaching over time.

ON-THE-JOB LEARNING: THE INSERVICE PHASE

Researchers and teacher educators have put forward a variety of descriptions of the "stages" teachers go through as they gain experience in teaching. Most of these descriptions posit three stages: a beginning stage of survival, a middle stage of consolidation, and a final stage of mastery. The stages are loosely tied to the amounts of teaching experience, even though there is a recognition of the first that teachers change at different rates. As one teacher put it: "I was a beginning teacher for three years."

The first stage is generally associated with the first year of teaching. Burden (1981) provides a useful summary of the characteristics of "first-stage" teachers:

1. Limited knowledge of teaching activities;
2. limited knowledge about the teaching environment;
3. conformity to an image of the teacher as authority;
4. subject-centered approach to curriculum and teaching;
5. limited professional insights and perceptions;
6. feelings of uncertainty, confusion and insecurity;
7. unwillingness to try new teaching methods. (p. 7)

The second stage generally extends through the third or fourth year of teaching. Growing confidence and mastery of basic teaching tasks enables teachers to concentrate less on themselves and more on their teaching. Concerns about "Can I?" change to questions about "How to." Increased self-confidence encourages feelings of worth, and success provides some appropriate and reliable solutions to problems. "Stage two" teachers have extended planning from one day at a time to weeks. They have a better grasp of long term goals, are more comfortable with the teacher's role, and their understanding of the problematics of teaching begins to grow.

The third stage is characterized by a sense of confidence and ease. The mechanics of teaching and classroom management are well under control. Teacher concerns center on whether pupils are learning what the teacher is teaching and whether the instructional content is appropriate for students. Whereas the beginning teacher focuses on the immediate problem—today, this child, that lesson—mature teachers are interested in the overall pattern. They can take in the whole room at once and have some sense of the relationship between their classroom and the rest of the school. Some teachers begin to think about the role of the teacher and the school in society.

First year teachers are confused and uncertain about many aspects of teaching. About five years later, if they are still teaching, most teachers feel confident, secure and professionally competent. They know how things are done in their school and they can function smoothly in the classroom. They have discovered that students are people and let students see their own personal side as well. They do not necessarily think that they know all the answers, but they feel more secure in what they are trying to do. The extent of these changes come through in the following retrospective observations about the first and fifth year of teaching taken from Burden's (1979) interviews with experienced teachers.

[My first year] was frightening. It was all of a sudden the feeling of bringing everything I was supposed to know altogether and really doing something with it. I had a great feeling of responsibility and a feeling of maybe not being able to handle it. It was a lot of apprehension and a lot of wanting to do well. I think there was a feeling that I couldn't measure up. (p. 122)

But over time, the picture changes.

I'm really feeling like I know what's going on and I feel that I am able to look more objectively at school and say this is where I want to go this year and with these kids. I'm able to do that now ahead of time a little more than before. And I'm able to 'read' my class a little more quickly and know what they're going to need. I feel like I have more resources to draw from in handling situations and knowing what to teach and how to deal with people. So I do feel kind of like a mature teacher. (p. 124)

The stage descriptions suggest that a major part of learning to teach occurs on the job, in the first five to seven years. During this segment of the inservice phase, teachers master the craft of teaching in one form or another and learn to live the life of a teacher. Missing from the formulations, however, is an understanding of how such changes come about and what happens once mastery is achieved. There is a notion that with time, experience and a little help, a natural process of improvement will occur. Actually, the stage descriptions reflect someone's view of an ideal path of professional growth, a path that some teachers may have taken. Characteristics associated with the "third stage" may be attainable, but their specification is conventional and their attainment not automatic (Floden and Feiman, 1981).

Basically two pictures have been painted of what happens to teachers once they master the tasks of teaching. According to one view, teachers stabilize their basic teaching style, setting into workable routines and resist efforts to change. According to a second view, teachers continue to change not only because they want to be more effective with students, but also because they need to have challenge and intellectual stimulation in their work. How can the latter view be fostered? What do we know about the conditions and strategies that promote teachers' continued learning and openness to new ideas?

There are basically two perspectives on how to support and stimulate professional development of teachers. One perspective focuses on the individual teacher. The underlying assumption is that teachers have the potential to achieve a professional level of practice if they have access to appropriate support and service. Teacher centers represent this perspective with their emphasis on work with individual teachers over time.

The second perspective looks at schools as a context for teachers' learning. The underlying assumption is that prevailing norms and patterns of interaction in schools can limit or promote opportunities for professional development. Recent research on successful schools and staff development suggests the kinds of expectations and practices that can promote on the job learning.

In combination, these perspectives blend formal and informal approaches to teacher development. They suggest that the alternatives of boredom and burnout or growth in effectiveness are less a function of individual characteristics and more a reflection of the opportunities and expectations that surround teachers in their work.

Inservice Programs Ignore Teacher Development

Schools have no well defined structures for helping teachers learn from the everyday experience of teaching, nor have they given priority to what teachers feel are their job-related needs. Most inservice programs are designed to help teachers meet certification requirements or comply with district objectives. Colleges and universities offer courses and schools support this form of continuing education by granting salary increases for advanced degrees. If teachers find intellectual stimulation in formal study, they often have trouble seeing the connection with their daily classroom work. Districts mount inservice training to put new curriculum or management systems into operation. Too often the training is perfunctory with no follow up help. As a result teachers do not adapt new approaches to their own teaching situation and school practices do not change. In short, improving the practice of experienced teachers has not been taken seriously as a legitimate inservice priority.

A Teacher Centered Approach to Teacher Development

What distinguishes teacher centers from most school district and university inservice programs is their responsiveness to teachers' self-defined needs and their faith in teachers' potential for professional growth. Devaney and Thorn (1975) summarize the basic premises that make teacher centers a genuine alternative to conventional forms of inservice education:

> Teachers must be more than technicians, must continue to be learners. Long lasting improvements in education will occur through inservice programs that identify individual starting points for learning, build on teachers' motivation to take more not less responsibility for curriculum and instruction decisions in the school and classroom, and welcome teachers to participate in the design of professional development programs. (p. 7)

Warmth, concreteness, time and thought—these are the enabling conditions that centers believe teachers need in order to develop (Devaney, 1977). Teaching has been called a lonely profession. Often teachers feel unsupported and ill-prepared to do the job expected of them. Teacher centers provide a responsive, nonjudgmental setting that promotes collegial sharing and provides support for the risks of change. "Concrete" refers to the hands-on curricular materials that teachers explore and construct in center workshops. From the center perspective, teachers must continuously create, adapt and collect curriculum materials to meet the diverse and changing needs of their students. "Concrete" also refers to a focus on the specific and particular in teaching. Many centers have advisory services, master teachers who consult on classroom problems either in the center or in the teacher's classroom. It takes time to learn new things. Genuine change comes from an awareness of needs that evolves over time. Centers structure activities to give teachers time to discover their needs and those of their students. Increased responsibility for curricular and instructional decisions require increased understanding. Centers try to engage teachers in serious study of subject matter and students.

Centers with a clear commitment to teacher development try to respond to immediate needs without losing sight of long-term goals. The strategy that typifies this developmental style is advisory work. Unlike inservice coordinators, the advisor is not responsible for implementing official policy. Unlike curriculum specialists and principals, the role carries no supervisory or evaluative functions. The focus is on concentrated work in the teacher's own situation with the purpose of helping teachers improve their practice. The long-term goal is to stimulate teachers' critical thinking about their work (Bussis, Chittenden, & Amarel, 1976).

This individualized form of inservice has something to offer teachers at every stage of development. Beginning teachers need support and advice from someone they trust as a mentor. Middle stage teachers want practical assistance, but they also need the encouragement to look closely at what they are doing and why. Watts (1980) observes that the most important role for advisors working with middle stage teachers is "to keep alive a vision of what education might become, far beyond what it is, and to insist on an attitude of inquiry, even when it is uncomfortable" (p. 8). Finally, the advisory role offers master teachers a chance to share their expertise with less experienced colleagues, which can also be a powerful form of professional development.

The teacher center concept represents a serious effort to identify conditions that support teachers' learning. Still, centers have been criticized for emphasizing individual work and paying less attention to the effects of schools on individuals. It appears that patterns of participation in center activities and teachers' latitude to experiment in their classrooms are influenced by expectations in the schools where they work. There is no getting around the fact that it is easier to be a learning teacher in some schools than in others.

The School as a Setting for On-the-Job Learning

The daily work of teaching shapes teachers' notions about how one becomes a good teacher. It would not be surprising, for example, if many teachers believed that learning to teach was a matter of independent trial and error with occasional assistance from others. This view is built into the typical conditions of the first years of teaching and reflected in the norms that govern both asking and offering help. Many teachers are cautious about revealing problems and reticent to enter the private domain of another teacher's classroom. Thus, the chance to see advice played out or get feedback on one's own progress is limited. The isolation of teachers in their classrooms also makes it easier to stick to comfortable practices without having to justify them in terms of students' learning.

Despite these dominant patterns, schools differ. Little (1981) has identified two powerful norms that appear to characterize schools where teachers view their own continued learning as part of the job of teaching. The "norm of collegiality" refers to the expectation that improving one's teaching is a collective undertaking. The "norm of continuous improvement" refers to expectations that analysis, evaluation and experimentation are tools of the profession that can help teachers be more effective. Both norms are shaped by the kinds of interactions that teachers have in the normal course of their work. These include:

1. Frequent talk among teachers about the practice of teaching
2. Frequent opportunities to observe and evaluate one another's teaching
3. Regular opportunities to design and evaluate teaching materials
4. Regular opportunities to teach and learn from one another

These interactions occur in various locations—training sessions, faculty meetings, teachers' lounges, hallways, and classrooms. They focus on specific practices as distinct from teachers, which helps to preserve self-respect and minimize barriers to discussion. They tend to involve a large portion of the faculty. In short, collegial experimentation is a way of life in these schools.

Little calls these "the critical practices of adaptability" because they enable schools to respond to changing social conditions, including changes in student populations. Not surprisingly, they coincide with the enabling conditions associated with teacher centers. What unifies these efforts at school improvement and teacher development is a shared perspective on teachers and how they can be helped to improve in their work. This perspective is relevant to various activities—curriculum development, inservice education, and innovation adoption.

A Point of View about Teacher/Staff Development

In studying effective inservice programs, researchers from the Rand Corporation discovered that successful districts did not have a *program* per se but a *point of view* which explictly acknowledged teachers as professionals and visibly supported their efforts to grow and learn. One tangible sign of this point of view was the existence of a teacher center which provided a context for "useful peer interaction, for cross-fertilization, and for peer evaluation." The researchers judged these informal activities as more important than any new technologies or formal center programs (McLaughlin, 1977, p. 80). In an earlier study of federally initiated change efforts, the same researchers found that successful projects emphasized local invention rather than the implementation of "validated products." From the start, teachers were involved in the planning, and local leaders were utilized more than outside experts. Frequent project meetings gave teachers a forum to relate the project to their own situation and to get support for trying new ideas. Classroom advising provided timely assistance. In short, the most successful projects were not "projects" at all, but an integral part of an ongoing process of problem solving and school improvement (McLaughlin & Marsh, 1978).

Successful change efforts like effective inservice education reflect an expectation that teachers can grow and improve in their work. They set into motion a process of professional learning that is adaptive, concrete, tied to ongoing activities. They give teachers the skills to identify and solve problems themselves.

Traditional approaches to inservice training and school reform reflect different expectations and practices. They try to eliminate the process of professional learning with teacher-proof packages and one-shot training by outside experts. They convey a message that teachers are deficient and that others (researchers, administrators, legislators) know better what teachers need to improve.

There is growing evidence that an approach which views teachers as professionals and visibly supports their efforts to learn is more effective and enduring. The capacities that enable teachers to make something work are not unique to a given program or innovation. They are the same capacities that teachers use when they develop and evaluate materials, adapt their instruction to fit the needs of individual students, monitor their teaching and make necessary changes. If schools were organized so that teachers engaged in these activities as part of their work, we would not have to mount special training efforts in response to every new social mandate. The structures to deal with social change would already be in place.

CONCLUSIONS

This journey along the learning to teach continuum lends support to the arguments advanced at the beginning of the chapter about the relationship between how teachers learn to teach and how they are taught. Despite the limitations of the knowledge-base, a broad perspective enables us to assess the relative contribution of formal and informal sources of teachers' learning and to see the mismatch between formal arrangements for teacher education and the actual processes of teacher learning. Adjusting this mismatch involves more than filling in the gaps or responding to immediate needs.

Learning to teach begins long before formal programs of teacher preparation. Its roots are personal experiences with parents and teachers and images and patterns of teaching shaped by the culture. Most preservice programs do not challenge these early influences which provide unexamined models of practice.

We know very little about what prospective teachers actually learn during the preservice phase of learning to teach, but what we know indicates that preservice programs are not very powerful interventions. If schools were organized to support on-the-job learning, perhaps expectations for preservice teacher education could be adjusted to fit more realistic and appropriate goals.

Whatever preservice preparation is or could be, a major part of learning to teach inevitably occurs on the job. Some have called the first year of teaching *the* formative phase in the teacher's career. Moreover, studies of teacher development suggest that teachers only *begin* to concentrate on the relation between what they do as teachers and what students learn *after* they master the basic tasks of teaching somewhere around their fifth year.

Despite the centrality of learning on the job, helping teachers study their practice and make appropriate changes has not been considered a legitimate priority for inservice programming. Even the current interest in induction programs for beginning teachers is short-sighted if the primary intent is to ease the trauma of the first year of teaching rather than to help teachers learn from their classroom behavior and its consequences.

Given the relative impotence of formal programs at both the preservice and inservice levels, learning to teach is mostly influenced by informal sources, especially the experience of teaching itself. Experience is not always a good or effective teacher, however, and the problematic role of first hand experience is apparent at every phase of the learning-to-teach continuum.

In the pretraining phase, prospective teachers store up countless impressions of teaching from more than 10,000 hours of teacher watching. Formal preparation does not offset these early experiences which contribute to the perpetuation of conservative school practice.

Teachers rate student teaching as the most valuable part of their preservice preparation. Research on student teaching suggests that the experience fosters a utilitarian perspective and a view of good teaching as a matter of maintaining order and keeping kids busy.

The first year of teaching is generally considered a critical time in learning to teach, but most beginning teachers have to flounder on their own. This strengthens their attachment to practices that helped them survive and reinforces a belief that learning to teach is a matter of independent trial and error.

In general, the isolation of teachers in their classrooms makes it easier to stick to comfortable practices without having to justify them. School norms often limit collegial interaction to giving advice and keep teachers from scrutinizing their own and each other's practice. Improvements in teaching are linked to ideas imported from the outside not to the ongoing responsibilities of teachers themselves.

Simple adjustments such as giving more time for classroom experience at the preservice level, providing support to beginning teachers, placing more importance on teachers' sharing their experiences with one another may appear to realign formal teacher education and actual processes of learning to teach. They are not likely to improve teaching or teacher education, however, unless we pay close attention to the content and context of these experiences. Furthermore without appropriate structures in formal teacher preparation and a school culture that supports learning from teaching, we cannot take advantage of the educative potential of teaching experience nor guard against its miseducative tendencies.

Learning to teach is a bigger job than universities, schools, experience or personal disposition alone can accomplish. Recognizing that fact, we can begin to develop a concept of learning to teach that fits the reality and fosters a vision of the possible.

BIBLIOGRAPHY

Becker, H. Personal change in adult life. *Sociometry*, 1964, *27*, 40–53.

Berman, P. and McLaughlin, M. *Federal programs supporting educational changes*, (Vol. IV). The findings in review. Santa Monica, CA: The Rand Corp., 1975.

Bolam, R. *Introduction programmes for probationary teachers*. Bristol, England: University of Bristol, 1973.

Bolam, R., Baker, K. and McMahon, A. *The T.I.P.S. project national evaluation report*. Bristol, England: University of Bristol, School of Education, 1979.

Burden, P. *Teacher's perceptions of the characteristics and influences on their personal and professional development* (Doctoral dissertation, The Ohio State University, 1979). University Microfilms International, 1979, No. 8008776.

Burden, P. *Teachers' perceptions of their personal and professional development*. Paper presented at the annual meeting of the Midwestern Educational Research Association. Des Moines, Nov. 1981.

Conant, J. *The education of American teachers*. New York: McGraw Hill, 1963.

Davies, D., and Amershek, K. Student teaching. In R. Ebel (Ed.), *The encyclopedia of educational research*. New York: Macmillan, 1969.

Devaney, K. Warmth, concreteness, time, and thought in teachers' learning. In K. Devaney (Ed.) *Essays on teachers' centers*. San Francisco, CA: Far West Laboratory for Educational Research and Development, 1977.

Dewey, J. The relation of theory to practice in education. In M. Borrowman (Ed.), *Teacher education in America: A documentary history* . New York: Teachers College Press, 1904/ 1965.

Feiman, S. Technique and inquiry in teacher education: A curricular case study. *Curriculum Inquiry*, *9*(1), 1979.

Feiman, S. Evaluating teacher centers. *School Review*, *85*(3), May 1977, 395–411.

Field, K. *Teacher development: A study of the stages in the development of teachers*. Brookline, MA: Brookline Teacher Center, 1979.

Floden, R., and Feiman, S. *A developmental approach to the study of teacher change: What's to be gained?* (Research Series No. 93). East Lansing: Michigan State University, Institute for Research on Teaching, Feb. 1981.

Fox, T., Grant, C., Popkewitz, T., Rombert, T., Tabachnick, B. and, Wehlage, G. *The CMTI impact study*. Technical Reports No's. 1–21, Madison, WI: USOE Teacher Corps., 1976.

Friebus, R. Agents of socialization involved in student teaching. *The Journal of Educational Research*, *70*, 1977.

Fuchs, E. *Teacher talk: Views from inside city schools*. New York: Anchor Books, 1969.

Fuller, F., and Bown, O. On becoming a teacher. In K. Ryan (Ed.), *Teacher education* (The 74th National Society for the Study of Education yearbook). Chicago: University of Chicago Press, 1975.

Grant, C., and Zeichner, K. Inservice support for first year teachers: The state of the scene. *Journal of Research and Development in Education*, 1981, *14*, 99–111.

Hawkins, D. What it means to teach. *Teachers College Record*, 1973, *75*(1), 7–16.

Howey, K. *School focused inservice education, clarification of a new concept and strategy:*

Synthesis report center for educational research and development. OECP, Paris, France, 1980.

Howey, K., and Bents, R. *Toward meeting the needs of the beginning teacher: Initial training/ induction/inservice.* Minneapolis, MN, 1979.

Howey, K., Yarger, S., and Joyce, B. *Improving teacher education.* Washington, D.C.: Association of Teacher Educators, 1978.

Hoy, W. Organizational socialization: The student teacher and pupil control ideology. *Journal of Educational Research*, 1967, *61*, 153–155.

Hoy, W. The influence of experience on the beginning teacher. *School Review*, 1968, *76*, 312–323.

Hoy, W. Pupil ideology and organizational socialization: A further examination of the influence of experience on the beginning teacher. *School Review*, 1969, *77*, 257–265.

Hoy, W., and Rees, R. The bureaucratic socialization of student teachers. *Journal of Teacher Education, 31*(1), 1977.

Iannaccone, L. Student teaching: A transitional stage in the making of a teacher. *Theory into Practice*, 1963, 2, 73–80.

James, W. *Talks to teachers.* New York: Norton, 1958. (Originally published, 1904).

Katz, L. Issues and problems in teacher education. In B. Spodek (Ed.), *Teacher Education: Of the teacher, by the teacher, for the child.* Washington, D.C.: NAEYC, 1974.

Kohl, H. *On teaching.* New York: Schocken Books, 1976.

Little, J. *School success and staff development: The role of staff development in urban desegregated schools* (Contract No. 400-79-0049). Boulder, CO: Center for Action Research, Inc., January 1981.

Lortie, D. *Teacher socialization: The Robinson Crusoe model.* The real world of the beginning teacher. Washington, D.C.: National Commission on Teacher Education and Professional Standards, 1966.

Lortie, D. *School teacher: A sociological study.* Chicago: The University of Chicago Press, 1975.

McDonald, F. The problems of beginning teachers: A crisis in training (Vol. 1). *Study of induction programs for beginning teachers.* Princeton, N.J.: Educational Testing Service, 1980.

McDonald, F. *Study of induction programs for beginning teachers.* (Contract No. 400-78-0069). Princeton, N.J.: Educational Testing Service for the National Institute of Education, 1982.

McLaughlin, M. Pygmalion in the school district. In K. Devaney (Ed.), *Essays on teachers' centers.* San Francisco, CA: Far West Laboratory for Educational Research and Development, 1977.

McLaughlin, M. and Marsh, D. Staff development and school change. In A. Lieberman and L. Miller (Eds.), *Staff development: New demands, new realities, new perspectives.* New York: Teachers College Press, 1979.

National Institute of Education. *Beginning teachers and internship programs.* (R.F.P. No. 78-0014) Washington, D.C.: NIE, 1978.

Newberry, J. *The first year of experience: Influences on the beginning teacher.* Paper presented at the annual meeting of the American Educational Research Association, New York, 1977.

O'Shea, D. *The experience of teacher training: A case study.* Paper presented at annual meeting of American Educational Research Association, Los Angeles, 1981.

Richardson, G. X is for the unknown: Accounts of the first year of teaching. In K. Ryan (Ed.), *Don't Smile until Christmas.* Chicago: The University of Chicago Press, 1970.

Ryan, K. *Don't smile until Christmas: Accounts of the first year of teaching.* Chicago: The University of Chicago Press, 1970.

Sarason, S. *The culture of the school and the problem of change.* Boston, MA: Allyn and Bacon, Inc., 1977.

Sarason, S., Davidson, K., and Blatt, B. *The preparation of teachers: An unstudied problem in education.* New York: John Wiley and Sons, Inc., 1962.

Stephens, J. Research in the preparation of teachers: Background factors that must be considered. In Herbert, J. and Ausubel, D.P. (Eds.), *Psychology in teacher preparation*. Toronto, Ontario: The Ontario Institute for Studies in Education Monograph Series No. 5, 1969.

Tabachnick, B., Popkewitz, T., Zeichner, K. *Teacher education and the professional perspectives of teachers*. Paper presented at the annual meeting of the American Educational Research Association, Toronto, March, 1978.

Tabachnick, B., Popkewitz, T. and Zeichner, K. Teacher education and the professional perspectives of student teachers. *Interchange*, 10(4), 1979/1980.

Tabachnick, R., Zeichner, K., Densmore, K., Adler, S., and Egan, K. *The impact of the student teaching experience on the development of teacher perspectives*. Paper presented at the annual meeting of the American Educational Research Association, New York City, March, 1982.

Waller, W. *The sociology of teaching*. New York: John Wiley and Sons, Inc., 1932.

Watts, H. *Starting out, moving on, running ahead or how the teachers' center can attend to stages in teachers' development*. Teacher's Centers Exchange (Occasional Paper No. 8) San Francisco: Far West Laboratory for Educational Research and Development, 1980.

Webb, C. Theoretical and empirical bases for early field experiences in teacher education. In C. Webb, N. Gehrke, P. Ishler and A. Mendoza (Eds.), *Exploratory field experiences in teacher education (Chap. 2)*. Provo, UT: 1981.

Weber, L. The teacher as learner. In R. Dropkin (Ed.), *The center and the summer institute*. New York: City College Workshop Center for Open Education, 1977.

Wright, B., and Tuska, S. From dream to life in the psychology of becoming a teacher. *School Review*, 1968, 253–293.

Wright, B. Identification and becoming a teacher. *Elementary School Journal*, April 1959, 361–73.

CHAPTER 7

State Regulation of Teacher Preparation

Joseph M. Cronin

State Senator Samuel Smith expressed his frustration with the principal witness of the day, Dean Ellwood of the College of Education at Regional State University: "Why have test scores in our state been going down for twelve straight years and why aren't our teachers more effective in the classroom? What help can we give you on improving teacher training so our schools will be more productive? Do you want a literacy exam required for entrance to your college or one upon graduation or after teaching from one and two years? Do you want us to mandate more liberal arts courses or more courses on how to teach effectively? Should we extend the time of student teaching and maybe add an internship after the course work is complete? Should we add a fifth year of study or a Master's degree as a requirement for all new classroom teachers?"

Then he moralized: "We have got to do something. The citizens, parents, and employees are losing patience. The costs of education have soared and so have our state appropriations for teaching salaries as well as teacher training. All we want are teachers who are competent to prepare pupils for work or college and to be good citizens! Maybe you don't have adequate evaluation of your teacher education programs, your prospective students, your graduates, and maybe of your faculty and their qualifications? If not, you can count on my filing the Teacher Education Omnibus Reform bill this year to add the review and quality checkpoints needed to shape up your program and your graduates!"

WHY REGULATE TEACHER EDUCATION?

Senator Smith was not the first legislator contemplating legislation to prescribe ways to improve or redesign teacher education. Five generations of legislators before him sought, at least since the 1830's, to try to guarantee that qualified teachers would instruct the boys and girls in public school classrooms.

What are the possible purposes of regulating teacher training?

1. *Recruitment*. We encourage literate, sensitive people to enter the teaching profession. We want them to feel that state laws and policy reach out to include competent, child-oriented, scholarly persons who are then properly trained and well suited to instruct young people in the schools.

2. *Screening*. We want to convey to the public and to those already teaching or running schools that stupid, careless, incompetent, lazy persons will not qualify for

teaching certificates because of the rigorous standards they must meet—academically and professionally—before attaining a degree and a certificate to teach in schools.

3. *Quality preparation.* We insist that prospective teachers understand the purpose of education, the psychology of learning and of human development, the methods of teaching and testing, and the content of the subject(s) to be taught. We require that inadequate teacher preparation programs be reviewed either by accrediting officials or by state inspectors and promptly put out of business if high standards are not achieved.

4. *Legitimacy.* One important social function of teacher certification is to suggest legitimacy, to reassure the public that the teacher is competent, properly trained, and thoroughly reliable. Parents want to believe that the adults to whose care they have entrusted their precious children truly are worthy of that responsibility, and the teaching certificate seems to confer that worthiness. Without this symbolic reassurance, many Americans would keep their children at home or try to withhold that portion of taxes that goes for public school expenses. Teachers, especially new teachers, themselves want personal reassurance of their readiness to teach. However flimsy a piece of paper, the teaching certificate appears to assure "competence" and legal respectability upon the practitioners. We want doctors and lawyers to "measure up." Why not teachers, counselors, school social workers, school administrators?

On occasion, teacher regulation performs other functions—to exclude or include certain social groups, to reward literacy or penalize the lack of a general education, to screen out social deviates, nonconformists, and troublesome persons from teaching, to make sure that all teachers are reasonably law-abiding, obedient, and conserving of traditional American values.

Meanwhile, Preston Ellwood, himself a rather new Education Dean at Regional State University, listened patiently back at his office to the briefing from the Associate and Assistant Deans.

"Eighteen months ago we worked very hard to prepare all the documents for the National Council on Accreditation of Teacher Education (NCATE) Self-Study and Visits. We prepared 1,000 pages of material, worked for many hundreds of hours, and spent $60,000 on the NCATE evaluation."

"Six months ago our university complied with the North Central Association visit. Our college prepared 500 pages of documents and spent about $40,000 on the process."

"Now we have begun to work on the State Teacher Certification and Professional Standards Review. This book is the total package of forms, checklists, and survey questionnaires the state office just sent us. Fortunately we have about ten months before the site visit by a professional review team from other universities and the state coordinators themselves. We figure this will cost another $50,000, which we have placed in the budget for that purpose."

Dean Ellwood arched an eyebrow as he learned of the schedule of evaluations. Earlier his secretary informed him of a State Human Relations Commission investigation of charges of discrimination against a minority student who received two failing grades last semester.

"Is there any good news?" the Dean wondered aloud. He was told, "Yes, the U.S. Department of Education, Office of Special Education, has just renewed the Dean's grant."

"What's the Dean's grant used for?"

"That's a grant to any dean of education who agrees to get the whole faculty involved in program revision so that all faculty and new teachers will know how to comply with the education of all handicapped children laws and regulations!"

Issues in the Regulation of Teacher Education

The new dean was not alone in wondering about the possible overlap of evaluation activities, the cost in terms of hours and dollars, and the purpose and benefits of all those reviews. He was discovering how complex these issues really are, especially when:

1. Traditional concerns for quality teacher preparation blend with new concerns such as sensitivity to the needs of the handicapped, racial and ethnic minorities, and women.

2. Educators blur and confuse the terms "accreditation," "certification," "licensure," and "program review."

3. The burdens of evaluation include not only cost but the time of accreditation teams, state agencies, and other external agents, and there is no guarantee that schools will follow up on recommendations or that teacher competency will be achieved.

4. The surplus of teacher candidates diminishes and superintendents ask for emergency certification to cope with spot shortages.

5. Legislators demand that teachers prove their competence beyond the shadow of a doubt, such as Senator Smith had proposed.

6. Pressure builds for fifth- and even sixth-year teacher preparation programs.

7. A well-educated public calls for additional quality control measures to regulate institutions of higher education, teacher education programs in particular, and individuals who aspire to teach.

8. Teachers and/or the public demand more of a say in teacher education curricula and program approval.

9. Educators protest the overloaded curriculum, the overreliance on testing, and the overatomization of objectives for teacher education.

This chapter intends not to build sympathy for education deans as much as to display the complexity of the issues of standard-setting and regulation. It will review both the traditional and recent concerns of teacher education reformers, will review prevailing practices as well as popular reforms, will examine their shortcomings, and will end with sober cautions over embracing any or all prescriptions. Again, the intended audience is not prospective college administrators but policymakers, legislators, researchers, and erstwhile reformers of teacher education. It is the purpose of this chapter to draw attention to and to delineate the ramifications of the overregulation of teacher education, accompanied by insufficient attention to the inspection of the quality of teacher preparation programs.

Traditional Concerns

Horace Mann, Secretary to the Massachusetts Board of Education in the 1830's, worried about the inadequate preparation of schoolteachers and raised money for the first public normal school in the nation, an approach to specialized teacher preparation at that time borrowed from the French. In each decade since that time educators have pursued three standard goals for prospective teachers:

1. Knowledge of subject matter, for elementary schoolteachers a breadth of knowledge (mathematics, social studies, science, and language) and for secondary schoolteachers some depth of knowledge (a major and possibly a minor in specific subject matter fields);
2. Knowledge of pedagogy, systematic study of the philosophy and methods of teaching including the evaluation of student needs and accomplishments; and
3. Actual practice of teaching, generally supervised or coached by one or more experienced teachers in an actual school for a period of weeks or months.

The actual mixture of courses to achieve these goals has generated much controversy especially since the end of World War II. Books with titles such as *Quackery in the Public Schools* (Lynd, 1953) or the *Miseducation of American Teachers* (Koerner, 1963) attacked "methods of teaching" courses for their superficial content. Other critics have called for longer and more closely supervised student teaching to teaching internship experiences evaluated both by university and school system staff. Dr. James B. Conant in his highly visible *Education of American Teachers*, for example, recommended for universities the priority of subject matter and the hiring of "clinical professors" who, like medical teachers, would keep one foot in practice and the other in the university while supervising the fieldwork for new practitioners (Conant, 1963).

The National Education Association (NEA) and the American Association of Colleges for Teacher Education (AACTE) have stressed long the need for thorough preparation in courses labeled professional education—the social, historical, and philosophical foundations of education, the theories and best practices of teaching each subject from reading to science, to music and health, the individual learner diagnosis and motivation toward achievement, and practical observation and experiences in the classroom. These are the traditional concerns of teachers and teacher educators.

The tension between these priorities has never been resolved. The issues of proper mixture usually get compromised by mandating "all of the above" and more of each.

New Concerns

Education can either transmit the prevailing culture or try to modify it. Teachers can perpetuate the values and practices of yesteryear or implement new laws or court decisions which change them. Three examples dramatize the significant new concerns for regulating teacher education:

1. Until the 1970's handicapped children traditionally were educated in institutions or classrooms separate from other "normal" children; now all but the most severely retarded or disturbed students may attend the community school where teachers generally must accept them. Experienced teachers never before trained to help the handicapped have been told to take special courses or attend workshops, e.g., on helping blind students use the abacus or typewriter to complete classroom assignments. Teacher training institutions have been directed to provide all new teachers instruction in the methods of handling handicapped children in the basic psychology of education courses or teaching methods courses.

Some teacher groups, especially the American Federation of Teachers, have protested the possibility of "dumping" numbers of hard-to-teach children on classrooms already burdened with discipline problems—especially in high-pupil-turnover urban schools. They do not believe one course or seminar in special education techniques will suffice and they call for more potent techniques such as reducing class size or total pupil load, adding psychologists and teacher aides, and other remedies.

2. Educational reformers suggest that schools and colleges of education commit themselves to recognizing diverse local and ethnic values and community and parent choice. For example, until recently Indian teachers were not allowed to teach children of their own tribes, and many Indian youths were sent away to residential schools to build new loyalties to the dominant culture. Until recently students who could speak Italian, Japanese, Spanish, Chinese, or other world languages were told in school to learn only English and forget the culture, history, and traditions of their parents and neighborhoods. Only a Supreme Court decision saved the Mennonite and Amish communities from learning in high schools the motorized, commercialized norms that those orderly and productive citizens by and large reject. Schools and teachers must show respect for virtue and new ideals dear to the local community—and not simply homogenize everyone into industrialized, bureaucratized white middle-class Americans.

3. Women until recently have been excluded from most vocational programs, from a full program of varsity sports, and from many administrative positions in American public schools. School counseling steered women into low-level secretarial and home economics fields and the college-bound into elementary school teaching and nursing. Now schools must admit young women into all trades and technical courses. Girls were offered limited athletic team choices and competed in far fewer numbers for shorter seasons under lower-paid coaches—until Title IX of the Elementary and Secondary Education Act was passed. For twenty-five years the number of female high school principals and school superintendents actually declined.

The handicapped, the minorities, and women each demand of teacher education new recognition of diversity and of varying needs not previously honored in the curriculum or in state regulations.

Accreditation, Certification, Licensure, and Program Areas

Who decides who can teach in a public school? What is the process called and how is it handled? The very terms "certification" and "accreditation" are improperly interchanged by otherwise knowledgeable people.

Certification is the process of deciding that an individual meets the minimum standards of competence in a profession. Licensing is the legal process of permitting a person to practice a trade or profession once he or she has met certification standards (Koff, Florio, and Cronin, 1976).

Certification is essentially for new teachers and only a few states require further course work as a condition for staying in the teaching profession. Thus a teacher trained in science in 1940 (before the atomic bomb, let alone nuclear energy) can round out his or her career in 1985 in most states without a challenge to his or her academic adequacy. Albert Shanker, President of the American Federation of Teachers, says the teacher unions should not object to safeguards against incompetence or defend it but that any retesting of mature teachers and their subject matter proficiency should be accompanied by parallel decisions by doctors and lawyers to submit to similar evaluations (Shanker, 1980).

Virtually every state establishes certification boards or commissions to review the criteria for entrance to the profession, which helps a designated state or local official award the certificate, or "license to teach." How well this is handled is subject to argument.

No two states agree on what should be the minimum entry standard. What bothered Dr. James B. Conant after a year of looking at sixteen of the larger states was the great disparity between New York State, which required 57 semester hours of math and science, and Georgia with only 30 hours of science. Most of all he complained about the number of "end runs," including escape clauses, provisions for waivers, or exceptions. He was especially shocked by the assignment of insufficiently trained persons to teach math or science. He felt enforcement of the "course credit hour" approach was scandalously weak in all states and that basing certification on transcript review of course requirements was a "bankrupt" policy (Conant, 1963).

Many states in the 1960's agreed to a policy of "program review" wherein a college could ask that their total program be approved rather than allowing students simply to shop around for various required courses and submit them to the state for review. The approved institutions, therefore, could require a sequence of courses from introductory to advanced, could weed out weaker candidates, and then would stand behind any graduate of the program. Conant questioned this approach as well—again because of interstate political squabbles and because "some of our generally best institutions do a very poor job of supervising practice teaching" (Conant, 1963, p. 55).

In recent years reformers have looked for some type of national review process, especially as federal grants and scholarships and loans have increased and many teachers moved from one state to another. Yet no one wants the federal government to assume the function of guaranteeing teacher competence, for the process may become even more bureaucratic, doctrinaire, and possibly even more expensive. Teacher education and the organized professional groups created a national accrediting council to provide for a voluntary review of program quality by one's peers—fellow teacher educators sent over from another university or college of education. Accreditation is a private process in that a university must pay fees to a council and prepare a self-study or report then reviewed by others. How widespread is the commitment to voluntary standards and to peer reviews? Less than half (537) of the 1,328 teacher education institutions belong to the National Council for Accreditation of Teacher Education (NCATE). So not every program will be evaluated and accredited and, in fact, many will never be reviewed.

The accreditation visits are spaced every ten years, although NCATE may decide on more frequent reviews in the future. Programs can rise and fall flat in that time. George Arnstein advised the federal government that the process of accreditation is carried out by "amateurs, that is professionals in their own disciplines (Ph.D. in statistics, for example) but unskilled, untrained part-time volunteers in their capacity of evaluation or inspection of a college department or college" (Arnstein, 1976, Chapter 1). He describes the evaluation process, which relies heavily on checklists, as more art than science.

The most recent report on NCATE evaluation, by Christopher Wheeler, praised several efforts since 1974 to define standards more rigorously, train the leaders of visiting teams more systematically, audit the term reports, and deny accreditation to more marginal schools. For example, the percentage of denials of teacher education programs rose from 10% (1954–73) to 19% between 1974 and 1978 (Wheeler, 1980).

However, Wheeler's study found that most teacher education evaluations simply summarize the "presence or absence" of requirements supposedly met rather than subject a college to an in-depth qualitative review. He noted that NCATE can only recommend and suggest, not require—which means a number of schools do not make the changes needed—and that NCATE essentially relies on volunteer help. Finally, NCATE relies for revenue on dues from the institutions it accredits, which he felt made a genuinely tough review less likely.

Wheeler urged that NCATE prepare a new policy manual with more specific examples for each quality standard, refuse to accept incomplete reports, and require more in-depth evaluations even if it meant a larger team or longer visits. He deplored the practice of allowing schools to veto the appointment as team leader of those evaluators known to be critical and who previously used the in-depth approach. Wheeler thought maybe the public and the legislature should receive copies of the evaluation reports. Without these indirect levers of public concern, the actual NCATE impact can be very slight.

Does NCATE denial assist a state in its regulatory role? Wheeler found 16 states where the 21 institutions denied NCATE approval actually continued to receive state recognition. Only 4 of the 16 states as a result of the NCATE denial took any action to suspend or further advise the institutions. State observers in most cases did not follow up on the negative reviews, thereby failing to use NCATE information to try to improve teacher education.

Wheeler concluded that many state evaluation procedures might therefore be even weaker than NCATE and that NCATE actually did little to share findings or involve the state. He recommends that the NCATE reports be made public and that cooperative relationships with state education departments be sought much more aggressively.

Therefore accreditation, the voluntary process, not only differs from certification, the legal process, but too few of the procedures either assure or reassure what the educational consumer might expect.

A Teacher Surplus?

During the 1970's many of us thought that the time was ideal for imposing new stricter, higher standards. The supply of teachers was finally outstripping demand. In fact, many city and suburban school districts in the North and the Midwest—and after Proposition 13 in California, districts including San Francisco and Los Angeles—actually reduced the size of the teaching force. What better time to raise standards and tighten up enforcement?

Over a period of two or three years, however, enrollments in many teaching specialties plummeted rather dramatically. The younger brothers and sisters of teachers laid off (most were young, untenured, or recently tenured teachers) voted with their feet and instead enrolled in business, journalism, or liberal arts majors. The number of new teachers each year dropped from 300,000 to 170,000 between 1972 and 1980. Education to some otherwise excellent professional prospects was seen as a career cul-de-sac.

By 1980 a few states reported growing shortages of qualified science and mathematics teachers. Reports were filed (Illinois) of an emerging shortage of high school English teachers. Industrial arts, other vocational, and agricultural teachers already were in short supply. The prospect of spot shortages and the specter of "provisional" or emergency credentials, so common in the 1950's, began to reappear.

If reform requires adding requirements, the best time may be during surpluses of enthusiastic prospects to a profession. But if candidates are in short supply, the addition of new hurdles or a longer training time may actually contribute to future shortages.

The payment of teachers by law and tradition and more recently by contract does not generally permit a "free market" type of competition. If math teachers can double their income by becoming computer programmers, few schools can alter the pay scales either to hold or to lure them back into the classroom. Economists deplore the rigidities of teacher salary scales for the lack of responsiveness to market requirements. The question is what types of reform can be made in the 1980's, when salaries lag behind cost-of-living increases and surpluses of qualified candidates fade away? (See Sykes, this volume.)

EFFORTS TO REFORM TEACHER EDUCATION

Make Teachers Pass a Test

The idea of a teacher exam has been debated for many years. Abraham Lincoln, as an Illinois legislator in the 1830's, voted in favor of the idea (Simon, 1970). Early in this century many cities established boards of examiners for the purpose of devising tests for teachers, counselors, and principals—largely as a civil service device to protect the city from charges of patronage, favoritism, and corruption. Scores on such tests also were used to sort out and rank from top to bottom all teaching candidates. Especially during the Depression this was useful in handling large surpluses and of informing disappointed job-seekers exactly how many persons were ahead of them on a presumably objective list. In 1979, 85% of those citizens answering the Gallup Poll agreed that teachers should be required to pass a state board examination and then be tested periodically to keep up to date with their field.

Entire states have imposed a test for new teachers as a condition of entry into the profession, states such as: Alabama, Arkansas, Florida, Georgia, Louisiana, Mississippi, North Carolina, South Carolina, and Virginia.

Florida will require both an entry-level exam for students wanting admission to collegiate teacher education programs and a comprehensive written test upon graduation. Candidates for the Florida teaching certificate must be able to write in a logical style; read, comprehend, and interpret orally as well as in writing; work with mathematical concepts; and comprehend patterns of social and academic development in students.

New York State, where New York City teachers for five decades have had to pass a test, will impose a testing requirement for all new teachers beginning in 1984. Five of the states (as of 1979) require new teachers to take the National Teacher Examination, a national test prepared by and marketed by the Educational Testing Service. Some city school systems require the NTE, while others use their own test.

Georgia decided to develop its own teacher test on specific objectives tied to a state program of competence-based education. Twenty percent of Georgia's new teacher candidates (800 of 4,000) failed the Georgia exam on the very first round in 1979. The state spent $800,000 to develop the tests and offers them in 17 teacher specialties at 17 assessment centers around the state.

Why test new teachers? Many citizens and teaching groups feel teachers should know basic skills and ought to prove this conclusively upon graduation from college. If student test scores have been dropping for 15 years, how well do their teachers score on basic literacy or other academic tests? If colleges did in fact lower the academic standards in the late 1960's, maybe a test is needed to see if their students know enough to teach.

Walter Hathaway of the Portland, Oregon, schools complained to universities in 1980 that "competent, marginally competent, and incompetent products of the teacher preparation and certification systems have all shown up at the school district office with similar diplomas, indistinguishable transcripts due to grade inflation, largely glowing and unhelpful recommendations, and a state certificate to teach" (Hathaway, 1980, p. 210). Maybe that is why a new consensus is developing around the testing of teachers.

Establish a Longer Trial Period

The possibility of a five-year program for prospective teachers has been debated since the 1930's. The Ford Foundation during the 1950's sponsored a Master of Arts in Teaching Program for three dozen liberal arts colleges and universities—from Harvard to Duke to Stanford and the University of Wisconsin. A five-year program allows an undergraduate student to major in an academic discipline without the need to take professional studies, which can be postponed to a graduate year. Since some students do not decide to teach until about the age of 20, this option is or was very attractive —especially for future secondary schoolteachers.

Now in the 1980's five years of training may be even more necessary for those who want to teach the handicapped or certain categories of disadvantaged children. The course requirements for teaching severely handicapped children consume more time than many colleges can provide on an undergraduate basis. However, the University of Kansas decided that all new teachers need five years to be liberally educated and properly trained as teachers (Scannell and Guenther, 1981).

Also, some teacher groups such as the American Federation of Teachers believe that a four-year program of studies is not sufficient to prepare a teacher adequately for a career in a metropolitan area school and an increasingly complex technological society. Many of the outstanding deans of education endorse the expansion to a five- or six-year program of liberal arts and professional teacher preparation (Denemark and Nutter, 1980).

New York State has decided that several reforms ought to be implemented simultaneously in order to protect the concepts of minimum standards and an adequate trial period:

1. Passage of an examination after completion of the baccalaureate degree, after which a certificate of qualification (CQ) would be issued so that a candidate might find an internship.

2. Completion of a very carefully supervised internship of one year in the classroom to qualify for a limited permit (LP) good for four years of teaching.

3. Completion of a Master's degree to qualify for a full and permanent teaching license.

Failure to pass the examination or to work during the internship or to complete the Master's degree each would be cause for disqualification from teaching. Buffalo and New York City teachers already must pass an exam. The internship teaching year could count for purposes of qualifying for tenure. The Master's degree could be obtained part-time and through summer study in an academic field such as English or in reading instruction and pedagogy. Certain visiting teachers would be exempted from degree requirements but not from the internship. Regional supervisors would visit and evaluate each intern, whose progress would also be assisted by local supervisors or mentors. A State Board for Teachers would recommend policies for waivers and exceptions.

Nor would the approval or review process end at year five. Each school district would be required to conduct periodic "performance reviews" of experienced, tenured teachers and to provide in-service education on new topics of concern, e.g., computer technology. Each local district teacher from out-of-state with a Master's degree and three years' teaching experience could waive the internship but must pass the exam. The exam would cost, in 1980 dollars, approximately $17–$19 per applicant.

The New York Regents blend in one package most of the safeguards advocated by reformers—a Master's degree, an exam, longer internships or practice, and stronger participation by school districts and university and state officials in defining satisfactory performance. Also provided for are waivers and exceptions for future Dr. Einsteins and other uniquely gifted individuals with the consent of the Board for Teachers.

More Teacher Public Participation

Myron Lieberman in the 1950's was the leading advocate for giving teachers control over entrance into the profession. He felt that any occupation whose members did not define criteria of entrance and the rules and standards by which competence was judged was most likely not a profession at all (Lieberman, 1956).

Amitai Etzioni and others have described nursing, social work, and teaching as "semi-professions" because others—usually doctors or administrators—set the criteria and approve the preparation programs (Etzioni, 1969).

Teachers resent this limited or lowly status and in several states have secured legislation to increase the number of teachers on certification boards. They want legislators and governors to mandate a much stronger role for classroom teachers in licensing their peers and regulating the colleges of education.

Nowhere were teachers more effective than in California, where the legislature agreed to take certification out from under the State Superintendent and to establish a separate teacher education commission as an independent entity with its own staff. Oregon and Minnesota also have virtually autonomous licensing or professional practice boards with a majority of teachers.

The Illinois Teacher Certification Board between 1965 and 1975 was changed to add three classroom teachers and to drop one of the two superintendents of schools. The Illinois Education Association subsequently proposed legislation to change the role of state Superintendent of Education from final decision maker to simply a staff advisor to the board. Surprising to many people, an independent analysis of the Illinois teacher certification board's voting trends revealed that administrators, teacher educators, and teachers on the board actually voted together most of the time.

One remedy more discussed than implemented is that of adding parents or consumer representatives to such boards. This is a "populist" reform in that noneducators will be less likely to be bound by professional courtesy or educator tradition. Of course there is no guarantee that parents won't be partisan, ideological, or show preference either to teachers or administrators. This proposal may parallel the "civilian review boards" designed to evaluate police brutality charges or other types of malpractice or damages panels.

Developing Teacher Competence

During the late 1960's and early 1970's teacher educators took note of several trends— the research on "individualization" and "mastery learning," the popularity of tighter "accountability" schemes including "management by objectives," and greater federal investment in school programs tied to specific goals and tasks.

California in 1971 approved the Stull Act, which required school districts to establish a teacher appraisal system, annual for probationary teachers and biennial for all others. The "objective system" called for was to include standard-setting and: (1) the assessment of student progress in each area of study; (2) the assessment of teacher competence as it relates to the established standards; (3) the assessment of duties performed by teachers as an adjunct to their regular assignments; and (4) established procedures for ascertaining that teachers are maintaining proper control and a suitable learning environment (Popham, 1971).

Gene Hall and Howard Jones define competencies as "composite skills, behavior, or knowledge that can be demonstrated by the learner and are derived from explicit conceptualizations of the desired outcomes to be learned" (Hall and Jones, 1976, p. 11). They insist that the objectives be known in advance by teacher and student, that the levels or criteria of success be made explicit, and that the assessment of student learning be achievable through direct observations. Clearly this suggests that learning and teaching be personalized on an individual basis as opposed to batch or group processing of students.

Competency-based education will only work if one can actually measure whether actual skills have been learned. "Friend and foe agree, a major problem in competence-based education is assessment of the acquisition of competences" (Hall and Jones, 1976, p. 59). However, this caveat did not prevent a dozen states from pledging all-out support for the evaluation of the dozens of specific skills required of a classroom teacher.

CRITIQUE OF STATE AND OTHER "REFORMS"

Almost every effort to improve and upgrade teacher education is proposed in a positive, constructive, even generous manner. Hardly anyone wants to tear down structures. Everyone wants to build up and refine further the quality and effectiveness of our teaching work force. What, then, goes wrong? Why do some of the solutions create new problems or even worse problems than anyone ever intended?

The Overloaded Curriculum

Teachers, of course, must know their subject matter. (For more on learning to teach, see Feiman, this volume.) Everyone agrees that teachers should have some math, some science, some English and history, and some art and music. What else? Colleges of education and state agencies generally ask for one or more introductory courses in professional education, philosophy and history, and purposes and ethics of education.

Teachers must know enough about psychology to evaluate children's needs and progress, to identify disabilities, to motivate children to learn, and to organize lessons and courses so that children will develop competence, skills, and values. Courses in the psychology of education, evaluation, and the sociology of education are generally required of all teacher education candidates.

A teacher must take one or more teaching methods courses needed, for example, if one wants to be able to teach math and science at a small high or junior high school. An elementary teacher may need four or more methods courses—one each in teaching reading and math and social studies and general science and possibly methods courses in music and art as well.

State teacher organizations have expressed concern over the inadequacy of student teaching experiences lasting in a few colleges for as little as six or eight weeks for one-half day. The regulatory solution has been to require ten weeks or a full semester of supervised practice for the full day. The student then finds it difficult or impossible to take any other courses that semester. Learning to teach is psychologically and physically very demanding for most people. Student teaching really dominates a full semester for the teacher candidate.

Student teaching is often one of the last courses one takes. This is too late to find out that one really doesn't like children or school very much or vice versa. One cure is to require systematic visits to classrooms in the sophomore year of college and a supervised teacher aide or "practicum" experience often during the junior year of college. This implements the "gradual immersion" theory of teacher education, which suggests that the initial shock is less if one wades into the adult classroom role step by step—first as a spectator, then as a helper, then as an apprentice teacher, then as a new teacher on one's own. Such a sequence is now required by law or regulation in many states. It helps weed out the "not so sure" prospects.

Big city teachers and their unions know that this sequence of preparation is not enough. A new teacher literally can be driven out of the classroom without substantial assistance in the often very difficult first year in teaching. Teacher groups propose for new teachers a reduced class load, extensive help and supervision by experienced teachers, and the delay of full certification until that successful first year of teaching is completed.

Groups concerned with education of the handicapped urge the requirement of additional courses for prospective teachers of the retarded or disabled or disturbed—additional field experience courses as well as methods courses. This may require a fifth year of collegiate study at least for more complex specialties such as the blind and deaf and multihandicapped.

Now many state legislators believe that *all* teachers should have a course on how to help handicapped children, since one may be discovered or assigned to any teacher's classroom—a more frequent occurrence since 94–142 defines "less restrictive" placements and the integration of able but handicapped children with other pupils.

Legislators shocked by reports of declining literacy now want *every* teacher to take a course in teaching reading. Writing may be the next such requirement, possibly mandated for teacher educators and university administrators as well as for future schoolteachers.

Health and survival advocates want new teachers to know first aid up to and including cardiopulmonary resuscitation (CPR) and the Heimlich maneuver to rescue those choking on food in homes or restaurants. Health educators in some states have won a victory by establishing methods courses separate from the traditional parent field of physical education. Driver educators now generally must take a methods course in automobile instruction over and above any other major field.

Some states require a course in audiovisual aids to help the less verbal pupils learn. California for many years asked this of every teacher.

Other proposals for additional *required* teacher preparation courses include: (1) a course in the history or the constitution in that state; (2) a course in futurism; and (3) a course on the free enterprise system.

Clearly the overloaded curriculum conflicts with and reduces the amount of time for liberal arts learning. If a university requires physical education or the history of the state or courses in philosophy and religion of all students, the typical education major will have little room for electives. State certification officials or legislators may have unintentionally but sharply squeezed the options and course choices for students over a period of years.

A corollary of the overloaded curriculum may be the underloaded syllabus. For a generation critics of pedagogical curricula have complained about the mediocre and less than challenging content, the thin academic gruel dished out in many methods courses. It is not necessarily true that one course is as good as another. Some courses are not much more than educational "junk food" with high fat and low protein content for the brain. Typically the College of Education only provides 30–50 credits of a student's 180-credit four-year program (quarter system), yet the Education School always catches the heat when teachers are considered inadequate. The problem is one of divided responsibility.

Overreliance on Testing

How good are these tests given to prospective classroom teachers? Do they predict who the good teachers are and weed out incompetent or insufficiently prepared teachers? Do high scores correlate with excellent classroom productivity? Or do they correlate, as do most tests, with a person's family income and level of education? Do the tests treat fairly minorities and those from low-income backgrounds?

The most comprehensive examination is that offered since 1950 by the Educational Testing Service in Princeton, New Jersey. The National Teacher Exam lasts 8½ hours and includes: a general education exam; special tests on subject matter knowledge; and professional education (90 minutes).

1. Teacher educators themselves are concerned about the validity of the NTE professional education test. It clearly has not demonstrated predictive validity; it claims "content validity," and over this there is controversy.

2. Are minorities treated fairly? In several states most of the minority candidates have had considerable difficulty passing the exam—compared to middle-class white candidates. Two explanations are possible: the preparation of minority college graduates was inadequate and/or the test is normed on the existing majority population and is biased in that direction—the net effect will be to screen out and exclude many prospects whose background is other than Anglo-Saxon.

3. Who makes up the test? ETS relies heavily on teacher educators to develop the professional education content. Practitioners—i.e., classroom teachers—are employed to look at test items but this is a very limited, after-the-fact role. The philosopher Mortimer Adler wants the tests prepared by neither group but "by the leading critics of our school system and of our teachers" (*Time*, September 29, 1980, p. 80). He

objects to teacher educator involvement in the test since most of the education schools or departments "are themselves the reason why our schools are staffed by woefully incompetent, uneducated, illiterate, unmotivated teachers." Again, Adler ignores the 1/6 to 1/4 contribution to the total undergraduate education of teachers made by education faculties, in contrast to 100% for four years in medicine.

As early as 1963 James Koerner dismissed the NTE as "wholly unsatisfactory" and called for "essay-demonstration exams" (although more expensive) as "the only way to test a person's grasp of most academic disciplines, his ability to reason logically in the field, to organize, relate, synthesize and give orderly expression to his thought" (Koerner, 1963, p. 257). He proposed, as did Myron Lieberman, that education specialty boards be roughly parallel to medical specialty boards. Koerner proposed that "established scholars" in the academic disciplines take on the responsibility for devising the exams and setting standards—both for initial certification and possibly for advanced career recognition later on.

Koerner was pessimistic about adoption of his proposal. He said, ". . . there is no chance at all that I can see of a *mandatory* system of qualifying examinations being adopted generally in teacher education" (Koerner, 1963, p. 261). He felt teacher groups, specifically the NEA, and educationists would block any qualifying exam system. No one in the early 1960's could have predicted the surge toward teacher competency testing that took hold in Southern states in the 1970's and will in 1984 take effect in New York State as well.

Needed is further research and evaluation of the validity of any teacher examinations, the extent to which minorities do poorly on Caucasian culture tests, and the control over test items, scholarly content, and standards.

Overextension of Teacher Training

Will adding a fifth and possibly a sixth year of teacher preparation actually improve education? The evidence is remarkably scanty and recent developments are not completely reassuring.

1. Many outstanding universities—Harvard, Stanford, Johns Hopkins, Claremont, Wesleyan—adopted fifth-year Master of Arts in Teaching Programs in the 1950's and 1960's, when the teaching shortage was severe and quality teachers were in demand. During the 1970's demand fell off sharply and many first-rate universities dropped these programs for lack of student (and sometimes faculty) interest.

2. Many students from blue-collar or disadvantaged backgrounds can hardly afford the costs of a four-year program, let alone a fifth year. Only the upper-middle class can wait an extra year or borrow the funds needed. Other students upon graduation from a four-year college may find themselves in debt for $7,500–$10,000 for undergraduate studies and then face another loan burden of up to $5,000 for the fifth year. The cost will discourage the economically disadvantaged and many minority candidates in particular from teaching careers.

3. "Moreover, the fifth year programs are frequently overrated, involving nothing more than the piling up of further education courses that might well be at the undergraduate level," Koerner complained at the outset of a movement he feared would sweep the nation (Koerner, 1963, p. 268). He proposed instead requiring all prospective teachers to achieve a B average or better in an academic major prior to

admission to a program with 18 hours of professional education for high school teachers and 24 hours for elementary school teachers. In other words, prune the excessive methods courses and attract a higher cut of prospective teachers and you won't need a fifth year. Even in five-year programs, Koerner favored the MAT program provided at least half of the work was in academic areas.

Overatomization of Teacher Competencies

It borders on the absurd to think that each and every facet of a teacher's performance can be broken down into bits and discretely measurable pieces. Teaching involves human motivation, rapport, and persuasion beyond a simple collection of atomistic instructional objectives and pedagogical tactics.

Harry Broudy in an early critique of Competency-Based Teacher Education (CBTE) suggested that the distinction between teacher and technician can be compared to that between artist and craftsman. A great painter does not apply oils by the numbers or break down each brush stroke according to a prearranged plan. Neither does a good craftsman.

The CBTE movement required the endless listing of very precise objectives and the search for checklists and plausible objective "measures" by which to ascertain gain. However, there are at least a dozen ways to teach and no one education scheme fits each one of them. The better writers acknowledge and respect the diversity of teaching styles but others look for packaged solutions and accept lengthy lists of prescriptions as a step forward.

Teachers, of course, need to develop confidence in their ability to carry out basic functions such as giving instructions, explaining concepts, asking questions, and measuring student achievement. But the complexity of many CBTE schemes makes feedback very difficult. As one text admits in suggesting the use of videotapes of a teacher teaching, "the instructional specialist obviously would not test the student to focus on 300 different skills at once" (Hall and Jones, p. 191).

Also, CBTE requires tremendous record keeping, close cooperation between professors, a large budget, and a very considerable time commitment. Bruce Joyce in 1973 carefully projected the costs of computerizing a total CBTE system and estimated $5 million or more for each local unit within a state, which figure Hall and Jones found to be possibly conservative (Joyce, 1973).

One early pioneer of CBTE reported considerable frustration with the complicated process and thought it might lead to staff "burnout," emotional and physical (Hall and Jones, p. 303).

The New York State Education Department early in the 1970's mandated "competency-based" and field-centered programs. One university reported many difficulties: "the lack of theory"; "the tendency to produce 'technicians' "; "political pressures"; and "political games" (Hall and Jones, p. 321).

One student in a CBTE program reported satisfaction but warned that

At times being in a CBTE program is like being in the middle of a desert. You have been told how many steps it will take you to reach the oasis. But you don't know until you take the steps how difficult each step will be. Some steps are short but you find yourself mired in sand drifts as you take them. As you make your way toward the oasis, it is often tempting to give up. Perseverance is a prerequisite for completion of a CBTE program (Hall and Jones, p. 344).

The Costs of Screening and Selection

One illusion is that more testing and more screening will upgrade the calibre of candidates for teaching. The marginal teacher prospect will be discovered and dropped or will drop out. Only the fittest presumably will survive. This is the hope behind many of the screening and testing and selection proposals. Will state examinations help upgrade the teaching profession as many citizens and some legislators hope?

Much has been made of Weaver's (1979) study of the low scholastic aptitude scores of teachers. He reported that in 1976 college seniors majoring in education ranked fourteenth of sixteen specialties on verbal measures (SAT) and next to last of sixteen fields on math scores. Groups such as the National Commission on the Humanities then published reports asserting that this confirms public suspicions about teacher incompetence. It may simply mean that the nation gets approximately what it pays for—the bottom third of the college-going population seeking positions paying salaries in the bottom third of the college-trained marketplace, almost always for less money than what other graduates will command.

Is this a recent development? Does it possibly account for the gradual decline in student test scores?

Actually the scores of young teachers may have changed very little over thirty years. The Selective Service College Qualification Test (1951–1953) showed these percentages of students exceeding the critical score of 70% for freshman and 75% for seniors:

SSCQ Test Scores 1951–53	Freshmen	Seniors
Engineering	68	67
Humanities	52	47
Agriculture	40	20
Business	38	43
Education	28	20

SOURCE: Educational Testing Service (SR-55-30, November, 1955), p. 89.

Traditionally the elite (and generally well-paid) professions of medicine and law have skimmed the best achievers among college graduates. Other top students in each field pursue scholarly disciplines—Ph.D.'s in a dozen academic specialities. Science and technology firms now bid very aggressively for top math and science majors. Business majors and journalism are popular fields either because of higher salaries, exciting careers, or the prestige accorded those occupations. Women college graduates now are much more likely than before to be welcomed by banks, accounting firms, and engineering enterprises with prospects for solid salaries for year-round work in interesting cities. Teaching has always had to compete with higher-paying and often more glamorous lines of work for college graduates.

Surpluses of teachers and job retention or relocation difficulties reported by young teachers have affected many university programs. Several prestigious universities actually cancelled their Master of Arts in Teaching Programs during the 1970's, reducing, for the teaching profession, the supply of well-prepared liberal arts students. This could further reduce the quality of the teaching force over time. Will these universities reestablish teacher education programs in the late 1980's when teachers are in scarce supply? How much will it cost to implement new programs at that time?

Henry Levin suggests we systematically examine the dollar costs and social utility of various approaches to improve certification. He contrasts the possible costs of program approval, testing, or more sophisticated observation of new teachers in a classroom. He points out the need for measuring the "economics of information" about the alternative methods, rather than assuming each checkpoint is inexpensive and equally useful (Levin, 1980). In fact, some of the solutions are very costly in time and dollars, and the responsible legislator properly asks, "How much does each checkpoint cost?" and "For what value?"

ANALYSIS AND SUMMARY

Most of the remedies proposed for the ailments of teacher education involve *more* of something:

- more teacher candidates of higher quality and test scores
- more frequent evaluation of teachers
- more years at the university
- more use of examinations
- more evaluators to review each College of Education for more days
- more teacher involvement in the process

Dr. James B. Conant, perhaps the most prestigious evaluator of teacher education programs, considered most of the arguments for additional components and came down generally for less, not more. Specifically he felt a baccalaureate degree from a first-rate college and successful performance as a student teacher with skillful "clinical professors" evaluating success in the classroom would constitute the most effective certification process. He felt NCATE should be simply advisory and ought to include more scholars and members of the lay public.

Now in the late 1970's and early 1980's his recommendations would be termed "deregulation," the simplification or reduction of rules and requirements. Of course, he wanted the short list of specifications much more systematically and uniformly enforced. He was emphatic about strengthening the general education or academic courses, especially in writing and mathematics, foreign languages, literature, art, and music. He deplored most of the educational "foundation" courses, the philosophy of education and methods courses, including audiovisual aids (at the time, a California state certification requirement). He urged that education students major in an academic discipline, not in methods of elementary education with all the duplication, dullness, and drivel so characteristic of these courses.

Conant, James Koerner, and other well-educated critics in the 1960's argued, then, for less pedagogy and fewer educational course requirements. This remains an option for state legislatures and education boards.

The alternative approach is that adopted by the New York State Board of Regents —a series of more stringent checkpoints. The New York board assumes that no one approval will suffice, so a college degree must be reaffirmed by an examination. Successful student teaching must be verified by a successful internship documented by a local mentor *and* a state education department visitor. Then, a four-year trial period follows and the bachelor's degree, deemed sufficient only for beginners, must be bolstered by a Master's degree for those who wish permanent career status. Then each school district must provide continuous performance reviews of each teacher, and the state will pay millions to support a local teacher in-service plan. Also, the state will further specify in detail the types of immoral, illegal, and incompetent behavior for which teachers can be dismissed. Like other professions, teachers will have a licensing board—actually two of them, one with a slight majority of teachers to advise on teacher criteria (and exceptions) and a separate professional board to advise on supervision-administration.

Economists complain that teachers are compensated, tenured, and reduced in force by measures unrelated to competence or performance. When a school district reduces the teaching force, union contracts usually require the dismissal first of the younger, more recently educated, and lower-paid teachers. It might be preferable simply to pay teachers another 25% and see whether and how many good math and science teachers stay in the classroom. If all the measures proposed were price-tagged, this recommendation might seem more practical than visionary.

FINALE

Dean Ellwood, in 1990 after nearly a decade of abuse, announced his resignation, "to return to a first love, the classroom." One course he intended to plan during a well-deserved sabbatical was "The Ethics of Evaluations by External Authorities."

First, he must brief his successor, a "new breed" educator committed to many of the new reforms. He told her:

1. You inherit as I did the NCATE, state, and regional evaluations. They each cost half-a-million dollars every three years. The results will be made public and you will have one year to correct any program deficiencies.

2. Your teacher education graduates will be tested twice—once by us to see if they can pass tests and then by the state (NTE) upon graduation. If they flunk, you will provide remediation. The price tag for the Project Retread is $100,000 each year.

3. You must administer the math, science, and vocational education "emergency certification program." For the next four years, the teaching career entrance exam requirement is waived for them. That will save $20,000 a year.

4. The fifth-year program requirement has created a great demand for a "Weekend University" except during Home Games and during the Blossom Festival in the summer. Fortunately this is a money-maker, and the older faculty love to teach the more mature students who become more reverent and deferential after a few years in the classroom. We make $250,000 on this one each semester!

5. A team from the joint NCATE and State Board of Teacher Regulation will visit you every third year. Provide $10,000 in the budget for lodging, meals, entertainment, and diversion for this group, including the teachers and scholars and lay citizens, all 25 of them. They will be here a week at a time.

The retiring dean was unwilling to say whether any of the above meant teachers would be any better than before. "We wear both belt and suspenders," he started to say to her but caught himself. "We have beefed up the remedial program for our own staff. Somehow we must find ways to stress the basics and avoid the illusion of improvement by always adding new procedures, checkpoints, and quality controls."

RECOMMENDATIONS FOR POLICYMAKERS

Each and every proposal to *add* to the laws on teacher education should first pass through a screening against these criteria:

1. *Proven Worth of the Remedy.* Has the proposed measure to upgrade teacher education actually been tested and proven to be worthwhile? Who says so, and what evidence of improvement was presented? Would a pilot program to demonstrate the value be a sensible first step in state X?

2. *Cost to Each Group Affected.* How much does it cost any or all parties—the student, the college or university, the state? Does it add to faculty load or the years of paying tuition and fees? Will the budget carry another requirement?

3. *Access to the Profession.* Does the measure make it easier or more difficult for a bright person to teach? For a poor person, for a minority educator, or, for that matter, a member of a majority? Can the requirement be waived for a person with a Ph.D. or brilliant record of performance in the field?

4. *Provision for a Balanced Program.* Does the measure reduce the number of hours for general education studies—or for advanced study in the major subject to be taught? Is a new course really needed or could the concern be handled in an existing course?

5. *Deregulation.* Can some other requirement be dropped at the same time? What is no longer needed or is even superseded by the new measure? Could time and money be saved?

Policymakers can learn from previous experiences, research, and writings:

1. The teacher education curriculum already is complicated and, especially at the elementary level, cluttered with separate, specific courses that crowd the time schedule. For thirty years, over and over again, new teachers have complained that the "method of teaching" courses are too many, too thin in content, and too repetitive. State laws and regulations ought to reduce sharply or consolidate these requirements. New specifications or courses should, as a rule, be resisted. Content such as methods of teaching the mildly handicapped, improving reading (or writing) skills, teaching cardiopulmonary resuscitation (or the Heimlich maneuver, etc.), presenting multicultural materials, and other reforms should ordinarily be incorporated into existing course outlines.

2. Program reviews by NCATE and by states should routinely be made available to state officials who should summarize the findings to the affected public, including school systems and to prospective consumers. Colleges of education should be given a choice of one or two years to clear up the program or faculty or facility shortcomings or else to cease offering a substandard program. States should take the NCATE reviews much more seriously than at present, and NCATE must sharpen the focus of program standards, impose the training of teams, cancel team visits when campuses have failed to complete the self-survey, and assign without veto threats academic "whistle-blowers" on the visiting teams to police properly the standards.

3. Academic scholars and articulate citizen consumers of education (parents, school board members) should be added to teacher certification and licensure boards—and to teacher education program review teams. Teacher licensure boards tend to be

closed to all but teacher educators, administrators, and the teacher organizations; this often leads to the exclusion of ideas which reform, open up, or revitalize the teaching profession. New requirements for teacher training are usually added and old ones rarely dropped or consolidated, in part for lack of questioning skeptics and consumer viewpoints.

4. State legislators and policymakers ought to treat teacher tests with the skepticism accorded any primitive instrument. Exams must be more rigorously validated and linked to expectations of classroom teaching in a community or state. Exams should be reviewed to make sure that minorities are not intentionally or accidentally excluded from teaching.

5. Longer student teaching periods and internships may help improve the initial preparation of teachers, especially for the most challenging assignments—inner cities, changing neighborhoods, mobile families, etc. However, increasing the quality of time "in training" will never substitute for the quality and appropriateness of supervision by both university personnel and experienced teachers in an effective school.

6. No set of reforms as simple as testing or more frequent evaluation or as complete as the New York Regents package of multiple checkpoints will guarantee that first-rate prospects enter the teaching profession. On the contrary, some very able persons will avoid all the bureaucratic harassment (forms, tests, more courses, longer trial periods) and choose to teach in less regimented private schools. Excessive regulations create problems as discouraging as low pay, inadequate state and local support, or poor discipline. Salaries in the computer or defense industries may attract those who otherwise may ordinarily have wished to teach math or science.

Most of all, legislators or study commission members should remember that any change not only may fail to solve the specific problem but may in fact create new problems not anticipated at present—e.g., a shortage of teachers in some specialty or unusual increases in costs per student.

Remember the immortal words of H. L. Mencken, those of you who would reform teacher education: "For every complicated problem there is a simple solution, and it is usually wrong." Too much may already have been required but too little expected of the actual performance of colleges and universities, too little paid to teachers, and too much reliance placed on complicated new laws that try to tell the teachers of teachers precisely how to discharge their duties. During the 1980's more attention should be paid to rigorous evaluations of existing programs and the reduction in the number of mediocre or substandard teacher education programs and courses.

REFERENCES

Arnstein, G. "Teacher Certification: Is It an Art or a Science?" in *The Illinois Policy Project: Accreditation, Certification, and Continuing Education*, Task Force Reports. Prepared for the National Institute of Education, Northwestern University Press, 1976, Chapter 1, pp. 4–32.

Conant, J. B. *The Education of American Teachers*. New York: McGraw-Hill Publishing Company, 1963.

Denemark, G. and Nutter, N. *The Case for Extended Programs of Initial Teacher Preparation*. Eric Clearinghouse on Teacher Education, Washington, D.C., February, 1980.

Etzioni, A. *Semi-Professionals and Their Organization*. Riverside, N.J.: The Free Press, 1969.

Hall, G. and Jones, H. L. *Competency-Based Education*. Englewood Cliffs, N.J.: Prentice-Hall, 1976.

Hathaway, W. "Testing Teachers." *Educational Leadership*, December, 1980, pp. 210–215.

Joyce, B. *Estimating Costs of Competency Orientation*. New York: Teachers College, Columbia University, 1973.

Koerner, J. D. *The Miseducation of American Teachers*. Boston: Houghton-Mifflin Company, 1963.

Koff, R., Florio, D. and Cronin, J. M. *The Illinois Policy Project: Accreditation, Certification, and Continuing Education*, Task Force Reports. Prepared for the National Institute of Education, Northwestern University Press, 1976, Three Volumes.

Levin, H. M. "Teacher Certification and the Economics of Education." *Educational Evaluation and Policy Analysis*, July–August, 1980, Vol. 2, No. 4, pp. 5–18.

Lieberman, M. *Education as a Profession*. Englewood Cliffs, N.J.: Prentice-Hall, 1956, pp. 157–184.

Lieberman, M. "Educational Specialty Boards." A memo (Appendix B) in Rosner, *The Power of Competency-Based Education*. Boston: Allyn and Bacon, 1972.

Lynd, A. *Quackery in the Public Schools*. Boston: Little, Brown and Company, 1953.

Popham, W. J. "Performance Tests of Teaching Proficiency." *A.E.R.A. Journal*, January, 1971, pp. 105–117.

Scannell, D. P. and Guenther, J. E. "The Development of an Extended Education Program." *Journal of Teacher Education*, January–February, 1981, Vol. 32, No. 1, pp. 7–12.

Shanker, A. "The Nonsense of Attacking Education Tests." *Washington Post*, October 19, 1980. Reprinted in *Commentaries on Testing*, Princeton: The College Board.

Simon, P. *Preparation for Greatness: Lincoln as a Legislator*. University of Illinois, 1970.

Time Magazine. "Licensing Plans." *Time*, September 29, 1980.

Weaver, W. T. "In Search of Quality: The Need for Talent in Teaching." *Phi Delta Kappan*, September, 1979.

Weiss, R. M. *The Current Controversy in Teacher Education*. New York: Random House, 1969.

Wheeler, C. W. *NCATE: Does it Matter*? Prepared for the Institute for Research on Teaching, Michigan State University, Research Series, November, 1980, No. 92.

Williams, J. *A Report on Teacher Competency Testing*. Prepared for the Resolutions Committee of the Illinois Association of School Boards, Springfield, Illinois, 1980, 16 pages.

CHAPTER 8

Demographic Aspects of the Supply and Demand for Teachers

James A. Sweet and Linda A. Jacobsen

During the 1950s and 1960s rising school enrollments contributed to the boom in American education. Enrollments during the 1970s stabilized and then began to decline. We moved quickly from a situation of teacher shortage and rapid expansion of physical plant to a general teacher surplus, layoffs, and contraction of physical plant. The market for teachers has, because of demographic changes, shifted very quickly from boom to bust. Projections for the 1980s and 1990s are somewhat more optimistic than the 1970s, but we are unlikely to return to the boom conditions of earlier decades.

In this chapter we will examine some of the demographic factors affecting the changing market for schoolteachers. Specifically we will:

1. Describe the change in the number of teachers during the boom and the bust and some of the processes underlying those changes.

2. Document some of the social and demographic trends affecting both the supply and demand for schoolteachers.

3. Describe the changing characteristics of American schoolteachers and some characteristics of the teacher labor market.

The changing market for teachers cannot be understood solely in terms of what is happening in American education. Many changes have been occurring in our society and economy which affect the market for teachers:

1. Throughout the twentieth century the great majority of teachers have been women. The teacher market must be seen in the context of the general factors affecting the labor market experience of women. More women are working and their work experience is less sporadic. However, occupational segregation by sex has persisted, and the earnings of female workers continue to be considerably below those of male workers.

2. Much of the discussion of the market for schoolteachers involves a concern over the employment prospects for young teachers. Part of this concern derives from the fact that the number of children to be educated has fallen off, and hence, the number of teachers needed will stablize or decline. However, equally important is the fact that the number of young adults who are potential teachers is at an all-time high and the rate of increase in recent years in the number of persons reaching adulthood has been phenomenal. In 1960, there were about 17 million persons aged 18–24. By 1980, this number was about 30 million.

3. The teacher work force is a part of the college-educated work force. In fact, a

surprisingly large share of all college-educated workers are schoolteachers. This is particularly true of college-educated women. The share of the total population with a college education has grown rapidly in recent years, and the rate of employment of college-educated women of all ages has risen. These changes occurred at the same time that the large baby boom cohorts reached adulthood and joined the work force. Hence there is now, more than ever before, a glut of college-educated workers in the labor market.

4. The condition of the market for teachers is not identical, or even similar, throughout the country. In addition to declining fertility, and the resultant decrease in the total number of children to be educated, there have been significant shifts in population distribution. In some parts of the country, the education boom of the 1960s has continued through the 1970s. Even in some states experiencing rapidly decreasing enrollments, there are subareas with persisting booms.

THE CHANGING MARKET FOR TEACHERS

The "Boom" of the 1950s and 1960s

In 1950 there were 28 million students in America's schools. Enrollment increased to 42 million in 1960 and to 51 million in 1970. Hence, in a period of 20 years the number of students increased by 23 million, or by an average of 1,150,000 per year. How did this growth in enrollment occur?

1. As a result of the baby boom, which followed on the heels of very low fertility during the Depression and World War II years, the population of school-age children grew. In 1950 the number of persons aged 5 to 17 was 30.8 million. By 1960 it had grown to 43.9 million, and in 1970 it was 52.5 million.

2. In addition, the fraction of school-age persons who were enrolled in schools was growing. In 1950, only about three-fifths of the five- and six-year-olds were attending school. The fraction rose to about four-fifths in 1960 and to nine-tenths by 1970. During all these years 99 percent of the 7- to 13-year-olds were enrolled. There was a rise from 83 to 90 to 94 percent of the 14- to 17-year-olds enrolled in school. If the age-specific rates of enrollment had not changed between 1950 and 1970, total enrollment would have been about 46.6 million rather than 51.3 million. There would have been nearly 5 million, or 10 percent, fewer students in the nation's schools.

During this same two-decade period, the number of public school teachers rose very rapidly. According to NCES figures the number of public school teachers rose from 914,000 in 1950 to 1,387,000 in 1960 and to 2,055,000 in 1970. In addition, the number of principals and other supervisory personnel rose from 49,000 in 1950 to 77,000 in 1960 and to 122,000 in 1970.

TABLE 8.1. Change in Number of Children, Students, and Teachers

Period	School-Age Children	Students	Public School Teachers
1950–1960	42%	47%	52%
1960–1970	20%	22%	54%

During the 1950s the number of students increased by 47 percent, while the number of teachers increased by 52 percent. In the 1960s the number of students increased by 22 percent, while the number of teachers rose by 54 percent (see Table 8.1). Hence, the ratio of students to teachers fell. In the public schools as a whole, the ratio of students to teachers fell from 27.5 in 1950, to 26.0 in 1960, and to 22.3 in 1970.*

The "Bust" of the 1970s

The total number of births in the United States began to decline beginning in 1961, when there were 4.3 million births. By 1973 the number of births had fallen to a level of slightly over 3 million. However, since that time the number has again increased to 3.5 million in 1979. Thus, there were 26 percent fewer births in 1973 than at the peak in 1961. Between 1970 and 1980, the number of 6- to 17-year-olds declined from 52.5 to 46.2 million.

What has happened to enrollments? In 1960 there were 42 million persons enrolled in elementary and secondary schools. This number continued to rise to a peak of 51.3 million in 1970. By 1979 total enrollment had fallen to 46.7 million. Projections indicate a further decline to a low of 43.6 million by 1984. Hence, if the projections for 1984 are correct, the bust of the 1970s and early 1980s will have consisted of:

- A decrease of 15.0 percent in the total number of children in all schools.
- A decrease of 16.3 percent in the total number of elementary school students.
- A decrease of 13.0 percent in the total number of high school students. High school enrollments will continue to decline for several years after 1984.

One might expect that the number of teachers would drop in proportion to the decline in the number of school children. In 1970 there were 2.06 million teachers. In 1980 there were 2.14 million public schoolteachers.† Obviously, the student-teacher ratio has continued to decrease. In the public schools the student to teacher ratio fell from 22.3 in 1970 to an estimated level of 19.0 in 1980.

The student-teacher ratio has decreased in part because of increased emphasis on highly labor (teacher) intensive educational programs—special education, vocational education, and to a lesser extent programming for the intellectually gifted. In part, the decline was a consequence of the increased fraction of all students who were in high school, where the ratio of students to teachers is lower. The fraction of all students in high schools rose from 30 to 33 percent between 1970 and 1978.

In the 1970s, for the first time in the history of American education, there was virtually no increase in age-specific enrollment rates (U.S. Census Bureau, 1979). The rates remained constant between 1970 and 1979 for all ages from 7 to 15 and declined slightly for males aged 16 and 17. Only for 5- and 6-year-olds was there any change in

---

* The ratio of the total number of students to the total number of teachers is often taken to represent average class size. This is not an appropriate interpretation of this ratio. It is, in part, a function of the average number of students in the average class, but it is also a function of the fraction of the school day that teachers are in the classroom as opposed to in preparation time or other nonclassroom activities; the fraction of the school day that students, particularly those in high school, spend in the classroom; and the number of teachers who work individually or in small groups with children outside of the normal classroom.

† NCES projections indicate a decrease from a peak 2.4 million teachers in 1978 to 2.36 million in about 1982 and a slow rise thereafter.

enrollment rates. In the future, enrollment rates cannot increase much at ages 5 to 17. Perhaps the rates will increase for 3- to 4-year-olds.*

In thinking about the character of the enrollment bust in the 1970s, it is important to understand the significance of the "momentum" of the growth of the 1950s and 1960s. The number of teachers had been expanding rapidly for many years. We developed institutions of higher education to produce large numbers of new teachers and the ability to recruit persons into those positions in order to meet the demand. School systems developed personnel procedures and policies to deal with growth and with conditions of scarcity of teachers. Collective bargaining relations developed in this context.

There is a second dimension to this momentum. The baby-boom babies have grown up and have now entered the work force. Hence, it is precisely at the time that the education system needs them least as teachers that they are most abundant.

Finally, because of the recency of the buildup of the teacher work force, there are very few teachers approaching retirement age.

RECENT SOCIAL TRENDS AFFECTING SUPPLY AND DEMAND FOR TEACHERS

As we emphasized in the introduction, it is impossible to adequately understand the changing market for schoolteachers by considering only trends within education. There are a number of recent social trends which affect the labor force in general and the college-educated, the female, and the young labor force in particular. In this section, we review several of these trends which seem to be of particular relevance to teachers.

Fertility

Fertility trends affect both the supply and the demand for schoolteachers. The number of births which occur within the population determines the number of children to be educated, while the reproductive pattern of teachers, a majority of whom are women, affects the supply of teachers. It is important, therefore, to understand the character of current low fertility.

Fertility levels fell continuously in the United States from about 1870 through the 1930s. The average completed family size of couples who married in the later 1920s and 1930s was about 2.5 children. During the postwar period, from roughly 1946 through the mid-1960s, there was a revival of high fertility. In response to the prosperous economic conditions, and for a variety of other reasons that we do not fully understand, couples began to marry at younger ages, to have more babies, and to have them earlier in their marriages. Although a large share of pregnancies during the baby boom were "unwanted" or accidental, it is not accurate to think of the baby boom as a phenomenon of uncontrolled fertility. In large part couples wanted more births than their predecessors and had them. The baby boom was clearly not primarily a result of uncontrolled fertility of the economically disadvantaged or of Catholics

---

* According to the October 1978 Current Population Survey the number of 3- to 4-year-olds enrolled in school (presumably mostly in sursery school) was 2.1 million or 34 percent of the entire age group. In 1970, the number was 1.5 million or 20 percent of the age group.

who were unable to or did not wish to control their fertility. It was a phenomenon which pervaded all segments of American society.

Beginning in the early 1960s and accelerating in the late 1960s and early 1970s, a new pattern of reproduction emerged:

- Family size goals and expectations were suddenly (and unexpectedly) revised downward.
- Couples began to delay marriage to later ages.
- After marriage, more couples began to delay births for longer periods.
- Highly effective birth control—the pill, the IUD, and surgical sterilization—replaced less effective and less desirable methods such as condoms, the rhythm method, and diaphragms.
- Unwanted, as well as ill-timed, births declined sharply.

By 1970 fertility reached a level consistent, in the long run, with zero population growth. Again, it is not accurate to think of the baby bust as a result simply of a revolution in contraceptive protection. Perhaps half of the overall decline in fertility levels was due to the reduction in unwanted births and half due to a reduction in the number of births that were desired. The baby bust was also pervasive throughout all of American society—the rich and poor, well-educated and less well-educated, rural and urban, black, white, and Hispanic. Larger shares of young women now report that they plan to remain voluntarily childless. Perhaps as many as one-fifth of all young women will choose to remain permanently childless.

Demographers are sharply divided as to their expectations for future fertility. Some expect a continuation of current low fertility levels or even a further decrease, particularly if barriers to full and equal participation of women in the work force begin to fall. Others feel that higher fertility, perhaps as high as that in the 1950s, will return. They would emphasize the persistence of strong normative pressures that define the adult role of women in terms of wife and mother. Still others expect sharp year-to-year and decade-to-decade fluctuations in birth rates in response to changing economic conditions faced by young men and women.

Changing Employment Patterns of American Women

Some of the most profound changes in American society during the 20th century have been those associated with the increased employment of women. The rate of employment of American women has been rising continuously for the past several decades. By 1979, 51 percent of all women aged 16 and over were in the labor force. This is nearly twice the level (26 percent) in 1940 and considerably higher than the 43 percent who were in the labor force in 1970. In the past decade or so, rates of employment rose very rapidly for young women. By the late 1970s, nearly two-thirds of women in their 20s were in the labor force.

To a certain extent, the increase in employment is the result of changes in reproductive behavior. To a large degree, however, it is independent of changes in fertility. As a result of fertility decline, more women spend more time with no child care responsibilities. However, employment rates have been rising continuously through the baby boom and the baby bust, and the employment rates of women with young children have risen very rapidly throughout the entire period.

About 40 percent of married women with children under 3 and nearly half of women with youngest child aged 3 to 5 were in the labor force in 1979. These compare to rates of 26 and 37 percent in 1970. Women are more likely to work further into their pregnancy and to return sooner after childbirth.

The rate of employment of college-educated women is higher than that of women with less education. In recent years the employment rate of college-educated women has risen at an especially rapid pace.

Of particular significance may be the tendency for increasing shares of young women to spend time "on their own" prior to marriage and prior to childbearing. During this time they gain work experience and probably a rather different self-image and set of priorities. During the baby boom the typical life cycle involved completing one's education, marrying immediately, and bearing children as soon as possible after marriage. American women tended to move immediately from a dependent relationship in the household of their parents to a dependent relationship as wife and mother. During the young adult years, few women spent much time working. Few had any experience of self-sufficiency. Today young American women tend to delay marriage and delay reproduction within marriage. They are more likely to develop nonfamilial interests and identities.

Occupational Segregation and Sex Differences in Earnings

For decades there has been a high degree of occupational segregation by sex. There are men's occupations in which relatively few women are found—plumber, dentist, banker, truck driver, and engineer. There are women's occupations which employ very few men—telephone operator, secretary, receptionist, nurse, and elementary school teacher. Studies have shown that there has been very little change in the degree of occupational segregation by sex, at least through 1970. Perhaps the 1970s will be the beginning of a reduction of this segregation, as legislation and judicial decisions begin to lead employers to consider only a person's ability to do the job in hiring, promotion, and job assignment, and as affirmative action plans are implemented in an attempt to overcome the effects of practices which have restricted entry into occupations on the basis of sex. To date we do not know the effect of these changes on aggregate employment patterns. This is one of the research topics that awaits the availability of data from the 1980 Census.

Not only has occupational segregation persisted, but the earnings of women relative to men have not improved. The economic value of women's time seems to be about three-fifths of the value of men's time. This does not seem to have changed very much over the past several decades. This ratio of .60 seems to be a fairly good description not only in the aggregate but for each education level. Evidently a majority of this earnings differential is due to occupational segregation—i.e., the concentration of women in low-paying occupations—rather than because women receive lower pay within occupations. A portion, perhaps as much as a third, of the sex differential in earnings is due to the fact that women have, because of childbearing and child care responsibilities, tended to be sporadic workers. Hence, at any given age women tend to have, on average, less life-time work experience and less experience on their current job than men.

The work lives of men, particularly men with college educations and men in craft occupations, tend to involve progression through career stages. The word "career" connotes the typical orderly progression from job to job with increasing responsibility, prestige, and earnings. The work lives of women are far less likely to be organized in this manner. A large share of women workers, including those with a college education, are not in such careers. It is hardly an exaggeration to say that they are in "dead-end" jobs with little prospect for upward mobility. Two of the reasons for this are: (1) Women tend to be employed in organizations such as schools and hospitals with rather restricted hierarchies. There are many teachers, but few principals and other supervisory personnel. There are few steps in the hierarchy. (2) In addition, the supervisory or higher-level positions in such organizations tend to be filled by men. Traditionally, elementary teachers are women, elementary principals are men. High school principals and school superintendents are almost always males.

Upgrading of Education Distribution

The education distribution of the American population has undergone a tremendous upgrading in recent decades. Among persons aged 25 to 34 in 1975, 35 percent had some college education. Twenty-one percent had completed college. The fraction of 25- to 34-year-olds with 13 or more years of education rose from 14 percent in 1940 to 15 percent in 1950, to 22 percent in 1960, and to 30 percent in 1970. By the late 1970s, the proportion of women attending college was as high as that of men.

According to the 1970 Census, there were about 2.5 million schoolteachers in the United States. There were, in addition, 170,000 educational administrators. These figures do not include school guidance and library personnel and probably exclude some other professional school staff. The total employed labor force was 77.6 million. Hence, teachers constitute about 3.5 percent of the total work force.

Teachers constitute a sizable share of the college-educated work force, particularly among women. In 1950 there were approximately 3 million males and 1.25 million females who were college graduates in the total U.S. labor force. Of them, about 8 percent of the men and 42 percent of the women were schoolteachers. By 1970 the total number of college-educated persons in the labor force was over 10 million—nearly 7 million men and over 3 million women. Of that number, 12 percent of the men and 50 percent of the women were schoolteachers. Thus, the share of schoolteachers in the total college-educated work force is very high and has increased in recent decades for both men and women.

Economic Position of Young Workers

During the 1970s, the economic position of young workers deteriorated greatly. Several of the recent social trends discussed above have combined to create a glut of young workers in the labor market:

- The baby boom babies have grown up and entered the work force.
- The rate at which women of all ages are working has increased.
- Employment rates of young women and of women of all ages with college educations have risen at very rapid rates.
- The education distribution has been upgraded, creating a particularly large growth in the number of employed, college-educated persons.
- Following the Vietnam War the number of persons entering the armed forces decreased.

Between 1970 and 1978, the total number of persons aged 25 to 34 increased by 35 percent, from 24 to 33 million. The labor force aged 25 to 34 increased by 51 percent from 17 to 26 million. The number of 25- to 34-year-olds with a college degree rose by 111 percent, while the 25- to 34-year-old labor force with a college degree rose by 129 percent.

As a result of this glut of young workers, a number of things have happened:

- Young workers are less likely to find jobs commensurate with their education than they were a decade ago.
- The fraction of young adults, particularly young men, who choose to go to college has stabilized or decreased after several decades of continuous rise.
- The rate of increase in starting salaries has slowed.
- The average earnings of young workers relative to older workers has decreased. According to Oppenheimer (1979) the ratio of the median income of males aged 25 to 34 to that of males aged 45 to 54 decreased from about 100 percent (equality) around 1960 to 90 percent in 1970 and to 81 percent in 1978.
- The economic position of young adults and young married couples has deteriorated.

Marriage and Divorce

Marriage ages have risen greatly in the past two decades. In 1960 about one-quarter of the 22-year-old women were single. By 1979, the fraction was almost one-half. There is no evidence that the fraction of persons who will never marry is increasing. Rather, the age at which persons marry has increased. One of the potential consequences of rising marriage ages for women is that they gain greater work experience and greater commitment to work and career in the early adult years.

The other major change in marriage behavior during the past few decades is the rise in separation and divorce. One-quarter of the marriages of 1965 were terminated by divorce by the tenth anniversary. It is estimated that nearly one-half of all marriages formed in the 1970s will eventually be terminated by divorce. Of course, most persons who divorce will remarry. However, many more men and women will spend a larger share of their adult years as separated and divorced individuals. Many young women will be "female family heads," supporting themselves and their children.

These changes in marriage ages and in the rate of divorce and separation have implications for the female work force. Larger fractions of women workers are the "primary earner" in their household. Employers have tended to treat female workers differently than male workers because they regarded them as merely "secondary earners" who did not "need" to earn enough to support themselves and their families. Such a view was probably never appropriate; it is clearly not appropriate today. The behavior of women workers themselves may also have changed. Women may now take their own careers more seriously. They may now be more likely to aspire to, and to prepare themselves for, promotion to higher-level positions.

Population Redistribution

One final social trend of relevance to the market for teachers is the redistribution of the population. The rate of aggregate population growth has slowed considerably in the past couple of decades. In addition, there are some important shifts in the location of the population. This redistribution of the population means that the condition of the market for teachers may vary widely from area to area.

There has been a movement toward the West and the South. During the first half of the 1970s, the population of the South grew by 5.1 million. In the West the growth was 2.9 million. By contrast the North Central region grew by 1.0 million, and the Northeast by only .3 million. During the 1970s, several states grew by over 30 percent, while the population of the country as a whole grew by only 12 percent.

	1970–80 *Population Growth* *(percent)*
Nevada	64
Arizona	53
Florida	41
Wyoming	41
Utah	37
Alaska	32
Idaho	32
Colorado	30

The populations of many of the older, large cities, particularly in the Northeast and North Central region, have fallen rapidly during the 1970s. Perhaps the most dramatic examples are the District of Columbia, which declined in population by 16 percent; Detroit, which lost 21 percent; and St. Louis, which lost 28 percent of its population over the 1970s. The rate of decline in the school-age population in these cities was often greater than the rate of total population decline.

There continues to be a net shift from central city to suburb. In many large metropolitan areas the population in the central city is falling while the suburban population is increasing.

The long-standing depletion of the rural population has reversed. In the 1970s, nonmetropolitan counties have begun to grow more rapidly than metropolitan areas. This is true both for nonmetropolitan counties that are near large cities and those that are more remote.

CHANGING CHARACTERISTICS OF TEACHERS

In the preceding sections we have described changes in the number of teachers over the past thirty years, as well as some of the major social and economic trends which have implications for the teacher work force. In this section, we examine some changes in the social, demographic, and economic characteristics of teachers from 1960 to 1979.

Age Distribution

The age distribution of the teacher work force has changed a great deal during the past two decades. In 1960, about 24 percent of all teachers were under the age of 30 (Table 8.2). By 1971, the fraction was about 35 percent. Since 1971, the fraction decreased to 28 percent. Of particular importance is the decreasing fraction under the age of 25 (8 percent in 1979; 19 percent in 1971). The fraction aged 45 and over has also changed a great deal, declining from 43 percent in 1960 to about one-third in 1970 to 28 percent in 1979.

In 1979 the fraction of female teachers under the age of 30 was about 31 percent, in comparison to 23 percent of male teachers. By contrast, in 1960 the fraction of

TABLE 8.2. Age Distribution of Teachers by Sex for Total, Elementary, Secondary; 1960 to 1979

Age	Total*				Men				Women			
	1960	1970	1971	1979	1960	1970	1971	1979	1960	1970	1971	1979
<25	10.8	17.3	19.2	8.2	8.3	17.1	16.0	6.5	11.8	17.4	20.8	9.1
25–29	13.0	17.5	16.9	20.0	19.9	20.0	20.6	16.9	10.4	16.4	15.0	21.5
30–34	11.5	12.1	12.3	18.5	18.8	18.4	13.9	23.0	8.7	9.4	11.5	16.2
35–44	21.3	19.2	19.7	25.1	24.6	19.8	23.8	25.4	20.1	19.0	17.6	25.0
45–54	25.5	17.2	16.8	18.5	17.4	13.1	15.5	19.0	28.6	19.0	17.4	18.2
55–64	14.7	14.0	13.1	8.2	9.0	10.7	9.5	8.1	16.9	15.4	14.9	8.3
65+	3.2	2.7	2.0	1.5	2.0	0.9	0.6	1.1	3.6	3.4	2.8	1.7
Total	100.0	100.0	100.0	100.0	100.0	100.0	100.0	100.0	100.0	100.0	100.0	100.0

Age	Elementary				Secondary			
	1960	1970	1971	1979	1960	1970	1971	1979
<25	11.4	17.1	20.9	9.0	9.6	17.6	20.9	9.4
25–29	12.1	16.2	17.3	22.5	14.7	19.5	18.6	19.6
30–34	10.8	10.3	11.3	16.9	13.0	14.8	14.1	21.9
35–44	20.2	19.1	17.4	24.6	23.5	19.4	18.5	24.8
45–54	26.8	18.3	15.7	16.9	23.0	15.5	16.6	16.9
55–64	15.3	15.5	14.9	8.5	13.6	11.6	9.8	6.0
65+	3.4	3.4	2.6	1.6	2.6	1.6	1.5	1.5
Total	100.0	100.0	100.0	100.0	100.0	100.0	100.0	100.0

* Total includes kindergarten and some nursery school teachers, guidance counselors, and school administrators.
NOTE: Because of a change in occupational classification, the data for the 1960–1970 period are not strictly comparable to those for the 1971–79 period. Hence change is best measured by comparing the 1969–70 segment and the 1971–79 segment.

female teachers under the age of 30 was smaller than the fraction of male teachers. This may reflect a decrease in attrition (temporary or permanent) of women teachers in connection with childrearing. In all years the age distributions of elementary and secondary teachers were quite similar.

Composition by Sex

Teaching is traditionally a predominantly female occupation. The fraction of female teachers rose from about 60 percent in 1870 to over 80 percent in 1910. It remained about 80 percent until about 1950. Since that time the fraction declined to its present level of about two-thirds (Ferris, 1969). According to NCES statistics, the fraction of male teachers in elementary schools rose from 7 percent in 1947–48 to its present level of about 17 percent (Dearman and Plisko, 1980). Most of the rise occurred in the late 1940s and early 1950s. Among secondary teachers, the fraction of male teachers rose from 40 to 50 percent in the ten years following World War II. Since 1957–58 the fraction moved up slightly from 50 to 54 percent.

Data from Census sources are consistent with these estimates. In Table 8.3 we show the percent female by various teacher types. Virtually all kindergarten and nursery school teachers continue to be female. There has been a trend toward a larger share of women among guidance personnel—rising from 41 to 65 percent during the 1970s. Administrators are slightly more likely to be female in 1979 than in 1971 (36 versus 29 percent). (Comparable data on guidance personnel or administrators are not available from Census sources prior to 1971.)

TABLE 8.3.   Percent of Teachers Who Are Women by Type of Teaching Position: 1960 to 1979

All Ages	1960	1970	1971	1979
Elementary	85.9	84.8	84.5	84.9
Secondary	46.4	46.5	46.6	49.7
Kindergarten–Nursery	NA	NA	100.0	97.5
Guidance	NA	NA	40.6	64.7
Administrator	NA	NA	28.9	36.0
Total	72.2	69.6	65.4	66.2

The fraction of female teachers decreases with age through the early 30s, then increases (see Table 8.4). This probably reflects attrition of women from the ranks of active teachers due to childbearing and childrearing and the return to teaching of women at ages 30 and beyond. It may also reflect the effects of attrition of men, about which little is known.

Educational Attainment

From the point of view of the profession at large the education distribution reflects the level of professional preparation. For an individual teacher, degrees and credits toward degrees influence both professional competence and salary, since most school districts pay higher salaries for both experience and greater educational credentials.

The education distribution of teachers changed over time. According to surveys done by the NEA, the fraction of all teachers with less than a college degree fell from

TABLE 8.4   Percent of Teachers Who Are Women, by Age and Occupation: 1960 to 1979

Age	Total			
	1960	1970	1971	1979
<25	78.8	69.9	71.2	73.3
25–29	57.5	65.2	58.0	71.3
30–34	54.6	53.9	60.9	57.9
35–44	68.0	68.7	58.3	65.9
45–54	81.0	76.8	68.1	65.3
55–64	83.0	76.8	74.8	66.6
65+	80.7	89.3	89.0	76.0
Total	72.2	69.6	65.4	66.2
	Elementary			
<25	88.0	80.2	85.0	82.4
25–29	75.0	83.3	74.8	84.0
30–34	71.1	75.2	81.5	81.8
35–44	83.8	81.8	84.1	84.8
45–54	92.4	91.0	30.5	86.7
55–64	93.3	92.1	89.4	92.7
65+	93.0	94.6	95.8	84.6
Total	85.9	84.8	84.5	84.9
	Secondary			
<25	58.2	54.8	50.9	61.6
25–29	30.3	42.4	36.7	52.8
30–34	28.8	31.1	43.4	37.1
35–44	42.4	49.1	45.1	51.9
45–54	55.9	51.4	50.2	50.5
55–64	61.3	45.5	52.1	50.7
65+	57.1	71.3	83.8	66.8
Total	46.4	46.5	46.6	49.7

about one-seventh in 1961 to virtually zero in 1976. During the same period, the fraction with Master's degrees rose from less than one-quarter to more than one-third (see Ream, 1977).

Educational data in the Census do not provide information on degrees attained. Instead, they provide information on years of schooling completed. Presumably persons (including teachers) who often add to their education a course at a time rather than a year at a time convert their educational credits to full-time equivalent years when responding to the survey. We use as an education index the fraction with 17 or more years of schooling. Note that many teachers with 17 and 18 years of education have not completed a Master's degree and would fall in the bachelor's degree category of the NEA data. According to these data there was a small increase between 1960 and 1970—from 34 to 38 percent—in the fraction with 17 or more years of schooling (see Table 8.5). Part of the reason for this slow increase was the rising fraction of very young teachers. At most ages the fraction with 17 or more years of education rose considerably, but this increase was swamped by the growing fraction of young teachers who were unlikely to have more than 16 years of education.

TABLE 8.5.   Percent of Teachers with 17 or More Years of Education Completed, by Age and Sex: 1960 to 1979

Age	Total			
	1960	*1970*	*1971*	*1979*
<25	8.2	6.1	9.4	8.2
25–29	26.8	31.6	35.6	36.7
30–34	40.2	43.5	43.9	55.6
35–44	44.3	50.2	52.8	57.8
45–54	37.6	48.1	49.8	63.0
55–64	34.5	49.2	46.1	60.6
65+	30.5	38.8	25.5	48.8
Total	34.0	37.7	38.7	50.2
	Male			
<25	18.5	7.0	14.7	6.0
25–29	37.3	48.0	44.3	41.8
30–34	59.3	64.0	56.8	65.8
35–44	72.7	70.6	75.7	72.8
45–54	73.6	79.6	69.0	82.9
55–64	64.2	89.4	74.5	79.0
65+	53.6	41.9	41.8	80.0
Total	57.7	56.9	55.4	64.2
	Female			
<25	5.4	5.7	7.2	9.1
25–29	19.0	22.8	29.2	34.6
30–34	22.4	26.0	35.6	48.3
35–44	30.9	40.9	36.5	50.0
45–54	29.1	38.6	40.8	52.5
55–64	28.5	37.1	37.8	51.4
65+	25.6	38.4	23.5	38.9
Total	25.0	29.3	29.8	43.1

During the 1970s the education distribution rose considerably. By 1979 one-half of all teachers had 17 or more years of schooling. Again, the changing age structure contributed to this trend. With relatively fewer young teachers, the education distribution would tend to increase.

There are large differences by sex in the fraction with at least 17 years of education. In 1971, 55 percent of the men and 30 percent of the women had some post-bachelor's degree education. This is not much different than it was in 1960. Between 1971 and 1979 the percentage increased for both men and women, but somewhat more for women. However, the differential remained quite large—64 versus 43 percent in 1979.

Percent of Teachers with 17 or More Years of Education

	1960	*1970*	*1971*	*1975*
Male	58	57	55	64
Female	25	29	30	43

Several factors may account for the sex differential in educational attainment:

1. Women are found predominantly in elementary education. Perhaps increases in education are not as important there as in secondary education. Of course, perhaps there is not as much continuing education among elementary teachers because elementary teachers are predominantly women.

2. Women tend to be secondary earners. Perhaps it is not regarded as so important to make the investment in continuing education.

3. Married women have the preponderance of child care and housekeeping responsibilities, and continuing education may be more difficult to "fit in' to their time schedule during the school year or in the summer than it is for men.

4. Economists would argue that workers who expect to work less over a life time will not have the same motivation to invest in continuing education as those who will be working continuously throughout their lifetime. The rate of return for such investment is lower. To the extent that women spend less of their lives working, they may invest less in further education.

Enrollment in School

The 1970 Decennial Census asked a question concerning school enrollment of all persons. The question was, "Since February 1, has the person been enrolled in school?" We have tabulated the fraction of schoolteachers who were enrolled in school at the time of the 1970 Census. (We have no information on enrollment during the summer months.)

Altogether one teacher in ten reported attending school. The fraction was higher for younger than for older teachers (Table 8.6). Of teachers under the age of 30, one in six were going to school. Of teachers aged 45–54, the fraction was 6 percent.

Men are more likely than women to be enrolled. Fourteen percent of the men and 9 percent of the women were going to school. The sex difference was particularly large among teachers under the age of 35. For example, 21 percent of the 25–29-year-old men and 11 percent of the 25–29-year-old women were attending school. Beyond the age of 35 there is no sex difference. This pattern of differences is consistent with the proposition that women do not enroll as often as men because of greater family and household responsibilities. There is virtually no difference in enrollment rates among elementary and secondary teachers, once age and sex are controlled. Men in all fields of

TABLE 8.6. Percent of Teachers Who Were Enrolled, by Age, Sex, and Level: 1970

Age	Male Elementary	Male Secondary	Total	Female Elementary	Female Secondary	Total
<25	26.3	22.4	24.9	14.4	14.0	15.2
25–29	19.4	21.4	21.0	10.4	12.6	10.9
30–34	17.9	15.4	16.0	9.4	10.8	9.7
35–44	11.1	10.1	10.0	9.2	8.1	8.7
45–54	5.7	7.4	5.9	7.2	4.8	6.2
55–64	1.4	1.9	1.8	2.6	2.1	2.5
65+	2.6	2.9	2.1	0.9	1.4	1.1
Total	15.4	14.3	13.7	8.7	9.0	8.7

* Total includes guidance and administration personnel.

education, including administration, are more likely to be enrolled than women. Seven percent of black teachers and 10 percent of white teachers are enrolled. Black teachers are less likely to be enrolled than white teachers at all ages.

GEOGRAPHIC VARIATION IN THE MARKET FOR TEACHERS

The condition of the market for teachers is not the same in all parts of the country. As we have already discussed, the population of the United States has been shifting from Northeast to South and West. Many large cities have lost a large share of their population, and some suburban areas continue to have rapid growth. There is also a resurgence of growth in nonmetropolitan areas. Space does not permit a review of the market for teachers on a state-by-state or substate basis. It is, however, informative to see how the number of teachers and the total population of major geographic regions have changed.

An indicator of changes in school enrollment in the recent past and near future is the change in the number of persons graduating from high school. According to one set of projections, the percentage change from 1979 to 1995 in the number of high school seniors will range from an increase of 58 percent in Utah to a decrease of 59 percent in the District of Columbia. The increases occur in the Pacific Northwest and Rocky Mountain states, as well as in Texas and Louisiana. The decreases are found primarily in the industrial states in the Northeast and the Great Lakes area. Column 1

TABLE 8.7.   Regional Differences in Change in High School Graduates and Total Teachers

Regions	Projected Change in Number of High School Graduates 1979–1995	Change in Number of Teachers 1971–1979
Pacific	− 8.0	+ 8.1
Mountain	+14.4	+18.5
West South Central	+ 6.2	+15.3
East South Central	−12.4	+10.8
South Atlantic	−18.4	+13.0
West North Central	−23.8	+ 5.9
East North Central	−30.3	+ 3.8
Middle Atlantic	−39.3	− 0.1
New England	−36.7	+15.0
U.S. Total	−19.9	+ 8.0

States in Census Regions:
    Pacific: Alaska, California, Hawaii, Oregon, Washington
    Mountain: Arizona, Colorado, Idaho, Montana, Nevada, New Mexico, Utah, Wyoming
    West South Central: Arkansas, Louisiana Oklahoma, Texas
    East South Central: Alabama, Mississippi, Kentucky, Tennessee
    South Atlantic: Delaware, D.C., Maryland, West Virginia, Virginia, North Carolina, South Carolina,
        Georgia, Florida
    West North Central: North Dakota, South Dakota, Nebraska, Kansas, Minnesota, Iowa, Missouri
    East North Central: Wisconsin, Michigan, Illinois, Indiana, Iowa
    Middle Atlantic: New York, New Jersey, Pennsylvania
    New England: Vermont, New Hampshire, Maine, Massachusetts, Connecticut, Rhode Island
SOURCE: Chronicle of Higher Education, 1980; Simon and Grant, 1973; Grant and Eiden, 1980.

of Table 8.7 shows a regional summary of rates of change in the projected number of persons graduating from high school between 1979 and 1985. The numbers range from a decrease of nearly 40 percent in New England and the Middle Atlantic region to an increase of 14 percent in the Mountain region. Nationally, there will be a 20 percent decline.

Similarly, there is considerable variability in the rate of change in the number of teachers. Between 1971 and 1977 the number of teachers in the United States as a whole increased by 8 percent. The percentage change ranged from a gain of 27 percent in Arizona to a decrease of 5 percent in New York State. The percentage changes were distributed across the states (including the District of Columbia) as follows:

Decrease	6
Increase	
0–4.9%	13
5–9.9%	8
10–14.9%	10
15–19.9%	8
20–24.9%	4
25+	2
TOTAL	51

Regionally, the change in the number of teachers ranged from a slight loss in the Middle Atlantic region to a gain of 18 percent in the Mountain states.

Regions are not homogeneous with respect to demographic change, nor are states. In Wisconsin, for example, there was a statewide decrease of 8.6 percent in the number of students enrolled in public and private schools between 1970–71 and 1977–78. Counties within the state had enrollment changes ranging from a loss of 21 percent in Milwaukee County to a gain of 16 percent in Washington County (a suburban county near Milwaukee). There was tremendous variability, with a number of isolated, northern counties and counties in the central part of the state gaining school population, and a number of the more urban areas, particularly in the southern part of the state, losing enrollment (see Sweet, 1979). Similar experience undoubtedly has occurred within other states.

PROJECTIONS OF TEACHER SUPPLY AND DEMAND

The National Center for Education Statistics biennially publishes ten-year projections of teacher supply and demand. For example, in 1980, NCES projected through the school year of 1988–89 (see Frankel and Gerald, 1980). This task begins with a projection of the number of students enrolled in schools, derived from the age distribution of the population and projections of the number of births to fill out the lower-grade levels at the end of the projection period. Age-specific enrollment rates are also projected forward by an unspecified procedure. Enrollment is projected separately by level (elementary and secondary) and by public and private schools.

Projected enrollments are converted into teacher demand by projecting forward student-teacher ratios. In the 1977 projections to 1985–86, the NCES comments that they expect student-teacher ratios to continue to decrease, but at a slower rate, and that a lower bound of 15 would be unlikely to be crossed. (Private schools are done separately with their higher student-teacher ratios.)

Next the total demand for teachers is converted to a demand for new teachers. The procedure used is quite simple:

$$T_2 = T_1 - T_L + T_N$$

where T_2 = Total number of teachers at Time 2
T_1 = Total number of teachers at Time 1
T_L = Teachers leaving teaching between Time 1 and Time 2
T_N = Teachers newly employed between Time 1 and Time 2

The number of new teachers (T_N) is equal to the change in the total number of teachers plus the number of teachers who leave the teaching profession.

$$T_N = (T_2 - T_1) + T_L$$

The (T_2-T_1) component is divided into two parts—increase (decrease) in teachers needed because of changing enrollments and an increase (decrease) in teachers needed because of declining (increasing) student-teacher ratios.

How does the NCES estimate the number of teachers leaving the profession because of deaths, retirement, occupational change, or whatever? According to the 1977 report, the historical experience has been that 8 percent of teachers leave per year. They assert that a minimum exit rate due to death, retirement, childrearing, and administrative promotions is 4.8 percent. No explanation is offered as to how this 4.8 percent was determined. The difference between the 8 percent and the 4.8 percent reflects teachers leaving the profession of teaching for other occupations or leaving the labor force entirely. The 1977 report suggests that 8 percent is too high for the present period and prefers a 6 percent "turnover" rate. It argues that:

1. In a tight job market, in general, fewer teachers will quit teaching to go to other fields, because there are few attractive jobs elsewhere.
2. In a tight market in teaching, fewer teachers will leave temporarily (presumably for childrearing) because they will have great difficulty returning.
3. The age structure is young, thereby reducing the fraction of teachers leaving because of retirement or death.

According to the projections made in 1980, there will be (between 1979–88) a need for 1.3 million new teachers in the public schools, if turnover is 6 percent. If turnover were 8 percent, 1.7 million would be needed, and if it were 4.8 percent, the need would be 1.0 million new teachers.

Assuming a 6 percent turnover rate, the following are the components of new demand estimated for the period 1979–1988:

Enrollment Change	−186,000	teachers
Change in Ratio of Students to Teachers	+181,000	
Turnover	+1,276,000	
TOTAL Demand for New Teachers	+1,271,000	

The actual experience between 1969 and 1978 was:

Increase in Number of
Teachers due to:

Enrollment Change	−95,000
Change in Ratio of Students to Teachers	+359,000
Turnover	+1,364,000
TOTAL	+1,628,000

What is the source of the 8 percent turnover figure, which has recently been adjusted downward to 6 percent for the preferred set of projections? In 1968–69 the NCES conducted a sample survey of principals in which they asked about the number of teachers who left their schools during the preceding year. At that time, the aggregate annual separation rate was 15 percent, of whom 6 percent were known to have taught in another district after separation, 7 percent were known to have not taught in another district, and 3 percent had unknown teaching status. A survey done a decade earlier produced similar estimates, as did two other surveys done by the NEA during the mid- to late-1960s. (See Metz and Fleischman, 1974.)

The 7 percent who were known to be no longer teaching were distributed as follows:

Changed to Nonteaching Job in Education	0.7%
Changed to Job outside Education	1.3
Left for Marriage, Pregnancy or Family Reasons	1.0
Leave of Absence	1.2
Retired	1.7
Other	0.8
TOTAL	6.6%

Is the turnover assumption adequate for projections? The projections summarized above show that in the next decade or so, virtually all the demand for new teachers will be due to turnover. In the period 1979–88, the projections indicate a turnover or replacement need of 1,276,000 out of a total need for new teachers of 1,271,000. The turnover assumption is, therefore, central to the projection of employment opportunities for new teachers.

The turnover assumption of 8 percent includes the 6.6 percent known not to be teaching and a share of the 3 percent whose teaching status was not known. If all of the 3 percent were not teaching, the turnover would be 9.6 percent, rather than 8 percent. We know nothing of the quality of the information obtained from principals for this sort of survey. The principals may or may not provide complete coverage of all turnovers. They may or may not have reliable information on the activities of departed teachers. A more adequate methodology would be to survey a sample of teachers about their own employment experience. Such a survey has never been conducted. Jacobsen and Sweet (1982) make estimates of five-year mobility of teachers for 1965–1970 from 1970 Census data. It appears that the annual turnover was over 8 percent.

There are several reasons to believe that changing conditions in the 1970s and 1980s may have affected the turnover of teachers.

1. The 1.3 percent who moved to a different job outside education may well be changing. It is true that the market is tight outside of education. If salaries in education have fallen relative to those outside education, particularly for younger persons, attrition may increase. In addition, teaching is a predominately female occupation. If better-paying opportunities for women open up outside of education, one might expect an increase in turnover of female teachers.

2. The fraction leaving for marriage, pregnancy, and other "family reasons" was 1 percent. This fraction might be expected to drop somewhat because fertility is low, marriage ages are rising, and the population of teachers is becoming more concentrated at the older ages. On the other hand, it is unlikely to be reduced to near zero.

3. As we have discussed earlier, the fraction leaving for retirement, death, or long-term disability will eventually rise as the fraction of teachers over the age of 45 rises. At some point, this will become a major source of attrition. Despite the future importance of this shift in age structure, we found no separate projections of this component.

4. "Early retirement" provisions are being included in negotiated teacher contracts all over the country. Often teachers are given a financial bonus for retiring early. The replacement of an older teacher at the top of the salary schedule with one at the bottom of the schedule may save school districts a good deal of money, some of which can be used to pay a bonus for early retirement. The diffusion of this practice could temporarily accelerate the rate of attrition from teaching. The effect would·be temporary since teachers who retire early this year are not around to retire in some future year.

Whether the 6 percent turnover assumption for the future is a good one or not is very difficult to assess. We simply do not know very much about the processes underlying turnover. A start would be to produce estimates of the age function of attrition from and addition to the teacher work force from various sources and estimates of how these functions may be changing. These could be combined with projections of the age structure of the active teacher work force, to provide a better basis for projection.

The Teacher Reserve

An additional source of confusion about the state of the market for new teachers is the size of the teacher reserve and its potential for adding to the teacher work force. According to a recent NEA publication, there may be as many as 1 million former teachers and teacher graduates making up a "teacher reserve." Of these, it is estimated that 120,000 former teachers actively sought teaching positions in 1978.

According to NCES, about three-quarters of new teacher graduates actively seek teaching positions. This implies that the teacher reserve is increasing each year by as much as one-quarter of the new graduates as well as the number of persons leaving teaching positions. It also increases whenever a newly trained teacher is unable to find a job and whenever a teacher is laid off.

Historically, the "reserve" was regarded as being made up primarily of female teachers who left the work force because of childbearing and childrearing. In recent years with the number of teacher graduates greatly exceeding the number of new jobs, the reserve may consist more of young, recent graduates. Similarly, in recent years fewer women have left the work force for childbearing-childrearing, and those who do leave tend to leave for a shorter period of time. According to recent NCES estimates, there were 862,000 graduates of teacher training programs in the 1970s who sought, but did not secure, teaching positions (Dearman and Plisko, 1980 p. 72).

Do the persons in the reserve who were unsuccessful first-job seekers remain potential teachers to the same degree as the women who left for childrearing? We do not know. However, it would appear that the answer to this question is of considerable import.

What do these new "reserve" teachers do if they are unable to find teaching jobs or if they do not seek them in the first place? Undoubtedly many of them seek and find alternative employment. Others obtain further training and secure employment in other fields.

To what extent could they be lured back into teaching? One consideration is salary. Persons who are working and accumulating work experience are probably earning a higher salary year by year. If they returned to teaching, they would probably enter at the bottom of the salary schedule for teachers. To the extent that *starting* teaching salaries are rising more slowly than the salary increment per year of experience in other fields, teaching may become relatively less financially attractive over time.

Similarly, many persons who are forced into other fields by the dearth of teaching jobs will find them quite satisfying and will lose interest in teaching. Some, however, may retain an interest in teaching and be willing to accept a teaching position, even if it involves a financial loss.

The "old" reserve of teachers consisted primarily of married women with young children. The new reserve teacher is more likely to be a male or an unmarried woman and to be a childless person. If we are to make satisfactory projections of teacher supply, we need to know more about the characteristics and experience of the members of this reserve of potential teachers and their potential willingness to reenter the teacher market.

CONCLUSION

In this paper, we have identified a number of demographic and social factors which have had an impact on the supply and demand for schoolteachers. We found that two social trends have had a primary impact on the rapid growth in the potential supply of teachers. The first is the entry into the work force of the large baby-boom cohorts, combined with the general rise in educational attainment. These changes have resulted in a glut of young, college-educated workers in the market in general; and because such a high proportion of college graduates, particularly females, go into teaching, a glut has occurred in the teacher market as well.

The second factor affecting the supply of teachers has been the change in women's patterns of labor force participation. The sheer number of women working has increased dramatically, and the propensity of women to work more continuously and to spend less time out of the labor force because of childbearing has also increased. Therefore, since such a large proportion of all teachers are female, this trend has served to increase the supply of potential schoolteachers. This is evidenced by the fact that despite postponement of marriage and declines in fertility, there was a higher proportion of employed women teachers who had children in 1979 than in 1960. These changes also imply that there should be less movement by females in and out of the "reserve" of teachers now than there was previously.

Two demographic factors have affected the demand for schoolteachers. The first is the decline in fertility, which over the period of the last 20 years has resulted in fewer children being enrolled in school. These declines in enrollment showed up on the elementary level first and are now being felt at the secondary level. Unless there is a dramatic increase in reproductive levels, the number of children enrolled in school will not increase very much in the future.

Concomitant with the decline in fertility has been a shift in the distribution of the population in the United States. There have been large movements of population out of the Northeast and into the South and the West. Hence the balance of supply and demand for teachers exhibits considerable regional and subregional variation.

We have also attempted to identify some important sociological factors which affect the conditions of working as a teacher. There is still a high degree of sex segregation in the United States occupational structure, and women typically have much lower earnings than men. Although women have increased as a share of counselors, secondary teachers, and administrators, they are still primarily located in kindergarten or elementary teaching. In comparison to men, they have low rates of mobility from teaching to other occupations (see Jacobsen and Sweet, 1982). If there were increased opportunities in other spheres of employment, teaching might become less attractive to female college graduates in the future, and this might lower the supply of both "new" teachers and those in the teacher reserve.

A part of the supply and demand picture we have not been able to consider in any detail is the utilization of persons trained as teachers. There is very little information available on either the career patterns of teachers or on attrition from teaching. These factors play an important role in determining teacher supply and demand, especially in their effect on the size of the teacher reserve. Data on these issues are essential to more reliable projections.

Specifically, the two areas in which we see the most need for further study are: (1) utilization and attrition of teaching personnel and (2) career opportunities and working conditions for teachers. With regard to the first area, the following questions should be investigated:

1. What are persons trained as teachers, but not currently teaching, doing? To what extent are they working in other occupations? To what extent are they out of the labor force? Is there a significant share of this population interested in returning to teaching? Have they "priced themselves out of the market" by gaining experience and seniority in other occupations?

2. What are the characteristics of "marginal" teachers—persons teaching part-time or temporarily, substitute teachers, and teacher aides with teaching credentials?

3. How many teachers are on leaves at any given time? What is the pattern of return from leaves? What are the characteristics and aspirations of teachers who take leaves of absence for continuing education?

4. When persons leave the teaching profession for other occupations, where do they go? How do they make the decision? To what extent are their new occupations related to their teacher training and experience?

5. What are the retirement patterns of teachers? How are they changing? What effect have early-retirement programs had on retirement of teachers? (This issue will assume increasing importance as the fraction of teachers aged 45 and over increases in the future.)

In relation to career opportunities, two additional questions should be addressed:

1. How have starting salaries of teachers changed over time? (They have un-doubtedly deteriorated in real dollars during the 1970s.) Have they deteriorated more than in other fields? What is an appropriate comparison, given that the teacher work year is only 9 or 10 months and that many teachers supplement their earnings with earnings from extracurricular assignments? How has the experience of young teachers differed from that of young persons in other occupations during the 1970s?

2. How have the changes in women's work patterns in the past decade affected teachers? Do female teachers have more work experience at a given age than they did a decade ago? Are female teachers more likely to invest in further education than in prior years? Do more women teachers aspire to and train for administrative positions? Will they be able to attain such positions if they have the appropriate aspirations, ex-perience, and training?

None of these questions can be addressed with information that is routinely col-lected by the National Center for Education Statistics, the National Educational Asso-ciation, or any other source. Research on these matters is essential to projections of teacher supply and demand and to the planning of educational policy.

REFERENCES

Changing numbers in high school graduating classes. *The Chronicle of Higher Education*, Janu-ary 7, 1980.

Dearman, N. B., and Plisko, V. W. The condition of education. *National Center for Education Statistics*, Publication #80–400, 1980.

Ferris, A. L. *Indicators of trends in American education*. New York: Russell Sage, 1969.

Frankel, M. M., and Gerald, D. E. Projections of education statistics to 1988–89. *National Center for Education Statistics*, Publication #80–402.

Frankel, M. M., and Gerald, D. E. Projections of education statistics to 1988–89. *National Center for Education Statistics*, Publication #77–402, 1977.

Grant, W. V., and Eiden, L. J. Digest of education statistics: 1980. *National Center for Edu-cation Statistics*. 1980.

Jacobsen, L. A., and Sweet, J. A. Mobility into and out of teaching: 1965–70. *Working Paper 82–8*, Center for Demography and Ecology, University of Wisconsin, Madison, Wisconsin 1982.

Metz, A. S., and Fleischman, H. L. Teacher turnover in the public schools: Fall 1968–Fall 1969. *National Center for Education Statistics*, Publication #OE 74–11115, 1969.

Oppenheimer, V. K. Structural sources of economic pressure for wives to work: An analytical framework. *Journal of Family History*, 199, (Summer): 177–197.

Ream, M. Status of the American public school teacher: 1975–76. National Education Associ-ation, 1977.

Simon, V. A., and W. V. Grant. Digest of educational statistics. *National Center for Health Statistics*, Publication OE 3-11103, 1973.

Sweet, J. A. Demographic aspects of education in Wisconsin. In D. P. Slesinger and P. R. Voss (eds.), *Recent trends in Wisconsin's population*. University of Wisconsin, Applied Popu-lation Laboratory, 1979.

CHAPTER 9

Labor Relations and Teacher Policy

Douglas E. Mitchell and Charles T. Kerchner

Collective bargaining is a major change in American education. In twenty years public school teachers have moved from an almost totally nonunion work force to one of the most completely unionized occupations in the United States. More than 2,100,000 school workers (91% of all teachers) belong to either the National Education Association (NEA) or the American Federation of Teachers (AFT). Approximately 89 percent of all school districts with more than 1,000 students bargain collectively with teachers. The NEA has more members than any labor organization except the Teamsters, and the AFT local in New York City is the largest in the AFL-CIO (Cresswell and Murphy, 1980, pp. 31, 105). Thus, by conventional standards of size and penetration into the industry, public education has become highly unionized.

This chapter explores the policy framework within which labor relations are conducted. Recent debate over labor relations policy, though intense, has been extremely limited. Most discussions have focused on the economic and political effects of teacher bargaining, but little attention has been given to the impacts of labor policy on the definition of teaching work. Managers have naively assumed that their interests are best protected by legally narrowing the scope of permissible bargaining (Kerchner, 1978). And teachers have tended to insist that virtually any expansion of their powers is a step toward liberation from arbitrary, insensitive, or irresponsible control over their work (see Mitchell, 1979). Both groups have neglected the redefinition of education implied in the selection of one labor policy over another.

This neglect by educators is compounded by the fact that most labor policies are actually written by labor professionals. These professionals, though avowedly neutral in the clashes between labor and management, are by no means "neutral with respect to collective bargaining *per se*" (Lieberman, 1980, p. 143). They embrace collective bargaining as an effective means for keeping labor strife under control. Typically, they make assertions such as, "Just as you wouldn't say that collective bargaining with auto workers has altered the product mix at General Motors very much, I don't think you will see very much impact on the way schools work" (Mitchell et al., 1981, p. 154). This professional enthusiasm for collective bargaining has been encouraged by the traditionally pragmatic thrust of the American labor movement, whose leaders generally embrace Samuel Gompers' (1919) advice to concentrate on immediate problems and avoid the European tendency toward radical political activism.

Taken together, these forces have resulted in a largely instrumental view of labor

This research is, in part, supported by National Institute of Education Grant No. NIE-G-79-0036. Exploratory research on the same subject was aided by a grant from the Eli Lilly Endowment to Charles Kerchner. However, the conclusions reached and the opinions offered do not necessarily reflect those of the Institute, the Endowment, or the staffs of either organization.

policy—a presumption that is only a matter of organizational housekeeping rather than a vehicle for shaping education or defining teaching. The time has come, however, to expand the public debate and to develop a fuller awareness of how labor policies impact on teaching.

The discussion of labor policy options presented in this chapter is largely theoretical and conceptual. We are, of course, sensitive to the many practical and political problems which will accompany any effort to redirect policy. Our primary concern here, however, is to stem the headlong rush of so many policymakers toward labor policies based entirely on their desire to control labor-management conflicts rather than improve school operations.

Our analysis is presented in three parts. First, an analytic framework for distinguishing among various conceptions of teaching is developed. This framework describes the relationship between labor, craft, professional, and artistic work structures and explores ways in which teaching includes elements of each type of work. Second, a detailed analysis of how collective bargaining has affected teacher work activities is presented. Finally, the relationships between support for the different teaching work structures and the selection of alternative policy choices in four basic arenas are explored.

Our analysis draws on both historical and empirical data. The empirical data are drawn from a two-year National Institute of Education–sponsored study of bargaining in California and Illinois and a series of interviews with leaders of the American Federation of Teachers (AFT), leaders of the National Education Association (NEA), and representatives of school administrator and school board organizations.

THE STRUCTURE OF TEACHING WORK

The activities of teachers can be compared with those of other workers along two dimensions. First, every job has some system of "task definition" to specify the particular activities workers are expected to perform. And second, all have some sort of "oversight mechanism" for monitoring the performance of these tasks. By distinguishing among various "ideal type" alternatives for defining tasks and overseeing worker performance, we can develop a framework for comparing teaching with other types of work in society.

Task Definition

There are two basic approaches to task definition. Some jobs are structured primarily through "rationalization." That is, specific tasks are preplanned (by either managers or the workers themselves) and then undertaken as a matter of routine enactment of standard operating procedures. Automobile assembly and building construction are typical examples of this approach to task definition. In other job settings, however, tasks are primarily adaptive—requiring accommodation to unexpected or unpredictable elements within the work situation. In this case, the task definitions cannot be embodied in a preplanned program. Instead, the emphasis must be on responding to conditions arising on the job, exercising proper judgment regarding what is needed, and maintaining intellectual and technical flexibility. Newspaper editors, firemen, and emergency room doctors all rely on this type of task definition.

FIGURE 9.1.   Task Definition and Oversight Structures.

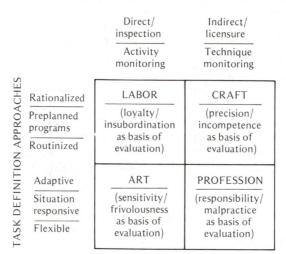

OVERSIGHT AND MONITORING MECHANISMS

	Direct/inspection Activity monitoring	Indirect/licensure Technique monitoring
Rationalized Preplanned programs Routinized	LABOR (loyalty/insubordination as basis of evaluation)	CRAFT (precision/incompetence as basis of evaluation)
Adaptive Situation responsive Flexible	ART (sensitivity/frivolousness as basis of evaluation)	PROFESSION (responsibility/malpractice as basis of evaluation)

TASK DEFINITION APPROACHES

Oversight Mechanisms

Monitoring or overseeing work performance is also typically structured in one of two basic ways. Some workers are subjected to direct oversight through close supervision (such as assembly line workers) or through stringent reporting requirements (such as policemen). For other workers (such as architects or accountants) oversight is indirect. Preparation and skill—that is, the *ability* to perform the work—are the prime considerations. In the first case, the work itself is "inspected." In the second, the work often goes unexamined while workers are certified or "licensed" to perform the work on their own.

The criteria used to evaluate these two different types of work are quite different. Licensed workers are expected to have at their disposal a set learned techniques for performing needed tasks, and they are held accountable for the care and precision with which they apply the appropriate techniques. Where work is inspected rather than licensed, however, a worker's cooperativeness, dedication, and overall level of effort are most important. If special skills or techniques are required, managers are expected to guide workers in their application through direct supervision and critical review.

As indicated in Figure 9.1, four distinctive work structures are created when the basic task definition systems and oversight mechanisms are combined. "Labor" (upper-left cell of Figure 9.1) is the term which best describes those work settings where tasks are rationally planned and oversight is undertaken by direct supervision. As used here, the word "labor" has a special meaning. All jobs involve labor to the extent that they all require an expenditure of effort directed at task accomplishment. In this sense the word "labor" often is used more broadly than we intend here to describe any job requiring concentrated effort and attention. As used by the Bureau of Labor Statistics, the word "laborer" refers to any unskilled or semiskilled worker. This use of the term often connotes a kind of denigration of workers as "merely laborers." While this usage captures the important sense that laboring jobs have limited technologies, it deflects attention away from the important structural and organizational differences between labor and other types of work. Laboring is not distinguished by its association with "low-level" jobs but rather by the rationalized and preplanned character of tasks and direct inspection of how those tasks are performed. While low-level jobs (such as those of sanitation or assembly line workers) are more frequently subjected to routinization and close supervision, there is no intrinsic reason why high-status jobs cannot also be so structured. William H. Whyte's *Organization Man* (1956) describes the work we are calling "labor" being performed by people holding executive job titles but confronted with a social ethic which "rationalizes the organization's demands for fealty and gives those who offer it wholeheartedly a sense of dedication in doing so . . ." (p. 6).

Loyalty and insubordination are the most important concepts in evaluating laboring work. It is very important for laborers to give allegiance to the organization for which they work and to respond energetically and promptly to directions given by superiors. This need for loyalty arises because laborers are not expected to take personal responsibility for the overall purposes toward which their efforts are being directed. As Frederick Taylor's *Principles of Scientific Management* (1911) makes abundantly clear, it is the manager, not the laborer, who must decide when, how, and for what purposes work effort should be directed. The worst offense of a laborer is insubordination to a supervisor—not inadequate results. Laborers need to do what they are told to do, when they are told to do it. If the result is unproductive, it is the manager's, not the worker's, fault.

Craft workers (upper-right cell of Figure 9.1) differ from labor workers. These workers are generally freed from direct supervision but held responsible for selecting and applying appropriate specialized techniques in order to realize the specific objectives of their work. In place of direct supervision, craft workers are licensed, certified, or otherwise explicitly identified as having special abilities. Managers (or clients in the case of craft workers who operate on a direct contract basis) establish the overall objectives of the work, but once craft specialists take an assignment, they are expected to carry it out without needing detailed instructions or close supervision. Licensure is a matter of public policy in many craft areas because incompetent or unscrupulous craft workers are difficult for unskilled clients to recognize. Thus the watchful eye of the state is often substituted for the *caveat emptor* of the marketplace when technical competence is crucial to adequate task performance.

Craft work (typified in tool making, routine computer programming, or electronic instrument repair) is evaluated on the basis of precision and competence. Craft workers are judged on how adequately they execute required tasks. They are even expected to risk insubordination toward their superiors in order to competently apply the techniques of their craft. While laborers are only expected to follow orders, craft workers are deemed incompetent if they are unable to recognize which techniques to use in the performance of particular tasks.

Rationalization and planning are important in both labor and craft work structures, but they take very different forms. For laboring work, rationalization is conventional and refers to *standardization* of procedures or *specificity* of managerial directions. For craft workers, however, rationalization is technical and refers to the *appropriateness* of the methods being used. For laborers, standard operating procedures are right because they are standardized. For craft workers, by contrast, they become standardized because they are technically correct (Gouldner, 1954, pp. 223–

224). As Parsons (1947) has noted, Weber's failure to understand this difference led him to an inadequate conception of modern bureaucracies—a conception that failed to properly incorporate expert craft or professional employees.

Professional workers (lower-right cell of Figure 9.1), like craft workers, are expected to possess a set of specialized techniques. Where professional work differs from craftsmanship, however, is in the way tasks are defined. While both craft and professional workers perform specialized tasks, professionals are expected to analyze or diagnose situational factors and adapt their working strategies to the true needs (not just the expressed wishes) of their clients. A craft worker has to know whether a particular task *can* be performed and how to perform it. But a professional is responsible for deciding whether the task *should* be performed. As craft workers, surgeons must know how to operate; as professionals, they must know whether an operation is needed.

Responsibility and malpractice are the key elements in evaluating professional work. Professionals (e.g., surgeons or architects) are expected to consider the implications of choosing a particular course of action, resisting interference and pressure from superiors or outsiders and accepting personal responsibility for the outcome. Thus, while the worst criticism to be leveled at a craft worker is incompetence, malpractice is the appropriate label for inadequate professional work. Malpractice differs from incompetence in two important ways. First, even if the execution of a task is completely competent, a professional worker is guilty of malpractice if it can be shown that the task was unnecessary or inappropriate to a particular case. Second, in a case of malpractice the judgments of professional *peers*, rather than those of supervisors or other superiors, are recognized as the basis for determining whether the work was properly executed.

We have given the label "art" (lower-left cell of Figure 9.1) to work characterized by both adaptive task definitions and direct monitoring of workers' activities. Although artistic work may require a high level of technical skill, the social organization of this type of work is not based on the possession of particular skills. Art is recognized in the products produced and by the quality of the artists' engagement in their work. When necessary for their work, artists are expected to rise above the limits of specific techniques or established conventions and to develop novel, unconventional, or unexpected techniques. Like professional workers, artists are expected to be flexible and adaptive in defining their work responsibilities. Like laborers, however, artists are not licensed. They are monitored and evaluated directly—by assessing whether their work is engaging, exciting, and creative.

Actors and musicians are prototypical artists. Key concepts in the evaluation of their work are sensitivity and frivolousness. Whereas the professional is required to be responsible, the craft worker to be competent, and the laborer to be loyal, the artist in an organizational setting is called upon to be sensitive to the need for integrity, creativity, and spontaneity. They are frequently granted a great deal of autonomy in order to allow for the exercise of this artistic sensitivity. There is no such thing as malpractice for the artist—only the frivolous use of talent or refusal to enter fully into the creative process. Genuine art work requires dedicated and serious effort. Loyalty to preplanned institutional programs, a basic requirement in laboring work settings, is often the enemy of great art.

The works of solitary artists (such as novelists or painters) are evaluated through inspection and critical review by individual consumers or by editors, juries, and reviewers in journals and newspapers. Organized artistic ventures, such as designing buildings or performing plays, are closer in form to teaching. Here the creation of an artistic masterpiece depends on adequate coordination or direction as well as sensitive review and critical evaluation.

The work structures presented in Figure 9.1 are "ideal types" in the sense in which Weber (1947) used that phrase. Real jobs will always involve a mixture of labor, craft, art, and professional work activities. Abstracting these four ideal types is helpful in the interpretation of teacher organizations and collective bargaining in two ways, however. First, by applying these analytic distinctions to teacher work, we are able to show how labor relations policies affect teachers' job responsibilities and influence the supervision systems used by school administrators to oversee their work. Second, they help us interpret the personal stresses and organizational tensions that arise when workers are confronted with multiple job responsibilities falling into several different ideal types simultaneously. When, for example, teachers are on lunchroom duty or are asked to report student attendance to the school office, they are performing tasks which closely fit the ideal definition of labor. No special skills are presumed, no advanced training for this work is offered, and the work is expected to be performed in strict accordance with preplanned guidelines. These tasks are generally defined and supervised in ways quite different from such craft or artistic tasks as planning curricula, leading discussions, or evaluating student achievements. If either teachers or their supervisors come to see lunchroom duty and attendance taking as the model for all teaching work responsibilities, we can expect substantial changes in how other tasks are defined and how day-to-day working relationships are structured. Similarly, if educators come to believe that all work activities are (or should be) essentially professional, craft, or artistic in character, pressures for organizational and job performance arrangements reflecting these assumptions will follow.

THE IMPACT OF LABOR RELATIONS ON TEACHER WORK STRUCTURES

The impact of teacher organization and collective bargaining on public education can be interpreted from the perspective of the four ideal-type work structures described above. Labor relation effects are complicated, however, and involve much more than how contracts are made or what's in them. As the Webbs (1903) remind us 80 years ago, in addition to contract negotiations, the collective efforts of workers include: (1) self-provision through worker-run organizations, (2) self-protection through insurance and job market control schemes, and (3) political action through lobbying, campaign work, and financial contributions. The contract is the cornerstone of labor relations, but it is by no means the whole picture. Organized teachers have proven themselves potent as a political force and as a vehicle for changing social relations within the schools. Nevertheless, without the right to contract, the rest of the relationship would likely come unraveled. As one teacher organization leader put it, "Without the right to contract, they wouldn't take us seriously when we came in to 'just talk.'"

Labor contracts themselves are more ambiguous than they appear. Very similar contract clauses—on evaluation procedures, for example—can have quite different impacts in different places. In part, this is due to the interdependence of work rules and the grievance mechanisms specified within a contract. "One is meaningless without the other," one Illinois labor leader told us. "You can have all the work rules you want, but without the means to grieve violations, those rules mean exactly what management wants them to mean." On the other hand, he continued, "the right to grieve an empty contract doesn't mean much either." The impact of a contract clause can be understood only when the ability to use it is considered.

Contract impacts also vary because their meaning depends on how they are interpreted. Consider, for example, two large school districts, each with a stormy labor history and grievance clauses leading to binding decisions by outside arbitrators. In the first district, principals had standing orders to "deny all first-step grievances." That district had more than 80 grievances filed, more than a dozen of which ended up in binding arbitration. There were two results: (1) the teacher organization found (with glee) that a law degree isn't necessary to win grievances, and (2) the school district's operating structure became more formal and bureaucratic. Because grievance decisions apply to all the schools in the district, there was a ballooning effect in the number of new rules, and principals came to be less concerned with solving problems and more with following rules and interpreting them.

In the second district, despite a substantially greater enrollment than the first, only four grievances had been filed. This district maintained a full-time employee whose primary function was to resolve disputes before they became formal grievances. The standing order to the principals was not to deny grievances but to call the district "grievance chaser." While the formal rule structure was left largely unchanged, social relationships changed substantially as teachers realized that even the *threat* of a grievance was sufficient to get the attention of a powerful central office staff member.

Labor relations in education are also influenced by school district politics. Teacher labor relations evolve through three distinct phases or "generations" separated by two periods of overt political conflict (Mitchell et al., 1981). Before the first conflict period, first-generation labor relations are characterized by an acceptance of the proposition that ultimate authority in all school policy matters rests with the board. "Meet and confer" sessions between a teacher committee and the school board may occur, but the board is recognized as having unilateral authority. First-generation labor relations end with the onset of a political struggle over the legitimacy of teachers' rights to organize and deal collectively with school systems. A second generation begins when the teacher organization is accepted as a legitimate interpreter of teacher interests. During this period labor relations are based on bilateral "good faith bargaining." Teacher interests are accepted as legitimate, but as inimical to those of management. During this period teacher "wins" are seen as management "losses." As the second-generation relationship matures, overt conflict generally subsides as each side develops ways of accommodating the essential interests of the other. In doing so, however, they tend to isolate school board and citizen groups from the process.

A second districtwide controversy erupts when disagreements over the propriety of teacher organizations' power and influence over matters of personnel and policy become politicized. The third generation in labor relations—which arises only after there has been an overt political rejection of the second-generation arrangement—involves teachers in the creation of "negotiated policy" for the school district. School boards and managers eventually come to recognize that working conditions for teachers are inextricably bound up with major educational policy decisions and that both are being hammered out at the bargaining table (Eberts and Pierce, 1980).

Unfortunately, except for the question of managerial authority, the significance of labor relations policy disputes is frequently unrecognized by the participants (McDonnell and Pascal, 1979, p. 80). The process tends to be seen as one of conflict management or coalition building rather than institutional policymaking. Settling the contract peacefully is frequently more important to both sides than the educational effects of the agreement. In several districts where we observed negotiations, there was little or no recognition that a money settlement with the teachers' organization has any impact on the mix of services that will be available to students. It was not unusual, for example, for management to figuratively "put its money on the table" and announce that it was a matter of indifference how the teachers divided it. When this happened, it was generally clear that management's goal was simply to get the contract signed and avoid public conflict.

Even when salary gains are explicitly traded for substantial changes in the mix of educational services, the policy implications frequently go unacknowledged. In one of our study districts, for example, there was a clear trade of educational support personnel jobs for larger salary increases for regular classroom teachers. Both labor and management understood, roughly the impact of the settlement. Being unwilling to undergo a strike, however, both sides simply declared "this was the best settlement possible under the circumstances," without acknowledging that they had reshaped the district's educational services.

In sum, then, teacher organization and bargaining have affected education through: (1) development of formal contracts, (2) changes in the social relationships between teachers and administrators, and (3) reshaping the political context of school policymaking. Each of these effects, as we discuss more fully below, tends to reinforce the laboring definition of teacher work.

How Labor Relations Support the Laboring Work Structure

Both rationalization (preplanning and routinization of activities) and inspection (close monitoring of teacher work performance) tend to be supported by the evolution of formal labor relations. Rationalization is encouraged as teachers attempt to protect themselves. Closer inspection is stimulated by management efforts to define and enforce their rights in responses to unionization.

While craft, professional, and artistic conceptions are abundant in the literature on teaching work, the labor definition is most compatible with collective bargaining. A craft conception, which encourages rationalization through improved techniques rather than standardization of practice, is most popular with the school administrations we studied. Traditionally, managers have believed that teacher training assures the development of needed skills and that certification means that teachers possess them. Recently, however, widespread doubt about the efficacy of specific techniques, combined with a lack of confidence in teacher dedication, has encouraged managers to feel that school programs—not individual teachers' skills—are what counts. Nationwide concern about student achievement has created a suspicion that

> Incompetent teachers wind up in the classroom because the state sets *virtually no standard of performance*. Most candidates become teachers after obtaining state certification, which simply means that the college student passed the required number of education courses at an accredited college or university. (*New York Times*, July 3, 1979, Section C, p. 4)

University training and teacher licensure were originally the keystones of a "craft movement" in teaching. They were used to break a political patronage system which subordinated teaching skill to political party allegiance. But these requirements are no longer viewed with confidence by school managers faced with rebellious teachers openly asserting the legitimacy of their own self-interests (Grimshaw, 1979). Inspection is a natural management strategy and the redefinition of teaching as labor an inevitable result.

The Mechanisms for Rationalization and Inspection

Figure 9.2 summarizes the ways in which current labor relations practices in education support a laboring conception of teaching. As indicated in the figure, contract language, social relationship changes, and new political decision-making mechanisms within the schools each contribute to the rationalization of teaching tasks and encourage increased inspection of teacher job performance.

The Contract.   As indicated in the first row of the figure, three aspects of typical teacher contracts encourage rationalization of the work. First, by specifying hours and duties, contracts encourage the general industrial-society drift from "mission-bounded" work to "time-bounded" work. As Bernstein (1977, p. 3) put it:

> From the Olduvai Gorge to the spinning jenny, in both primitive and preindustrial societies, man's work was task-oriented. He picked nuts and berries until a sufficient number had been gathered for the meal; he hunted until the kill was made; he tended the cows until the milking was done; he worked from dawn to dusk in the harvest and hardly at all in the winter; and so on. He often measured time by the task....
>
> In the last two centuries, at first in Europe and by now in much of the rest of the world, work has become time-oriented. It has been divorced from the task. For those who are employed the amount of work to be performed is endless.... Time is traded for money.

Whereas the "school day" has always been time-bounded, the teacher's day has been ambiguous. Classes begin and end at set hours, but an undefined duty extends beyond those hours for grading and preparing lessons and nonclass interactions with students and parents. Through collective bargaining, teachers have asked that previously undefined hours and duty requirements be specified—when teachers are to be on campus and when they are to be available for after-school activities, meetings with parents, open houses, and the like.

In addition to specifying hours and duties, contracts formalize the distinction between teachers' "regular" and "extra" duties. Regular duties are largely limited to classroom instruction while extra duties cover most extra-curricular and student supervision responsibilities. Also by contract, many teachers have been relieved of onerous lunchroom and playground supervision duties. By making this separation obvious, contracts encourage teachers to narrow their sense of responsibility for outcomes and concentrate on explicitly stated (i.e., rationalized) tasks.

Less rationalized, spontaneous, and extra-curricular forms of teacher-student interaction receive little support from contract language. Moreover, where they are contractually specified, the stipends and other rewards offered for after-school and extra-curricular work are so low that teachers frequently turn them down.

The propensity for negotiators to develop elaborate procedural rules to cover all adjustments in teacher job definitions and assignments represents a third source of work rationalization. By expanding requirements for notification, consultation, and

FIGURE 9.2.   How Labor Relations Support Labor Work Structures.

THE LABOR PARADIGM SUPPORTED THROUGH

	Rationalization	Inspection
SUPPORT PROVIDED THROUGH CONTRACT LANGUAGE: (primary motivation)	1. Specifying hours and duties. 2. Separating regular and extra duties. 3. Elaborating procedural rules. (protecting teacher interests)	1. Creating grievance processes. 2. Requiring standard practices. 3. Defining evaluation procedures. (enforcing management rights)
SUPPORT PROVIDED BY CHANGES IN THE SOCIAL SYSTEM: (changed principal work roles) (emergent teacher leader roles)	1. Dual organization system. 2. Homogenization of work roles. (manager) (policymaker)	1. Need to demonstrate power. 2. Intervention by labor pros. (supervisor) (advocate)
SUPPORT PROVIDED BY CHANGES IN THE POLITICAL SYSTEM: (dominated by)	1. Need for support coalitions. 2. Lobbying for remote control. (group solidarity building)	1. Breakdown in the "logic of confidence." 2. Evaluation–based politics. (winning elections)

review of work assignments (through layoff and transfer policies, curriculum planning councils, etc.) contracts encourage planning and rationalization for every aspect of a teacher's job.

As indicated in Figure 9.2, the primary motivation for using contract language to rationalize tasks rests with teachers who perceive rationalization as a mechanism for securing and protecting their interests. By contrast, inspection is a management concern. Three elements found in most contracts support increased inspection of teacher job performance.

First, because arbitration proceedings require school site managers to show a contractual basis for their orders and to show that they have enforced the same work rules for all employees, grievance clauses encourage inspection of teacher job performance. Grievance threats force management to give attention to situations that they might have preferred to ignore. When a grievance is filed, managerial attention is quickly focused on the problem area involved and, particularly in smaller school districts, prompt action by the superintendent and the school board is assured. Thus grievance mechanisms encourage closer inspection of teachers and their task performance at the expense of other management functions.

Second, managers are motivated to inspect teacher job performance because contract administration requires standardization of practice in all buildings and classrooms (Gonder, 1981, p. 41). As principals come to accept their role as contract administrators, they also tend to adopt a diminished definition of management, confining their oversight to those work rules explicitly set forth in the contract.

Third, evaluation clauses found in many contracts encourage inspection by linking evaluation more closely with teacher discipline and discharge. Quite apart from the matter of difficulty in dismissing teachers, collective contracts have changed the definition of legitimate causes for dismissal. Judgments of technical competence or personal adequacy by superiors have been largely replaced by a factual assessment of whether a teacher did or did not follow rules. For example, in the celebrated case of Cyril Lang, an English teacher in Rockville, Maryland, a suspension for misconduct and insubordination was ordered because Lang exposed tenth-graders to Aristotle's *Poetics* and Machiavelli's *The Prince*—books not on the approved reading list. To school officials, the issue was not learning but whether rules were followed. As superintendent Edward Andrews said, "I don't know whether Lang is right or wrong about the books, but in a public school system, you have to have reasonable procedures to determine what is to be used and the superintendent has to uphold them" (*Time*, 1980, p. 77).

The Lang case illustrates the application of an explicitly laboring standard to the evaluation of teachers. If Lang were treated as a craft worker, the question would have been whether the children learned, not whether orders and procedures had been followed. If he were viewed as an artist, the assignment of Aristotle and Machiavelli might be subject to criticism, but with the improvement of instruction, not employee discipline, as the central concern of the critics. If he were viewed as a professional, selection of course material would have been recognized as something only other English teachers (as professionals) could adequately evaluate.

Evaluation abuses, through capricious or irrelevant standards, have been among the most important causes of teacher organizations (Corwin, 1970). Teacher leaders in interview after interview pointed to their conversion to militancy after experiencing one of their coworkers being "screwed by the system." Union response to these abuses has been to insist upon narrow standards and explicit procedural due process. These procedural standards, in and of themselves, have become an important value for teachers.

Increased labor power has encouraged some teacher union leaders to be more open to the idea of inspection. As AFT president Albert Shanker (Interview, 1981) puts it, current pressures for educational vouchers and tuition tax credits require union leaders to

> turn to the members and say, "Look, you may not like evaluations, you may not like testing, you may not like to do things that will involve some discomfort. . . . But unless we in the public schools respond in a very strong and obvious way, a way which is visible to the public, a way that turns around the present weaknesses and balance; then at the end of the decade there is going to be no such thing as public education left in this country."

The Social Organization.   As shown in the second row of Figure 9.2, changes in the social organization of the school have also contributed to the rationalization and inspection of teachers' work. In some respects these social system changes are more dramatic than those resulting from written contracts. As one national teacher organization staff number told us, "Schools changed a lot when senior teachers shifted from bringing the younger ones into line with what principals wanted to adopting the ideology that any grievant is right."

Most school districts now contain two distinct social organizations—each competing for the loyalty and cooperation of teachers. The administrative organization, led by the superintendent, wants teachers to adopt district goals as their own and to pursue those goals diligently. The teacher organization, led by the union president or staff executive, needs teachers to be willing to challenge the legitimacy of management directives and perhaps even withdraw services if a suitable accommodation to their demands is not forthcoming. The integration of these two social systems is accomplished largely by rationalizing each of them—that is, by circumscribing the powers of each system and emphasizing the importance of formal "official" interpretations of all rules and organizational practices. As a result principals face sharply increased pressures to treat all teachers alike and teachers find that "peer pressure" from colleagues becomes very intense whenever labor tensions are high. These pressures are kept under control by formulating explicit rules for behavior and encouraging all teachers to follow them closely.

While competition for teacher loyalty encourages rationalization, the need for both social systems to demonstrate their vitality and power increases the level of inspection. Administrators feel a great need to show that they are willing and able to monitor and enforce the rules governing teacher behavior. At the same time, although they often do not recognize it, teacher organizations need to call attention to the behavior of their members. As teachers try to show that they are serious about demands for improved working conditions, they invariably go out of their way to attract attention to their work. In one district we studied, teachers opted for "teachless Wednesdays." They continued to meet their classes, but lessons were not taught. The principals found themselves spending a great deal of time in classrooms monitoring teacher performance; futilely trying to ensure that instruction was taking place. Even when less dramatic demonstrations of power are needed, teacher organizations will often publicly remind members to "work to rule"—doing only explicitly mandated tasks. In 1980, the House of Delegates of the Los Angeles teacher organization opted for this strategy by voting to recommend that teachers refuse "extra volunteer work at their school site until the present crisis is past" (*United Teacher*, 1980, p. 4).

Grievances are frequently used to express the power of the teacher organization, and the process has the effect of socializing both teachers and administrators. For teachers, using the grievance process is generally the first expression of militancy. As one grandmotherly type was overheard to say in a teacher's lounge, "Honey, you don't have to put up with that horse poo anymore; you can file a grievance." School principals respond to a grievance with immediate attention to the specific problem and a general skepticism of teachers who are now regarded as "them" in an "us or them" power struggle.

The existence of strong grievance clauses also enables teachers to exercise their power through what Kuhn (1961) calls "fractional bargaining"—modifying contractual rules through direct informal negotiations with middle managers. Since virtually any complaint can be linked to health and safety violations or unilateral changes in working conditions—items that are nearly always grievable—teachers can easily threaten a grievance in order to get a principal's attention.

Rationalization of teaching work is further encouraged by surprisingly strong pressures for the homogenization of teacher job definitions. Both teachers and administrators have generally come to believe that collective bargaining requires identical working conditions for all teachers. Teachers tend to be suspicious that administrators only try to differentiate work roles in order to control teachers rather than to improve education. Moreover, the political structure of teacher organizations and the dynamics of collective bargaining make the homogenization of teacher work roles attractive. During contract negotiations demands and proposals by specialist teachers are frequently put forward in initial proposals but are rarely embodied in completed contracts. Specialist teachers generally lack political influence because they are relatively small in numbers and tend to feel that they have already moved out of the classroom proper to embark on new careers. The numerically stronger ordinary classroom teachers often suspect that specialists have less demanding jobs, are protected by law from economic risks, or are doing nonessential tasks. School managers also find it difficult to support special work rules for specialist teachers. They find that any offer to accommodate the needs of specialists is immediately seized on by teacher negotiators as an indication that management "has something to give." Thus specialists are seldom able to obtain contractual protections and frequently find their programs traded off as "frills" when finances become tight.

Labor professionals contribute substantially to both rationalization and inspection of teachers' jobs. These professionals generally bring with them the ethos and assumptions of private sector labor relations. Within this frame of reference, workers are thought to be motivated primarily by salary incentives and to need close supervision in order to work productively. Such a view encourages the belief that close inspection and performance evaluation are the primary vehicles for controlling educational outcomes.

The overall impact of these various changes in the social system of the school can be summarized in terms of changes in the roles of two groups of key actors: principals and teacher organization leaders. For school principals, collective bargaining has meant giving greater attention to two concepts that have recently been receiving increased attention in both professional and scholarly circles: *management* and *supervision*. Widespread use of "management by objectives" (MBO) techniques and recent enthusiasm for "clinical supervision" are only the most obvious indicators of this new emphasis on the principal as manager and supervisor. As managers, principals are expected to help rationalize the teaching process. As supervisors they are asked to increase the level of inspection in the system. Further evidence of these new role expectations for school principals is reflected in the opinions of 1,500 school board members who in substantial majority (63 percent) felt that collective bargaining would force school districts to adopt more effective management and budgeting practices, to be more informed about school operations (65 percent), and to take a more aggressive role in planning, goal setting, and the like (78 percent) (Gonder, 1981, p. 12).

Teacher organization leaders have emerged as important educational "policy makers" and "advocates" for fellow teachers. As policymakers, they help to rationalize the system through salary setting, curriculum planning, and day-to-day management of tensions and problems. As advocates, teacher leaders stimulate inspection by challenging the status quo and thus drawing attention to teacher activities that would otherwise go unnoticed.

The Political System.   Though economic factors are important, public sector labor relations are more political than economic. Achieving a satisfactory contract settlement in education depends heavily on the ability of each side to form and sustain strong political support coalitions. While solidarity within labor and management groups is necessary for effective bargaining, attracting and holding the support of politically active citizens is also a critical element. Since teachers rarely have powerful economic sanctions to use against school managers and managers have political survival or personal pride—not economic benefit—at stake in trying to resist teacher demands, political support from citizens (especially in the matter of voting for school board members) sets the overall direction in /labor relations as in other areas of school policy (Lutz and Iannaccone, 1978).

Enhancing the importance of the political coalitions with citizens is a weakening of what Meyer and Rowan (1978) have called the "logic of confidence." They argue that schools have traditionally operated on the basis of "ritual" classifications rather than closely inspected work performances. For example, special requirements for certifying mathematics teachers are scrupulously followed—but then almost no attention is paid to what they actually do once certified (see Schwille and Porter, this volume). Ritual classification is applied to both students and teachers. It enables schools to assure themselves of at least the appearance of success by simply declaring that teachers are fully certified or that students have "passed" from one classification to another. Maintenance of these ritual classifications is perilous, however. They can be sustained only if

> Parties bring to each other the taken-for-granted, good-faith assumption that the other is, in fact, carrying out his or her defined activity. The community and the board have confidence in the superintendent, who has confidence in the principal, who has confidence in the teachers. None of these people can say what the other does or produces, but the plausibility of their activity requires that they have confidence in each other. (Meyer and Rowan, 1978, pp. 101–102)

By formalizing conflict, bargaining weakens this logic of confidence and encourages school board suspicion of teacher dedication and loyalty. Consequently, an interest in the inspection of teacher work is easily triggered once negotiations have been institutionalized. School managers are fond of saying that teacher unionization robs them of their ability to manage. That is importantly wrong. The politics of unionization forces school managers to act more like managers than they ever have. They are forced to plan programs more carefully, inspect how well teachers execute these plans, and give a more detailed accounting of both to school board trustees. Unionization has made it more difficult, however, for school administrators to socialize teachers, to create internal cohesion within school sites, and to rely on mutual confidence.

There are two other aspects of school politics which interact with labor relations to encourage the adoption of a laboring conception of teaching. One is the emergence of teacher organizations as lobbyists and major political contributors at the state and federal levels. Teachers rank among the largest political contributors in some states. The California Teachers' Association, for example, ranked ninth in lobbying activity in 1978 (FPPC, 1978) and was first among campaign contributors. The Michigan Education Association outspent the United Autoworkers in Michigan's 1978 state legislative elections, and the NEA's political action committee raised more than $3 million for 1976 state and federal elections (Herndon, 1979).

In appealing to state and federal policymakers for support, teachers have endorsed the belief that education can be rationalized and controlled through program structures, funding categories, and procedural regulations. While this belief, taken by itself, would tend to support the craft rather than the labor paradigm, it has interacted with a second factor—a widespread demand for accountability and assessment underlying the "politics of evaluation" which has dominated most recent state and federal initiatives (House, 1974). The interaction between teacher power and evaluation politics has led to a climate in which state and federal policy frequently encourages compliance rather than excellence, maintenance of effort rather than appropriateness of service, and following guidelines rather than responding to needs.

Teacher organizations have influenced numerous local and state elections. They have recently become visible in national politics. There has, however, been a significant backlash against teacher involvement in politics in some communities. As one teacher organization president in a large California city said, "When the newspaper came out with a headline saying, 'Teachers Major Force in Local Politics,' I knew that we no longer were.'"

POLICY IMPLICATIONS

The general effects of teacher unionization and bargaining described in the previous section are not, of course, either universal or inevitable. Labor relations in education are influenced by a broad array of public policy choices—choices that interact with each other, sometimes reinforcing and sometimes inhibiting the overall drift toward a laboring paradigm. Two areas—teacher *organization powers* and *bargaining content* determination—are treated explicitly in all labor relations statutes. Two others—educational *finance and budget* arrangements and *management staff development* policies—are not generally thought of as labor relations policies at all. They are basic education policies, however, and we will examine how they interact with labor relations policy choices.

Empowering Worker Organizations

At root, labor policy involves creating a balance of powers between labor, management, and the public interest (Mitchell, 1979). Historically, labor laws have developed in response to the realization that individual workers are at a disadvantage in coping with the corporate giants for whom they work. How great that disadvantage is and how it can be corrected are, of course, matters of intense disagreement and debate. It is clear, however, that collective bargaining shifts power into the hands of workers and that this shift of power rests on empowering worker organization to represent the *collective* interests of their members—thus overcoming individual weakness with organized strength.

Debate over the powers given to worker organizations tends to be centered on the magnitude of their strength. In our view, however, the *nature* of the powers given workers needs more careful scrutiny. The redefinition of teaching being produced by contemporary labor policies arises primarily from the *types* of powers teacher organizations have acquired—not from their having become either too strong or too weak.

As indicated in Figure 9.3, various labor relations policies and practices generally provide worker organizations with specific powers in four broad arenas. They give unions: (1) a voice in defining workers' job responsibilities, (2) control over worker access to employment or to specific jobs, (3) power over the membership in the union, and/or (4) mechanisms for strengthening worker influence over the work itself.

FIGURE 9.3.   Labor Relations Policy Strategies for Empowering Teacher Organizations.

WORK STRUCTURE TO BE SUPPORTED

	LABOR	CRAFT	PROFESSION	ART
WORKER ORGANIZATIONS EMPHASIZE: WHEN THEY ARE EMPOWERED TO:	Bargaining with management	Organizing workers	Certifying practitioners	Evaluating products
1. Define work based on:	Working conditions	Task definition	Public policy	Product distribution
2. Control worker access to:	Terms of employment	The guild	Client treatment	Specific jobs
3. Define membership based on:	Employment	Apprenticeship	Examination and license	Recognition of talent
4. Give workers control by:	Limiting management rights	Expanding autonomy	High social status	Product ownership

$\longrightarrow$————MORE CONTROL OVER THE WORK ITSELF————$\longrightarrow$
$\longleftarrow$——MORE CONTROL OVER PRODUCTION PROCESSES——$\longleftarrow$

By allocating a specific mixture of these powers, policymakers can significantly influence the degree to which work in any industry will be structured as a labor, a craft, a profession, or an art.

As shown in the left column of Figure 9.3, the laboring paradigm is supported when unions are organized around plants, firms, or specific agencies. This occurs when unions concentrate on the bargaining process and are granted the power to: (1) define working conditions for all employees within a firm or plant through *good faith bargaining* of contracts, (2) prevent managers from negotiating separately with individual employees through the right of *exclusive representation*, (3) prevent access to work by workers who do not contribute to the union through the right of *agency shop*, and (4) support individual workers and limit the rights of managers by *representing workers* during contract disputes and grievances.

Craft Organizations.   The relevance of this particular mix of powers becomes clearer if we contrast them with those that are more central to workers engaged in craft, professional, or artistic work activities. Craft unions, for example, generally find that integrating workers into a strong organization is a greater problem than succeeding at the bargaining table. This is so because, once a group of craft workers is adequately organized (and so long as the craft is vital to production), they find it fairly easy to press their demands on managers. The 1981 air traffic controllers' strike illuminates the craft union situation. Because the FAA was able to find an adequate supply of skilled traffic controllers willing to cross a picket line, the traffic controllers' union had little capacity to negotiate. To strengthen their position, craft unions have to secure the cooperation and support of virtually all practitioners of the craft. They cannot rely, as labor unions do, on getting the cooperation of all the workers in a single firm.

In order to solve its organizational problems and succeed in dealing with employers, craft unions need the power to: (1) define specific tasks for union members by being able to *negotiate task assignments*, (2) control worker access to the union or guild independently of their employment by any particular firm by being able to operate a *hiring hall*, (3) establish criteria for membership in the worker organization by controlling *apprenticeship* or other certification mechanisms, and (4) expand worker *autonomy* by keeping nonunion workers from performing craft tasks and limiting supervisors' rights to direct the work.

Professional Organizations. Professional workers find the certification of practitioners to be central to their power needs. Generally speaking, professional organizations are more concerned with controlling the legal system which grants them specific rights and protections than with bargaining. This is partly because professionals tend to value autonomy more than job security and partly because most professionals are self-employed and therefore must rely on statutory rather than contractual definitions of their working conditions. Autonomous control over the work (as well as needed job security) are gained by professional worker organizations when they are given the power to: (1) use *statutory policies* (rather than written contracts) to define their work responsibilities, (2) control *access to the treatment of clients* by making it illegal to practice the profession without a license, (3) make membership in the profession depend upon an extended period of rigorous training and *formal examination*, and (4) increase worker autonomy by assuring that *high social status* accrues to members of the profession.

Obviously the power of professional organizations depends greatly on their social prestige and status. Public policymakers frequently do not recognize, however, the extent to which they influence the granting of this status. By establishing professional licenses, funding training programs, defining standards of performance, and relying on members of the profession for development and enforcement of these standards, policymakers greatly influence the overall prestige of a profession.

Artist Organizations. Artist unions need powers focused largely on the evaluation of art products rather than on bargaining, organizing, or certifying members. By equating union membership with creativity, artistic unions are able to both establish minimum pay scales and give individual artists a starting point for personal contract negotiations. Artistic worker organizations are supported in the pursuit of these interests if they are empowered to: (1) *control the distribution and use of their products* through royalties, copyrights, residuals, etc., (2) *limit worker access to certain jobs* by requiring producers to hire only union members, (3) *define artistic talent* by granting membership in the worker organizations only to individuals who have achieved public recognition of their work (such as limiting membership in the Screen Writers' Guild to writers who have had a manuscript accepted), and (4) empowering individual workers to *negotiate the value or ownership of their artistic creations*.

The extent to which teacher work will be structured as a labor, a craft, a profession, or an art depends to some degree on the particular mix of powers given to teacher organizations. It also depends, however, on factors completely beyond the control of teachers themselves. The destruction of craft unions in railroads and newspaper typography, for example, resulted from technological developments. These unions became powerless because their craft skills were no longer necessary to production—not because union powers were inappropriate or inadequate. The grant of specific powers to a worker organization can encourage, but it cannot command, the adoption of any specific work structure.

As suggested by the arrows in Figure 9.3, labor, craft, professional and artistic worker organizations can be thought of as lying along a continuum. At one end are the labor organizations, seeking to control production processes in the firms for their members' work. At the other extreme are the artistic unions, trying to gain control over the work itself. Craft and professional worker organizations occupy the middle ground. Craft workers want unilateral control over the exercise of craft techniques, but they collectively negotiate other aspects of their work. Professional employees insist on controlling both the particular techniques which they use and decisions regarding when and how to apply those techniques.

Shaping the Content of Bargaining

As indicated in Figure 9.4, the development of specific teaching work structures can also be influenced by controlling the *content* of bargaining and the basis on which settlements are to be reached at the bargaining table. A labor paradigm is encouraged when negotiations are concentrated on teacher work role definitions. This is so because written work rules can only be formulated if work is preplanned, and these rules can only be adequately enforced through direct inspection of the work process. If the labor paradigm is dominant, settlement is reached when a satisfactory "wage/effort" bargain has been struck. Management negotiators concentrate on the wage costs while labor representatives look at the effort costs involved in contract proposals. If the wage offered is high enough or the effort demanded low enough, agreement can be reached.

If negotiations are directed toward the definition of specific tasks for which teachers are to be held accountable, a craft paradigm is encouraged. If, for example, contract negotiations focus on questions of curriculum selection procedures, extra duty assignments, or classroom management requirements (rather than on the length of the school day, class size, or duty-free lunch and preparation periods), they presume that all certified teachers will be able to bring specific technical skills to bear on their work. Under the craft work paradigm, a bargain is struck when a suitable "compensation/performance" balance is reached. Negotiators for both sides recognize that

FIGURE 9.4.   Labor Relations Policy Strategies for Limiting the Content of Teacher Bargaining.

WORK STRUCTURE TO BE SUPPORTED

	LABOR	CRAFT	PROFESSION	ART
LIMIT THE CONTENT OF BARGAINING TO:	Defining work roles	Specifying tasks	Identifying clients	Determining product value
LET SETTLEMENTS BALANCE BETWEEN:	Wage/ effort	Compensation/ performance	Fee/ service	Commission/ product use

⟶———WORKER AUTONOMY AND PRODUCT CONTROL ⟶

⟵———MONETARY REWARD AND PROCESS CONTROL ———⟨

union members will be expected to perform specified tasks competently and that they are being paid for performance—not just for effort.

The content of negotiation shifts again when a professional work paradigm is being supported. Professional workers seek to retain control over when to use specific work techniques as well as the assignment of work responsibilities. Thus professional negotiations emphasize the identification of clients rather than the responsibilities of workers. For teachers, this would mean negotiating such matters as staffing ratios (e.g., the number of special education, music, or physical education teachers) and the assignment of students to various programs (e.g., vocational, remedial, or college preparatory programs). To maintain a professional work structure, individual teachers need to maintain control over what material they will teach, and when or how they will teach it, once staffing patterns and program assignments have been agreed to. Professional negotiations do not usually touch on questions of compensation, but when they do, the settlement represents a "fee/service" agreement. Professional workers accept with their fees an obligation to fully serve client needs—not just to follow supervisory instructions or perform certain technical operations. Accepting a professional work assignment means being committed to "seeing it through."

In order to support an artistic work structure, negotiations must shift completely away from the specification of worker behavior and focus instead on the ways in which the outcomes of their work are to be recognized and used. Artistic contract negotiations can proceed only if both managers and union representatives truly believe that membership in the worker organization assures a capacity for competent and creative work. If this presupposition is shared, worker representatives can demand and get control over their work and can win for union members the right to continuing control of the products of their work. If the artistic paradigm is operative, teachers should control their own curriculum materials, have guarantees of academic freedom, and be evaluated on the basis of results rather than on the curricular materials covered or the techniques used in their teaching.

For artists, the labor contract strikes a "commission/product usage" balance. Negotiators for artist unions concentrate on specifying the minimum commission which must be paid for the right to have their artistic talents displayed or used. Beyond this minimum scale, artists are expected to negotiate individual contracts to determine the commissions to be paid for specific products or performances.

As indicated at the bottom of Figure 9.4, the scope of contractual negotiations becomes narrower and is aimed at securing greater individual worker autonomy as we move from labor through craft and professional to artistic work structures. Similarly, the more workers are presumed to be motivated by purely monetary incentives rather than by intrinsic work satisfactions, the more there will be a tendency to adopt the labor paradigm and to conceptualize bargaining as a matter of reaching a wage/effort agreement.

Non-Labor Relations Policy Strategies

In addition to providing direct support for one of the basic work-structure paradigms through worker power and bargaining content policies, policymakers can provide indirect support through a wide range of other policy actions. Two important policy areas currently receiving widespread attention are: (1) school finance and budget policies and the related market or pseudo-market mechanisms aimed at controlling when and how educational services are purchased and (2) staff development policies aimed at influencing the work orientations of principals and other middle managers.

School Finance and the Educational Marketplace.   Current public interest in educational vouchers, tuition tax credits, and support for private or parochial school systems reflects serious interest in the role of market forces in shaping the delivery of educational services. These forces interact strongly with school tax and budget policies, which are also being debated and implemented at all governmental levels. Thus, for example, the development of block grants interacts with other mechanisms for raising and allocating resources to alter both the level of funding and the patterns of expenditure in most school districts. Debate over the desirability of strengthening the role of the marketplace in education is both intense and confusing. The most serious confusion in the debate springs from a general failure to recognize that there are many different types of market mechanisms. The market for professional services (such as medical care or legal assistance) is very different from that associated with the purchase of relatively low technology products (such as staple foodstuffs or furniture), high technology products (such as home appliances or automobiles), or artistic objects (such as records, high-fashion clothing, or Broadway plays).

As indicated in Figure 9.5, each of the four basic work structures is most compatible with one particular type of market mechanism. Each also presumes a very different basis for choice on the part of consumers. Products created through labor, for example, are best suited to a classical "commodity" market system. In a commodity market, consumers assume that quality is generally standardized; they make choices based primarily on the *price* charged for the good (or services) being purchased.

Commodity markets are not, however, best suited to the distribution of high-technology craft-based products. Craft-based production presents high risks to both investors and consumers. Investors seek a market mechanism that will protect the large capital investments needed to sustain a craft industry. Consumers seek a market where *value* rather than price forms the basis for decisions to buy. Autos and home appliances illustrate these problems clearly. In these industries brand names, a small number of large-scale producers (i.e., oligopolies), and consumer research and edu-

FIGURE 9.5.   Non-Labor Relations Policy Strategies Related to Marketing and Financing Educational Services.

WORK STRUCTURE TO BE SUPPORTED

	LABOR	CRAFT	PROFESSION	ART
MARKET AND PSEUDO–MARKET CONTROL THROUGH:	Free trade	Competitive commerce	Established clientele	Personal patronage
(Market choice based on)	(Price)	(Value)	(Trust)	(Taste)
FISCAL ALLOCATION MECHANISMS:	Block grants to local districts	Categorical aids to specific programs	Categorical aids to specialist groups	Block grants to individual schools

cation systems play a prominent role in marketing. It is appropriate to say, therefore, that craft industries involve "competitive commerce" rather than commodity markets. Competitive commerce markets are characterized by intense product differentiation efforts and value-oriented advertising rather than simple price competition. The "human capital" approach to analyzing educational productivity reflects an adoption of this perspective.

Professional markets are even less competitive than craft markets. In this case, constraint on competition springs from the fact that consumers select professional services on the basis of whether they feel they can *trust* the professionals. That is, professional markets create "established clienteles" which are carefully cultivated by professional workers and are even passed from one professional to another through various systems of referrals. Prestige private schools clearly illustrate this market mechanism in education. The impact of school quality on neighborhood housing values reflects a similar market process for public school services.

Art markets are controlled by choices based on *taste*. Whatever one may think of designer blue jeans or Broadway musicals, it is clear that such art products acquire their worth to consumers through critical review and acclaim, not through any calculation of the labor costs of producing them. Thus art consumers develop a market structure organized around the personal patronage of recognized art producers and dealers. Art markets are also highly fragmented and pluralistic. One consumer's masterpiece is another's kitsch. To sell an art product one must locate consumers who have the appropriate inclinations and tastes. In public education, this type of market structure is implicit in the fact that parents express great concern over which teachers their children will receive. The artistic (taste) rather than craft (value) basis to this concern is reflected in the fact that parents with very similar educational values will still demand that their children be placed with *different* teachers.

At present, education, like other governmental services, has a rather weak market system. To be sure, homes are frequently purchased on the basis of the school systems which serve them, and private education is frequently purchased by those who can afford it. Financial support for education, however, is largely controlled through legislative tax and budget decisions which have a powerful but indirect impact on educational market processes and work structures. These finance policies also differentially support specific teaching work structures. For example, although research evidence is lacking, it appears likely that the laboring paradigm is well served if block grant funding is combined with typical collective bargaining policies. District-level block grants provide maximum flexibility at the point where work rules are being negotiated and thus allow for the closest possible linkage between rationalization of work rules and allocation of expenditures. Especially if the grants are accompanied by an overall reduction in funding, they encourage managers to become price conscious and to treat teaching as a standardized commodity.

By contrast, craft work is encouraged by making categorical grants to specific programs. Categorical grants help to reinforce local commitment to the use of specialized techniques in the treatment of children and protect specialist teachers from being sacrificed at the bargaining table as union leaders try to win benefits that can be distributed equally to all members and managers try to keep labor tension to a minimum. The support offered by categorical program grants is strengthened if a system of program budgeting is adopted to monitor and evaluate the expenditure of these categorical funds.

The professional work paradigm is supported if categorical aids are distributed to specialist groups rather than to programs. It is rare for this approach to funding to be explicitly adopted in education, but it is implicit in tutoring systems which permit families to select trusted teachers for their children. Implicit professional control over finances is also generated when accreditation or other certification requirements are attached to working in programs such as special education or vocational training. Specially certified workers are encouraged to adopt the professional paradigm when they are paid in ways which insulate them from oversight and program planning processes used to direct the work of other employees.

The artistic work paradigm is best supported by allocating funds to the smallest unit of production (which in the case of education is the school site—or perhaps even the classroom). Artistic freedom and creativity are encouraged when a grant-in-aid rather than contract approach is used to establish budgetary control. If funding agencies adopt a policy of supporting promising educational projects through grants based on a careful screening of project proposals, but allow clients to participate on the basis of interest and approval of project goals, artistic freedom will be given substantial encouragement.

Management Staff Development Options.   Figure 9.6 outlines alternative staff development and training approaches that can be used to help principals and other middle managers support particular teaching work structures. As the arrows on this figure suggest, the relationships between managerial style and work structure fall along a continuum. Laboring work structures call for an emphasis on *direct control* of teacher work activities. The more the work is structured along artistic lines, however, the more managers must concentrate on stimulation, encouragement, or *socialization*.

When teaching is conceptualized as a laboring activity, the word "supervisor" captures the essence of the principal's work role. Supervision involves direct oversight of teacher work performance. To be effective, principals must learn to concentrate on consistency and stability in the interpretation and application of work rules. If they allow work expectations to vary greatly from day to day or from school to school, teachers can be expected to become confused and resentful of supervision.

"Manager" describes the principal's role when teaching is seen as a skilled craft. Management by principals is improved if they are trained in skillful definition of work

FIGURE 9.6.   Non-Labor Relations Policy Strategies Related to Staff Development for Principals and Middle Managers.

WORK STRUCTURE TO BE SUPPORTED

	LABOR	CRAFT	PROFESSION	ART
ENCOURAGE PRINCIPALS TO BE:	Supervisors	Managers	Administrators	Leaders
(Emphasizing)	(Consistency and stability)	(Skill and coordination)	(Ethics and support services)	(Sensitivity and spontaneity)
Enhance the quality and importance of:	Direct oversight	Technique application	Peer review	Critical review

⟶ ———— MORE EMPHASIS ON SOCIALIZATION ———— ⟶

⟵ ———— MORE EMPHASIS ON DIRECT CONTROL ———— ⟵

goals and careful coordination of work activities to reach those goals. Thus, management training for principals must include thorough grounding in the techniques of effective teaching and knowledge of how to assist teachers in applying these techniques in the classroom.

For teachers to work as professionals, principals need to view themselves as "administrators." Effective administration involves the maintenance of adequate support services (such as budget making, food services, transportation, etc.) and the articulation of a system of ethical norms which are expected to guide professionals in the conduct of their work. Principals expected to support a professional work structure need to understand the details of support service operations and to know how to keep these support services functioning efficiently. Rather than personally evaluating teacher job performance, principals being asked to adopt this view of teaching need to be trained to organize and implement a system of *peer* review. Professional teachers need to believe that they have a formal responsibility for evaluation of their peers in order to prevent malpractice and secure public respect for the profession.

In order for teaching to be seen as an art, principals need to see themselves primarily as "leaders." They must learn how to encourage sensitivity and spontaneous creativity among teachers and will need to express these qualities in their own work. Leadership in the art of teaching means providing effective critical reviews of teacher performance. Quality art is stimulated and improved when talented performances are given critical acclaim and when uninspired work is explicitly recognized as such. Criticism is a particularly difficult social process to institutionalize. A delicate balance must be maintained between the need for public reviews, which help to define the meaning of good art for everyone, and private criticism, which helps the individual performer to recognize strengths and weaknesses. In the fine arts (music, drama, painting, etc.) public criticism is usually undertaken by individuals not directly involved in the creation of the art products. Private criticism is undertaken by directors, teachers, and fellow performers in order to improve the product, but usually without an attempt being made to influence public acceptance of it. School principals, unfortunately, have been cast in a role which requires them to both nurture public support and stimulate teacher excellence. It is important for them to learn, therefore, to distinguish help for individual teachers from efforts aimed at shaping the overall quality of school programs. For the artistic teacher, principals must learn to become connoisseurs of live performances and critics of artistic technique. For the public, the principal is a reviewer and critical evaluator—one who defines "good taste" in educational services.

CONCLUSION

In this chapter we have argued that labor, craft, professional, and artistic work structures rely on different approaches to task definition and worker oversight. We have described the ways in which teacher organizations and collective bargaining encourage the adoption of a laboring conception of teaching work. And we have indicated how this tendency toward a laboring paradigm can be either strengthened or ameliorated by key public policy choices.

In closing we want to underscore two obvious facts about the relationship between making policy and educating children. First, policymakers may influence teachers, but they do not control the learning process. If policies are based on an inadequate understanding of learning processes, education will be hampered rather than facilitated. Policies that encourage laboring behavior will not help children who need the services of craft, professional, or artistic teachers. Second, policy analyses such as the one presented here can help to clarify what *will* happen if different policy decisions are taken, but they cannot determine what *ought* to happen in society. If policymakers encourage craftsmanship among teachers when the public is seeking a more artistic approach to education, the result will be deflection of effort rather than realization of the public interest. In short, policy analysis is no substitute for either a knowledge of how children learn or an understanding of the goals of public education. In the final analysis, no policy can be better than the statesmanship of political leaders or the wisdom of educational scholars.

Our analysis suggests that careful attention to the implicit assumptions and natural consequences of specific choices is necessary if policymakers are to avoid damaging the capacity of the schools to educate or breaking the fragile link between public goals and the intrinsic character of teaching and learning processes. Care must be taken to ensure that policies do not become mutually contradictory and self-destructive. Supporting a proper balance of labor, craft, art, and professional work structures requires that tough-minded and careful political choices be made.

REFERENCES

Bernstein, I. Time and work. *Proceedings of the 25th annual winter meeting*. Madison, Wis.: Industrial Relations Research Association, 1977, pp. 1–8

Callahan, R. E. *Education and the cult of efficiency*. Chicago: University of Chicago Press, 1962.

Chambers, M. Teacher licensing considered. *New York Times*; July 3, 1979, Section III, page 1.

Corwin, R. G. Teacher militancy in the United States: Reflections on its sources and prospects. *Theory into practice*, 1968, *7*, 96–102.

Corwin, R. G. *Militant professionalism: A study of organizational conflict in high schools*. New York: Appleton-Century-Crofts, 1970.

Cresswell, A. M. and Murphy, M. J. (with Kerchner, C.). *Teachers, unions, and collective bargaining in public education*. Berkeley: McCutchan, 1980.

Eberts, R. W. and Pierce, L. C. *The effect of collective bargaining in public schools*. Eugene, OR: University of Oregon, College of Education, 1980.

Fair Political Practices Commission, State of California, 1978. (Annual Report)

Gompers, S. *Labor and the common welfare*. New York: Dutton, 1919. Reprinted in E. W. J., Bakke, C., Kerr, and C. W. Anrod, (eds.), *Unions, management and the public*, (3rd ed.). New York: Harcourt, Brace and World, 1967.

Gonder, P. O. *Collective bargaining problems and solutions*. Arlington, VA: American Assn. of School Administrators, 1981.

Gouldner, A. *Patterns of industrial bureaucracy*. New York: Free Press, 1954.

Grimshaw, W. J. *Union rule in the schools*. Lexington, MA: Lexington Books, D. C. Heath, 1979.

Herndon, T. Annotating a *Reader's Digest* article: The NEA a Washington lobby run rampant. *Phi Delta Kappan*, February 1979, *60*, 420–423.

House, E. R. *The politics of educational evaluation*. Berkeley, CA: McCutchan Publishing Company, 1974.

Kerchner, C. T. From scopes to scope: The genetic mutation of the school control issue. *Educational Administration Quarterly*, 1978, *14*, 64–79.

Kochan, T. A. Correlates of state public employee bargaining laws. *Industrial Relations*, October 1973, *12*, 322–37.

Kuhn, J. *Bargaining in grievance settlement.* New York: Columbia University Press, 1961.

Lieberman, M. *Public sector bargaining.* Lexington, MA: Lexington Books, D. C. Heath, 1981.

Lutz, F. W. and Iannaccone, L. *Public participation in local school districts.* Lexington, MA: Lexington Books, D. C. Heath, 1978.

McDonnell, L. and Pascal, A. *Organized teachers in American schools.* Santa Monica, CA: Rand Corporation, 1979.

Meyer, J. W. and Rowan, B. The structure of educational organizations. In M. W. Meyer and Associates, *Environments and organizations.* San Francisco: Jossey-Bass, 1978, pp. 79–109.

Mitchell, D. E. The impact of collective bargaining on public and client interests in education. *Teachers College Record*, 1979, *4*, 695–717.

Mitchell, D. E., Kerchner, C. T., Erck, W., and Pryor, G. The impact of collective bargaining on school management and policy. *American Journal of Education*, 1981, *89*, 147–188.

National School Boards Association Research Report 1977–2. *Collective bargaining—Practices and attitudes of school management.* Washington, D.C.: NSBA, 1977.

Parsons, T. *The social system.* Glencoe, IL: The Free Press, 1957.

Taylor, F. W. *Principles of scientific management.* New York: Harper, 1911.

Time. How to protect tender minds. *Time*, December 15, 1980, *116* (24), 77.

United Teacher. Don't volunteer reps advise. *United Teacher*, December 1, 1980, *12*, (4).

Webb, S. and Webb, B. *Industrial democracy.* London: Longmans, Green, 1903.

Weber, M. *The theory of social and economic organization.* New York: Oxford University Press, 1947. Translation by A. M. Henderson and T. Parsons.

Whyte, W. H. *The organization man.* New York: Simon and Schuster, 1956.

PART III

Teaching from the Perspectives of Teachers

In the previous part the authors discussed teaching as work, but from the perspective of outsiders analyzing a way of life. In this part we move inside the lives of teachers and attempt to understand teaching as it is experienced and lived by those who engage in it. Much of the narrative of this section is told in the first person. And much of it describes the pain and frustration of individuals who feel unappreciated, unrewarded, and powerless. It is ironic that the motivation behind much of contemporary school reform and federal educational policy has been to improve the conditions of education for those Americans who are relatively powerless. Yet the feelings of impotence are also experienced by teachers, whether trying to introduce innovations into their systems, to practice excellently in their classrooms, or simply to survive the daily rigors of the job. Any attempts to improve the quality of schooling will have to take account of these impacts of teaching on teachers.

In the opening chapter of this section, Sara Lawrence Lightfoot discusses the lives of teachers, the relationships between their activities and feelings as teachers in classrooms and the lives they lead outside of school as spouses, parents, community members, and simply as individuals. She weaves a fascinating portrait as she moves between the theoretical literature on the sociology of teaching and personal accounts of how teaching is.

The Boston Women's Teachers' Group was formed by a group of teachers who were interested in understanding the conditions of teaching more fully and in attempting to assist one another in coping with the strains of the job. Freedman, Jackson, and Boles are the three teachers who formed the cooperative, and they have been conducting a study among women teachers in the Boston area. The purpose of the study is to understand the effects of teaching on teachers throughout their professional careers. They have conducted a continuing series of interviews with fellow teachers to identify a set of themes that capture the culture shared by teachers. Their interview protocols and the analysis that accompanies them vividly communicate the ways in which teachers experience the struggles and triumphs of classrooms and schools. Facile references to "teacher burnout" become rather empty as we read these moving first-person accounts of teaching. This chapter is also important because it reports research on teachers conducted and written by teachers. One of the ways in which members of this profession may begin to exercise power is to participate in the activity of studying the profession themselves.

Many educational policies mandate innovations or changes in school programs. Teachers often complain about the "top-down" character of such innovations and argue that they should be the initiators of "bottom-up" changes. Weinshank, Trumbull, and Daly are teachers in two different Michigan school districts. They teach at the junior high, elementary, and high school level, respectively. They discuss the role of the teacher in school change, alternating between first-person accounts of attempts at teacher-initiated innovation and analyses of the research literature on teacher roles in school change.

CHAPTER 10

The Lives of Teachers

Sara Lawrence Lightfoot

As the cultural priorities and norms of American society are rapidly being transformed, the images and expectations of our country's teachers seem strangely anachronistic and one-dimensional. A recent leading article in *Time* magazine presented two primary portraits of teachers. One shows a burnt-out, hassled, contemporary teacher who expresses boredom and fear in her face and no longer has energy to teach or commitment to children. Another, more traditional, picture portrays a dedicated schoolmarm, firm in manner, consistent in her caring, and sustained by her commitment to children. She is homely, single-minded, and protected from the harsh realities of the world. She is a good teacher because teaching is not merely a job for her. It is her life's work. No other duties intrude on her classroom responsibilities. No other relationships capture her emotions as strongly as those she has with her charges.

The opposite extreme is expressed in the contemporary teacher portrait. Here the teacher is vulnerable to the violence, ambiguities, and decadence of the society that intrudes into the daily life of her classroom. She is weary and discouraged by the multiple demands of her job, the overwhelming needs of her children, and the unsupportive quality of her relations with her principal and colleagues. Public criticism undergirds this image. This burnt-out teacher is seen as lazy, distant, not caring enough, not dedicated enough, and too concerned with self.

The *Time* article does admit that there are a few outstanding examples of exemplary modern teachers who show the historic dedication of the idealized schoolmarm.

> Lillian Becker wanted to teach so much that she went to college for her degree at age 42 and graduated from the City College of New York as a Phi Beta Kappa. Today, at Intermediate School 70 in Manhattan's Chelsea district, Becker scrubs the desks in her classroom herself and sweeps the floor three times each day. Says she: "Kids sense the order, and they like it. They behave differently in a clean classroom."
>
> She has other practical suggestions. "You have to keep calling parents. You have to keep trying to get homework done." She also believes in sentence diagramming and drill. "They can disregard it later on, but it only becomes part of you later on if you drill now." To discourage predictable student alibis like "I forgot my book" or "I lost my pencil," Becker spends her own money to keep an extra supply of paper and pencils on hand. She always has extra textbooks on her desk.[1]

These caricatures presented in the popular press echo many of the stereotypic perceptions of teachers left over from our childhood memories and experiences in school. Our adult recollections of teachers exaggerate the extremes. We yearn for and idealize the special teacher who changed our life and gave it purpose, and we denigrate the memory of poor teachers who wasted our time and damaged our spirits. The variations, the subtleties, the strengths, and the limitations of the real alive teachers are forgotten over time as the caricatures become fixed.

Literature on teachers often seems to suffer the same reductionism. Teachers are described in simplistic ways and given one-dimensional labels that are often heavily judgmental. Caught between lofty, idealized visions of their work and their low professional status, perceptions of teachers reflect a severe case of cultural ambivalence and uncertainty.[2]

On the one hand, teachers are seen as all-powerful, central forces who determine the life chances of defenseless children. On the other hand, we see them as helpless, impotent victims; empty vessels who must merely react to the constraints and inhibitions of the social, economic, and political systems of which they are a part. The conflicting images, often espoused in the same breath, are distortions of a much more complex reality. Both images portray relatively static conceptions that ignore change within teachers and change in the school system and society that surrounds them. The images also reduce the teacher to those behaviors and verbalizations expressed within classrooms. Rarely do researchers and observers recognize the multiple roles the teacher plays beyond the walls of the school or try to chart the ways in which the teacher seeks to integrate the myriad roles. Teachers, therefore, are seen as strangely presentist characters—without past or future—and without life beyond the classroom. Ironically, it is a view that is profoundly childlike. Many young children believe that their teachers never leave school, remain there overnight and on the weekends, and exist solely for them. Potentially competitive realities are denied or ignored by children who want their teacher all for themselves. They do not want to hear about sons and daughters, grandchildren, spouses, or other sources of attachment that their teachers might have.

Willard Waller speaks about adult perceptions of teachers as extensions of childlike fantasies and images. The issue of dominance and subordination, for example, that shapes the nature of relationships between teachers and students in school is unconsciously repeated by adults unable to escape the deeply rooted childhood conceptions. Parents are likely to approach their child's teacher with the same fears and inhibitions that they felt when they approached their own teacher thirty years earlier.

> This is an idealized and not a factual portrait [of the teacher], because the memory will not hold all the flesh and blood of human beings for so long a time; the general impressions remain, but the details fade. The idealized conception tends to become a caricature, because a real enmity exists between teacher and taught, and the memory transmutes the work of memory into irony.[3]

Perhaps it is an overstatement to suggest that researchers who study teachers and teaching might suffer from the same persistent retrospective distortions, but it does seem likely that social scientists, educational researchers, and policymakers would not completely escape the stereotypic images of teachers that are so commonly held in this society.

In this essay I will explore some of the views of teachers' lives presented in the literature. I will search out those pieces of work that attempt to portray teachers as whole beings, as more than technicians, pedagogues, or caretakers. In the process, I will report on studies that have described teachers from different angles of vision.

Methodological strategies, theoretical formulations, and research goals shape the image of teachers that investigators delineate in their studies. And inevitably, the portraits, evolving from the research, are abstractions and economies of thought that do not convey (nor should they convey) all the subtlety of individual variation.

There is a complex and diffuse connection between these research portrayals of teachers' lives and public policies regarding the work of teachers. The correspondence between research findings and policy remedies is rarely found to be linear or unidirectional. Empirical evidence is just one source used by policy analysts in shaping their views of social problems and needed solutions. Moral judgments, political negotiations, and economic repercussions are three other compelling dimensions that influence policy choices. But when research findings are clearly articulated, highly visible, and appear during a "receptive" socio-political moment, they become part of public discourse. A conversation begins that is often fuelled by research evidence. In turn, research data are also used to rationalize, justify, and defend policy choices.

In the areas of education and teaching one would certainly anticipate interactions between portraits derived from research, prevailing cultural images, and policy formulations. After all, everyone feels a certain legitimacy and authority in commenting on education, derived from their many years in school and the experiences of their offspring. Public officials and lay people are rarely reluctant to express passionate views on the structures and quality of education. Additionally, schools are highly visible institutions. Historically, schools have been the stages on which the social conflicts and dramas of society have been played out.[4] As the primary adult actors in schools, teachers have been the focus of intense concern, lingering dissatisfaction, and some subtle abuse. Their high visibility and centrality in the educational process makes them easy symbols and subjects for researchers and policy analysts, who are not only influenced by one another but also by prevailing cultural views.

This paper will begin by reviewing some of the classic studies on the character of teachers. I will look at how views of teachers' personalities have been influenced by their peculiar status as "professional adults" in our society ("Teachers and Adulthood"); by their special role as objective and fair judges of student abilities ('Teachers and Equality"); and by the personal and subjective quality of their work ("The Self and Career of Teachers"). The final section of this essay will offer contrasting perspectives on teachers' work and search for the connections between researchers' views and policy formulations ("Teachers and Change"). I will be arguing that narrowly constructed, one-dimensional views of teachers found in the literature not only misrepresent teachers and their work but also lead to misdirected public policies. As long as teachers are denigrated or idealized, as long as our images imprison them in constricting roles, the educational policies directed at their support will be misplaced and poorly designed. Policies must be focused on images that come closest to conveying the complexities, uncertainties, and processes of teachers' lives in "real" settings.

THE CHARACTER OF TEACHERS

Throughout the literature, teachers are described as basically conservative—personally, politically, and professionally. Teachers are said to lack spontaneity, imagination, flexibility, and intellectual rigor. Politically and professionally, teachers are described as myopic, with a limited vision that permits them to ignore important questions in favor of considering the pragmatic, presentist concerns of the classroom.[5] Most researchers have searched for the origins of teacher conservatism by investigating how teachers' personalities are determined by recruitment and the nature of the job.

Lortie discusses the recruitment of teachers, noting the ease of entry despite the fact that the profession requires a college degree. It can be entered at different times in a person's life and it does not require a long apprenticeship or rigorous special training. For many applicants, teaching feels like a continuation of their own schooling, requiring similar talents, commitments, and life rhythms. And for women "the subjective warrant comes closer to matching feminine than masculine ideals as defined by our society; it emphasizes qualities which are more widely reinforced for girls than for boys."[6] Entering teaching does not require a radical choice for women because teaching fits what they have always been told is appropriate behavior for women.

It is not only that teaching tends to attract non-risk takers but also that the recruitment process further encourages later conservatism. Lortie points to two major ways recruitment fosters a conservative outlook among entrants. First, the young people who choose teaching tend to be favorably disposed toward the status quo. For the most part, they identify with traditional views and rarely confront opposing perspectives that might challenge the existing system. Second, recruitment tends to attract people who have only limited interest in the "occupational affairs" of teaching. Lortie uses the case of time compatibility as an example of teachers' interest in the nonsubstantive, peripheral aspects of their work. Teachers who choose the profession for the convenient time schedule it permits would not be expected to challenge either the context or the conduct of classroom teaching. Men tend to be transient members of the occupation—both literally and psychologically—and are loathe to invest their energies in a setting that will not embody their futures.

> It is considerably easier, then, to see recruitment into teaching as leading to reaffirmation than as leading to challenging the past. Recruitment is one of the key processes in any occupation; in teaching, it tips toward continuity rather than change.[7]

Some scholars go beyond Lortie's assertion that teachers' recruitment encourages conservatism and self-protective tendencies and claim that even within their classrooms, teachers behave conservatively; leaning toward restrictive routines and discipline, rather than toward a real interest in learning.[8] After all, the process of learning is inherently chaotic in the sense that it demands confronting new, and often, contradictory data and means rearranging one's established view of the world. Teacher conservatism inhibits this potentially volatile process and therefore restricts real learning in the classroom.

Except for classifying teachers as conservative, most analysts scrupulously avoid describing a typical teacher personality. Lortie cautiously declines by saying, "It is important to note that efforts to find a single teacher personality have not been successful."[9] But with typical boldness and insight, Waller describes the characteristics of the modal teacher. His characterizations are vividly negative, and it would be tempting to dismiss them as "dated." But we find the description of the "retrogressing personality" compelling because he traces the causes of personality change and because, frankly, his words "ring true."

Waller identifies four factors affecting teacher personality:

1. self-selection influencing the composition of the profession,
2. the set of roles, often conflicting, that teachers must juggle,
3. external community views which influence teacher self-perception, and
4. traumatic experiences connected with the work.[10]

Waller is hesitant only in the first area, claiming that there is not enough information about why and how people select any career, even teaching. He recognizes the failure of the profession to attract highly capable people but doubts that raising salaries would solve the problem. He sees the problems in larger terms: "The social standing of the profession is unfortunately low and this excludes more capable than incapable persons. Particularly damaging, probably, is the belief that is abroad in the community that only persons incapable of success in other lines become teachers, that teaching is a failure belt, the refuge of unsalable men and unmarriageable women."[11] He goes on to say that the drudgery of the work and the restrictions placed on the teacher by the community probably drive off more talented people who have little respect for oppressive morality and react strongly to the rigid stereotypes of teachers.

With these observations, Waller does begin to sound dated and regional. That is, one would expect the community restrictions on teachers to be exaggerated in the early 1930's, in the small midwestern town from which Waller drew most of his data. Although it is clear that restrictions have eased over the past fifty years and there is more autonomy and anonymity for urban teachers, there are vestiges of inhibiting morality that remain today. The recent struggles in Dade County, Florida, over the hiring of a homosexual teacher point to the narrow roles in which teachers continue to get cast. Communities still expect teachers to conform to more traditional and conservative norms of behavior.

Most observers admit that decisions for entering the profession are varied and not necessarily rational. Personal history, early identifications with respected teachers, perceptions of appropriate women's work, and fears of institutional barriers all combine to shape decision making. Teachers may be influenced by a need to be in a managerial mode or have unquestioned authority. Others have been blocked from the professions of their choice and compromise on teaching; while still others are influenced by the desire for ready money in a profession which offers immediate benefits to newcomers.

Beyond the self-selection of teachers into the profession, their personalities are influenced by the special nature of their work. Waller, who is most interested in how teacher character is influenced by teaching, recognizes that "There are some persons whom teaching liberates, and these sense during their first few months of teaching a rapid growth and expansion of personality."[12] But he believes these people are rare. He indulges in one of his few moments of sarcasm when he says, "Teaching affords a splendid opportunity for self-sacrificing persons (how many of these are there?)."[13] Generally though, most analysts see the role of teacher as constricting the personality.

The relationship between student and teacher is based on a special form of dominance and subordination and this leads to many negative characteristics. First, a teacher must always keep a consistent pose with his students which results in an "inflexibility and unbendingness of personality."[14] The authority role becomes formalized and grows into "flatness and dullness."[15] Waller refers to this defense of the authority role as the embodiment of "dignity." Fear of losing one's dignity is "the landmark of one's assimilation to the profession... according to the teacher code there is no worse offense than failure to deport oneself with dignity.... He must learn to be dignified without the slightest effort."[16]

Teachers and Adulthood

Indeed, this must be a fragile and superficial dignity if it derives from an automatic and protective response and a fear of losing one's precarious position. Perhaps a better word for Waller's description of teacher character might be "decorum" rather than the calm self-possession and self-respect that "dignity" implies. Decorum connotes propriety and the requirements of polite behavior, which match the masking of emotion and the dullness to which Waller refers. It would be misleading, I think, to view teachers' preoccupations with decorum as merely a response to their struggle for securing power and dominance over their charges. Certainly the problem of establishing order in the classroom is a primary agenda for large numbers of teachers. But I suspect that the quest for decorum has more complicated origins that relate to the peculiar status that teachers have in our society as guardians of morality, as caricatures of virtue, and as symbols of traditionalism.

This societal charge to teachers demands that they be representatives of the adult world—interpreting the diverse, and often conflicting, norms and values of our society and protecting idealized notions of fairness, equality, and justice, central themes of democratic life. In order to accomplish these purposes, the teacher is often caught between the ideal and the reality. In his analysis of the occupational status of teachers, Frederic Terrien concludes that "teachers constitute a kind of conscience in society, and their status is that of the conscience—recognized as fundamentally important but neglected as much as possible."[17] The position of the teacher is ambiguous. She has the power of one on whom the stability of society somehow depends and is thus more "adult" than any ordinary individual adult; yet her competence is judged by her ability to live by, and teach children to believe in, values that other adults cannot or do not actually take too seriously.

In addition, students recognize that real-life does not match the idealized portrayal their teachers seek to communicate. Even within their own classrooms, pupils may experience the profound dissonance between the actual behaviors and practices of their teacher and what he claims are his purposes and goals. Children learn to incorporate these contradictions as part of school life and teachers seem to continually accommodate to the discrepancies in the immediacy of practice. I would suspect that over time these accommodations become increasingly routinized and unconscious and lead to the fragile and brittle dignity that Waller describes. It is not a quality that emerges out of self-discovery through one's work, but rather one that quickly develops in order to protect the vulnerabilities of the role.

Teachers have reported that these kinds of social expectations affect their lives outside of school as well as their image inside of classrooms. Clearly schools are no longer regarded as "museums of virtue" and "repositories" for high ideals in the sense that Waller described them fifty years ago, but teachers still experience the normative constraints on their behavior beyond the walls of school. In a National Education Association survey taken twenty years ago, teachers were asked to assess the public attitudes regarding their out-of-school conduct. Although a large majority asserted that there were no restrictions on their behavior,[18] it is difficult to interpret the meaning of that response. Perhaps these teachers had so fully incorporated societal norms that they did not perceive community expectations as inappropriate and would not have classified them as restrictive.

Lortie found that single, female teachers were most vocal and annoyed about the occupational constraints on their social lives. Said a thirty-four-year-old, fifth grade teacher; "Teaching is confining, emotionally and socially. I mean a teacher has to be a Caesar's wife, beyond reproach, particularly in the eyes of the community. You think twice about doing things." A second grade teacher, also in her thirties, complained; "Teaching is too confining.... You find that you're always watching who is around who might know you from school, and how you have to behave and who shouldn't I be seen with here and see this and that."[19]

One would expect that the pressures of scrutiny would be most severe in small towns where teachers tend to both live and work and where they are more incorporated into community life. A loss of prestige, a tarnishing of ideal images might spread to the other roles that teachers play in the community and diminish their general social standing. The value structures of small towns also tend to be relatively discernable and monolithic—providing a single standard by which to measure teacher conduct. Urban teachers, on the other hand, face a more ambiguous and inconsistent set of community values. School neighborhoods tend to be less stable and more pluralistic. Along with the anonymity of big city life, urban teachers would seem to enjoy more freedom from occupational expectations and stereotypes. In her study of small town teachers, McPherson described their great concern for establishing an image that was thrifty, clean, and respectable—an image that would counteract the belief that teaching is a job for the unambitious and lazy. McPherson speculated that their preoccupation with image-making served to alleviate their anxieties about whether or not they were accomplishing anything in the classroom.[20]

The moral righteousness of teachers is not only a community requirement; it is self-imposed. Within a particular school, teachers exert pressures on one another to maintain the idealized image. They believe that a collective image of good and moral teachers is necessary for the maintenance of their individual status. A lowering of collective standards, they fear, might lead to chaos and disruption among students and might present a less than united front to intrusive parents. In her study of junior high schools, Mary Haywood Metz reports on this mode of peer restrictiveness among teachers. Older teachers expressed concern when some of the younger teachers wore buttons protesting the imprisonment of a local black militant. They considered this an open flouting of the due process of law and worried that the young teachers would indulge in this "in front of students." The casual, contemporary dress of the younger teachers also offended their older colleagues, who criticized them for "denying their adulthood."[21]

A more troublesome problem that arises for teachers, confronted with idealized expectations, is that the occupational restrictions may have an indirect impact on the multiple roles they play in their lives beyond school. Getzels and Guba speak of this when they analyze the conflicts between the role expectations of teachers and the expectations that go along with other roles that teachers fill as parents, citizens, consumers, and even as children and students of others. They find that although "the adult members of a community are generally assumed to be responsible citizens whose judgment regarding their own conduct may be trusted."[22] teachers are in effect "second-class" citizens having less than a full adult status. The restrictions associated with their role as teachers are transposed to their other adult roles, limiting their freedom and autonomy in other settings and relationships. There is a kind of "guilt by association." Since they spend most of their time with children, they too must be, in some profound way, childlike. Their conduct must also need to be monitored in the same way that we watch over children.

Teachers often express dismay over this infantilization by the wider society and long for the opposite response. Their intense association with children makes them hungry for "adult conversations" and the full range of expression in the other areas of their lives. In some sense, they yearn both to be "taken seriously" and to be permitted to indulge their childlike urges after performing the burdensome and inhibiting role of superadult in school. It would seem that our cultural definitions of the teacher role pose an inherent contradiction that claims that in order to communicate effectively with children, teachers must exhibit the nurturant, receptive qualities of the female character ideal and the expressive, adaptive qualities of the child. Ironically, these same qualities are regarded as inferior and of low status when one conceives of the teacher in relation to the social and occupational structure of society.

TEACHERS AND EQUALITY

The idealized views of teachers, which inhibit their full development as persons, may be further amplified by the expectation that they treat children equally, distantly, and rationally. In preparing children for life beyond their families, teachers purposefully establish relationships with children that are less passionate than parent-child bonds. In contrast to families, schools and society are supposed to value uniformity of production and consistent methods of assessing quality and competence. Neither schools nor society are expected to bend to the peculiarities of the individual with the flexibility of the family.

According to Parsons, the primary responsibility of teachers is to evaluate students "along a single continuum of achievement." Acting as "an agent of adult society," the teacher makes broad-based judgments of the students' capacity to act in accordance with society's values.[23] Schools are organized to support these judgments with visible and explicit criteria for success and failure, with a limited set of tasks that all children must perform, and with large numbers of children reacting to a single adult. These are all in contrast to the more intimate, passionate associations within families and are designed to ensure that teachers will not show special favors to individual children. In Parson's view, the teacher evaluations are meaningful to children not because of any personal attachments but because they are the authorized representatives of adult society.

In their interactions with children teachers seek to establish "universalistic" relationships that will support fair treatment and social equality. The teachers in Gertrude McPherson's study interpreted this view as a warning to keep their emotions in check and maintain their distance from students. "Even the kindergarten teacher saw herself as standing apart from any individual pupil, trying to teach him, not to love him if to love him meant to accept him as he was. Teachers did not want to destroy the classroom uniformity even if that meant subduing the singular achievements of a talented or gifted child."[24] Each pupil had to be judged in relation to other pupils and a pupil who stood too far ahead posed as great a problem to the teacher as one who stood too far behind. Thus the Adams teacher might find herself in conflict with the parents who demanded more progress for the child who was, in the teacher's eyes, "proceeding at a normal rate."[25]

Establishing distant relationships with children is often associated with the masking of emotions and affect by teachers. They must keep passion down, fearing that deep commitments will grow that diminish the chances for the successful socialization of children to group norms. Sometimes teachers protect themselves from the emotional content of children's messages by interpreting the affect impersonally. "Mrs. Merrick quoted in dismay the second grader who said to her, 'I hate this rotten work, I hate you,' but she quickly consoled herself with 'of course, he didn't mean it, he was just angry.'"[26] Strict control over emotionalism is thought to be particularly important in defending against parental intrusions.

> The teacher should above all avoid allowing emotions to become aroused in the process. If the teacher's own emotions are involved the procedure will denigrate into a personal quarrel, and the possibilities for a constructive attitude on either side will be immeasurably decreased. While the angry parent states his grievance, the teacher should remain silent, respectful, sympathetic enough to allow the cathartic procedure its full emotional value for the other person, but aloof enough to prevent becoming personally involved in the situation.[27]

Although teachers often internalize their dispassionate, objectifying role, they also recognize the individual, negotiating quality of an educational experience. In order to teach well, they must see individual faces in the crowd and discern differences among students. In tailoring their responses to the individual needs of children, teachers are likely to develop "special" relationships with individual children in the class—relationships of greater intensity, commitment, and depth. The special quality of this relationship may be reflected in the teacher's giving the child more attention, more positive reinforcement, more privileges and affection, but the relationship itself may depend on complex and subtle *matches* between the personalities, styles, values, and histories of teacher and child. It would be unrealistic to expect that even the most reflective and sensitive teacher would develop relationships of equal intensity with all the children in the classroom. Building and sustaining human relationships is a complex and dynamic process that requires a great deal of commitment and energy on the part of both participants. Rather than developing equal and similar relationships with all children, it is more likely that the teacher will feel closer and more committed to a few children—often children who have pursued and initiated contacts with her or worked hard at becoming the focus of her special attention and favors. The teacher's relationships with "special" children should be viewed as one of the inevitable consequences of a single person relating to a large group of persons (i.e., the limits of individual energy and the unique dynamics of deep commitment) and not necessarily perceived as dysfunctional to the creation of a just and comfortable classroom environment.[28]

In *Life in Classrooms*, Jackson describes the complex negotiations between teachers and children and the problems teachers face in resolving the contradictions between group life and individuality in the classroom. The dynamic culture of classrooms presents teachers and children with a unique set of influences that require accommodation and change. Children must learn to adapt to *crowds, praise,* and *power.*[29] And teachers experience the ambiguities and tensions of their "individual-istic" orientation. On the one hand, they perceive the class as a group of individuals with differential needs, competencies, and personalities, while on the other hand, they recognize that their social and cultural role requires that they harness and constrain in-dividual differences and create a smoothly functioning and relatively stable and homogeneous social group. Despite the conflicts created by the institutional and societal demands, teachers perceive the individuality of their work as the source of greatest pleasure. Responding to individual needs and watching the progress of particular children is especially exciting within the context of *group* experiences in classrooms.

> Thus, paralleling the teacher's delight in observing the progress of individuals is his insistence on having a group with which to work. At first glance these con-ditions may appear contradictory, but on further reflection the apparent contradic-tion disappears. . . . They do not talk about their class as if it comprised a social unit with integrated parts and differentiated functions. Rather, they seem to be calling for a collection of individuals; a collection large enough to preserve the visibility of individual members. Stable social relations commonly develop within these collections of students, and classes surely evolve into groups in the func-tional sense of the term. But the primary unit of the elementary school teacher's concern and the major source of his satisfaction remains the individual and his development.[30]

THE SELF AND CAREER OF TEACHERS

Teachers' lives are shaped not only by their peculiar status as "professional adults" and purveyors of justice but also by the special quality of their work—a work that cannot be reduced to rules, competencies, techniques, or attributes. David Cohen, for example, has analyzed teaching practice in terms of its lack of specificity. He observes that not only are the outcomes of the teacher's efforts all encompassing and vaguely defined, but also there are no readily agreed upon strategies for producing even the more explicit outcomes such as reading and writing. Cohen labels teaching an "inde-terminate" practice because the desired outcome is personal change and because it re-quires both technical skill and a kind of social competency which must incorporate the values and personalities of both the "producer' and the "product."[31]

It is difficult, therefore, to disentangle teacher character from teacher competence. The teacher is deeply engaged in his work as a whole person because an effect is re-quired on the student as a whole person. In his analysis of the organization of teaching, Charles Bidwell recognizes the personal character of teaching and suggests that teachers make use of powerful affective resources to motivate learning by de-veloping emphathetic relationships with students.[32] Lortie also suggests that teachers become self-conscious and disciplined about using the "self" as a tool of the trade.[33]

But most observers view the uncertainties of the work and the necessary involve-ment of self as a liability, a source of distraction and difficulty, and finally routiniza-tion. Beyond the uncertainties of the task, the teacher's work is made even more burdensome by the large number of students in each class and the lack of time to cover the required material. Teachers also experience constant tension over their in-ability to reach every student. Teachers know that no matter how much they do, more could be done. No student, lesson, or course is ever "finished." The guilt about not being able to do enough for each child is exacerbated by the "realization that part of the problem resides in the teacher's inadequacies in knowledge, understanding, and technique."[34]

Feelings of isolation fill the daily experiences of teachers. Behind closed doors, they are asked to perform a complex and demanding job alone, without companionship and supportive criticism, often without reinforcement and reward; and their lack of adult contact and interaction gives them a distorted view of their own power and maturity.[35] The distortions are further amplified by the nonreciprocal quality of classroom life. Sarason, for example, focuses on the inherent "giving nature" of teaching:

> Constant giving in the context of constant vigilance required by the presence of many children is a demanding, draining, taxing affair that cannot be easily sustained. . . . To sustain the giving at a high level requires that the teacher experience getting. The sources for getting are surprisingly infrequent and indirect.[36]

Closely tied to the demands of giving are the constant shifts in demands—all students do not want or need the same thing. The teacher may resort to routine to minimize the onslaught of conflicting demands on her time and patience. Though the routine may be necessary for the survival of the teacher, it may be to the detriment of the children.[37] The rapid pace of classroom events, the simultaneous nature of many ongoing activities, and the sheer numbers of children may allow the teacher little time for diagnosis, evaluation, or reflection. One way of adapting to the situational demands of the classroom is to keep talking, lecturing, demonstrating, questioning. Another is to simply react to events as they unfold, abandoning the role of initiator and shaper of student behavior.[38]

Ironically, analysts' descriptions of the extraordinary emotional demands of teacher work have not led them to focus much attention on *the teacher's* needs and development. For the most part they recognize that the teacher's self is central to his work, yet they tend to focus on the patterns of his career.

Teachers' careers are seen as having three distinct stages: training (education courses and practice teaching), untenured novices (the first three years), and veteran teachers (everything after that). The literature abounds in its descriptions of teachers' discontent with their training—the irrelevance of their curriculum to the pragmatic world of schools and the lack of intellectual stimulation in education courses. Descriptions of novice teachers center on the loneliness of the ordeal despite high initial enthusiasm.[39] The disillusionment starts early, leading to a wish to escape.

> One young teacher (aged 26) told of the attitudes of himself and his friends as follows: "Every summer when you come back to summer school after a winter of teaching, you see your old friends and go through the same ceremony of explaining why you are still teaching. Each one tells of flattering offers that he has had to go into business but explains that he can't quite make as much at the start of business so he has decided to teach another year and save his money. Each one ends by saying, 'Well, I thought I'd teach another year, but I'm pretty sure that another year will find me doing something else.' Sometimes hints are dropped about splendid opportunities one is hoping to take up—usually based upon circulars from life insurance companies. But every year it's the same old story.[40]

McPherson also reports this tentativeness about teaching in veteran teachers who continue to fantasize about the great escape. But for the teachers she describes there is another edge to the problem. As middle-aged women in a small town, most of them assume they are unqualified for anything but teaching.

> The dissatisfaction of the Adams teacher was frequently expressed in her posing of alternatives, references to the possibilities of resigning, leaving the job, abandoning the status. Sometimes the teacher threatened to give up teaching altogether; sometimes she merely suggested leaving Adams and trying again in another community. . . . For the most part these (alternatives) were not intended as realistic alternatives; the complaining and the dissatisfaction were real, the alternatives were window dressing. The Old Guard teacher had no real alternatives. The work she suggested as an alternative would pay her less and give her even less status than teaching did. She would have to give up her salary, her retirement benefits, her tenure, at an age when she believed she must provide for her old age.[41]

The persistent complaints and lingering fantasies across many years of teaching point to continuities, and perhaps sameness, of the career. The fact that teaching is an unstaged career is central to understanding the nature of the job. Teachers do not get promoted based on classroom excellence, except to be transferred to another school or level. Instead, successful teachers are moved out of the classroom into administration or guidance. The work assigned to the first-year teacher is essentially identical to the job description of a thirty-year veteran. "But in contrast to the larger packages of money, prestige, and power usually found in other careers, the typical career line of the classroom teacher is a gentle incline rather than a steep ascent. The status of a young tenured teacher is not appreciably different from that of the highly experienced old-timer."[42] Although outstanding achievement may be recognized and appreciated by students and administrators, exceptional talent is not rewarded with career advancement.

The negative consequences of an unstaged career, claims Lortie, are that teachers become very present-oriented and feel depreciated if they persist at teaching above the average level of effort.[43] Male teachers expect to be promoted out of the classroom and into administration. But if this does not happen, most men become involved in a strong avocational interest or supplementary job.[44] Women teachers expect to teach until they marry or have children. If they do not marry, they tend to become more involved with teaching, although they are still seen by society as someone who was "passed over." These career patterns, he concludes, "favor recruitment rather than retention and low rather than high involvement."[45]

Observers agree that women and men view teaching as a career very differently. Despite the recognition that teachers' sense of their futures tend to vary according to sex and marital status, analysts tend to ignore other sources of contrasting views among teachers. The unstaged career leads observers to stress the sameness, rather than the changes, in experience over time. Waller is typically bold when he points to significant, though negative, shifts in perspective between new and veteran teachers. He observes the "reduction of personality" as teachers progress through their career, moving from initial idealism to decisive realism, and finally to impassivity and inflexibility.[46]

Although Waller's portrayal seems overly pessimistic and generalized, it begins to illuminate the processes of change within teachers and the interaction between the teacher's psyche and the social environment. In his view, teachers do not merely react to the institutional and cultural constraints; they are involved in their construction, as actors. But Waller's characterization is still defined by organizational stages and only points to the extremes of the continuum of teacher socialization. The emotional stages of teaching can, of course, be divided into "beginning/novice" and "experienced/ veteran" but these categories are too crude to reveal much of the inner life of the teacher. Even though society does not recognize or reward steps in a teacher's career, that does not mean that teachers do not understand their lives as having different, though blurred, stages.

The following exerpt is from the journal of a veteran public high school teacher in the urban Northeast. Written in 1980 as part of a research project in which I was involved, her introspective account dramatically tells the story of professional evolution, personal change, and the emerging conceptions of her own adulthood.

For many of us, our first year of teaching had the trappings of adulthood, but no inner core. We received a paycheck; younger people (not much younger) treated us as older than we felt; and we were expected to identify with teachers, not with the students we had been two months before. When I began teaching, I played teacher, so I imitated my past teachers, or at least my memory of them. My classes were simplified versions of recent college courses. I bought dowdy suits and sensible shoes; I prepared lengthy lectures; I talked severely; and I laughed little. The strain of playing adult was so great that when I returned home from school, I resorted to baby-talk with my new husband.

Because I had no sense of myself as a teacher, I took my cues from the people above and below me. I mimicked older teachers, when I wasn't arrogantly telling them how much I knew. I followed all the rules of the administrators and worried about my supervisor. If a student said, "but this is not the way we did it last year," I would change the procedure. Much of what I did was determined by fear that I would look like a fool in front of my students.

At the same time that I was filling everyone else's expectations, I was exhilarated by teaching. I loved interacting with so many students; I loved to think and write and talk about teaching; and I loved being in control.

In fact, control was the central issue. I solved the problem of discipline within two years of adopting the fashionable pose of being permissive and sympathetic (this was the mid-sixties and again I was following the dictates of the time, not of myself). But control was a much larger issue than discipline. I thought that I could control everyone's learning. If I prepared the perfect lesson, or devised the perfect exercise, every student would learn. I controlled discussions, tests, assignments, everything.

I enjoyed being the center of attention, and I worked hard at giving a good performance. Even when students worked in groups, I prided myself on my ability to "keep an eye on everyone" and squelch any "irrelevant" talk.

I was also extremely, almost pathologically, nurturing. I wanted to "reach" every student, and I was willing to expend enormous amounts of time conferencing, tutoring, and counseling students. Because I thought I should be responsible (control?) for the whole child, I was involved in their social lives, cultural enrichment, academic futures and private lives. I saw no boundaries between myself and the students. Even now, sixteen years later, I can name most of the 135 students I had in my first year of teaching.

Five years later, I began to feel competent, not just flashy, in a classroom. Because I was building a stronger sense of myself as a teacher (and as an adult outside of school), I could shed the external definitions of myself. I did not need student or administrative approval for what I did, and I could act and judge independently. As my competence grew, the loneliness and isolation of the classroom began to feel like an opportunity for freedom.

I became less obsessive about my students. I lectured less, spent less time on lesson planning and paper grading, and no longer took students to cultural events in the city every Friday night. I began to build clearer boundaries between myself and my students. They were getting younger and younger!

My own limitations were more acceptable to me. I realized that I could not reach every student, that I could not be witty every hour or insightful on every paper. And, that felt fine. I admitted to myself that I had no idea of how anyone learned anything, but instead of feeling demoralized by the uncertainty, I felt a quiet awe at the mystery of teaching and learning. I gained a bit of humility.

After I taught for ten years, I had a baby. This affected my teaching more than any other event in my life. From the outside, it might appear that his birth took my attention away from teaching because I taught part-time for a few years. But, in fact, my new role as mother intensified and clarified my relationship with my students. I learned through mothering that nurturing means holding on *and* letting go, and that my son only learned when I gave him enough freedom to learn. I could not teach him anything; I could only provide him with love and support so that he would have the courage to experiment. I could not mold him into some preconceived ideal because he was born with a personality of his own, beyond my control.

As I returned to teaching, I carried with me a new understanding of what it meant to nurture others. Although I had less time to be obsessed about teaching, the time I spent thinking about classrooms was focused differently from before. I no longer thought so much about myself—what I would say, how I would appear, how I would judge and correct. Instead I thought about the students and what I could do to allow them to take more responsibility for their own learning. I wanted to accompany them through learning.

Because I was so overwhelmed by the depth of my love for my infant, I began to use him as a kind of ultimate test about how I should behave in a classroom. For several years, whenever I felt tense about a class or irritable towards a student or uncertain about a lesson, I would consciously ask myself, "How would I want my son to be treated in this situation?" In some ways, this test took the brusque edge off my teaching—I became gentler. And in other ways, it made me far more responsible to the students because I hoped that my son would seldom be bored, unchallenged, or ignored in school.

The influence of his birth might make it seem that the stakes became very high for me again in my teaching, that I was overly intense about my relationship with each student. But, in fact, that's not quite accurate because the constantness of my child's needs tempered my desire to nurture my students. Because so much nurturing was going into my infant, I would not spend the time I had previously spent with each student. I no longer needed or used my students as surrogate children.

I also felt humbled by the realization that no matter how much affection I had for any student or class, I was only a fleeting influence in a small segment of their lives. I knew—and am now ashamed that I never understood it before—that the parents loved their children far, far more than I ever would, and that I was not central to their lives. My new awe of the parental role changed my relationship with parents. I called them more often when their children were doing well in school; I no longer dreaded parent-teacher meetings, and I respected their knowledge of their children.

The most liberating stage of my career was when I could allow not only my students, but also myself to be a whole person in the classroom. I was no longer hesitant to admit to students that I was baffled by some pieces of literature; I didn't try to hide my idiosyncrasies (I had to put up with some of their nuttiness, they might as well adjust to some of mine); I tried to show students how I thought through academic problems, instead of just showing them the "right answer"; I listened to students tell me about what learning was like for them; and I laughed a lot more.

My teacher-personality and my private-personality finally merged. I no longer felt the strain of "keeping up appearances" in a classroom. Part of this, of course, is just the result of aging—one becomes more comfortable with oneself, and the distance between teacher and student age increases, so the teacher does not need the false pretenses of distance. At age thirty-five, I do not need to prove to students that I am an adult, and I am not conscious of needing to prove my dominance.

TEACHERS AND CHANGE

The images presented at the beginning of this essay are strikingly different from this self-portrait. It is not only that the latter account has more flesh and blood and the former is bare-boned, but also that the cultural stereotypes are single snapshots—taken out of context, at one moment in time—and the teacher's journal is an introspective film showing complex changes in perspective. The self-portrait is a view from the inside, complex and subjective; while the teacher caricatures are external images, made simple and distant. The personal account of one teacher certainly does not tell us about the universal patterns of most teachers. It does, however, point to differences in external and internal perspectives, challenge simple caricatures, and hint at dimensions of teachers' lives that are often neglected by social scientists and policymakers. We recognize the value of perceiving teachers as knowledge bearers, as important sources for understanding their own experience.

Teacher's voices deny easy categorization. Cracks appear in the facile and anachronistic caricatures. A central aspect of most teacher stereotypes is the notion of female identity. Social science perspectives on teachers have been confused with and shaped by views regarding women in American society. When Waller and Lortie, for example, report on teachers' attitudes toward career, they make interesting assumptions about categories of women. In 1932, Waller assumed that women teachers were either young and unmarried or older and "spinsters." Lortie, forty years later, adds another category of "married teachers," but hints that these women are over forty and have returned to teaching having raised their children. Both analysts conclude that women have less stake in the economic rewards of teaching because either the women are single and have only themselves to support or they are married and using their income to supplement their husband's. As Jessie Bernard points out, this is an increasingly inaccurate portrayal of women and work:

> The rather astonishing change which is taking place in the work lives of women is that the effects of the birth of a child on work life continuity is rapidly diminishing. Increasingly women work right through their pregnancies and are then returning to work after a lapse hardly longer than a somewhat lengthy vacation. . . . Indeed, the most dramatic growth in the labor force during the current decade will occur among persons twenty-five to thirty-four . . . the steepest rise in work propensity has been among women with children under three, whose labor-force participation rate increased from 14.3 percent in 1960 to 26.9 percent in 1972 . . . the importance of this phenomenon of increased work participation by young mothers cannot be overemphasized.[47]

These emerging statistics fly in the face of past notions concerning the place of teaching in women's lives and point to the need to consider their work as not only central to their livelihood but also basic to their self-definitions. For decades, women have had to justify their choice of life style, and the locus of this justification has rested in the family rather than in their professional work. Traditionally it has been her ability to supervise a household, have a happy marriage, and bring up well-behaved children that has served as the real justification for a woman's life rather than her success and satisfaction in her profession.

> The professional woman with a family meets requirements in her work that are covered by values quite different from those that organize her home life, and she is faced with the necessity of learning to tolerate such contradictions or of extemporizing an integration of her own.[48]

One of the ways women seek an integration of their domestic and professional roles is to find work in the fields traditionally conceived as feminine—work devoted to problems and concerns that the women herself faces within the private capacity of her family. Choosing a profession such as teaching provides a continuity of this sort because it supports a special form of integration in the woman's life.[49] Lessening the distance between her two roles reduces contradictions in her self-image.

Interestingly enough, the blurring of distinctions between family life and work has provided social scientists and policymakers with an opportunity to give less attention to the characteristics and qualities of professional and work roles. Such a continuity has led analysts to assert the lack of commitment and attachment that women feel toward their work lives. The teaching profession has been regarded as a woman's secondary role which competes with her primary role as mother of a family. It has received, therefore, only peripheral attention from the social scientists, who do not seem to be interested in the teacher's conceptions of her work, her professional goals, and her maturation.

Recently, in response to blurred boundaries between family and work, and in reaction to the devaluation of professional roles traditionally chosen by women, a growing body of feminists have stressed the need for women to do work that is counter to "female tendencies." No longer are successful and achieving young women counselled to enter teaching, nursing, and social work. They are urged to go into law, business, and medicine; fields traditionally associated with men and the masculine' stereotypes of rationality, hierarchy, and order. This not only has meant a loss of good talent, but it has also led to a strange, and often painful, battle among women. A perceptive and intelligent teacher from a Northeastern city spoke of her responses to the strident feminism:

> For myself, feminism always lurked in the background—often to the detriment of my self-concept as a teacher. As women began to talk about working and as the promises of Affirmative Action beckoned, women began to expect important, ambitious careers. But to hold a traditionally "woman's job" was perceived by many of my friends as a step backwards. Women thought I should be more ambitious, more career oriented, more professional than I was by being "just a teacher." One of my most strident friends said, in 1975, "you're capable, you should do more than teach. Women should refuse to be exploited in low-paying women's work. You're a bad role model for your girl students—a woman doing women's work." She was not alone, many of my friends were slightly embarrassed by my teaching. Even some of my teacher friends argued that feminism and teaching were incompatible.
>
> As feminism became more flexible, my teaching was tolerated as though I were a housewife—I was given token respect for my right to choose, even though I had chosen the wrong job. At times I felt undermined by others' opinions of my work, but often I just knew that they were wrong. Teaching was honorable, I insisted to myself defensively. I began to wonder if I should "do more." I applied for an administrative position and felt relieved when I didn't get it. I began to read the articles in teachers' journals about how to disguise teaching skills on job resumes. I considered going to business school. But I knew that all these options weren't what I wanted. I remembered that every year, about mid-August, I began to dream about going back into a classroom—and the dreams were almost always happy.
>
> By now, I think, women are beginning to see some value in traditional female virtues such as nurturing, affiliation, and vulnerability. I sense that these new attitudes are affecting how my peers see my work.

The shifts in cultural values and the reigning ideology clearly have an impact on teachers' lives—both male and female. In order to gain a more authentic view of the constraints and barriers within which teachers function, they must be seen in action and in context. Attention must be focused on the changing social and political views and the shifting economic realities.

The external constraints, which shape teachers' lives, have never been more evident. With diminishing public resources for education, increasing public disregard for schools, rising inflation, and decreasing birth rates teachers feel more beleaguered and chronically dissatisfied with their work. The 1981 NEA Survey on "The Status of the American Teacher" shows that the average public school teacher was older (i.e., thirty-nine years), had spent more time in college, was relatively less well paid, and was far less likely to choose teaching as a career if given a second chance than was the case in 1976. School staffs, once relatively mobile, are becoming static and teachers are having to cope with the pressures of a demanding and unchanging environment. There is minimal opportunity for criticism and renewal from new colleagues. No longer are bright, young idealistic teachers being hired with new ideas and promising dreams; with energy to do the daily, extracurricular chores.

Policies must be directed toward teacher sustenance at a time of retrenchment. This requires a clear view of the socioeconomic barriers as well as a recognition of the potential for teacher inspiration and renewal. Those whose primary job it is to nurture and stimulate inquiring young minds must themselves be offered rewards and nurturance. They too must experience the difficulties and exhilaration of confronting new ideas, and occasionally be once again in touch with the vulnerable and subordinate role of student. Sabbaticals and study leaves provide a good opportunity for these kinds of role shifts and invigoration. But if teachers return from these sojourns to a stagnant, uninspired environment, to the cellular, isolated life of classrooms, their renewed mission will soon fade.

It is important to not only consider *individual* teachers but also think about restructuring the social contexts and networks in which teachers function. In order to increase collegiality and mutual support among faculty, schools will have to provide more opportunities for co-teaching, encourage collective curriculum development, and redefine status hierarchies between administrators and teachers that typically infantilize the latter. The inevitable distortions of power and authority that come with living in a world full of children must be tempered by more authentic and productive interactions among adults. Schools need to be thought of as environments that not only inspire the learning and socialization of children but also encourage the development of adults. The intellectual and psychic growth of teachers will inevitably have repercussions on their confidence, risk-taking, and creativity in approaching pedagogical tasks.

The rejuvenation of teachers will only emerge with their increased involvement. Many perceive the persistent complaints of teachers as laziness, malaise, and requests for less work. These critics point to teachers' preoccupations with noneducational issues—contract negotiations over vacations, release time, salaries, and protection from student assaults. But my interviews and observations of teachers in recent years reveal a malaise that comes not from overwork, but from feelings of disconnection with the intellectual and psychic center of the educational process. Their complaints can be interpreted as requests for greater *participation* in school life, greater *ownership* of their work, and support from sources beyond the school. They seem to be asking, therefore, to be regarded as adults with human needs, not paragons of virtue; to have responsibility *and* power; to join *with others* in defining contemporary values for students.

Public policies, shaped by these teacher needs, must be directed at reducing the social status distinctions and categories that inhibit communication, collaboration, and criticism among the people involved in educating children. Teachers must not be seen as empty vessels or mouthpieces for curriculum developers, but be intimately involved in shaping, developing, and interpreting the curriculum. They have a perspective on children and classroom life that is more subjective, more complex, and more intimate than the distant stance of policymakers and academic specialists. Teachers must directly mediate between intellectual substance and interactional processes in school. They must, through their own approach to knowledge and inquiry, model attitudes and behaviors for children.

If teachers are to be regarded as a powerful educational resource, reformulations of policy will have to recognize the shaping influence of local context. Policy initiatives at the federal and state levels should invite reinterpretations at the local and school level. The culture and tone of individual schools will require different strategies for collaboration and initiative among teachers.

The structure and norms of most of today's schools do not allow for these participational and developmental supports. Traditionally, schools have been organized around the developmental needs of children. We assume that children will grow and change, and we offer different tasks to match their skills, competencies, and stages of development. For many the match is imperfect; children are often put in the wrong box; and stages tend to become unmoving categories rather than transitions. But the notion of child growth prevails. I would argue that teachers should be given the same regard; that we should assume that they will change and need guidance, support, and relief from the heavy burdens. Their careers, like their lives, are not static, but highly complex and transforming. Policies and structures must be developed to support the integration of roles, to smooth the basic contradictions of imagery, and to encourage movement toward a fulfilling adulthood.

NOTES

1. *Time*, June 16, 1980, pp. 56–57.
2. For a more thorough discussion of the idealized images and real-life status of teachers, see Sara Lawrence Lightfoot, *Worlds Apart: Relationships Between Families and Schools*, New York: Basic Books, Chapter 2.
3. Willard Waller, *The Sociology of Teaching*, New York: John Wiley and Sons, 1932, p. 59.
4. See Joseph Featherstone, *What Schools Can Do*, New York: Liveright, 1976, and Diane Ravitch, *The Great School Wars: New York City 1805–1973: The History of the Public Schools as Battlefields of Social Change*, New York: Basic Books, 1974.
5. See Willard Waller, *Sociology of Teaching*, New York: John Wiley and Sons, 1932; Dan Lortie, *School Teacher: A Sociological Study*, Chicago: University of Chicago Press, 1975; Gertrude McPherson, *Smalltown Teacher*, Cambridge, MA: Harvard University Press, 1972; Seymour Sarason, *The Culture of School and the Problem of Change*, Boston: Allyn and Bacon, 1972; Myron Brenton, *What's Happened to Teacher?* New York: Avon Books, 1970.
6. Lortie, *op. cit.*, p. 53.
7. *Ibid.*, p. 54.
8. For an elaboration of this point of view, see Seymour Sarason, *The Culture of School and the Problem of Change*.
9. Lortie, *op. cit.*, p. 53.
10. Waller, *op. cit.*, p. 376.
11. Waller, *op. cit.*, p. 379.
12. *Ibid.*, p. 383.
13. *Ibid.*, p. 383.
14. *Ibid.*, p. 384.
15. *Ibid.*, p. 387.
16. *Ibid.*, p. 389.
17. Frederic Terrien, "The Occupational Role of Teachers," in *Journal of Educational Sociology*, 1955, Voo. 29, p. 20.
18. W. W. Charters, "The Social Background of Teaching," in N. L. Gage (ed.), *The Handbook of Research on Teaching*, Chicago: Rand McNally, 1963, p. 770.
19. Lortie, *op. cit.*, p. 97.
20. McPherson, *op. cit.*, p. 42.
21. Mary Haywood Metz, *Classrooms and Corridors*, Berkeley, Cal.: University of California Press, 1978, p. 178.

22. J. W. Getzels and E. G. Guba, "The Structure of Roles and Role Conflict in the Teaching Situation," in *Journal of Educational Sociology*, 1955, Vol. 29, p. 32.
23. Talcott Parsons, "The School Class as a Social System: Some of Its Functions in American Society," in *Harvard Educational Review*, 1959, Vol. 29, p. 303. Also see Robert Dreeben, *On What Is Learned in School*, Reading, MA: Addison-Wesley, 1968.
24. McPherson, *op. cit.*, p. 36.
25. *Ibid.*, p. 29.
26. *Ibid.*, p. 105.
27. Waller, *op. cit.*, p. 75.
28. See Jean V. Carew and Sara Lawrence Lightfoot, *Beyond Bias: Perspectives on Classrooms*, Cambridge, MA: Harvard University Press, 1979, Chapter 1.
29. Philip Jackson, *Life in Classrooms*, New York: Holt, Rinehart and Winston, 1968, pp. 3–37.
30. *Ibid.*, p. 143.
31. David Cohen, "Commitment and Uncertainty—A Study of Practice," unpublished monograph, Spring 1979. Also see Bryan Wilson, "The Teacher's Role—A Sociological Analysis," in *The British Journal of Sociology*, 1962, Vol. 13, pp. 15–32, and Robert Dreeben, *The Nature of Teaching*, Glenville, IL: Scott Foresman, 1970.
32. Charles Bidwell, "The School as a Formal Organization," in James March (ed.), *Handbook of Organization*, Chicago: Rand McNally and Company, 1965, p. 925.
33. Lortie, *op. cit.*, p. 156.
34. *Ibid.*, p. 155.
35. *Ibid.*, pp. 134–161.
36. Sarason, *op. cit.*, p. 167.
37. *Ibid.*, p. 168.
38. Robert Dreeben, *The Nature of Teaching*, Glenview, IL: Scott Foresman, 1970.
39. See Lortie, *op. cit.*, pp. 73–74; Sarason, *op. cit.*, p. 171; McPherson, *op. cit.*, pp. 61–71; Waller, *op. cit.*, Part V.
40. Waller, *op. cit.*, p. 422.
41. McPherson, *op. cit.*, p. 204.
42. Lortie, *op. cit.*, p. 85.
43. *Ibid.*, p. 86.
44. *Ibid.*, p. 95.
45. *Ibid.*, p. 99.
46. Waller, *op. cit.*, pp. 435–436.
47. Jessie Bernard, *The Future of Motherhood*, New York: Penguin Books, 1974, p. 144.
48. Lotte Bailyn, "Notes on the Role of Choice in the Psychology of Professional Women," in Robert Lifton (ed.), *The Women in America*, Boston: Beacon Press, 1967, p. 242.
49. See Jean Baker Miller, *Toward a New Psychology of Women*, Boston: Beacon Press, 1976.

CHAPTER 11

Teaching: An Imperilled "Profession"

Boston Women's Teachers' Group (Sara Freedman, Jane Jackson, and Katherine Boles)

INTRODUCTION

We are a group of public school elementary teachers who are studying the effects of teaching on teachers throughout their professional careers. We believe that the work situation of elementary school teachers intrinsically creates a culture whose aspects are overwhelmingly shared by all the teachers at this level, no matter what their present teaching situation or what background they have brought to teaching. The superstars and the weary, the inquisitive and the smug—we all make up the image of the elementary school teacher. Every one of us shares basic concerns and problems and it is these common issues we are addressing.

> When I was a kid in the 50's I went to a strict, traditional school. The teachers were thirty and forty year veterans. They never varied from plans written many years ago. In September the same pictures were posted on the blackboard. The construction paper borders were replaced each year but the paper faded early in November and was a dull sheen by March. I loved those teachers. They conformed to many of the stereotypes of longtime women schoolmarms—stern, swift in justice, unimaginative, inflexible, sure of their methods. They praised the docile, hard-working, quick-to-grasp pupil and were alternately punishing or neglectful of the silent majority. The wicked were quickly subdued.
>
> In fifth grade a spate of male teachers arrived, returning GI's straight out of college, who had a fertile field in the burgeoning school industry. They were different—young, creative, with lots of energy. They introduced SCIENCE!, giant papier-mache animals, and new seating patterns. We all wanted to be in their classrooms. Most of them soon moved to other positions in the quickly expanding system—principal, science co-ordinator, creative arts department. The children were left with the old women teachers—and with a disdain of old women teachers.
>
> When I began teaching ten years ago, I had a clear image of the kind of teacher I wanted to be—Mr. Williams, the fifth grade teacher who had introduced the most daring educational experiments and who worked tirelessly, coming to school on Saturday. He was the closest person I actually knew to the figures portrayed by Jonathan Kozol, Herb Kohl, and John Holt in those books coming out of the 60's. And I managed. I worked tirelessly, tried all kinds of experiments, came in on Saturdays. It was exhilarating—for the first few years. But at the years wore

on and on, I began to notice that the drive was being replaced by myriad frustrations. Many teachers who arrived with me on the crest of the 60's waves, felt tethered in place. We became less experimental, angrier, more isolated. In my voice, face and walk I was watching a metamorphosis. I was turning into my present perception of one of them—those female teachers of long ago who worked year after year in a closed space, each class merging into the next, stale ideas, frayed construction paper. (Freedman, 1979)

Many teachers in suburban systems as well as inner-city schools are leaving or would like to leave teaching, despite a tight job market outside of education and what has been until recently perceived as a secure job within the field. It is vital that we examine why and how within the institutional structure of schools some teachers continue to grow intellectually and emotionally in teaching, while others become stultified or, sensing the approach of stultification, leave. For can we expect schools to educate, encourage, and expand the horizons of our children if those same institutions serve to restrict and retard the growth of teachers?

"Burnout" is the term now popular to describe the phenomenon. The term has begun to appear regularly in the magazines directed to the teaching profession to explain widespread feelings among teachers of inadequacy, listlessness, and decreased dedication to teaching.

We question the implications of using such a term to explain teacher frustration. "Burnout" implies that at some point a finite amount of energy has been consumed. It does not acknowledge the reservoirs of strength and the varied sources of that strength from which teachers draw in the continuous challenge to help children in their common day-to-day work. Many teachers continue to be renewed by their work and gain a sense of self-fulfillment from the profession. However, the number of articles and workshops that explore the issue of teacher burnout has greatly increased during the past few years. This is occurring at the same time in which many teachers face layoffs and a shrinking job market. Yet it is not only the teachers most likely to face the end of their teaching careers who experience the attitudes described as "burnout." It is a malaise that can be found throughout the teaching profession, among teachers secure in their positions, well-respected, and with many years of proven ability.

Our project is an attempt to analyze why teachers change. For we do not believe that anyone changes from a dynamic teacher into a conservative pedagogue out of mysterious personal reasons. And the discontent expressed by the teacher in the opening statement is often echoed by others. It is not the despair of teachers working in ghetto schools with "deprived" children, few supplies, and racist administrations. The fear and anger arising from this situation have always been acknowledged. The anger we are addressing is found in urban *and* suburban schools, in affluent *and* poor neighborhoods, among men *and* women teachers.

Over a two-year period we have conducted biweekly interviews with elementary school teachers. We restricted our choice of participants to women elementary school teachers because the working conditions and role expectations of elementary teachers differ significantly from teachers of secondary students. We restricted our subjects to women because of the overwhelming representation of women within the occupation of elementary school teacher (87%) and the equally skewed percentage of men in administrative positions in elementary schools (83%). (N.E.A., 1978)

Our two interview groups were composed according to length of teaching: half have taught 3 to 8 years, and half over 15 years. We were able to select 14 participants for biweekly interviews and 11 participants for bimonthly interviews. Their teaching situations encompass a variety of institutional configurations, from large urban inner-city systems to very small affluent systems.

Indeed, as we investigated the views held by teachers, we came to see that schools as institutions create contradictory feelings and demand contradictory actions from teachers. The rhetoric surrounding the institution of public education often proves to be in direct conflict with the function a teacher finds herself required to perform. The dissonance between the goals teachers presume they are striving for and the realities they encounter may be more or less pronounced depending on where they teach, but the contradictory requirements of schools have always existed.

In this paper we intend to show how the currently acknowledged phenomenon of teacher burnout is a result of historical and institutional factors. First we will use selections from our teacher interviews to illustrate several of the main conflicts inherent in public education today. Then we will show how conflicting demands have been an integral part of public schools since their inception.

We will outline the rise of the "professional teacher," a fairly recent development which increases the contradictory nature of the teacher's role. Attempts to improve schools offered today, as in the past, do not address these contradictions—the inherent barriers to the growth of teachers within the structure of schools. Rather the solutions buttress the "blame-the-victim" approach. This approach defines the problem as an aggregate of disaffected or incapable teachers whose deficiencies are seen as personal rather than as a reflection of the failure of the educational system to grapple with and confront these contradictory demands. Through teachers' descriptions of the effects of such solutions, we will demonstrate the bankrupt nature of this virtually unchallenged approach. We will argue for the imperative need to look at the institutional nature of schools and how the structure of schools creates such contradictions and prevents their resolutions.

Examples of the main conflicts inherent in public education are:

- Teachers work in an institution which supposedly prepares its clients for adulthood, but which views those entrusted with this task, the teachers themselves, as incapable of mature judgment.
- Education is an institution which holds that questioning and debating, risk and error develop one's thinking ability. But learning situations are structured to lead to one right answer, and both teachers and students are evaluated in ways that emphasize only quantifiable results.
- The schools have the responsibility of developing the whole child. But the structure of the institution constricts the types of behavior acceptable in teachers and students.
- Education is charged with the social task of providing equal opportunity for the school-age population of a pluralistic, multilevel society. But the structure of schools emphasizes comparative worth and increases competition not only among the pupils but also among parents, teachers, and administrators.
- Public education is charged with upholding democracy by developing an electorate capable of critical thinking and the intelligent balancing of alternatives, but teachers are required to pursue this goal by increasingly mechanical, technical means.

CONFLICTS INHERENT IN PUBLIC EDUCATION

Teachers work in an institution which supposedly prepares its clients for adulthood, but which views those entrusted with this task, the teachers themselves, as incapable of mature judgment.

When our principal is talking to a first, or second, or third grade teacher, . . . I find that she's repeating directions one, two, or three times, almost as you would to a first-, second-, or third-grader. When you get higher up, fourth, fifth, and sixth, the directions are not repeated as much, but they're more done in like an outline form as you would give to kids who are a little bit older. (AA, 1980)*

Even when the teachers' work has created a major program, their contribution appears publicly as negligible and secondary. Their isolation from each other and the need to funnel any request and information up through the levels of the hierarchy and back down again rather than directly to each other has not allowed them to use their unique knowledge of classroom life, which they alone possess, as a basis for determining systemwide, or even schoolwide, policies.

After working for months on the fourth grade reading curriculum, we brought it up to the Assistant Superintendent. We had put a blanket statement at the beginning stating that we would assume that the teachers would be responsible by consulting the textbooks and other resource materials and their expertise and so on and so forth. . . . He made it quite clear that he didn't think they were capable of going over anything by themselves, finding the materials, using them appropriately. . . . We're smart enough to do all the busy work but not smart enough to carry it out. (D, 1980)

Professional development courses for teachers are frequently planned by others in the school hierarchy and dictated to the teacher, whose concerns and opinions are disregarded. Faculty meetings, which could provide a forum for issues and ideas, a place where group discussion and decision making might be encouraged, are more likely to be organized for the presentation of previously made decisions to the assembled teaching staff.

Every Tuesday is a half day for faculty meeting. The boss does all the talking. They are just sit-and-listen types of things. . . . If he asks for suggestions on things, it usually is put like this, "Now this is what I have planned. If there's anybody who wishes to disagree or there's anybody who doesn't care to go along with that . . ." That might not be his exact words, but he really doesn't care to open anything to discussion. People sit there with a deadpan because they don't want to commit themselves, you know, get themselves into any kind of hot water, a little afraid sometimes, depends on who the principal is. (E, 1979)

When the weekly faculty meeting is replaced or supplemented by a list of notices prepared and disseminated by the principal's office, the message is that teacher input is

---

* Letters are used to indicate specific teachers interviewed by the Boston Women's Teachers' Group. Single letters indicate teachers interviewed biweekly over a year's teaching schedule. Double letters indicate teachers interviewed bimonthly over a school year calendar.

unnecessary, a discussion of issues is not called for—and the teacher's control of her work environment is further limited.

Anger and resentment build as the teacher realizes that the control she wields over her work place and her working conditions is being sharply limited by restrictive administrative policies and practices.

> That's the thing that really kind of aggravates me about education: we as educators are not treated as adults. I feel that administrators still look upon us as being one of the children. So you teach elementary education, so you have an elementary education mind, and we can tell you just about anything and you will believe us. And at this point I would like to get into a situation where... I would be respected for *my* thinking as a person, as an individual, and I find that in this particular field, I'm not always treated that way, and I resent it and I'm angered by it, too. (AA, 1980)

Fostering independence in children has always been an avowed goal of our educational system.

> When we have our break in winter and we don't go out in the yard, the children have twenty minutes, and they become very, very social. I'm gone like five or six minutes and then I come in and I don't butt into anything unless there's a problem. And they get very, very close to each other in that way. It really is the best thing for developing some sort of a social attitude. You're trying to develop some kind of independence and they really get it from each other. (E, 1979)

Too frequently, however, the teacher is told to encourage independent thought and action in her pupils, while at the same time being cautioned never to leave her charges unattended. The same lack of trust implied here is mirrored in the school's careful monitoring and control over the teacher within her classroom.

> We have been told that we were never to leave our classrooms. We are never to leave those children *for one moment* unless we open our doors, go across the hall, and tell another teacher that we had left. And if something, God forbid, happened, it is *our fault*. That is insane. Children should be able to be left alone. By the time they are 12 and they cannot be left alone it is a tremendous failure of the educational institution. It sets up this dynamic between you and them that you can't trust them, you can't allow them to grow up because you're not allowed to grow. (G, 1981)

> The intercom is something that many people have been paranoid about. There is a button on this that can be pushed to Privacy, which means the office can talk to you, but they can't *hear* you unless you press it onto Open. . . . It has been rumored . . . I believe the rumor . . . that the principal can in fact override that and listen to anyone he chooses. And that's something that has upset people at different times. Yeah, I mean if you're a teacher who's having problems, that is definitely something that you're very aware of. . . . (C, 1980)

Education is an institution which holds that questioning and debating, risk and error develop one's thinking ability. But learning situations are structured to lead to one right answer, and both teachers and students are evaluated in ways that emphasize only quantifiable results.

> The principal was a marvelous person for handling the paper work, organizing the building, but when it came right down to the individual child, I think sometimes he missed the point a little. Once I remember he came into the classroom and said, "Look at that, and that, and that." He was pointing to the reading scores of three children. And these children were so, so unbelievably slow. I thought they were doing beautifully. They really sustained their interest to the end of the year and slow children don't *do* that. And I was enthusiastic. I was pushing a new program in reading for all it was worth. I can remember feeling awful, just awful when he said that. I felt I had been put down, a terrible put-down. I used to work like a son of a gun, always that push to do your best. And I felt awful. I don't think I dwelt on it forever, but I can remember getting feelings of like what a thankless job, you know. Really. (E, 1980)

A teacher who works day by day alongside a youngster knows which words a child will more likely stumble over, what words must be introduced in several different contexts, and which stories excite interest or increase the shuffling of feet and emergency trips to the bathroom.

> I can learn something by the papers that a kid turns in but I learn more by watching them do it, and that's particularly useful with kids. . . . When kids really know something, I know it. They have a confidence about it. When they do it, they make the comment, "Oh, boy, I love doing it," or "this is easy," . . . I have to hear that or see that. (B, 1979)

Parents, school committee members, researchers, and future employers would like to have the same information the teacher has without spending six hours every day in the classroom reading stories and learning times tables. If the teacher's own description of the child's progress is dismissed as too biased and personal, the only way to communicate what a child knows to those outside the classroom is to abstract that experience by quantifying the results.

> A couple of years ago they developed a reading checklist in this district. Each year you are supposed to check off what the child has accomplished during that year in your classroom. They developed a math checklist, and we have to give what is called a test of essential skills in reading, and that's supposed to measure their progress. Then we enter all the stuff on the checklist. And they have these little punch cards that during the year you're supposed to punch out each time they've learned something in math, and then you fill out the little checklist at the end of the year. I piloted one in writing last year, and writing is too subjective to evaluate in that way. All of these things are absolute killers for teachers, and personally, I don't think they are valid. (Y, 1981)

This involves a distortion. The teacher, who knows the children as idiosyncratic, highly individual people, must administer tests that yield quantifiable results easily transferable to charts and tables. The teacher cannot simply stop to share a child's joy over her accomplishments or commiserate with her in her problems. The teacher must first officially "translate" the pupil's progress as defined by test makers and publishers. Only then can it be officially recorded that the pupil has learned a fact or is able to reach an opinion. The role of comforter and educator yields to that of recorder and judge.

> We were all so very conscious of teaching subject matter that we were not teaching the children; we were just teaching the subject. I had made the determination, "I'm not going to teach like that." I almost don't care if a kid doesn't know how to add if he knows how to be nice to another human being and if he respects himself. I think that's very important. (W, 1980)

The same teacher in a later interview:

> I think the happiest day of my life was when I got back the reading tests and found out that the exact percentage of kids in the other two first grades were all reading on the same level. They had 25% of the kids who were below grade level and so did I. (W, 1981)

Once she has entered the child's progress into her book or on the blackboard, both the teacher and her pupils are easily understood and evaluated. The desire to nurture and support students, a major reason for many to enter teaching, is transformed into the drive to keep each student on a predetermined grade level.

> My principal gets upset because he doesn't see enough low science and social studies marks that should correlate well with reading. . . . He complains about this in general. . . . if they don't read well, how could they be doing well in science and social studies. He's also the same person who told us that . . . if they're in the 8th or 9th stanine that means they're an A or B student and their report card marks should reflect this. (C, 1980)

Parents, particularly those of working-class and minority children, know that rank order and grade-level achievement will be used to justify the kind of treatment their child receives, from the welcome in the first grade to the expression on a personnel manager's face. When teachers and parents discuss a child's progress, they both understand that a careful fostering of a child's uniqueness will have no place in a bell curve of national test scores; nor will it accrue to the teacher's or parent's benefit. Both the mother and the teacher know that to a large extent *their* life's work is judged by the immediate performance of the child in question.

> I always got the feeling that a mother came up to kindergarten just looking at her child in a very, very loving way. There's always this hope that this child may be somebody, you know, amount to something. And the minute you tag them in first grade as being top group, middle group, lower group, it took a little something from the child, it took a little spirit out of the mother. You know, they have a very positive approach to the child until he gets labeled as a G or an S. I think they get a little saddened by it. "This is not my hope; this is not my great hope." (E, 1979)

The teacher, under attack for failing to help children reach arbitrary grade-level goals, accedes to the greater wisdom of the commercial test makers and the research academics. Once started on the road to quantification, the method becomes addictive, even for attributes other than achievement.

> I went to a very exciting convention about learning style. They have been doing a lot of research on it and finally validated a reliable test so that you can give it to kids so that you can determine learning style.... It's a multiple choice test of a hundred questions, just very simple questions.... It's like the Stanford Diagnostic that tells you exactly what you need to know about a kid and all. Even if you did it yourself you wouldn't really figure it out—what the computer can do, put all the little things together. (F, 1979)

Principals and school board members then use the same types of evaluation created by the researcher to evaluate the teachers. The new "objective" type of teacher evaluations that have recently been introduced into the schools are examples of such quantitative methods. They take great pains to code and enumerate the type, number, and direction of the interactions of the teacher with her pupils within the classroom. She is not evaluated outside the classroom because presumably these contributions to the school as a whole, enhancing the sense of community of the school, are not properly considered her responsibility or, more strongly, not really "her business."

> The principal called us in one by one to tell us what our assignments would be next year when our school closed and we would be consolidated with another school. I knew I would be vying for a spot with three other nontenured teachers. All of them have taught in the school more years than I have. One is a widow with five kids. She teaches down the hall from me and is a good, decent, caring teacher. When it was my turn, I said, "Please don't consider me. It will ruin the rest of my year to feel that everything I do will be toted up in consideration for that job. It would demoralize everyone and they would resent me. I just don't want to compete with Sue and her five kids." The principal turned to me and snapped, "That's what I get *my* green check for." (G, 1979)

When she helps a teacher reorganize her classroom, when she "takes in" a difficult child so that teacher and child can have a rest from teach other, she is simply being nice. She is not being "professional" and no professional benefits will accrue.

What is left for the evaluator to write down are the concrete manifestations of the interactions of the teacher with her pupils that can be observed by the examiner himself. Only those moments become part of the meticulously documented, seemingly exhaustive evaluation of the teacher. It seems as though the examiner is riveted to the teacher, but it is actually the teacher who in a more important way is focused on the principal. What the principal does not see or is not done for his eyes becomes irrelevant, even counterproductive.

> My principal says, you know, he could look in the room and in one second he knows everything that's going on. Well, yeah, he might get an idea of what's going on, but that doesn't mean it's the right idea, and you know, sometimes it's not.... One day...I came back to my room after dittoing off papers, and there I am sorting my papers out on the table, and all of a sudden I realize there's a presence in my room—my kids are all at art or music or something. And I look up, and there's the principal sitting in my room, with an evaluation sheet...writing

down—he's looking at the questions on the board, he's looking at the bulletin boards I've got up, he's looking at everything around and he wrote me up a detailed evaluation based on what he saw in my classroom when my kids weren't there and I wasn't there. (C, 1980)

The more quantitative measures and national exams are used to evaluate the teacher, the more she will feel the need to use such quantitative methods to judge her students and other teachers. She is now the in-class representative of the national norms and countrywide bell curves. Once she has entered the child's progress into her books or on the blackboard, both she and her pupils are assured to be easily understood and evaluated.

The schools have the responsibility of developing the whole child. But the structure of the institution constricts the types of behavior acceptable in teachers and pupils.

Teachers, especially those in less affluent districts, often feel that they and their colleagues are encouraged to show only a few facets of their personalities within the confines of school.

I don't think that there are people who are really close. I can just not picture one teacher going to another one in tears. I really can't. There's no one to run to. Not just for me. People really just don't get that close. And I think part of it is working in an impersonal system. You do what the boss tells you. You don't have choices. You file at 10:10, whether you like it or not. . . . Everything is impersonally handled—time, bells. (A, 1979)

The message quickly gets across that order and quiet are the primary goals, leaving teachers to stifle, in themselves and their students, any activities that might be disruptive.

Teachers of working-class children are not surrounded by the many signs of their pupils' affluence—and probable future success—that bolster the teachers' and the students' sense of worth. It is difficult for such a teacher to justify "developing the whole child" when the local paper publishes yearly standardized test scores. The teacher's ability to identify with her job and with her students is threatened.

A retired friend of the principal's said last year that down at Central Administration they have a list and next to your name is how well your kids did on the ICRT. They're holding you accountable. If you go down to the bulletin board on the first floor you'll see the scores posted. (M, 1981)

When I changed from kindergarten to first grade teaching, it was a whole new scene. I just seemed to take on a first-grade personality. I think you just become a different type of person because you're more instructor and you don't have time to develop their personalities. The whole point in kindergarten was to develop this child so he's happy and likes school. If he's uncomfortable about something in his life, you try to make him loved. You get to first grade, forget it. I haven't got time for you. You've got to learn to read. You've got to finish that book before the second grade teacher sees you. . . . Somebody raises their hand, in kindergarten you would listen. You're hoping to develop their language, and you listen. . . . You got to first grade, it was, "Put your hand down. That's all the stories for now. Pay attention. Sit up." And they go to talk to you, "I don't want to hear your story. We're lining up. You have to go out. The clock doesn't wait for any-body. Be quiet. We have to leave the room." A whole new emphasis. (E, 1980)

The definition of "skills for life" varies according to the social class of the school and the teacher. A teacher in a working-class school:

In my school it's a luxury to think about those things—interpersonal relation-ships, how to encourage spontaneity—we have to teach the basic skills for life. Basic skills, that's the most important thing I teach them. Reading and math be-cause those are the tools to succeed in life, you know, to help you live. (H, 1980)

A teacher in a middle-class school:

One parent said, "What's important is the tools that you are giving kids to be ex-cited about finding out things and feeling okay about being wrong, too. You're just giving them lots of tools for the future and how you look at things and find things out." I felt very good about that. (B, 1979)

Sometimes areas which a teacher might consider very important are dropped or ignored because they are not part of the mandated curriculum which takes up more and more of the day's schedule.

I've learned a lot about how scapegoating needs to be stopped at the first possible opportunity. My first instinct is to say, "stop the world, we're going to talk about this." But in this school I can't suspend the schedule. So there's not any time for soul-searching, heart to heart. I could stick a little in that 25 minute math block. I could stick a little in that one-half hour when you get to passing papers. So I'm really stifled in handling things my way by that. Yet I'm not placing a whole lot of faith in traditional discipline. So I'm in a real conflict—I'm doing what I feel is wrong. (A, 1980)

Ironically, those teachers who want to provide "enrichment activities"—creative writ-ing, improvisational dramatics—must increase the pace and pressure of the classroom in order to cover the real work already established by the basal reader. The extras can be added only by a furious winding-up of prescribed work.

Education is charged with the social task of providing equal opportunity for the school-age population of a pluralistic, multilevel society. But the structure of schools empha-sizes comparative worth and increases competition not only among the pupils but also among parents, teachers, and administrators.

We never had any administrative encouragement to work together. There was never any time, there was never any made, there were very few group decisions. It's a very individual thing, if you found someone you wanted to share materials with, you did it on your own. No, nobody has ever encouraged that route. . . . It only comes from the individual teachers in our building. None of it is encouraged by the principal. (D, 1979)

The goal of the best education for each child is thwarted when feelings of envy and competition divide a school staff.

> The teacher in the room next to me seemed to be very friendly. I'd been in and out of her classroom, sort of looked around and made some nice comments about it. I asked her once if she would mind sharing a ditto sheet or something. . . . She said, "No! You come in here and you look around the room." She was really, I mean I couldn't believe it. . . . I don't know why she felt threatened. What was I going to do with this paper? Do one better? Put it up on the wall? I don't know. But it was a terrible, terrible feeling. (B, 1980)

Rather than working on problems together, teachers—and pupils—are labeled, categorized, and divided. Ironically, the desire to ensure equal opportunity to what have been termed disadvantaged children has led in practical terms to an increasing reliance on abstract quantifications that document inadequacy and focus the attention on what the child does not know.

> If there's a kid in the classroom that a teacher is having a problem with, and it looks like there might be something the matter, they go through the core evaluation process, and they discover that he does, he has an auditory figure ground problem, so automatically he's going to get picked up by the person in charge of auditory figure-ground problems. So now we've created a label for a kid and a person to deal with that label. There's a pattern and the pattern is they're minority kids, they are ESL kids, they are the kids who walk to the beat of a different drummer. (W, 1980)

For teachers caught up in the demands of school there is no time to think about the divisions among the staff and how these divisions often undermine the school's atmosphere and educational effectiveness. Resentment and competition can split teachers along many lines—older vs. younger, traditional vs. innovative, classroom teacher vs. specialist, those whose jobs are "safe" vs. those threatened by layoffs, those teachers requested by parents vs. those who are not, those who are given aides vs. those who aren't.

> We have to have kids till the last day of school. Why doesn't everybody have to have kids? Now people who are specialists in tutoring kids have to do a lot of testing and writing of reports. We have to write reports four times a year. We have report cards. I have to write my core. I have three of those to write. I realized I was really pissed. (B, 1979)

The competition among children in the classroom and among teachers in the school building is often echoed in the antagonistic feelings fostered among schools in a district.

> The superintendent made it very clear that the quote-unquote more aggressive schools would get funding and materials for the programs they wanted. . . . He said, "The more aggressive buildings will get the money. If there's something you want to do in your building and you can give us a good reason for it, then you'll

get the money. . . . If you really push for it, then we may be able to make it available to you." Some schools took advantage of that, like the _____ School. They have a lot of parents who know how to write proposals and they always get their way. (W, 1981)

Public education is charged with upholding democracy by developing an electorate capable of critical thinking and the intelligent balancing of alternatives; but teachers are required to pursue this goal by increasingly mechanical, technical means.

Until recently the teacher's recommendation was all that was needed to get a child into the Gifted and Talented program. You had a form you had to fill out, but it was a pretty liberal form. It was all comments. And you could comment on the fact that the child was a plugger, and he didn't necessarily have to have a totally super high I.Q. But now they won't even let you recommend a kid if he hasn't done well on these stupid CTBS's. This kid has to have scored beyond a certain point before they'll even take him and test him. (R, 1980)

The principal started another program in kindergarten that he wanted to adopt, working with small groups, using electronic equipment like head sets and things, very carefully planned individualized instruction with the children. He was structuring, planning 15 minute segments. He wanted to try something new. We would have a half-hour of concentrated teaching in small groups. . . . So you worked on listening to sounds or you worked on your workbooks in small groups and then after 15 minutes it was [clap hands] change groups. And no matter what you had to stop at that point. There was one little girl who had had kidney surgery in my room who really wasn't learning and had a lot of problems and I felt couldn't sit and do the work like that. And I remember one day when I said, "You know, she just had kidney surgery," he said, "I'm tired of hearing about her kidney surgery. I'm tired of hearing emotional things blamed for reading problems." (H, 1981)

In poorer and working-class schools, where standardized test scores provide the major indicator of how much a pupil has learned, the teaching of discrete mechanical skills takes on primary importance. Expertise is seen to lie in the books, not in the teacher. These tools are seen as the crucial determining factor in the education or miseducation of the child. If the teacher adheres strictly to the text, the child should learn.

We can't use any supplementary materials until we've finished all the textbook work. . . . I can show you the memo. [The memo read: "Teachers are reminded that only materials found in the adopted textbooks can be duplicated. (Supplementary materials are not to be stenciled and duplicated.) It is the feeling of the administration that materials in the textbooks are adequate and must be completed before other materials are to be introduced in the curriculum."] Even the kids who are repeating go back through the same materials. . . . Last week I was teaching a reading lesson and the story was about Galileo. Now I have a wonderful ditto about Galileo and telescopes. But it's from the science unit, so I couldn't use it. The administrator's aide controls the ditto machine and files all the dittos that are run off. If we have any supplementary dittos, they have to be cleared first. (McCutcheon, 1980)

Computers and other advanced technical equipment, supposedly designed to make the classroom a more productive place, reflect an assumption built into the newly acquired equipment of what is considered "productive." By establishing a centralized control developed from abstractions of "real" students, helping a child become "productive" means asking the child to compete with a pre-set standard rather than developing the unique skills and qualities of each pupil. For the teacher, these types of equipment limit the teacher's control over the pace and manner in which the skills are presented far more narrowly than possible by using only the basal reader.

> I'm not a machine-oriented person, for one thing. Not a bit. Not at all. And I just cannot see feeding stuff into a machine and have it talk back to me. I know what's going on in my room. With a small class, I'm getting to know them better and better, and I'm much more sensitive to them, it being a small class. And I've done it with bigger classes, too. I don't need a machine to tell me this child doesn't know this or doesn't understand that. (E, 1979)

Teachers also recognize that this equipment is not introduced to enhance their capabilities, nor those of their pupils. Richard Bueschel of Time Share Corporation which prepares materials for Houghton Mifflin said, "The approach in the 60's was to replace the teacher. Technically it was correct . . . the computer can replace the teacher. But it missed the practicalities, missed the point that education is student interaction with the teacher. . . . Besides, teachers weren't going to go for it." J. Kenrich Noble, Jr., publishing analyst for Paine, Webber, Mitchell, Hutchins notes: "Though student enrollments have dropped 5.5 percent since 1969, largely among elementary and high schools, there are segments, particularly in the earlier grades, that are flattening or rising. Several years from now declining numbers of teachers may cross rising student numbers, making any instructional tools that make the teacher more efficient high priorities."

Knowledge is, therefore, seen as residing in the machine, not the person.

> I think these diagnostic tests are another one of these things where somebody came up with the idea. Somebody who has a little empire to run sold somebody in the school department. Descriptively it sounds wonderful. You test each child and you know exactly what they need. It's a prescriptive thing. You look at their profile and you say, "Oh good, this child needs to study this and this and this." It sounds wonderful. Now that's based on two assumptions. One is that we don't know ourselves how the children are doing. Secondly, the other assumption is that the kinds of things that are being tested there are more important than the kinds of things such as general comprehension and following directions and understanding that the whole thing has to hang together. The whole paragraph or sentence has to hang together to mean something. The tests simply don't test for that kind of general reading ability. (Y, 1981)

Retaining teachers then becomes a question of choosing the person who will most strictly adhere to that mechanical solution, rather than the one who will weigh and discuss, choose and implement.

> I'm realizing that the other third grade teacher who is my colleague, with whom I exchange children for reading, has what is presumably the middle group. I have

presumably the top group and bottom group. I find out that her top group is almost where my top group is, and we've been on our book since the beginning of the year, and she didn't start it until just two months ago. It makes me feel that maybe I'm holding these kids back, but consensus is that these books are pretty hard. They've got some rather intriguing stories, ones that are not just run of the mill ordinary kind of stories, with a lot of metaphorical language and different kinds of fiction and fantasy. We do a lot with that sort of thing. I just feel really that I don't know if I'm doing the right thing in spending all that time on each story and having the children do a lot of things with each story. She's just obviously bombing through this book. A story a day, I guess. It makes me nervous that somebody is going to say I'm not a very good teacher. I really feel as though my kids are getting a great deal out of their reading. But it's one of those things that doesn't look good on paper. (Y, 1980)

The roots of these conflicts have never been addressed within the context of analyzing classroom issues. Rather, critics have focused teachers' attention on the failure of the individual—the teacher, the student, and the student's parent—and his or her inability to adjust to the established system. Understanding how life inside the classroom is crucially affected by the structure of the school system as a whole is considered counterproductive to a teacher's career.

Maybe teachers are hired to do their thing in the classroom, but that's as far as they're supposed to go. They're not really part of policy or curriculum in very meaningful ways. I think that's what a lot of the isolation is about. I certainly have the feeling—I know I'm not alone in this—there's a lot of futility in that and frustration. (B, 1979)

HISTORICAL ROOTS OF CONFLICTING DEMANDS ON TEACHERS

The present-day discovery of teacher dissatisfaction as a recently recognized phenomenon obscures the fact that the basic contradictory demands on teachers have been present since the doors of the brick grammar school first closed behind a staff of schoolmarms, a male principal, and a rush of youngsters. The emphases on individual response, implicit in current discussions on teacher burnout, deadwood, professionalization, and effective schools have had their ideological and structural counterparts from the inception of teaching in our public schools. For each new level of control that has been introduced—the switch from the model of the one-room school to a centralized urban bureaucracy, the introduction of intelligence tests and experts to interpret them, the present-day use of computers to diagnose and prescribe "enhanced individualized learning modes" to both teachers and students—a concomitant new ideology and rationale have been added to obscure the increased tensions that such divisions create.

The basic work situation of the elementary school teacher was first established by the "common school" movement of the mid-1800's.

Women filled a desperate need created by the challenge of the common schools, the ever-increasing size of the student body, and the westward growth of the nation. America was committed to educating its children in public schools, but it was insistent on doing so as cheaply as possible. Women were available in great numbers, and they were willing to work cheaply. The result was another ideological adaptation: in the very period when the gospel of the home as woman's only proper sphere was preached most loudly, it was discovered that women were the natural teachers of youth, could do the job even better than men, and were to be preferred for such employment. This was always provided, of course, that they would work at the proper wage differential—30 to 50 percent of the wages paid male teachers was considered appropriate. (Lerner, 1980)

The common school movement broadened the conception of school from the colonial pattern of privately funded academies responsible for the intellectual development of selected students to publicly supported institutions through which the government would provide opportunities to overcome socially inherited disadvantages. Education was to be the great equalizer.

By declaring the goal of equal opportunity, society also recognized that children entered schools with a wide range of needs. While charged with promoting individual intellectual development of each child, the teacher took on the additional role of the soothing, regulating, and resolution of the frictions that developed when children became aware of these differences. The contradictory nature of these two roles was institutionally resolved by allocating to the master and the normal school dean the task of devising curriculum materials and establishing institutional procedures while delegating to the teacher the responsibility for reconciling children to their disparate needs.

Disciplining children to an acceptance of institutional roles and standards, always a problematic and tension-ridden task, was one administrators willingly appropriated to the teacher on a daily, six-hour-a-day basis. Teachers were recruited to this essentially "disciplinarian" role by defining their sphere of influence not in the pejorative term of "discipline" but in the more positive sense of exercising their natural talents of empathy and nurturance. The administrative dichotomy masked teachers' lack of control over curriculum policies and management decisions. Teachers did not question the trade-off, accepting their lack of control over systemwide policies for the announced moral superiority inherent in their gender. Teaching was heralded as "women's true profession," but not because teaching followed the classic definition of a profession whose members controlled a shared body of specialized knowledge. Instead, the claim to professionalism of a 19th-century teacher rested on the ideology of women's birthright of maternal solicitude. Women were encouraged to believe that the management of schools was of a lower order.

From the beginning, sex segregation was part of the design of the urban graded school. Women's supposed comparative advantage in nurturance, patience and understanding of children led the architects of the urban school system to slot women in primary school teaching. . . . By structuring jobs to take advantage of sex-role stereotypes about women's responsiveness to rules and male authority, and men's presumed ability to manage women, urban school boards were able to enhance their ability to control the curriculum, students and personnel. Male managers in the 19th century urban schools regulated the core activities of instruction through standardized promotional examinations on the content of the prescribed curriculum and strict supervision to ensure that teachers were following mandated techniques. Rules were highly prescriptive. Given this purpose of tight control, women were ideal employees. With few alternative occupations and accustomed to patriarchical authority, they mostly did what their male superiors ordered. Differences of gender provided an important form of social control. (Strober and Tyack, 1980)

Highly prescriptive methods were at the core of teacher training since it was in the area of curriculum that teachers presumably required careful guidance and monitoring.

What I mean is, you know, there's sort of a picture, sort of your old schoolmarm, old maid teacher. They're strict but they teach you so well. They know everything. They've been teaching for years. They know all the ropes. They know the technical part of teaching. They know how to write a lesson plan. They know how to organize a room. They know phonics, in and out. They can give you any rule of phonics. There's some training there they can refer to. There's a lot of strength there. But sometimes I feel that they're one track. They all come along the same track and there's not a lot of creativity. In their training they have to go step by step. And you cannot jump from step two to step four. You have to go step two, three, four, five, and six. And that if they were allowed to feel their way along a little bit more, it would be more exciting. (Z, 1980)

They [state teachers colleges] only had one goal, and that was to turn out fellows and girls that would step right into a classroom and know what they were doing. They achieved that, they really did. Blackboard writing, attendance register. There was nothing about the running of the classroom that they hadn't covered, really. (V, 1980)

To question these methods would mean rebelling against accepted gender roles and the strongly socialized belief that those in positions of authority were inherently wiser. It would also mean losing the protection of following an approved model.

I used to have a much better tolerance for noise, but the principal has a very low tolerance and I sort of absorbed that. I can't tell you, all these years later, how very nervous it makes me when there's noise. So a lot of the times I can't allow a lot of things in the room to get used because they talk while they're using them. So I'm just a lot more directive and authoritarian. Once I asked a teacher, "How do you keep your kids under control?" and she said, "Well, you have to be a dictator." And it took me about two or three years to understand what that meant. (C, 1980)

The structure of the school and school system are thus reflected in the structure of the individual classroom. Within the given of a carefully controlled set of work restrictions, the teacher's institutional style tended to become more authoritarian as she sought control over student behavior, the only task that was hers alone and the only means by which she was considered unique.

Any classroom tension that developed from such a rigidly predetermined system was to be eased by improving the teacher's ability to sooth children when their inability to meet standards caused problems. Gaining collective control over curriculum decisions or systemwide policies, the basis of such competitive tensions, was discouraged.

We don't have any choice when they give you those books. . . . They want everyone in this system to be in this . . . I felt you had to cover them by hook or by
crook. It didn't mean everybody knew it or was able to learn it. . . . We had only
the hardest of books and workbooks to work with. . . . We're practically killing
ourselves trying to get enough reading into the low group. . . . You get very frustrated trying to teach it. . . . The expectations were absolutely way out of line.
And that's why the frustration on our part, and the youngsters. (D, 1980)

The highly prescriptive nature of teaching—in which neither teacher nor student
could deviate from a set norm—exonerated both of them from responsibility for upgrading the education of pupils. The assumption by school boards that all "qualified"
teachers would approach their classrooms in essentially the same manner, strengthened by the school board's knowledge that teachers had little selection of materials
and texts, paradoxically freed teachers from competitive comparisons with their colleagues. If a student could not read in the fourth grade reader, it was simply accepted
as an immutable fact that neither teacher nor pupil could change. As yet there was no
finely graded system of specialists and curriculum advisors to interpret such deviations. Once a teacher finished the "basic subjects" each day, the less loosely defined
attributes of nurturance for which she was hired could be exercised without fear of
falling behind an adjusted norm. Teachers put on plays, directed marching bands, and
spent whole afternoons with their classrooms drawing clouds or leading their pupils in
Halloween parades through town.

I had a self-contained classroom. I just remember glorious afternoons where you
would have like an hour and a half to do anything you wanted to do. I didn't have
specialists. So we could meander through the day and if we wanted to do more
reading we could do more reading. If we wanted to do a special project, we'd
just kick math out. And you could make a huge mess of the room and invite people
in. . . . There was just more of a family feeling with your own class. (Z, 1981)

In addition, teachers also regularly and creatively adjusted prescribed curriculum
methods and schoolwide policies to meet the needs of individual pupils. Many
teachers knew that strict adherence to administrative fiat would create unbearable tensions and considerable boredom for both themselves and their pupils. But they were
careful to make sure that their own modifications were not seen as too original by
their administrators, nor to give any signal that they considered their judgment to be
equal to their superiors.

There is no facility for ever discussing anything. The former principal pretty much
handled things his own way. If you knew how to handle him, you would go with
whatever your problem was or whatever your suggestion was and be very clever
about it and discuss it with him when he's in a very good mood and give him the
answer and let him think that he solved the whole problem. And if you could do
that, it worked out fine. If you just say, "The children in the cafeteria are behaving terribly. Something has to be done, they just can't run any old place. Okay,
Bill, I'll sit down and I'll draw a picture of the tables and I'll write down just how
many children sit in each room and number the tables and then we'll have a dia-
gram of just exactly where everybody goes." "Oh, that's a good idea"—and then
we'll have a meeting and he tells everybody of how he thought about this idea.
(D, 1980)

Ironically, combining the qualities of nurturance and self-sacrifice of woman's role in the home with the wage-earning position forced women in many school districts to choose between the two life choices. If women were expected to be truly self-sacrificing, they could hardly be expected to serve two masters. Married women, and later women who married and became pregnant, were forced to leave the field. Men were not required to make such choices as they were not hired for the same reasons. A 50-year-old teacher speaking of her childhood aspirations:

> I sort of always wanted to teach ever since I was a little girl and had any idea of the future. I always wanted very much to have children. When I was a little girl ... if you were a teacher you sort of had to be an old maid. All of my teachers, they were all unmarried. I think, in fact, that if it wasn't an actual rule, that is, written in the contract, it was an unwritten rule that a woman had to be able to devote her whole self to the job. Otherwise, she could not possibly handle it, right? A man could be a provider and a husband and everything else and run a profession, but a woman couldn't possibly handle it. So I was really broken up about that when I was a young girl, a teenager and thinking of my future. And my career and my desire for children. (Y, 1980)

As Lortie (Lortie, 1975) has pointed out, working in schools was a one-step career, a least for women and those men who chose to remain in such a woman-identified role. For most men, it was merely one step in a multileveled career as an educator, one that often expanded to include principal, district supervisor, and perhaps superintendent.

> Men in elementary education back in the early, middle fifties were a rarity. Those fellows had been told they probably would be principals very quickly if they went into elementary. ... Most of the fellows had intended to be junior high teachers but they were told at that juncture that if they went into the elementary program they could practically guarantee them they would be principals within two or three years and they were. (V, 1981)

What is not recognized is that the one dimensionality of teaching was the result of the 19th-century structuring of the schools which separated the intellectual and managerial functions of the school as a whole—the pace and scope of curriculum, the allocation of budget, the hiring of staff—from the day-to-day running of individual classrooms.

> You have to make yourself very well known to get any recognition in this system. I've decided that. You have to belong to the teachers' union and the negotiating team and negotiate with these people. Then I think they get a feeling of your strengths and weaknesses and get to know you. ... I was just thinking the other day, who are the busy little bees that do all the dirty work, put together minimum competency standards and tests, do all background work for curriculum decisions? Women. Who's on the negotiating team? Men. And I think if you don't do those things there is no other way they get to know you because they certainly don't go in classrooms. No one would ever recognize you for that. And that's what I've done all my life and I don't think they know me from a hole in the wall. Of if they did, it doesn't really count. (D, 1979)

Dividing these functions in two allowed for a narrowing of the job description of the teacher with the result that following one's job description leads to feelings of stagnation.

Elementary school teachers, each working in a separate room, were told that they had an enormous impact on the life of each of their students. But working in such isolation prevents teachers from influencing adults and pupils outside the classroom.

> It's a vacuum. It's a vacuum. You come in here and you close the door. And what goes on in here, goes on in here, and it doesn't in any way seem to affect anything that goes on outside the classroom. And I wish that it could. I really do. (W, 1981)

THE NEW IDEOLOGY OF PROFESSIONALISM

Within the working lives of today's teachers, a series of divisions within the school staff has created an increasingly hierarchical and segmented working force that has been added to the formal structure of the 19th century. The framework erected in the past provides the infrastructure of today.

A new type of teacher began entering the field in the 1950's when the postwar baby boom created an unprecedented strain on existing facilities and staff. While Rosie the Riveters were forced to relinquish positions they had attained in male-dominated occupations in order to make way for returning GI's, married women were assured that teaching would be one field where they would not be accused of upsetting the division of sex roles. Many barriers to the profession were dropped, and a whole segment of potential teaching candidates who had previously been excluded from the profession were now encouraged to apply. The desire to perform a socially approved task appealed to many women who were entering the work force in increasing numbers from liberal arts colleges. Unlike their normal-school predecessors, they had not all originally conceived of themselves as teachers but often were unable to find work in other fields. The prohibition against hiring married women was dropped in an all-out scramble to recruit large numbers to teaching. Thus, to the teacher college graduate was added a new group of teachers—those who had received their education in liberal arts colleges where teacher training was only a part of their degree seeking. Three out of five female employed university graduates of the 1950's entered teaching. (Oakley, 1974) This figure reflects both discriminatory bias in other occupations and an intense ideological campaign to lure them to the field.

The ideology of a liberal arts background allowed teachers to resist seeing their education as a vocational training ground for a prescribed task. The prescriptive methods and specific classroom management techniques of the teacher colleges were not emphasized to liberal arts students. Instead, the education courses offered to liberal arts students underscored the importance of entering schools with a distinct philosophy of education that was not to be found in a static model of classroom life. The approach to understanding and handling the child was reformulated in terms of the new professional careers emerging from the rising sciences of psychology and sociology. Teachers were trained in analyzing the child as a distinct personality and developing a curriculum that would be tailored to individual needs.

A lot was coming out at that time about how important it was, developmentally, for children to learn certain things at certain phases of their growth. Otherwise, they would never learn them as well. I started thinking about it rationally and sort of professionally. So this sort of meshed with my own feelings and my love for children and that I was able to deal with them well. I felt that that was an accomplishment that I had. (Y, 1980)

When the liberal arts graduate began her career, she discovered that the position of teacher was not reformulated to accommodate her training. The structure of the school itself changed little, but the upgrading of the description lured middle-class teachers into the field. Through the design of its courses, normal school had adjusted its graduates to the institutional constraints on teachers and pupils found in public schools. The training of liberal arts graduates did not prepare them for these constraints.

My first year I had the extra class. There were just too many kids which is why they hired me. I was isolated from other teachers, so I didn't have them for support. I didn't know how I was supposed to know what to teach in the grade. I had very few books, and I was too embarrassed to ask anybody, "What should I teach in the second grade?" I thought, "What's wrong with me that I didn't learn this in college, what to teach in every grade?" And I was absolutely made to feel by the principal that it was my fault. Absolutely. And I'd say that has never stopped influencing me (C, 1980)

A new philosophy of education which emphasized a more affective approach to cognitive development had come hard up against the inherent competitive nature of schooling and the structural barriers that emphasized relative worth for both teacher and pupil. Veteran teachers pulled new recruits through the first traumatic years by explaining the methods that were tailored to life inside the bureaucracy of schools.

I taught across the hall from someone who was a good disciplinarian, very well organized, and she took me by the hand. She knew I was young, the type of teacher who wasn't "well-trained." She wasn't saying, "You're doing a crummy job," but her attitude was, "Well, why don't we do it this way, dear?" She would like team teach. "This is how you teach second grade." She gave me materials. She just set me up. She was wonderful. I just thought she was the most marvelous thing because she led me through my second year teaching. These people just took me under their wing and, you know, just laid it all out for me. (Z, 1980)

Others learned through the chaos and confusion of their first years when they struggled to adjust to the established order as the only way to provide evidence of competency.

I became *really* skills oriented. I really feel that is terribly, terribly important, and that every time I think of myself going off the track I have to remember, "Well, look, what I can give these children. The best thing I can do for them is to provide them with skills that they are going to need to face a very difficult world." That's technique, that's technology. That's all it is, but I can do that. The affection will come along with it, and the affirmation will come along with their feeling good about themselves and having success. So I think one thing that I was a little less muddy in my mind as I went along about what I really wanted to achieve. I went in. I wanted to change the world. Everybody does, I guess. Your own little world. Not only can you not do that, but it's not even desirable. (Y, 1980)

Teachers were able to exchange techniques as long as the competency of one did not imply the failure of the other. During the 50's the liberal arts graduates recruited to teaching were not threatening to their colleagues or threatened by them. Married women did not see their job as their major source of self-definition. They viewed themselves and were viewed primarily as wives and mothers.

I think that I went through a period of time where, the period we're talking about, I really didn't get that much, what I really would have liked to have gotten from my profession personally. I guess during those years as a typical female I sublimated that. I wasn't supposed to get that much. I had my kids at home to think about and that was paramount. And my job was really secondary, so I didn't really look to it to get the kind of stuff that I would perhaps expect from it. (OO, 1980)

The ability to find another teaching job easily or to leave for a socially approved feminine alternative, either in the home or the work place, dissipated much of the teacher's anger or dissatisfaction.

I was in _____ only that year. Halfway through the year I was contacted by an assistant superintendent in another town who had my application, and, to make a long story short, he asked if I would come to his system right then and there, and I said I would not because I already had this class and it was December. He said, "I don't know what we can find in the spring. We may not have it." But I took my chances and come spring there was still a job. So I came here. (BB, 1979)

Schools had solved the problem of finding people willing to teach the expanding school population of the 50's and 60's. But the international event—the launching of Sputnik—and the domestic issue—the demand for civil rights among minorities— were telling reminders that recruitment of large numbers of teachers alone would not ensure the proper education of children. There was no discussion of substantive changes in the scope of teachers' responsibilities that might lead to a more effective staffing of schools. Instead, superintendents decreed the need to enlist a different type of personnel who viewed their job as one without set hours, who would take risks, whose allegiance to their pupils and a belief in their pupils' potential were paramount. Married women with children were no longer the ideal employees. A teacher in an alternative elementary school:

You have to be in there with those kids no matter what. Most of the teachers are single or divorced women. I think that the commitment you have to make to this school is such that it's easier if you're not married. You don't have a heavy family demand. (KK, 1980)

What was required was a redefinition of teaching as "women's true profession."

The emphasis in that phrase was no longer on the word *women*, but on the word *profession*, which implies "special expertise based on broad theoretical knowledge and an extended training." The new definition did not discard the nurturance of women, for that quality was needed even more in schools that now were asked to rededicate themselves to facing racial and economic differences within a highly competitive society. The ideal professional teacher combined the previous role of nurturer with a new awareness of cognitive development and technique. This new emphasis permitted incorporating the older definition of women's true profession within the new. The two-pronged criticism of schooling—that it perpetuated societal inequities while deadening the minds of all—could be solved by recruiting teachers who viewed their task from a "professional" perspective. They could and would solve such issues through a combination of diligence and strength of personality along with adherence to scientifically derived sources of information.

> The education department here had big illusions of changing the whole world. They told us that everything we ever knew about teaching and the experiences we had had as students were wrong. Everything was wrong. It was pretty traumatic. Pretty soon, I was writing 20 lesson plans a night with behavioral objectives. I was also supposed to be writing manipulative materials for kids to use because books were out. I mean you were really supposed to turn up your nose at that. You were supposed to write your own things. It was supposed to come from within, based on the children's needs, based on what you felt would be valid for them to learn. This was expected of undergraduate teachers and we were expected to create from a vacuum. That's about what it amounted to. (HH, 1981)

A number of books written in the 60's had an enormous impact in advancing this belief. Many of the authors were new to teaching and maintained a psychological distance from the vast army of public school teachers. Each of these authors was determined not to become one of "them." Most of these critics were men, they were generally young, they were often educated at prestigious universities, and they had "chosen" teaching.

Their books expressed the paradoxical feelings of despair and hope. Despair was voiced in the descriptions of schools' mindlessness, their racism and class bias. The effects of the school's environment upon children were mercilessly exposed. Nothing was said about the school's effect on teachers or on the relationship between what happens to the child and what happens to the teacher.

Out of the despair of these authors, however, emerged a hope that the efforts of people such as themselves could create a humane enclave for children within a hostile environment.

> In my training in Teacher Corps, I think there was a lot of energy there, a lot of excitement about what could be done, although I was never placed in a classroom that made me feel really good about what was going on there. I just remember at the time just wanting to read anything I could get my hands on in relation to teaching and learning and education. I went through a whole thing of reading Herbert Kohl and a whole rack of them that are very similar. And even up to this year that would be something that I would find really pleasurable to just read about things people had tried and that you could do and I'd sort of get a rush. (J, 1980)

The books gave hope to teachers—to new teachers the hope that they too could be forces of change; to veteran teachers the idea that while others surrounding them were easily identifiable as insensitive or unwilling to "give," those who were willing could maintain a higher degree of dedication and continue to find meaning in their field. It was up to the individual teacher.

> There's a sixties urge toward social reform which I think is where I still am—I accepted the whole notion of pulling up the culturally deprived—getting the kids early enough, intervening in lives, cutting the cycle of failure. So that's one of the reasons I think I entered teaching. I have a gut commitment somewhere to working in a helping field. (A, 1979)

Staff development often meant hiring a new person who would "show" the old timers how it should be done. These new teachers expected that adherence to curriculum innovations and new teaching styles would gain them independence from the school system's hierarchy. The recruits were often dramatically different in class background and training from the other teachers, yet once placed found themselves no more powerful than their peers.

> I took a classroom in a school where I had worked with the entire staff as a consultant. The principal said that if I was there, "Maybe you'll be able to keep things going." They gave me all the bad guys or at least it seemed that way. It was very frustrating because I knew too much. I expected way too much of myself. I expected to be able to go in there and do all these wonderful things all of a sudden. I also found a lot of things there that I hadn't been aware of as a consulting teacher the two previous years. What I found was that on the surface everything was cooperative and beautiful, but underneath there was a lot of grumbling and dissension about what he was doing. He would have us attend these lengthy meetings where he would expound and he would ask for our input and then he'd make the decision and would completely ignore any input that we might have given him. (HH, 1980)

For the children in those classes, school may have been a very different experience, but for the teachers it was much the same.

Teachers entered schools wanting to grapple with the effects of societal tensions as they affected the children in their classrooms, but the methods promoted by such books focused their efforts on individual solutions by individual teachers. A minority teacher:

> I went to the district superintendent, who happened to be a minority himself, to ask for a transfer because after six years of being in that building, I felt the school had taken a toll on me. What he said to me in essence was, "We need you there, so if there's any way that you can reconcile yourself to the difficulties on a personal basis, I really wish you would because at this time I would not consider your request for transfer from that building." My feeling was when I left his office that whatever was to be done was to be done by me. I just really felt very locked in. So, what is typical of my behavior, I just went back to my classroom and redoubled my efforts to deal with the kids, and I guess to a certain extent to isolate myself from some of the current that existed in the building, so that I

wouldn't constantly feel the undercurrent that did exist. But it didn't work. I mean you can't be in the building and not be a part of what's going on. (W, 1981)

To be a professional, therefore, placed the teacher in a very lonely position.

There were attempts to "restructure" schools. The open space concept, generally introduced by administrative fiat as a way of "freeing teachers and pupils," frequently pitted teachers against each other for use of centralized resources. The openness of the space belied the fact that teachers were still placed in competition by the pace of workbooks and national norms.

I think you have to be so inflexible in an open space. It's like with a lot of people in the same bed. It's crowded. If you want to turn over, everybody has got to turn over. You can't do things that you feel you need to do spontaneously. If you feel like your kids need to do something active, it's going to disturb the other people in the open space. You've got to do this at this time because other people are doing this at this time. You can't just be spontaneous and change and do something else. (HH, 1981)

Teachers were often eager to apply new methods but recognized that would require new resources if traditional standards were still to be met. A teacher in a working-class district:

The building was specifically built for open classroom. All the teachers who were assigned to this building when it was opened opted for working in open space. They all took courses in it and were all told they would have learning resource centers, aides, a lot of equipment. They did get a lot of equipment ordered by central office. They never got the aides. I think after two or three years of going on the open space concept, they just said, "It's not working. We never got aides. We can't do learning centers when we're the only adults in the classroom with kids zipping around us." So we all sat down and took a vote that we wanted to go back. (Z, 1981)

Affluent districts provided such resources and encouraged teachers' creativity in implementing new programs. A teacher in an affluent suburb:

People believed in innovation, and one of the major changes I would say that's really come across to me in my years in education is that in those years we really believed that innovations could make a difference, that a new way of organizing ourselves and a new way of organizing children and a new way of teaching them this and a new book or a new machine to help them do this—it was going to make a difference. And all those problems, reading problems and behavior problems, would be helped and cured. (BB, 1980)

The classroom door closed when teachers realized they were being asked to react to schoolwide policies, not create them.

What I think happens around here from what I've been able to gather asking people is that people come in and after a few years they just sort of pull in. I don't know how much I can keep growing in that atmosphere. It's too isolating. There is no flow. It's not that peole are nasty cause they're not. They're nice people, and they're friendly, but one of the problems is the downstairs which is K through 2 and one third grade never sees the upstairs teachers. The most we ever have might be 15 minutes once a week. The secrecy is another thing. You go up to the office and you ask questions. "It's okay. Don't worry about it." "Well, what about it?" "Don't worry. Just go back to your room. We'll let you know." My hunch is that the whole school system has the germs of it, and they filter down. So what do you do? You shut up and you run your own show. I just turn to my kids and that's great, that's fantastic, but for me that's not the whole picture. You miss out on the stuff that could be done with cooperation with other people at any level whether they're administrators or teachers. (B, 1980)

Again, teachers in more affluent areas were able to carve out greater structural changes, while those working in poorer sections had only the label of professional as reward.

In the past we have had $100,000 worth of summer work allotted for program planning and this is essential to carry on a cohesive program throughout the year. You can't do long range planning when you're teaching. . . . For instance, long range—if we're revising social studies in the elementary school, we'll have representation from each grade level. It might be that we are going to do an electricity unit in science and that it really needs individual work projects for kids to do. Teacher time will be given to plan out what those projects will be and to get the materials and the instructions, etc., etc. So, it's for really in-depth planning. Sometimes, it's for resolving issues that seem to be blocking us in some way. We've had a number of workshops on what is the relationship between the races—black and white kids, black and white teachers in the schools. What are the problems that come up? What are we doing to block solutions to these problems? What is the atmosphere? Quite intensive workshops. (BB, 1980)

A 29-year veteran of teaching equates the uncritical acceptance of changes in teaching to the pressure to appear as "professional" as the more affluent school systems, who readily yielded to the campaigns of textbook publishers. She speaks of her own community:

I really truly think that an awful lot of the fads came down to us through big businesses who wanted to sell books and sell kits and sell this and sell that and also from people who really, if you go right back to it, who wanted to make money on their ideas, like the publishers. You know if they could say everything in the old books was out of date and old hat and they could convince a few towns, the so-called leaders like Newton and Brookline and Lincoln, everyone followed suit. You didn't want to be considered old-fashioned. (V, 1979)

A teacher from a wealthy suburb concurs:

Administrators who are in curriculum positions, well some—I'm generalizing— are under pressure to produce and to show that curriculum and development is being done in the schools. They need something to run up the flagpole, to show the community that this is what we're doing. Some neat things might be happening next door with two teachers, but you can't sort of run this up. This is what we're doing for the whole school or the whole town, so it doesn't have as much value. So, they're under pressure to show the community that this is how we are handling curriculum development. The easiest way is to use commercial materials such as a beautiful SKIS kit, lovely, big expensive kits, and it's easier to do it like that. (OO, 1979)

The training of teachers as professionals, a term originally applied to private entrepreneurs who worked on a fee-per-client basis, also encouraged prospective teachers to see each pupil as a separate client whose needs and "problems" were to be intensively and expertly analyzed using the newer, more specialized and up-to-date methods.

I've told my student teacher that some of the things that she has done, she would never be able to do if she were the only teacher in the classroom. She's only been able to do it because I've taken part of the class or because I've been there to help her. They require her to do work with an individual child and do individual assessment of that child. She is required to work with small groups. She is required to do a special unit with a whole class. She is required to do something in all these specific fields—in art, in language arts, in math and science and so on. But she isn't required to do the meat and potatoes of classroom teaching. (Y, 1981)

The designation and training of teachers as professionals, a necessary lure for recruiting liberal arts graduates, thus served to confuse the label with the reality. Teachers were continually perplexed by the admonition to be "professional" while the area to which their expertise could be applied became narrower and narrower.

We're all professionals and our job is to educate children and it just seems to me that we ought not to exhaust any avenue that is available to us to get the quality education that the kids in our classroom deserve. I'll never understand whose idea it was, and maybe it wasn't anyone's idea, to set up a kind of adversary role between administrators and teachers, but it seems that every administrator has a vested interest in keeping his faculty at an arm's length, even the best administrators like to remind their faculty from time to time that they're the boss. And my attitude is that we're all in this together. So maybe you are the person in charge but do not let your in-chargeness stand in the way of your fairness so that the job that we're supposed to be doing can get done. That really bothers me. (W, 1981)

Salary increments were tied to professional development as incentives to teachers to go back to school and earn Master's degrees in remedial reading and new math. Teachers were persuaded to use their new expertise by serving on curriculum committees which would decide systemwide policies. Yet case after case confirms the frustration of those prepared for added responsibilities, but prevented from realizing them.

There were two people in my school, myself and a sixth grade teacher, who piloted social studies texts. We were not the only teachers who piloted the texts. I'm sure several teachers in other schools did too. The teachers who piloted the different programs never met together. Now they go and say, "We had this piloted and here is all the information and here is the text." But you wonder whether the text had already been chosen and this rigamarole had to be gone through. I just wonder how much of that goes on ahead of time. They have to cover themselves. You get kind of jaded. You think why bother. It was the same with the report card committee. You knew in the end it was going to be the way the people in charge really wanted it although I was on that committee and it lasted two years. They took an afternoon of your time once a week for two years. They pretty much shot down what we did and it got revamped right back to what it had been in the first place except for a little philosophy that was on the front of the card, and I noticed on the new batch of cards that we got that that isn't even there anymore. (R, 1981)

As teachers' own education increased, the disparity between their professional attainment and the inability to translate that new expertise to a strong position with the school increased teacher alienation. There developed an inverse ratio between the level of education demanded to retain the job and the level of education needed to work well at the job. A teacher with a Master's in reading:

What I'm required to teach is predetermined. The equipment I use is predetermined, all the books are predetermined and we just get a certain series. Being able to order an extra workbook or two probably is as much extra anything that you can do or one of the decisions you make on your own or if your books fall apart you can make a decision on your own that you can order those same books. (D, 1979)

The term "professional" was used to encourage teachers to participate in the running of the school, now larger and increasingly more difficult to manage. In fact, teachers were generally given only those tasks which reinforced the teachers' position but did not challenge it.

As Chair of the Faculty Senate, I'm having a lot of responsibility for writing, for getting the proposals prepared and everything. Partly, it's because the faculty senate is being specifically asked to participate in all of these meetings and stuff. Of course, you understand that the faculty senate has no authority whatsoever. I mean I can't initiate anything. I can't give out directives. We the faculty are advisory to the principal. Because she is pretty inefficient and pretty overwhelmed by everything and also isn't very enthusiastic about the job, so she's perfectly happy to let us handle a lot of these things because she feels as though, this is my own feeling, that she can't or she doesn't want to get into all that. (Y, 1981)

Minority teachers and parents found themselves caught between the desire to accept professional standards and the understanding that this perspective was often used to continue discriminatory treatment. A minority teacher speaks of her own ambivalence:

I think in terms of teachers we may have done ourselves once again a terrible disservice in that before 766 if there were children in your classroom that you had problems with, my God, you worked with them. You provided individualized instruction and you found the time to sit down and work with these kids who were not the middle-of-the-road average. And it was harder and it was frustrating, but you did make the time for it. Then came 766 and along came the opportunity for quote unquote specialists working with these kids, and all of a sudden there was a proliferation of kids with special needs. . . . Minority parents for a while thought that the system worked for their kids because of so many 766 referrals. On the one hand, they are somewhat resentful that their kid is being singled out, but then on the other hand, they said, "Well, at least someone has noticed my kid and he's getting this kind of help and that kind of special service." (W, 1981)

As the system becomes more oriented to the individual client model of traditional private sector professions, teachers are pressured to use set curricula originally created by fellow teachers to suit a particular classroom. Now seen as "professionally" produced, these curricula can be taken as expert advice for meeting another classroom's needs. Administrative attempts to collect their work and display the "best results" are resisted by teachers who otherwise willingly shared resources and ideas.

I think teachers resent that administrators who are supposed to be helping us come in and ask us to give them copies of things we've done in our room. They want to see all the stuff that we've done and share it with other teachers. I think generally teachers would want to share with other teachers and feel good about and do. I think next door or even in another school somebody is doing something, and they become very excited about it and that excitement is transmitted to another person, and I think they're very apt to try it. My own feeling when I get a pile of things that somebody else has made is that it's lovely and I may use some of it, but it's not mine. But their assumption is that now I'm going to become committed to it—the whole curriculum—that you will go and you will sit and you will listen and you'll learn and you'll go back to your classroom and you'll implement. (OO, 1980)

The sense of competition inherent in such appropriations robs the teacher of controlling the product of her labors. She may have created a game to help children learn, but it is now being used as a means of judging her among her fellow teachers. Others embrace such means, spurred by the knowledge that teacher evaluations often now include the number of parental letters of praise and requests for class placement.

We got a teacher from an involuntary transfer a couple of years ago. She's been there six years now. She does marvelous things. I've never seen such big candy bars. She gives the kids tons of big candy bars. Everything they do, they get a prize and a party at least three times a week with a big cake and soda and everything. She puts ads in the papers to thank the parents for their children. On Valentine's Day she puts ads in the paper thanking the parents for letting her have their precious possessions. I showed it to the teacher who teaches beside me. She died and said, "How can you compete with that?" (CC, 1979)

The acceptance of the term "professional" by the teacher includes the understanding that the more specifically trained one is in a particular field, the more highly regarded one's opinion should be. The desire by teachers themselves to be called professionals obscures the growing levels of control in schools by using one term to describe all teachers. The friction between specialists and classroom teachers is derived from the greater authority accorded the "true" professionals, the specialists, while the greater responsibility for each child is still charged to the classroom teacher.

> I hate to have them get up and walk out of the room. They can't leave without missing something, and it's something you have to make up or you have to sit down specially with them. The part that really annoys me is that in the very end of it all whether they do well or they don't do well on the achievement tests—and I know that they shouldn't put so much stock in achievement tests but I'm sure they do, they being the administrators and the parents too—in the end you're responsible for that child for his reading and his English and math and all that and yet if they haven't been there in front of you, how the heck can you really be responsible for them? How can you be held responsible for it? That does bother me. (V, 1981)

When the classroom teacher has less control over the educational program of an individual child than specialists or administrators do, while still being held responsible for the general well-being and instruction of the child, the teacher experiences demoralization, a sense of impotency, and resentment when progress is ascribed to specialists. The practical results are an unwillingness to follow the program dictated by the specialists and a resentment toward the individual child who represents a mark of the teacher's professional inadequacy. The issue of scheduling becomes the locus for the anger of classroom teachers toward specialists.

> One of the things that has bothered me about these constant interruptions and the pace of teaching today is that a lot of that is taken away from you—the creativeness, the feeling that I know what I'm doing, I'm going ahead and I'm going to do such and such, think of a new, fresh way to do it. There doesn't seem to be that kind of time anymore. This is not just a complaint of mine. I've heard it from other teachers. I know one teacher said the other day, "I want to teach science today and I don't care *who* comes and asks for my kids, they're not going to get them." I look back on the things that I used to do and I no longer have the time to do them anymore. The math program, for instance, took from 12:30 to 2:00 when they went to gym. They got back from gym at 2:30 and there goes the afternoon. I don't seem to paint anymore. I don't do music anymore. My science is hit or miss. I grabbed them when they came back from gym because we had the science teacher in to talk about vegetables. I grabbed them and I had bought garlic and onions and we jammed them in a pot. Literally. That's science. (L, 1980)

MODERN DAY "SOLUTIONS"

Today when teachers turn to educational literature for advice and explanations for dealing with intransigent problems, they discover meticulously documented studies of their own inabilities to cope with such concerns. Time and again studies and evaluations confirm that the individual teacher is not perfect.

> This year my principal's evaluation said, "Five kids looked up from their work

and looked out of the window within a five minute period. Now if you multiply five kids and five minutes in a period and you place it in an hour, this percentage are not doing their work and are not involved." (F, 1980)

As remedies, these studies urge the teacher to study herself, to ceaselessly examine her faults in order to better serve her pupils. They zero in on the teacher and demand that the teacher do the same if she and her pupils are to improve.

> I used to get terrible headaches. I cried all the time. I remember once the principal told me that I'd better start thinking about this class and what I was going to do about it. I was shocked that he could say this to me because that's all I *did* think about. (C, 1979)

> I usually have some behavior problems. Possibly I'm not structured enough, I don't know. My first principal used to say, "Isn't it funny? The difficult children always seem to be in your class." That's another thing—instead of the principal supporting us in our problems, they turn it right back and they say it's our fault. So that we're a little bit afraid to go to them for help because they say, "Well, you're doing something wrong." (A, 1979)

The teacher discriminates, is consciously or unconsciously racist or sexist, is more involved in the "here and now" than with global concerns. If she is indulgent to girls, she retards their growth and accustoms them to unquestioningly respect authority; if she is demanding of boys, she reinforces their importance and sense of rebelliousness.

If year after year she is unable to recreate the miraculous conversion of a depressed, poor AFDC child into a passionately curious, on-reading-level plugger, she is not fulfilling every child's potential. She is by definition failing—the child, the school, herself, and society's hopes for the future.

> "It's tempting to write that you had a bad class, or one could write that you had a very bad class and you handled it well." But he said, "Other people expect when you're looking for a job that you're a superteacher. They want to hire super-teachers who never have any problems and that's not realistic. If anybody writes that she had a terrible class but she came through with flying colors, somebody could say, 'If she's such a superteacher, her class shouldn't be terrible.'" (B, 1979)

The popular press increasingly reinforces these negative images of teachers. Two of the common stereotypes of veteran teachers described in the press and held by the public are: the lazy, superficial, tenured public servant, uninvolved in her work, getting away with as little as possible; and the embittered, rigidly inflexible battleax whose class resembles army bootcamp in atmosphere.

> I have some very mixed feelings about the role of order in classrooms. There's a teacher at this school who I look at with a mixture of awe and contempt. She has absolute iron control over her class—control that is so good and so consistent that she very rarely raises her voice, she very rarely keeps anyone after school, but you don't move from your seat until you raise your hand and get permission. On the other hand, I have her with 32 kids on one side of me, and on the other side there's another teacher with 32 kids. This other teacher is screaming. The kids are

screaming. And I started thinking, "Is it better to be a kid in this class where the teacher is always at the end of her rope—yelling, screaming; or is it better to be this other teachers' kids—not allowed to get out of their chairs, but doing marvelous art projects, doing a lot of positive stuff?" She can do it because she has absolute total control, and everybody does the same thing at the same time. (A, 1980)

Juxtaposed to these negative images is the ideal of the nurturant, understanding, patient teacher to whom every child is entitled.

I think you have to be pretty kind to them yourself. I'm a head-patter. I stroke and I pat. Somebody fell down and I'd say, "Are you all right, honey?" You have to be kind, firm, and fair. You give a child what he needs when he needs it.

If every teacher would only be perfect—responding fairly, efficiently, and effectively with infinite wisdom and tact to every child and exigency, we would have the perfect system. Teachers know that they are incapable of such persistent perfection. They often react in ways that increase their sense of isolation and reinforce their powerlessness in the institution. When confronted with stereotyped choices that deny or obscure the conflicting demands placed on teachers, teachers frequently lash out in angry denial while internalizing the negative message. They are told, and have come to believe, they have "burned out."

I had found that toward the middle of last year I was beginning to feel—dead. And I was beginning to feel frustrated and I was beginning to feel sort of like this was a drudgery. And I had never felt like that before—I mean, classroom teaching was my thing. I really loved it. Then this year coming into the situation and getting such a difficult class, I started off the year with a tremendous sense of frustration. I thought, "My God, what am I going to do with these kids?" I kept thinking, "I'm not really, really happy with what's happening in this class and I wonder how much of it is my own fault." (W, 1981)

BURNOUT—THE RESULT OF "PROFESSIONALISM"

What has been labelled "burnout" is, in fact, anger and frustration not easily or without fear of censure expressed in schools. The concept of "burnout" is the natural result of the ideology of professionalism which encourages teachers to see themselves as more powerful than they actually are and, therefore, more responsible alone to correct complex societal and institutional dilemmas. The coining of the term "burnout" at the same time that teachers are threatened with the loss of their jobs serves to direct the focus of each teacher's growing anger away from a critical analysis of schools as institutions to a preoccupation with her own failure. Curiously the preoccupation with describing teachers as burned out or deadwood has become a way of using these terms of deviance to represent the "true identity" of all teachers, by which every dedicated teacher will eventually be defined. It encompasses even those who haven't burned out because if burnout is the natural end to a dedicated teacher, those who have managed to survive are seen as callous, self-serving.

The two labels of "burnout" and "deadwood" further divide the teaching work force. Younger teachers or those still with other career options are told they have worked too hard and have therefore "burned out." Older teachers are told they aren't working hard enough and have become "deadwood." The fact that both are demoralized points to similar concerns, but the labels obscure the commonalities.

Those people who are visibly upset, who are willing to go to battle for a child, still believe in the possibility of change within their work situation and in the value of education as a tool for achieving equal opportunity. They continue to believe in the system's ability to respond to logical, reasonable, and justified criticism.

> They treat you at central office as though you don't know anything. You go down and you say, "I'd like to discuss the 766 process because I don't understand it quite and I don't think the kids are getting serviced." People give you all this runaround, rigamarole, and it becomes so complicated that you want to say, "Okay, you do it." But I'm not listening to that anymore. I've struggled through a lot my first four years and, hell, now I'm a damn good teacher and I know what my kids need. What happens is that then they become kind of frightened of you, as the individual who is going after them and saying, "Wait a minute, you're responsible for this." It makes me angry because it's taking so much time, and I shouldn't have to do the pushing. (G, 1980)

As long as influential segments of the community actively support efforts to improve the public school, the teacher feels some degree of comfort with her position of change-maker. If these groups no longer see teaching as politically correct, if they can no longer pressure the federal government or the school system for funds, or if they now see the role of the teacher as a glamorless one for women, the teacher is left extremely vulnerable. When and if these support groups withdraw, the teacher's attempts at change become more difficult, begin to appear useless, if not destructive to her own job security.

> They [the school administration] go out of their way to sabotage their own affirmative action program.... If they intend in good faith to make this thing work, then they have to find ways to do it so it's not going to make people feel like the Bakkes. You don't want that kind of feeling, and it exists.... People began to look to see who is disappearing and who's staying and I heard comments passed like, "Well, you don't have anything to worry about. You can go anyplace you want." Actually, I was thinking I probably do have something to worry about, plenty. Because if they do intend to let people go to make room for minorities, that means that all minority teachers in the system are going to have a pretty hard way, too, 'cause it's going to create a lot of feelings, hard feelings, and a lot of rancor that doesn't necessarily have to be there if it's done in a fair and equitable way. (W, 1981)

The teacher cannot help noticing the areas she is not able to change, the emotions in her and her pupils she has difficulty controlling.

> I've been thinking a lot about my own survival, how I can get through the year in a way that helps me keep my sanity and helps the kids learn and I think my priorities deal with (1) my sanity, because without it there's nothing else; (2) the kids' learning; (3) the kids' heads and social change comes after all those things

and I don't know when I'm going to get there. I would definitely like to leave my mark, but given my personality structure, it's hard. (A, 1980)

The disturbing fact is that admitting her mistakes does not prevent her from continuing to make them. The school provides no constructive place for teachers' legitimate anger to be channeled. The anger turns inward or is directed at her fellow teachers who represent what she is fearful of becoming and feels helpless to prevent.

I guess what I'm saying is that sometimes I just feel aggravated by picky little things. I just feel like I'm a nag, not directly to the people maybe but just thinking, "That bugs me and that bugged me and that bugged me," which is not a healthy kind of way. The avenues for communication are just so nonexistent or so skewed, it's really hard to get above that. (J, 1981)

I think I tend to get angrier inside than I otherwise would because you really can't talk about things. They throw them right back at you. "Well, that's the way it's always been. . ." In this place there is no outlet for anger and it's really been hard to know what to do with it. The whole business of having to psych things out, do I go to the office? Why can't this be straight? That doesn't bring out the best in me. I don't like the feelings I have when I'm acting that way. (B, 1980)

The teacher can either accept the label of burnout and leave, or she can retreat even further emotionally and physically. Experts on burnout and teacher effectiveness, by zeroing in on the individual teacher and her classroom to explain education's increasingly documented failures, have chosen to scrutinize the most vulnerable member of the school system's hierarchy—the classroom teacher, 87 percent of whom are women on the elementary school level. (N.E.A., 1978). Those teachers are the people least critical of the investigators' findings because they confirm the teacher's own lack of self-esteem. Documentation of teachers' failures without linking individual problems to institutional roadblocks does not spur the teacher to rededicate herself to the profession. She has now become convinced of her own worthlessness and is sure she will simply continue to fail.

The funny thing is that I'm a good teacher and a good teacher can teach in almost intolerable situations. . . . I see so many not bad teachers, just people who should not be teaching and it's important to me that if I thought I wasn't doing a good job at it, I wasn't helping the kids, I would get out of it right away. It's beginning to feel that way. I guess the term is burned out. The ideas, the spontaneity wasn't coming. I wasn't feeling fresh or excited when I was coming into the classroom. (W, 1981)

I assimilated into my surroundings. I'm a reasonably good mimic and I also needed models of success since I was getting poor feedback and I was isolated my first year, and I needed to succeed very badly. So that's what I did—I studied models of success and they were authoritarian, and I learned. . . I recognized that I was somebody that I didn't want to be, and that—it just brought home to me a personal dissatisfaction that I hadn't stuck to my ideas, that I had given them up. (C, 1979)

Once the teacher is convinced that she has burned out, she has admitted that she has used up her inner resources, that she is personally deficient, and that she must leave the occupation for her own good and that of her pupils.

Parents, many of whom have experienced bitter frustration and conflicts with individual teachers, accept the definitions of burnout and deadwood as labels easily affixed to troublesome teachers, much as teachers label parents as deficient or school phobic to explain a child's lack of progress or unruly behavior. Neither side is encouraged to look at the parallels between their situations and the institutional barriers that create and sustain these conflicts.

> I always used to say, "As a teacher I hate parents and as a parent I hate teachers." I didn't want to go up to school if my kids were having problems. I think some teachers make you feel like an intruder and they probably are threatened by parents being around. At the end of the day you get very business-like and either the youngster reads or he doesn't, and when you say it to a parent that way, it doesn't always come across too well, you know, (D, 1980)

> Today this mother came in. In the course of talking with her, I said, "You know, I'm the teacher who called you the first day your son was here" because I wanted to find out if he was in Title I reading or any of these special programs. She said, "Oh, yes. I remember." After school the principal comes up to me and says, "You know, I need to know whenever you make a telephone call to a parent." I just looked at him and took a deep breath. I said, "Any phone call?" And he said, "Yes, just in case something comes up, so I'll know what's coming out of this school." I swallowed what he said and I walked away. I wanted to tell somebody but I realized that all those people had probably been living under the same thing forever. I mean, this is their idea of the role of the principal, which is to control. (A, 1980)

The teacher begins to devalue and doubt the existence of those qualities in herself which were her reasons for entering teaching. She is not sure they ever existed in her co-workers.

> He said, "Look around this room. Those over there and those over there are typical . . . public school teachers." He was stereotyping these people in their 30's and 40's but not 30's new but 30's old style. They tended to be overdressed, over weight lumps. . . . They all looked rather vacant. . . . I looked around and I saw some of these people and heard some of the questions they were asking. I wouldn't have anything to talk with those people about and I know that's important to me, that kind of sharing. (B, 1979)

The teacher's own past accomplishments appear inconsequential.

> I walked into a supermarket the other day and the boy who was checking out my groceries said, "Hello, Mrs. _____!" with such love. They recognize me. And he's 18 years old, and they remember me. A lot of the kids that I meet years later have wonderful memories. . . . So I wonder, is it just—I feel that I give them a good start. I give them a belief in themselves. . . I make them think they can do it rather than my doing it for them. And I try to build up their self-image. I think I

do it all right, and then all of a sudden, these people come in and say, "You're no good." So it's hard, you know, it's hard. So now I'm thinking already, you know, I could retire in about 2½ years, maybe I'll retire. I used to think I wouldn't want to retire so soon and I enjoyed my job. . . . This fall I thought to myself, "Maybe I'm really not such a good teacher, you know. Maybe I'm really not that good. Maybe I should never have gone into teaching." (H, 1980)

What continually strikes us as significant in the use of the term "burnout" to describe teacher discontent is the implicit assumption that teachers are responsible for their own departures and that it is an act of benevolence on the part of school systems to let them go at the very time that Reduction in Force allows these teachers no choice in their departure from teaching. For those teachers who are being laid off, "burnout" encourages a teacher to feel grateful for losing her paycheck rather than directing her anger in a fight for an equitable system of RIF for all teachers and a healthier and more productive work environment for those who remain.

By concentrating criticism for classroom failures on individual performance, *all* teachers, including "superteachers," become timorous. They, too, refrain from taking risks.

My school is closing. There's a lot of tension over that. Plus the fact that they're getting rid of teachers now. Everything becomes magnified, everything is much more frightening, anything the child does is much more frightening, because somebody could come into your classroom at any moment and see that and that would be the reason—that would be seen as your evaluation. It distorts your relationship with children, with your peers. (G, 1981)

The self-hate and self-doubt that follow are the roots of an anxiety that is projected out as hating the people you are afraid of becoming.

I started looking at the other teachers I was teaching with and seeing myself retrenching, not taking the risks, the educational risks that I used to take. I used to do all kinds of interesting things with my students, go places with them, get involved with all kinds of projects, build things but every once in a while someone would notice that the classroom wasn't as neat as it should be or if that wasn't a factor with one principal then something else would be and since everything is cumulative and anything can be pointed to to get rid of you now, you start to retrench and you start to become conservative. You feel a lack of growth and you look around. Everyone has a stereotype of those 30 year veterans and I found myself becoming exactly the same way and it really frightened me. (G, 1981)

The current debate over seniority versus merit in deciding layoffs rests on this assumption—that schools as institutions cannot and will not revitalize a teacher of several years' service. It is all too easily accepted by policymakers, as well as teachers, that the institutions will deaden those who work in them if they do not receive new infusions of energy—"new blood"—from some outside source. Further, the debate over seniority versus merit is never discussed within the context of teaching as an occupation requiring less and less critical thinking, originality, and creativity. As more and more administrative decisions are made for the teacher by the school or the school system, the teacher's role is returned to that of dispenser of various prepackaged curriculum systems. "Merit" in such situations can only mean adherence to pre-established dicta.

> A friend of mine went to teach in ———. She had taught with me for five years. She's a wonderful teacher, super teacher, very conscientious and very organized. She lasted three months there. It was a disaster. For one thing, the curriculum was deadly. "Here is a book and teach it. You should be on page 200 by such and such a date." It has nothing to do with your kids and nothing to do with whatever ideas you might want to bring in. Just do it and be on that page. That was their approach. Deadly. Secondly, she had a classroom with nine kids with hyperactivity. Very disruptive. No support from the principal, a sort of wishy-washy, incompetent man. She said it was a travesty of learning. Here she had probably 18 kids who to one degree or another were interested in learning, some very interested, and nine kids turned that class into total chaos. And she is no pushover as far as discipline goes. She is a very competent teacher. Well, she was getting an ulcer. She came to school nauseated every day and was throwing up before she left the house because it was such an uncontrolled situation. There was no one to turn to, no one. To her amazement, she ended up writing a letter of resignation, and she left after Thanksgiving. She felt really sick about it, but knew that her mental health would not take it. It was really sad because she was a super teacher. (BB, 1979)

THE NEED FOR AN INSTITUTIONAL APPROACH

The books and magazine articles of today, unlike those in the 60's, now concentrate on shoring up the coping skills of isolated teachers. These writings consist of short articles addressed to the teacher as an individual citing specific ideas he or she can take to cope with the problems of teaching. Issues are discussed in terms of the individuals involved. Conflict is described in terms of the conflict between teacher and the parent, colleague, custodian, or secretary. The school environment is thus fragmented and the the solutions suggested are often contradictory. The suggestions for improvement do not take into account how change in one sphere may affect relationships in another sphere. Teachers are never urged to look beyond the classroom, to search for similarities and differences between themselves and others, either within the structure of schools or in other institutions of society. Teachers who one by one enter the profession remain largely unaware of the institutional nature of school systems and are therefore ill-prepared to handle the conflicts that arise from the nature of that institutional structure. The teacher's position within the school system as a whole is not seen as a "professional" concern and the institutional conflicts inherent in the role of teacher remain unchallenged.

We have shown that the image of the "all-powerful schoolmarm" is a myth. It is created by a system which has isolated individual teachers, granting each teacher autonomy to make and carry out the difficult decisions herself while the real agenda is determined outside the classroom.

> You have a great deal of autonomy about what goes on in your classroom within those four walls, but at the same time you have to be sure that it looks a certain way, that it appears to be the way that it's supposed to be on the outside. In other

words, you can't do anything that is too apparently outré without bumping up against things. So the fact that we quote unquote control 25 or so little people is a very small compensation for not feeling as though we can control the kind of books we can order, have the kinds of programs we want, the kind of feeling of friendliness throughout the school. Each classroom seems to be the kids' turf and there's a lot of competitiveness and aggressiveness about that. All those things that a teacher feels bad about and with no control over. (Y, 1981)

Therefore, we are not arguing that each teacher would wish or would benefit from a reassertion of her role as the individual arbiter of children's lives within an isolated classroom. However, without understanding how the structure of the school creates these tensions, a teacher may acquiesce to the demands to work ever harder while growing increasingly frustrated with her own efforts and those of her fellow teachers. She may become competitive with other teachers in lobbying her principal for favored pupils, preference in assignments, or more supplies. She may voluntarily seek autonomy and shut her door in the hopes that a rise in reading scores will be directly attributable to her abilities.

All of these individual attempts to ameliorate teachers' sense of frustration may well contribute to its increase. Solutions encouraging individual negotiation for control of greatly circumscribed, if not clearly articulated, boundaries neglect the area teachers consistently noted as helpful to their particular teaching situation. Many teachers reported that their most reliable source for new techniques and strategies, as well as feedback for confirmation of their own solutions, are the discussions they hold with other teachers during breaktime, between speakers at an in-service workshop, at crosstown meetings with teachers of the same grade level, or by a frank request for help in the teachers' room.

Our interviews revealed that these "hands on" discussions, while alleviating specific problem areas, were not the only type of discussions necessary to break the isolation and accompanying loss of self-esteem reported by many of them. Teachers frequently expressed a general sense of efficacy in their classrooms, amply documented by anecdotes and test score verification, that was lacking or allowed to go unnoticed in the area beyond the classroom. In fact, for many teachers, the more grounded and sure they were in classroom issues, the less they were assumed to contribute to or be valued by life outside the classroom.

It was in their attempt to extend the discussion into the areas outside the classroom walls that teachers experienced the greatest resistance—whether this referred to community meetings with parents, whole-school discussions of school climate, or attempts to link one teacher's issues with another's. Pressure from outside support groups, and federal and state programs mandating teacher involvement, afforded the few possibilities for leverage teachers experienced in confronting systemwide reform.

The school district was newly Federally redeveloped so there have been a lot of changes. . . . The point is that we really didn't know how to solve these problems. Teacher Corps became a vehicle to help us solve these problems by showing us unity as parents and teachers. The parent coordinator worked very hard to get good relationships between the parents and the teacher and we got to know each other as people and friends and not just in that relationship where it is so stand-offish. "Don't you attack my child or I'm going to attack you" bit. . . We went from talking to taking action. Parents and teachers began working with each other, learning how to go about problem solving, gathering the correct statistics and presenting them in a correct manner, not just going up to City Hall and yelling and screaming. (D, 1980)

These opportunities were not frequent and they were not encouraged. Involvement in communitywide efforts and programs to increase staff morale were necessary to engage both staff and parents in federal programs. Once these programs withdrew or became part of the general administrative structure, the roles of teacher and parent were relegated to carrying out the decision mandated by the school hierarchy.

At the early release days when we had Teacher Corps we got to stay in our own building and work out issues. We had much more communication. We could stay in our building and talk over programs. You'd know an issue was coming up and it would be decided. Now that Teacher Corps is gone, all our early release days are taken up with superintendent's meetings. (D, 1980)

Communication among teachers and parents was modified from establishing a consensus of concerns in communitywide meetings to defining schoolwide tensions as problems of specific individuals to be handled in isolation. The mass movements of the 60's that had propelled many teachers and parents to take a more activist stance in education were consistently translated by administrative design to programs in which individuals were pitted against each other—parent vs. parent, teacher vs. teacher, parent vs. teacher—for the right to participate in and control the few reforms allowed.
Our schools will not be served by counselling teachers to minimize or block out their frustrations. Nor will our schools be improved by a mass exodus of teachers, whether they leave as a result of reduction in force, a purging of the "deadwood," or their own personal considerations, and their replacement by a new batch of teachers who will inevitably face the same problems when they too have "burned out" or become desensitized.

What's so easy to fall into is to say, "Oh, the primary team has been frustrating because of that personality or that style or whatever when I also at the same time have to sort of believe that there are certain things that at least could be tried to draw some of it out, to draw those people out. I really feel in a lot of ways the staff is flat and yet I feel like there are dynamic natures sleeping there just waiting to be tapped. (J, 1979)

Teachers sense that being a good "professional"—facing the issues alone—frequently ends in bitter self-recrimination or alienation from teachers, parents, and students. The crisis of declining enrollments and of reductions in force can be seen as a demoralizing period for teachers but also as an invigorating one, for it uncovers a latent anger and its resultant energy. It makes obvious the contradictions present for teachers that have been smoothed over in preceding eras of increased enrollments and flowing federal funds.

I think there is a responsibility for every teacher to be involved as greatly as they can in matters other than what's in the classroom. Very often when you are in the classroom with kids you do get sort of jaded and isolated from the mainstream of the world but if you at the same time are simultaneously working outside the class-room, still dealing with education but maybe talking about it in a different light or working from the standpoint of teacher advocacy, you continue to grow and you don't get so stultified like you would if you just closed your classroom door every day and spent 25 years in the classroom. (W, 1981)

Probably for the first time in my school we have not talked specifically about the kids and subject matter and school problems. We've been talking about political things and how it affects our personal life, too. I think it's taught me a lesson that you cannot hide your head in the sand. I'm not just fighting for me either. Yeah, I'm fighting for my job, but I'm fighting for the kids, too. I think it's going to help my awareness of things and help me maybe stick through it a little bit. That I'm not alone in this and I've got other people to talk with and see how it is going to affect other people. I think it has already made me mentally and also just in action make more of a commitment to my work. (Z, 1981)

Teachers must now begin to turn the investigation of schools away from scapegoating individual teachers, students, parents, and administrators toward a sys-temwide approach. Teachers must recognize how the structure of schools controls their work and deeply affects their relationships with their fellow teachers, their stu-dents, and their students' families. Teachers must feel free to express these insights and publicly voice their concerns. Only with this knowledge can they grow into wisdom and help others to grow.

REFERENCES

Fitzgerald, J. "From script to screen." *Boston Globe*, August 25, 1980, 25.

Freedman, S. Personal journal. January 29, 1979.

Lerner, G. "The lady and the mill girl: Changes in the status of women in the age of Jackson, 1800–1840," *A heritage of her own*. New York: Simon and Schuster, 1979, 182–196.

Lortie, D. C. *Schoolteacher, a sociological survey*. Chicago: University of Chicago, 1975.

McCutcheon, G. "How do elementary school teachers plan?" *The Elementary School Journal*, September, 1980, *8*, 4–23.

National Education Association. *Estimates of school statistics*. Washington, D.C.: National Education Association, 1978.

Oakley, A. *Woman's work, the housewife, past and present*. New York: Vintage Books, 1974.

Strober, M. H., and Tyack, D. *Why do women teach and men manage? Signs*, 5 (3), Spring 1980.

CHAPTER 12

The Role of the Teacher in School Change

Annette B. Weinshank, Emily S. Trumbull, and Patrick L. Daly

INTRODUCTION

I'm a person who enjoys teaching. Each summer I attend workshops, I read, I think. I come up with new ideas to help my students. It doesn't take long after each school year begins, though, before my enthusiasm starts to diminish. For example, last year declining enrollment in our district resulted in personnel changes within my team. This may sound minor but my plan for last year was to integrate social studies, science, and English. Because of the decline in enrollment, though, my new teammate was someone who was involuntarily transferred from a secondary school where she had taught social studies and science. She had no interest in integrating English with her speciality. That effectively ended one carefully planned program.

I had also looked forward to devoting time to creative writing. I planned at least a half hour a day of peer evaluated writing, the best of which would be reproduced for all the students in the school. My first shock when school began was learning that innovative or not I, like every other teacher in my school, was going to be limited to one pack of ditto paper and lined composition paper per week. Next I realized that mandated state and federal programs had drastically changed the composition of my class: two blind children, one deaf child, and an emotionally impaired child had been mainstreamed into my class. I found that it now took longer to get lessons started because I had to keep the special needs of these students in mind. The methods that I had originally devised for teaching how to edit and evaluate took so much longer than planned that the attention and interest of the class as a whole waned. Added to this, when we did get going, students were continually being pulled out for state and federally mandated tutorial programs. When they would return I had to catch them up, which diverted the attention of those who had finally begun to write.

Two years ago when I reported back to school in September, I found out that there would no longer be an art teacher in our building. Instead we had a consultant who we could talk to once a month. Last year we had been back to school just a few days when we were informed that the district could no longer supply our half-hour-per-week music teacher. Instead, there would be large assemblies

The authors acknowledge with gratitude the valuable comments of Sharon Feiman Nemser.

four times a year in which the children would sing or be introduced to an instrument. Since state law requires weekly music and art instructions, I found myself abandoning many of my innovations and using the time for planning my weekly art and music lessons.

This summer I am again attending workshops but in all honesty, I only go to those for which I will be paid. The reason in obvious: I don't know if anything I'm working on will survive in September. At least I've done something for my family with the money I'll get. (Interview with elementary teacher)

Schools are changing and will continue to do so. Teachers perforce are changing with them. This career teacher's account traces a steady erosion of energy, emotional investment, and curricular coherence in the face of mutually antagonistic requirements imposed by mandated state and federal programs designed to promote educational equity on the one hand and budgetary constraints and retrenchment on the other. These opposing political and fiscal forces operate beyond any individual teacher's control and adversely effect even the most conscientious attempts at constructively managing change.

Will teachers come to play an acknowledged central role in mediating change or will their autonomy be increasingly constrained and their professional status increasingly diminished? The possibilities for both outcomes exist. The authors contend that in the current climate of retrenchment it is imperative that policymakers accord the teacher a central place in the process of change lest we find that our profession attracts only the passive, the unimaginative, and the unlettered which simultaneously depleting the vitality and commitment of the best practitioners now serving.

The teacher's role in successfully managing school change is generally acknowledged to be central. However, the acknowledgement obscures much that currently interferes with realizing this role. Selected literature dealing with planned change is helpful in generally characterizing some of the conditions that support teachers' successfully accommodating change: time for planning, collegial involvement, expanded professional contacts, and continuing administrative support. But this literature does not lay bare troublesome modal conditions which are debilitating the profession. These include allienation that increases with length of service, professional isolation, inadequate training, and unsatisfactory reward systems, all of which adversely effect the role of the teacher in successfully managing school change. Neither does the literature make explicit how teachers are to deal with the complexities of implementing change given the problematic conditions of teaching and classroom life.

In the first section of this chapter, descriptions of conditions that support the teacher's role in school change are drawn from the literature on planned change and from the personal testimony of teachers. The next section details the modal conditions of the teaching profession that act as obstacles to enhancing the teacher's role in school change. In the third section, the effects on teachers of the collision between the requirements of mandated programs and the constraints of modal conditions are presented. The final section invites policymakers to consider what might be involved in changing problematic modal conditions. Failure to address this overriding professional issue will ensure that egregious errors in policy relating to the classroom will continue to be made.

CONDITIONS THAT SUPPORT THE TEACHER'S ROLE IN SCHOOL CHANGE

Evaluations of the impact of the Elementary and Secondary Education Act (ESEA), which controls more than 90 percent of the federal aid that flows to school districts (Carter, 1978), have provided important insights into the centrality of the teacher's role in determining the fate of planned change.

The Rand Corporation (Berman and McLaughlin, 1975; Berman and McLaughlin, 1978) studied federally sponsored techniques, multi-age grouping in elementary schools, staff development and training, and curriculum projects in reading, math, environmental studies, etc. The projects varied in setting and scope. Some were ambitious (open education, schools without walls), others straightforward (addition of material to the standard curriculum). Some spanned all schools in a district, others focused on one grade in one school.

The investigators concluded that the net return on the federal government's investment was: adoption (initiation) of many innovations, successful implementation of few, and long-run continuation of still fewer. Projects could be initiated in response to local problems or because of opportunism (the money was there). Opportunistically initiated projects tended to undergo symbolic or pro forma implementation. Goals were reportedly met, but there were no concomitant changes in teacher behavior. In contrast, successful implementation, though not easily come by, resulted after a process of mutual adaptation in which both project and setting were altered. Teachers changed as they, and only they, worked to modify the project's design to suit their particular school or classroom. Conditions that promoted teacher change and feelings of efficacy were (1) staff training, (2) frequent and regular meetings, (3) local materials development, (4) strong principal support, and (5) establishing of a critical mass of project participants so the involved teachers did not seem deviant.

Another series of studies concluded that implementing complex innovations (such as team teaching) takes several years and that administrators who ignore this endanger the innovative thrust (Hall and Rutherford, 1975; Hall and Loucks, 1976; Hall, Wallace, and Dossett, 1973; Hall, 1975). Those contemplating innovation (e.g., teaming, individualized instruction, changed subject matter curriculum, etc.) need to take into account the likelihood that significant increases in feelings of insecurity will have to be dealt with over a span of time before a teacher can move forward from routine use to more sophisticated implementation of an innovation. Evaluation data collected at the end of the first year of implementation usually show no significant differences between users and nonusers of an innovation precisely because most users would at best be coping with the mechanics of the innovation and outcomes would likely be worse, at least initially, than they would have been if the innovation had not been implemented at all. Broadly speaking, the above authors argue that change is a process whose key elements are collegiality, principal support, accessibility of materials, and continual consultation and collaboration with co-workers.

All of these key elements can be seen in the following two vignettes. The first is an account of a unique ongoing experiment in educational change at Edsel Ford High School in Dearborn, Michigan. The story is told by one of the teachers who joined the staff of Edsel Ford in the early years of the experiment and who is still teaching there today. The second vignette is also by a career teacher who has been a catalyst for change in her school and her district for many years. Together the vignettess show that change on either a broad or more restricted scale requires a set of common conditions to increase the likelihood of successful implementation.

In the mid 1950's Dearborn, Michigan was a growing community with a burgeoning school age population and in need of a new high school. The Dearborn Superintendent of Schools at that time approached the Ford Foundation for a grant to release a number of teachers and administrators from all regular duties so that they could devote full time to finding answers to such questions as: What kind of school does the community want? What kind of education do students need? What should be taught and why? How shall it be taught? The grant totalling approximately $250,000 was awarded and 24 teachers and three administrators were chosen as a planning group for the new Edsel Fort High School. The teachers spent January to June, 1953, on the campus of the University of Chicago examining educational trends and educational practices in Dearborn, and developing a rationale for curriculum development. One of the most important results of the work at Chicago was the development of a process for continuous revision and refinement of the program that was finally adopted. During the early part of the Chicago period, team visits were made to 60 of the nation's leading high schools. Upon completion of the work in Chicago, the group returned to Dearborn where meetings were held daily over the next 18 months. During this time teachers were assigned only afternoon classes. High teacher morale and enthusiasm was generated by giving teachers ample resources and time to examine some basic questions regarding education.

There are three major features of Edsel Ford's program that continue to be unique today even after the passage of 25 years and the inevitable adjustments and refinements that have been made to adapt to changing conditions. First, English Humanities was and is part of the curriculum that differs in significant ways from the traditional English program in American high schools. *All* students take English Humanities at Edsel Ford. The typical student has three periods of English per week, one period of art and one period of music. In this integrated program of English, art and music the emphasis is on both communication and appreciation. In the English classes, in addition to the study of literature, there has been unusually strong emphasis on writing. It has become quite common for graduates to do very well on English advanced placement examinations in college and to express gratitude for the writing skills that they developed at Edsel Ford. The guidance program is a second unique feature of Edsel Ford. Each class (freshman, sophomore, junior) is organized into classes of approximately 25–30 students for group guidance. These classes meet on a regular basis of two days one week and three days the following week. The human relations classes are taught by the student's counselor. To those familiar with traditional guidance programs in American high schools the most striking departure from tradition is that guidance counselors teach classes on a regularly scheduled basis on topics such as growth and development of personality, marriage and family life, career guidance, reading improvement and other topics related to the field of guidance and counseling. As a result of the way that the Human Relations program is organized, a student will usually see his counselor two or three times a week rather than once or twice a semester, a not uncommon situation in large high schools where many counselors have such large students loads that they are only able to see students when an emergency arises, or when the student is called in to plan his next semester's schedule.

Finally, the Social Studies Department at Edsel Ford is a good example of a department that pioneered a curriculum development that was a major departure from tradition in 1955 but which has become a regular feature in the curriculum of many high schools and junior high schools in the past 25 years. Edsel Ford's Social Studies Department developed an introductory class that represented different degrees of exposure to political, social and economic change. By studying these smaller, less complex societies than our own it was hoped that students might gain greater understanding of how societies are organized and the impact that cultural change can bring about within the institutions created by a society. The principles learned within this introductory course were to be used in succeeding semesters when studying the infinitely more complex and rapidly changing American society. The introductory course was to have an anthropological emphasis but was to rely heavily upon a broad fields approach and utilize concepts drawn from all the other social science disciplines. At the time that the program was first taught, and for quite a few years thereafter, all materials had to be created by the staff, because appropriate commercial materials did not exist. In the past 25 years it has been interesting to watch many high schools adopt introductory social studies classes similar to Edsel Ford's and to note the steady growth in the number, variety and quality of commercially produced materials which may be used in such courses.

Last year we had a 25th anniversary celebration. Former Edsel Ford teachers came from all over the country to share in the pleasure and satisfaction of having been part of such an enduring venture.

What enabled such a major departure from traditional educational practice to be sustained over a 25-year period? First, according to the teacher interviewed, the participating faculty believed strongly in the worth of what they were doing and were articulate in its defense. Second, those who were recruited to work on the project had every expectation that a tangible product, namely a new curriculum, would result from their labors and that they would benefit directly from this outcome. Third, resources were available that helped to provide the time and materials that were needed to produce change. Fourth, the administration and school board of the district made a clear and firm commitment of long-range support to those engaged in promoting the change.

The career elementary teacher who provided the second vignette derived from her own experience the elements necessary to facilitate change.

I feel quite comfortable about my ability to effect change in my elementary building. It does take a certain amount of skill however. The climate for innovation has to be just right. It must be set very carefully. The principal is a key variable. Therefore, make sure feedback received about you from the community and others is positive. Satisfy parents. Handle your own problems. When the secretary says the fourth Friday count is due, hand it in. Never end up on a list of those who have not done their paper work. If the custodian asks that all chairs be put up on desks at the end of the day, get them up. No negative reports about *you*. Mix with your staff. Try to do or say something nice to each person at least every three months. This is much easier, of course, if you are in a smaller building. At staff meetings don't disagree when the issue isn't the battle you really want to fight. Be supportive when you recognize that something is important to your co-worker. Never present a new idea fifteen minutes from the end of a meeting or be the one that asks the question that makes the meeting last fifteen minutes longer. With the groundwork laid you're just about ready to come up with that innovation you know will make a difference.

Ideas for change have to come from different people, not the same person all of the time. That gets wearisome very quickly. So, first, mention your concerns quietly to one or two staff members who probably will agree with you. Don't dwell on it. Mention it again next week and maybe the following one also. Do a mental sociogram concerning the people in your building. You are not looking just for a leader. The right person to carry your innovation has to relate well with the principal and at least some of the upper level administrators. That person must also not have been involved in programs that resulted in regular contacts with Central Administration in the last two years. New faces are refreshing! When that person comes to mind, you present your concern and solution in a dynamic fashion. If you see that proper spark of enthusiasm, leave quickly on some pretense and come back to it a few days later. You don't want to overwhelm people. The next time offer to write all the proposals and gather needed information. Have many good reasons why it will make the existing program better, make management easier, and enhance the reputation of the school. You also think there might be some money available to get paid for doing some of the organizing during the summer. You know some people who would be happy to help. Have them talk to friends among the staff and join with you at some common time. You'll supply the coffee and doughnuts. Perhaps they would like to mention the idea to the building principal. State that you would be glad to accompany them or jot down some pertinent notes beforehand. If they accept your invitation you are on your way. Be prepared, however, for many hours of work. Not just then but for the next few *years*! The hardest part is keeping a good thing going. Some one has to encourage the project at all times. Enthusiasm dwindles easily as pressures mount. Thus, it needs to be rekindled often. Design evaluations that don't take a lot of time to fill out by the teacher. Necessary revisions will become apparent. Your help must be subtle and materials should be gathered and placed in an easily accessible spot. Over the next few years you will have to keep reminding yourself, and that person who is hopefully still aiding you, that it really is all worth it. Allow yourself only one other major innovation during that time period or you will loose steam. If the project is going well never gloat or remind anyone that you were the initiator. Compliment anyone and everyone else. With luck and a lot of hard work the project may still be going in some fashion in five years.

These teachers are in agreement about the conditions which enhance the possibility that proposed changes will be successfully managed. Both emphasized the need for (1) having time to plan, implement, and evaluate new projects; (2) promoting collegial involvement and cooperation; (3) establishing ongoing contact with professionals outside the immediate school settings; and (4) securing continuing administrator support for the goals of the project.

While the literature and the vignettes cited share common views about the institutional conditions necessary to support change, it is unfortunately the case that actual conditions are problematic; they do not facilitate but rather tend to thwart teachers' attempts to change.

OBSTACLES TO ENHANCING THE TEACHER'S ROLE IN SCHOOL CHANGE

Jackson (1968), Sarason (1971), and Lortie (1975) provide some of the most perceptive and salient observations on what life is like "for the modal teacher in the modal classroom" (Sarason, p. 172).

> The teacher does much the same thing on each of the 180 plus days of the school year with much the same children and in exactly the same classroom. From the rituals associated with the beginning of the school day to those associated with the end, it is very much like every other day.... Without exception those who have been teaching for five or more years admitted that they no longer experienced their work with the enthusiasm, excitement, sense of mission, and challenge that they once did. (Sarason, p. 163)

The Rand study, too, found that length of teaching career was negatively correlated with successful implementation of changes; that teachers with many years on the job were less likely to change their own practice or to continue using project methods after the end of federal funding (Berman and McLaughlin, 1978).

More recently, the results of a study on the relationship of teacher alienation to workplace characteristics and to stage of career (Vavrus, 1979) strongly suggested that the longer teachers stayed in the profession the more alienated and less involved they were with their work, suggesting that teaching appears to become an increasingly frustrating occupation.

What is it about the nature of the profession that creates these attitudes?

First, teaching can be characterized as "front-loaded." A beginning teacher knows exactly what will be earned after long service and sees that such service brings limited reward. "Earnings are 'front-loaded' in the sense that one begins at a high level relative to one's ultimate earning potential" (Lortie, p. 84). The lack of continued progress constitutes one chief difficulty in establishing teaching as a professional career. Ambitious classroom teachers cannot look forward to an increase in responsibility and influence without somehow leaving the classroom (Cohen, 1973).

Second, there is less opportunity for movement upward. In contrast to the larger packages of money, prestige, and power usually found in other careers, the typical career line of the classroom teacher is a gentle incline rather than a steep ascent. The status of the young tenured teacher is not appreciably different from that of the highly experienced old-timer (Lortie, p. 85). As one teacher asked, "How many jobs are there that you can do for 35 years and still have the same job description?"

Third, teachers are extremely dependent on what they learned through their own experience. Professional training typically is not rigorous, and the metamorphosis from college student to fully responsible classroom teacher can take place literally overnight, throwing the new teacher immediately on his/her own resources (Lortie, p. 79). One result of this compressed socialization into the profession is that teachers rarely, if ever, turn to evidence beyond their own personal experience to justify concrete experience with particular students in fixed locales.

> The teacher's concern with the here and now and her emotional attachment to her world was often accompanied . . . by an accepting attitude toward educational conditions as they presently exist. Interest in educational change was usually mild and typically was restricted to ideas about how to rearrange her room or how to regroup her students. (Jackson, p. 148)

There is little, then, in the structure of the profession or the socialization of its members to cast the teacher in the role of a change agent. As Sussman (1977) notes, "Teacher-as-innovator is not part of the usual definition of the teacher's role."

The teacher's everyday role in the classroom presents an extraordinarily complex picture, which is only recently receiving the careful research attention it merits. The picture that emerges helps us to see more clearly why it is so hard for many teachers to support changes, even if they want to.

Doyle (1979) concluded on the basis of extended classroom observation that teachers are preeminently concerned with gaining and maintaining cooperation in classroom activities. "If any learning is to occur, the teacher must sustain the cooperation of the student in an activity" (p. 48). Securing cooperation is not a once-a-year proposition but a daily concern. The beginning of the year is a particularly crucial time because if a class is "lost" then, obtaining cooperation for the remainder of the year is next to impossible.

Studies of teacher planning by Clark and Yinger (1979) confirm that planning throughout the year is continually influenced by decisions made early in the fall. Two major goals are to establish a routine daily and weekly schedule for different activities and to train students to follow rules and procedures for these activities. It turns out that routinizing activities makes classroom management feasible; that routines confer predictability. In the unstable environment which is the classroom, routines allow the teacher partially to "go on automatic" so that some attentional capacity is released to monitor individual students and deal with unexpected events. Management and planning routines are powerful lenses through which teachers will view the feasibility of implementing innovation, or even consider their use at all.

> The introduction of innovations is likely to increase the frequency and intensity (of misbehavior initiations) and thus produce high management demands for teachers. . . . Since many innovations are not designed on the basis of classroom knowledge, some may be very difficult to implement. It is understandable, then, that more innovations are proposed than are implemented. Indeed, teacher resistance may often be a realistic reaction to many innovation schemes. (Doyle, p. 73)

Time is a fixed resource affected by change. Time must be allocated to existing subjects within the school day. Incorporating an innovation means that the teacher must not only decide how to redistribute time allotments to various activities but must also devote personal time to learning about the new program. "To overburdened teachers and administrators trying to arrange local staff development activities, the very willingness of each to participate, not to mention the motivation to continue, often depends upon time available" (Corno, 1979, p. 249).

To review the literature surveyed and the teachers interviewed, there is agreement that the likelihood of educational innovations being successfully implemented depends on (1) having enough time to plan, implement, and evaluate new projects, (2) promoting collegial involvement and cooperation, (3) establishing links with outside professionals, and (4) securing long-term project support from administrators. Unfortunately, the organization of schooling itself presents obstacles even to teachers who want very much to participate in the change process. Teachers work in isolation, depending almost entirely on personal experience to justify professional decisions. They work in a setting that rewards little else besides longevity. They must daily secure student cooperation primarily via well-established rules and procedures that govern daily and weekly activities. Finally, they must depend for support and encouragement on building administrators who deal continuously with multiple and competing demands, instructional leadership being only one among many.

Modal conditions in general, then, are not conducive to supporting change, but change has nevertheless been legislated. The specific requirements of mandated state and federal change programs interact with existing institutional problems to the teacher's detriment. Predictably, decrements in morale and feelings of professional competence result.

COLLISION BETWEEN MANDATED CHANGE AND MODAL CONDITIONS

The following series of interviews show teachers who want to comply with mandated change but find themselves facing conditions which make compliance difficult and success problematic. The first set of interviews is with teachers working with students mainstreamed under the provisions of the Education for All Handicapped Children Act (Public Law 94–142). The second interview is with a bilingual specialist funded under Title VII of the Elementary and Secondary Education Act. The final interview reports the experiences of a classroom teacher working in a school that receives funds under Title I of the Elementary and Secondary Education Act.

The Education for All Handicapped Children Act, passed in 1975, is designed to extend educational equity to children with physical, emotional, intellectual, and learning handicaps by placing them in the least restrictive educational environment consonant with their special needs. In many cases this means they will be mainstreamed into regular classrooms for most of the day, receiving intermittent services from relevant specialists. There are numerous regulations governing the referral and placement of these students and the subsequent formulation of an individual education plan (IEP) for each child.

> As a vocational education teacher I have great concern about the placement of special education students in my shop classes. The student's handicap makes him much more prone than non-handicapped students to accidents with the tools and machines. In my school district they relieve the special education teacher by sending approximately ten emotionally disturbed students to our shop classes for the whole period. (Interview with a junior high school shop teacher)

> Maintenance of academic standards in classes with handicapped students causes concern for many of us. If the nature of the handicap makes it necessary for us to spend a great deal of extra time with the handicapped student, then that is time

taken away from the majority of our students whose academic achievement may suffer. If there are one or more hyperactive or emotionally disturbed children in a class where basic skills are being taught, it makes it impossible for us to spend the time that is necessary for non-handicapped pupils in the class to learn. We may be forced to decide whether the handicapped student or the rest of the class should receive the limited time and energy we have. Sometimes it seems like the more conscientious the teacher the greater the guilt and the anxiety that we feel. (Interview with a group of elementary school teachers)

As a classroom teacher I feel that even when in-service is offered by my school system I am really being asked to learn skills in one afternoon that it may have taken a special education teacher months or even years to acquire. Most of us have had no in-service training to cope with the demands of implementing 94–142. Where in-service has been offered it is usually superficial and not helpful to what we need for day to day work with our students. (Interview with an elementary teacher)

For these teachers, complying with the mandated changes of PL 94–142 has meant reallocating time in ways felt to be inimical to the majority of students; has meant stretching supervisory ability beyond perceived safe limits for the children; has meant trying to fulfill the mandates of the program and finding that doing so engenders feelings of professional inadequacy.

The next interview is with a bilingual education specialist. Bilingual education projects funded under Title VII of the Elementary and Secondary Education Act (ESEA) are designed to equalize the educational opportunity of minority group children from environments where the dominant language is not English. The intricacies of this program are well illustrated by the interchange between an elementary school teacher and the specialist.

Teacher: By the end of September, at the latest, we've established our flow for the year. Why is it October or later before we know what your role in our school is going to be? You want to see children during times that have already been established for gym, library, art—the very activities that they will resent leaving. It now means getting together all the teachers involved to reshuffle schedules that took weeks to establish in the first place.

Specialist: Funding is never secure. The local district has made only minimal commitment to funding bilingual education which means that we rely almost entirely on state and federal funding. Those amounts or, in the case of federal funding, the certainty of funding is not known until mid-fall.

Different agencies get into the act. In the case of our district, we must meet requirements of federal regulation because we receive money under ESEA Title VII (bilingual), Title I (migrant), and Title VI (bilingual) of the Emergency School Assistance Act (ESAA). We receive state funding under section 41A of the State School Aid Act and the requirements for that funding have changed annually since the funding was made available in 1976.

A few years ago we moved to consolidate funding and service for students who are bilingual. Migrant and bilingual monies were combined so that a student who was a migrant bilingual would be seen by one person only. This move was a good one I think. What has not yet been consolidated is the in-service and evaluation procedure required of staff. I must go to lengthy in-services sponsored by migrant, others sponsored by the Emergency School Assistance Act, others by bilingual. Last year I filled out three lengthy questionnaires on my job, one for migrant, one for ESAA and one for our education association. The three surveys were virtually the same. Another thought: The U.S. Office of Civil Rights places requirements (such as the full Language Assessment Battery) on the district because they want to ensure that students who are monolingual non-English speakers do not have their rights violated. These requirements have meant that actual services to youngsters and permanent placing of staff in buildings gets postponed at least a month, if not longer. This makes it difficult for me to work into a school's program, and for the staff to take me into account when doing much of their beginning of the year planning. When I'm assigned to a new building it means I arrive after everyone is settled into routines. Supplies, rooms, and so on are spoken for. To make matters even worse I have moved from working half-time in one building with 20 students to working with more than 80 students in 3 buildings full-time. No wonder the quality of the in-building program suffers. (Interview with elementary bilingual specialist)

This specialist also voices doubts about the possibility of simultaneously fulfilling her mandated responsibilities and maintaining her own professional standards. Compliance with mandated change has put her at odds with the classroom teachers' needs for stable routines and plans. Her problem is further complicated by the unpredictable funding cycles and redundant requirements of the change program itself, both of which she sees as having eroded her instructional impact.

Title I (disadvantaged) funds are distributed according to the number of low-income children aged 5–17 within a school district who are (1) from poor families as defined by the U.S. Census, (2) from families receiving Aid for Dependent Children payments but which are above the poverty line, (3) living in institutions for the neglected and delinquent, and (4) living in foster homes (General Accounting Office Report, 1980). The funds are typically used for remedial reading and mathematics at the elementary school level. In the final interview, an elementary classroom teacher muses about some unintended consequences of the Title I program.

At this point, many of the teachers in my building would rather not participate in Title I. It has become extremely frustrating. The Title I aides can only work with Title I children. If we assign the aide to the 40 Title I children who are distributed among five different teachers, the aide is accountable to everyone and no one. There is no preplanning time with individual teachers since the aide is obliged to follow the students from class to class. Often it is the aide who decides who will be served each day, and this often means that the least disruptive children are seen more than the more difficult students. If the aide is assigned to one out of the five teachers though, that teacher is most likely to determine the priorities of her own classes and not act as a coordinator on behalf of the other teachers.

In complying with the regulations the aides can only spend ten percent of their time doing non-tutorial tasks. However, students resent being pulled out for tutoring when there are guest speakers, or when they have art, music, phys ed, and library. All this means that if their ten percent is used up and they are not tutoring at the moment, they are not allowed to help the teacher with any activities that might benefit the entire class.

When we're introducing new material—and only the teacher is allowed to do that—the aides keep their eyes on how their Title I students are doing. In the process of heading over to help one who is having problems, the aide will be asked by non-Title I students for help. She must, according to the regulations, ignore those students. It's just awful. The aides resent it, the children can't understand it, and teacher's hands are tied. What should we do?

I can't believe we're the only school with this set of problems. If there is time and money for auditors to show up twice a year to audit the aides' plan books and interview them, why isn't there any time or money for someone with some national perspective to share with us the Title I success stories? We need to know about how successful schools are handling those problems we have. Some of us are beginning to wonder if there *are* any Title I success stories. Maybe there is no way to do it right. (Interview with elementary teacher)

For this teacher, Title I requirements have drastically curtailed her right as a professional to allocate time and instructional resources (aides in this case) to the maximum benefit of her students.

In all, the tone of these interviews is one of anxiety, even gloom. While the schools were to be instruments for ensuring equity in educational opportunity—surely a legitimate outcome—the teachers charged with implementing various policies were relegated to the role of faithful subordinate: their complex responsibilities misunderstood or ignored, their expertise unenlisted. Not a single condition for ensuring the possibility of successful coping with change can be found here. There is no mention of positive collegial collaboration or consultation, of principal support, of time to plan, implement, and take stock, of in-service training substantive and credible enough to vie with personal experience as a guide for making professional decisions, or of rewards of any kind that could accrue to exemplary implementation and maintenance of the required changes. Overall, these practitioners feel powerless, isolated, and ill-prepared.

IMPLICATIONS FOR POLICYMAKERS

Teachers are acknowledged to play a central role in successfully managing school change but their role is an ambiguous one. The literature on planned change and the testimony of teachers indicate that collegiality, expanded professional contacts, substantive in-service training, principal support, local adaptation of materials, and time to plan, implement, and evaluate are essential ingredients in sustaining change.

At present, much mitigates against full realization of the central place that the teacher must take in any implementation of school change. Teaching is largely a solitary profession and one's own experience, not that of colleagues, is the touchstone for action. In-service training is generally perfunctory and often disregarded if it is in conflict with one's own experiences. As some interviews showed, it can also fall woefully short of the required level of usefulness. Often changes are imposed quickly with the inevitable result that teachers feel inadequate and anxious about the effectiveness of their teaching. Further, effective management and planning routines so essential to the orderly process of instruction often fall victim to hastily enacted programs and policies, or to the effects of the most recent round of budget reductions. In short, research and teacher testimony point to the centrality of the teacher in the change process, but modal conditions and the specific requirements of mandated programs militate against successful change.

While successful change requires committed, experienced teachers, the fact is that teachers become more alienated the longer they teach. "Front-loaded" earnings and the absence of clear career stages act as severe disincentives for the very teachers the profession wishes to reinvigorate and retain. Until very recently, the deficiencies in the holding power of the profession and the consequences of losing good people were easily masked. First, talented women were streamed into a small number of "acceptable" professions, and teaching ranked at the top. Many taught for a few years before starting families, but they were bright and enthusiastic (having left before the onset of the five-year effect noted by Sarason) and were replaced by fresh graduates. Second, rising enrollments in the 1950's and 60's put teachers on the correct side of the supply and demand equation, thus boosting salaries. Third, a growing education industry opened up administrative and academic positions which required but a few token years of classroom teaching for entrance. The paths away from the classroom were well marked and well traveled. All that has changed for both men and women. Ambitious women go into every profession except teaching, salaries are no longer competitive, and declining enrollments and budgetary constraints at all levels of the educational ladder have effectively closed down the traditional administrative/academic escape routes out of the classroom. The alternative to classroom teaching now is to leave the field of education entirely. (See Chapters 4 and 5 of this volume.)

The drab underside of classroom teaching, well documented in the past ten years, must be confronted; new professional roles requiring new skills and responsibilities and conferring recognition and reward need to be piloted. For example, at the Institute for Research on Teaching at Michigan State University, the study of teaching is a collaborative enterprise conducted by researchers together with teachers who work half-time in their classrooms and half-time at the Institute. Over the past six years the teachers involved have participated in all phases of the research process: initial formulation of questions, data collection, analysis and interpretation of findings, and documentation and dissemination of the studies. Disappointingly, the teachers' home districts have been notably silent, apparently at a loss as to how to enlist the new and varied skills these practitioners have developed and which they are eager to use and extend.

Successful change requires collegial cooperation and involvement. In fact, though, teachers spend most of their professional lives locked into a rigid working day, isolated from their colleagues both in and outside of the school. What reorganization of the school day or the academic year might promote and reward the active collaboration and communication of teachers with other professionals and other institutions?

It is incumbent upon policymakers to find ways of staging the profession, of piloting new professional classifications and arrangements so that teachers do not have to leave the classroom entirely in order to fulfill intellectual and financial ambitions. Teacher organizations for their part need to go beyond bargaining for traditional issues of wages, hours, and working conditions, to basic considerations of job redefinition and recognized professional alternatives within the framework of classroom teaching.

Successful change requires long-term administrator interest, commitment, and involvement. In fact, however, principals typically spend about 25 minutes a day on instruction-related tasks. The hectic pace of their jobs leaves them with little time for involvement with the instructional program. Their main function appears to be maintaining the smooth operation of school routines (Boyd and Crowson, 1981). What structural changes within a system would make it possible for a principal, particularly at the elementary level, to act as the building's instructional leader? How would improved building outcomes be rewarded?

Successful change programs require several years for implementation since established routines must be altered and new ones perfected. In fact, however, mandated programs are typically thrust onto teachers with only the briefest prior in-service, often resulting in disrupted classroom routines and diminished outcomes, at least in the short run. How can policymakers ensure that new programs be given time to be evaluated fairly and that programs currently being implemented not be terminated or altered before a fair evaluation can take place?

Responsibility, recognition, and achievement are the work features most valued by satisfied teachers (Fuller and Miskel, 1972). Yet the structure of the teaching profession itself is cited repeatedly as being inimical to the long-term satisfaction of its practitioners. As Sarason observed:

> Discussions of new programs provide only the most superficial recognition of the problem of the effects of teaching on the modal teacher in the modal classroom. There was much talk about the need for teachers to be flexible, creative, stimulating—everyone was against sin and for virtue—but no one asked the question: to what extent may the development and maintenance of these virtues be hindered by what we know about the modal teacher in the modal classroom. (p. 172)

We have tried to show that we are beginning to know quite a bit about prevailing conditions in teaching and how they work against sustaining change. And none too soon. The profession stands at a crossroads today as perhaps never before in the history of public education in this country, faced with declining resources, retrenchment, growing demands for accountability, an increasing incidence of classroom violence and vandalism, exaggerated public expectations of what schools can do, and confusion over the future place of public education itself in American life. The teacher's role in school change is inevitably wedded to the teacher's role itself. To the extent that the difficulties associated with that role go unaddressed, the frequency of successful change will remain as it has been: rare. Programs and policies must begin addressing themselves to the needs of teachers as well as those of the students they serve.

REFERENCES

Berman, P. and McLaughlin, M. W. *Federal programs supporting educational change, Vol. IV: The findings in review.* Santa Monica, CA: Rand Corporation, 1975.

Berman, P. and McLaughlin, M. W. *Federal programs supporting educational change, Vol. VIII: Implementing and sustaining innovations.* Santa Monica, CA: Rand Corporation, 1978.

Boyd, W. and Crowson, R. The changing conception and practice of public school administration. In D. Berliner (ed.), *Review of research in education, vol. 9.* American Educational Research Association, 1981.

Carter, C. A. *An analysis of the education amendments of 1978.* Washington, D.C.: Educational Funding Research Council, 1978.

Clark, C. and Yinger, R. J. Teachers' thinking. In P. Peterson and H. J. Walberg (eds.), *Re-

search on teaching: Concepts, findings, and implications. Berkeley, CA: McCuthan Pub. Corp., 1979.

Cohen, E. Open space schools: The opportunity to become ambitious. *Sociology of Education,* 46, Spring, 1973, 143–161.

Corno, L. Classroom instruction and the matter of time. In D. Duke (ed.), *Classroom management: The seventy-eighth yearbook of the National Society for the Study of Education* (Part 2). Chicago: University of Chicago Press, 1979.

Doyle, W. Making managerial decisions in classrooms. In D. Duke (ed.), *Classroom management: The seventy-eighth yearbook of the National Society for the Study of Education* (Part 2). Chicago: University of Chicago Press, 1979.

Fuller, M. and Miskel, C. *Sources of work attachment among public school teachers.* Lawrence, KA: Kansas University, April, 1972, EDO61171.

General Accounting Office, Comptroller General. *An analysis of concerns in federal education programs: Duplication of services and administrative costs.* Washington, D.C.: Report to the Congress of the United States, 1980.

Hall, G. E. and Loucks, S. F. *A developmental model for determining whether or not the treatment really is implemented.* Austin: Research and Development Center for Teacher Education, University of Texas, 1976.

Hall, G. E. and Rutherford, W. L. *Concerns of teachers about implementing the innovation of team teaching.* Austin: Research and Development Center for Teacher Education, University of Texas, 1975.

Hall G. E., Wallace, R. C., and Dossett, W. F. *A developmental conceptualization of the adoption process within educational institutions.* Austin: Research and Development Center for Teacher Education, University of Texas, 1973.

Jackson, P. W. *Life in classrooms.* Chicago: Holt, Rinehart and Winston, Inc., 1968.

Lortie, D. C. *Schoolteacher.* Chicago: University of Chicago Press, 1975.

Sarason, S. *The culture of the school and the problem of change.* Boston: Allyn and Bacon, Inc., 1971.

Sussman, L. *Tales out of school: Implementing organizational change in elementary grades.* Philadelphia: Temple University Press, 1977.

Vavrus, M. *The relationship of teacher alienation to school workplace characteristics and career stages of teachers.* (Res. Ser. No. 36). East Lansing: Institute for Research on Teaching, Michigan State University, 1979.

Teaching and Educational Policy

The eight chapters making up Part IV of the handbook address the issue of government in the classroom. Over the last two decades federal and state governments have expanded and intensified their efforts to influence what goes on in schools and classrooms. This turn to policy as a means to influence education has raised a number of issues. One concerns value conflicts. Policy interventions in the schools have occurred in the name of such cherished ideals as equity and the protection of individual and minority rights. Yet pursuit of these ideals has led to conflict with other equally important values and has raised questions about utilizing education as the engine for social reform. Several of the chapters which follow explore the sources and nature of these value conflicts. Those by Green, Fenstermacher and Amarel, and Greenstone and Peterson examine from a philosophical point of view how the values and interests of agents external to the classroom (e.g., state policymakers, school administrators) are likely to differ from and contend with teacher concerns. This largely inevitable divergence in concerns produces a dilemma for policymakers, who must rely on teacher actions to realize the intent of their mandates. Elmore focuses centrally on this dilemma of policy implementation in his chapter, while Clune also notes the dependency of courts on teachers to carry out both the spirit and the letter of the law.

A second issue concerns the actual effects which policy has had on teaching. Chapters by Schwille et al., Kirst, and Clune take up this question while acknowledging the difficulties of conducting empirical research on the subject. Contentions range from the claim that policy has had little or no impact owing to local actors' capacity to ignore, blunt, or distort external mandates, to evidence of specific, direct and indirect effects, to claims about diffuse, global trends (e.g., legalization of dispute resolution or delegitimating teacher professionalism). These and other arguments the authors weigh against the evidence available.

A final paramount issue in a number of these chapters (as well as in chapters throughout the handbook) concerns the relationship of external policy to teacher autonomy. Policies seek to constrain teachers in a variety of ways and in the service of important values, yet teaching is an activity requiring discretion and the capacity to adapt. How to reconcile this fundamental aspect of teaching with the trend toward remote control is perhaps the central issue in this volume, highlighted in Shulman's concluding chapter.

Thomas Green's chapter examines the relationship among three central values—excellence, equity, and equality—which have figured largely in educational policy-making. He argues that these ideals will conflict with one another and that the essence of policy is to resolve conflicts among ideals all of which must be honored. Green distinguishes inequalities in educational achievement or attainment which result from choice, ability, or virtue from those attributable to differences in sex, social class, race, and the like, arguing that only the latter inequalities are inequitable. In practice these factors are difficult to disentangle, but large inequalities generally constitute evidence of inequity. Regarding excellence and equity, he claims the former has priority over and to an extent implies the latter insofar as criteria for excellence are universal and apply to all. While acknowledging that pursuit of excellence through policy is very difficult, he urges that such a pursuit in the long run will be the best guarantor of equity.

Richard Elmore addresses the implementation problem in his chapter, urging legislators to rethink their approach to legislative and administrative control. He contrasts two broad approaches to the implementation of policy. One, the regulatory view, is compliance-oriented and seeks to establish tight hierarchical controls via specific regulations and close monitoring. The other, the programmatic view, seeks to improve local capacity to deliver services. Local variation in response to central policies presents a puzzle for policymakers. Is it a sign of noncompliance or of healthy adaptation to local circumstance? Ultimately Elmore argues that in education delegated authority and a capacity-building approach is preferable given the decentralized, loosely coupled nature of the educational system and the need to rely on teachers' judgment in instruction.

The chapter by John Schwille, Andrew Porter, and colleagues reports on a research project exploring the determinants of curriculum content, specifically the content of elementary mathematics. Their chapter views teachers as brokering a variety of influences on the curriculum including external mandates in the form of district policies and state tests, the demands and needs of students, and their own preferences and repertoires. Teachers, their research indicates, vary in their responses to policy, but they find no evidence that prescriptive policy is harmful. Contrary to the view most strongly expressed by Fenstermacher and Amarel, they argue that curriculum policy does not unduly constrain teacher autonomy and that in fact many teachers appreciate the guidance provided by policy.

Gary Fenstermacher and Marianne Amarel seek to establish a strong case in favor of teacher autonomy. They ground their argument in a conception of teaching and learning which emphasizes the subtly idiosyncratic nature of human development and the corresponding necessity for teachers to respond sensitively to individual differences in learning styles. External mandates which prescribe for the general case, they argue, will inevitably interfere with teachers' finely tuned intentions for their students. While acknowledging the state's interest in education, they give priority to the teacher as representing both the student's interest and the interest of humanity. In their view increased state intervention even to protect individual and minority rights will in the long run distort teacher intentions for students and so jeopardize the interests of humanity.

In their chapter, David Greenstone and Paul Peterson locate a pervasive tension between two views of education in our society. The inquiry view stresses the transmission of culture and the development of each individual's faculties according to communal standards. The social functional view regards education as serving societal functions while protecting the rights and satisfying the preferences of individuals within a community of interest. The former orientation tends to regard education as an end and to favor teacher autonomy in fostering learning. The latter view emphasizes education as a means to societal ends which set limits on teacher discretion. This tension plays out in educational policy, in the relationship between teachers and administrators whose role norms conflict, and in American cultural ideas. From World War II onward, they judge, the social functional perspective has dominated, and they argue for the need to establish a better balance in public policy, according renewed weight to education as inquiry.

Michael Kirst's chapter provides a review of evidence on the impact of one type of policy—federal and state categorical programs. Kirst reviews the growth of such programs, noting the American reformist tendency to rely on legal procedures and bureaucratic standards rather than on professionalism. What reforms last? Those, he answers, which are structural in nature, create a new constituency, and are easily monitored. Categorical programs have added new layers of administration and new categories of personnel, have influenced pupil classification and the structure of instruction through pull-out and the introduction into the classroom of specialists and aides, and have expanded participation in educational governance. On the other hand, reforms aimed at the methods and substance of instruction such as the National Science Foundation's curriculum reforms have had little lasting impact. Kirst concludes by noting that the Reagan Administration's policy priorities in education may significantly alter these patterns via deregulation and the shift away from federal categoricals.

William Clune provides a parallel treatment of the influence of the courts on teaching. Courts, he argues, have had a major impact on teaching although often indirectly. For example, school finance reform pursued through the courts has affected the allocation of funds to districts and centralized educational funding within the states. Other major court impacts include desegregation, the expansion of student rights, and bilingual and special education. In the second section of the chapter Clune reflects on the experience of court-initiated educational change and notes a number of paradoxes. Along with Elmore, Kirst, and other authors he recognizes the power of "the bottom" over "the top" in the educational system, so that court decisions can at most initiate a complicated process of social and organizational change which ultimately requires the cooperation of teachers, administrators, and community members.

In the handbook's concluding chapter Lee Shulman identifies a central tension in the regulation and conduct of teaching—that between autonomy and obligation. Teacher autonomy is a value in service to enhanced learning for children, implying the conscientious exercise of discretion. Yet as Shulman points out, behind prescriptive policy lurks the suspicion that teachers may not fulfill their professional obligations. Confronting such fears, policymakers often turn to research for definitive prescriptions on school or teaching effectiveness, yet the impediments to any simple research-inspired solution are many. While the very complexity of teaching provides autonomy through the possibility of multiple interpretations of the role, the proper aim for policy and for research, he argues, is to allow and encourage the responsible exercise of autonomy.

CHAPTER 13

Excellence, Equity, and Equality

Thomas F. Green

I. THE CONFLICT OF IDEALS

Consider the educational ideals of excellence, equity, and equality. It may be doubted that any society can realize all of these ideals at once. But it cannot be doubted that we must try. The possibility of their joint realization is an open question because ideals inevitably conflict. In a single-minded pursuit of one, we may create conditions inhibiting the advancement of another. When we seek to forge a practical fit between two ideals by the adjustment of one, we are likely to discover that some other adjustment is needed for the promotion of a third ideal. It is such a conflict between ideals that I wish to explore in this essay. The question is not whether excellence, equity, and equality are all deserving ideals. They are. The question is whether they can exist at the same time, and especially whether public policy is uniformly an appropriate tool for their advancement.

This emphasis upon policy, moreover, is important. In what follows, I offer no advice as to how teachers may better judge the excellence of their educative efforts. Instead, I assume the burden of a more modest problem—namely, to determine the extent to which these three educational ideals, including their impact upon practice, are jointly attainable through the tools of public policy. Thus, the emphasis falls not on excellence in educational practice, but on determining the extent to which policy can rightfully impinge on practice and which of these ideals should have priority in the formation of policy.

Our ideals may clash in at least three ways. First, there are conflicts inherent in their meaning and, secondly, those arising from the presence of different levels of social aggregation. Finally, there are conflicts of implementation, those resulting from our choice of tools in making our ideals actual. These three modes of conflict do much to account for the difficulties inherent in attempts to secure equity, excellence, and equality through public policy. Consider each.

Conflicts of Meaning

Every ideal is likely to have several meanings. In short, ideals are not univocal. They do not speak with a single voice, and it is not transparent that all meanings of a single ideal can coexist in the same social state of affairs.

A social ideal, in contrast to a personal ideal, is describable always as a particular social state of affairs that would exist if we succeed in attaining that ideal. That desired state of affairs, moreover, will always consist in a definite frequency or distribution of some good—income, achievement, health, or whatever. For example, if we entertain the ideal that all citizens should have equal access to the institutions of justice, then we can examine court dockets, trial delays, and the like to uncover the frequencies, the social distribution of crimes, arrests, dismissals, convictions, acquittals, and suspended sentences. Given that information, then we can form a judgment as to whether or in what degree the statistical description of what exists conforms or departs from the ideal.

To say, therefore, that social ideals are not univocal is to say simply that there are many states of affairs all of which may count toward our estimate as to how well we are doing. And to say that these multiple meanings may conflict is to say simply that these different states of affairs may not be capable of existing all at the same time. For example, we probably cannot get an education that (1) is uniquely suited and best for each individual and at the same time (2) give to each an education that is as good as that provided for everyone else.[1] Yet, both of these conditions belong to the ideal of equal educational opportunity. Because of the multiple meanings contained in any one ideal, conflicts may arise.

But conflict can also occur between the meanings of different ideals. If in any social institution, for example, we get as much efficiency as we can, then we are unlikely to have as much community as we desire. The state of affairs statistically describable as the achievement of the one ideal is likely to conflict with the state of affairs implied by the other. If we ask, for example, "How efficient can a school or college be?" then we might also ask, "How inefficient must it be in order to secure its educational aims?" The ideals of efficiency and excellence of education may conflict.

Conflicts of Aggregation

Ideals may conflict also because of the different levels of social aggregation to which they appropriately belong. This kind of conflict has also two varieties. Isn't it clear that what is good among persons in general is sometimes not very good in specific cases? In the moral alchemy of bureaucratic organizations, for example, the general rules that mandate treating every case alike are intended to inhibit animosities, preferences, and personal prejudices from any easy passage into action. Such rules are necessary. But when they are applied in specific cases, they may also suppress the consideration due to individuals and even obstruct the achievement of efficiency[2] Justice in general is achieved but justice in particular cases is not.

We can recognize this kind of conflict in a second form. Some ideals make sense only when we consider large aggregations and others only when we consider small ones. For example, with respect to the general populace, we must conduct ourselves according to rules of justice, treating no one with preference except in unusual cases. But try that with your friends. Deal with them according to the standards of indifference required for justice within large groups. Ask them to stand in line for your attention, waiting their turn, and you will have no friends.[3] The ideals of friendship are not at home among large numbers. Such ideals do not reside there. The rules of conduct that must prevail in the case of large numbers should not prevail among friends. So ideals can conflict not simply by virtue of their social ambiguity but also because of the different levels of aggregation to which they apply.

This form of conflict between ideals is especially important to note when we consider the joint achievement of equity and excellence in education through the tools of public policy. The educational establishment is everywhere organized by levels of aggregation. It could hardly be otherwise. It seems inescapable that there will be students, aggregations of students in classrooms, aggregations of classrooms in schools, aggregations of schools to form districts, and even regional aggregations of districts in many states. But then there exists also the aggregation of districts within states and, of course, states within the federal system of government. These are such obvious facts that it is easy to overlook their importance.

It might turn out, however, that the ideal of equality in education is statistically describable and can become a source of human motivaion only at a fairly high level of social aggregation—say, at the state or federal levels of policy. But, at the same time, educational excellence may be an ideal that can motivate people only at a very low level of aggregation—say, the level of the school or classroom. So the joint realization of equity and excellence may produce conflict not because there is any logical difficulty in their joint realization, but simply because what we do at one level to secure the one ideal may conflict with what we need to do at another to secure the other ideal.

We may take it as intractable fact, for example, that parents love their children. Some parents some of the time may be inept, or even foolish, in the expression of that love. But ineptness and folly never suffice to cancel out the fact of love. As parents, hardly anyone will be satisfied to seek for their own just what others have. Their aim, instead, will be to secure the best that they can get—as they see the best. And that will mean, usually, trying to get something better than most others get. Equal opportunity is hardly ever a parental aim. The interests of the state may be secured if those interests are secured on the whole, in general, and for the most part. But even when the interests of parents coincide with those of the state in substance, they will never be secured if they are merely secured in general, on the whole, and for the most part. In other words, the interests of the State in education are aggregate interests. The interests of parents are specific. The State may wish to ensure the minimum essential, even in the distribution of rights and social benefits. But parents typically aspire to the best that they can get; and they seek not simply the best that is possible on the whole, but the best that is possible for their own children.[4]

Consider a further example of the difference made by levels of aggregation. In order to promote the cause of educational equity for children, some have proposed the need for a ceiling on the amount per student that can be spent by wealthy districts. Viewed from the vantage of one level of aggregation, I can see it as my civic duty to advance such measures. But from my vantage as a parent, I can view that kind of action to be a legally imposed limitation on my capacity to love my children and to express that love in practical ways. The very same action can be seen, on the one hand, as my civic duty to promote and, on the other hand, as an abridgement of my parental rights. The difference in view is a difference in levels of social aggregation.

Conflicts of Implementation

These points will become more vivid if we turn to a third source of conflicts in our ideals, those arising from the sheer necessities of implementation. Let us grant that all persons should be afforded an equal chance in life and that by "equal chance" we mean to include an equal chance at a good education. Our convictions combine the ideals of excellence and equity. But we know that certain groups in America do not have as good a chance as others. We have the statistical evidence in hand. In short, we know that our ideals of equity remain unsatisfied.

How shall we remedy this failure? Suppose we accept also the belief that those who are "disadvantaged" would benefit more from education if more resources were targeted especially to them. And so we seek an explicit federal policy. We enact Title I of ESEA. Never mind, for the moment, the actual history of such legislation.[5] We are, after all, only supposing.

In this way we embody our collective intentions into law, and in doing so we express certain ideals and beliefs, the belief, for example, that education is a significant path toward more equal participation in the fruits of American society and that, by increasing the excellence of education for some, we will increase equality. Excellence and equity are jointly affirmed. So we embody our convictions in policy, in legislation, and in guidelines for implementation.

But this decision to express our ideals in public policy has its own consequences. If public funds are used, then decency demands a public accounting. There is nothing wrong in that. Indeed, such a demand flows from another ideal of government sometimes called "responsibility." If we take a step with public funds, then we must leave in the files a footprint. There must be, as we say, "an accounting track."

And so, in this chain from federal policy to classroom conduct, we must be able to track the Federal Dollar. We must be able to trace it from its origin to its mandated destination. The accountant, at this point, overrules the moralist and does so, moreover, on moral grounds. And so, for perfectly inescapable reasons we must be able to identify which specific persons were to be aided and to certify that such funds were used to benefit no one else.[6]

What does this technical, but morally impeccable, demand impose upon us as we pass from the realm of policy at one level of aggregation to practice at another level? It means just this! We must identify those authorized to receive such assistance and either withdraw them from the normal classroom or segregate them within the classroom.[7] Otherwise, the accounting track is blemished. Given such measures, however, we could readily identify the destination of all costs from salary and paper to the provision of heat and rent.

But repeat this act of charity five times over and the problems of implementation alone will mandate the movement of students in and out, from class to special classroom, with sufficient frequency to defeat what anyone would offer as a statistical description of excellence in education.[8] What started as the joint pursuit of excellence and equity may end by producing a conflict merely because of what is required for implementation. The two ideals are logically compatible, but the tools of action can place them at odds.

Still, we cannot allow this conclusion to rest without amendment. We cannot abandon such multiple aspirations merely because their attainment is difficult. Our task is not to say "We can't get both" but to explore the path by which we can. The conclusion, so far, is morally repugnant. But it is also conceptually incomplete. It describes only a portion of the itinerary we must travel in the effort to transform our ideals into daily experience.

Let us therefore break the problem into manageable segments and examine each step. The path we seek must begin with a clearer grasp of the tools at our disposal and a more modest view of what they are good for. (1) What is the nature of policy and what are its limits in the case of education? That may well be the first question. But we must also ask what our ideals require and how they may conflict. (2) What is the ideal of educational equity? (3) What can we reasonably intend by the ideal of educational excellence? Where can it be found and what does it require? These are enough to provide a second and a third question. In short, we want to know whether policy (Q: 1) for equity (Q: 2) can be made to advance the pursuit of excellence (Q: 3). Let us begin by assessing the nature and limits of policy in the case of education.

II. THE NATURE AND REACH OF POLICY

Policy Limits

Public policy is a crude instrument for securing social ideals. We would not use a drop-forge to quarter a pound of butter or an axe to perform heart surgery. Public policy is the drop-forge or the axe of social change. It is not the knife or scalpel. That is to say, public policy deals with gross values. It deals with the common good, not with my good in particular or my neighbor's or even with the good of us both together. Policy deals always with what is good in general, on the whole, and for the most part.

No doubt public policy always actually benefits specific individuals. But we never formulate policy on the grounds that it will secure the good of specific individuals. If I seek my own good exclusively in the formulation of public policy, then I must nevertheless frame my case and defend it always as advancing the good of all or most.

Whenever a particular legislative benefit is granted by the collective for the specific good of some specific natural individuals, then we adopt a rather rare procedure. We call for passage of a "private bill," and the term "private" in this context is not an incidental term. It expresses the fact that private bills are never construed as formulating public policy. They are construed rather as the formulation of a private remedy of a public omission. A private bill frames always an exception to policy, where "policy" is construed as the formulation of the general case. And so, for example, no school board can afford to take action improving the quality of one school within its district without considering the need to treat all other schools in like manner. Such grand impartiality is required by the nature of public policy. That is one feature of its essential generality.

But the tools of policy are limited in another way. They are best construed as aimed not at the advancement of specific benefits, but at the prevention of specific evils. Injustice is always present to our conscience with more definiteness than justice. Injustices are nearly always specific. Justices seldom are. It is true that government can't do everything that we desire, and therefore, it is equally true that public policy is not the fit instrument to secure all our desires. For example, even if we knew what is needed to make every school excellent and every teacher a paradigm of wisdom in the care of children, it would remain doubtful that we could express this knowledge in public policy and thus secure the good we seek. If we could ascertain beyond all doubt that excellence of schools requires the presence of firm moral leadership, we might still be ill-advised to mandate such a thing as a policy prescription.

Still, from the fact that government can't do everything, it does not follow that government can or ought to do nothing. If the tools of policy are limited, then where shall we draw the line? Just here! The utility of policy for the advancement of the common good is best discovered not in the effort to maximize every good for everyone—even everyone in general. It will be found, rather, in the effort to minimize the harm that can be done to anyone in particular.

It may seem a small matter to thus emphasize the prevention of evil over the maximization of good. But this is a small distinction that makes a large difference. Those gentle and charitable souls who seek to do good to everyone—even to those who do not want it done to them—are more to be feared than those more cautious and humble souls who, with a sense of tragedy, perhaps, are willing to live in public office with the aim of preventing as much harm as possible instead of doing as much good as is conceivable. Minimizing evil is a proper aim of public policy. Maximizing good is probably not. The latter assumes that we may shape the axe into a scalpel. Perhaps the needed line can be cast in a single maxim: "Act so as to lower the levels of misfortune and you may find the ideals of equity and excellence jointly more compatible and more suitable to pursuit through public policy."

Such a maxim looks more toward minimizing evil than toward maximizing good. It is not a maxim of laissez-faire, one that would pardon doing nothing. It is rather a rule that encourages care in choosing the tool to fit the task. It is a maxim that, in pursuit of general equity, might mandate the formulation of policies reaching less remotely into the lower levels of social aggregation, such as the classroom, where decisions bearing upon educational excellence predominate in practice.

All this implies, of course, another limitation on the uses of policy. The general rule is that policy is a suitable tool only when fairly large marginal improvements are likely at fairly high levels of aggregation. In short, the benefit sought must be large in magnitude and widespread in its distribution or else the policy choice will be a "toss-up." That is a peculiarity of policy considerations. It is easy to elaborate the rank order generated by these variables. Policy that makes a large difference with small effort will always be preferable to policy that needs a large effort to make a small difference, whatever their relative moral value.

To this general rule, there is one exception, and it may prove or overriding importance. Any policy that can be framed as an issue of civil rights will gain some hearing even when disproportionate effort is needed to secure the benefits. Because of the enormous moral magnitude often attached to securing civil rights, policies that promise to secure such rights can be advanced whatever other social costs may be incurred.

There are obvious limitations to this rule also. But, in general, the typical policy constraint to weigh the effort against the magnitude of benefit has some likelihood of being suspended on issues of civil rights. Thus, policies that promise small aggregate marginal benefits proportionate to the effort required or that promise benefits long deferred—such measures are more likely to gain a hearing if they are framed as issues of civil rights than if they are framed as problems of educational excellence—and deservedly so.

Policy as Ideals in Conflict

These may be limits on the reach of policy, but we have yet to identify the nature of public policy itself. The term is used to cover everything from personal decisions to governmental actions. We will do well to alter the question. Let us ask, "What is a policy question?" How do such questions arise? To this question the elements of an answer are readily at hand.

A policy question is a request for a line of action to optimally resolve a conflict between different ideals all of which must be accepted but which, taken together, cannot all be maximized. That is to say, we do not have a well-formed policy question, a fully formulated statement of a policy problem, until we are able to state the set of ideals or goods from which the question arises, and state them so that their mutual inconsistency is evident.

The contemporary quest for financial equity in education provides about as clear a model of policy questions generally as it is possible to shape. Such issues are always "nested" within a set of mutually incompatible ideals. We seek:

1. Equal educational opportunity for children.
2. An equitable distribution of the tax burden.
3. Local control of education.
4. Responsible management of the state budget.

Maximizing any one of these goods, i.e., getting as much of it as we can, will damage the advancement of the others. The policy problem is generated by the fact that we accept all four of these aims and yet they cannot be jointly maximized. We cannot have all the local control possible because doing so will probably mean getting less than would be good in the way of equity for children and taxpayers and less than is needed in control of the public budget. On the other hand, if we maximize equity for children, then we are likely to get more inequity in the tax burden and less local control. The problems of educational finance policy, in short, do not arise merely from the need to establish a more equitable system for taxpayers and children. They arise rather from the need to do so within a system of ideals that demand both local control and responsible public management.

All issues of public (or even personal) policy have this feature. They are always "nested" in a set of social (or personal) ideals which must all be considered but which, taken together, are more or less mutually incompatible.

III. EQUITY AND EQUALITY

The Principle of Equity

Consider the next step, the nature of educational equity. It is a point of first importance to note that by "inequity" we do not mean "inequality." "Inequity" always implies "injustice." "Inequality" does not. Persons may be treated and rewarded unequally and also justly. But they cannot be treated or rewarded inequitably and also justly. In short, when we think of equity, we are concerned with a version of educational justice, and equality is only a part, not the whole, of justice. Justice requires that persons be treated alike or differently according to their likenesses and differences. But not all likenesses and differences count. Which are relevant, and in what degree? These become the central problems and the debatable issues.

If we could secure the ideal of educational equity, without cost to any other ideals, then we would have secured a statistically describable social condition within which there is:

A random distribution of resources, attainment, and educational achievement in respect to variables irrelevant to educational justice together with a predictable distribution in respect to variables relevant to educational justice.

This statement is tautological. I shall refer to it as the principle of educational equity. It is, of course, a principle that is like a blank check. It needs to be filled in to have any cash value. What are the relevant and irrelevant variables referred to?

We may consult our conscience for an answer. We are normally undisturbed by educational inequalities as long as they arise from differences of choice, ability, or virtue. These may be regarded as "educationally relevant" attributes in the sense that these are the variables we appeal to whenever we argue that educational inequalities are nevertheless fair.

In other words, these are variables that, on the whole, should make a difference. On the other hand, most people would not appeal to such attributes as sex, social class, race, or geography in this way. If inequalities arise from these variables, then, on the whole, our conscience informs us that they are probably also inequities. There is some injustice in permitting them to rule. These are differences that should not make a difference.[9]

The principle of equity is, therefore, easily discernable in the voice of conscience, even though its application in specific cases is not always clear. That voice informs us that educational results (or access or resources) should be distributed predictably with respect to educationally relevant variables, since they are the ones that should matter, and randomly with respect to educationally irrelevant variables, since they are the ones that shouldn't matter. Furthermore, we know approximately what the important variables are, even though we are not always able to give them univocal definition. In short, there is no disagreement on the bare principle of educational equity. Disagreement arises on the precise definition and application of its respective variables.

So, for example, if inequalities arising from differences of choice are acceptable— as they are in the Amish choice to pursue education somewhat less than is typical of other groups in America—then we are obliged to give some definition of what we mean by "choice" and when such inequalities are the result of choice rather than of necessity, ignorance, or something else.

On such applications of the principle, there will always be disagreement. After all, education itself should be one of the factors shaping the boundaries of the choices we can and do make. So if there is some initial inequality in the education provided different persons, then how can we ever say that subsequent inequalities have arisen from the exercise of choice and are therefore acceptable? They must have stemmed instead from previous inequalities of education. What increments of health, wealth, and discernment must we seek to be sure that educational inequalities result from choice and therefore are not inequities?

If a child never sees, hears, or handles a·violin and hence does not become a violinist, we attribute the result to environmental lack, not to choice. And likewise, if a child never encounters professionals and thus does not become one, we do not say the result is a matter of choice. When we think of such cases, we realize that it is not merely choice that limits education. It can be that inequalities, or differences, of education limit choice. So it is hard to know in all cases when inequalities of education arise from the exercise of choice, and are therefore acceptable, and when they do not, and are therefore unacceptable.

The same can be said of other variables in the principle of equity—ability, tenacity, and other virtues. We must either believe that they too are shaped by education or else confess that the pursuit of education has no truly educational consequences. And so in these cases too, we cannot be certain that inequalities of education are the work of acceptable or unacceptable variables. We cannot always be sure that educational inequalities are inequities or that they are not.

That we cannot always be sure, however, does not imply that we can never be sure. There are clear cases where, by choice, persons elect to secure less education or a lesser education than they could have secured. There are also clear cases in which persons of high and low ability receive more or less and better or worse because of their abilities. And there are also clear cases in which persons who by sheer force of effort, courage, and tenacity receive more in the way of education than, on other grounds, we might have expected. In none of these cases are the resulting inequalities unfair or inequitable.

There are clear cases where inequalities are inequities, clear cases where they are not, and cases where we may have strong debate. But if there is debate, the principle of equity will inform us on what the debate is about. So the fact that these matters are not always clear in application does nothing to detract from the validity of these summary points:

1. Educational inequalities are not prima facie inequities. Some are and some are not.
2. The principle of equity is insufficient to tell us which is which in every case. But nonetheless, it specifies what we have to look for in every case to get an answer. And that is all that such a principle is intended to or can provide.
3. The claim that there are inequalities in the distribution of resources, achievement, and benefits is hardly ever enough for us to conclude that such inequalities are also inequities. To derive such a conclusion, the principle of equity demands that we produce an independent demonstration that such inequalities do not arise from the educationally relevant variables of choice, ability, or the exercise of sheer tenacity.

The "Nested" Values of Equality and Equity

If policy questions are always "nested" in some set of ideals all of which are accepted but not all of which can be maximized at once, then we must ask how issues of educational equity are "nested." In addition to the preservation of excellence and the attainment of universality, I believe we seek educational equity always within the following additional ideals:

1. Apply the principle of equity.
2. Secure the fundamental interests of the State.
3. Maintain the educational authority of the family.
4. Preserve cultural pluralism of religious and ethnic communities.
5. Reward selected kinds of abilities.
6. Secure the civil rights of individuals.

When the list is visibly exposed in this way, then we can readily discern a conflict of ideals typical of the sort that produces policy questions. Neither educational equality nor educational equity can be obtained in any pure form without some costs in advancing the other ideals.

For example, if we obtain the uniform results of educational atainment as would be required by the ideal of equality, then we would have eliminated the differential educational effects of families. We would either have abridged the authority of the family or else developed a school powerful enough to overcome the educational effects of that authority. But we would also have aborted the educational effects of religious and cultural communities. It is probably also true that we would have greatly expanded the kinds of abilities legitimated by the educational process and thus would have introduced, once again, a source of inequality. In short, some, getting an education different from others, would probably also get an education superior or inferior to others.

We should be keenly aware that social status, an educationally irrelevant variable in the principle of equity, is probably a more exact proxy for family even than income is for social class, especially when we are concerned with the intergenerational effects of education. Thus, unless we are able to "secularize" the differential effects of family, religion, and culture—that is, render them inconsequential—then we must expect to see inequalities appearing again in close relation to differences of social status. Any pure attainment of educational equality (and perhaps even equity) will put us on a collision course with the ideals of pluralism and the educational authority of the family, and doing so is likely to reproduce still another form of inequity, one requiring public policies that treat different family and cultural groups differently, favoring some over others.

A Case

To make these points more vivid, let us consider a single case drawn from data on college attendance. This data is summarized in Table 13.1.

There are two immediate questions that we should ask about this table. First, does it document the existence of inequalities in educational participation? It does. But, secondly, does it document the existence of inequities in educational participation? To this question, the response is less clear. The answer lies somewhere in a range between "probably," "probably not," and "no." A clear "yes" is not in the range of possible responses.

But how can we be so unsure? Consider the following observations.

1. If there were no inequalities whatever displayed in this table, then the probabilities in each cell of the cross-tabulation would have to be identical. In that case, the table would show no distinction in college attendance between differences of ability (assuming that aptitude is an adequate proxy for ability) and also none between differences of status (assuming that SES is an adequate proxy for social status). So the table reveals inequality. No doubt about it. There would be no inequality whatever in such a table only if it showed that neither ability nor family—nor for that matter anything else—influences college participation with the exception of personal decision which, in turn, would have to be construed as uninfluenced by family, status, or anything else.

Under those conditions, the table would clearly display the presence of equality.

TABLE 13.1   Probability of Entering College Five Years after High School: Males, 1960 High School Class

		Socioeconomic Status				
		Lowest Quartile	*Second Quartile*	*Third Quartile*	*Highest Quartile*	*TOTAL*
	Lowest	.14	.29	.35	.42	.25
Academic	*Second*	.34	.45	.47	.76	.48
Aptitude	*Third*	.59	.65	.78	.90	.74
	Highest	.81	.81	.95	.96	.91
	TOTAL	.32	.53	.69	.86	.58

Probabilities are based upon weighted N's.

SOURCE: John C. Flanagan et al., *Five Years after High School*, Projects Talent, five-year follow-up, (American Institutes for Research and Pittsburgh University, 1971), p. 2–7. Reproduced in Stephen Michelson, "The Further Responsibilities of Intellectuals," *Harvard Educational Review*, Vol. 43, No. 1, February 1973, p. 100.

But perhaps this is too stringent a condition to impose as exemplification of such an ideal. We could say instead that equality would be present if Table 13.1 displayed differences of probabilities in the columns and none in the rows. In that case, we would know that ability, but not SES, has an impact on college attendance. We could call this "equality," however, only if by "equality" we mean "equity." We would be saying that even though inequalities exist, they are acceptable because they relate only to the educationally relevant attributes of ability.

But let us adhere, instead, to whatever clarity we may have reached. Pure equality would exist in such a table only on the condition that the probabilities are the same in each cell. But pure equity can exist on condition that different probabilities occur in the columns, but never in the rows. The ideals of equity and equality do not have the same statistical definition. They are not the same reality.

2. But if we now read across the rows in Table 13.1, we discover that there is a marked and regular impact of lower SES upon lower probabilities of participation. There is clearly some impact of family background or social class, and it appears to be substantial. Hence, the table shows that an educationally irrelevant variable does in fact influence the distribution of educational access and benefits. There is, therefore, a degree of inequity as well as inequality as defined in the principle of equity.

3. But if we read upward or downward in the columns, then we can see that differences of merit also have their impact, and merit is an educationally relevant attribute. Such inequalities are not prima facie inequities.

4. Consider, therefore, the magnitude of the interior marginal increments, or decrements, from cell to cell, by column and row, as presented in Table 13.2.

We observe that with two exceptions, the difference that merit makes in any two adjacent cells is greater than the incremental or decremental difference that SES makes. In short, the differences made by educationally irrelevant variables are less than the differences made by educationally relevant ones. In balance, then, does the table document the presence of inequity? We cannot say, without reservation, "Yes, it does." But neither can we say, without reservation, "No, it doesn't." Is the answer then, "Probably yes," or "Probably no"; or is it, "Both of the above?" We might say that the table shows the presence of more equity than inequity.

5. We might assume—that is, it would be understandable if someone did—that

TABLE 13.2.   Probability of Entering College Five Years after High School: Males, 1960 High School Class Decrements by Cell: Column and Row

		Socioeconomic Status				
		Lowest Quartile	Second Quartile	Third Quartile	Highest Quartile	
		Column	Column	Column	Column	
	Lowest	N −.15	N −.06	N −.07	N	← Row —
		−.2	−.16	−.12	−.34	
Academic Apititude	Second	N −.11	N −.02	N −.29	N	← Row —
		−.25	−.20	−.31	−.14	
	Third	N −.06	N −.13	N −.12	N	← Row —
		−.22	−.16	−.17	−.06	
	Highest	N −.00	N −.14	N −.01	N	← Row —

Derived from Table 13.1 by reading from right to left in rows and from bottom to top in columns recording the decrement between cells.

among those of highest SES and highest ability, .04 chose not to attend college. We might say, "They could have gone, but they didn't." What else could operate, but choice?[10] This is surely the group that could attend college at a rate of 100%. And so Table 13.1 underesimates the freedom of persons in this group to attend college. But, it probably also underestimates the compulsion they feel to do so. Because we assume they are free to go, we assume that they are free not to go. In short, the table may overestimate the freedom of this group to choose not to go to college.[11]

Let us extend this presumption from those of highest SES and highest ability to those of lowest SES and highest ability. If there are .04 of the former group who choose not to attend, then surely we must assume also that there are a least .04 of the latter group who choose not to attend.

My point is not to close the gap in the observed inequality among high ability students. I wish only to point out the minimal plausible parameters of the exercise of choice because choice is an educationally relevant attribute in the principle of equity. Those minimal parameters are just that—minimal. The actual exercise of choice would have to be much larger, especially among the lower, if not the lowest, SES groups. In other words, if SES is an adequate surrogate for family, then we must assume that the compulsion to seek further education is greater among higher SES groups than among lower because we suspect that they are more likely to come from families of higher education.

But let us persist in this concern with the dimensions of choice. Instead of examining the high ability cells between lowest and highest SES, let us consider the frequencies in the lower-right-hand and upper-right-hand cells. If there are .04 of the former group who choose not to attend when they could, then how many of the latter group attend, when they shouldn't? If we could answer this question with some precision, then we would have still another measure of the parameters of choice. How much does compulsion figure in this comparison? The bare inequalities reported in the data provide virtually no information on these questions relevant to the measurement of inequity.

But extend these considerations still another step. Compare the low ability frequencies between those of highest and lowest SES. The conventional wisdom has it that participation will be most strongly influenced by SES among those of lowest ability. But the data do not say so. The impact of SES is next to lowest for the low ability groups, and the impact of ability on participation is greatest for the lowest SES group.

Let us conjecture. The less able sons and daughters of the rich attend probably more often they they should. The compulsion to go, or the inability to choose not to, operates strongly together with their parents' ability to simply buy on the market what they probably don't deserve and what they would benefit from less than others might if those others were there. On the other hand, the less talented sons of the poor probably participate less then they could. The compulsion not to go, among them, is strong because of the often severe psychological and social costs in familial values incurred by the decision to go on. And this operates together with the fact that the economic freedom for them to go is also less. In short, for both groups choice operates, but with the same utilities pressing in opposite directions. For many youngsters of lower SES the choice to participate can entail a repudiation of familial values just as the choice not to participate can be a repudiation of familial values for many of higher SES.[12]

So do these data record the presence of inequity? Well, no doubt there is some, but no doubt there is less than the bare inequalities suggest. The single most significant inequity arises, no doubt, from the uneven distribution of direct economic costs, narrowly defined. But when we consider the dynamics of choice and compulsion unnoted in the observed frequencies, then we have reason to believe that even under conditions in which educational participation imposes no opportunity costs at all, still, we would probably get a distribution very like the one reported in Table 13.1. But in that case the inequalities reported would not reflect inequities because they would clearly arise as a consequence of educationally relevant attributes as specified in the principle of equity. In short, the issues of equity have to do less with reducing the recorded inequalities in frequencies of participation and more to do with reducing compulsion in the exercise of choice which, even if unconstrained, would probably still produce inequalities. Again, inequality and inequity are ideals that do not have the same statistical definition.

Equity and Large Inequalities

No doubt there must always be some effects of social status on the aggregate distribution of educational participation. Such a necessity is required by three of the six "nested ideals" in the total set listed above. These differences, however, will always show up in the distributional data as inequities because they will appear always as determined by educationally irrelevant attributes—class, race, sex, and the like. But even so, we cannot admit that these effects should be very large.[13] The question reduces to a judgment as to what is the best we can get—ideally and practically—in adjusting the entire set of social ideals. There is no technical solution to such a question. It is a problem of social philosophy, not sociology, and certainly not policy science.

The impact of large margins must be noted. Aggregate inequality is not, by itself, sufficient evidence of inequity. But large inequalities are. In short, equity is quite compatible with some inequalities in the aggregate distributions and frequencies that we observe. But beyond some point, such inequalities are clear evidence that something is wrong. Given large inequality, we may presume that inequity exists, even if we do not know its sources. Hence, even though equality and equity are not the same thing, claims of inequity are strong when inequalities are very large.

For example, we may be unable to agree on a definition of "adequate funding" for education per pupil. But we can agree on when there is not enough, and therefore, we may agree when problems of inequity appear. There will probably always be some unobjectionable inequality in the per pupil expenditures of different school districts. But if a child lives in a district where only $300 is provided in a state where the average is $3,000, then we are likely to agree that some inequity exists. Three-hundred dollars is not relatively enough. And if the range in the distribution between the ninetieth and the tenth percentile of districts is forty to one, then we may be even more convinced. In short, as the margins increase, so does our assurance that there is inequity for children. Both reason and conscience inform us that the principle of equity becomes more plainly applicable until finally a threshold is reached where no doubt remains; inequality is then proof of inequity. This partially explains why in public policy the pursuit of equity is so easily confused with the pursuit of equality. There is a threshold where the presence of one is proof of the other and so, under certain conditions, they may seem the same. The relevance of such thresholds for policy will be examined in detail in the next section.

But, for the moment, the impact of the point can be summarized in two claims. First, no doubt there is less inequity when inequalities are small than when they are large. But secondly, there may be more inequity when inequalities are nonexistent than when they are small. Equality is not what issues of equity are about. The problem is rather to recognize those inequalities that are morally acceptable, socially beneficial, and at the same time fair—those, in other words, that are justified by the principle of equity. Again, equality and equity are not, statistically, the same ideals.

IV. EQUITY AND EDUCATIONAL EXCELLENCE

How do the ideals of excellence and equity interact when they are "nested" in an appropriate set, and therefore how do they enter into the formation of public policy? To deal with these matters, let us reassemble the argument. Three claims need elaboration. The first is simply the reminder that our ideals are appropriately lodged at different levels of social aggregation. Educational equality is an ideal of high aggregation, educational excellence an ideal of low aggregation, and educational equity—an ideal of fair treatment or justified inequality—may "fit" at various levels of social aggregation. This difference in their "natural residence," as it were, has substantial bearing upon whether these different ideals are equally suitable objects for policy intervention.

The second proposition may seem to contradict the first. It is the claim that though educational excellence is a goal less easily touched by public policy than the ideal of equality, still, policies in pursuit of educational excellence are more likely to produce gains in equity than policies in pursuit of equality are likely to produce gains in excellence. Thus, it is better to pursue the ideal of equity through the pursuit of excellence than to pursue excellence through the advancement of equality. If that is true, then it is better in the long run to formulate policy for the advancement of excellence than to formulate policy for the advancement of equality, because in doing so we will come closer to satisfying several ideals together (even though we may get less of each) than we would if we pursued each ideal separately. This is a complex claim. It requires explication. It is, nevertheless, a direct consequence of the already familiar notion that the ideals we seek to realize through policy are always "nested" in a set.

The third proposition is, in some respects, a mere extension of the second. The claim is that educational excellence is already a "universalistic" rather than a "particularistic" value, in the sociological sense of the term "universalistic." In short, the achievement of educational excellence, by itself, entails the achievement of equity—of a certain kind—even though its attainment may not produce greater social equality. The concept of "educational excellence" entails a certain kind of equity, but the concept of "equality" does not entail "excellence." This conceptual relationship is precisely why the second of these three propositions can be sustained. It is why the more fruitful, though more difficult, path of public policy is to pursue the attainment of equity through the advancement of excellence rather than through the pursuit of equality. Clearly, this proposition is also complex.

But before turning directly to these crucial claims, let us make the points explicit in a series of direct and simple propositions. What, after all, does it really mean to speak of policies that emphasize the pursuit of excellence over the pursuit of equality and in the process achieve equity? Is there any evidence, drawn from experience and from our common conscience in the matter, that would demonstrate the priority of one ideal over the others?

1. Not many years ago, in the effort to secure more racially balanced schools in urban districts, it was often proposed to create "magnet schools." The idea was that if

schools in the "inner city" were truly excellent, including programs of high quality in the arts, sciences, and languages not available at other schools, then persons not already resident in the inner city would seek to have their children "bused" there. Here, then, was a line of policy favoring the advancement of excellence over the mere attainment of equal racial distributions or frequencies of participation in schools. Through the "focused" promotion of excellence, we would secure greater equality, a racially more balanced distribution of enrollments. It is irrelevant, at this point, to consider whether such efforts actually reduced racial inequalities more than would have occurred otherwise. My point is only to offer an example of what it means to speak of policies that give priority to the pursuit of excellence over the mere attainment of equal distributions in educational participation.

This policy priority was evident on all sides of the controversy over issues of racial balance. During the same period, the claim was also advanced that "busing is no good unless there is something worthwhile at the end of the route!" The implication was that busing is acceptable if excellence is assured. Again, the suggestion was that policies in pursuit of educational excellence must be given greater weight than those advanced in the mere pursuit of equal racial distributions in schools.

Often, in response to this suggestion, the slogan was pronounced that " 'quality education' means 'integrated education' " or "integrated education just *is* quality education!" Here again, the policy slogan drew its presumed strength from an appeal to conscience giving priority to excellence over equality as a policy goal. In short, the claim was that more equal distributions are good simply because that's what we mean by "excellence."

Even when different policy conclusions were drawn, the presumption was the same. Excellence of education is what we seek. Inequalities in the distributions of participation and achievement are taken as evidence (but not proof) that excellence is not uniformly attained.

2. But this implies that differential frequencies of participation, achievement, and resources are evidence of inequality even when the achievement of equal frequencies is not really the remedy being sought. Documenting the presence of such inequalities is simply our method—and possibly the only method we have—of establishing the presence or absence of inequity. But eradicating those inequalities is, nevertheless, not the presumed aim of policy. It is simply the sole means we have of monitoring our progress toward a stronger presumption of equity. The aim is the achievement of excellence.

3. But to this aim, beyond any doubt, we must add the phrase "excellence for all." And we need to add this phrase, because the aims of equality and equity are inextricably tied to the priority we grant in conscience to excellence as our primary policy goal. Here again we make a number of assumptions. Principal among them is the assumption that children of deprived or even impoverished backgrounds can achieve. If education provided for children of disadvantaged backgrounds were truly excellent, then—we assume—they would achieve.

To speak of giving policy priority to excellence over equality is, therefore, to speak of policies whose aim, among other things, is to provide such children with truly excellent education—not in preference to others, but not in deference to others either. If such children can be assured of truly excellent education, then they are likely to achieve more and to attain higher levels of education than they would if we were content simply to provide them with "equal" education. By focusing attention upon the excellence of their education, we are more likely to raise their levels of achievement and attainment and that would be a good thing to do even if doing so did not reduce the range in the observed rates of inequality. On the other hand, if our aim of policy were merely to reduce the observed unequal frequencies of participation and attainment, then, conceptually speaking, we can accomplish that aim, and probably will if we achieve it at all, without any increase in educational excellence at all.

We may see the point in still another way. If educational excellence were given policy priority and vigorously pursued, then we would have increased assurance that resulting inequalities are not inequities, i.e., are fair. But if our primary aim is merely to reduce differences in the frequencies and distributions used to monitor the matter in public policy, then we can accomplish our goal more easily and directly by simply making schools uniformly bad. Bare equality, in other words, can be achieved with a decline and even an abandonment of the ideal of excellence for all or even excellence for any. That is why we are more likely to get equity by policies in pursuit of excellence than we are likely to get either excellence or equity by policies in pursuit of equality. Let us turn then to the detailed exposition of the argument.

Levels of Aggregation

Educational equality can be a primary ideal and concern of persons only at a high level of social aggregation where public policy, being a tool of aggregate social control, is a "fit" instrument of intervention. That is what makes equality such a natural, and perhaps even uniquely suited, aim of public policy. Educational excellence, on the other hand, is something that occurs and is paradigmatically a central concern only at a very low level of aggregation. Therefore, if we are to frame policies in direct pursuit of educational excellence, we would have to frame measures that powerfully control the behavior of persons at a very low level of social aggregation. It is not clear that this can be done or that if it could, it would be good to do. The very concepts of "policy" and "educational equality," in other words, belong to the vantage point of high levels of social aggregation. The concept of "educational excellence," in contrast, does not.

Now in saying this I do not mean that considerations of equality or fairness of treatment never arise within the classroom. Clearly, they do. "Equity" is an ideal or concern that can be present across the range of social aggregation. Nor do I mean that educational excellence cannot be a concern of governmental actions. Sometimes it is. I mean only that educational equality—especially as it has been embodied in public policy—cannot be a foreground concern of the practicing teacher or school principal in conducting the day-to-day affairs of the classroom or the school. It can be, however, and often is, a substantive, even daily concern of government officials.

To say this is perhaps to point out the obvious. For example, no teacher worthy of the name would hold back certain able students, purposefully producing confusion in their minds, just in order to contribute to a socially more balanced range of school achievement. Neither would any teacher purposefully give special attention to certain children simply in order to improve the distribution of achievement. Achieving the social goal of equal distributions may be a consequence, but it cannot be a central concern in the actions of the practicing teacher. The advancement of education excellence, however, can and should be a central concern.

In like manner, issues of equalizing resources between schools or balancing enrollments of ethnic and racial subpopulations is not and cannot be an appropriate concern of teachers in their classroom practice. For the teacher or the principal in the daily affairs of the classroom or the school, such concerns, if ever elevated to the level of serious attention, would constitute a sheer distraction. But for the government official or the legislator concerned with basic policy, these matters are not distractions. They are, on the contrary, central problems. They may even be the substance of constitutional duties. These are the facts I wish to point to in the claim that these two ideals—excellence and equality—reside at different levels of social aggregation.

The same point is evident in the discontinuities of discourse and rhetoric that occur when we shift discussion from problems of equality to concerns of educational excellence. The discourse unremittingly employed to this point in the argument has all been "policy talk." Virtually none of it has been "educational talk." It has been the kind of talk that engages the concerns of persons at the district, state, and federal levels of social aggregation. Virtually none of it is the kind that one would hear in homes, in classrooms, or in schools where considerations of excellence and practice find their natural residence.

The rhetoric of public policy is the language of what happens in general, on the whole, for the most part, and only in relation to differences of rather large magnitude. But the educational rhetoric of the classroom and the home is not that kind of talk at all. It has to do with particular persons in particular settings and with differences that demand attention even though they may be quite minute. Surely, as any teacher might reflect, "All this talk of public policy cannot bear upon tomorrow's class because in tomorrow's class children 'in general, on the whole, and for the most part,' simply do not appear."

There is, in short, this discontinuity between the discourse, rhetoric, and concepts of educational equality and public policy, on the one hand, and of educational excellence, on the other. The one mirrors the character of thought and action at a high level of aggregation. The other reflects the quality of thought and action at a low level of aggregation. Excellence and equality are educational ideals that belong at different social levels. Public policy is a social tool clearly suited to promote the one, but not so clearly suited to promote the other.

Consider this discontinuity of discourse in an actual case. I refer to the words of Philip Jackson speaking as an educator when confronted with a work of policy import on the presence and dimensions of educational inequality. He says:

> Knowing that apples grow on trees need not, on the one hand, increase a child's happiness nor, on the other, increase the likelihood of his becoming a well-paid adult. Yet somehow it does seem like a good thing to know, as do most of life's learnings that have little bearing on whether we feel good at the moment or are able to pay our bills at the end of the month. . . .
>
> Most educators know . . . that some experiences are superior to others regardless of whether they are accompanied by heightened enjoyment. They also know that the defense of most school-sponsored activities cannot even rest with the argument that the activities themselves were intrinsically valuable in the sense of supplying worthwhile knowledge. . . .
>
> From an educational viewpoint, the potential of any experience is gauged by the answers to two questions: are participants prepared to make the most of it? and where does the experience lead in a developmental sense?[14]

All talk of aggregate frequencies, distributions, and conditional probabilities—so convenient for policy discourse and so essential for discussion of educational equality—

is alien to the problems confronted where excellence is really pursued. It is the kind of talk that probably cannot and should not even enter the minds of those actually engaged in the pursuit of educational excellence as they practice their craft and exercise their judgment. The intellectual gymnastics required to leap such a chasm of discontinuity must surely make policy pronouncements appear to the practicing educator as either "strictly academic" or "strictly governmental"—either as the expression of empty idealism or as the intrusion of governmental power. How can—indeed, why should—anyone attend to the kind of "on the whole" considerations so characteristic of public policy when every ounce of energy is required to discern what is educationally valuable in the quite specific (not general) case of these quite specific (not general) students?

From the vantage where excellence in education can be authentically pursued, one should not be surprised if the pursuit of equality is perceived as an irrelevance. Indeed, it would be amazing were it not discerned as an intrusion, or even an obstacle to the educational task of seeking excellence. As educational practitioner (as contrasted with administrator), one is required never to ask whether outcomes can be more equal in general and, at the same time, never to doubt that things must be fair in specific cases. Where educational excellence is truly pursued, aggregate educational equality is never the salient problem. The central problems have always to do with whether the participants are ready "to make the most of this experience" and where the next step may lead "in a developmental sense."

This distinction between the policy pursuit of excellence and equality is derived from the location of these different ideals at different levels of aggregation. It is an inexact distinction; it is not precise; but it is a point of depth and importance. It implies that the quest for equality is a more suitable aim of public policy, but educationally less weighty than the quest for excellence.

The Priority of Excellence over Equality

Nevertheless, policies in pursuit of educational excellence are more likely to produce gains in equity than policies in pursuit of equality are likely to produce gains in excellence. That is my second proposition.

The salient point to observe in this formulation is its careful employment of the term "equity." Equity, more than equality, is an ideal whose realization is spread widely over the range of discontinuities in social aggregation. Considerations of equity, unlike considerations of equality and excellence, are appropriate at every level of social aggregation. Fairness of treatment is always relevant to the quality of human relations. In contrast, concerns of educational equality are not even discernable except at high levels of aggregation. And considerations of educational excellence are salient only at low levels of aggregation.

However, if we could achieve uniform excellence of education, then whatever social inequalities remain could not be unfair, or if unfair, then the lack of equity could not be attributable to inequity in education. In this sense, the attainment of universal excellence entails a certain kind of equity, even though it might not erase all social inequality. The achievement of equality, on the other hand, has no such beneficent implications for the promotion of excellence. That is the essential reason why the pursuit of educational excellence for all is a more serious and more important aim of public policy than the pursuit of bare equality.

Thresholds

To this general conclusion, we must add three threshold conditions any one of which may drastically alter our priorities. If, in the formation of policy, our ideals are always "nested" in a set, then we should expect that at some times one and at other times another ideal will prevail. The saying is that "circumstances alter things." And indeed, they do. In arguing for the policy priority of excellence over equality, I have not meant that issues of equality should never assume a paramount position. I have argued only that within the limits of the usual caveat— "all other things being equal"—the pursuit of excellence should receive the more serious attention. But there are clearly thresholds at which this priority will be transformed.

First of all, recall that public policy is a relatively crude tool. It is an instrument of control most appropriately invoked when attention is focused on what is happening on the whole and in general and when the promised changes, being proportionate to the magnitude of evil, are large. For the correction of small evils or the advancement of marginal gains, we typically, and quite rightly, employ the "private bill" or other means to slightly modify the social structure of incentives. But such measures always fall short of formulating basic public policy. And so in the case of education some inequalities are inescapable. However real they are, if they are small, their presence does not constitute even presumptive grounds for fresh formulations of general policy. Under such conditions, policies in pursuit of excellence may assume their rightful priority.

In the table examined earlier, for example, undoubted inequalities are displayed. But they are fairly small—at least for youth of high ability. They do not, it was argued, add up to clear claims of inequity. Under such conditions, it was argued, the advancement of policies aimed at removing the observed inequality might place us on a collision course with the maintenance of other "nested" ideals. By pursuing greater equality, we risk abridging the educational authority of the family and constraining the expression of pluralism. So here is a case in which the pursuit of educational excellence may assume its presumed priority.

But if, on the other hand, those observed inequalities were very large, then the situation would be drastically altered. Large inequalities, truly blatant and gross ones, must be taken as presumptive proof not simply of inequality, but of inequity. Under such conditions, the priorities within our "nested ideals" would have to shift. The quest for excellence would have to yield to the restoration of bare equality. Similar remarks would apply when issues of civil rights arise. Their preservation must receive the highest priority even when the policy arguments have no foundation whatsoever in the quest for educational excellence.

Here then are two threshold conditions under which the normal priorities of our "nested ideals" would be modified. Thus, under certain threshold conditions the redress of gross injustices can become more important even than the pursuit of educational excellence. But not even under these conditions can we suppose that justice is always the highest among our ideals of public policy. For example, it would probably be easier for most of us to live in a society where we are openly treated unjustly (at least we would know where to focus our indignation), than it would be to live in a society where we are fairly, justly, exactly, and openly declared to be inadequate. And so, we may find that in a world where the quest for educational excellence takes sometimes the form of "competency tests," even the demand for justice may yield to a loud "hurrah!" in defense of murky, inconclusive, and even unjust devices of human assessment. Is it so outrageous to suppose that a society in which some are granted what they do not merit may be better than one in which each is given exactly what he deserves? In short, this view concerning the "natural priority" of the pursuit of excellence has its own dynamics.

The central problem is to determine when the transforming thresholds of policy priorities have been breached. To this question again there is no technical answer. Nevertheless, the question will be answered. It will be answered, however, through a political process and not through any increase in our capacity for measurement, our skills of policy analysis, or our tools of social control. It is likely to be answered rather by the sensibilities of politicians who, by some Byzantine black magic, will undertake to feel the public pulse. The agenda will change when the public's sensibilities are too severely strained. In short, in any free society, determining when the transforming thresholds in the priorities of our values have been reached is a political rather than a conceptual or scientific problem.

There is, however, one final threshold in these dynamics, one more closely related to the problem of educational utility. From the aggregate perspective that policy demands, educational excellence is likely to be defined as mastery of those segments of the school curriculum whose social utility is most transparent. Satisfying those requirements is admittedly a kind of need. But it seldom adds up to what anyone means by "educational excellence."

For example, it is often, and rightfully, a public complaint that schools, too often, fail to teach the basic skills of reading. And, it is said, this failure is crucial because we live in a world requiring that directions are read, forms completed, and citizens are informed. To fail generally in these matters, or even very often, is to risk the future of society itself. That would be no mere failure to satisfy our dearest aspirations. On the contrary, it would be a failure to meet the most basic social functions of education.

Now I do not care to dispute these facts or even to speculate whether they describe a present state of affairs. My point is rather that when such extremities are believed to exist, then any society would be justified in displacing the quest for excellence with policies aimed at satisfying basic needs. And so we reach another threshold transforming the priorities of policy.

But this transformation is likely not only to alter the rank order of our ideals, but to alter the very meaning of "educational excellence" itself. These are the conditions when we are most likely to replace maximums with minimums, talk of excellence with talk of elementary basics. But these are also the transforming conditions within which educational excellence is most likely to be confused with social utility. Even if we lived in a world where nobody had to read directions or complete applications for any life purpose whatever, still, we would have to teach reading and literature for educational reasons alone. There would be educational value in such activities even if they had no social utility at all. Acquiring the skills of reading is useful to those who acquire them, and no doubt also it is useful for any modern society that lots of persons acquire them. So these utilities add up to a kind of social value, but they do not add up to what anyone ordinarily means by "educational excellence." Education is a failure when it does not satisfy certain aggregate social functions; but even when it does, it may not be excellent.

Such threshold circumstances alter our policy priorities. But they do more. They also clarify and crystallize our aims. They are, as it were, the boundary conditions within which the pursuit of educational excellence can continue and beyond which concerns of excellence will be displaced. Such boundary conditions, whenever reached, produce clarity partly because it is easier to gain agreement on what to do when we are faced with large injustices and blatant failures than it is to reach agreement on small improvements or on standards of excellence. In the face of flood, fire, and other natural disasters, what to do is clear. Needs are near at hand. Concerns of excellence then take a back seat in the priorities of action. And so it is with educational policy. Aims are always clearer, less subject to debate, when we pass the thresholds that define failure.

Educational policy is most clearly defined on a continuum extending from "bad," to "worse," to "absolutely intolerable." But excellence is an ideal lying always on a continuum running from "good," to "better," to "best." The first of these continua moves on a line toward increasing clarity, the second on a line toward increasing difficulty.

And so we see, in still another way, the sense of the maxim that public policy is a tool of action better aimed at minimizing evil than at maximizing good. Remedying inequality is an aim more suited to the tools of policy than promoting excellence. Nevertheless, given the distinction between "equality" and "equity," policies in pursuit of excellence are more likely to advance the ideal of equity than policies in pursuit of equality are likely to advance the ideal of excellence. I have already advanced reasons to support this claim. Let us turn to a concluding consideration in its support.

The Equity of Excellence

Some inequalities are fair and some are not. That is implied by the principle of equity itself. We have passed through a period when the claims of equality have substantially defined the terms of American educational policy. We may now be entering a period when the more salient problem is to specify which inequalities are justified. That is a vastly more difficult, more perilous, and morally more ambiguous path for public policy. Yet, equality is easily monitored in suitably aggregate ways. Equity is not. How, therefore, can such a path of action be defended?

In the first place, it ought to be pursued only if we are convinced that the boundaries of injustice marked by the transforming thresholds of policy are no longer flagrantly breached, and whether those conditions are satisfied will always be partly a matter of fact and partly a matter of opinion. But there is another justification derived from the ideal of educational excellence itself. Throughout this argument, the claim has been implicit that the ideal of educational excellence entails its own peculiar kind of equity. The central point is that the concept of educational excellence is inherently a universalistic ideal. Its achievement would satisfy the requirements of equity but not equality.

Whenever education is truly excellent, it is always totally indifferent to every educationally irrelevant variable expressed in the principle of equity. A good inference, a good act, a good insight—these are always excellent regardless of the social class, the sex, the ethnic origin or religious convictions of the person whose mind and action they express. That is a true of excellence in graduate studies as it is of fifth-grade studies. There is no Presbyterian plumbing system, no Jewish algebra, no racial criteria for the assessment of belief, no social class barriers to the intellectual recovery of tradition and the human response to literature.

In short, there is such a thing as "the house of intellect." The criteria for entrance into it and for status within it are not grounded in distinctions of class, ethnicity, sex, or religious conviction. They are grounded rather in criteria, always debatable, always open to amendment, that express the qualities of mind, the acquired disciplines of thought and reflection that constitute the stigmata of those we call well-educated. Excellence in the exercise of intellectual powers, in the disciplines of craft and emotion, is always expressed by human beings as humans and not as members of a social class, sex, race, or as inheritors of a specific religious tradition. That is what I mean by saying that such criteria are universalistic. They are not sectarian.

Excellence of education should be measured never by the satisfaction of our basic social needs. Its excellence resides always in its capacity to arouse and cultivate those capabilities for memory, action, and emotional discipline that are ours as human beings. Excellence of education rests always in the quite specific questions as to whether these specific children are "prepared to make the most of" this specific experience and where it leads next "in a developmental sense."

We have some difficulty in grasping how our ideals of equity and excellence are to be adjusted in educational policy. But that difficulty does not arise from any lack of clarity on the demands of educational equality. The search for educational equality, whether in resources or in outcomes, has been the most studied, the most publicized, the most debated issue of recent years. It may be that the problem arises because we have not debated, with anything resembling equal intensity, our confused images of educational excellence. The path of public policy best designed to satisfy our yearnings for equity is the one path we have studied least and have debated hardly at all.

For example, there is, right now, increasing concern among reflective observers of education that the practice of curricular tracking is the source of dangerous inequality, even inequity. And so we are likely to hear more strident calls for its abolishment. Yet, this pleading, too, is likely to prove illusory unless it results also in a reconsideration of our views of educational excellence.

Let us suppose that some children, on grounds that violate the principle of equity, are "persuaded" at an early stage to take the curricular path of business arithmetic. And let us suppose further that, as a consequence, they are forbidden the chance to take algebra. They are "closed off" from the "higher curriculum." What is wrong about this is not merely that it throws up artificial barriers to educational progress and thus unfairly predetermines the social destiny of youth. It is more seriously wrong because it prepares them neither for any decent life in business, nor in industry, nor in the crafts. What is wrong, in short, is not that there is tracking, but that there is a denial of educational excellence. And what is doubly wrong is that such a result is created in the name of excellence.

Why? Because if there is any property whatever that for whatever reason is differentially distributed among children and is relevant in determining the kind of education they should receive, then we are obliged to take that difference into account. That differential property can be anything from a handicap to a special talent. For the sake of educational excellence, grouping is probably required. But the more inequitable consequences of tracking are not required.

These practices, however, are double-edged. If some are denied access to the "higher curriculum" by the practices of tracking, others in the "higher curriculum" are denied the chance to learn those skills and disciplines of art and craft that can contribute to their respect for labor and arouse their talent. If we object to the one kind of tracking, we must object to the other. Both are wrong, not because they are instances of tracking, not because they produce social inequality, but because they are equally a denial of educational excellence. The pursuit of excellence, its very definition, is what, as a nation, we have not debated. It is, nonetheless, the most direct path toward equity in education.

It is worth a reminder that those who go to MIT and get C's in physics may decide that they are no good at it and give up, whereas, if they had gone elsewhere, they may have gotten A's, persisted in their studies, and persevered to distinguished careers. In these respects, institutions of so-called excellence may do greater damage educationally than institutions of the second-rank. But this again is merely another mark of our confusion in the images of excellence we uncritically possess. In short, by "educational excellence" we cannot mean "exclusive," "selective," or "elite." Residence in the "house of intellect" is not limited to the Professoriate or to graduates of "elite" institutions any more than participation in what Butler called "the moral institution of life" is limited to saints.

Educational excellence is present whenever and wherever there are those activities that nurture the capacities of mind that we share as humans, the memory of the traditions that we share as those with a common history, and the allegiances that we share as those who have a common membership. In its pursuit we do not ask whether those participating will end up with equal status in the eyes of other human beings. We ask instead whether those who participate are prepared "to make the most of it" and where it leads next "in a developmental sense." If we ever get good at this effort, then inequality will persist, but there will be less inequity in it. In other words, if we are confused about the place of equity in educational policy, it is because we are confused about our ideals of educational excellence. The pursuit of equality, though sometimes demanded by the priorities of policy, is neither the clearest path toward equity nor a direct path toward educational excellence.

NOTES

1. A fuller treatment of this value conflict, its dynamics, complexities, and influence on the transformation of educational policy is given in Thomas F. Green, *Predicting the Behavior of the Educational System* (Syracuse University Press, Syracuse, N.Y., 1980), Chapt. VII.

2. See Robert K. Merton, *Social Theory and Social Structure* (The Free Press, New York, 1964), Chapter VI, "Bureaucratic Structure and Personality."

3. See John H. Schaar, "Some Ways of Thinking about Equality," *The Journal of Politics*, Vol. 26, No. 4, 1964, pp. 869–870. "What is justice for all others is injustice for your friend. To treat those closest to us by a rule applicable to everyone would amount to an insane cruelty.... That is why the maxim has it that there is no justice among friends. (It is) because justice is blind.... In our higher courts this ideal becomes literal reality: the concrete individual for whom justice must be done does not even appear before the judges. The judges see only lawyers, craftsmen trained in what Blackstone called 'the mysterious science of the law.' Any intrusion of the human and personal violates the whole process and threatens its validity."

4. For a more extended analysis on how parental and State interests interact in the case of education, see also Thomas F. Green, *Predicting the Behavior of the Educational System*, (Syracuse University Press, 1980), Chapter II, "Control."

5. ESEA was originally intended to remedy interstate inequities in the allocation of resources. This is true especially of Title I. Only later, in its legislative history, did the act become a tool for the advancement of intrastate equality.

6. See in this volume the article by Michael Kirst in which the necessity of such an "accounting track" is stressed and its implications traced.

7. See again the article in this volume by Kirst in which it is documented that this is indeed a

dominant consequence of such legislation in practice. When the intent is transferred from the level of aggregation where it is conceived to another where it must be executed, then through the process of implementation, there is created a conflict of ideals.

It may be that the solution to this policy problem is to cease framing policy that requires the "tracking" of the Federal Dollar and to call instead for the capacity to monitor the provision of services. But this would constitute a somewhat weakened version of the ideal of public accountability. And besides, even with this radical transformation of federal practice, it is not obvious that the accountants' problem would be sufficiently altered to change the impact of implementation on the expression of our ideals in practice.

8. See Gerald Grant, *Authority, Equality and the Nature of the Crisis in American Education* (forthcoming), particularly Chapter 4, "The Rise of Specialists and a Technicist Spirit," for an account of the paradoxical impacts of the increased number of specialists who have taken an often ambivalent place next to the classroom teacher.

9. In this discussion, the concepts of "educationally relevant" and "educationally irrelevant" variables can be defined precisely, but not without some technical rendering.

An educationally relevant variable is any variable x, such that if educational resources and benefits are distributed unequally to accord with the unequal distribution of x in the population, then that inequality cannot be regarded as unjust. An educationally irrelevant variable can be defined as any variable x, such that if educational resources and benefits are distributed unequally to accord with the distribution of x in the society, then that unequal distribution will also be inequitable or unjust.

10. Actually, there are several things that might operate instead of choice. Among them would be incarceration, military service, and disabilities of various kinds. The probability of .96 in this group may actually be the real-life equivalent of 1.0.

11. The usual claim is that children of highest SES try harder to keep from falling in status than those of lower SES try to rise in status. See Jencks and Riesman, *The Academic Revolution*, Chapter III, "Social Stratification and Mass Higher Education"; and Stephen Michelson, "The Further Responsibilities of Intellectuals", *Harvard Educational Review*, Vol. 43, No. 1, February 1973, p. 101. But this is an imperceptive observation. In this case, the claim that such persons "try harder" is the literal as well as social equivalent of saying "they don't have to try as hard" or "they have to actually try if they are to fall in status."

12. It is worth nothing that there was a time in the United States when college attendance was more common not among the most able sons of the rich, but among the second and third most able. The really capable ones had better things to do—the family business, work, the farm, and so forth. The compulsion to go was less, but the economic freedom to go was not less.

13. However, if the data considered are the kind of highly aggregated distributional data (as they must be in order to be policy relevant) compiled and displayed as they are for the table already examined, then the inequalities are likely to be larger than an egalitarian would like and smaller than a true proponent of an inegalitarian status quo would desire. A thorough defense of this point would require, however, a rather intricate exploration of the sheer logic of such tables.

Such a study, I believe, would prove that, on grounds of logic alone, if there is any effect at all of family upon frequencies of college attendance, then the diagonal from high SES and high ability to low SES and low ability would have to be not only the largest inequality in the table but also a substantial one.

The significant point in this conjecture is the proviso "if there is any effect at all of family. . . ." In short, the very logic of such tables contains an inherent conflict between the ideals of the educational authority of the family, on the one hand, and the demands of social equality, on the other hand. In short, no matter what probabilities are recorded in such a table, if the numbers satisfy the conditions of the one ideal, they will record a severe abridgement in the other.

14. Philip W. Jackson, "After Apple-Picking," from a series of commentaries on Christopher Jencks' *Inequality, Harvard Educational Review*, Vol. 43, No. 1, February 1973, pp. 57–58.

CHAPTER 14

Complexity and Control

What Legislators and Administrators Can Do about Implementing Public Policy[1]

Richard F. Elmore

> ...*there are limits to the human capacity to design and manage, by the political process, huge, complex, interdependent human and ecological systems, and...we are now pressing against those limits.*
>
> RUFUS MILES

Complexity is probably the most troubling aspect of modern government. Nowhere is the effect of complexity more apparent than in the translation of legislation into administrative action—what we have come to call "the implementation problem." Most policies have their origin in a piece of legislation. Following on the heels of the legislation are a series of administrative actions—regulations, guidelines, budget decisions, reorganizations, and so forth—that express legislators' and administrators' expectations. As the complexity of government increases, the connection between legislative intent and administrative action becomes more difficult to follow.

This paper is intended to demonstrate how legislators and administrators can develop a common language for dealing effectively with the complexity of implementation. The paper is addressed primarily to an audience of practitioners—legislators, administrators, and their staffs—and only secondarily to an academic audience. It is written, to the best of my ability, in standard English rather than academic jargon, and it summarizes and amplifies recent research on the implementation of public policy. The major purpose, though, is not to review research but to turn that research into something useful for people who deal with implementation problems in their daily work.

The paper is structured around a series of exchanges between legislators and administrators. I have chosen this technique because it effectively demonstrates their shared responsibilty for the success or failure of policy implementation. The exchanges are all fictitious, but I think they illustrate problems that are familiar to anyone who has worked on either side of the legislative oversight process.

The major theme of the paper is that the complexity of implementation requires a substantial rethinking of legislative and administrative control. The traditional devices that legislators have relied upon to control policy implementation—more specific legislation, tighter regulations and procedures, centralized authority, and closer monitoring of compliance—probably have an effect opposite of that intended. Rather than increasing control, they increase complexity. And as complexity increases, control itself is threatened. Thus, this paper represents an attempt to develop alternatives to the traditional techniques of legislative and administrative control.

The signs of increasing complexity in policy implementation are clear to legislators and administrators in their daily work. The number of concurrences, signoffs, and agreements necessary to set a policy in motion increases as layers of policy accumulate. The number of individuals whose actions must be coordinated increases as new responsibilities are added to administrative agencies. Lines of responsibility become more difficult to follow, and the causes of failure become more difficult to trace. Complexity, in its most basic terms, is a function both of the *number of actors* and the *number of transactions among actors* required to accomplish a given task. Complexity stems not just from the sheer *size* of government but also from the *interdependence* of people within it.[2]

When we speak of government agencies or programs being "out of control," we generally mean that they are aimless, unresponsive to policymakers and clients, sluggish, uncoordinated, or self-serving. Control, then, consists of bringing administrative actions into line with the expectations of policymakers and citizens. But this general notion of control conceals two very different meanings: one meaning is the *control that superiors exercise over subordinates*, and the other is the *control that individuals exercise over their own actions*. In the first instance we are talking about *hierarchical control*—authority, supervision, regulation, and coercion—and in the second we are talking about *delegated control*—individual responsibility, initiative, and discretion. Common sense tells us that both kinds of control are required for successful implementation. Hierarchical control is the means by which policymakers (legislators and high-level administrators) affect the actions of subordinates (mid-level managers and service deliverers). But the administrative structure would soon collapse if individuals did not exercise some degree of responsibility, initiative, and control over their own actions. Imagine a group of policymakers presiding over a bureaucracy in which no one acted unless they were explicitly told to do something. The success of policymakers depends, to a very large degree, on the skill and initiative of policy implementors.

Hierarchical control and delegated control have very different effects on administrative complexity: the former leads to greater complexity, the latter to less. The more a government invests in hierarchical control, the more effort it devotes to writing regulations, specifying procedures, monitoring performance, and enforcing compliance. The more a government invests in delegated control, the more it relies on individual judgment as a substitute for complex administrative procedure, but the less assurance it has of strict compliance. The crucial trade-off for policymakers is between more complexity with greater hierarchical control and less complexity with greater delegated control.

In the discussion that follows, I suggest ways that legislators and administrators can attack problems of complexity and control in policy implementation. The discussion demonstrates, I think, that policymakers can become very skilled analysts of implementation problems without radically altering their established roles. The basic meaning of implementation analysis (as used in the context of this paper) is best captured by "foresight," which means simply "thinking and planning beforehand" or "previous consideration."[3] The analysis that we observe policymakers engaging in consists of reasoning through implementation problems *before policy* decisions are firmly made.

My purpose is *not* to convince legislators and administrators that they need another contingent of expert consultants, but rather to show how a systematic discussion of implementation issues can be introduced, without much trouble, into routine legislative oversight hearings. An important part of my argument is that responsibility for implementation rests jointly with legislators and administrators. The formal doctrine of separation of powers encourages us to think of implementation as purely an executive responsibility. But experience with the implementation of large-scale programs demonstrates that there is no clear boundary separating legislative and administrative responsibility. If legislators show a lack of concern for administrative feasibility in the drafting of legislation, or if adminstrators fail to communicate practical problems to legislators, or if administrators and legislators fail to address implementation issues in the oversight process, then the complexity of implementation will almost certainly overwhelm the intent of policy. For this reason, I do not treat implementation analysis as a special, highly refined area of expertise, but as a part of the ongoing interaction between legislators and administrators. The central focus of the discussion is the relationship between policymakers (legislators and high-level administrators) and service deliverers (mid-level managers and direct service personnel). Implementation analysis consists, for our purposes, of systematically discovering ways to make effective connections between policymakers and service deliverers.

REGULATORY AND PROGRAMMATIC VIEWS OF IMPLEMENTATION

To begin with a fairly common implementation problem that surfaces in a legislative hearing, we interrupt an exchange between the chairperson of a legislative committee and the head (commissioner) of a large executive agency. The chair has been reviewing a number of programs in the commissioner's agency and has come to one that has been the subject of some criticism—call it the 320(d) program. The person who is directly responsible for administering the 320(d) program—call this person the program director—does not participate in this exchange, but is involved in subsequent exchanges.

> **Chair.** As you're probably aware, Commissioner, we've heard testimony from a number of people that funds from the 320(d) program are being misspent by local agencies—they're being used to fund questionable activities and they're not effectively reaching the target population. What is your estimate of the situation?
>
> **Commissioner.** I am as concerned as you are about these criticisms of the program. I've asked for a complete review. You must understand our problem here, though. We're dealing with independent units of local government and they have ideas of their own about how to spend program funds. The 320(d) program gives local agencies a fair amount of discretion in the use of funds. We've written the regulations so as to spell out the purposes and activities that we have determined are consistent with legislative intent. But the law says that each agency is to construct its own program consistent with its own local needs.
>
> **Chair.** Well what's the difficulty then? Why are we getting complaints? Do we need to amend the legislation to give your agency more control over local decisions? Do you need to rewrite the regulations? Or do you just need to tighten up your enforcement of existing regulations?
>
> **Commissioner.** We're not absolutely certain ourselves what the solution is, but I expect the director's review will produce some recommendations that will help us decide what to do. I don't think I'm incorrect in saying, am I, that the intent of

the legislation is not to preempt local decisions but to encourage local agencies to develop their own programs?

Chair. I think that is a correct statement of the intent. But it's also true, is it not, that when we find evidence that the program is not reaching the target population, we ought to do something about it?

Commissioner. Yes. If we find that agencies are not complying with the regulations and the intent of the law, we will act on those cases. Also, if we find that we need additional authority, we will ask for legislative amendments. Is that satisfactory?

Chair. Fair enough. We'll expect to hear from you in the near future.

Commissioner. As soon as the director's review is completed.

This exchange illustrates most of the factors that define an implementation problem: the program has somehow missed its mark; the evidence that most troubles the chair is that local agencies are not serving the people whom the legislature intended them to serve. Is there something that can be done, either to the legislation or to the administration of the program, to remedy this problem? The commissioner is carefully trying to establish two basic points with the chair. The first is that responsibility for operating the 320(d) program is lodged with the program director; it is the director's responsibility to determine whether the program is missing its mark and, if a problem is actually found to exist, to develop a solution. The second point is that the operation of the program depends, in a very basic sense, on local agencies' taking responsibility for the program at the delivery level; if local agencies fail, the program fails.

Notice how the complexity develops. The chair and the commissioner are sitting at the top of a very tall pyramid trying to diagnose a problem that is occurring at the bottom. Between the top and the bottom are at least two levels of administrative machinery: the director's office and a large number of local agencies. The complexity of the problem is a function of both the distance from the top to the bottom—the number of levels—and the number of actors at each level. The further down the pyramid we go, the larger the number of transactions necessary to get anything done. It is for this reason that delegated control is so important. The chair and the commissioner cannot pretend to manage the director's program, nor can the director pretend to manage the wide variety of programs at the local level. Policy—legislation, regulations, guidelines, and informal agreements—is what holds the levels together, but delegated control is what makes the policy work at any given level.

Observe, also, that the chair and the commissioner seem to have agreed already on the solution to the problem—tighter regulation and more hierarchical control. Imagine the following scenario: The program director's study reveals that, indeed, there are examples of questionable local decisions. The chair, the commissioner, and the director agree that no new legislative authority is required but that the director needs to tighten up monitoring of local spending. In operational terms, this means that the director's staff will spend a larger proportion of their time questioning local administrators about their program decisions. It also means that the regulations and guidelines that define legitimate local expenditures will become more complex and detailed, requiring more attention to compliance. As questions of compliance increase, the director's staff and local administrators will focus a larger proportion of their conversations with each other on interpretation of the rules.

The element that is missing in this scenario is any direct concern for *whether the program is actually working*. After all the rules and regulations are complied with, do we actually know that the beneficiaries of the program are better off? Does compliance ensure success?

The chair and the commissioner, without really intending to, have taken a *regulatory view* of implementation. They have, for the sake of simplifying their problem, chosen to equate success with tighter hierarchical control and greater compliance. The problem with this view is that, while we can demonstrate that greater hierarchical control produces greater compliance, we cannot assure that greater compliance produces better results. In fact, we could argue that, in some instances, there is a negative relationship between compliance and better results because resources used for regulation cannot be used for service delivery. Regulation constitutes a diversion of resources from substance to surveillance.[4]

There is an alternative to the regulatory view that I call the *programmatic view*. This view focuses on delegated control instead of hierarchical control, and it defines the important issue not as compliance but as the *capacity to deliver a service*. To decide whether tighter regulation will solve their problem, the chair and the commissioner first must decide whether they are interested in compliance as an end in itself or whether they are interested in compliance as a means of improving the performance of the 320(d) program.

In some instances, it makes sense to view compliance as the primary goal. Certain types of policies are primarily regulatory in intent, such as those dealing with school desegregation, affirmative action, auto emission standards, pure food and drug laws, and occupational safety and health standards. These policies exist to regulate private choices in accordance with public standards of equity and safety. Other policies, however, are not primarily regulatory in intent. Housing, education, social service, and health policies, for example, exist primarily to deliver services rather than to regulate private choices. For such policies, compliance is secondary to *improving and supporting the capacity of public organizations to deliver services*. The quality of public services depends heavily on delegated control; the choices that go into constructing an effective health care delivery program or an education program are too complex to be entirely structured by a uniform set of regulations. In fact, the quality of service and the capacity of the program to respond to human needs are often hindered rather than helped by hierarchical control.

In reality, all policies have elements of both compliance and capacity-building. Affirmative action is an essentially regulatory policy. Its objective is to hold employers to certain standards of equity in hiring and promotion. But affirmative action will fail as a policy if all it produces is compliance with regulations. If the net effect of affirmative action is to increase the body-count of certain types of people, without fully utilizing the skills and talents of these people, one could hardly say that the policy has been effective. Evidence of underemployment of skilled personnel would be a signal that affirmative action is not working in the programmatic sense, even though it might be working very well in the regulatory sense.

If regulatory policies have a programmatic component, the reverse is also true. Health care, social service, and education policies, for example, have to contain certain rules of financial accountability to guard against corruption and misuse of funds. Regulations are also necessary in service delivery programs as a way of establishing common ground rules for eligibility and termination of government grants. But we would not say that a service delivery program was effective simply because it produced compliance with these rules. More importantly, legislators and high-level administrators cannot improve the quality or capacity of service delivery organizations simply by regulating them. Quality depends mainly on the skills and competence of the people who actually deliver the service and only secondarily on their compliance with rules and regulations.

For most legislators and administrators, implementation means writing and enforcing regulations. My aim is to demonstrate that solving implementation problems requires a broader, programmatic view. How would the exchange between the chair and the commissioner differ if they took a programmatic rather than a regulatory view of the problem?

The most obvious difference would be that the discussion would focus much more on service delivery than on regulation. So, in order to proceed, we need some more information about the 320(d) program. Assume the following: The 320(d) program grew out of concern by the State Legislature over declining test scores in reading and math achievement. After hearing testimony from a number of experts on testing, basic skills, and teaching, the Legislature's Education Committee settled upon a strategy. Local school districts would be asked to survey their student populations, using whatever instruments the districts felt were appropriate, and develop a plan for improving performance in reading and math. The state would offer supplementary grants to local districts, through the State Department of Education, for the purposes of assessing student needs, developing basic skill programs, and implementing them. To qualify for support, a local district would be required to submit a plan describing how it would identify students needing help and what services it would provide to those students. The State Department of Education would review the plans to ensure their consistency with the law and would provide assistance to local districts requesting help in starting programs. (In an effort to hold local districts accountable, the law required that "renewal of grants to local districts shall be conditioned on demonstrated progress in achieving the objectives of the local plan" and gave the State Commissioner of Education the authority to establish criteria for determining whether local districts were making adequate progress.)

TAKING THE PROGRAMMATIC VIEW

Imagine one year later. Virtually every school system in the state is participating in the 320(d) program, and the State Department of Education has established an office, headed by the director, to administer the program. In a routine legislative oversight hearing involving a general review of the department's programs, the Education Committee hears testimony from parent representatives and an advocacy group representing disadvantaged children that local education agencies are "abusing" the 320(d) program by using it to support their general education program, rather than focusing the funds on children with serious problems in reading and math. Local school system representatives counter this criticism by arguing that local plans have been reviewed by the State Department of Education and found consistent with the law. The chairperson of the Education Committee asks the Commissioner of Education to present the department's case.

The following exchange—a replay of the first dialogue—shows how the chair and the commissioner might attack the problem in a programmatic rather than a regulatory way.

Chair. As you're probably aware, Commissioner, we've heard testimony from United Parents for Education and the Children's Advocacy Group alleging that 320(d) funds are not reaching children with the greatest need for help in reading and math. Can you confirm or deny these reports? And can you explain why this appears to be happening?

Commissioner. I've asked the director of the 320(d) program to investigate this problem, and we've spoken at some length prior to this hearing. I've also asked the director to conduct a study and report back to me as soon as possible. At this point, we have several alternative explanations, and we're not sure which of them is correct.

One explanation might be that local administrators are simply not paying adequate attention to the way they use 320(d) funds. If this is true, our program staff simply has not been vigilant enough in monitoring compliance with program regulations. But I would stress that this is only one possible explanation.

Another one might be that some dispersion of funds is unavoidable if reasonably sound educational practice is followed. For example, the only way to ensure that the funds are targeted exclusively on children with serious basic skills problems is to isolate those children completely from the regular school program for all or part of the school day. But many teachers and school administrators would argue that we shouldn't isolate these children from the regular school program. This is a matter of professional judgment, and there's no real agreement on which is the best strategy. We know for sure, though, that if kids with basic skills problems are left in regular classrooms, there will at least be the appearance of diluting program funds.

Still another explanation might be that there aren't any clear-cut standards for what constitutes a basic skills deficit. Each school system has a different set of standards for deciding who needs help. Some systems concentrate on the fewest kids with the greatest needs. Some try to help everyone who falls below the national norm on a reading or math test. And some try to help those kids who are most likely to improve, which means less attention for the kids with the toughest problems. Again, these are professional judgments for which there aren't necessarily any correct answers.

So when you look at the program as a whole, you see a lot of variation in how local systems approach the problem of basic skills. Some of the variation may be due to poor administration, and some may be due to equally legitimate differences of approach.

Chair. If I hear you correctly, then, you're saying that the basic issue is how much local autonomy we're willing to permit in their program. Is that correct?

Commissioner. That's correct.

Chair. But if we allow local school systems complete freedom to decide who needs help, aren't we bound to see abuses and sloppy administration?

Commissioner. I'd like to think that our department can distinguish poor administration from legitimate professional judgments by local school people. I think the way to make that distinction is to look at the local program and ask administration why they've chosen to design it one way or another.

Chair. Would it help to have clearer standards in the law about what kind of children should be served by the program?

Commissioner. It might. But I think we also ought to allow for the possibility that clearer standards might hurt the program. Right now we've got a lot of interesting and promising local programs going, largely as a result of the autonomy we've given local districts. I wouldn't like to see us restrict that diversity because of some standard we've established. Also, it's not clear to me that we know enough to say exactly who should be served by the program. I'm more comfortable giving that decision mainly to the people who are closest to the problem.

Chair. You seem to be telling me that there's nothing we can do to respond to criticisms coming from parents and other people who are also very close to the problem. With all due respect, I'm not sure I can accept that.

Commissioner. I'd like to be able to respond to those criticisms too, but I want to respond in a way that preserves the quality of local programs, rather than in a way that imposes our standards on local districts. If the program is going to work, the responsibility for evaluating performance and deciding what to do has to reside with those who are closest to the problem. We at the state level can support them. We can connect them with others who have experience and help them clarify what they're trying to do. But we can't make the program work. I'd like to be able to respond to criticisms of the program by putting the department in the role of supporting effective practices in local districts, rather than just policing them.

Chair. Let's agree, though, that we've got to do something to respond to these criticisms and do it fairly quickly. We'll expect to hear from you in the near future.

Commissioner. As soon as the director's review is completed.

What distinguishes this exchange from the previous one is its concern with program operations rather than regulation, with delegated control rather than hierarchical control. The chair is no less insistent on the seriousness of the problem; in fact, questions raised by the chair are sharper because they focus more specifically on program operations. Furthermore, the chair has not sacrificed the central legislative concern, constituent complaints. Nor can the chair be expected to care as much about administrative problems as the commissioner. The chair's major concern is political issues that arise in the implementation process. An important constituency has raised a question about the department's implementation strategy. The chair wants a satisfactory answer from the commissioner because—as a legislator and committee head—the chair's political survival depends largely on his ability to respond effectively to constituent claims. The chair's approach to questioning the commissioner demonstrates that legislators can take an aggressive programmatic stance on implementation issues without departing from their role as adjudicators of conflicting political interests.

The commissioner has managed to give a relatively complete account of the administrative problems raised by the 320(d) program, without suggesting that they are susceptible to a simple regulatory solution. The commissioner has also managed to communicate that the Education Department's interest in the program involves more than just policing compliance; it also involves supporting and guiding the development of effective, local programs, which is a much more demanding (and, incidentally, more interesting) task. The commissioner is concerned about the stakes involved in the trade-off between hierarchical and delegated control. The commissioner understands that the more effort the department invests in enforcing compliance, the less resources it will be able to focus on program substance. It is also clear to the commissioner that variation in the way local districts respond to the legislation can be an advantage as well as a disadvantage, that it can be a source of ideas for improving the program rather than a threat to authority.

Neither the chair nor the commissioner has compromised any essential responsibilities. But both have agreed to treat the issue as something more than a matter of regulation and compliance. They have demonstrated an implicit understanding of the costs of hierarchical control and the benefits of delegated control, without losing track of the essential purpose of the program.

COPING WITH VARIATIONS IN IMPLEMENTATION

We have left the chair, the commissioner, and the director with a difficult problem: how to distinguish legitimate variations in the way local districts implement the 320(d) program from outright failures of implementation. The director will have to come to terms with this problem in reviewing the program. Any time a policy is implemented by more than one actor, we can expect some variability. Whether we regard variability as good or bad depends on the standard we use. If we take a strictly regulatory view, our standard of success is compliance, and all variability is suspect because it suggests noncompliance. But if we take a programmatic view, our standard of success is the capacity of program participants to produce desired effects. If variability enhances the likelihood of program effectiveness, it is good; if it does not, it is bad. The important issue, then, is when does variability support and when does it undermine successful program operations.

We are tempted to say that the more implementors agree with the intent of a policy, the less variability we would expect in the way the policy is implemented. In fact, research on implementation suggests otherwise. We have already described one circumstance under which we would expect wide variations in the implementation of a policy, even when implementors agree on the intent—where there are legitimate professional differences on the most effective way to address a problem at the operating level. There are at least five additional circumstances under which we would expect variability in the presence of agreement.[5]

- *Incompatibility with other commitments.* Implementors typically have multiple responsibilities. No matter how much they agree with the intent of a policy, they may have other responsibilities that conflict with or divert attention from it. How these conflicts and diversions are handled will vary among individuals and organizations. In the 320(d) program, school board members, administrators, curriculum specialists, and teachers are responsible for the total school program, one element of which is the state's basic skills program. They cannot all be expected to sort out competing commitments in the same way.
- *Variation in the sense of urgency.* People cannot be expected to share the same sense of urgency in implementing a policy, even if they agree on its intent. The ability of individuals and organizations to focus on a policy depends on the immediacy of other problems competing for their attention. In the 320(d) program, for example, one would not expect a school system dealing with the effects of six successive tax levy failures to bring the same sense of urgency to the program as a system without serious financial difficulties.
- *Existing policies that slow or deflect implementation.* Policies are implemented in the

context of other policies, and their mutual effects produce variations in implementation. Personnel policies, for example, affect virtually all other policies. In the 320(d) program, one would expect local collective bargaining agreements to affect the way teachers are trained and given responsibilities.

- *Disagreements over the assignment of organizational responsibilities.* Over a period of time, administrative agencies develop stable relationships with each other. A new policy often disrupts these relationships. New patterns of relationships develop slowly and vary widely. If, for example, local school systems are accustomed to dealing with the State Department's Division of Curriculum and Instruction on issues related to the teaching of reading and math, the establishment of a new office to administer the 320(d) program would require a realignment of these relationships.
- *Lack of resources.* One of the touchiest issues of federally and state-mandated policies is the resources they bring with them. Regardless of how well-funded a new program is, it exacts some cost from implementing agencies. The availability of local resources to supplement outside resources varies widely from setting to setting. School systems with declining revenue bases cannot be expected to implement the 320(d) program in the same way as those with stable or increasing revenue bases.

Notice that, in all cases, variability in implementation has been explained without accusing state and local administrators of deliberately undermining the intent of the legislature. Observe, also, that none of the problems can really be solved by focusing more resources on regulation and compliance. We cannot *require* all implementors to resolve conflicting commitments in the same way. We cannot require administrators to ignore urgent problems that deflect their attention from programs that policymakers consider important. We cannot create constructive working relationships between state and local agencies simply by requiring them to work together. Nor can we increase the level of resources available for a program by increasing regulations. In short, all of these problems require programmatic rather than regulatory solutions.

Some proportion of variability in implementation can, however, be explained by disagreement and ambiguity over the aims of policy. Administrators and constituency groups often use the implementation process as a way of demonstrating their opposition to a policy. By exploiting ambiguities in legislative intent, by pointing to particularly glaring practical problems in adjusting to a new policy, and by skillfully exercising delegated control, actors who disagree with the intent of a policy can blunt its impact. Alert legislators and high-level administrators understand that implementation is the continuation of policymaking by other means, and they are wise to the political effect of implementing decisions.[6] It is possible to categorize the variety of ways that disagreements with policy are expressed in the implementation process.

- *Diversion of resources.* When the implementation of a policy requires the transfer of money from one agency to another, a certain proportion of the funds will be used to support existing or new activities that have no direct relationship to the purposes of the policy. New funds are sometimes used to increase administrative staff and reduce workloads, to mollify important constituency groups, or to free-up existing funds for other purposes. In the 320(d) program, we might find, for example, that local districts used program funds to pay some portion of the salaries of curriculum supervisors who had been on the payroll prior to the beginning of the program. While the curriculum supervisors themselves might work directly on the teaching of basic skills, the funds that previously paid their salaries can now be diverted to purposes completely unrelated to those of the 320(d) program. The effect of the transfer of funds is not to increase activity related to the teaching of basic skills, but simply to increase administrative slack at the local level.

- *Deflection of goals.* As implementation progresses, policies attract the attention of constituencies with their own objectives and their own visions of what a good program should be. These groups view success or failure of the policy in terms of their own objectives rather than those of the legislature or the administrative agency. As a consequence, program activities become directed at goals that have little or no relationship to what legislators and high-level administrators consider to be the central objective of the program. With regard to the 320(d) program, parent groups might argue that the effective administration of the program requires the establishment of parent advisory committees. Teachers might argue for teacher-run advisory and training groups. These groups then become ends in themselves because they are important to parents and teachers, and the program at the local level begins to focus increasingly on the mechanics of teacher and parent participation rather than on the teaching of basic skills.

- *Outright resistance.* In the final analysis, policies may require implementors to do things that they oppose and are able to resist. In some instances, opposition takes the form of tokenism or passive resistance. If a local school administration sees the 320(d) program as an infringement on its prerogatives, it might designate a former football coach as "Basic Skills Coordinator" and locate the coordination office next to the locker room. In some instances, opposition takes the form of active resistance. School systems may simply refuse to participate or test the department's mettle by openly refusing to implement certain requirements.

All of these actions can, to a degree, be countered with tighter regulation. Administrators can prescribe more detailed rules for expenditure of funds, they can require that certain organizational features be part of every local project, and they can devote additional time to direct surveillance and to actions designed to demonstrate their willingness to enforce compliance. All of these devices are part of the administrative machinery of virtually every service delivery program. But each of these devices has a tangible cost associated with it.

Each additional increment of regulation brings an increment of administrative complexity—an additional step in the grant application process, another person responsible for monitoring compliance, a more elaborate system of checks and sign-offs, and the like. There are practical limits on the amount of administrative complexity a program can bear and still focus on its capacity to deliver tangible benefits. At some point, the investment in regulatory machinery becomes greater than the investment in service delivery, and, at that point, the emphasis shifts from producing an effect to maintaining a complex surveillance and enforcement system.

Surveillance and enforcement can elicit conformity, but they cannot elicit cooperation and commitment. The more rule-bound and compliance-oriented the implementation process becomes, the less one would expect administrators to use their own abilities and the more one would expect them to rely on other people's guidance. Increased enforcement enhances opportunities for passive resistance: "I'm sorry," the local administrator argues, "but we can't proceed until we get clarification on this issue from the state director." It also creates abundant opportunities for the deflection of goals: "Before we can deal effectively with local agencies," the state director argues, "we've got to have a clear-cut process for resolving these compliance issues." Increased enforcement also diverts resources away from program substance and toward compliance: "We would like to spend more time with teachers," the local curriculum supervisor argues, "but we've got to do the paperwork for the state department."

ASSESSING VARIATIONS IN IMPLEMENTATION

If the 320(d) director is smart, the program review will be designed around the issue of local capacity, rather than compliance. If he focuses on compliance, the director risks increasing the complexity of his task. If the focus is on local capacity, the director looks for opportunities to increase delegated control and hence to reduce the complexity of the task. But the director also has to attend to the chair's concern for whether the program is successfully reaching its target group. One solution to this problem is to design the review around the question, "Which variations in local projects seem to enhance their capacity to reach their target groups successfully, and which seem to undermine their capacity?" Designing the review around this question does several things. First, it accepts local variability as a fact. Second, it establishes a relationship between variability and program success in each local setting, allowing local programs to be judged on their own terms. And third, it puts a premium on *diagnosing* the causes of noncompliance and failure to perform, rather than enforcing uniform compliance. By stating the purpose of the review in this way, the director has effectively said that *variability of implementation will be used as a device for improving the program.*

Suppose now that the director's review is completed. Being alert to the distinction between capacity and compliance, the director has designed the review around a series of questions that relate 320(d) funds to evidence of change in local practice and to locally generated information on student outcomes. With the assistance of an outside contractor, 60 local districts out of the roughly 200 in the state receiving 320(d) funds have been sampled. The major findings of the review are as follows.

1. Use of teacher-generated curriculum materials seems to be associated with greater change in teaching practice. Where teachers have worked together compiling and adapting curriculum materials, rather than simply using standard materials, there is evidence that 320(d) funds have had greater influence on their classroom practice.[7]

2. First-year test results at the local level indicate that evidence of improvement in basic skills is positively related to the amount of time teachers report they spend on focused instructional activity in reading and math. A rough count of the time teachers report they spend on basic skills instruction is positively related to differences in classroom performance on standardized achievement tests.

3. In 12 of the 60 local districts, more than 30 percent of 320(d) funds were used for activities that could not be related directly to instruction. A review of local project budgets showed that most local districts spent between 15 and 25 percent of their 320(d) funds on activities not directly related to classroom instruction; in 12 of the 60, however, this proportion was 30 percent or greater.

4. Ten of the 60 local districts followed the practice of removing students from regular classrooms for basic skills instruction; 40 of the 60 made some form of individualized instruction available; and 10 made all basic skills instruction available

only through group instruction in the regular classroom. No systematic relationship could be found between these grouping practices and student outcomes on standardized achievement tests.

5. Five of the 60 local districts were unable to provide an explicit statement of how students were selected for basic skills instruction; 30 of the 60 indicated that their criteria for selection were based primarily on teachers' evaluations; and the remaining 25 relied primarily on standardized tests.

Allowing for the tentativity of results like these, we can begin to piece together a crude picture of how much variability there is in local practice and the degree to which variability represents intentional noncompliance or local adaptation. One might want to look more closely, for example, at the 12 districts that spent more than 30 percent of their 320(d) funds on noninstructional activities and at the 5 districts that could not explain their selection procedures. Simple indicators like these can be used to sort out serious compliance problems.

But the other evidence indicates considerable diversity in local practice that can be used to focus on more-or-less successful variations. Findings 1 and 5, for example, indicate a heavy reliance on teacher judgment in the selection of children and curriculum materials. One might want to take a closer look at how teachers exercise this judgment, with an eye to informing other teachers of apparently successful practices. Findings 2 and 4 give some hints about practices that local administrators can affect—instructional time and grouping practices—and their relationship to student success. In short, the review speaks both to issues of compliance and capacity, and it does at least a crude justice to local variability.

The important question is how the director, the commissioner, and the chair can address these issues in a constructive way. The following exchange takes place after the director's review is completed.[8]

Chair. I've looked at your review of the 320(d) program and I have a number of questions to ask you. Perhaps the best place to start is to ask whether your review has given you any clearer idea of how many local districts have just plain failed to do anything useful for children with basic skills problems.

Director. Let me begin by saying that I think there are few, if any, districts that have failed to do anything useful. But our review has led us to focus more sharply on those districts that seem to be having the greatest difficulty getting programs underway. We found that 5 of the 60 districts we surveyed were unable to state how they selected students for attention; these districts are out of compliance with the law and regulations, which say very clearly that recipients of 320(d) funds must state their selection criteria. So we intend to take a close look at the remaining districts in the state to discover how many of them have the same problem. When we've identified this group of districts, we'll focus a portion of our staff time on working with them to assure that their programs meet minimum standards of compliance.

Chair. That sounds reasonable. What about districts that meet the minimum requirements but still aren't teaching kids reading and math? Is there anything you can do about that?

Director. I think there are a couple of ways to get at that problem. One way is to take a closer look at how 320(d) funds are being used by local districts. Our finding, for example, that about one-fifth of the districts we surveyed use more than 30 percent of the funds for noninstructional purposes suggests that we've got some kind of problem getting the resources to the kids. We may need some new legislative authority. If we do, we'll ask for it.

Another way to approach the problem is to look for particularly outstanding programs or practices and find some way of communicating these to the districts that need them. We've started to get a handle on that with our findings about teacher-developed materials, instructional time, and grouping practices. But it's become clear to us that we need to know a lot more about local programs before we start publicizing ways of improving local practices. That's why I'd like to focus most of our effort on identifying and understanding successful programs, rather than enforcing compliance with the regulations. It just seems to me that the payoff is potentially greater when you try to understand what makes programs work.

Chair. If you're prepared to demonstrate to me that you've got the compliance issue under control, I agree that it makes sense to work on identifying successful programs. I guess I'm not clear where all this leads, though. When we understand a few things about successful programs, what do we do next? Do we write them into the law?

Commissioner. I have great difficulties with the idea of requiring all local districts to do things that we find are associated with success in a few settings. In the first place, we can never be sure about the conditions that make for local success; they're probably much more complicated than our data tell us they are. Second, I'm very concerned about the effect of mandating practice on local initiative and invention. How much inventive ability do we lose by telling people how to do their jobs? As a policy matter, I would argue that the more we can hold local people to their own standards of performance—get them to do their own diagnosis and evaluation—the better off we'll be. The purpose of collecting information on successful practices is to stimulate local invention, not to mandate that things be done a certain way.

Director. I agree with the commissioner. The last thing I want to do as an administrator is to tell teachers how to teach reading and math. That seems to me to defeat the purpose of having a solid group of professionals in the classrooms. What we can do, though, is increase the level of information on successful practices and increase the opportunities for exchange of that information. It seems to me that we are uniquely well-situated to do that.

Chair. I'm generally pleased with the responsiveness of the review and with your comments about how you intend to proceed. I still have questions about this issue of how to improve local practice, but they're better saved until you have more information. Can we agree to get together again and focus primarily on that issue?

Commissioner. I certainly would welcome the opportunity.

Director. As would I.

Notice how the ground has shifted from the first two exchanges. The central issue of the first two exchanges—why aren't 320(d) funds getting to the kids who need them most?—has now been broken down into three more precise questions: How are districts selecting children for participation in the program? How are districts allocating 320(d) funds between instructional and noninstructional costs? And how do local instructional practices relate to the benefits children gain from the program? The chair, the director, and the commissioner understand the difference between regulatory and programmatic issues and have used this distinction to isolate problems that can be solved with compliance from those that have more complex programmatic solutions. Furthermore, they have dealt very gracefully with the complexity of their problem. They have begun to distinguish instances where hierarchical control is appropriate from those where delegated control is appropriate. They have begun to narrow the domain of hierarchical control to a certain set of minimum conditions that all local programs must meet in order to receive funds. And they have begun to specify the limits of their ability to control certain important activities, notably the process of classroom instruction. In short, their recognition of the complexity of the problem has given them more, rather than less, competence in dealing with the problem.

THE POWER OF THE BOTTOM OVER THE TOP

Up to this point, the implementation problem has been defined exclusively from the point of view of policymakers and high-level administrators. We have been concerned with the ability of people at the top of the pyramid to understand and control the actions of people at the bottom. Shift positions now, and try to see the problem from the point of view of those at the bottom.

In a very basic sense, the most important actors in the 320(d) program are individual teachers and students. An enduring fact of all service delivery programs—education, health care, social services, manpower, and so forth—is that they depend heavily on the quality of the interaction between service-giver and client. If we isolate the factors that have the greatest effect on the quality of this interaction, we quickly discover that very few, if any, of them are subject to direct administrative control.

School administrators simply cannnot supervise the work of teachers in the same way as, say, a shop superintendent might supervise machinists or a floor manager might supervise clerks in a department store. Much of the success of the service in education depends on the sensitivity of the teacher to the individual attributes of students and on the teacher's ability to maintain a well-organized, task-oriented classroom. The role of administrators in the instructional process is necessarily marginal. Teachers work almost exclusively in self-contained classrooms, exercising a high degree of discretion in the management of classroom activities. Direct administrative control over classroom behavior is not only extraordinary difficult but also very risky. Administrators simply do not command enough specific information about teacher-student interactions to be effective supervisors of instruction, even if they are so inclined.

To be sure, many things that school administrators do can influence classroom instruction in positive and negative ways. Administrators can select teachers, reward them in modest ways, establish schoolwide or districtwide performance goals, focus public attention on certain parts of the school program, and mobilize outside financial support for innovative projects. All of these things can have a positive effect on classroom instruction. But administrators can also select and reward teachers on completely arbitrary criteria that have no direct relationship to the quality of classroom instruction. They can create activities in schools that divert energy and attention away from classroom instruction; writing instructional objectives might be one of these activities. And they can expose certain parts of the school program to public criticism, leaving teachers to fend for themselves. In other words, administrators can do many things to obstruct or enhance classroom instruction, but they cannot directly control it. All of the things that administrators do are at least one step removed from the critical face-to-face transaction between teacher and student.[9]

Think for a moment about the individual teacher's role in the 320(d) program. Word comes to the teacher from a variety of sources—state and local school administration, parents, newspapers—that something needs to be done to improve reading and math skills. The teacher searches his or her experience for clues as to the accuracy of this conclusion and forms a positive or negative attitude toward it. The district then formulates a program in response to the 320(d) legislation and guidelines; maybe teachers are involved in formulating the program, maybe not. Teachers will judge the net effect of the program by whether it enhances or obstructs the instructional process in the classroom. Training, special materials, and advice on classroom organization can be delivered to teachers as part of the implementation process, but if these things are not translated into tangible classroom behavior and if that behavior does not contribute to the teacher's sense of control over his or her own classroom, the program is a diversion of resources and a waste of teachers' time.

Teachers receive a variety of signals about what to do in the classroom. In addition to the signals they receive from the 320(d) program about reading and math skills, they hear about their responsibility for teaching democratic values, discipline, the free enterprise system, health and nutrition, career choice, and the history of western civilization, to mention but a few topics. It is the teachers' responsibility to turn these signals into a well-organized strategy of instruction that responds to the range of skills and abilities they find among students in the classroom. In short, *teachers will make most of the important discretionary choices in the implementation of the 320(d) program.*

If school district administrators are smart, they will recognize this fact and *design their implementation strategy around maximizing the individual teacher's control of the instructional process.* But to do this, they, like the chair, the commissioner, and the program director, must recognize the difference between compliance and capacity. Teachers can be required to perform certain activities—attend training sessions, develop instructional goals, use certain materials—but the performance of these activities does not assure success. In fact, if it diverts too much attention away from the classroom, it will virtually guarantee failure. So the essential problem for local school administrators is how to direct teachers' attention to the basic skills problem and then provide the resources to respond to the problem in a way that acknowledges teacher control.

Another important feature of the teacher's role is that teachers work in a physically isolated environment, the classroom, with little opportunity for routine interaction with other teachers. Yet when teachers are asked where they get most of their ideas for new instructional practices, they reply that they rely mainly on other teachers.[10] This suggests that the way to reach teachers is to put them in touch with other teachers, not to have administrators tell them what to do.

INEFFICIENCY, REDUNDANCY, AND PROTECTING THE INEPT

Back away from the specifics of the 320(d) program for a moment and think about the general features of the system we have been describing. The system is *bottom heavy* and *loosely coupled*.[11] It is bottom heavy because the closer we get to the bottom of the pyramid, the closer we get to the factors that have the greatest effect on the program's success or failure. The system is loosely coupled because the ability of one level to control the behavior of another is weak and largely negative. This characterization is true, in varying degrees, of all the relationships examined thus far: the chair's ability to control the commissioner, the commissioner's ability to control the director, the director's ability to control local school administrators, and the local school administrator's ability to control teachers. The skillful use of delegated control is central to making implementation work in bottom-heavy, loosely coupled systems. *When it becomes necessary to rely mainly on hierarchical control, regulation, and compliance to achieve results, the game is essentially lost.* Moving from delegated control to hierarchical control means moving from reliance on existing capacity, ingenuity, and judgment to reliance on rules, surveillance, and enforcement procedures. Regulation increases complexity and invites subversion; it diverts attention from accomplishing the task to understanding and manipulating rules.

Two criticisms are commonly levelled at bottom-heavy, loosely coupled systems: they are inefficient, and they protect incompetence. Inefficiency, the critics argue, stems from redundancy. Too many people making autonomous choices, with no rational division of labor, results in overlap, duplication, and a general confusion of functions. In the 320(d) program, the critics would argue that it is absurd to think of each teacher essentially inventing his or her own reading and math curriculum; the inefficiencies would be enormous. It would be much more sensible to develop a few model curricula from the best available sources and train teachers in how to use them.

Likewise, the critics argue, not everyone can be trusted to exercise autonomy in the correct way; lack of central control allows pockets of incompetence to develop and remain essentially immune from discovery. Some teachers and administrators are simply incapable of performing adequately without close supervision. To the extent that bottom-heavy, loosely coupled systems protect the inept, they reinforce inefficiency.

These criticisms point to simple, straightforward solutions. We should streamline administrative structures, eliminating overlap and duplication, tightening coordination and control. We should hold people accountable for the results they produce, stating clear performance standards and regularly evaluating them.

Proposals of the above type stem from a set of assumptions about the operation of complex administrative structures that do not stand up in the face of accumulating evidence. First, take the notion that redundant systems are inefficient and streamlined systems are efficient.[12] Do we say that a commercial aircraft with a triple-redundant landing gear system is inefficient? Of course not. Redundancy is a powerfully efficient device for increasing the reliability and safety of the aircraft. Would we say that a house wired in series is more efficient than one wired in parallel? Series wiring uses roughly half the amount of wiring material, but the result is that each connection is wholly dependent on the preceding one for its electrical current. In contrast, parallel wiring allows each connection to function independently of others. Thus, redundancy dramatically increases the reliability of an electrical system at a relatively modest additional cost. To say that redundant systems are inefficient is not only superficial but largely false.

Tightly coupled, highly centralized administrative structures are like houses wired in series; there is so little redundancy that the failure of one unit means the collapse of the whole system. If the organization's task is relatively simple, say brickmaking, the system's failure is of little consequence and can be remedied easily. But if the task is complex, like the implementation of the 320(d) program, the absence of redundancy can be disastrous; a small failure anywhere in the system can disrupt a long, inter-dependent line of relationships, creating confusion and disorder. Bottom-heavy, loosely coupled systems are difficult to administer, but they are extraordinarily rich and robust because they are redundant. *The more complex the task, the more import-ant redundancy is to the efficient accomplishment of the task.*

Furthermore, *most of the redundancies that we observe in the implementation of policy are the result of deliberate political choices.* The division of authority between federal, state, and local government is highly redundant; these relations are charac-terized by enormous overlap of functions, continual dispute over the proper boundaries of authority, and a high level of ambiguity over who is responsible for what function. The complexity of these relations makes implementation difficult, but a more stream-lined, rationalized system would not necessarily be more effective. Existing jurisdic-tional boundaries, in effect, protect us against too heavy a reliance on the competence or incompetence of any single level of government. The political genius of federalism stems from its skillful reliance on redundancy.

Returning to the 320(d) example, the redundancy of delegated control can be seen as a fail-safe device: The more responsibility is devolved toward the bottom of the sys-tem, the greater the number of people who will be actively involved in searching for a solution to the reading and math problem and the higher the likelihood that more effective programs will be designed and implemented at the local level. The more re-sponsibility is centralized, the more people will rely on direction from above, and, as a result, fewer people will be actively engaged in searching for solutions to the problem. Moreover, hierarchical control puts the responsibility for finding solutions to the read-ing and math problem in the hands of those who are least likely to discover them—administrators. Alert administrators understand that delegated control and redun-dancy are an important form of insurance against organizational failure.

But what about the argument that bottom-heavy, loosely coupled systems protect the incompetent? There is no question that errors are more visible in tightly coupled, centralized systems. What could be more visible than one individual or one unit of an organization bringing the entire system to a grinding halt? The more redundant the system, the more difficult it is to find ineffective parts because errors are less visible. But suppose our purpose was not to ferret out and penalize incompetence as much as it was to improve the overall performance of the system. If we define our purpose this way, redundancy becomes a powerful asset rather than a liability. Instead of investing organizational resources in making errors more visible—that is, in constructing accountability systems—we can invest them in increasing the exchange of information about more and less effective practices. The information would then be accessible to everyone, competents and incompetents alike. This does not ensure that the people who need the information most will get it. But it does at least play to the strength of bottom-heavy, loosely coupled systems: they are extraordinarily rich in specific in-formation about essential tasks. We can then say that the responsibility of adminis-trators is not to ferret out and penalize incompetents, but rather to devise ingenious ways of putting information and experiences that will improve their performance in the path of incompetents.

Research on the implementation of new educational programs consistently finds that peer relationships—teachers training teachers, teachers working jointly on the de-velopment of materials, and so forth—are strongly related to success of implementation and continuation of programs. It has also been found that implementation and continuation are strongly related to the individual teacher's sense of efficacy and control in the classroom.[13] Administrative actions that are designed to increase the density of interaction at the delivery level, rather than increase the dependence of the delivery level on hierarchical control, are more likely to have a positive effect. Furthermore, such actions capitalize on the most prominent attribute of complex systems, their redundancy.

Where does this leave the chair, the commissioner, and the program director? It seemingly leaves them in a very difficult position. To the extent that they acknowledge that they are operating in a bottom-heavy, loosely coupled system, there appears to be little for them to do. The standard devices of administrative control—regulation, streamlining, accountability—appear to have limited or perverse effects. We seem to have relegated policymakers to a helpless and largely peripheral role in the implementation of the 320(d) program.

The situation is actually quite the contrary. What we have done is to pare away the easy, superficial solutions to implementation problems and focus on the more difficult, challenging ones. Legislators and high-level administrators have a significant role in these solutions, but that role requires them to adopt a somewhat different view of the process than the one they conventionally hold. Recall that we opened the discussion of bottom-heavy, loosely coupled systems by flipping the system on its head and asking what we needed to know about the delivery level in order to make intelligent policy decisions.[14] With some elaboration, this is exactly the process of reasoning that legislators and high-level administrators can use to affect implementation.

BACKWARD MAPPING

People at the top of the system tend to think of themselves as initiators of the implementation process; for them, implementation consists of a series of actions emanating from the top and reaching to the bottom. Suppose, for purposes of discussion, we simply reverse this logic. *Begin with the assumption that implementation begins at the bottom, not at the top.*[15] At first this sounds like nonsense. It upsets our whole notion of the relationship between policymaking and administration. But with a little thought it turns out not to be such an alien idea.

It is clear that the success of policy depends heavily on the capacity of people at the delivery level. This is true in two senses. First, many policies originate with perceived failures of the delivery system. The 320(d) program was based on the perceived inability of schools to teach reading and math adequately. Second, even those policies that do not originate with delivery system problems require some form of organization to implement them. Eventually all policies require some form of organization, and that organization constrains and determines, in certain important ways, how the policy will be implemented. Understanding what is good policy depends, to some degree, on understanding the mechanism for its implementation. We might even say that *we do not clearly understand what a policy should be until we have thought about how it will be implemented.* This kind of reasoning tracks with the commonsense intuition of legislators and high-level administrators. The smart policymaker will say early in any discussion of a new policy, "Before we go too far with this idea, can you tell me what it will look like in practice?" This is often an embarrassing question that sends staff scurrying back to the drawingboard, because, as they begin to describe what the idea will look like in practice, they discover that it was not a very good idea to start with.

So it is not nonsensical to say that, in some ways, implementation begins at the bottom of the system. If a policy does not make sense at the delivery level, it is not going to make sense at the top of the system.

How, then, can policymakers protect themselves against ideas that make no sense at the delivery level? One way is by using a form of reasoning called "backward mapping."[16] Instead of beginning at the top of the system with a new policy and reasoning through a series of actions required to implement it, begin at the bottom of the system, with the most concrete set of actions, and reason backward to the policy. In the case of the 320(d) program, the reasoning process might look something like this:

- *What is the problem?* Poor performance by children on standardized measures of reading and math skills.
- *Where do we attack the problem?* In the classroom.
- *What has to happen in the classroom to improve reading and math performance?* Teachers: more instructional time on reading and math, better instructional skills, materials closely related to the teacher's strategy and style of instruction, access to other teachers confronted with the same problem. Students: motivation to master the content, reward for learning.
- *What can the local school system do to increase the likelihood that these things will happen in the classroom?* Remove conflicting instructional requirements, provide access to training for teachers, provide resources (released time, extra compensation, production of materials, etc.) for teachers to develop reading and math instruction, identify students with the greatest need, communicate program to parents.
- *What can the state education department do to increase the likelihood that these things will happen in local districts?* Remove conflicting policy requirements (with legislative concurrence), transfer information on unusually successful practices from one setting to another, assure fiscal responsibility of local districts receiving state support for basic skills programs.
- *What can the legislature do to increase the likelihood that the state education department and local school districts will successfully address the basic skills problem?* Remove conflicting policy requirements, authorize and appropriate funds, establish rules of fiscal responsibility, establish basic elements of program design: classroom as the basic delivery unit, local district support for teacher-produced curriculum, state support for transfer of unusually successful practices.

This is a very crude version of backward mapping, but it demonstrates how closely the reasoning process accords with commonsense intuitions about policy implementation. It simply formalizes the thinking that follows from the question, "What will this idea look like in practice?"

But it also forces an analytic structure on discussions of implementation: Begin with a definition of the problem, define the delivery-level unit with the greatest effect on the problem, describe what needs to happen in that unit to solve the problem, then describe for each successive level above that unit what needs to be done to support activity at the delivery level. Notice that the process of reasoning is driven not by the policymaker's limited understanding of the problem, but by the mobilization of delivery-level expertise.[17] Policymakers do not have to pretend, as they so often do, that they know how to solve the problem. But they do have to understand *where* in the system to focus the resources necessary for solving the problem. The role of policymakers is far from marginal. They are responsible for finding the critical transactions in the system and for ensuring that the largest proportion of resources reaches them.

Control has a new meaning if we take this point of view. The ability of one level of the system to control the behavior of the next is no longer the central issue. Instead, we are thinking of *where to locate the maximum amount of delegated control, how to get resources into the hands of those who exercise it, and what forms of organization enhance the likelihood of success at the delivery level.* Control exercised in this way minimizes investment in surveillance and maximizes investment in the capacity to exercise discretionary choices that directly affect quality of service. In this sense, delegated control is more efficient than hierarchical control.

Another way of thinking about this strategy of control is in terms of a contract between policymakers and service deliverers. Contracts turn liabilities into assets: each party to a contract lacks something that the other possesses. The contract allows each to capitalize on the assets of the other. Legislators and high-level administrators can make decisions that have systemwide effects. If they are skillful and clever, they can use their breadth of understanding to shift resources from one part of the system to another. But legislators and administrators cannot pretend to understand, in anything other than a superficial way, what makes the system work at the delivery level.

Moving down the delivery system from top to bottom, you make important trade-offs. You trade breadth of understanding for depth, and you trade the ability to make large allocation decisions for the ability to make small, but very significant, delivery-level choices. Delivery-level choices are very complex. The information needed to improve delivery-level performance is dense, specific, and situational. It is not the sort of information that can be easily understood and assimilated by people at the top of the system. But policymakers rely very heavily on performance at the delivery level for their own success.

So we have the makings of a very strong contract. Legislators and agency heads cannot teach reading. Teachers cannot increase the amount of money the government spends on reading instruction. But policymakers can trade—bargain—resources for increased attention to reading instruction and for information on the effects of that attention. And teachers can trade delivery-level performance for increased resources and the ability to make discretionary choices. This bargain is a two-way affair, inherently different from hierarchical control. A contract is not an instrument of coercion. Rather, it is an efficient instrument of harnessing delegated control to policy objectives.

How would all this look in practice? Suppose there has been a full authorization cycle of the 320(d) program, and it is now time for the legislature to consider whether the program should be renewed and what changes should be made if it is renewed. The commissioner and the director have prepared a package of legislative amendments for which they would like the Education Committee's endorsement. These amendments include authority for:

- The State Department of Education to make grants to groups of teachers for curriculum development;
- Teachers to contract, independently of the school system, for inservice training with state support;

- Local school districts to contract with other school systems for the transfer of exemplary practices; and
- The state department to identify and disseminate information on exemplary practices.

In addition, the commissioner and director have prepared some administrative regulations that do not require new legislative authority. They have forwarded the regulations to the Education Committee for review and comment. These include:

- A limit of 20 percent on 320(d) funds that can be used by local districts for activities not directly related to classroom instruction (instructional activities are defined as materials, teacher training, and released time for training); and
- A requirement that local districts make available for public comment criteria for selection of children for special instruction using 320(d) funds.

The following exchange explores the rationale for these amendments and regulations.

> **Chair**. I've reviewed your proposed changes for the 320(d) program, and I have a number of questions to ask you. The best place to start, I think, is with the basic question of how you expect these proposals to affect the performance of the individual student in the classroom. Commissioner?

> **Commissioner**. The 320(d) program rises or falls on the quality of instruction in classrooms. We're not certain, and we probably never will be, what creates a productive level of interaction between teacher and student. It's not so important that we know, but it's very important that teachers know. So the department has deliberately settled on a strategy of putting resources where they are most likely to affect quality of instruction; this means putting them largely in the hands of teachers. We expect that by focusing teachers' attention on the problem of instruction in reading and math and by increasing interaction among teachers on this subject, we will enhance their ability to respond to individual students with reading and math problems. We don't expect to generate a few "big solutions" to these problems, but we do expect to increase the level of attention focused on the problems at the classroom level.

> **Chair**. Director?

> **Director**. You'll recall that our interim review of the program showed a positive relationship between teacher involvement in curriculum-building and changes in classroom practice. We intend to test whether this relationship holds over the long run. In order to test it, we've got to increase the level of activity at the classroom level and create more opportunities for teachers to interact on curriculum matters. We're betting that this will have a pay-off for students with reading and math problems.

> **Chair**. We've heard testimony from a number of people who don't share your view. Yesterday we heard from the Council of Local School Administrators. Their representative said that the proposals "make the job of districtwide coordination of reading and math instruction more difficult" and that they "constitute a direct intervention by the state in local school affairs." We also heard from a local superintendent who said that the proposals are "a direct attempt to undermine the chain of command in school district administration." Don't these people have

a point? Aren't you short-circuiting a lot of administrative relationships by increasing the control of teachers over program resources?

Director. I think it's important to put our recommendations in the context of the whole program. The school system is still the administering agency for the 320(d) program at the local level. Local school systems are responsible for selecting and assigning teachers and for designing the local program. We've taken extra care to give local districts maximum flexibility in administering program funds. We haven't required them to select or assign students who receive 320(d) benefits in a certain way; we've simply said they should publicize their criteria for selection. We've only resorted to explicit regulations where we have found that local practices sometimes keep funds from reaching teachers and students. Our proposal to limit noninstructional expenditures to 20 percent is designed to limit the amount of money local districts can use to support administrators who have no direct instructional role. For districts that have taken the task of improving classroom instruction seriously, this requirement poses no particular difficulty.

We view the proposals for support of teacher-initiated curriculum development and training not as an intervention in local district decisions, but as a direct investment in activity that is likely to improve the quality of instruction. All we've done is to assure that some fraction of program funds is available for problem-solving and information-sharing at the delivery level, where the need is greatest. If increasing teachers' access to practical information threatens districtwide coordination or supervisory relationships, then it seems to me the district has a problem that goes beyond the 320(d) program. We don't expect teacher-initiated projects to cause problems in districts that have a strong commitment to the support of classroom instruction.

Chair. Don't the proposals create a lot of overlap and confusion at the local level, though? If everything works as planned, there will probably be district-sponsored training of teachers, training initiated by teachers themselves, and training that results from cross-district exchanges of information about successful practices. Isn't there a more efficient way of getting at the problem?

Director. If you mean, "Is there a simpler way to deliver training?" I think the answer is "Yes." We could locate all the responsibility for training in one place, with the state or with local districts. But this would restrict the number of possibilities for exchanging information and locate responsibility in the hands of people who don't necessarily understand the problems at the classroom level. We think the pay-off is likely to be greater if we increase the frequency of contact among those closest to the problem, providing them with a lot of options for access to information. If we increase the likelihood of successful classroom programs, then the strategy isn't necessarily inefficient.

Commissioner. As a matter of policy, I'm uncomfortable with the idea of locating sole responsibility for training in the hands of any single authority. It doesn't seem to me a good way to increase the inventive ability that is applied to a problem. I'm more interested in ways of capitalizing on diversity rather than controlling it.

Chair. The committee has also heard testimony from the Children's Advocacy Group that is somewhat critical of your proposals. They've said, "The department stops short of using its full regulatory authority to assure that the neediest children get the greatest access to 320(d) funds." Your proposals don't seem to speak to this issue, do they, Commissioner?

Commissioner. We're faced with a fairly difficult choice here. As I see it, we've got to decide whether to define the department's role primarily in regulatory terms or primarily in terms of enhancing local capacity. I've said a number of times that I prefer the latter. But issues like the one raised by the Children's Advocacy Group make my position difficult to argue. We've thought a great deal about whether we want to use the department's regulatory power to require local districts to select students for the 320(d) program in a certain way. We've decided that we're not in favor of it for two reasons. First, we think our resources are better used in activities that affect the quality of local programs rather than in those that assure local compliance with state guidelines. Second, we don't feel confident deciding how students should be selected, and we're more comfortable leaving that decision in the hands of local districts. So we've settled on a fairly straightforward requirement that districts should publicize their selection criteria. That at least gives local groups a chance to influence the local district's decision.

Chair. Thank you. We'll look carefully at your proposals.

This exchange demonstrates the essential logic of backward mapping. The chair's first concern is the effect of department proposals at the delivery level. Then, using previous testimony of school administrators and advocacy groups, the chair backs through to consider the administrative consequences of the department's proposals at the local and state levels. This approach means that the discussion will center on delivery-level problems rather than on the competing claims of rival bureaucracies. The chair, given the committee's responsibility to weigh competing political claims, may well reject the department's proposals on essentially political grounds. But the logic of the chair's questioning shows sensitivity to the delivery-level effects of political choices.

For their part, the commissioner and the 320(d) director have made a number of strategic choices in assembling their package of proposals. They have decided to bet that shifting resources toward the delivery level and increasing interaction among teachers at that level, even when this results in redundancy and overlap, will increase the likelihood that the program will affect students. They have decided to minimize the department's regulatory role and to focus regulatory attention only on those matters in which it is relatively easy to determine compliance. The 20 percent requirement can be enforced simply by checking local applications for funds against expenditure reports filed by local districts. On the sensitive issue of how students should be selected for attention, they have decided to rely on local politics.

The strategy is far from foolproof. There is no guarantee that teachers will capitalize on the availability of funds for training and curriculum-building. Local districts will, no doubt, invent ingenious ways of asserting control over teacher-initiated projects. Where districts are given wide latitude by the department, there will be failures as well as successes. And the department's ability to initiate exchange relationships between weak districts and strong ones will depend on its cleverness and diplomacy. But, despite the obvious problems, the major strength of the strategy lies in the fact that it is predicated on the principle of increasing capacity at the delivery level. If the strategy fails to do that, then it needs to be revised.

CONCLUSION

Complexity can work both for and against successful implementation. When complexity results from hierarchical control within organizations and across levels of government, it diverts resources from problem-solving and focuses them on surveillance and compliance, it increases the number of steps required to translate a policy into action, and it constrains the inventive capacity of delivery-level personnel. In this sense, hierarchical control *reduces* the likelihood that policies will result in delivery-level effects. But delegated control allows policymakers to capitalize on complexity at the delivery level, using it as a source of ideas for *increasing* the capacity to deliver services. Out of delivery-level complexity grows variability in the way implementors respond to policy. Variability, far from being a threat to successful implementation, produces valuable information about more and less successful practices. If some mechanism exists for capitalizing on variability at the delivery level, then complexity operates to raise the level of knowledge required for successful implementation.

Out of this basic understanding of complexity and control come a few prescriptions on how legislators and administrators can deal effectively with implementation problems:

- *Distinguish between compliance and capacity.* There is a critical difference between the ability or willingness of implementors to comply with rules and their capacity to successfully deliver a service. Implementation depends more on capacity than it does on compliance. A large part of the skill required to solve implementation problems depends on the ability of policymakers to determine where compliance is required and where success depends on enhancing delegated control.
- *Distinguish between implementation variations that result from a failure to comply with basic regulations and those that result from differences in capacity.* The two sources of variation require completely different responses. Variability, in and of itself, does not prove either the success or failure of implementation. The portion of variability that results from a failure to comply with basic regulations can be addressed with surveillance and enforcement. But variability that results from differences among implementors in their ability to define and solve delivery problems is a major resource in improving delivery-level performance. If policymakers view all variability as suspect, they not only increase the complexity of their regulatory task, they also eliminate the main source of ideas for successful implementation.
- *Regulate only those activities for which it is possible to specify a clear standard of performance and which constitute minimum prior conditions for successful implementation.* If a certain proportion of a local project's budget is not spent on activities directly related to the delivery of services, one can say that some defensible minimum condition for successful implementation has not been met. The more vague the standard of performance, the greater the effort required to enforce the standard and the less likely that resources will be targeted at the delivery level. Standards that go beyond minimum conditions of successful implementation effectively put decision-making responsibility in the hands of people with limited knowledge of delivery-level problems.
- *Focus resources as close as possible to the point of delivery.* Policies designed to improve the delivery of services depend heavily on discretionary choices at the delivery level. To have maximum effect, resources have to flow primarily to those points in the delivery system where they are most likely to affect discretionary choices.

The farther away from the point of delivery, the less the likelihood that resources will affect the capacity to deliver, and the greater the complexity of the administrative mechanism required to move resources. The practical effect of this strategy is to increase the complexity of interaction among those closest to the delivery level and to decrease the complexity of mechanisms designed to control their behavior from above.

- *Evaluate policy alternatives by mapping backwards from the point of delivery to the point where policy decisions are made.* If delivery-level performance is the basic determinant of successful implementation, then consideration of policies ought to start with their delivery-level effect. Begin with a statement of the problem to which the policy is addressed, define the delivery-level unit with the greatest effect on the problem, describe what needs to happen in that unit to solve the problem, and then describe for each successive level above that unit what needs to be done to support activity at the delivery level.

NOTES

1. This paper was written for the School Management and Organization Studies Team at the National Institute of Education, Department of Health, Education, and Welfare. It will be followed by another paper, "Complexity and Control: Theory and Action in Policy Implementation," which gives a more detailed presentation of the difficult theoretical issues raised here. Special thanks to Marc Tucker and Fritz Mulhauser of NIE for initiating the paper and for their kind support and patience while it was being written. Thanks also to Walter Williams, my colleague at the Institute of Governmental Research, for his assistance in editing and circulating an earlier version. During my work on the paper, I was also engaged, with Milbrey McLaughlin of the Rand Corporation, in a study of state education agencies. The paper shows the influence of our extended conversations about that project, and I am indebted to her for her help in framing a number of ideas. Useful and detailed comments on an earlier draft were given by Chris Argyris, Robert Levine, Jerry Murphy, Alan Rosenthal, and Don Sloma, all of whom have grappled with the problems discussed here, both as practitioners and researchers. The paper also benefited from a discussion, in May 1979, with NIE's Study Group for Research on Law and Government in Education. Thanks go to members of the committee and to Don Burnes, head of the Legal and Governmental Studies Team, for their useful critical comments. The epigraph is from Rufus E. Miles, Jr., *Awakening from the American Dream: The Social and Political Limits to Growth* (New York: Universe Books, 1976), 170.

2. Webster's dictionary says that something is complex if it "is made up of many elaborately interrelated or interconnected parts, so that much study of knowledge is needed to understand or operate it." Herbert Simon describes a complex system (circularly) as "one made up of a large number of parts that interact in a non-simple way," adding that "given the properties of the parts and the laws of their interaction it is not a trivial matter to infer the properties of the whole." [Herbert Simon, "The Architecture of Complexity," in Joseph Litterer, ed., *Organizations: Systems, Control, and Adaptation* (New York: Wiley, 1969, 2d ed.), 99.] Todd LaPorte argues that "the degree of complexity of organized social systems . . . is a function of the *number* of system components . . ., the relative *differentiation* or variety of these components . . ., and the degree of *interdependence* among these components." [Todd LaPorte, "Organized Social Complexity: Explication of a Concept," in LaPorte, ed., *Organized Social Complexity* (Princeton: Princeton University Press, 1975), 6.] Related sources on the meaning of complexity are: Ronald Brunner and Garry Brewer, *Organized Complexity: Empirical Theories of Political Development* (New York: Free

Press, 1971), and Paul Lawrence and Jay Lorsch, "Differentiation and Integration in Complex Organizations," *Administrative Science Quarterly*, Vol. 12 (1967), 1–47.

3. For more detailed discussions of the meaning of implementation analysis see: Paul Berman, "The Study of Macro- and Micro-Implementation," *Public Policy*, Vol. 28 (1978), 157–184; and Walter Williams, "Implementation Analysis and Assessment," in Walter Williams and Richard Elmore, eds., *Social Program Implementation* (New York: Academic Press, 1976), 267–292.

4. For a fuller treatment of the regulatory view of implementation see: Francine Rabinovitz, Jeffrey Pressman, and Martin Rein, "Guidelines: A Plethora of Forms, Authors, and Functions," *Policy Sciences*, Vol. 7 (1976), 399–416, and the accompanying articles in that number of the journal. The growing antiregulation literature includes: James Q. Wilson and Patricia Rachal, "Can Government Regulate itself?" *Public Interest*, No. 46 (Winter 1977), 3–14; Eugene Bardach and Lucian Pugliaresi, "The Environmental Impact Statement vs. The Real World," *ibid.*, No. 49 (Fall 1977), 22–38; and Albert Nichols and Richard Zeckhauser, "Government Comes to the Workplace: An Assessment of OSHA," *ibid.*, 39–69.

5. The following discussion is adapted from Pressman and Wildavsky's analysis of "The Complexity of Joint Action" in Jeffrey Pressman and Aaron Wildavsky, *Implementation* (Berkeley: University of California Press, 1973), 87–124.

6. The following discussion is adapted from Eugene Bardach, *The Implementation Game* (Cambridge, Mass.: MIT Press, 1977), 65–177.

7. This was an actual finding of the Rand Corporation's study of federally mandated education programs. See Milbrey McLaughlin, "Implementation as Mutual Adaptation: Change in Classroom Organization," in Williams and Elmore, eds., *Social Program Implementation* (New York: Academic Press, 1976), 167–180.

8. I have skipped over the important topic of how one would actually go about designing and conducting a review of program implementation. The best recent source on that subject is Jerome T. Murphy, *Getting the Facts* (Santa Monica, Calif.: Goodyear Publishing, 1980).

9. One ought not assume that this lack of connection between administrators and service deliverers is characteristic only of social service organizations. A fascinating example of the same problem in sanitation services comes from Jerry Mechling's analysis of New York City's Environmental Protection Agency. Mechling argues that a number of high-level decisions on sanitation—increasing the size of garbage trucks, changing shift patterns, et cetera—depended for their success or failure on the work patterns, aspirations, discretionary choices of garbage collectors. His message is that analysts ignore these things at their own peril. Jerry Mechling, *The Roles of Policy Analysts in Large Public Organizations: A Case Study of the New York Environmental Protection Agency* (unpublished doctoral dissertation, Woodrow Wilson School, Princeton University, 1974), quoted in Erwin C. Hargrove, *The Missing Link: The Study of the Implementation of Social Policy* (Washington, D.C.: Urban Institute, 1975), 28–31.

10. Dan Lortie, *Schoolteacher: A Sociological Study* (Chicago: University of Chicago Press, 1975), 70.

11. For a fuller discussion of bottom-heavy and loosely coupled systems see: Richard Weatherly and Michael Lipsky, "Street-Level Bureaucrats and Institutional Innovation: Implementing Special Education Reform," *Harvard Educational Review*, Vol. 47 (1977), 171–197; and Karl Weick, "Educational Organizations as Loosely Coupled Systems," *Administrative Science Quarterly*, Vol. 21 (1976), 1–18.

12. The following discussion is drawn from Martin Landau, "Redundancy, Rationality, and the Problem of Duplication and Overlap," *Public Administration Review*, July/August 1969, 346–358.

13. Paul Berman, Milbrey McLaughlin, et al., *Federal Programs Supporting Educational Change, Vol. VII: Factors Affecting Implementation and Continuation* (Santa Monica, California: The Rand Corporation, 1977); and Michael Fullan and Alan Pomfret, "Research on

Curriculum and Instruction Implementation," *Review of Educational Research*, Vol. 47 (1977), 335–397, especially 375ff.

14. Another statement of this point of view can be found in Eleanor Farrar, John DeSanctis, and David Cohen, "Alternative Conceptions of Implementation," unpublished paper, Huron Institute, Cambridge, Massachusetts, October 1978.

15. For a fuller statement of the theory lying behind this argument see: Richard Elmore, "Organizational Models of Social Program Implementation," *Public Policy*, Vol. 26 (1978), 209–217.

16. The term "backward mapping" and the logic of analysis come from Mark Moore at the Kennedy School of Government, Harvard University. I am indebted to him for sharing these thoughts with me. For a more extended treatment of this idea, see: Richard Elmore, "Backward Mapping: Using Implementation Analysis to Structure Program Decisions," *Political Science Quarterly*, Vol. 94 (1979–80), 601–616.

17. A fuller statement of this argument can be found in Dale Mann, "The User-Driven System and a Modest Proposal," in Dale Mann, ed., *Making Change Happen* (New York: Teachers College Press, 1978), 285–307.

CHAPTER 15

Teachers as Policy Brokers in the Content of Elementary School Mathematics

John Schwille, Andrew Porter, Gabriella Belli, Robert Floden, Donald Freeman, Lucy Knappen, Therese Kuhs, and William Schmidt

No one has ever said to me, "Why aren't you teaching this?" or "Why are you teaching this?" I like the flexibility. I guess if I didn't have that, I would probably be upset. But yet ... I think it is important that you do have some kind of a guide, with some flexibility within it. I wouldn't mind somebody saying, "Why are you teaching this?" It would make me stop and think, "Why am I?"

JACQUELINE, 18 JUNE 1980

Jacqueline is one of seven teachers (grades 3–5 in six schools and three districts) whom we studied throughout the school year 1979–80 to find out exactly what mathematics they covered, why they taught the topics they did, and why they did not teach other topics. Our aim in doing this study was not to learn about mathematics teaching per se. Instead, it was to find out how teachers make content decisions. We considered a variety of potential influences on these decisions, including not only hierarchical factors, such as district test and textbook policies, but also interpersonal factors such as advice from other teachers and parents.

Mathematics is a good starting point for this inquiry. Even though it is a subject critical to many high-status occupations, it is treated as less important in elementary school than one might expect. Less time is typically devoted to mathematics than to language arts and reading. Our research raises questions of why this imbalance exists and how one might change either the time spent on mathematics or the nature of what is taught during that time.

Fenstermacher and Amarel, in Chapter 16 of this volume, argue that the autonomy of teachers to make content and other instructional decisions is essential to the good education of students. Prescriptive curriculum policy they view as harmful. They argue against rules and regulations whose "purpose is to instruct teachers on what and how to teach."

Not all teachers with reputations for excellence agree with this extreme position. Jacqueline, for example, was an assiduous follower of the new district-mandated textbook for fourth grade mathematics. She argued that students would benefit if all the district teachers followed the book closely. Yet she was a teacher who had confidence in her ability to teach mathematics. She reported having had good mathematics teachers throughout her own schooling and, in a previous year, had even developed her own unit to teach geometry, a topic that many elementary school teachers skip.

As researchers, we wanted to know how much the characteristics of district policy had to do with Jacqueline's decisions to follow the textbook so closely. In particular, how did these policies interact with Jacqueline's own convictions and other possible influences in making the textbook almost her sole source of content? Although the cases we studied may be exceptional—a possibility to be addressed in further research— our studies thus far have led us to question various beliefs about teachers as well as certain assumptions about educational policies. For example, how much truth is there to the notion that teachers resist outside guidance in curriculum matters? Under what conditions does textbook following reflect commitment, not lack of commitment to the subject matter or content of instruction? Does lack of autonomy lead to abdication of responsibility on the part of teachers, as Fenstermacher and Amarel suggest?

Research has not yet shown that either autonomy or lack of autonomy invariably contributes to better-educated students. In part, the absence of such evidence is due to the fact that public school teachers are virtually never completely autonomous nor are they completely subordinate to prescriptive curriculum policy. Through continued research, it should be possible to learn to what extent and under what conditions students benefit from teacher autonomy.

The extreme position that Fenstermacher and Amarel take derives in part from their beliefs about the proper content of education. In their view, subject matter is subordinate to other educational goals, which require teacher autonomy for their realization: "The exploration of subject matter should permit the teacher [as model] to demonstrate an inquiring mind, a critical and creative orientation to ideas, a respect for evidence, a tolerance for beliefs, a regard for truth, and a degree of detachment from the immediate times." In our research, subject matter itself—the structure and content of a particular discipline—plays a more important role. Rather than assume that teachers need great freedom to pursue the goals listed by Fenstermacher and Amarel, we remain open to the posssbility that, under certain conditions, prescriptive curriculum policy may embody these goals. We are thereby relieved of putting as much faith as Fenstermacher and Amarel on the ability and motivation of each teacher to rediscover the more or less well defined paths that scholars have already taken toward the goals advocated in Chapter 16.

In contrast to Fenstermacher and Amarel, the chapter we have written is less marked by advocacy. Still it does argue that empirical research can be relevant and useful in addressing issues of teacher autonomy. This argument begins with the assertion that content has received too little attention in studies of what teachers do and how schools are governed. Studies of governance have neglected the capacity that teachers have for influencing the content of instruction. Studies of teachers have emphasized teaching methods to the neglect of content. Yet, even in a highly developed and logically organized field such as mathematics, there are issues of content selection that teachers cannot easily resolve by themselves. Policies may help teachers, but they are no panacea. No external policy can anticipate all the conditions that diverse teachers of diverse students face. In the study of curriculum policy, therefore, it is necessary to deal not only with the characteristics of policies but also with the characteristics of teachers and students with which these policies are confronted. Current policies are policies of ignorance in the sense that they do not rest on an adequate understanding of how external policies affect what teachers and students do. Examples from our research underscore the importance of teacher convictions in increasing or decreasing the effect of district policies.

Just as it is questionable whether the individual teacher can deal adequately with all issues of curriculum decision making, it is impossible for us as researchers to deal with all curriculum content (where content is defined inclusively as the cognitive, social, psychomotor, and affective outcomes of education). For this reason we limit ourselves to the cognitive content of elementary school mathematics. Our points do not necessarily apply to either secondary school mathematics or other subject matters. The issues raised, however, warrant being addressed in each of the other subject matters taught in school.

ASSUMPTIONS ABOUT CONTENT AND METHOD

Bronfenbrenner (1970) has suggested that there has been too much preoccupation in the United States with the teacher as purveyor of subject matter. But, in our view, researchers and educators have frequently taken content for granted.[1] For example, among the decisions studied by specialists in the politics of education, content decisions do not loom large (Schwille, Porter, and Gant, 1980). Content is less salient in the literature than such matters as collective bargaining, school finance, school desegregation, and changes in enrollment. School finance studies use as measures of output, not learning outcomes but expenditures, which give little indication of what is being purchased for this money.

Content (in the sense of acquisition of knowledge) has not been of much interest to sociologists either. They have been more concerned about the control of students and the learning of values. Spady and Mitchell (Reference Note 2) cite ten works, including those of such well-known sociologists as Becker, Parsons, Stinchcombe, and Waller, in support of the contention that "control of students is at the center of school system concerns." A collection of syllabi for the sociology of education, published in 1978 by a section of the American Sociological Association, gives no emphasis to the cognitive content of instruction (Persell, Hammack, and Thielens, 1978). Likewise, the Marxist point of view exemplified by Bowles and Gintis (1976) gives less emphasis to content than to the organization of instruction—the correspondence between the hierarchies of school and the work place.

Even among educationists, content has often been taken for granted. For years, the dominant school of research on teaching looked for methods of teaching that would be more or less equally effective across subject matters. Subject-specific skills were assumed to be of less interest (e.g., Rosenshine, 1971). Similarly, among teacher educators and practicing teachers, questions of content have often been eclipsed by questions of instructional strategy or method (cf. Buchmann, 1982).[2]

Whatever the reason, the taking of content for granted continues. In this volume, Elmore appears to subsume the selection of content under problems of choosing an appropriate instructional strategy. For example, he treats poor performance on standardized tests in mathematics and reading as a problem to be resolved by the teachers' choice of strategy (with support from the school system and other authorities). We would ask instead if the content of these tests is appropriate and if teachers have taught this appropriate content (as well as selected an appropriate strategy). Similarly, in the paragraph quoted below, Elmore assumes that teachers are able and willing to turn utopian content demands into a "well-organized strategy of instruction":

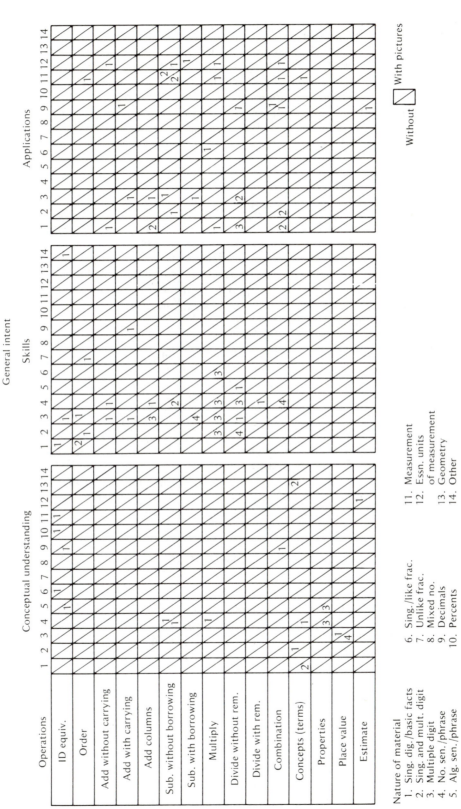

FIGURE 15.1. Content Analysis of Stanford Achievement Test (Intermediate Level/Grades 4.5–5.6), 1973.

373

Teachers receive a variety of signals about what to do in the classroom. In addition to the signals they receive from the [mandated] program about reading and math skills, they hear about their responsibility for teaching democratic values, discipline, the free enterprise system, health and nutrition, career choice, and the history of western civilization, to mention but a few topics. It is the teachers' responsibility to turn these signals into a well-organized strategy of instruction that responds to the range of skills and abilities they find among students in the classroom (p. 357).

We would ask whether it is justifiable to ask teachers to make the difficult content choices that this example implies.

In the last decade a new school of sociology has developed in Britain to challenge the taking of content for granted. According to this school, claims that some kinds of knowledge are worth more than other kinds have reinforced social inequality and posed an obstacle to social justice. Members of this school of thought follow Pierre Bourdieu, a French sociologist who sees schools as helping privileged families pass on their cultural capital and legitimating this inheritance under the guise of meritocracy.[3] According to an exponent of the "new" sociology of education, the experience of mathematics is an example in point:

Pupils have the chance to see that there is a high status group of those who can "do" mathematics and another, often larger group of lower status people who, though they appear to have had the chance to join the high status group, have failed to make it. Differentiation in such circumstances appears to be not only fair but also objective (Eggleston, 1977).

Our own approach to this issue does not presume that variation in content coverage always reinforces social stratification. Variation in content and its implications are matters for empirical investigation. We are therefore committed to measuring content coverage and to the investigation of the causes and consequences of teachers' content decisions.

PUZZLES OF CONTENT COVERAGE IN ELEMENTARY SCHOOL MATHEMATICS

Content coverage in American schools is a bit like a jigsaw puzzle. It is easy to put together a few pieces, based on personal knowledge and experience. But a national scene of content variation, in all its detail, is a challenge to assemble.

For many, to be sure, the content of elementary school mathematics is cut and dried. It is almost entirely computational skills with whole numbers and fractions. This point of view, however, is but one of several in a history of disagreement over what to teach (National Council of Teachers of Mathematics, 1970).

In the early part of this century there were frequent demands for the *reduction* of time on elementary school mathematics and the *elimination* of topics (Metter, 1934). Guy Wilson (1926) carried out surveys of how adults use mathematics and drew on the results to justify confining the mathematics curriculum to the most commonly used computational skills—addition, subtraction, multiplication, and division of whole numbers; simple fractions; percentage; and interest.[4] Although Wilson (1926) proposed to supplement drill with "meaning and understanding," his main concern was with computational skill. He declared that "the emphasis on one hundred percent accuracy is an important emphasis and should not require explanation.... Letter perfect results are the only results that are wanted in the business world."

A sharply contrasting point of view is represented by a group of university mathematicians and scientists who met in Cambridge, Massachusetts, in 1963. They attempted to give direction to the school mathematics reform movement then gaining momentum. This group justified its recommendations through reference to the discipline of mathematics, saying that they wanted "to make students familiar with part of the global structure of mathematics."

> ... Mathematics is a growing subject and all students should be aware of this fact.
> ... The knowledge that there are unsolved problems and that they are gradually being solved puts mathematics in a new light, strips away some of its mystique, and serves to undermine the authoritarianism which has long dominated elementary teaching in the area (Cambridge Conference Report, 1963, pp. 8–9).

According to recent reports on U.S. schools (NACOME, Reference Note 3; Suydam and Osborne, Reference Note 4), this history of competing points of view has led to consensus on the teaching of whole-number computational skills but considerable variation in the coverage of such peripheral topics as metric measurement, geometry, graphs, statistics, probability, relations and functions.

In the future, even the core whole-number skills may come under increasing attack. Already, the availability of calculators leads Wheatley (1980) to propose that schools discontinue the teaching of long division with two-digit divisors.

A National Curriculum That Vanishes upon Examination

The content of elementary school mathematics would not be so problematic, at least in practice, if there were agreement on a national syllabus, such as exists in other countries. It might be said that in the United States there is such a curriculum, one that is implicitly defined by widely used textbooks and standardized tests. To examine this claim, we have analyzed the content of five of the standardized tests and three of the textbooks most widely used in elementary school at fourth grade. This analysis is based on a three-dimensional classification or taxonomy developed for the purpose (Kuhs, Schmidt, Porter, Floden, Freeman, and Schwille, Reference Note 5).

Figure 15.1 contains the results of this analysis for the Stanford Achievement Test (STAN) and illustrates how this approach can be used to represent content at different levels of detail. The three dimensions of this classification matrix are (1) general intent (i.e., conceptual understanding, computational skills, applications), (2) nature of the material (e.g., whole numbers, common fractions, decimals), and (3) mathematical operations the student must perform (e.g., multiplication, estimation, ordering). Specific topics are represented by the cells of the classification matrix (e.g., 3 of the 112 STAN items are devoted to skill in multiplying a multiple-digit number by a single-digit number). More general topics can be addressed by summing across cells to obtain marginal totals (e.g., 17 items on the STAN deal with multiplication).

The claim of an implicit national curriculum was supported in the analysis, but only at a fairly high level of generality. All the textbooks and tests we analyzed contained material on addition, subtraction, multiplication, division, and geometry. Beyond these general areas of agreement, however, there was little evidence to support the concept of a national curriculum. Outside whole-number computation, we found substantial variation even at the marginal level of the classification (e.g., variation of emphasis on fractions, number sentences, estimation, and metric measurement). Still more variation could be seen at the specific or cell level. In the three textbooks, for example, over half the 290 cell-level topics covered (by one or more items in one or more books) were unique to a single book. Only twenty-eight percent of these topics were covered in all three books.

In examining the consistency between tests and textbooks, we found that only six cell-level topics were emphasized in all three books and five tests (Freeman, Kuhs, Porter, Knappen, Floden, Schmidt, and Schwille, Reference Note 6). The match in content covered was better for some textbook-test pairs than others. However, even for the best matched pair, no more than fifty percent of the topics on the test were covered by the equivalent of one lesson or more in the textbook.

Thus, there is a good deal of variation in what might be taught in elementary school mathematics.[5] Our research asks how teachers react to this variation. Who selects the content that is ultimately taught?

THE RESOLUTION OF CONTENT DILEMMAS: TEACHER POLICIES VS. EXTERNAL POLICIES

Teachers Make Policy

Teachers often face incompatible demands. They are subject to conflicting pressures from administrators, parents, and interest groups. In mathematics, for example, parents may want more emphasis on long division while mathematics educators ask for less.

In principle, the policies adopted by boards and legislatures might resolve many of the conflicts and inconsistencies which teachers face. Teachers would have only to implement these policies. But in practice the educational policies of districts, states, and the federal government are often ambiguous or weak. Even where clear and strong, such policies may promote the interests of particular groups, often for good reasons (e.g., in the case of the handicapped, low-income children, the gifted), but nevertheless leaving teachers and local administrators to arbitrate among competing interests.

We therefore consider two types of policy: *teacher policy* as the definitive allocation of public resources by working-level personnel in education (Schwille, Porter, and Gant, 1980; cf. Lipsky, 1980; Elmore, this volume); *external policy* as policy in the usual sense—the laws, regulations, and other directives of boards, legislatures, and executive departments.

A Framework for Teacher Policies about Content

Teachers ultimately decide what is covered in the classroom. That is, they specify *how much* time will be devoted to a subject, *what topics* will be taught, *to whom* these topics will be taught, *when* and *how long* each topic will be taught, and *how well* topics are to be learned. In principle, it is possible for all these decisions to be made autonomously by the teacher, but in practice there is usually leverage exercised by external policies (formal or informal) at the school or district level.[6] In addition, teachers are exposed to a variety of external influences which have nothing to do with external policies (e.g., another teacher, parent requests, newspaper articles).

In this semi-autonomous role, teachers are better understood as political brokers than as implementors. They enjoy considerable discretion, being influenced by their own ideas of what schooling ought to be as well as persuaded by external pressures. This view represents a middle ground in the classic sociological contrast between professional autonomy and bureaucratic subordination. It pictures teachers as more or less rational decision makers who take higher-level policies and other pressures into consideration in their calculation of benefits and costs.

Teacher Repertoire and the Effects of External Policies on Content and Method. In the absence of external policies and other pressures, teachers are likely to select topics from their repertoire, that is, the topics they have taught in the past. Within this repertoire, we expect that the more a teacher regards a topic as appropriate for students and one that (s)he is ready to teach, the more likely it is to be taught.

The teacher's beliefs about appropriateness and readiness may, in turn, be influenced by external policies, but the manner and extent of this influence is not well understood. It is commonly thought that external policies do not have much influence on teachers' beliefs about content, presumably because in the short run policies which run contrary to teacher beliefs engender considerable resistance (e.g., Oldham, Reference Note 10). If a call for new content is not too esoteric, however, it may cause less resistance than calls for change in a teacher's instructional strategies. It is important to remember that instructional strategies are the focus of much of the innovations literature which has led us to expect teacher resistance (e.g., the Rand change agent study as reported in Berman and McLaughlin, 1978). In the long run, we expect that external policies do gradually change teacher beliefs about content as these policies gradually gain more and more acceptance.

Students and Their Effect on Teacher Policies. Students, we believe, have a continual, though perhaps small effect on teachers' content decisions. For example, although teachers select instructional materials without being acquainted with the particular students who will be using the materials, teachers can evaluate the materials in terms of both students they have had in the past and students they expect to have in the future. Subsequently, when important decisions about grouping and classroom assignment are made at the beginning of the year, actual student characteristics can inform teacher decisions about who gets what content.

During the course of the year, teachers monitor the response of students and may modify content decisions as a result. The Dahllöf-Lundgren steering group hypothesis suggests that teachers pick out particular students to pace the class, students at the borderline between those who are expected to learn the content covered and those who are not (Lundgren, 1972).

Students may also actively influence the content of instruction by making suggestions or requests which are taken into account by the teacher. In our case study of Jacqueline, such requests occasionally came to our attention (e.g., students asking for things they could do for extra credit, students asking to repeat a mathematical game). After one such request, Jacqueline went so far as to make a substantial change in the assignment of students to groups.

External policies give the teacher more or less leeway to respond to student differences. On the one hand, adoption of a districtwide textbook puts little constraint upon teachers. They can delete topics that they consider inappropriate for students. On the other hand, a requirement to record student achievement on a set of district objectives discourages teachers from skipping topics. An external policy which mandates individualized, self-paced instruction can take much of the control over pacing decisions away from the teacher and give it to students. Such a mandate allows highly motivated students to move ahead quickly, but it also permits unmotivated students to lag behind more than they might in group teaching.

A Parallel Framework for External Policies

External policies which are likely to affect teachers' content decisions can be sorted into categories which, for the most part, parallel the teacher decisions discussed above (how much time, what topics, to whom, etc.):

1. *Mandated or recommended time allocations.* According to a national survey sponsored by the National Science Foundation (Weiss, Reference Note 11), forty percent of the school districts sampled had guidelines for the minimum number of minutes to be spent per day on fourth grade mathematics (an average of 38 minutes recommended or required).
2. *Press for specific topics.* Written objectives, textbook adoptions, and testing programs make it possible for schools or districts to influence, intentionally or unintentionally, the choice of topics to be taught. For example, according to Weiss (Reference Note 11), ninety-three percent of U.S. school districts use standardized tests in K–6 mathematics. Of these districts, fifty-four percent report making moderate or great use of these tests in revising the curriculum, while thirty percent report small use and ten percent no use (six percent no response).
3. *Press for differentiating content among students.* Grouping policies (including assignments to classrooms), pull-out programs with either a compensatory or gifted focus, and district adoption of individualized systems of instruction can affect the extent to which students of the same age are taught different content.
4. *Press for standards.* Tests required for graduation, tests for mastery of objectives, policies on retention in grade and mandated remediation all set standards for student learning and thereby foster persistent coverage of certain topics.

Giving Weight to External Policies

In addition to the four categories just listed, external policies have other attributes that may have an effect on content coverage. For example, some content-relevant policies reflect an intent to prescribe content, some do not. A district textbook adoption may or may not be intended as a prescription for content. Some teachers, especially those who are aware of a prescriptive intent, may perceive the text as a weak press for specific topics. Others may see the mandated text as nothing more than a pool of topics which they draw upon to fit (a) their own repertoire or (b) the content others (e.g., upper-grade teachers, parents) want them to teach.

The consistency of pressures on any given teacher is also important. In schools with heterogeneous clientele, ambiguities and inconsistencies in content messages are likely to be common (Lortie, 1969). To the extent that pressures are consistent, their impact will be enhanced (Floden, Porter, Schmidt, Freeman, and Schwille, 1981). Where consistency is lacking, teacher autonomy may be increased.

Still another means of giving an external policy more weight is to see that it has one or more of the following attributes of *authority*: the invoking of law or law-like rules, legitimation by a body of teachers, endorsement by experts or charismatic individuals, and consistency with social norms (e.g., the belief that a topic should always be taught at a certain grade level). Likewise the *power* of a policy can be increased through use of rewards and sanctions.[7] One particular category of rewards which the Rand change agent study has shown to be important is support to teachers for implementation of a policy (Berman and McLaughlin, 1978). In the case of content-relevant policies such support might include teacher training on unfamiliar subject matter, provision of paraprofessional aides, and automated record keeping.

Presumably, comprehensive external content policies could be given great weight if all the above attributes were present and taken into account by teachers. Policies of this nature probably do not exist in the United States. Closer approximations can be found in other countries (e.g., France) where hierarchical control of content is accepted and teacher autonomy is, for the most part, limited to instructional strategy.

Top-Down vs. Bottom-Up Studies of Content Policies

Implementation, a word made fashionable by policy analysts (e.g., Mazmanian and Sabatier, 1980), can be misleading if it leads us to look at external policies solely from the top down.[8] From this perspective, the study of implementation starts with policy directives, derives intended outputs from these directives, and then assesses the extent to which the directives are carried out and the intended outputs realized.

The difficulties with this top-down approach, especially when applied to education, are now widely discussed in the literature. A top-down approach emphasizes hierarchical control, but hierarchical control plays a limited role in the loosely coupled world of schools (Bidwell, 1965; Weick, 1976; March, 1978). Teachers and building administrators have enough discretion to be able to adapt external policies to their own priorities as well as to pressures from their clients (Lipsky, 1980). Weatherley's (1979) study of the Massachusetts mandatory special education law illustrates both the impact and the limits of hierarchical control. This law and its regulations, strictly interpreted, required the immediate evaluation of many more children than could be handled. The lack of priorities in the law forced administrators and teachers to set their own priorities, to develop unofficial rationing techniques, and to use their own criteria for weighing the costs and benefits of making a referral.

Teachers may even have views of schooling that are incompatible with the views implicit in external policies. For example, Darling-Hammond and Wise (1981) discuss views of teaching which are opposed to the "rationalistic" views of teaching assumed by external policymakers. The rationalistic view, as they define it, assumes that schools can be assigned clear-cut goals and that teacher activities can be prescribed, evaluated, and ultimately controlled in terms of those goals. Such a view is still very much a part of top-down studies of implementation even when many variables which interfere with implementation are taken into account (Mazmanian and Sabatier, 1980).

The top-down approach is particularly problematic for the study of content decisions. In this case, even external policies are not particularly "rationalistic," at least in the United States, where there is a reluctance to be clearly and specifically prescriptive about what teachers teach. For example, in developing curricula for natural and social science the National Science Foundation was criticized for infringing on local autonomy and in 1976 was forced by Congress to stop funding implementation of its projects (Nelkin, 1978; Welch, 1979).

As a result of this ambivalence at district, state, and national levels, existing external policies are often unclear or weak as far as content is concerned. Nevertheless, such policies can still have an effect on teachers' content decisions, an effect which may or may not reflect the policymaker's intent. To understand this effect, the bottom-up approach exemplified by our case studies of seven teachers is useful. This approach starts with an analysis of what happens in classrooms and works back to see to what extent these happenings are influenced by external policies, together with other factors. Such an analysis will turn up (a) long-standing ways of doing things which are not subject to scrutiny by higher authority, (b) anticipated and unanticipated effects of hierarchical pressures, and (c) the teacher's response to nonhierarchical influences (e.g., student pressures, pressures attributable to school norms, and the teacher's own views of what is desirable and feasible).

ILLUSTRATIONS FROM STUDIES OF TEACHERS' CONTENT DECISION MAKING

Teacher Policies, Given Six Simulated Pressures

In one of our earlier studies (Floden et al., 1981), sixty-six teachers from five areas in Michigan indicated how they would respond to various combinations of pressures to change the content of fourth grade mathematics. The six pressures came from (1) parents, (2) upper-grade teachers, (3) the school principal, (4) district instructional objectives, (5) textbook supplied to the teacher, and (6) standardized test results reported in the local newspaper.

The following example of these hypothetical situations is a mix of pressures from objectives, tests, and other teachers:

> In Wakita the central administration has published, for fourth grade mathematics, a set of objectives which all teachers have been directed to follow. At the end of the year, a standardized test in mathematics is administered in each grade. The test results for each school are published, by grade level, in the local newspaper.

> Shortly after your arrival, you study the set of objectives and the test which is used. You realize that these materials do not deal with five topics you have been accustomed to teaching in fourth grade. You also note that they do include material on five topics you have never taught to fourth graders.

> Also imagine that the teachers in your school express a particular interest in mathematics at staff meetings and in conversations in the teachers' room. During these discussions you find that the fifth and sixth grade teachers feel you should teach five topics you have not taught to fourth graders in the past. They also question the value for fourth graders of five topics you have been used to teaching. The topics mentioned in each case are the same as those you noted in your examination of the test and the objectives.

In all the hypothetical situations, the pressures were limited to content decisions about specific topics. While the pressures were always consistent, they were not always clearly prescriptive in intent nor was there much attempt to give them authority.

No explicit reference was made to rewards for compliance or sanctions for noncompliance. In particular, no help was promised for putting into practice the changes in instruction that would be required. In short, when the hypothetical situations referred to external policies, these policies were not given much weight.

Nevertheless, the most striking aspect of the teachers' responses to the pressures was their reported willingness to add topics to their instructional content, whatever the source of pressure for change. In other words, teachers presented themselves more as potential implementors than as autonomous decision makers. The teachers seemed less willing to give up topics currently taught and did not seem to consider the new topics as necessarily supplanting the old ones.[9]

Objectives and published test results stood out as the most powerful pressures to affect teacher content decisions. Textbooks were the least powerful pressure for adding content.

Our Design for Seven Bottom-Up Studies

In our case studies of seven teachers, the outcome of primary interest was the mathematics covered in each of the classrooms, as recorded in daily logs kept by each teacher. In weekly interviews, we discussed the logs; the use of textbooks, tests, objectives, or other materials; and any conversations or newly received documents relating to mathematics. In addition, we interviewed the teacher at the beginning of the year to ascertain his or her intentions and priorities and at the end of the year to probe the teacher's reaction to possible curriculum influences. A limited amount of classroom observation was also scheduled. Independent information on content-relevant policies and other attempts to influence content were obtained through (a) interviews with principals and other district personnel and (b) observation of meetings (e.g., building staff meetings, in-service workshops to explain test scores, open houses for parents).

The six schools and three districts in which these teachers taught were selected for differences in (a) external policies for the control of mathematics content (centralized vs. decentralized), (b) urban vs. small-town location, and (c) extent of teacher isolation within schools (e.g., self-contained classroom vs. open schools). The most centralized district (which we call Knoxport) was an urban district with a management-by-objectives system, districtwide standardized testing, and guidelines for time spent on mathematics (forty-five minutes per day in fourth grade). Finn, the least centralized district, was a small-town district with a strict policy of building autonomy in curriculum matters. The only breach in this autonomy was districtwide standardized testing, initiated one year before our study began. Sawyer, the third district, was also a small-town district but with somewhat less building autonomy. Following appointment of the district's first curriculum director one year before our study, a districtwide mathematics textbook was adopted and a districtwide standardized testing program initiated. To get some sense for variation in content decision making within the districts, two schools were selected in each district. The two schools varied in the extent to which the classrooms were self-contained.[10]

Two Teacher Policies in the Aftermath of a District Textbook Adoption

Our case studies have a good deal to say about whether and why the seven teachers followed their textbooks. For illustration, we can take two Sawyer teachers, Jacqueline and Wilma, and their response to the district textbook adoption. The district began to use a new mathematics textbook series in all its elementary schools the year of our study. The series was chosen a year earlier by a committee of teachers, together with the curriculum director. Although the committee later gave precedence to the textbook as the primary authority for what to teach (over district scope-and-sequence chart and Michigan Assessment tests), it never resolved the question of how much of the textbook teachers should cover. In fact, at the very last meeting in the year of our study, one of Jacqueline's colleagues once again asked whether the committee was going to decide what was important in the textbook. She declared that the teachers did not all know what they were supposed to be teaching.

The Sawyer textbook policy should thus be viewed as a weak policy for influencing teacher content decisions. According to our informants, it was recommended that teachers follow the textbook, but no one recalled specific examples of this recommendation being communicated to teachers. Rewards for following and sanctions for not following the textbook were little in evidence. For most teachers, including the two we studied, in-service assistance on the new textbook was very limited, in part because teachers did not express much need for this assistance. Hence, it is not surprising to find that the two teachers in our study relied principally on their own judgment in deciding how much to use the textbook.

Determinants of Jacqueline's Use of Textbook. For most of the year, Jacqueline taught two groups in mathematics. With only minor deviations, she led one group consecutively through the first nine of the thirteen chapters in the fourth grade mathematics text. When Jacqueline spoke of the changes in content she made between the year of our study and the year before, she attributed these changes more to differences in students than to differences in textbooks. Jacqueline perceived the students as high ability (relative both to another group taught by her team and to a group she had the year before).

We also studied Jacqueline's work with a remedial group of three students who were using the third grade textbook. Here again Jacqueline followed the text closely, though not as closely as with the higher group. In so doing, she taught content that other teachers might well have skipped in a remedial group (e.g., writing number sentences for word problems, rounding to nearest ten and nearest hundred, using estimation in word problems).

Our interviews throughout the year dealt frequently with Jacqueline's reasons for following these textbooks so closely.[11] In responding to these questions, Jacqueline pointed to benefits for students in following the textbook. She held that the text ensures "continuity" in subject matter. Teachers who follow the textbook do not skip important topics; they do not teach topics out of appropriate sequence. According to Jacqueline, teachers who did not like the old textbook did pick and choose. They left out important chapters (e.g., number theory). In contrast, Jacqueline maintained that other teachers in her school and district liked the new textbook. She therefore predicted that they would follow it more closely than they had the old book, thereby increasing continuity across grades.

Following the textbook was seen not only as beneficial to the students, it also benefitted the teacher by saving planning time. Time was important to Jacqueline, a very busy member of a team of four teachers. The team held planning meetings, but they were devoted in large part to science and social studies, the two subjects that were taught in tightest coordination among the four teachers. Outside these meetings, Jacqueline was a demanding teacher who spent much time working with students. She was also an active participant in the local teacher organization and in university courses.

In spite of these advantages of following the textbook, Jacqueline's commitment to the new book was provisional. During a district curriculum committee meeting, Jacqueline told the committee that, after using a textbook for the first time, a teacher may find parts inappropriate. Later Jacqueline did object to parts of the text and even deviated to some extent. Most of these objections were not so much a matter of content as of strategy, that is, the method of teaching a topic. On rare occasions she did skip some peripheral content (e.g., use of flow charts). At times she also supplemented the text to put more emphasis on conceptual understanding.

Her criticisms were usually based on the observed or inferred response of students. For example, the text did not break the various multiplication facts into separate lessons as much as she had in the past. Although this lack of separation posed no problem for her current high-ability class, she repeatedly criticized this part of the text as unsuitable for students of lower ability.

Jacqueline did not consider skipping geometry with her high-ability group. But, although she was distressed that teachers might skip geometry without good reason, she did consider geometry expendable for any class that was well below average in achievement.

Jacqueline's use of textbooks also varied across subject matters. In science, she conjectured that if a new textbook did not compare favorably with units already developed by her team, the team would probably continue to use their own units. Jacqueline reported that she did not use the district textbook in language arts. She and other teachers regarded this textbook as deficient in both content and strategy.

In short, Jacqueline considered many factors in her decisions of how much to follow the text: the desirability of giving the book a fair trial, benefits of continuity to students, the opinions of other teachers, the characteristics of the text once she tried it, the time she had available. In the year of our study, these considerations led the district textbook to figure very prominently in Jacqueline's content decisions. However, this effect of the district adoption was so bound up in Jacqueline's personal policy that other teachers might respond to the same external policy in very different ways.

Determinants of Wilma's Use of Textbook. During our study Wilma taught fourth grade in the same district as Jacqueline, but in another building. Her conception of what was basic and what was peripheral in fourth grade mathematics was neatly packaged in what she termed a "subject clock." The subject clock was limited to basic content: (a) addition, (b) subtraction, (c) multiplication, (d) division, and (e) fractions. Topics such as geometry, measurement, and estimation were considered "frills." Wilma strongly believed that the five subject-clock topics should help children deal with real-life activities, such as collecting a pay check, purchasing things in a store, and determining what an item costs when it has been marked off a certain percent.

Wilma also had a personal view of learning which she called her "internal clock." According to this point of view, there are optimal periods during the year for learning new content, periods which are least disrupted by long breaks or by children's anticipation of some upcoming event. Wilma asserted that the greatest learning occurs in the period from January to spring break. Before January, the year is increasingly disrupted by Christmas. After spring break the students' thoughts turn more and more to summer, play, and getting outside.

Hence, according to Wilma, September through mid-November should be chiefly devoted to review of addition and subtraction. From mid-November through January the main topic to be covered is multiplication, and then from February to Easter students should concentrate on division. After Easter the important topic is fractions. Once fractions have been adequately taught, peripheral topics can be included in whatever time remains.

Wilma's conception was carried out in practice. In almost all cases actual instruction on topics began no more than a week later than predicted earlier in the year.

Since all widely used fourth grade textbooks cover the five topics in Wilma's subject clock, she could make extensive use of any textbook. However, if a textbook were to follow the suggestion to delete the teaching of long division with two-digit divisors (see, e.g., Wheatley, 1980), we would predict that Wilma would follow her clock rather than the text. In several conversations, Wilma indicated that if the approach suggested by the textbook were not consistent with her thinking, she would ignore the book. In fact, Wilma did omit the geometry chapter, saying that it was not part of her subject clock. Unlike Jacqueline, Wilma did not follow the pages or sections of the new textbook in the order given. She rearranged the sequence to fit her internal clock. Even within topics, such as addition, she did not follow the textbook sequence.

Wilma was ready to consider topics in the textbook that she had not taught previously, but that fit her subject clock. For example, the new textbook included averaging, which Wilma had not taught before. She taught this topic because it fit well under division, one of her core topics. She admitted that in earlier years, she had never thought about teaching averages.

In short, unlike Jacqueline, Wilma was from the beginning convinced that following her own repertoire and priorities was better than sticking closely to the text. Both teachers ultimately decided how they would use the district-adopted text. But Wilma's strong commitment to her repertoire resulted in a continuation of earlier practices, whereas Jacqueline was more willing to give the text a try to see what advantages it offered.

A Teacher Policy in the Context of State and District Testing Programs

In the Finn district where buildings have enjoyed almost complete curriculum autonomy, the use of standardized tests was one possible exception to this lack of external control. In the fall of our study, the Michigan Assessment (MEAP) was administered to all fourth graders, here as elsewhere in the state. In addition, a widely used standardized test (we can call it the WUST) was given in each grade. This external policy for the use of the WUST was adopted by the district one year before our study on the initiative of the curriculum director, who had been impressed with the test while taking a course from an author of the WUST. However, in conformity with the district philosophy of building autonomy, the policy was not initiated until key building principals had also attended this course and been similarly convinced.

The curriculum director viewed the WUST as the district prescription for what to teach. However, as far as we could tell, there were no rewards or sanctions to be given teachers for performance on this test. Nor was the content message of the WUST entirely consistent with the messages communicated by the MEAP, the state-mandated test.

In Finn, WUST results were carefully reviewed in a meeting of school principals, which was followed by staff meetings in each building. In one of the schools we studied, the principal circled all items on the WUST where the proportion of correct answers was not as high as district or national norms. But at the meeting he deferred to the teachers as authorities, asking them to determine whether the topic covered by each of these items represented something they should be teaching.

Donna, a teacher in this school, was closely monitored throughout the year. She did not increase her emphasis on any of these areas of relatively low student achievement. When asked if the staff meeting on WUST results had been valuable, Donna made no reference to the analysis of strengths and weaknesses.

Although specific feedback from the WUST did not appear to affect Donna's teaching, she and other teachers in her school repeatedly expressed concern for why the WUST scores in reading were so much higher than in mathematics. According to Donna, the other teachers attributed the lower scores in mathematics to earlier use of an individualized program. Donna disagreed, believing that this difference was the result of (a) the fact that the teachers had placed so much emphasis on reading in recent years, (b) the use of different textbooks in mathematics in different grades, and (c) the lack of communication across grades. In Donna's words teachers should "know exactly what (other teachers) have covered and are covering." Thus, the effect of the WUST was not to cause Donna to give more emphasis to specific topics, but rather to raise teacher concern for overall mathematics performance and to give Donna an occasion for discussing the lack of articulation across grades.

In contrast, neither Donna nor her principal paid much attention to the MEAP results. In the principal's words:

> For this particular school in mathematics... [the MEAP] goals are worthless because our students function at a much higher rate than what they want as minimal objectives.... It is utterly ridiculous, ninety-three to ninety-seven percent attainment... [and] doesn't tell me my real needs for this building as far as individual kids are concerned.

A Teacher Policy within a District Management-by-Objectives System

In Knoxport, a district with more than thirty thousand students, all teachers in grades one through six were required to follow a management-by-objectives (MBO) system. In mathematics, the system included over one hundred objectives which were to be mastered in a prescribed order. The objectives were narrow in definition and focused on computational skills. For example, there was one objective for two-digit by two-digit multiplication and another for two-digit by three-digit. There was a district goal that each student master at least sixteen objectives each year, and district-level records of student progress were kept on all compensatory education students. However, we found no evidence of sanctions for teachers whose students did not reach sixteen objectives.

To facilitate use of the MBO system, there were tests for student placement at the beginning of the year, mastery tests for each objective, review tests for subsets of objectives, end-of-year tests for grades four through six, and forms for recording student achievement. In addition and of key importance were the assignment sheets, which tied each objective to relevant pages from each of several textbooks in use within the district.

The MBO system began to take shape eight years before our study. At the beginning it was a pilot project to evaluate federal and state compensatory education programs. It was formally adopted and required of all teachers three years later. The number of objectives achieved by students in the MBO system continued to serve as the basis for evaluating nearly all categorical programs in the Knoxport district. By virtue of the MBO system and without direct intent to prescribe content, federal and state categorical programs have had an important effect on the choice of mathematics content in this district.

At the time of adoption, the MBO system was strongly opposed by many teachers despite its having been created by a committee with substantial teacher representation. However, Andy (our case study teacher) started using the system before it was mandated by the district. He was the first in his building and one of the first in the district, although he had no involvement in the development or revision of the system. When he began using the system, he was a member of the district mathematics committee. Dissatisfied with his approach to mathematics at the time, he accepted the district mathematics specialist's request to give the system a try. In general, our evidence suggests that this specialist had a major influence on the mathematics taught by Andy.

Later, Andy tried to persuade other teachers to use the system. His recollection is that eight or so teachers in his building were using the system by the time it was mandated by the district. Even so, according to Andy, it was never followed closely by all teachers, even at his school.

Andy himself allowed almost no exceptions to the system. Only two students in his class were allowed to skip any objectives during our study. When asked if he would like to see any changes in the content of the objectives, Andy responded, "No additions, no deletions, [only] the re-ordering of [objectives] numbers 57 and 58."

Given Andy's policy, delivery of content was almost entirely in the hands of the materials, not the teacher. In contrast, another teacher we studied in the same district gave two periods of mathematics for her students, one for working individually on the MBO system and one for whole-group instruction on a textbook. We were also aware of teachers who made little use of the system.

In brief, Andy was a voluntary implementor who used the MBO system in much the way it was designed. Still, his own decisions at points not prescribed by the system partially determined the content covered by students in his classroom. For example, he decided not to let students do as many objectives as they could without interruption. Instead, once they had progressed to a point in the objectives that he had selected, they were given enrichment assignments in the fourth grade textbook. Andy reorganized this textbook material and had all enrichment students proceed in fixed order. Students who completed this textbook enrichment were returned to the objectives. In addition, the quickest to finish the complete textbook were given a unit on metric measurement.

Andy chose assignments from the assignment sheets which tied textbooks to objectives. He rarely used knowledge of students in making these assignments. As far as we could tell, the primary consideration was whether the old or new textbook was on the shelf at the moment the assignment was made.

Still other teacher decisions influenced the pace at which students completed steps in the system. The system itself provided no advice on when a student should be permitted to take the mastery test. At the beginning of the year, Andy let students decide when they were ready. Dissatisfied with this aspect of his policy, Andy later tried other procedures (limiting testing to certain days, making the decision himself, setting goal dates for mastery). But when none of these procedures resulted in a better trade-off between pace and content learned, they were progressively abandoned.

In short, district policies had a major impact on the mathematics content covered in Andy's class. Nevertheless, factors other than district policy were important as well in determining what topics were taught, in what order they were taught, and how long was spent on each topic. In this semi-autonomous role, Andy was no mere implementor, but rather a booster and a broker for the system.

MISSING PIECES

The history of elementary school mathematics in the United States, together with our content analyses of present-day instructional materials, reveal important differences of opinion, even in this traditional subject, about what should be taught and tested. These differences surface from time to time in public debate but are rarely settled to the point of providing clear guidance to teachers. Teachers are expected to deal with predicaments that makers of external policy are unable or unwilling to resolve.

It is not our purpose here to take a position on control of the curriculum. It is rather to provide evidence that might be used in arguments *for or against* greater control. Fenstermacher and Amarel in this volume do take a stand. They argue for autonomy, but their case rests on hypotheses about the effects of greater autonomy which are yet to be substantiated.

However, their assumptions and our studies are consistent in one respect. They suggest that external policies do influence teachers' content decisions—despite the absence of many of the attributes that make for strong policies. The sixty-six Michigan teachers in our simulation study hypothetically abdicated their role of autonomous decision makers even when confronted with what we would judge as weak attempts to influence them. In each of the three districts we studied over the course of a year, policies did have a notable impact on individual teachers. Nevertheless, the seven teachers also exercised much discretion. These teachers were indeed political brokers, arbitrating between their own priorities and the implied priorities of external policies.

As for teachers in general, we do not know exactly what mathematics they cover, how autonomous they are in their content decisions, or whether their autonomy is of particular benefit to students. Moreover, what little we know of other subjects suggests that the effects of autonomy may differ from subject to subject. Given this state of ignorance, it is premature to argue that the present trend toward more prescriptive curriculum policies on the part of districts and states has entirely and necessarily negative consequences.

Few would say that what children are now taught in school is optimal. In our judgment, teachers can be persuaded to change content more readily than one might think in the wake of federal curriculum development that did not live up to expectations (Welch, 1979). We recognize that teachers have and no doubt will continue to resist proposals for content that they have not been given the opportunity to learn thoroughly themselves or that they find too difficult to teach. But virtually all teachers do teach difficult content (e.g., long division) and many teach peripheral content that was once unfamiliar in elementary school (e.g., geometry, metric measurement, inequalities). Given our research and literature review, we believe that a large proportion of teachers would readily make changes in the content of their instruction when such changes are consistent with their repertoire. Our conceptual framework leads us to predict that a great many teachers would even make changes which are inconsistent with their repertoire, provided that these changes came from persons with perceived legal and expert authority and that the teachers receive ample training and other help in making the changes. In short, the "new" mathematics reform, in our opinion, fell short not because of irreducible teacher resistance but rather because of inadequate external policies in general and inadequate support for teaching in particular.[12]

National policies to control content prevail in many countries. We may find that these policies increase continuity from grade to grade and from school to school and that this continuity is beneficial to students. If so, this sort of benefit has to be weighed against the disadvantages of prescriptive external policies. Fenstermacher and Amarel, for example, assert that prescriptive policies lead teachers to put too much value on indoctrination and compliance. Weinshank, Trumbull, and Daly (this volume) contend that diminished autonomy may result in the teaching professions attracting "only the passive, the unimaginative, and the unlettered while simultaneously depleting the vitality and commitment of the best practitioners now serving." These contentions deserve serious, empirical study. In this way we can better understand under what conditions external policies have such consequences and when they do not.

Educational research has had the salutary and chastening effect of showing that grand generalizations about education are generally unwarranted. Broad claims for the benefits of autonomy or control are not likely to be the "exception which proves the rule"—the logically required counter to this generalization about generalizations. It will take many pieces of evidence and much analysis to solve the puzzles of content decision making.

NOTES

1. We follow the "new" British sociology of education in calling for analysis of what educators take for granted. Similarities and differences between their work and ours are discussed in Schwille, Porter, and Gant (Reference Note 1).
2. As one explanation for this state of affairs, Apple (1978) paraphrases recent comments of Stanwood Cobb, one of the early organizers of the Progressive Education Association: "Many progressive educators throughout the early decades of this century were quite cautious about even raising the question of what actual content should be taught and evaluated in schools. They often preferred to concern themselves primarily with teaching methods, in part because the determination of curriculum was perceived as inherently a political issue which could split the movement." Apple, however, cautions us that Cobb's recent recollection of what happened many years ago may not be accurate.
3. "Prior acquisition of cultural capital through osmosis in the family environment creates the impression of ease and brilliance in school whereas having to make up ground through methodical effort is seen as laborious striving that indicates lack of ability.
    "By treating socially conditioned capacities as if they were differences in native ability, the school legitimates ascribed inequalities and masks the differential transmission of cultural heritage. It serves to convince the lower social classes that they owe their destiny to their lack of individual ability and that they have chosen their fate" (Bourdieu's position as summarized in Murphy, 1979, p. 25).
4. "Ninety percent of adult figuring is covered by the four fundamental processes: addition, subtraction, multiplication, and division [of whole numbers]. Simple fractions, percentage, and interest, if added to the four fundamental processes, will raise the percentage to over ninety-five percent. Mastery of these essentials becomes the drill load in arithmetic for the

grades. Beyond that, the work is informational problem work adjusted to child interests" (Wilson, Stone, and Dalrymple, 1939; also quoted in National Council of Teachers of Mathematics Yearbook, 1970, p. 122).

5. For another example of core consensus and peripheral variation in mathematics content, this time as described by nineteen teachers of grades three to five in a single district, see Kuhs, Reference Note 7.

6. The teacher Liz, described by Fenstermacher and Amarel in this volume, is an example of an autonomous teacher. For examples of a high degree of curriculum autonomy among teachers at the high school level, see Cusick (Reference Note 8) and McNeil (Reference Note 9).

7. These definitions of power and authority are adapted from the Spady-Mitchell revision of Weber's classic formulation (Spady and Mitchell, 1979).

8. The following statement by Edwards and Sharkansky (1978) is a good example of this perspective:

"Top officials must take several steps to assure proper implementation. They must issue policy directives that are clear and consistent; hire adequate staff and provide them with the information and authority necessary to carry out their orders; offer incentives for staff to execute policy as decision-makers intended and effectively follow up on the implemental actions of subordinates" (p. 321).

9. The same sort of accretion without deletion has been documented in a content analysis of geometry in German mathematics textbooks (Damerow, Reference Note 12).

10. Elizabeth Cohen (Reference Note 13) suggested to us that susceptibility to external pressures would be partially determined by the nature of collegial relationships within each school (assessed at the point of selection by the use vs. nonuse of teaming, resource teachers, instructional aides, and open-space building).

11. However, to avoid influencing the teachers unduly, we were careful about how we probed into such issues before the end of the year since content decisions were still being made.

12. See the Weinshank, Trumbull, and Daly chapter in this volume for further discussion of these inadequacies and the need for supportive policies.

REFERENCE NOTES

1. Schwille, J., Porter, A. and Gant, M. *Factors influencing teachers' decisions of what to teach: Sociological perspectives* (Research Series No. 62). East Lansing, MI: Institute for Research on Teaching, Michigan State University, 1979.

2. Spady, W. G. and Mitchell, D. E. *Authority and the functional structuring of social action in the schools.* Unpublished manuscript, 1977.

3. National Advisory Committee on Mathematical Education (NACOME). *Overview and analysis of school mathematics, grades K–12.* Washington, D.C.: Conference Board of the Mathematical Sciences, 1975.

4. Suydam, M. N. and Osborne, A. *The status of pre-college science education: 1955–1975; Vol. II: Mathematics education.* Columbus, OH: Center for Science and Mathematics Education, Ohio State University, 1977.

5. Kuhs, T., Schmidt, W., Porter, A., Floden, R., Freeman, D. and Schwille, J. *A taxonomy for classifying elementary school mathematics content* (Research Series No. 4). East Lansing, MI: Institute for Research on Teaching, Michigan State University, 1979.

6. Freeman, D. J., Kuhs, T. M., Porter, A. C., Knappen, L. B., Floden, R. E., Schmidt, W. H. and Schwille, J. R. *The fourth-grade mathematics curriculum as inferred from textbooks and tests* (Research Series No. 82). East Lansing, MI: Institute for Research on Teaching, Michigan State University, 1980.

7. Kuhs, T. M. *Elementary school teachers' conceptions of mathematics content as a potential*

influence on classroom instruction. Unpublished doctoral dissertation, Michigan State University, 1980.

8. Cusick, P. A. *A study of networks among staffs of two large comprehensive secondary schools.* Final report, NIE contract 400–79–0004. East Lansing, MI: Institute for Research on Teaching, Michigan State University, 1980.

9. McNeil, L. *Economic dimensions of social studies curricula: Curriculum as institutionalized knowledge.* Unpublished doctoral dissertation, University of Wisconsin, 1977.

10. Oldham, E. Case studies in geometry education: Ireland. In *Comparative studies of mathematics curricula: Change and stability, 1960–1980.* Proceedings of a conference organized jointly by the Institute for Mathematical Didactics, University of Bielefeld, and the International Association for the Evaluation of Educational Achievement, Osnabruck, January, 1980.

11. Weiss, I. R. *Report of the 1977 national survey of science, mathematics, and social studies.* RTI/1266/06-01F. Research Triangle Park, NC: Research Triangle Institute, 1978.

12. Damerow, P. Concepts of geometry in German textbooks. In *Comparative studies of mathematics curricula: Change and stability, 1960–1980.* Proceedings of a conference organized jointly by the Institute for Mathematical Didactics, University of Bielefeld, and the International Association for the Evaluation of Educational Achievement, Osnabruck, January, 1980.

13. Cohen, E. Personal communication, July, 1979.

REFERENCES

Apple, M. W. Ideology, reproduction, and educational reform. *Comparative Education Review*, 1978, *22*, 367–387.

Berman, P. and McLaughlin, M. W. *Federal programs supporting educational change; Vol. VIII: Implementing and sustaining innovations.* R-1589/8-HEW. Santa Monica, CA: Rand Corporation, 1978.

Bidwell, C. E. The school as a formal organization. In J. G. March (ed.), *Handbook of organizations.* Chicago: Rand McNally, 1965.

Bowles, S. and Gintis, H. *Schooling in capitalist America: Educational reform and the contradictions of economic life.* New York: Basic Books, 1976.

Bronfenbrenner, U. *Two worlds of childhood: U.S. and U.S.S.R.* New York: Russell Sage Foundation, 1970.

Buchmann, M. The flight away from content in teacher education and teaching. *Journal of Curriculum Studies*, 1982, *14*, 61–68.

Cambridge Conference on School Mathematics. *Goals for school mathematics.* Boston: Houghton Mifflin Co., 1963.

Darling-Hammond, L. and Wise, A. E. *A conceptual framework for examining teachers' views of teaching and educational policies.* Washington, D. C.: Rand Corporation, 1981.

Edwards, G. C., III and Sharkansky, I. *Policy predicament: Making and implementing public policy.* San Francisco: W. H. Freeman and Co., 1978.

Eggleston, J. *The sociology of the school curriculum.* London: Routledge and Kegan Paul, 1977.

Floden R., Porter, A., Schmidt, W., Freeman, D. and Schwille, J. Responses to curriculum pressures: A policy-capturing study of teacher decisions about content. *Journal of Educational Psychology*, 1981, *73*, 129–141.

Lipsky, M. *Street-level bureaucracy: Dilemmas of the individual in public services.* New York: Russell Sage Foundation, 1980.

Lortie, D. C. The balance of control and autonomy in elementary school teaching. In A. Etzioni (ed.), *The semi-professions and their organization.* New York: The Free Press, 1969.

Lundgren, U. P. *Frame factors and the teaching process*. Stockholm: Almqvist and Wiksell, 1972.

March, J. G. American public school administration: A short analysis. *School Review*, 1978, *86*, 217–250.

Mazmanian, D. and Sabatier, P. (eds.). Symposium on successful policy implementation. *Policy Studies Journal* (special issue), 1980, *8*, 531–651 (to be published in expanded form by Lexington Books).

Metter, H. L. Trends in the emphasis on various topics of arithmetic since 1860. *Elementary School Journal*, 1934, *34*, 767–775.

Murphy, R. *Sociological theories of education*. Toronto: McGraw-Hill Ryerson, Ltd., 1979.

National Council of Teachers of Mathematics (NCTM). *History of mathematics education in the United States and Canada: Thirty-second yearbook*. Washington, D. C., 1970.

Nelkin, D. *Science textbook controversies and the politics of equal time*. Cambridge, MA: MIT Press, 1978.

Persell, C. H., Hammack, F. M. and Thielens, W. *Teaching sociology of education*. Washington, D.C.: American Sociological Association, 1978.

Rosenshine, B. *Teaching behaviors and student achievement*. Slough: National Foundation for Educational Research in England and Wales, 1971.

Schwille, J., Porter, A. and Gant, M. Content decision-making and the politics of education. *Educational Administration Quarterly*, 1980, *16*, 21–40.

Spady, W. G. and Mitchell, D. E. Authority and the management of classroom activities. In D. L. Duke (ed.), *Classroom management: The seventy-eighth yearbook of the National Society for the Study of Education*. Chicago: University of Chicago Press, 1979.

Weatherley, R. A. *Reforming special education: Policy implementation from state level to street level*. Cambridge, MA: MIT Press, 1979.

Weick, K. E. Educational organizations as loosely coupled systems. *Administrative Science Quarterly*, 1976, *21*, 1–18.

Welch, W. W. Twenty years of science curriculum development: A look back. In D. C. Berliner (ed.), *Review of research in education* (Vol. 7), American Educational Research Association, 1979.

Wheatley, G. H. Calculators in the classroom: A proposal for curricular change. *Arithmetic Teacher*, 1980, *28* (4), 37–39.

Wilson, G. M. *What arithmetic shall we teach?* Boston: Houghton-Mifflin Co., 1926.

Wilson, G. M., Stone, M. B. and Dalrymple, C. O. *Teaching the new arithmetic*. New York: McGraw-Hill Book Co., 1939.

CHAPTER 16

The Interests of the Student, the State, and Humanity in Education

Gary D. Fenstermacher and Marianne Amarel

The education of the young has long been contested ground. Any design for formal education requires alignment of at least three separate interests: those of the young, those of the state, and those of humankind. These interests embody the commonly conflicting demands of the present and the future, the needs of the individual and the community, the expediencies of the immediate political and social conditions and the requirements of planned change. While often in conflict, these separate interests rarely present clear choices, nor are there certain means to realize one or another of the plausible claims. Educational choices may, in fact, be best construed as a series of dilemmas calling for reasoned intentions, informed judgments, and principled actions on the part of practitioners.

The underlying theme of our argument is that the conflict created among the means and ends of education in the effort to align the interests of the student, the state, and humanity falls most heavily on the teacher. It is the teacher who must ultimately forge a working resolution among competing claims, and it is the teacher who habitually perches on the horns of dilemmas. It is our belief that these responsibilities are inherent in the teaching role.

They arise directly from the nature of human learning and the characteristic features of the most common educational setting, the classroom. We believe that teachers *ought* to be responsible for the day-to-day resolution of dilemmas implicated in educational encounters, for, as we will try to show, attempts to prefabricate resolutions stand to distort, even debase, the interests of all who have a stake in education. We also believe that teachers must be prepared for, and supported in their efforts to take, the principled actions their role entails.

In developing our position, we will make the case for the students' interests by offering a view of human learning that is theoretically credible and increasingly fortified by empirical evidence. We depict our points through vignettes of children learning in elementary classrooms. We have taken our illustrations from primary schools because we understand the workings of this setting best and in the belief that primary grades afford the clearest view of the competing interests. The young age of the students renders particularly acute the tensions between the goals of induction (the need to inculcate children with the ethos and received knowledge of the prevailing culture) and the goals of personal autonomy (the obligation to enable students to ultimately rethink the norms and forms of their world and participate in maintaining and reshaping it).

We will go on to describe the interest of the state in educating the young and provide an historical context for these claims. In this discussion, by "state" is meant the federal and state governments and their agents in the executive, legislative, and judicial branches. It is assumed that the state's interest is expressed through the policies it promulgates and the ways it undertakes to implement and enforce these policies. Laws, court decisions, and administrative regulations are all viewed as means of shaping and expressing policy. In this second section we point to misalignments between the interests of the students and the state and express our belief that increasingly, the state is compelling teachers to resolve the conflict of interests in its favor.

In the third section of this essay we place the argument in the broadest and more abstracted context of the interest of humankind and attempt a more detailed analysis of the problematic consequences of tilting the balance of resolutions in favor of the state's interest.

It is important, for the purposes of our arguments, that the subtleties of the word "interest" be respected. There is a difference between what a person believes is in his or her interest and what others believe is in that person's interest. This difference is critical in discussions of the education of the young, for here it is tempting to think only of what is *in their interest* and not of *what their interests are*. At issue are the multiple perspectives implicated in the educative endeavor—the very source of incipient and actual conflict of interests.

THE STUDENTS' INTEREST

This is Paul's second year in a combined first and second grade classroom.[1] He entered first grade unobtrusively, remaining at the periphery of classroom life at first. Gradually, he established working and social connections with several of his classmates and became an integral member of the class.

Paul makes acceptable headway in schoolwork, his progress marked by a gradual, cumulative sequence of steps. He attends to the assigned tasks, becomes engrossed in the optional projects available in the room, and proves himself responsible and planful, able to make choices, to exercise judgment, and to express his preferences. For all this, Paul is not a strongly felt presence in the classroom. His even temperament, measured pace, and responsive manner exemplify moderation; he is an apt, but not exceptional, pupil who makes no undue demands and gives little cause for concern. Were it not for his teacher's probing observations, the pedagogical challenge that Paul poses would remain obscured. More likely still, were it not for the range of learning opportunities she provides, Paul would be a less productive and more troublesome student.

The instructional program in Paul's class is a balance of prescribed and self-selected work. The traditional curriculum is augmented by a variety of activities: at various times, provisions are available to paint or draw; to work with wood, clay, and sand; to undertake construction projects; to engage in dramatic play; word and number games are on hand; children can dip or dig into the well-stocked class library; individual or communal writing projects are encouraged; field trips are documented. The students are responsible for and may conduct studies of the class menagerie, which includes the regulation guinea pig, along with seasonal tenants such as worms, spiders, the odd turtle or snake, and assorted creatures small and smaller. These activities are reserved for the daily "choice time," when children can select or initiate activities in pursuit of their own interests. They are, however, expected to approach these projects in the same spirit as they do the more traditional assignments.

Paul's choices reveal decided preferences, and his manner of work bears a distinct personal stamp. There is, in fact, remarkable congruence between Paul's way of doing things and his choice of things to do. He regularly embarks on construction projects. Typically, he proceeds incrementally, step-by-step. The materials he favors most—Lego and blocks—are assembled by adding discrete elements one at a time. In this fashion, he constructs models of real-life objects, most often cars, planes, and heavy machinery. Working without the aid of pictures or blueprints, he is apparently guided by well-remembered images, for his vehicles are accurate in essential detail; he is often seen rummaging intently among the large supply of components he likes to keep about for the one piece that is "just right" for his purpose. His projects become more elaborate and ambitious over the year, as he undertakes to design facilities for housing and repairing the equipment he builds. Combining meticulously realistic detail with a hint of fantasy, these structures are not without panache; his grand opus in second grade is a service station with a flat roof that doubles as an airfield for small planes, controlled from an adjacent tower. The project occupies Paul for several weeks as he gradually realizes his plans.

Faced with materials or tasks that do not come in ready-made units, Paul will section them into discrete parts if at all possible. He passes over materials such as clay, sand, and water that do not easily segment. He rarely paints, cooks, or participates in plays. Even his choice of construction materials is highly discriminating; he favors small components, interlocking rather than free-standing units, and straight-edged more than rounded pieces. Lego embodies the features that are particularly hospitable to his way of working, and it is his consistent choice over large blocks, tinker toys, rods, straws, and other modular materials.

On the few occasions that Paul puts pencil or magic marker to paper, he draws recognizable objects and creatures or records an actual event, expressing a preference for the concrete and familiar. His best effects are achieved by a grouping of elements; a drawing of nine bees, arranged as if in a phalanx, with a lead bee followed by three rows of bees all flying in the same direction, projects a rather menacing image, reinforced by the caption: I hate bees, I hate bees.

Paul's stylistic hallmark has considerable integrity across settings and specific content. His early reading efforts are a case in point: he learns to read much the same way he learns everything else, by focusing his attention narrowly and advancing step-by-step. He treats letters and words as discrete units, trying to string them together in sequence. His strategies for dealing with print are also acquired in additive fashion: relying mostly on sight recognition at the beginning of first grade, he begins to use his knowledge of phonetics by the middle of the year; he adds picture cues in the fall of second grade, expanding his repertoire to include context cues later that year.

Paul segments reading by setting boundaries around component activities. He learns the letters and words he is taught, but not others. He does not look ahead in his reader, nor does he try to decipher the writing that surrounds him in the classroom and outside. His particular style enables his teacher to track his progress in uncommon detail: on a particular day in October of first grade she is aware that he knows all the upper-case letters and the lower-case letters save g, v, d, and b and that he does not recognize beginning sounds but has a sight vocabulary of five words, *one, two, three, house,* and *street.*

The sequential, narrowly focused approach that Paul prefers inhibits such strategies as guessing, skipping words, scanning ahead, or repeating a phrase in order to recoup meaning lost in the decoding effort; his capacity to anticipate meaning and to maintain the forward momentum that skilled reading entails is thus impeded. His teacher's encouragement to sound out an unfamiliar word, to venture a guess, to try and err are to little avail. He plods along in reading, unable to make productive use of his extensive vocabulary, good memory for the stories his teacher reads to the class, and sensitive grasp of their more subtle implications. As such capacities generally are powerful supports for beginning reading, Paul's teacher is puzzled by his unexpectedly slow progress.

During the better part of first grade, reading in his instructional text is effortful and largely unrewarding work for Paul. Yet, he does not lose heart and, better still, does not lose interest in books. He will pour over the accurate and detailed illustrations of "machine books," disregarding the accompanying text he cannot begin to tackle. He discovers mix-and-match books with their segmented pages and gets absorbed in rearranging the heads, torsos, and feet of the human, animal, and mythical figures they depict. He is attracted by dictionaries and riddle books that feature single words rather than connected prose. In short, Paul's discerning eye has identified the books that are analogous in form to the modular materials he prefers.

Close observation of Paul adds confirmation to the emerging view that learning is a constructive, purposeful act. Knowledge supplied by textbooks and teachers is not absorbed and accumulated intact; all learners, even very young children, actively select, organize, interpret, and integrate the "facts" of the world, so as to make sense of the universe within their ken. Observing learners over time reveals different, even idiosyncratic approaches to making and stating sense, of bringing order to and deriving meaning from experience. Paul's responses to the prescribed program, and the curriculum he designs for himself out of the optional activities in the room, make visible his particular and preferred way of working, the strength and limitation of his approach, and the degree to which it is adaptive and elastic. It appears that for Paul, the construction projects he undertakes represent a productive nexus of his interests, his style of thought and work. For him, they are a good vehicle of posing, clarifying, and working through problems, for seeking knowledge and understanding of aspects of the world that now engage him. His predominant approach to learning is, however, less compatible with the demands of learning to read. Deriving meaning from text requires integrative as well as analytic skills, parallel rather than sequential thought. In learning to read, Paul is at a disadvantage.

Paul exemplifies the numbers of children who, for various reasons, are slow to establish an easy relationship with print. More intense and concentrated instruction—a common response to their plight—all too often proves ineffective. In the numerous classrooms where learning to read not only is an overarching goal but is actually made a condition of access to learning opportunities, such children are doubly disadvantaged. In Paul's case alternative means for engaging his surroundings were provided, and he could apply his considerable cache of resources to expand his world while he was learning to read.

Carrie presents a very different case. She entered kindergarten giving no indication of being able to read. Around February of that year, she apparently decided to learn to read. She began in a way quite common to nonreaders, retelling stories from memory while turning the pages of the book. By late spring, she was working with beginning readers. She still "read" much of the story from memory but was now clearly paying attention to the printed text. By fall of first grade, she was fully engaged in beginning readers, and by mid-year she read entire stories on her own.

In contrast to Paul, Carrie made up her mind to learn to read, and in the shortest possible time. Her approach indicated that she believed from the beginning that she was a reader, and her subsequent behavior was designed to fulfill this view of herself.

She sought the assistance of anyone close to her, including the teacher, her parents, classmates, visitors, and even members of the research team. She grabbed, pestered, and insisted that others read to her and listen to her read. From the time of her first serious attempts, her reading demonstrated flow and continuity, quite different from the halting, segmented, reluctant approach taken by Paul. At one point, her teacher remarked: "If she doesn't know the words, she will make them up. Nothing gets in her way." The pattern of her effort varied little. She gained familiarity with a story by having someone read it to her or by going through it herself, asking for help whenever necessary. Then she worked through the story repeatedly, practicing on her own. Finally she mastered it and read with fluency.

Carrie's progress was fluid, continuous, and integrated. She did not learn to read piecemeal, but went after everything at once. What sight words or decoding strategies were part of her repertoire at any one time is hard to say; she never slowed enough for anyone to make a definite assessment. A keen interest in stories propelled her effort, and an early understanding of the narrative form, along with a good sense of the rhythm of written language, enabled her to make sense of texts she could not fully decipher. For Carrie learning to decode words on a page seemed a kind of by-product of the act of reading itself, whereas for Paul reading proficiency hinged on mastering the printed code.

Carrie's clear intention and subsequent success in reading represents a happy intersection of interests and stylistic resources: her consuming interest in stories is directly served by reading. Her efforts immediately rewarded, her momentum never flags, as she rapidly becomes the reader she believes herself to be from the very start. Still, on closer look, Carrie reveals a pedagogical challenge well handled and suggests that the actual outcome was by no means inevitable. For Carrie learned to read in a rather unorthodox fashion when contrasted with the pedagogy inherent in most reading programs. She had access to books across a broad range of difficulty, rather than being restricted to basals at some arbitrary "instructional level"; she was permitted to "read" from books, when she was clearly relying on memory, a practice frowned upon in many programs; she was allowed to skip, to invent, to treat individual words rather cavalierly, as long as she demonstrated a reasonable understanding of the text she was reading. For Carrie the leeway in forging her own method of self-instruction worked; it is more than likely that harnessing her to preordained skill hierarchies would have brought her quickly to heel and dampened the zeal and broken the momentum that carried her forward so rapidly.

Paul, in his way, is also intent on reading, but for him the urgency is somewhat muted by the disjunction of his interests and the purposes to which reading can be put. He can live with his plodding reading, for it does not keep him from absorbing, satisfying activities. The challenge to his teacher is how to provide for the cultivation of his interests and the broadening of his perspectives as he learns to read. In the meantime, foisting a preordained timetable on him and depriving him of alternative paths to express his interests or to acquire new knowledge cannot but prove debilitating to his overall development and most likely to his reading efforts as well.

Both children, differences in their early progress notwithstanding, were proficient readers by the end of second grade. Their distinct approaches to the task were respected by their teachers, each supporting their students' strength and counterbalancing, without assaulting, the less productive aspects of their manner of work. Both teachers recognized that while they may compel the children to modify their overt behavior, or induce them to memorize material insistently presented, they cannot command them to *learn*, to work ideas and facts into their understandings, to make them their own.

Viewed this way, learning cannot be mandated or forced, as it requires the active participation of the learner. It is in this sense that learning is an intentional act, under the ultimate control of the student. Teaching, viewed this way, is a negotiated, interactive process, where the teacher, in parallel with traditional responsibilities, needs to gain the students' consent, must enlist their collaboration in a mutual endeavor.

This is not the view of teaching that predominates in schools today. Teachers are given reading programs, prescribed diagnostic instruments that suggest a student in the second grade ought to be reading at a particular level. Should the student fall short, he or she may be thought to be recalcitrant, an underachiever, or perhaps learning-disabled. Often the student with other interests is penalized for lack of accomplishment by a report card mark that notes the discrepancy between actual and expected performance. A teacher might choose to make allowances for the interests of the students, realizing that translating probabilistic expectations into demands for individual achievement violates the one immutable norm of human behavior—that it is idiosyncratic. Contemporary testing and accountability procedures, however, deter many teachers from attending to the interest of the students. Why this may be the case takes us to the second major area.

THE STATE'S INTEREST

In theory, the primary educational interest of the democratic state is the preparation of the young for responsible citizenship. This notion was clearly set forth by Jefferson in "Notes on Virginia":

> Every government degenerates when trusted to the rulers of the people alone. The people themselves therefore are its only safe depositories. And to render even them safe, their minds must be improved to a certain degree. . . . An amendment to our constitution must here come in aid of the public education. (quoted in Calhoun, 1969, pp. 108–109)

Though public education never was mentioned in the federal constitution, it appeared prominently in many of the early federal statutes. Among the more significant of these were the acts designating sections of public lands for the support of schooling. Article III of the Northwest Ordinance of 1787 begins, "Religion, morality, and knowledge being necessary to good government and the happiness of mankind, schools and the means of education shall forever be encouraged."

Under the general rubric of citizenship the state places a demand on the young to learn to read and, to a somewhat lesser extent, write and calculate. Also included here is some knowledge of the nature of law, the development of attitudes of regard for the law, and a sense of how laws should be made and changed. By making education compulsory and justifying this compulsion in the name of citizenship, the state is exerting a sovereign right over its youth. By requiring persons like Paul and Carrie to attend school, the state attempts to abridge their freedom to choose ignorance over knowledge, lawlessness over lawfulness, and injustice over justice. In the democratic state, the sovereign exercises the right to compel education as a means of preserving democratic government and ideals.

In the United States the government has economic as well as political interests in education. Recognizing that the health of the state is correlated with the health of the state's economy, the government looks to schools to provide training and education supportive of continued economic well-being, for the individual, the marketplace, and the state itself. The state's economic interest expands its entitlement in education, justifying such curricular additions as mathematics, science, and vocational-industrial education. As the state's interest in education enlarges, it may begin to compete with the interests of learners and of humanity. In *Democracy and Education*, John Dewey struggled profoundly with this possibility. His words are as relevant now as 65 years ago:

> Is it possible for an educational system to be conducted by a national state and yet the full social ends of the educative process not be restricted, constrained, and corrupted? Internally, the question has to face the tendencies... which split society into classes some of which are made merely tools for the higher culture of others. Externally, the question is concerned with the reconciliation of national loyalty, of patriotism, with superior devotion to the things which unite men in common ends, irrespective of national political boundaries. (Dewey, 1916, pp. 97–98)

For Dewey, there was no essential, necessary conflict between the ultimate interests of the students, the democratic state, and humanity. He argued that

> a society which makes provision for participation in its good of all its members on equal terms and which secures flexible readjustment of its institutions through interaction of the different forms of associated life is in so far democratic. Such a society must have a type of education which gives individuals a personal interest in social relationships and control, and the habits of mind which secure social change without introducing disorder. (1916, p. 99)

Though there is, in principle, no necessary conflict between the ultimate interests of students, the democratic state, and humanity, in practice, the situation may be otherwise. If the state, through its policymaking apparatus, sets minimum standards of accomplishment, stated by age and grade level, then it may come into conflict with the interests of both students and humanity. Paul is a case in point. The combined effect of how he learns and what engages his interests is a relatively slow start in reading. Should the state demand a particular level of achievement from Paul, it compromises both Paul's intention and Paul's teacher's intention to pursue what is in Paul's interest.

Just how this conflict arises, and the seriousness of its possible consequences, is worth elaborating in some detail. To grasp the force of the potential conflict, a distinction between agents of the school and agents of the state is needed. Agents of the school are proximal actors. They are in both the spatial and psychological proximity of students, in the sense that they share a setting for learning and in the more important sense that the relationship between teachers and students is of a special kind. By virtue of an implicit social contract, mutual privileges, responsibilities, and obligations are assumed. For the teacher to fulfill her responsibilities, she is permitted and (we would argue) is obliged to try and discern the meanings and intentions students bring to instructional events. Teachers, in effect, become participants in children's learning and privy to their thinking in a way barred to others.

Specialist teachers, school counselors, and principals also need and gain various knowledge of individual students. But the further from the classroom, the more distal agents become; the unique characteristics of children will be less available and of less interest to them.

Agents of the state are distal actors in educational affairs. They are far from the educational life of the students and must, perforce, deal with students, teachers, and schools in the aggregate. As such, these agents become concerned with gross effects of patterns of treatment. For example, differential treatment based upon sex, race, mental impairment, or physical handicap becomes prominent in the affairs of distal agents. Insofar as distal agents become involved in educational affairs, they become involved in the only aspects of these affairs that are open to them: aggregate phenomena dealing with patterns of treatment and their effects.

Should distal agents find it necessary to intervene in order to adjust unwarranted patterns of treatment, they confront the problem of how to do so lacking the essential knowledge about students, teachers, and their circumstances. This problem can be resolved in several different ways. The first is not to become involved at all, recognizing that only proximal agents are positioned to assist in the education of the young. During the last few decades, the state has found this approach unacceptable. A policy of noninvolvement permitted racial discrimination, sex discrimination, and discrimination by economic status and physical handicap. An alternative to noninvolvement is a kind of limited-inducement approach. Here distal agents offer needed resources, such as money, in exchange for changing practices considered unjustified in a democratic state. A third approach is a restricted statutory and case-law procedure, whereby distal agents specify what proximal agents cannot do, but do not stipulate what they must do. Finally, there is an all-out statutory and case-law intervention, specifying in a fairly high degree of detail what proximal agents shall do to properly educate the young. The United States has used all four approaches, with contemporary policy initiatives falling into the second, third, and fourth categories. The Elementary and Secondary Education Act of 1965 is an example of the second, the reward-for-doing-the-right-thing approach. The 1954 *Brown* decision, outlawing racial discrimination, is an example of the third approach, telling schools what they cannot do. The Education For All The Handicapped Act (PL 94–142), popularly known as the "mainstreaming" legislation, falls into the fourth category, wherein educators are instructed in how they shall treat certain classes of schoolchildren.

Expanded distal intervention in educational affairs has consequences for proximal agents; most often it curtails their decision authority. In some cases, this is exactly the effect that is intended: distal agents desire proximal agents to desist from unjustified and discriminatory practices. Yet it remains unclear how much intervention distal agents may undertake without beginning to compromise the purpose and effectiveness of proximal agents. The proximal agent's sense of what the student's interest are and what is in the best interest of the students begins to be eroded by excessive distal intervention. Proximal agents who resist the constriction of their purview often do so in defense of the students' interests, or they may in fact be resisting ameliorative action. From the vantage point of the distal agent, the source of the resistance is difficult to identify, for the same reasons that distal agents are unable to provide prescriptive remedies: they have no access to the context-bound information required for appropriate decisions.

Just how deleterious policy initiatives that undertake to ameliorate through explicit prescription of instructional goals and practices can be is seen by examining the case of an elementary school teacher. Ann Simon works in a setting that, like nearly all school settings in the United States, has been engulfed with distal demands for equality of educational opportunity, accountability, performance testing, and mandated evaluation of student outcomes. Note the extent to which her thinking is couched in the rhetoric of the times and the extent her sentiments have been influenced by the circumstances surrounding her.

> I usually teach one math skill for a whole week. The skills I teach are from the text, which are related to the learning expectations given by the district. Also, the principal decides on a skill-of-the-month that should be taught. After I teach the skill, there is class work, doing the exercises in the math book and work sheets, all in the skill being taught. Then the kids copy the homework problems off the board.
>
> At the end of the week, I give a test, and grade the students on percent of correct answers. There was a memo that came around early this year on how you pass and how you flunk kids; 70% is passing. This way, if a parent comes in complaining, you can show them that their kid got 68% on the test... sorry, he didn't pass.[2]

This teacher's conception of what it means to teach math is built almost exclusively on influences from outside her classroom. The textbook and district learning expectations list controls what she teaches. The interests of her students are not mentioned. Her appraisal of student progress is based solely on test performance, and the meaning of test scores is determined by distal agents deciding on what shall count as a passing score. The passing-score directive is welcomed for the protection it offers from angry parents. In short, Ann Simon's sentiments, her general dispositions to act in certain ways, have been put there by the exercise of distal prerogative. She approaches the teaching of reading in the same way.

> I begin my reading lessons by introducing the new vocabulary in the story we are reading. Then the children read the story and fill out a comprehension sheet about it. Then they work on whatever skill is included in the lesson, doing work sheets on that. Sometimes I have sentence writing. They work on their own; I sit back at my desk and answer questions.
>
> The whole class is reading the same book. We have the Ginn series. It's all right; sometimes when you teach level 5 five times a year you get tired of reading about raccoons. I have other books in the room, but I don't use them for teaching.

Imagine Paul as Ms. Simon's student. Would he have the opportunity to exercise his preferences in her classroom? Probably not. Would he learn to read in her class? Probably. But this learning would not be learning in the sense described earlier, a purposeful action undertaken to bring meaning to one's experience and increase the learner's power to control events in his or her immediate environment. If Paul complied with this teacher's wishes, it would be for something of the same reason she appears to be complying with distal wishes: as an expression of obedience to authority. Assuming that Paul is not able to make sense of his teacher's instructional methods as being in his interest, what he may really *learn* from her is that learning itself is something one does in response to authority.

The destructive consequences of this view of learning will be explored in the next section of this essay. For the moment, we will return to Ann Simon one last time, as she expresses her view of the district's learning-outcomes list:

> I like the learning expectations list. It is a good list to keep you on track, so you don't get stuck teaching multiplication too carefully. The list reminds you that there are fifty other things you have to cover; you can only devote so much time to any one thing. The kids who don't get it, well... they just don't get it. If there is time at the end of the year, we can go back and review.

From Ann's description of her work, it seems that students are in school to meet the expectations set forth by agents external to her classroom. If they do not meet these expectations, "well... they just don't get it." By articulating policy in explicit, procedural terms, the distal agencies strip Ann Simon of her pedagogical intentions; her own priorities thus annexed, she defines her teaching activities according to the sentiment and rhetoric of distal agents. She illustrates a particularly pernicious consequence of intervention—the assumption of a distal perspective by the proximal agents themselves. Given the hierarchical organization of school systems, with diminishing power and status at the broad base of the pyramid, it is not surprising that under sufficient pressure, some teachers will become persuaded to look through the wrong end of the telescope and view their students as they are seen from the vantage point of the district or state administrator. Principals, trying to balance their teaching and administrative roles, are particularly vulnerable to becoming exclusively identified with the latter function. Representing an extreme example of the teachers that Schwille and Porter (this volume) found to be operating as "political brokers, arbitrating between their own priorities and the implied priorities of external policies," Ann Simon suggests that explicit prescriptions regarding the ends and means of schooling will undermine considered and principled instruction. Denied a purposeful posture, teachers are unlikely to respect, or even acknowledge, the intentionality of their students.

Distal agents, acting on behalf of the state's interest, may not find it altogether troublesome that their policy efforts infringe on the full expression of students' interests. Public schools are, after all, state agencies and as such are no more entitled to be unjust or inefficient than state hospitals, prisons, asylums, parks, or regulatory agencies. Regardless of the mission of any state agency, it may not act so as to abridge personal and civil liberties or rights. Thus the state may justify its intervention into the affairs of education on the same grounds it justifies its intervention into the affairs of welfare, health care, criminal justice, recreation, and conservation. Herein lies the rub, for it is conceivable that the mission of education is in fact sufficiently different from other legitimate activities of the state that it deserves a very different form of consideration. To determine whether or not there is a fundamental difference between the state's interest in education and its interest in other activities, it is necessary to consider the larger ends of education.

THE INTEREST OF HUMANITY

There are many ways to conceive of the ends of education. Among these, one appears particularly helpful in these times. It rests upon a distinction between liberal and specialist education. Liberal education is education undertaken primarily to free (liberate) the mind. Specialist education is designed to prepare persons for specific tasks in life, usually those that are defined by such economic and social roles as worker, parent, student, consumer. Liberal education is also intended to prepare persons, but not for certain roles in the society; rather, for being persons in a highly developed sense. The two kinds of education are not linked to any particular discipline or specific subject matter. Art may be taught in the spirit of specialization, and instruction in the sciences may be directed toward liberal ends. Nor are the two kinds of education, in principle, in conflict with one another. Specialized knowledge, with its implication of depth and expertise, is as clearly indispensable for the pragmatic endeavors of contemporary society as it is required by scholarly pursuits. It is when specialized education is so construed that individuals become but carriers of expertise, to be used as tools in the service of interests they do not determine, that the essence of liberal education is placed in jeopardy.

Seeking to ensure a sufficient pool of expertise and to guarantee an acceptable level of attainment across groups, distal agents, using the only mechanisms available to them, e.g., generalized dicta and uniform criteria, have increasingly promulgated the aims of this less benign construction of specialist education, with the result that the aims of liberal education are being excluded from consideration.

Perhaps the clearest example of how the spirit of either liberal or specialist education can imbue and guide instruction in any topic or discipline, with markedly different results, is the teaching of reading. Recent years have witnessed the transformation of reading from an enabling skill to a specialized subject, from a means to an end. Reading as an end has become reified in specified hierarchies of subskills that are tested independently from the capacity to derive meaning from text. It has created a paradoxical situation in many classrooms, where reading instruction is largely devoted to the acquisition of component skills presumed necessary for reading and entails hardly any reading of connected text. It has led to the regimentation of both the instruction and the assessment of reading, raising the possibility that readers like Paul would receive, at certain points in time, higher reading scores than readers like Carrie, with the result that instructional directives would confront Paul with curricular materials that he could make little sense of and restrict Carrie to drill and practice materials that have virtually none of the meaningful content that propels her interest in reading. Inducing teachers to conform to distal prescriptions will, at the very least, impede the optimal progress of many students; at worst, it will deprive students of a conception of reading as an omnibus skill, as a key to many doors, some clearly marked as to the content they open up, others unmarked, inviting exploration and promising the unexpected.

State intervention can go awry even when the problems it seeks to rectify appear only to be secondarily educational, as when they pertain to the inequitable distribution of educational resources and opportunities or to discriminatory practices affecting particular groups of students. A telling example is the taxing problem of racial equality, which, on closer examination, turns out to be both a legal and an educational problem. There is a major difference, we have come to understand, between desegregating a school and intergrating a school. To desegregate, one need only take away the physical barriers that create racial isolation. To integrate, the psychological barriers must also be removed. Laws and regulatory policies may effect desegregation, but they alone cannot effect integration. The removal of psychological barriers is a distinctly educational problem. It rests on human beings becoming the kinds of persons who see racial isolation as morally unjustified action. Education, in its broadest conception, is the means for becoming persons of this kind. No law alone can make us morally indignant about racial discrimination; this is uniquely a task of education, and this education must be the kind that liberates the mind from dogma, bias, and conformity.

Distal agents, confined to their singular perspective, may lose sight of the limits of law and policy. They may come to rely on legal and political intervention where educational intervention is also required. Heavy-handed state intervention, however just the cause it means to serve, may arrogate the considered action genuine change entails. For paradoxically, the more distal authorities intervene to regulate the processes and procedures of school practice, the greater the risk to humanity's interest. It turns out this way because the sentiments and rhetoric needed to support liberal education are supplanted by the sentiments and rhetoric of state policy, as is clear from examining Ann Simon's conception of her work. The impact of all the external forces impinging on her is to relieve her of the necessity to act autonomously; the state has effectively excused her from confronting the great issues of our times as educational issues and from treating these issues in ways that model for her students the manner of free and concerned citizens in a democracy. The state has created the conditions that enable her to act only as its agent.

Another example of the ineffectiveness of the state's policy apparatus to remedy can be seen in a recent study of gender stereotyping (Eisenhart and Holland, 1981). In response to state directives to desist from practices implying sex discrimination, a district enacted specific provisions against gender stereotyping. Teachers responded to this policy by adopting an almost completely neutral stance on the matter of gender. They rarely used it as a basis for deciding anything and limited discussion of gender differences in their classes and in extracurricular events. This left the students to deal with gender as they wished. Their speech and actions turned out to be rife with gender referencing and stereotyping, none of which was attenuated by school personnel because of their neutral stance on the issues. The net effect of the policy was to place the topic almost completely in the hands of the students' peer groups, where it received highly prejudicial and comformist treatment. A great educational opportunity was missed, and the situation the policies were designed to correct was intensified.

As in the case of integration, the policy prohibiting gender referencing made it possible for the school staff to wash their hands of the matter. It is not difficult to extrapolate from these cases the effects of policies dealing with affirmative action, the handicapped, minimum competencies for graduation, and the use of standardized tests to judge the performance of groups of students and their teachers. Each of these usurps decision authority and more. Each relieves teachers from confronting the issues for themselves and with their students. Each carries a set of sentiments and a body of rhetoric that influences teachers' conceptions of their work. Each makes it more difficult for teachers to act purposefully and intentionally, mindful of the interests of their students and humankind. These consequences make liberal education more difficult to promote.

The heaviest cost of imperious policymaking and enforcement occurs in the area of the teacher as model for his or her learners. We speak here of traits of character, such as justice, compassion, integrity, responsiveness, and the capacity to wonder and the desire to know. These are not acquired by direct instruction, in the way that one learns to ride a bicycle, fix a leaky faucet, or fill out a job application. Rather they are acquired by modeling those who already possess such traits. Children learn compassion by first witnessing it in others, then imitating it, then appraising the effects of the imitation on themselves as well as on others, then considering its full adoption as a feature of their own character. Human beings are in a state of civilization precisely because there are civilized human beings. These persons serve as models for others. They must be witnessed and imitated in order to continue and refine the heritage they represent. The *sine qua non* of the liberally educated person is his or her intentionality.

Intentionality is the foundation of humanity's interest. To act on the basis of one's own thoughts and values defines the condition and the potential of humankind. Intentional action is preceded by deliberation and reflection. It is the essential ingredient in our plans, choices, decisions, and aspirations. Remove it and a human being is little more than an automaton, a creature of another's will.

If intentionality is the foundation of liberation of the mind from dogma and conformity, then what is it that persons should intend to do? This question is perhaps the central question of education. It asks how shall we live and what shall we do? The answer all of us hope for is that the person will do what is right and good. How does one know what is right and good to do? By learning from teachers, books, other persons, and experience. In order for students to learn how to think about their world and act upon it, their teachers must be free to confront the perennial questions of human existence. They must be free to serve as models and guides, using subject matter in ways that prompt and sustain the search for meaning. To the extent that teachers are relieved from dealing with humanity's interest, to that extent they are mere servants of the intentions of others. In turn, servility is all they can model for their students. Under these conditions, schooling is little more than an occasion for obedience and conformity. Without teachers and students whose actions are based upon their own well-founded intentions, the interest of humanity is unserved.

What of teachers who seem unfit for their work? What of teachers who are deficient in their craft and are unable to translate their intentions into effective pedagogy? What of teachers whose intentions conflict with the interests of students? Is not one purpose of good policy to restrict the range of harm they may do to students? We have been asserting that positioned as they are, distal agents are categorically unsuited to formulate ameliorative prescriptions to counter the effects of unfit teachers. We have tried to show, through the descriptions of students learning in classrooms, how critical close observation of learners is to making instructional decisions in their behalf. However well-intentioned, distal agents cannot make these decisions; the most productive role they can play is to enable teachers to acquire the personal and curricular resources effective pedagogues need and to provide a political setting and moral climate that will have an educative influence on teachers whose intentions are at cross-purposes with their students' interests. Ultimately, only policies that support action grounded in the intentions of students and teachers will sustain a coherent educational system. The imposition of rules and procedures will not change teachers' intentions, it will only transform teachers into functionaries, as is the case with Ann Simon, or lead them to engage in the kind of guerrilla warfare with distal agencies so well documented by the Boston Women's Teacher's Group (this volume).

Exemplifying a teacher who is supported in her effort to think deeply about what and how she teaches, and to act on the basis of these deliberations, Liz Grey's conception of her work places her in stark contrast to Ann Simon:

> My greatest concern is that children develop a good approach to problem solving. . . . I use two or three math texts; I want them to see that there is more than one

way to solve a problem. I like to have a balance between abstract manipulations and real life applications. Sometimes I have the kids make up their own problems.

Numeration is not just naming numbers. At one point they have to realize that this is a group of ones, tens, hundreds, and when they are doing subtractions, they can say, looking at an answer, "This can't be, . . . it doesn't make sense."

I want them to be able to show the process in their thinking, not just give answers. I want them to be able to explain what they are doing, how their mind works. I try to understand their thinking by talking to them. I take them aside and say, "This doesn't look quite right. What were you thinking about?"

What Liz Grey does is based on her ideas about education. Almost no distal considerations intrude into her thinking about her work. There are no references to learning expectations other than those she herself holds for her students. There is no sense that she is trapped by the texts she uses. There is no underlying concern for how she will justify her instruction to school administrators.

A teacher with convictions about her work, Liz Grey is employed in a setting that honors these convictions and functions to protect them. It is a place where current distal actions are moderated by an overriding concern for the interests of students. It might be different if she were to move to an environment that insisted she use one set of textbooks, that she meet a defined list of performance outcomes for all students, that she set herself before her students as an expert and taskmaster, and that she concentrate on her students' getting the right answers rather than on the process used to get whatever answer is obtained.

One critical task of educational policy is to enable and sustain environments that permit the expression of their participants' intentionality. Current policy initiatives, especially the means used to implement and enforce them, diminish the intentional character of instruction. They do so by insisting on sentiments of standardization, compliance, measurable performance, and detachment from the life experience of learners. They do so by promoting a rhetoric that focuses attention on the observable and measurable properties of persons, such as their outward behavior, their skin color, their performance relative to some standard. So much of the rhetoric of contemporary policy has little to do with the essence of education, yet, by promulgating policy in this rhetoric, it is made highly salient in the thoughts and actions of teachers.

We do not claim that teachers always know best or that decentralized decision structures will invariably serve the best balance of interests; rather we assert that even when distal agents know best, they cannot realize their aims and values directly, but must engage the minds and intentions of the teachers in a mutual enterprise.

EDUCATIONAL POLICY IN THE INTERESTS OF STUDENTS, THE STATE, AND HUMANITY

What, exactly, is involved in the promulgation, implementation, and enforcement of policy that meets the interests of students, the state, and humanity? The preceding discussion forms the basis for an answer to this question. The first part of the answer describes what teachers need in order to serve the three major interests in any conception of education. Teachers must have (1) the time and opportunity to come to know their students well; (2) curricula that create opportunities to build upon the experiences of students and offer occasions for modeling traits of character which mark a civilized person; (3) freedom from processes and procedures that classify and group students in educationally irrelevant ways; and above all, (4) a work environment conducive of their deliberation on the means and ends of education and supportive of instruction based on this deliberation.

The first three requirements are subsumed under the fourth; it calls for freedom for teachers to plan and act autonomously and implies thereby the obligation on their part to do so. It is a conception of teaching that precludes the settling of the means and ends of education outside the classroom and their subsequent importation in the form of dicta or prescriptions. Teachers, like learners, may be advised, encouraged, offered evidence, asked to consider possibilities, and questioned; but commanding, mandating, or insisting on compliance does not aid their understanding of their work, nor does it permit them to learn from their work. Granted there are some areas that require mandates; the intentional exclusion of minorities from certain schools requires straightforward application of the law. However, compulsion and compliance should be subject to a strong principle of restraint, for each occasion of their use detracts from the capacity of teachers and learners to act in accord with their intentions.

It is a conception of teaching, in short, that calls for policy which does not relieve teachers from confronting for themselves and in their classrooms the issues that perplex and confound humanity. For teaching of this kind to be realized, distal authorities cannot make or enforce policy that leaves teachers and students with no choices about its application in the classroom. Instead, the critical task of policymaking and enforcement would be to create or enable the conditions that allowed deliberation and responsible choice on the complex questions at issue.

As we noted before, classroom teachers bear the major burden of day-to-day, moment-to-moment responses that require weighing and resolving the claims of legitimate multiple interests. In addition to the broad interests of students, the state, and humanity, dilemmas endemic to the classroom setting itself demand attention: faced with necessarily diverse groups of students, teachers must balance the claims of individuals for finite communal resources and, more difficult perhaps, the claims of individuals against the requirements of maintaining a working community. All teachers confront the choice of enabling students to acquire specific skills and bodies of knowledge efficiently or supporting independent efforts that trade short-term gains for more slowly developing competencies. Responses to such myriad routine predicaments may be made haphazardly, without deliberation, or on the basis of ill-conceived principles, but they will be made—they must be made.

In contrast to the insistent demands of the classroom setting, teachers bear a disproportionately light share of the decisions that frame and determine the conditions of their work. The control they may have over classroom practices is theirs more by default than by design; typically, policies intended to improve schooling constrain the discretionary domain of the teacher, rather than provide for the wise and just use of that discretion.

This misalignment of the obligation to act and the responsibility to decide has long and complex roots. Lightfoot (this volume) reminds us that the image of the teacher has been consistently simplified and distorted, just as the requirements of the teaching role have been persistently underestimated and deprofessionalized. This state of affairs is both perpetuated and compounded by the comparatively thin resources provided for the education of teachers and the relatively undemanding and largely mediocre preparation they receive before they undertake their responsibilities.

The opportunities of teachers for professional growth in any of its forms is equally wanting. The school as a workplace has few occasions for reflection, for colleagueship, or for a tradition for the systematic observation and modification of instructional practices. Perhaps the ultimate challenge for ameliorative policy is to support the transformation of schools so that they become educative institutions for teachers as they are for students, where teachers become learners just as their students are, only the content and the way they receive it differs. Like students, teachers are entitled to instruction that bears on their experience and aids them in bringing meaning to this experience.

Policy and the rules and regulations that flow from it are misused if their purpose is to instruct teachers on what and how to teach. Policy is neither the instrument nor the content of education. It is a temporary resolution of competing potentials and demands to optimize the attainment of the ends we seek. The ends we seek for schooling are the education of teachers and their students; the purpose of policy is to enable attainment of these ends in the most equitable and excellent way. Policy that is well formulated and thoughtfully implemented fosters the creation of schools that are good places for teachers and students to learn.

NOTES

1. The student vignettes are taken from a study of beginning reading, conducted by the Early Education Group at Educational Testing Service, reported in:
   Bussis, A., Chittenden, E. A., Amarel, M., and Klausner, E. *Inquiry into meaning: An investigation of learning to read.* Final report submitted to NIE, Washington, D.C., 1982.
   Amarel, M. *Qualities of literacy.* A collaborative study of beginning readers. 35th Distinguished Scholar Lecture, Kent State University, Kent State, 1981.
2. The teachers' comments are excerpted from interviews conducted in the course of a study of teachers' centers and an evaluation of a computer-aided instruction program reported in:
   Amarel, M. *The intersection of teaching roles and the use of teachers' centers.* Far West Laboratory of Educational Research and Development, San Francisco, CA, 1981.
   Amarel, M. The classroom: An instructional setting for teachers, students and the computer. In A. Cherry Wilkinson (ed.), *Classroom computers and cognitive science* (in press).

REFERENCES

Calhoun, D. *The educating of Americans: A documentary history.* Boston: Houghton Mifflin, 1969.

Dewey, J. My pedagogic creed. In M. S. Dworkin (ed.), *Dewey on education.* New York: Teachers College, (1897) 1959.

Dewey, J. *Democracy and education.* New York: Macmillan, (1916) 1961.

Eisenhart, M. A., and Holland, D.C. Learning gender from peers. Unpublished manuscript. Blacksburg, Va.: Virginia Polytechnic Institute and State University, 1981.

CHAPTER 17

Inquiry and Social Function

Two Views of Educational Practice and Policy

J. David Greenstone and Paul E. Peterson

The condition of American public education is often described in terms of its impact on teachers. From one increasingly influential perspective, government efforts to achieve educational equality and excellence have often been self-defeating because they rest upon a "rationalistic" assumption that laws, administrative regulations, and general policy directives can readily and predictably modify the behavior of teachers and students. This rationalistic model, Wise asserts, is too simple: "To understand teaching is at least as difficult as understanding human behavior in general. Like any human being, a teacher's purposive behavior is governed... by individual disposition, social circumstances, and institutional factors" (1979, p. 101). Although Barr and Dreeben address the problem differently, they too are skeptical about our capacity to understand and control what happens in classrooms:

> [A]lthough economists and sociologists have investigated the transformation of school resources into outputs (usually rates of achievement),... the transformational technology by which inputs are turned into outputs is largely unknown... (1977, pp. 150–151).

Such educational complexity, it is urged, often confounds both the generalizations of theorists and the interventions of policymakers. To use Weick's (1976) celebrated phrase, school systems are so "loosely coupled" that policies, rules, and instructions issued from outside the school are ignored, subverted, or implemented in ways unintended by their authors. Indeed, educational leaders are "hard pressed either to find actual instances of rational practices... whose outcomes have been as beneficent as predicted, or to feel that these rational occasions explain much" of the processes of education (p. 1). Even apparently attractive and well-intentioned policies may have little beneficial impact. As Stephens (1967, pp. 9–11, quoted by Weick, 1976) observes:

> Every so often we adopt new approaches or new methodologies and place our reliance on new panaceas.... Yet the academic growth within the classroom continues at the same rate, stubbornly refusing to cooperate with the bright new dicta (p. 2).

This assessment remains relevant even in the 1980s. State and federal laws now require that children in special education, for example, must receive attention and instruction. Although these laws—and administrative regulations implementing them—focus on the features of student and teacher behavior that can be easily monitored, they at times seem to be of little additional educational value. Psychologists and special educators may develop Individual Educational Plans (IEPs) for these students that merely include readily available services (Lipsky, 1980). More serious efforts to address the needs of handicapped children can prove extremely costly to local school districts. In addition, the process of drafting and approving IEPs can be so burdensome that substantial teacher time and energy is diverted to administrative processes. In some cases, actual compliance may be counterproductive. If marginally handicapped students are "pulled out" of regular classrooms for enriched instruction, the continuity of the students' learning experience may be disrupted while the regular teachers are encouraged to treat these students as someone else's responsibility. Each of these responses suggests a different way in which extremely complex, loosely coupled educational organizations react to general policy directives. In effect, teachers and school administrators adjust their behavior in ways that frustrate broader policy objectives — even when the teachers themselves strongly share the basic objectives of special education.

Yet for all its cogency, an analysis of "complexity" and "loose coupling" does not fully describe the obstacles to effective policy implementation. For one thing, these two concepts do not specify particular problems to be addressed but tend instead to depict an educational reality too chaotic and disorderly to permit any effective policy innovations. In fact, "complexity" refers to symptoms rather than basic educational pathologies. Underlying the loosely coupled structure of the school system organization are two very different conceptions of the nature and meaning of public education. The inability of educators either to resolve or at least to recognize and understand the conflict and tension between these two views perpetuates a pattern of school organization that is intricately complex and hard to coordinate.

According to one of these views, education is primarily an intrinsically important process of *inquiry*, valuable because it contributes to the transmission of culture from one generation to the next. According to the other, public education is mainly a process of training, important because of the variety of *functions* it performs for the larger *society*. These two contrasting perspectives pervade all of American education, including discussions of complexity and loose coupling themselves. Whereas Barr and Dreeben seem to stress a functional view in their discussion of the "transformational technologies" which turn inputs into educational outputs, Stephens emphasizes education as inquiry when he refers to "academic growth" as an "autonomous process" (1967, p. 1). Indeed, Wise himself identifies the two alternative perspectives when he contrasts teaching "basic skills" for "vocational and career preparation" with instilling "a desire to learn" that contributes to the "generation or transmission of one's cultural heritage" (1979, pp. 101 and 59–61).

Differences between the inquiry and functionalist perspectives manifest themselves at three distinct levels of the educational process:

1. In the *policy arena*, the social function position seeks to improve education by changing the allocation of organizational resources to shape student and teacher behavior, while an inquiry approach emphasizes teacher and administrator motivation, insight, and capacities.
2. At the level of educational *role norms or expectations*, the role of teacher involves a commitment to inquiry values, such as transmitting intellectual skills and broad cultural traditions. This teacher commitment stands in contrast to the administrators' obligation to perform the services or social functions desired by the larger community.

3. At the level of *cultural commitments*, we find basic assumptions or presuppositions about both the individual personality and the social community. The inquiry tradition emphasizes the development of each individual's faculties according to communally prescribed standards of competence and excellence. By contrast, the social functional view is concerned with protecting the rights and satisfying the preferences of individuals living within a community of interest.

That these competing perspectives appear in three such different forms suggests that each view identifies important features of public education in the United States. But we must emphasize that these contrasting views identify underlying tendencies in American education rather than characterize overt patterns of debate and conflict. For example, we cannot divide all teachers from all administrators into two neatly separated groups, one espousing an inquiry perspective, the other a functionalist. Indeed, we shall see that particular individuals can have inquiry values at one level (e.g., with respect to classroom teaching), while adopting social function views at another (e.g., on policy questions). At the same time, we shall argue that as school systems have become more elaborately organized, and as American culture has become more secularized, the social function position has steadily increased its influence over educational policy. This trend toward social functionalism has made the school increasingly resistant to current policy innovations, increasing the complex, loosely coupled structure of the educational system as a whole.

Two initial objections may be offered to these observations. First, it may be argued that American educational beliefs do not exhibit this internal dissonance but contain instead a broad agreement on the purposes of education, namely, the teaching of mathematics, language arts, natural science, history, and other crucial skills. This contention is valid but beside the point. The inquiry–social function dichotomy is not mainly concerned with curriculum or subject matters. The central issue that divides these two perspectives is, instead, whether teaching of whatever subject is, or ought to be, a mainly autonomous activity valued for its own sake or is substantially influenced by, and instrumentally important for, important activities and projects in the larger society. The educational policy process, in other words, divides along inquiry–social functional lines over what accounts for good teaching and how it can be justified.

According to a second objection, if the inquiry–social function opposition is so fundamental to the loose coupling of educational organizations, why has it been largely ignored in policy discussions? This question contains its own answer: the most familiar and fundamental features of a social practice or situation are taken for granted precisely because they are often the hardest to observe and analyze. In daily life, for example, we often do not pay explicit attention to how interactions with members of our family, or the placement of living room furniture, affects conversation patterns. We take these patterning features for granted not because they are unimportant but because they provide stable frameworks for those activities to which we do attend, e.g., having a child run an errand or entertaining guests. The most basic relationships or patterns, then, are tools we use in pursuing conscious objectives, much as chemistry teachers and students use test tubes to help examine compounds, but not as objects to be examined in their own right.

The same tendency to take basic elements for granted occurs in education. When administrators consider how they can obtain better teaching, or teachers think of ways they can better use the resources administrators provide, they typically assume the basic patterns of teacher and administrative roles and responsibilities. To the extent one begins with assumptions about teaching and administrative role norms, they themselves do not become principal objects of analysis. Yet just these assumptions, and the role differences they help sustain, contribute to the fundamental opposition between social function and inquiry perspectives.

INQUIRY AND SOCIAL FUNCTIONAL APPROACHES TO EDUCATIONAL POLICIES

Given substantial agreement on the schools' specific aim of teaching important skills, the decisive issue for educational policy seems simple enough: What steps will most effectively promote student learning? But this straightforward question has been answered very differently, depending on whether one's perspective is social functional or is concerned with educational inquiry.

From the social function perspective, the steps needed to improve education involve the organization and allocation of overall societal resources. Social functionalists may argue that more money should be spent on education, or it should be allocated more equitably, or it should be used more efficiently by, for example, paying teachers on a merit basis instead of on the basis of education and seniority. Sophisticated research projects examine which, if any, of these social functionalist claims is supported by existing data, and the results of these studies are used to promote organizational or financial reforms.

This social functional view is most appropriately applied where there is both enough agreement on the specific social functions to be realized and sufficient information about the learning process to warrant national standards for educational practice. For example, the national government has found that effective, equitable education cannot proceed where school systems are formally segregated, where a handicap precludes educational opportunity, or where schools ignore the language problems of non-English-speaking children. Educational policies are now committed to a set of social functions that just a generation ago were often simply overlooked.

The social functional perspective is applied much more widely than just the mere enunciation of the national priorities, however. In its extreme version it tries to identify the exact impact of financial, organizational, curricular, and other school resources on the learning of children. This tradition typically takes two forms. On the one side, some of the most influential studies make the unlikely claim that school resources (money, personnel, organization, and time) have no effect at all (Coleman, 1966; Jencks, 1972). Other studies believe their regression analyses of patterns in one school system yield results that should be the basis for national policy. Summers and Wolfe (1977), for example, claim that their study has substantial policy relevance: "Perhaps [the] most interesting... finding," they write, is "that there appear to be school inputs which help the disadvantaged do better." Thus they urge "targetting" school resources that "are specifically helpful to the disadvantaged" (p. 69; see also Summers and Wolfe, 1974).

Researchers have made strenuous efforts to identify the effects of financial and other resources on learning in large part because these are the factors policymakers can most easily change. Indeed, the most widely known policy innovations in education have focused on structural and resource constraints that bear only indirectly on educational activities within classrooms. School finance reform has sought to equalize expenditures for education among school districts; school desegregation has altered the pupil composition of classrooms; and ESEA Title I has dramatically increased resources available for the socially and educationally disadvantaged. But for all the policy analysts' emphasis on these factors, the impact of financial and other resources on student performance remains unclear. In the United States, variations in monies expended, size of classes, equipment available, facilities enjoyed, materials supplied, and formal teacher credentials have not been shown to be consistently related to variations in pupil performance (Boocock, 1980). Even fifteen years after the original Coleman study, which questioned the effects of school resources on learning, we do not have a body of research that social functionalists can confidently draw upon in making their policy recommendations.

In part because of these findings, another social function tradition has concentrated on changing the learning process in the classroom. As Smith and Geoffrey (1968) put it, the first step is to build "a more general theory of teaching" as a guide to "the collection of data" (p. 13) about curricula presentation and content. In the same vein, Barr and Dreeben (1977) view the school as an economic firm and "assume that instruction is a technology . . . [for allocating] time, materials, and people under prevailing constraints and opportunities" (p. 126).

With these attempts to define precisely the classroom technology that works best, the social functional perspective pursues its understanding of education to its logical conclusion. Education can be planned, predicted, controlled, and made to work effectively. Only current limits on our research knowledge preclude the provision of more efficient, more effective school services. When further breakthroughs are achieved, well-informed central decision makers will be able to issue regulations and offer financial incentives or establish new teaching methods and curricula that will decisively change educational practice. To the extent that this social functional understanding of educational processes is correct, power and control need to be centralized and hierarchical. Key societal resources that affect learning must be disseminated fairly and widely; only central institutions—the federal and state governments, for example—have the capacity to do this. Also, decisions need to be handed down an administrative chain of command so that each and every local school does the best by its pupils.

On some policy questions, such centralization of direction and control seems so sensible that the social functionalist view appears entirely warranted. One obvious, but seldom appreciated, example should be sufficient to demonstrate our point. A century ago American schools varied widely in their provision of textbooks to pupils. Some schools provided none, some required students to pay for them, and other schools made them available free of charge. As a result, pupils had widely varying access to the material they were asked to study. Educational reformers, applying a social functional view, encouraged state legislatures to mandate the provision of free textbooks in all local school districts, and today Americans take for granted a policy that was only won at considerable political effort. In less favored nations, great variation in the availability of textbooks continues to this very day, and, as a result, careful research has been able to document what educators had long known intuitively. Without textbooks, students learn much less. Indeed, in some studies this factor explains more of the difference in what children learn in school than any other school-related variable. At least in this policy arena, then, central control and directions seem both possible and desirable.

While there are undoubtedly other policy areas where a social functionalist view is equally applicable, it encounters greater difficulties when central decision makers attempt policy changes in areas where a consensus on effective teaching methods is less clear. Do children learn better by remaining in a single classroom with one teacher or by being "pulled out" for special tutoring? What kinds of educational contexts are best for children with certain kinds of handicaps? How quickly should children be moved from bilingual settings? On these questions, as several of the papers in this volume suggest, opinion varies dramatically, research suggests diverse answers, and the effects of varying classroom technologies remain unknown. Here it seems, classroom teachers rather than central decision makers are likely to be given considerable choice and autonomy.

Because not all policies can be easily determined centrally, the inquiry approach to educational policy emphasizes instead the causal importance of teachers interacting with students. Although this perspective recognizes the many factors that constrain teacher behavior, it insists that individual classes, and the students within them, are both so numerous and subtly differentiated that no general formula can fully explain or account for differences in student performance. Even the best research on teaching technologies yields (and is likely to continue to yield) such tentative conclusions that the effects of varying teacher methods remain basically unknown. The educator's task, therefore, remains one of active and creative problem solving, i.e., an essentially autonomous activity that will fail if teacher-student relations are decisively subordinated to centrally shaped policy considerations. From the inquiry perspective, the real question, then, is how one best helps each student master a certain subject matter when individuals learn in very different ways that cannot be readily or straightforwardly described (Jackson, 1968, p. 136ff). Teachers in this view, must rely on insight and intuition, on expertise and experience, in order to recognize their students' varied problems and then flexibly adjust their methods and behaviors.

To employ the terms Mitchell and Kerchner (1983) use in this volume, whatever the extent to which the classroom process can be directly supervised by administrators, good teaching must be "adaptive" rather than "preplanned." From the inquiry point of view, whether teaching is closer to an art or to a profession, educating children surely resembles one of these forms more than it does an applied science. Just as there is no unequivocal standard for good art, there is no indisputable definition of good teaching and no perfect unanimity in the ranking of teachers. Yet some teachers are widely considered to be better than others. Just as art, or the work of gifted practitioners in a profession, can be judged by knowledgeable critics, excellent teaching can be spotted by administrators skilled in perceiving these abilities. The inquiry policy approach accordingly emphasizes the teachers' need for freedom and autonomy within the classroom; the recommendations of experts should be incorporated into practice only when teachers, as professionals, find the idea useful. For their part, administrators are essential for recruiting teachers, identifying talent, weeding out incompetence, and, above all, for inspiring professional dedication. But to be effective these educational officials must be close enough to the classroom to take specific situations into account.

The consequence of this understanding is a substantially different view of the policy process. Control must be sufficiently decentralized so that teachers can be free to engage in the same deliberate, reflective problem solving with which policymakers and administrators approach their tasks. Rather than controlling what happens in schools, state and federal officials ought to provide local administrators with necessary resources. Administrators, in turn, should identify able practitioners, place them in key positions, motivate them to use their skills, and supply them with the means to teach effectively. By the same token, school boards and superintendents wishing to help educationally disadvantaged schools and neighborhoods should locate gifted teachers, support them administratively—and then leave them alone.

It is not easy to choose decisively between these two understandings of appropriate educational policy. While in some policy domains, one or another view seems decidedly preferable, the grey areas that will be disputed by the contending views are likely to continue to be large and important. The dispute on policy questions is especially difficult to resolve because it parallels tensions between teacher and administrative role relationships. It is to this level of the conflict between social functional and inquiry views that we now turn.

THE OPPOSITION BETWEEN TEACHER AND ADMINISTRATOR ROLE NORMS

Quite apart from these policy issues, the level of educational practice exhibits a conflict of values between the teacher's obligation to help students master the central skills of their culture and the administrator's obligation to fulfill broader social, economic, or political objectives. "Obligation" here refers to the norms and expectations that pattern these two roles, i.e., the criteria that specify what ordinarily counts as successful role performance, whether in teaching or administration.

In our society, "good teaching" has generally been defined as helping each student reach his or her highest possible level of development. Because this process is cooperative, with each child contributing his or her own information and insight to the common task, it has moral and social as well as intellectual dimensions. Jackson (1968), for example, reports that his sample of widely respected teachers knew they had succeeded when their students were "willing to work above and beyond the minimal expectations," when they brought "things to you like articles out of magazines or pictures they have drawn" (p. 122). McPherson (1972) voiced very similar sentiments in concluding her otherwise pessimistic study of elementary classroom teaching in a New England school: "When I was most discouraged . . . I would recall what one teacher said: 'it is wonderful when everyone is working toward the same goal . . . they're learning and you're learning, too. . . . Then it is worth it, being a teacher'" (p. 215).

Stated positively, these expectations affirm the role responsibilities, the standards of performance, that good teachers are expected to meet. Precisely because teachers must impart a body of knowledge and socially prescribed skills that students do not have, their primary goal cannot be to please or entertain or satisfy pupils' preferences. Nor does this commitment require either intellectual conformity or educational elitism. "Good teaching" can be understood as educating every child, and it surely can mean stimulating students to ask critical, challenging questions. But "good teaching" almost certainly requires different responses to different groups of students and changing classroom situations. It is for this reason that teacher role norms lend clear support to those inquiry-oriented policies that stress the educator's insight and discretion.

Role norms or expectations, it must be emphasized, may not be recognized overtly by every individual in the role. Not all teachers, not even all "good" teachers, will necessarily articulate an inquiry understanding of their task. Lightfoot (1969) describes a successful first grade teacher (Ms. Sarni) whose general attitudes toward education were closer to a social function perspective. Unlike the teachers Jackson describes, and unlike another teacher whom Lightfoot studies, Ms. Sarni stresses the acquisition of specific, vocationally useful skills, especially reading and writing, rather than broader intellectual growth. (Somewhat similarly, many special education teachers have become advocates of a rather different social function, the more equitable treatment of their students.) Nevertheless, Ms. Sarni's success as a good teacher—it is said that she regularly teaches every one of her students to read—seems to reflect, at least in part, her adherence to inquiry norms. Not only does she insist on her own autonomy in the classroom, rejecting the intrusions of all other adults, but she dismisses as irrelevant to learning such broader social goals or functions as equalizing opportunity (cf. Good, 1983).

The role obligations of educational administrators and policymakers follow from their specific responsibilities in an industrial democracy. Once again the issue is role norms, not preferences. Personally, many administrators are devoted to both the students' total intellectual development and the teachers' autonomy, expertise, and creativity. But in their capacity as government officials, administrators are expected to try to carry out the directives of a school board, the state's laws and regulations, and various federal and constitutional requirements. In addition, administrations are pressured by various group demands. Many businesses want the schools to teach the values and skills appropriate for participation in the labor market. In Katz's (1968) view, these pressures are so great that "the school became the means of instilling in the population the qualities necessary for success in industrial society..." (p. 43 and pp. 59–60). From another perspective, the schools' proper social function is to combat "the perceived threat of barbarism and severe disorganization" by socializing children into values that reflect the nation's dominant morality and lifestyle (Bailyn, 1960, p. 73; see also Bobbit, 1915, p. 16). Again, labor leaders and minority groups have looked to the schools to provide genuine equality of opportunity and thus avenues of social mobility to each and every child (Bowers, 1969 pp. 48–49). Finally, others have sought procedural fairness as a way of securing the right or entitlement of each student to an effective education.

These conflicting views of the schools' social functions continually press upon school administrators. Although the dominant perspective will vary with time, place, and level of government, all conscientious administrators, whatever their own sympathies, must try to mediate these competing group demands in order to regularize and sustain the school system's relationships to the larger community. To ignore this concern, to emphasize inquiry values at all costs, would be irresponsible in a democratic polity. For this reason, administrators have a strong incentive to adopt a social functional approach to educational policy precisely because it justifies manipulating organizational resources and structures in order to implement the demands of the larger community.

As Barr and Dreeben's paper (1983) in this volume helps make clear, these very different role norms have led teachers and administrators at the school site to create two distinct domains that almost physically decouple educational organizations. The "public places" within the school, the hallways, playgrounds, washrooms, and lunchroom, fall rather directly under a principal's supervision with little teacher protest (McPherson, 1972). But within the classroom, the teacher's prerogatives are seldom challenged. Principals may visit, inspect, and evaluate, but in general, they interfere only if behavior has disruptive effects elsewhere in the school.

Less tangibly, perhaps, while administrators establish the structures, context, and resources that facilitate learning, teachers employ these same resources in the actual learning process. Once again, participants in each role act with greatest authority on matters clearly within their domain. Administrators (at the school site and at school district, state, and national levels) decide on the length and shape of the school day, allocate books, equipment, materials, and supplies, assign students to each classroom, and recruit teachers and other staff. But teachers rather than administrators must decide how much time is to be spent on reading and spelling or on art and music, whether to teach the class as a whole or in subgroups, if discipline should be strict or lax, and how to allocate time among students who differ in ability and responsiveness.

Some decisions, though, do not fit neatly into the administrator's or the teacher's domain, producing the recurring tensions between teachers and principals. In particular, principals are often upset by collective bargaining agreements that reduce their capacity to assign staff for hall and luncheon duties and for extracurricular activities. For their part, teachers especially resent the principals' requests to examine their lesson plans or within-term grading sheets. They resist external attempts to specify particular components of the year's curriculum; they are often disturbed by interruptions of class periods by the principal, the school staff, or outside visitors; and increasingly they have complained about interruptions required by federal programs.

Here, indeed, is the source of much of the disagreement, uncoordinated behavior, and outright conflict that make schools so loosely coupled. Each party clearly begins with a valid insight. Conscientious administrators must try to control (rather than simply support and encourage) their teachers' activities on certain issues. However valuable a teacher's spontaneity, creativity, and experience, these virtues are sometimes invoked to justify the exercise of discretion in ways that discriminate against students who are poor, who come from particular ethnic backgrounds, or whose personality happens to clash with the teacher's. On the other side, equally conscientious teachers must resist outside interventions that detract from the central business of teaching and learning, for even the most discreet and tactful administrators may in fact become so intrusive that they disrupt the classroom.

As we shall make clear in our conclusion, the point here is by no means to dismiss efforts at compromise and accommodation as hopeless, but to ask why so many well-intentioned efforts to surmount the two conflicting understandings of education have failed—why loose coupling has so stubbornly persisted. One answer is that tensions between teacher and administrator role norms reflect a still more fundamental value conflict that pervades all of our civic and political culture.

THE OPPOSITION BETWEEN AMERICAN CULTURAL IDEOLOGIES

By "cultural ideologies" we mean those "cultural systems" (Geertz, 1964) or interpretive frameworks with which members of a society render their experience meaningful. These ideologies are so fundamental that they include both disagreements over the most effective educational policies and conflicts over the objectives teachers, policymakers, or administrators should pursue. Because they try to describe the basic realities on which social life rests, these ideologies are simultaneously empirical and value-laden: they refer to "facts" so important that they create moral obligations (Taylor, 1973).

The two cultural ideologies share some crucially important beliefs, including the liberal commitment to both individual liberty and equality of opportunity (Hartz, 1955). But they have disagreed for nearly two centuries over such basic questions as the character of human cognition, the nature of the individual personality, and the ordering of the political and social community. The social functional ideology stresses the interests and rights of individuals, looks for ways that individuals can best achieve their wants and desires, and identifies the good of all with the sum total of each person's well-being. The inquiry ideology stresses the social conditions that shape individual faculties, hopes, and desires and searches for a substantive, communally prescribed standard against which the behavior of each member is to be measured. Although these large philosophical questions may seem far from everyday educational practice, they are hardly irrelevant to the way a society views the teaching of its young.

To take one revealing example, Jackson's study of outstanding teachers found both an emphasis on intellectual growth: "helping young people . . . teaching them something new all the time . . ." (1968, p. 134) and a stress on the "moral attribute" of "patience," a "desirable balance between impulsive action and apathetic withdrawal" (p. 18). As he put it, good teaching resembles "missionary work" in which an "almost spiritual calling" moves good teachers, especially those who awaken a student whom other adults "have given up for lost" (pp. 134, 138). This statement is revealing on three counts. *First,* Jackson's respondents articulated inquiry rather than the social function values. *Second,* these same values remarkably parallel the pre-Civil War cultural ideology of evangelical Northern Whigs. As Howe notes, their crucial value "was not freedom per se but freedom to shape one's life rationally and religiously . . . [a] freedom . . . equivalent to self-discipline" (Howe, 1979, p. 159). Most Whigs, moreover, sought "not self-indulgence . . . [but a] striving to shape the self according to an approved plan" (Howe, 1979, p. 301). This Whig creed diverged from the Jacksonian Democrats' interest-oriented liberalism which emphasized freedom from those constraints that interfered with satisfying one's preferences. *Third,* Horace Mann and other ante bellum founders of American public education came almost entirely out of just this evangelical Whig culture. These Whig leaders, in other words, may have introduced the role norms of contemporary classroom teachers at just that point when they helped inaugurate American public education at the time of its founding.

Philosophically, the inquiry-oriented side of this ideological division can be formulated in broadly Kantian terms (as did Mann's Transcendentalist contemporaries (Miller, 1950)). But as Mann's own evangelical sentiments suggest, it received a major impetus from the Second Great Awakening in American Protestantism early in the nineteenth century and thus from the liberal Calvinist belief in the cultivation of each and every individual's rational and moral faculties. This position was substantive, and thus connected with inquiry values, because its standards had a specific content, i.e., they required the mastery of socially established, culturally prescribed skills and traditions. In Mann's words, "The seeds of knowledge, of refinement, and of literary excellence are implanted, with a liberality nearly or completely equal, in the mind of the ignorant peasant, and in the mind of the most profound philosopher" (quoted by Thayer and Levit, 1966, pp. 4–5).

Two generations later, John Dewey elaborated a pragmatist, explicitly antiutilitarian variation of this same general theme (Bowers, 1969, p. 21; Cremin, 1961, p. 123). In epistemology and aesthetics, Dewey propounded a highly activist view of human cognition (rather than an exclusive stress on sensation); in ethics and philosophy of science, he assigned a central place to collective inquiry; in his social and political thought, he emphasized opportunities for individual growth and achievement rather than just instruments for the satisfaction of desires: "Nature . . . [only] supplies [the] potential material embodiment of ideals.... It lends itself to operations by which it is perfected. The process is not a passive one.... It depends upon the choice of man whether he employs what nature provides and for what ends he uses it" (Dewey, 1929, p. 302). Given these views, Dewey insisted on a central role for the classroom teacher in guiding the child's intellectual development according to culturally determined, socially shared standards. For him, the school was not an institution for training, but a "house of reason" (D'Amico, 1978).

More recently, a number of radical teachers, reflecting on their teaching experiences during the 1960s, have more pessimistically expressed similar substantive standards commitments:

> For poetry, in place of the recommended memory gems...you...introduce a poem of William Yeats.... The children do not all go crazy about it, but a number of them...become more intrigued...and many of them grow more curious... than they appeared at first. There again, however, you are advised by older teachers that...Yeats is too difficult for children (Kozol, 1967 pp. 186–87; see also Kohl, 1967).

Implicitly or explicitly, each of these educators asserts the two tenets central to an inquiry oriented cultural ideology. First, the idea of self-development (notably through education) is intelligible only if there are substantive criteria for determining whether an individual has mastered a culturally central skill. Equally important, if these standards are to be genuinely meaningful, they must be the socially shared commitments of a moral community that sustains the public schools. As Mann himself put it, he "abandoned jurisprudence" for "the larger sphere of mind and morals" (Messerli, 1972, p. 249); in the words of a recent biographer, Mann thought that the schools "provided the best means to maintain a set of common values and reestablish the older ...consensus on a newer urban and industrial foundation" (Ibid.). Early in this century, as Bowers (1969) observes, "educators were deeply committed to Dewey's idea that the school must deliberately improve society" in part because "they possessed the sense of mission that comes from a feeling of guardianship for the present and future well-being of their students" (pp. 13–14).

The contrasting liberal tradition which supports the social functional understanding can be traced to utilitarian philosophic roots. It aims less at the cultivation of human faculties than at the protection of individual rights and the satisfaction of individual preferences. Thus, its standards are typically procedural, i.e., concerned with fairness and equity and the right to pursue one's own goals. From this perspective society is not a moral community but a community of group and individual interests. Given the diversity of important interests in American public life, policy advocates of this tradition have moved in highly varied political directions. Some use liberal ideals to justify a laissez-faire approach to education that allows each individual family to spend as much as it wishes for their children's education. Critics of Horace Mann objected that his "whole scheme was utopian and visionary and that it was wrong...to take a man's property to educate his neighbor's child...[and to have] the state... interfere in the education of the child" (Callahan, 1957, pp. 128–29). Others have seen the public schools as useful instruments for satisfying individual and group interests. Mann's conservative contemporary, Edward Everett, observed that "we can, from our surplus, contribute toward the establishment and endowment of the seminaries" in order "to give security to our property, by diffusing the means of light and truth..." (quoted in Thayer and Levit, 1966, p. 63). The purpose of education, from this vantage point, was simply to protect existing rights and privileges.

During the Progressive Era, Cubberley (1909) argued in a similar vein that "the school is essentially a time and labor saving device, created by democracy to... prepare the future citizen for the tomorrow of our complex life...[thus] its real worth and its hope of adequate reward lies in its social efficiency" (p. 54; see also Bagley, 1926, p. 126). Even within the progressive education movement itself, the increasingly influential child-centered wing stressed the satisfaction of the student's desires, rather than the mastery of culturally transmitted and intellectually demanding skills. Railing against this view, Dewey denounced the "absurd" claim "that children are individuals whose freedom should be respected while the more mature person should have no freedom." Instead he insisted on teachers having a positive and "leading share" in the direction of the "classroom" (Dewey, 1938, pp. 58–59; see also Bowers, 1969, pp. 5–11).

More recently, the broadly utilitarian ideology has supported two basically egalitarian perspectives. First, because all students are entitled to equitable treatment, the schools should be governed by norms of fairness and procedural due process. Second, the schools must provide effective vocational or prevocational training in order to help all their students achieve their goals once they graduate. Jencks et. al. (1972) have put the utilitarian position forcefully: "We begin with the premise that every individual's happiness is of equal value. From this it is a short step to Bentham's dictum that society should be organized so as to provide the greatest good for the greatest number.... To this end we prefer monetary incentives to social or moral incentives, which tend to be inflexible and very coercive..." (p. 9–11).

This conflict between cultural ideologies parallels the split between the role norms of educational administrators and classroom teachers. On one side, a utilitarian or interest-oriented ideology emphasizes the importance of individual preferences and incentives. Accordingly, it reinforces a conception of schools as institutions that should respond throughout the nation to group demands and pressures. On the other side, a substantive standards ideology emphasizes the intrinsic (rather than simply instrumental) importance of the students' self-development. Consequently, it favors the teacher role norms, i.e., helping students acquire culturally important skills—and it sustains a policy perspective that also emphasizes the importance of creative, autonomous classroom teaching.

INQUIRY, SOCIAL FUNCTION, AND THE TRANSFORMATION OF EDUCATIONAL POLICY

The conflict between the inquiry and social functional approaches have not remained constant over the century and one half since the time of Horace Mann. While the tension between teacher and administrator has continued unabated, and the clash between the two cultural ideologies has not changed very much, the situation at the policy level has been transformed. Consider the complex case of Horace Mann. Even before the Civil War, Mann and his colleagues labored to establish a stable organizational context for public education. As this framework gradually became more bureaucratized, it added administrative and supervisory positions whose occupants were necessarily concerned with the schools' social functions. "Through his efforts," Messerli writes, "Mann was laying the basis...for a centralized and rationalized educational system,

complete with prescribed curricula, licensed teachers and hierarchial administration"
(1972, pp. 341, 346–347). Thus, even as Mann remained committed to inquiry values,
he helped found an institution whose very structure encouraged it to attend primarily
to the social functions of education. Beginning with these administrative changes, the
inquiry perspective has gradually declined from apparent dominance in the policy
arena to a primarily dissenting position that, until recently, has attracted relatively
few important new adherents.

These changes had already become clear by the end of the Progressive Era. While
the inquiry tradition dominated policy discussions in Mann's time, by World War I
social and economic changes had created powerful countervailing pressures. As complex school systems required more administrative coordination and control, the quest
for efficiency manifested the enthusiasm of a cult (Callahan, 1962). According to one
disciple of the new creed:

> The fundamental demand in education, as in everything else, is for efficiency—
> physical efficiency, mental efficiency, moral efficiency.... The potential econ-
> omic worth of each school pupil, to say nothing of his moral value as a householder
> and as a citizen, is enormous... (Munroe, 1912, pp. v–vi; cf. Spaulding, 1922,
> and Bobbit, 1915).

This gospel of efficiency can be understood as the triumph of business values or as
legitimating the new profession of educational administration. But in either case, it
signaled the eclipse of inquiry values in favor of social control over teacher discretion.

From this perspective, Dewey's pragmatist philosophy attempted to resist these
new educational trends by providing a viable new meaning for the crucial concepts of
moral community and thus of educational inquiry. With respect to the school's social
functions, to be sure, Dewey's pragmatism was still more complex than Mann's liberal
Calvinism—witness his instrumentalism, his (nonpositivist) enthusiasm for science,
and most importantly, his belief that education could further social reconstruction
(Dewey, 1934a; Dewey, 1934b). To Bowers (1969), Dewey failed "to resolve the internal conflict between his own idealistic desire to let people decide for themselves the
kind of society they wanted and his own deep commitment to a socialist society"
(p. 155). Yet in terms of educational policy, Dewey's efforts are notable less because
they were ambiguous than because they were ineffectual. His insistence on individual
growth and development according to communal standards articulated and imparted
by the teacher and even his subsequent break with the child-centered version of the
progressive education movement were rearguard actions (D'Amico, 1978, pp. 35 and
44–45). They could stave off but not reverse a growing belief that educators must
train their students to participate in a society marked by rapid economic growth,
countless technological innovations, sophisticated organizational systems, and a competitive labor market.

These economic trends were reinforced by the gradual secularization of public
life. For Mann, all participants in the educational process belonged to, or could be expected to join, a genuinely moral community. But by the Progressive Era, moral and
religious values, while by no means entirely abandoned, were for the most part pursued socially—outside the public and civic realm—by a plurality of religious and
ethnic groups. Given their differences, one could not know that education would have
the same meaning to all who participated. Even in the nineteenth century, both the
growing parochial school movement and the increasing ethnic and cultural diversity

of the urban public schools had challenged a monolithic, Protestant conception of American society (Kleppner, 1970).

Most of these trends have continued. The concern with increasing efficiency and economic productivity has, if anything, increased. At least since the Sputnik crisis, advancing technology, improvements in communication and organizational control, and continuing specialization have all generated demands that the schools provide the training in new skills. More recently, a trend toward accountability, competency-based education laws, and elaborate national and statewide assessment programs has even more directly affected classroom practices. Meanwhile, the United States appears to have a still less widely accepted unifying "civil religion" than it enjoyed even as late as the Progressive Era. As public life has become increasingly secularized, religious orientations have become more private, diverse, and separatist. The political arena is now the stage for "single-issue" campaigns by sectarian factions, including an increasing interest in tuition vouchers and tax credits for private education.

Finally, increasingly persuasive social functionalist arguments demand more equal educational treatment of blacks, women, linguistic minorities, the handicapped, and low-income groups. Since many believe that local and state governments often favor the socially advantaged (McConnell, 1966; Peterson, 1980) and that administrative discretion works against the interests of the poor (Lowi, 1969), it is widely thought that only through central controls can egalitarian reforms be achieved. Teacher autonomy itself is suspect, in part because some teachers are said to defer almost instinctively to better-educated, economically successful parents (McPherson, 1972, p. 139 ff), while others concentrate their energies on "rewarding" those students whose schoolwork reflects educationally advantaged backgrounds (Lightfoot, 1969, p. 112). As a result, each effort to increase educational equity has typically meant a new set of federal regulations and increased administrative impact on the classroom—witness Title I of the Elementary and Secondary Education Act, bilingual education, the All Handicapped Childrens Act, laws and regulations eliminating sex discrimination in vocational education and extracurricular activities, as well as measures to protect the students' (and teachers') entitlement to procedurally fair treatment.

As we have already noted, educational theory and policy discussions have responded to these developments by becoming increasingly functionalist. Not only do Jencks et al. (as quoted above) justify their analysis in explicitly utilitarian terms, but Barr and Dreeben (1977), who remain intensely interested in the practice of teaching, also take an essentially social functionalist view of the enterprise. These last two authors, to be sure, criticize the production function literature's concentration on changing financial allocations and approvingly refer to Jackson's (1968) portrayal of "the teacher as one whose many diverse activities keep the complex classroom system functioning (p. 148)." But instead of Jackson's stress on teacher discretion in a process of inquiry, their largely behavioral perspective emphasizes instead a change in classroom teaching technologies.

That sociologists such as Jencks and Dreeben can be taken as representative figures in current educational thought illustrates the inquiry perspective's loss of influence. While philosophy, once the queen of the academy, has been pushed to the margins in most of the leading schools of education, the nature and meaning of education has increasingly been defined by economists, social scientists, and policy analysts primarily concerned with social functional approaches.

Yet as many of the papers in this volume point out, these changes may in fact have weakened the connection between educational theory and the actual process of teaching and learning, whether in educationally disadvantaged or in socially privileged settings (Green, 1983). Power may become more centralized, administration may proliferate, evaluation procedures may become more complex, yet the connection between these changes and student performance continues to remain unclear. One may plausibly reply, of course, that important progress in the public schools awaits new technological breakthroughs or even more subtle control mechanisms. But it may well be that a concern for these measures has encouraged some of the most gifted educators to retreat during the 1960s and 1970s to those private and parochial schools whose homogeneous, if not explicitly religious, constituencies could sustain some equivalent of Mann's or perhaps Dewey's moral community. From their perspective, surely, American public education has tested the limits of useful centralized policymaking and administrative control.

At first, the advocates of inquiry values were mainly antiestablishment writers such as Kohl and Kozol, who wrote out of their direct experience with classroom teaching. Increasingly, however, others have made the same point in more general terms—including writers as diverse as Jackson and McPherson (in their analyses of the classroom), Callahan and Wise (in discussions of educational administration), and Lightfoot (in her study of educational issues in the black community). Recently, Dean Myron Atkins concisely summed up this whole perspective:

> The government supported curriculum movement, with its attendant proliferation of specialties, may have contributed to "deskilling" and "deprofessionalizing," because the act of teaching is not seen as requiring skilled selections from a broad repertoire of possible actions . . . this governmentally inspired redefinition of schooling and professional practice . . . will lead, in my opinion at least, to further decline (Atkins, 1980, pp. 94–95, 97).

INQUIRY, SOCIAL FUNCTION, AND AMERICAN EDUCATIONAL POLICY

This claim, that American educational policy has tilted much too sharply against inquiry values, seems persuasive to us on two major counts. First, much of educational practice must continue to be described in inquiry rather than social functional terms. The way children learn still seems highly dependent on interactions within specific classrooms at particular moments in time, partly because certain crucial features of the learning experience simply "happen" and are not reducible to any set of behavioral relations that can be scientifically modeled. Teaching, in other words, continues to remain an art form, whose practitioners are responsible for transmitting our society's culture from one generation to the next.

One can rightly respond, of course, that these "happenings" occur more frequently in some contexts than in others. While learning can occur anywhere at any time (and, in one way or another, does occur everywhere in all conscious moments), it is surely more likely to occur if facilities are pleasant, books are available, supplies are adequate, teachers are well paid and competently trained, and fellow students have been appropriately selected. To the extent that education is the product of these structural and contextual factors, there are strong reasons for advocating a behavioral policy approach which relies on careful, systematic research.

But insofar as this reply succeeds in reproducing the inquiry—social function debate, it suggests a second reason for returning to an inquiry understanding. Whatever their intrinsic merits, both these understandings are so deeply entrenched in our educational thought and practice—in the role norms of educators and the fundamental ideologies of our culture—that to consider only one will almost certainly be self-defeating. In other words, educational policies encounter such resistance, such loose coupling, because the contemporary policy process has so ignored the inquiry side of the basic division in American education. In particular, social functional policies that try to reallocate resources and improve teaching methods to help the disadvantaged may well be resisted *not* because they are egalitarian, but because they appear to disturb teaching and learning in the classroom.

In short, educational policy must pay more attention to inquiry values. Yet we will commit the same mistake in reverse if we then ignore the schools' social functions. Policies that concentrate entirely on engaging children intellectually may appear to be so rarified, so irrelevant either to the students' present social and cultural situation or their realistic future prospects, that they will be dismissed as too abstract and impractical. The most obvious move therefore might seem to be to seek policies that maximize both inquiry and social functional values.

Here, we believe, one might profit from Lightfoot's (1969) discussion of teachers and parents in minority communities. Lightfoot recognizes that American public education has failed many of its students, particularly in low-income or minority communities. Her analysis suggests that the social function of promoting genuine equity and equality of opportunity in the public schools can be linked to inquiry values—but only if this effort recognizes the diversity of American culture and society. As she points out, the staffs of some of the most successful public schools take into account the parents' aspirations through tacit understandings that reflect a shared, often upper-middle-class culture. Parents in minority, lower-income schools, of course, share with other parents the social functional concern with training their children for adult life. These districts, however, must overcome not only their students' social and economic inequalities, but subcultural differences between teachers, students, and parents that preclude such tacit cooperation. Although there is no certain solution to this problem, Lightfoot's answer is to substitute for tacit cooperation the *overt* involvement of the parents (and the community) in the life of the schools. The point is not to eliminate all disagreement and conflict—for the inquiry–social function tension remains fundamental—but to add the parents' social functional concerns to a discourse that already reflects the faculty's inquiry commitments.

If this step inserts social functional values into the inquiry-dominated context of the individual school, another must insert inquiry considerations into an educational policy process by now too thoroughly dominated by social functional concerns. This move means the participation of articulate representatives of local administrators, principals, and especially classroom teachers. Here, too, the objective must be less to seek compromise and consensus than to bring to the fore the fundamental issues that so pervasively shape our educational practice, in part because these are not explicitly acknowledged. As we have tried to show, such genuine, creative debate is an essential precondition if American public education is to recognize and act on its complex heritage and responsibilities.

REFERENCES

Atkin, J. Myron. The government in the classroom. *Daedalus*, 1980, 109: 85–97.

Bagley, William C. *Educational values*. New York: The Macmillan Co., 1926.

Bailyn, Bernard. *Education in the forming of American society*. Caravelle Ed. New York: Vintage Books, 1960.

Barr, Rebecca, and Dreeben, Robert. Instruction in classroom. *Review of Research in Education*, 1977, 5: 89–162.

Bobbitt, Franklin. *What the schools teach and might teach*. Cleveland, Ohio: The Survey Committee of the Cleveland Foundation, 1915.

Boocock, Sarane, *Sociology of education: An introduction*. Boston: Houghton Mifflin, 1980.

Bowers, C. A. *The progressive educator and the depression: The radical years*. New York: Random House, 1969.

Callahan, Raymond E. *An introduction to education in American society*. New York: Alfred A. Knopf, 1957.

Callahan, Raymond E. *Education and the cult of efficiency*. Chicago: The University of Chicago Press, 1962.

Coleman, James, et al. *Equality of educational opportunity*, Vol. 1. Washington, D. C.: U.S. Government Printing Office, 1966.

Cremin, Lawrence A. *The transformation of the school*. New York: Alfred A. Knopf, 1961.

Cubberley, Elwood P. *Changing conceptions of education*. Riverside Educational Monographs. Boston: Houghton Mifflin Co., 1909.

D'Amico, Alfonso. *Individuality and community: The social and political thought of John Dewey*. Gainesville, Fla: The University Presses of Florida, 1978.

Dewey, John. *The quest for certainty*. New York: Paragon Books, 1929.

Dewey, John. Can education share in social reconstruction? *Social Frontier*, 1934a, 1: 12.

Dewey, John. Educating for tommorrow. *Social Frontier*, 1934b, 1: 5–7.

Dewey, John. *Experience and education*. New York: Collier Books, 1938.

Geertz, C. *The interpretation of cultures*. New York: Basic Books, 1973.

Hartz, Louis. *The liberal tradition in America*. New York: Harcourt Brace, 1955.

Howe, Daniel Walker. *The political culture of the American Whigs*. Chicago: The University of Chicago Press, 1979.

Jackson, Philip W. *Life in classrooms*. New York: Holt, Rinehart and Winston, 1968.

Jencks, Christopher, et al. *Inequality*. New York: Harper & Row, 1972.

Katz, Michael B. *The irony of early school reform*. Boston: Beacon Press, 1968.

Kleppner, Paul. *The cross of culture*. New York: The Free Press, 1970.

Kohl, Herbert R. *Teaching the "unteachable."* New York: The New York Review, 1967.

Kozol, Jonathan. *Death at an early age*. Boston: Houghton Mifflin, 1967.

Lightfoot, Sara L. *Worlds apart*. New York: W. W. Norton & Co, 1969.

Lipsky, Michael. *Street-level bureaucracy*. New York: Russell Sage, 1980.

Lowi, Theodore J. *The end of liberalism*. New York: W. W. Norton & Co., 1969.

McConnell, Grant. *Private power and American democracy*. New York: Random House, Vintage Books, 1969.

McPherson, Gertrude H. *Small town teacher*. Cambridge, Mass.: Harvard University Press, 1972.

Messerli, Jonathan. *Horace Mann: A biography*. New York: Alfred A. Knopf, 1972.

Miller, Perry (ed.). *The transcendentalists*. Cambridge, Mass.: Harvard University Press, 1950.

Munroe, James P. *New demands in education*. Garden City, N.Y.: Doubleday, Page & Co., 1912.

Peterson, Paul E. *City limits*. Chicago, Ill.: University of Chicago Press, 1980.

Smith, Louis, and Geoffrey, William. *The complexities of an urban classroom*. New York: Holt, Rinehart and Winston, 1968.

Spaulding, Frank E. *Principles, policies and plans for the improvement of the New Bedford public schools*. New Bedford, Mass.: n.p., 1922.

Stephens, John M. *The process of schooling*. New York: Holt, Rinehart and Winston, 1967.

Summers, A. S., and Wolfe, B. L. Equality of educational opportunity quantified: A production function approach. Mimeo. Philadelphia: Federal Reserve Bank of Philadelphia, 1974.

Summers, A. S., and Wolfe, B. L. Do schools make a difference? *The American Economic Review*, 1977, 67: 639–52.

Taylor, Charles. Neutrality in political science. In Alan Ryan (ed.), *The philosophy of social explanation*, Oxford: Oxford University Press, 1973, pp. 139–170.

Thayer, V. T., and Levit, Martin. *The role of the school in American society*. New York: Dodd, Mead & Co., 1966.

Weber, Max. *From Max Weber*. H. Gerth and C. W. Mills (eds.). New York: Oxford University Press, 1958.

Weick, Karl E. Educational organizations as loosely coupled systems. *Administrative Science Quarterly*, 1976, 21(1): 1–19.

Wise, Arthur E. *Legislated learning*. Berkeley: The University of California Press, 1979.

CHAPTER 18

Teaching Policy and Federal Categorical Programs

Michael Kirst

The Reagan Administration proposes to change fundamentally the impact of federal categorical programs on teaching policy. Reagan's education leaders contend that federal aid causes costly, needless, and harmful classroom intrusions. One way to illuminate this debate is to examine the teaching policy impact of current (1981) federal policy. Evidence presented here demonstrates that there is a substantial categorical impact that could be lasting. But federal policy changes such as bloc grants could alter the nature of the impact, and particularly affect some of those with a potential for a long-term deposit.

There is widespread agreement that the classroom teacher is the key to the success of federal categorical programs. Most federal categorical efforts, however, are focused on the early grades, where the classroom teacher influence ranges over many subjects and is particularly difficult to discover. Although 80 percent of Title I ESEA is spent for preschool through grade 6, little research has focused on changed teacher behavior or attitudes. Indeed, the burgeoning implementation literature is concentrated overwhelmingly on levels above the classroom (Benson, 1980, pp. 169–206).

This paucity of research is understandable given the time, expense, and complexity of classroom observation (Carew and Lightfoot, 1979; Kirst and Jung, 1980, pp. 17–34). Many classes for a long period of time must be observed and prior studies indicate that the variation among classrooms is very large. Studies of the longitudinal evolution of federal programs indicate that observation results in year one and year ten of implementation would be quite different, suggesting that long-term studies are necessary (Kirst and Jung, 1980, pp. 17–35). There has been no self-reporting by teachers that goes much beyond complaints about federal paperwork. The interaction effects within the classroom have proven especially troublesome, because federal categorical programs mingle with state categories and a myriad of other local influences. We are unsure how to separate second-order consequences, indirect effects, and the impact of time spent on categorical tasks that might have been spent on some other teaching activity.

This paper focuses on the more direct classroom impacts of federal and state categorical programs, and not the cultural or social forces (e.g., affirmative action, civil rights) that orient teaching policy. The author will speculate on classroom impact from what is known concerning teaching policy components that surround and intrude into the classroom. Caution is necessary because many claims about the impact of categoricals are unproven and value-laden (Kirst, 1980, pp. 705–708). Sweeping proposals of grant consolidation by the Reagan Administration are likely to heat up this philosophic debate, but not illuminate classroom behavior. Given this state of the art, we will begin with assumptions that orient the federal role with respect to teaching policy, then produce what evidence exists, and conclude with projections about future policy changes. Before analyzing the teaching policy impact of federal categorical programs, it is useful to outline the overall federal role and the intergovernmental administrative system.

THE FEDERAL ROLE: AN OVERVIEW

In the last two decades the federal government has expanded its monetary commitment to elementary and secondary education in a striking manner, as indicated by the growth of the Office of Education's budget from $377 million in 1960 to $8 billion in 1981. The federal share of overall education expenditure at all levels, however, has undergone only a slight increase from 4.4 percent to 9 percent. But federal funds of elementary and secondary education are primarily earmarked for categories such as vocational education, special compensatory programs, and environmental education. Consequently, they have a more precise impact than unrestricted aid. This targeting of federal resources has endowed federal funds with more leverage than a 9 percent increase in total expenditures would cause if federal officials merely "put money on the stump and ran."

Many recent studies, however, have tended to deflate some claims concerning the impact of the increased federal categorical funds (Timpane, 1979). For example, state and local funds have often been distributed in such an inequitable manner that a relatively modest increase in federal aid has not been able to overcome the expenditure disadvantage of low-expenditure districts. Indeed, federal aid itself works at cross-purposes—the bulk of it is equalizing (Title I ESEA Elementary and Secondary Education Act), but large programs (impact aid) operate to give wealthier school districts or schools a larger share than poorer ones. Finally, the categorical intent of federal funds is blunted by the various mechanisms for substituting local priorities for federal ones as the money flows from Washington to local classrooms. For example, the impressive growth of federally supported research has been offset in part by the difficulty of installing the research products in local schools.

There have been basically six alternative modes of federal action for public schools:

1. *General aid.* Provide no-strings aid to state and local education agencies or minimal earmarks such as teacher salaries. A modified form of general aid was proposed by President Reagan in 1981. He would consolidate numerous categories into a single bloc grant for local education purposes. No general aid bill has ever been approved by the Congress.
2. *Stimulate through differential funding.* Earmarked categories of aid provide financial incentives through matching grants, fund demonstration projects, and purchase specific services. This is the approach of ESEA.
3. *Regulate.* Legally specify behavior, impose standards, certify and license, and enforce accountability procedures. The bilingual regulations proposed by the Carter Administration and rescinded by President Reagan are a good example.
4. *Discover knowledge and make it available.* Have research performed and gather and make other statistical data available. The National Institute of Education performs the first function and the National Center for Education Statistics, the second.

5. *Provide services.* Furnish technical assistance and consultants in specialized areas or subjects. The Office of Civil Rights will advise school districts who design voluntary desegregation plans.
6. *Exert moral suasion.* Develop vision and question assumptions through publication and speeches by top officials. Secretary of Education Hufstedler stressed the shortage of science teachers.

The ill-defined value of promoting equal educational opportunity has been the most pervasive theme of federal education policy. Its most obvious expression is through numerous categorical grants targeted to students not adequately served by state and local programs (e.g., disadvantaged, handicapped). The federal government has also attempted to stimulate educational reform through the Teacher Corps or demonstration programs such as women's equity and career education. The Reagan Administration will attempt to scale back aggressive federal activity in such areas. The interest groups that are the recipients of federal policy will resist, but the key will be whether they can form coalitions. The Reagan Administration will promote the following basic changes in the federal educational policy of the past twenty years:

1. from minimal support of private education to significant support through tuition tax credits,
2. from a prime concern with equity to more concern with efficiency and state and local freedom to choose,
3. from a larger and more influential federal role to a mitigated federal role,
4. from mistrust of the motives and capacity of state and local educators to a renewed faith in governing units outside of Washington, and
5. from detailed and prescriptive regulations to deregulation.

In 1950 when USOE was transferred to the Federal Security Agency, forerunner to the Department of Health, Education, and Welfare (HEW), it had a staff of three hundred to spend $40 million. Growth was slow and largely unrecognized. By 1963 forty-two departments, agencies, and bureaus of the government were involved in education to some degree. The Department of Defense and the Veterans Administration spent more on educational programs than the USOE and the NSF (National Science Foundation) combined. In 1963 the Office of Education appointed personnel who were specialists and consultants in such areas as mathematics, libraries, and school buses and who identified primarily with the National Education Association (NEA). Grant programs operated through deference to state priorities and judgments. State administrators were regarded by USOE as colleagues who should have the maximum decision-making discretion permitted by categorical laws.

While the era of 1963–1972 brought dramatic increases in federal activity, the essential mode of delivering services for USOE remained the same. The differential funding route was the key mode with bigger and bolder categorical programs and demonstrations. The delivery system for these categories continued to stress the superior ability of state departments to review local projects. Indeed, the current collection of overlapping and complex categorical aids is a mode of federal action about which a number of otherwise dissenting educational interests could agree (Wirt and Kirst, 1975, pp. 153–170). It was not the result of any rational plan for federal intervention but an outcome of political bargaining and coalition formation.

In addition to expanded categories came an incremental shift in the style of USOE administration. The traditional provision of specialized consultants and the employment of subject matter specialists were ended in favor of "managers" and generalists who had public administration rather than professional education backgrounds. These newer federal administrators have been more aggressive and created a political backlash against federal regulation that President Reagan was able to highlight in his 1980 campaign.

AN OVERVIEW OF FEDERAL FUNDING

Alongside the USOE program growth from 1964 to 1980, there was a new aggressive strategy of federal-local categorical grants (bypassing the states) through such federal agencies as the Office of Economic Opportunity (Head Start, migrant education, Follow Through) and the Department of Labor (Jobs Corps, CETA). These federal-local grants could be accompanied by more explicit federal controls than those that employed general guidelines for states to interpret. The Office of Economic Opportunity (OEO) and the Labor Department funded or created agencies supplementing the K–12 educational system, such as Head Start, child care centers, and CETA skill centers. These programs were operated by mayors and city councils rather than by the school systems. It has been traditional for educators to acknowledge the curriculum outside the K–12 system and then to ignore it in their analyses. Indeed, federally funded public TV broadcasting such as *Sesame Street* might have a more profound and pervasive impact on teaching policy than any categorical program.

A breakdown of Labor Department and Education Department funds for education including higher education is presented in Table 18.1.

The consolidated budget obscures the numerous separate categorical programs. Since no one was sure what type of federal intervention would be effective, the con-

TABLE 18.1. Federal Funds for Education and Training (Departments of Education and Labor) *Outlays (in millions of dollars)*

	1980 actual	1981 estimate	1982 estimate	1983 estimate	1984 estimate
Education:					
Elementary, secondary, & vocational:					
Elementary & secondary education:					
Existing law	3,569	3,371	3,942	4,185	4,509
Proposed legislation			50	900	900
Indian education	395	294	332	368	383
Impact aid	690	799	443	425	455
Education for the handicapped	822	1,074	1,088	1,258	1,359
Vocational & adult education	863	937	1,092	980	996
Other	393	466	419	471	517
Subtotal, elementary, secondary, & vocational education	6,732	6,942	7,366	8,588	9,119

TABLE 18.1   con't

	1980 actual	1981 estimate	1982 estimate	1983 estimate	1984 estimate
Higher education:					
Student financial assistance	3,683	3,743	3,947	2,600	2,472
Loan guarantees for students & parents	1,408	2,109	2,350	3,172	3,600
Higher & continuing education	410	452	384	430	457
Special institutions	193	212	246	281	291
Subtotal, higher education	5,694	6,516	6,927	6,483	6,820
Research & general education aids:					
Educational research & improvement	401	394	387	411	441
Unallocated salaries & overhead	170	234	249	261	270
Cultural activities	632	671	745	781	826
Other	154	173	157	157	161
Subtotal, research & general education aids	1,357	1,473	1,539	1,610	1,698
Subtotal, education	13,783	14,931	15,832	16,681	17,637
Training, employment, & labor services:					
Training & employment:					
General training & employment programs	2,932	2,851	2,995	3,004	2,928
Public service employment	3,697	3,088	3,772	4,078	4,408
Youth programs:					
Existing Law	2,330	2,536	1,782	1,551	1,588
Proposed legislation			875	1,100	1,125
Older workers	235	265	277	277	277
Work incentive program	395	365	385	385	385
Federal-State employment service	756	831	904	981	1,065
Subtotal, training & employment	10,345	9,935	20,989	11,375	11,776
	551	605	664	695	716
Other labor services					
Subtotal, training, employment, & labor services	10,896	10,540	11,653	12,070	12,492

SOURCE: Office of Management and Budget, 1981.

gressional view was to try almost any politically palatable program. President Reagan would reverse this trend through massive consolidation into two bloc grants—one for LEA's and another for SEA's.

FEDERAL INFLUENCE ON LOCAL SCHOOL OPERATIONS

The impressive growth of federal funds has not automatically been translated into commensurate influence on local education. Except for the impacted areas program, large-scale federal programs stress the promotion of innovation or change in state and local programs, priorities, and teaching policy. For instance, NDEA of 1967 stimulated more science and math courses, a new science curriculum, and more guidance counselors. The recent Vocational Educational Acts emphasize reorienting local vocational education programs so that they match the large-scale transformation in labor force needs—e.g., from agriculture to computer technology. ESEA Title I was not to provide "more of the same" educational approaches for disadvantaged children, but special programs for special needs.

For our purposes here, it is important to realize that federal aid is change-oriented money that is being filtered through a rather rigid local educational organization (Berke and Kirst, 1972). Indeed, federal leverage should extend to the locus of where the child comes in contact with education services—at the classroom level. Have the services purchased with federal aid reached the classroom level or been diverted? Has federal aid altered the process of education in a large number of classrooms?

Despite uncertainty and frequent policy changes, the federal government has been the only public agency supporting large-scale demonstrations. Very few local districts have the discretionary money to support demonstrations, and states have only minor programs. Local funds are programmed often into standard operating procedures and routine efforts that are stressed by theories of organizational rigidity and choice.

The numerous constraints on effective and focused implementation (at each level of the political system) are indeed disconcerting. It is a long delivery chain from Washington to a classroom in Houston. When one aggregates the various structures and individuals at all three levels that must be changed or overcome by categorical aid (that asserts the primacy of federal goals), implementation appears to be an awesome task. Essentially, federal aid relies on a top-down delivery mechanism to ensure that its objectives are accomplished. This top-down strategy (operating largely through administrators wielding federal-state regulations and guidelines) requires sanctions, incentives, and local acceptance of federal goals, to ensure that the aid reaches the intended targets or reorients classroom practice.

FEDERAL CATEGORICAL ASSUMPTIONS AND THE TEACHING PROFESSION

The way a policy problem gets defined says a great deal about how it will be implemented. A policy question may be treated as best settled through reliance on professional expertise—professionalism orients the formulation and implementation stages. Or, policy resolution may rely on political concepts such as bargaining coalitions and participation of conflicting interest groups. A widely used American option is recourse to legal norms and procedures including fair decisional process (Kirst, 1980, pp. 705–708). Two other possibilities are bureaucratic consistency and private market determinations of the contours of policy. The choice of these policy orientations embodies alternative values—politically neutral competence, expertise, choice in free markets, and so on. The consequences are many, as Kirp describes:

> These distinctions among frameworks matter a great deal. They determine what will be provided, by whom, and on what terms. They fix the nature and extent of regulatory control. They shape the extent of variability; they identify who will benefit. Defining a policy problem primarily in terms of rights creates a different client class, with a different stake, than does treating the issue as one lodged fittingly within the discretion of a professional class or as the ministerial responsibility of a bureaucratic agency. Choices among frameworks embody choices about the allocation of power. How these choices are made thus becomes itself a significant policy question.
>
> Once a policy question has been framed in a certain way, change usually comes slowly and at the margin. Professional judgment may count for somewhat less or somewhat more, procedural protections may have modestly more or less effect (Kirp, 1980, pp. 3–4).

Federal and state programs embody a conceptualization that does *not* rely heavily on professional expertise and experience. The approach of U.S. categoricals has been to stress legal procedures and bureaucratic standard setting. The contrast on this dimension with Britain and Australia is striking (Blackburn, 1981). Australia's program for the disadvantaged allocates money to specific schools, but includes little prescription after that. Britain expanded the domain of the professional in its recent special education initiative. In these nations, courts and legislatures rarely act to fix policy, and the degree of professional flexibility among local schools is noteworthy by U.S. standards.

In the United States, categorical programs are mounted with a presumption that the professional educator cannot be trusted and has helped cause the problem through neglect or bad practice. The concept of rights and due process in special education provides legitimacy for the rejection of teacher judgment. Mainstreaming and IEP's are legislatively dictated, and federal categories have considerable bureaucratic consistency and internal accountability embedded in regulations and guidelines. Elaborate due process procedures are triggered when either the school system or parent reach an impasse. In sum, teaching policy in the United States is constrained and oriented by nonprofessional policy concepts. The ultimate impact of federal categories on teaching policy is the outcome between the contending forces of teachers' behavior and the enforcement of legal, political, and bureaucratic influence external to the classroom. This author concurs with Schwille et al. (this volume) that teachers are "policy brokers" who take higher-level policies and pressures into consideration, but also enjoy considerable discretion.

In this semi-autonomous role, teachers are better understood as political brokers than as implementors. They enjoy considerable discretion, being influenced by their own ideas of what schooling ought to be as well as persuaded by external pressures. This view represents a middle ground in the classic sociological contrast between professional autonomy and bureaucratic subordination. It pictures teachers as more or less rational decision makers who take higher-level policies and other pressures into consideration in their calculation of benefits and costs (p. 377).

The Loosely Coupled System: Implications for Federal Impact

Classroom outcome from categoricals is unknown because of the organizational structure of schooling. The concept of "loose coupling" has become a widespread descriptor for the education implementation process and need not be reviewed in depth here (Weick, 1976, pp. 1–19). While theoretical and empirical gaps abound in loose coupling analysis, the basic notion is the tendency of educational organizations to disconnect policies from outcomes, means from ends, and structure or rules from actual activity. The hierarchy of central control in a federal system does not imply central control over actual work processes. Teacher behavior is delegated beyond the control of the formal organization control envisioned in categorical programs. The federal and state administrators, local superintendents, and school site principals do not comprise a command structure with straight line and precise directions for teaching policy. Meyer goes even further:

> But this [education] organizational structure is imposed on an extraordinarily chaotic domain:. . . technologies of instruction are nonexistent or variable . . . outputs are unpredictable and uncertain in measurement, and an organizational system of controls over all this would be impossibly expensive. The real world of the educational domain is, as the current phrase in organizational theory has it, "loosely coupled." . . . In this situation, the rationalized educational order has a highly ritualized character, disconnected at every point of technical substance from the variability of the domain over which it exercises control. . . . The order in the classification of pupils is achieved by ignoring their substantive properties and attending to ritual ones: they are admitted to Algebra II because they "had had" Algebra I, not because they know it. They enter college because they "have graduated" from high school, not by virtue of substantive properties or competencies (Meyer, 1981, p. 9).

The existing fragmented structure of federal and state categories intensifies this inherent educational organization tendency toward loose coupling. Meyer describes this in graphic terms:

> Consider the practical situation of a school principal or superintendent. The state will provide extra funds for a special program for handicapped students; the federal government will provide further funds if there is no special program (i.e., for mainstreaming). The parents insist that funds be managed equitably within the school and district. But both state and federal governments provide special funds which must be spent only within a few schools, or even for a few students within a school.
>
> What is the administrator to do? The answer is simple. Have a differentiated subunit for each funding or authority program. Let these subunits report as best they can in conformity with requirements. Avoid having the subunits brought in

contact with each other (so as to avoid explicit conflict or inconsistency), and remain in ignorance of the exact content of the various programs, reports, and budgets . . . (Meyer, 1981, pp. 16–17).

All of these problems are magnified in large school districts that receive forty or more categorical programs and have eighty separate sources of income. California has over twenty large state categorical programs of its own! Loose coupling does not imply that there is no classroom impact, but it does imply that this impact will be nonuniform, cumulative, and primarily indirect. Indeed, the major federal categories do not attempt to prescribe classroom teaching methodologies or curricula.

Federal categorical programs, however, can influence teaching policy in specific directions. Kirst and Jung conducted a synthesis of thirteen years of studies on Title I ESEA annual appropriations ($3.2 billion). This longitudinal view found that federal efforts to target more Title I dollars to participating students were successful (Kirst and Jung, 1980). Federal objectives were gradually embedded in the local education agencies' standard operating procedures. Program design elements specified in federal Title I regulations are implemented in 1980 with much greater fidelity to federal regulation than in 1965. This impact grows incrementally and is not easy to find in early cross-sectional data. Persistent federal categorical enforcement and persuasion pays off over time. The loosely coupled system is not completely disconnected.

In sum, the federal government's major policy goal is more attention to the needs of pupils in particular categories—handicapped, disadvantaged, bilingual, and so on. This federal goal is to be accomplished through a top-down delivery system relying on regulation. The federal government employs very few subject matter or teaching methods specialists who can advise on classroom practices. The federal government does hire a great many grant administrators and compliance officers. There is miniscule federal interest in teacher training, in-service, or curriculum development. Only very small categories such as the Teacher Corps relate to these issues.

WHAT FEDERAL TEACHING POLICIES PERSIST

Since we have little observational data about classroom teaching behavior, we must explore federal teaching policy impact through forces that intrude into the classroom. For example, if federally funded teacher aides are placed in classrooms, then some impact will take place on teacher behavior. Someone else in the room will upset teaching routines. Which federal influences are most likely to persist and which ones will disappear quickly? Tyack, Kirst, and Hansot examined and classified education reforms that left a long-term deposit and compared their characteristics to ephemeral reforms.

They researched the common characteristics of such varied reforms as:

- Graded school
- Consolidation of rural elementary schools
- Abolishing ward school boards and cutting central urban boards in size
- Carnegie unit
- Cutting class sizes
- Raising educational requirements for teachers
- School lunch programs
- Creating vocational courses and tracks in high schools

- Intelligence and other forms of standardized testing
- Guidance counselors
- Adding other specialists to school staff

They found that the lasting changes tended to have these common characteristics: (1) they were structural in nature, (2) they created new constituencies, and (3) they were easily monitored (1980). In particular, changes that added new functions or new layers of specialized personnel persisted. Examples of such changes include school lunches, vocational education, and separate classes for handicapped children. It was easy to monitor the existence of such structural reforms and to identify the people who had strong motives for retaining them. Many of these reforms added functions to the school such as guidance. Other reforms such as graded schools, Carnegie units, and raising education requirements for teachers were easily monitored. By contrast reforms calling for new skills or added effort on the part of existing staff have had a more checkered fate. Team teaching, inquiry learning, core curriculum, and individualized instruction are cases in point.

Given this historical analysis, what types of federal interventions will most likely have a long-term impact on teaching policy? This question can best be answered by differentiating various dimensions of teaching policy.

Dimensions of High Impact (followed by examples of federal intervention):
1. Policies that promote change in organizational structure including added personnel layers (vocational specialists or aides) or "pull-out" teaching structures under Title I (e.g., pupil is pulled out of a regular classroom for intensive work with a remedial specialist). These instructional methods or organizational changes require a new layer of specialists. These specialists can be organized into a constituency for the maintenance of the "program."
2. Pupil classification, e.g., limited English-speaking, handicapped, or gifted. The classification system can be monitored and creates a constituency of teacher or specialist credentials.
3. Certificates for teaching remedial reading or bilingual education. These differentiate the specialist from the regular classroom teacher. They are necessary to assure that federal funds are used for special programs and constituencies.
4. Compensatory rights and procedures, e.g., due process for pupil placement in a handicapped program. The individualized education plan (IEP) can be easily monitored, and due process rights create a separate legal structure.

Dimensions of Moderate Impact:
1. Testing policies—that teachers must administer. While Title I requires a test be given, LEA's may use a long-standing instrument. Consequently there may not be a new test given. *Test taking is easily monitored.*
2. Differentiation of content among students—e.g., a new curriculum for Title I–identified children. Federal aid stimulated much new remedial curriculum development and encouraged materials purchases. In these areas, the teacher feels somewhat constrained by federal rules but can ignore or greatly change the general statement of federal intent. There is no constituency to lobby for longevity, and monitoring is difficult. Both these high- and moderate-impact interventions can be weakened greatly by substituting bloc grants for the 1980 categorical structure.

Dimensions of Low Impact:
1. Time on specific instructional tasks—e.g., minutes per day on math or reading.
2. Curricular coverage of specific topics—such as fractions.
3. Tests for graduation or retention in grade. The federal government requires sorting of pupils, but not pass or fail policies.
4. Teaching methods or strategies—e.g., individualization of instruction or inquiry methods. A 1976 NSF study found that new math concepts and science inquiry methods promoted in the 1960s had vanished from the vast majority of schools (Stake and Easley, 1978).
5. Curricular linkage and cohesion—e.g., core courses or sequential curriculum development that arranges topics, concepts, or courses in some order.

These probable low-impact areas are the most difficult to monitor or create constituencies for. The organizational changes are within the traditional classroom instructional mode and can be eliminated without consultation with administrators.

Other dimensions such as federally sponsored in-service training could have some impact or leave a residue but have never been stressed since NSF programs in the mid-1960s. The next section will provide more detail on several of the issues sketched above.

Organizational Structure for Teaching

A major federal residue has added layers of administrators, specialists, and aides. In 1971 federal vocational education aid helped create a new layer of structure, especially credentialled teachers for areas such as agriculture and trades. While teacher credentials and new courses can be attributed to federal vocational education aid, the influence on classroom teachers from Title I and PL 94–142 is more problematic. As early as 1971–72 SRI researchers noted the trend across all types of instructional staff (see Table 18.2) and attributed the increase in classroom personnel to ESEA (Thomas and Larson, 1976, p. 12; NIE, 1977). It is easier to convince federal auditors that there is a special federal program if special personnel are hired from earmarked federal funds. Moreover, federal rules against supplanting encourage "pull-out programs" staffed by remedial specialists charged to federal grants.

TABLE 18.2. Instructional Staff in Public Elementary and Secondary Schools, by Type of Position (full-time equivalents)

Position	1961–62	1971–72	Percent Change
Principal (including assistant principal)	67,249	97,211	44.5
Consultant/Supervisor of instruction	16,169	37,495	131.9
Classroom Teacher	1,457,964	2,069,838	41.9
Librarian	19,603	41,954	140.2
Guidance & Counseling Personnel	21,152	52,368	147.6
Psychological Personnel	2,409	7,376	206.2
Other Nonsupervisory Personnel	3,215	15,365	377.9
Total Instructional Staff	1,587,761	2,321,607	46.2

SOURCE: Office of Education, Statistics of State School Assistance.

NIE's 1977 study of Title I ESEA unearthed some noteworthy impacts on teaching policy. Most Title I students received pull-out services where they are removed temporarily from the classroom. Students in pull-out programs are more likely to miss regular instruction than students in regular classroom programs. However, they have the advantage of being more likely to receive compensatory instruction from a subject area specialist. Specifically, NIE found in its congressionally mandated study of Compensatory Education Services:

- Class sizes are small. They average 9 students in compensatory reading and 12 in mathematics and language arts, compared with 27 in homeroom classes.
- Compensatory education students spend an average of 5½ hours per week in special instruction. That amounts to 29% of total instructional time for students in reading, 22% for students in language arts, and 27% for those in mathematics.
- Professional teachers who deliver compensatory instruction are often highly qualified: 67% have graduate training beyond a bachelor's degree, and 62% specialize in teaching one subject. This confirms the high impact of federal policy on easily monitored credentials.
- Teachers' aides deliver a substantial portion of compensatory education. More than half the aides employed nationwide are paid from Title I funds.
- Many school districts attempt to individualize their instruction, although few districts offer instruction that could be considered individualized in all respects.

Seventy-five percent of the children in compensatory reading programs are pulled out of their regular classrooms, while somewhat smaller proportions are pulled out in other aspects of language arts (41%) and mathematics (44%). Though they often miss instruction in their regular classrooms, these students generally receive different content or teaching methods from subject area specialists in the pull-out setting.

California with its twenty or more state categoricals on top of the federal programs is an extreme case of specialized personnel expansion. In 1980 the California Legislative Analyst reported:

> Since 1970–71 the number of full-time equivalent (FTE) positions in school districts has increased by 17%. Average daily attendance has declined by 9 percent over the same period. As a result, the number of FTE positions has increased by 28 percent per unit of student attendance.
>
> The overall growth in school personnel since 1970–71 reflects the following:
> (a) noncertificated or classified employees increased by 43 percent, primarily due to the growth in the number of full-time teacher aides;
> (b) teachers increased by 4 percent;
> (c) administrators (FTE) increased by 6.1 percent. Among these, full-time central administrators increased by 12.8 percent and site administrators increased by 1.0 percent;
> (d) pupil service personnel (FTE) increased by 27 percent. Among these, full-time counselors increased by 30 percent and psychologists increased by 83 percent.
>
> Availability of state and federal categorical aid appears to be the major reason for the growth in nonteaching staff. School districts reporting very high administrative ratios received double the amount of categorical aid per student received by

TABLE 18.3.   Changes in the Ratio of Teachers to Pupils by Racial and Ethnic Group in California: 1967 to 1977

Ratio of Teachers to Pupils	1967	1977
White Teachers to White Pupils	1 to 20	1 to 19
Hispanic Teachers to Hispanic Pupils	1 to 147	1 to 108
Black Teachers to Black Pupils	1 to 48	1 to 45
All Minority Teachers to Minority Pupils	1 to 69	1 to 64
All Teachers to All Pupils	1 to 25	1 to 25

SOURCE: California State Department of Education, "Racial and Ethnic Distribution of Students and Staff in California Public Schools, Fall 1977," mimeographed, table 15. Analysis was done by Dennis Encarnation of the Institute for Research on Educational Finance and Governance, Stanford.

districts reporting very low administrative ratios (California Legislative Analyst, 1980).

Categorical programs change not only the teaching structure but also the racial mix. For example, Hispanic teachers in California increased at a rate twice that of Hispanic students (96 percent versus 45 percent) from 1967 to 1977, the period marked by rapid proliferation of state and federal categorical mandates targeted for a large majority of Hispanic students. Consequently, as shown in Table 18.3, the ratio of Hispanic teachers to Hispanic students narrowed significantly during this period. Similar gains, however, were not recorded for Black teachers, whose growth barely kept pace with the growth of Black students. Instead, a reanalysis of 1978 survey data on a statewide sample of California public school teachers suggests that Blacks entered the teaching profession and stayed there in fewer numbers than did Hispanics, while the reverse appears to be true during the mid-to-late 1960s. A preliminary conclusion, a working hypothesis for subsequent research, is that the restructuring of the labor market over the last decade has not only shifted new jobs away from white to minority teachers, but also away from Blacks to Hispanics. As a result according to Table 18.3, minorities generally and Hispanics particularly have grown in absolute and relative terms over the past decade. In part, this shift resulted from California's state law requiring a bilingual person (teacher or aide) in any class where there are ten or more limited English-speaking students. Blacks have been employed by federal and state compensatory education funds that have not grown much.

Just as categorical programs have spurred growth in the number and types of professional subspecialties within the ranks of certified teachers, so too these programs have stimulated growth in the size and scope of the paraprofessional sector (i.e., instructional aides). As shown in Table 18.4, in 1967 equal numbers of Blacks and Hispanics were instructional aides, but by 1977 the ratio was two Blacks for every five Hispanic paraprofessionals. Moreover, by 1977 there were more Hispanic paraprofessionals than Hispanic certified teachers in the labor force; the same could not be said for Blacks, whose rate of growth in the paraprofessional sector was less than that for minorities generally or for whites.

Meyer has explored the layers of administration added by categorical programs. He emphasizes that one of the distinguishing characteristics of American school districts and SEAs is the *small number* of administrators who have direct line authority and the *large number* of administrators and units with specialized functions. These specialized units have created an explosion in administrators to the point where Han-

TABLE 18.4.   Changes in the Racial and Ethnic Distribution of Credentialed Teachers and Paraprofessional Personnel Employed in California: 1967 to 1977

		Minorities			Whites	Total
			Of Which			
		Total	Blacks	Hispanics		
Fall 1967	Teachers	16,152	8,137	4,189	163,523	179,852
	(%)	(9.1)	(4.5)	(2.3)	(90.9)	(100)
	Aides	4,137	1,933	1,933	12,073	16,210
	(%)	(25.5)	(11.9)	(11.9)	(74.5)	(100)
Fall 1977	Teachers	24,514	9,645	8,227	146,195	170,709
	(%)	(14.4)	(5.6)	(4.8)	(85.6)	(100)
	Aides	20,238	5,204	12,972	36,318	56,556
	(%)	(35.8)	(9.2)	(22.9)	(64.2)	(100)
Change 1967 to 1977	Teachers	8,185	1,508	4,038	−17,328	−9,143
	(%)	(50.7)	(18.5)	(96.4)	(−10.6)	(−5.1)
	Aides	16,101	3,271	11,039	24,245	40,346
	(%)	(389.2)	(169.2)	(571.1)	(200.8)	(248.9)

SOURCE: California State Department of Education, "Racial and Ethnic Distribution of Students and Staff in California Public Schools, Fall 1977," mimeographed, Tables 13 and 14. Analysis was done by Dennis Encarnation of the Institute for Research on Educational Finance and Governance, Stanford. Encarnation is completing a major research analysis of this topic.

nan and Freeman estimate that each dollar of federal funds creates nine times the increase in administrative personnel that each new dollar of local money creates (Meyer, 1981, p. 33).

One impact of this added number of aides, specialists, and administrative layers is that there is more role complexity and hierarchy. Teachers must relate to specialists through lesson plans. The aides' duties must be routinized. The Title I central office coordinator is an added supervisor. This change in roles results in a different sequencing of activities for pupils. Does the teacher introduce an item and then let the specialist reinforce it—or vice versa?

There are some indicators that these aides and specialists are having an impact on students. For example, recent Title I achievement studies display significant positive pupil gains which suggest a revised teaching policy could be one of the factors causing such gains (Kirst and Jung, 1980, p. 24). The introduction of aides and specialists might assist the regular classroom teacher through: cutting down on the variation of pupil attainment in the classroom, permitting the use of higher-level curricular materials, removing the more difficult pupils for part of the day, and consulting on strategies with low-achieving pupils. But the added personnel might make the classroom teacher more cautious because many people are reviewing the teacher's work. Given the large expenditure of Title I for aides and specialists, more research on such speculations should be a high priority. One strategy would be a pre- and postanalysis of teacher time allocations in the classroom. Such studies have been made by college presidents and business executives, but no time budget studies exist for a large sample of teachers.

Pupil Classification: A High-Impact Dimension

Federal regulations and compliance mechanisms can check effectively for pupil procedural rights including screening, sorting, and formulating educational plans. Atkin characterizes such practices in PL 94–142 this way:

> One has only to talk with the teachers involved—and most particularly with special education teachers—to learn of their frustration over the fact that effective special education has come to be associated with a properly constructed Individualized Education Plan. Teachers tend to derive their satisfaction from fulfilling of a new procedural requirement since this is the element of their sional activity that is most subject to external scrutiny.
>
> Many special education teachers and administrators have come to see themselves as compliance officers rather than as providers of educational services.
>
> We learn once again that any well-intentioned action has side effects, and not all the side-effects are beneficial. A pronounced result of the new law is that teachers and others spend enormous amounts of time writing plans, conducting conferences, and preparing reports (Atkin, 1980, p. 25).

These procedural rights are also enforced through elaborate due process appeal panels and the potential agitation by groups of parents. Moore et al. analyzed student classification in eight Illinois LEAs. He discovered large variations among districts and schools depending in large part on how detailed the federal and state regulations were.

> The quality of student assessment standards and the resulting care with which assessment was carried out varied from program to program, primarily reflecting the specificity of external mandates for that program. For instance, bilingual education placement in Elgin was based on what one instructor described as "a ten-minute quick and dirty test," while special education placements usually required extensive testing. The districts lacked *general* criteria for the assessment process to protect the quality of placement decisions.
>
> Further, once specific assessment procedures were adopted as part of district policy, they quickly became (as the organizational patterns perspective suggests) part of the institutional woodwork; there was no systematic effort to review established cutoff scores, testing instruments, etc., even when these procedures were creating obvious problems (such as substantial racial disproportions) in classifying students (Moore et al., 1981, pp. 12–13).

Changes in Governance and Participation: A Residue of Federal Categories

Numerous federal categories require parent advisory councils (PAC) at the district and/or school level. The clash between lay and professional interests has been complicated by the split between organized teachers and community groups with different priorities. Federal policy specifies various parent decision-making structures and the decisions such structures must make. For example, Title I PAC's have sign-off power on LEA applications for federal funds, while parents under PL 94–142 have appeal rights under due process. The PAC parents become a constituency for continuation of their role.

Teachers are constrained somewhat by these new parent participation structures, but probably not very much. Davies suggests parent councils are evolving into more cooperative reinforcement efforts with teachers and moving away from the account-ability mentality (Institute for Responsive Education, 1980). Duke et al. stress that teacher participation in various school site councils is enhanced by principal leadership styles, training in collaborative problem solving, and an expectation of efficiency by teachers (Showers, 1980, p. 2). What impact these school site councils have had on classroom practices is not widely known. Cohen et al. found, however, that California's Early Childhood Education Program (ECE) had a number of impacts that stemmed in part from the requirement of a school site council (parents, school staff, and the principal) to work out a plan for individualized instruction. Indeed, her findings summarize well that interaction effect of a number of these high-impact dimensions of categorical teaching policy.

> The need for more formal and informal meetings in the ECE schools was an obvious consequence of the program. Just to list a few of the reasons for meetings and increased interaction: teachers had to learn how to work with aides; parent volunteers had to be incorporated and made to feel significant and useful; teachers in the affected grades had to coordinate their record keeping and direct their teaching and testing program to the same instructional objectives; coincidental with the implementation of the plan in Grade 1, there was a mandated state-funded planning process with parents and teachers for Grade 2. Principals had to deal with sticky problems of the jealousy of teachers in Grades 4–6 who did not stand to benefit directly from the program funds; he or she also had to work with informal leaders in the faculty who could either sabotage the whole effort or make it successful. Principals fought rear guard actions at the district level to prevent the district from trying to use program funds to pay for budgeting items ordinarily paid for by the central office (Cohen and Miller, 1979, p. 5).

The individualized instruction components of ECE caused so much resistance by teachers that the state dropped this focus after the first three years in its revised effort called School Improvement. The emphasis on joint planning through a multirepresentative school site council remains, however.

Dimensions of Low Impact: The Methods and Substance of Instruction

Federal aid is largely silent on teaching methods or prescribing curricular content. Consequently teachers do not feel constrained in these areas. Although straight line hierarchical impacts are unlikely, the indirect effect on teaching methods could be significant. The various federal rules and procedures introduce new lexicons and concepts such as mainstreaming, IEP's, and compensatory education. The publicity surrounding the new lexicon seeps into the teachers' customs and orientation. The federal government does not specify teaching methods or materials, but sets up procedures (e.g., IEP) that cause rethinking of teaching strategies. A common ethos might eventually permeate the classroom because new approaches such as DISTAR become fashionable. The impact is likely to be short-term, however, compared to the added structure of vocational education or remedial reading teachers that creates a separate constituency of employees. Federal impact on teaching methods and content will be cyclical, faddish, and ephemeral because there is no consistent federal policy or enforcement mechanism and bottom-up teacher support appears to be short-lived. The NSF experience with science inquiry methods is a good case of the short-lived impact (Stake and Easley, 1978).

TABLE 18.5.   Techniques Characterizing Individualization of Instruction in Regular and Compensatory Language Arts Programs in the Demonstration Districts (for Title I students only)

Instructional Characteristics	Average Percent of Teachers Employing Characteristics			
	Regular Classes		Compensatory Classes	
	Mean	Range	Mean	Range
Alternative Learning Paths and Sequencing				
1. How materials are used:				
a. Different materials for different children	30	7 to 47	51	0 to 100
b. Same materials, different sequence	17	0 to 40	18	0 to 60
c. Same materials, same order, different rate	35	0 to 47	5	0 to 45
d. Same materials, same order, same rate	16	0 to 47	5	0 to 45
Individual or Small Group Pacing				
2. How tasks are assigned:				
a. To individual students	26	19 to 42	55	30 to 100
b. To small groups	27	14 to 44	27	0 to 52
c. To whole class	49	27 to 67	19	0 to 46
Specific Learning Objectives				
3. Use of performance objectives:				
a. Specific performance objectives used	87	72 to 100	90	56 to 100
b. Of those using specific objectives goals are set for:				
Each child	13	0 to 33	65	0 to 100
Small groups	20	0 to 45	19	0 to 83
Total group	66	42 to 100	16	0 to 100
c. Of those using specific objectives, access to materials keyed to those objectives	64	43 to 88	94	57 to 100
Diagnostic and Prescriptive Activities				
4. Tests used to assess performance level at beginning of instruction:				
a. Standardized achievement test scores	54	20 to 80	86	30 to 100
b. Standardized diagnostic test scores	39	20 to 60	71	40 to 100
c. Scores on district-, school-, or program-developed tests keyed to instructional objectives	51	22 to 97	64	33 to 100
d. Scores on teaching staff-developed tests keyed to instructional objectives	57	20 to 80	52	0 to 100
e. Informal testing	82	50 to 100	74	33 to 100
5. Frequency of recording students' progress:				
a. 5 times a week	2	0 to 7	28	0 to 100
b. 1–4 times a week	16	6 to 40	36	10 to 59
c. 1–3 times a month	58	27 to 93	25	0 to 67
d. Less than 1–3 times a month	23	0 to 60	10	0 to 70

SOURCE: National Institute of Education, Compensatory Education Services (Washington: NIE, 1977), p. 51.

In sum, what classroom evidence we have does not indicate significant impact on classroom teaching methods from federal or state categoricals. From sparse and fragmented evidence, Cuban discovered a stubborn continuity in "teacher-centered instruction" as the dominant pattern.

> I mean the common method by which teachers teach to the whole group of students in a class, show high concern for whether or not students are listening to them, concentrate mostly on subject matter and academic skills, and in general control what is taught, when it is taught, and under what conditions it is taught. As a result most of the teachers' questions call for students' reciting factual information, the teacher relies most of the time on a single textbook for information, and it is likely that rows of desks will be placed facing a blackboard with a teacher's desk probably at or near the front of the room (Cuban, 1980, pp. 33–34).

In 1978, NIE conducted a congressionally mandated study of Title I. A survey of 12 districts revealed that compensatory education teachers in special classes are more likely than regular teachers to:

- Use different materials for different children
- Assign tasks to individual children
- Set specific performance objectives for children and have access to materials oriented to these objectives
- Use standardized achievement or diagnostic tests
- Record children's progress at frequent intervals

Table 18.5 displays the survey results and highlights the differences between pullout compensatory classes and regular classes.

Added federal rules have affected teaching policy through the changed role of the principal. Rand reports that principals mentioned increases in their activities caused in large part by federal categoricals—paperwork, consultation, and coping with students' noninstructional needs.

> A majority of the respondents reported that they now spend less time supervising instruction. However, many reported that the decreases were small, and that they were still able to meet the minimal requirements of the job (Hill et al., 1980).

TEACHER UNIONS AND CATEGORICAL AID

From the perspective of teacher unions, categorical aid is viewed as a mixed blessing. Categorical programs expand the total demand for instructional personnel. On the other hand, enrollment decline and severe fiscal crises have resulted in a loss of jobs for teachers and, ultimately, in a weakening of the unions' bargaining position. In this context, federal aid becomes a constraint during reduction-in-force negotiations. Since federally funded employees cannot be laid off, federal mandates have worked to further constrain the increasingly limited bargaining options available to local union leaders. By boosting the relative demand for educational personnel qualified to satisfy program mandates such as specialists, categorical programs often restructure the labor market in ways inimical to the seniority and tenure provisions recently secured by unions through collective bargaining. Consequently, the interaction between categorical mandates and the unions is changing:

> Different types of specialists have different interests and problems and thus cannot generate cohesive support for particular proposals. At least as important as this divergence in interest, however, is the fact that regular classroom teachers tend to resent specialists whom they see as having protected, less demanding, and less productive jobs. Moreover, they find that specialists in specially funded categorical programs (e.g., special education teachers) benefit from negotiated salary and fringe benefit increases but are not subjected to the same risks of job loss from declining enrollment.
>
> Secondly, we learned that—contrary to our expectations–the specialist teachers themselves tend to be less active and influential in teacher organization policy formation than regular classroom teachers. Instead, we discovered that, largely because they think of themselves as already having left the tedious rigors of the classroom, the specialists do not frequently seek or acquire leadership positions within the teachers' organization. Thus, they invite the union to bypass their complex and varied interests in order to win basic benefits (Mitchell, 1980, pp. 12–13).

Mitchell's data are limited to eight LEA's (four in California and four in Illinois). But he concluded that there is a "serious and permanent contradiction between collective bargaining and the creation of specialist teacher roles in the school." If economic hard times cause pressure to reduce school budgets, then tension will rise between classroom teachers who must absorb the brunt of personnel cutbacks. Specialists are protected by federal/state categorical restrictions. In Mitchell's words, teachers resent specialists' "protected status and cushy jobs."

Categorical programs have stipulated that bilingual teachers' aides be hired from Title VII money. By 1977 there were more Hispanic paraprofessionals than Hispanic teachers in the California labor force. Since these categorically funded teachers have organized politically, they have become an important internal and external force within the teachers' union. It is difficult to unite paraprofessionals and teachers in one union. Moreover, Mitchell et al. found that union leaders have little sympathy for federally funded specialists such as remedial reading experts (Mitchell et al., 1980, pp. 12–13). This lack of union support could result in a lack of protection of specialist jobs under Reagan's bloc grant proposals.

IN-SERVICE TRAINING AND LEGISLATION: AN UNTRIED AREA

The amount of time explicitly set aside for in-service training of teachers involved with federal categorical programs is surprisingly low. In 1970 Title I devoted only $20 million of its $1.02 billion to in-service. In California, so little in-service was provided for education of the handicapped (PL 94–142) that the legislature mandated one day.

A study of three large U.S. city districts found that a large number of LEA personnel were involved in staff development, and it is expanding. Staff development is characterized as a dispersed and largely invisible collection of activities with not much impact (Moore and Hyde, 1980). Categorical programs and regulations are not likely to change dramatically the low level of staff development impact.

> In all three districts, the actual costs of staff development were fifty times more than most school district staff estimated. These significant costs resulted partly from the "hidden cost" of teacher administrator time for staff development activity—time that was seen by school district staff as part of the school district's regular budget. Another factor obscuring the extent of staff development activity was that responsibility for staff development in each district was dispersed among a large number of people and departments.
>
> Staff development activities in each district had accumulated over time, often in response to other factors (federal funding opportunities, fund cutbacks, organizational politics, teacher contract negotiations, etc.). Thus, the nature of staff development activity in each district was not primarily the result of conscious policy (Moore and Hyde, 1980), pp. 131–132.

> The report's overall conclusion for changing the current status of in-service was that the weak political position of staff development and the constraints operating on school districts make substantial reform of actual staff development practice unlikely in the near future (Moore and Hyde, 1980, p. 132).

It is probable that the federal categorical structure helps cause the lack of coordination in LEA in-service efforts, but most of the money came from local sources. Hyde and Moore stress that there is an increasing local interest in staff development, but no consensus about what it is or what constitutes effectiveness. Consequently, categorical legislation cannot solve such basic conceptual problems. It can only create more activity and exploration. A precondition to federal intervention would be a better understanding of what organizational structures and incentives could be used to improve the use of present resources and ensure that added resources will not be deployed in the same unsatisfactory way.

CONCLUDING THOUGHTS

The effect of legislative policy on teaching depends on numerous factors. Some of these are:

1. Whether the legislation is properly formulated to secure compliance from the teachers whose behavior it is intended to influence.
2. Whether legislative policy interacts with other legislative acts in ways that are mutually supportive or that are divergent and contradictory.
3. Whether the legislation impacts the internal control systems that influence teaching.
4. Whether the effects of changes in one teaching control system are offset by countervailing pressures of other internal standard operating procedures or mechanisms (at the district or state level).

The teaching policy impact of categorical programs is not uniform across classrooms and LEAs. There are some positive achievement results from Title I ESEA. Parents of handicapped children ardently support PL 94–142. Consequently, there must be some beneficial effects on teaching policy, but we are unsure of their precise nature or causes.

It is unlikely that future federal or state reforms will be similar to the expensive added structure and layers involved with vocational education or school lunch. Kirst and Garms (1980) project an increasingly competitive environment for public school funding with the probable outcome of steady state funding (increases equal to inflation but no real growth). Consequently, future teaching policy changes will stem primarily from inexpensive reforms that have not left a long-run residue or deposit—curriculum, changes in classroom teaching techniques or strategies, and an increased level of teacher effort. The themes of the 1980s should feature obtaining more from existing teaching resources and reducing the number of inconsistent objectives teachers must cope with. Almost any major problem that confronts U.S. society is attacked in part by adding an element to the school curriculum or structure—environment, sex, driver safety, and the decline of free enterprise. Moreover, mainstreaming and bilingual mandates add to the variation and multiple demands in the classroom. It is difficult to see how the teacher can meet all these societal expectations in a steady state or declining funding situation. Teachers become frustrated and see themselves as victims of an overloaded demand system.

Duke (1980) has studied school retrenchment in California and New York City. If these conditions become widespread, federal categorical programs will be endangered by the slow erosion of the teaching policy infrastructure. Cutbacks create uncertainty, job insecurity, low morale, and the exit of some teachers for other jobs. Duke documents how the 8 percent federal share through categoricals can be undermined by a decline in the 92 percent state and local base.

> As a consequence of retrenchment, the number, morale, and commitment of personnal at San Jose High dropped, and many elective and special programs were cut. The changes led to a decline in the quality of education provided by the school and a fall in student achievement. Some of the better students and those who could afford nonpublic alternatives left (Duke and Meckel, 1980, p. 676).

President Reagan's proposals for bloc grants, federal deregulation, and budget cuts would probably undercut many of the potential long-term areas of high categorical impacts discussed in this paper. For instance, deregulation and categorical budget cuts would cause many LEA's to eliminate categorically funded aides and instructional specialists. The key variables for long-term deposit of added structure, layers, procedures, and pupil classification are under attack by the "New Federalism." "Pull-out" programs under Title I would be less used because regular classroom instruction would pass federal audits. Procedures for pupil classification could be simplified and less identifiable. Indeed, the entire added layer and structural deposit of Title I or vocational education would be threatened and specialized personnel reduced. Fewer achievement tests would be required for federal evaluation purposes. There would be no requirement to buy special remedial, vocational materials, or texts in order to show federal auditors that a categorical program is in place. The requirement to group categorical target pupils for special instruction would be dropped by Reagan and have a significant impact on the instructional organization discussed above. In sum, while we have identified characteristics that promote a lasting federal categorical impact, many of these characteristics would be eliminated by the President's proposals. If his proposals are adopted, more state and local discretion will make it very difficult to identify specific federal impacts.

REFERENCES

Atkin, J. M. Judges' rulings put limits on education reform. *Stanford Campus Report*, October 29, 1980, p. 25.

Benson, C. A new view of school efficiency. In J. Guthrie (ed.), *School finance policies and practice*. Cambridge: Ballinger, 1980.

Berke, J. S., and Kirst, M. W. *Federal aid to education*. Lexington: D.C. Heath, 1972.

Blackburn, J. *The disadvantaged child: Education policy in the U.S. and Australia*. Stanford: School of Education, 1981.

California Legislative Analyst. *Administrative and pupil service personnel*. Sacramento: Author, 1980.

Carew, J. V., and Lightfoot, S. *Beyond bias: Perspectives on classrooms*. Cambridge: Harvard, 1979.

Citizen action in education. *Monograph of the Institute for Responsive Education*, 1980, 7(2).

Cohen, E., and Miller, V. Increased accountability and the organization of schools. *Program Report of the Institute for Research on Educational Finance and Governance*, May 1979 (79–A2).

Cuban, L. Durable instruction. *Education Digest*, December 1980, pp. 33–34.

Duke, D., and Meckel, A. M. The slow death of a public high school. *Phi Delta Kappan*, June 1980, *61*(10), 674–677.

Hill, P., Werchitech, J., and Williams, R. *The effects of federal education programs on school principals*. Santa Monica: Rand, 1980.

Kirp, David. *Professionalization as policy choice*. Berkeley: Graduate School of Public Policy, 1980.

Kirst, M. W. A review of legislated learning. *Administrative Science Quarterly*, December 1980, *25*(4), 705–708.

Kirst, M. W., and Garms, W. The fiscal, demographic, and political context of public school finance in the 1980's. In J. Guthrie (ed.), *School finance policies and practice*. Cambridge: Ballinger, 1980.

Kirst, M. W., and Jung, R. The utility of a longitudinal approach in assessing implementation: A thirteen year view of Title I, ESEA. *Educational Evaluation and Policy Analysis*, 1980, *3*(5), 17–34.

Meyer, J. W. The impact of the centralization of education funding and control in state and local organizational governance. *Draft Report for the Institute for Research on Educational Finance and Governance*, 1980 (79–C5).

Meyer, J. W. Organizational factors affecting legalization in education. *Program Report for the Institute for Research on Educational Finance and Governance*, 1981 (81–B10).

Mitchell, D., et al. *The impact of collective bargaining on school management and policy*. Claremont: Claremont Graduate School, 1980.

Moore, D., and Hyde, A. *An analysis of staff development and its costs in three urban school districts*. Chicago: Designs for Change, 1980.

Moore, D. R., Hyde, A., Blair, K., and Weitzman, S. *Student classification and right to read*. Chicago: Designs for Change, 1981.

National Institute of Education. *Compensatory education services*. Washington, D.C.: Author, 1977.

Showers, B. Teachers as school decision makers. *IF Policy Notes*, 1980, *1*(3), 2.

Stake, R., and Easley, J., Jr. *Case studies in science education.* Washington, D.C.: National Science Foundation, 1978.

Thomas, C. T., and Larson, M. Education indicators and education policy. *Monograph for the Institute for Humanistic Studies,* 1976.

Timpane, Michael. *The federal interest in financing education.* Cambridge: Ballinger, 1979.

Tyack, D., Kirst, M. W., and Hansot, E. Educational reform: Retrospect and prospect. *Teachers College Record,* 1980, *81*(3).

Weick, K. Educational organizations as loosely coupled systems. *Administrative Science Quarterley,* 1976, *21*, 1–19.

Wirt, F., and Kirst, M. W. *The political and social foundations of education.* Berkeley: McCutchan, 1975.

CHAPTER 19

Courts and Teaching

William Clune

INTRODUCTION

This paper is about the effects of courts on teaching. It begins with a discussion of some difficulties in what is meant by the topic. Distinguishing courts from other agencies of government and teaching from other aspects of schooling is easier to do conceptually than in the real world of government policies affecting schools.

Then, turning to the substance, the paper divides into two broad approaches. In the first, a kind of inventory of judicial activism is taken. As to each area substantively identified—school finance, desegregation, and so on—the question is what were the idiosyncratic effects on teaching of that particular substantive goal. In other words, the question in the inventory section is not so much about the effect of courts as about the effects of the substantively specific things courts have done (the idea being, for example, that many of the effects of desegregation would occur no matter what agency of government was responsible).

The second approach is more organizational and generic. It looks *across* the substantive areas and tries to develop some generalizations about the prospects for, and dynamics of, educational reform through law.

What Do We Mean by "Courts"?

We know what we mean by courts as institutions. Although arbitrators, neighborhood courts, and other court-like mechanisms of dispute resolution may indeed have an effect on schools, clearly the interest here is on official state and federal courts whose edicts and decrees have affected the life of schools. Moreover, other topics on the agenda deal with legislation and administration, both activities of government with which the courts are involved. Is there some special province of courts distinct from these other activities of government?

The source of the difficulty is in a static vs. dynamic view of courts. In a static sense, we have been taught that there are "three branches" of government each with distinct functions; hence, it seems logical to ask what the distinct impact of the judicial branch is on schools. On the other hand, in the dynamic world of social change, courts usually are involved with the other branches of government. I would like to point out some of the complexities and ambiguities in our thinking about courts as agents of social change and then adopt a rather simple working definition for purposes of the paper. The simplicity of the definition is justified, in a sense, only to the extent that one realizes what it is a simplification of.

One common idea of the scope of a paper on courts and schools would exclude courts in their role of applying legislation or administrative rules. This would narrow attention to constitutional law (state or federal) and common law (almost all state).

School finance, desegregation, and due process litigation have been constitutionally based. Teacher and school competency litigation may be based on tort liability, a species of the common law.

There are some problems with this limited definition, however. If the notion is to isolate cases in which the courts act independently as policymakers, we would have to include those in which they have been very "adventurous" with statutes (implying private rights of action, broadening or narrowing a statutory right, etc.).[1] Moreover, where the court "gets" its law is rather an independent question from how much other branches of government are involved in the whole litigation. Litigation over a statutory right may be brought by an individual plaintiff and may terminate in a very simple, very discrete order to a school or a school district to admit a certain student, reinstate a particular employee with back pay, etc.[2] On the other hand, constitutional litigation may involve dozens of governmental entities as parties or participants and may be the overture to a panoramic governmentwide policy struggle, involving the legislature and many parts of the bureaucracy. Think of *Serrano v. Priest* and *Robinson v. Cahill*.[3] Both cases touched off a series of major legislative packages at the state level and sweeping administrative changes in state and local educational administrations. Another weakness of the statutory/constitutional distinction is that major legislative packages enacted by Congress have been stimulated by and modelled upon judicial decrees. Indeed, it would not be exaggerating to say that practically the entire federal legislative intervention in education is "civil rights" in nature. (The part that stirs up controversy anyway—there are federal interventions on a completely different model, such as loans for college students).[4]

It might be possible to take a completely different approach which ignores the constitutional/statutory distinction. We could ask, "What distinctive effects do courts as institutions have on schools, regardless of the source of the decree?" This is not an entirely barren line of inquiry. Much thought has been given to the special characteristics of courts, their limited powers of negotiation, their need for particularly clear standards, and so on.[5] Too much of such thinking is polemical, the desire to make a point distorting the authors' logic and judgment.[6] However, there certainly are salient differences between courts and legislatures as institutions.

But there are problems with this "institutional" view as well. The greatest is that what people say is wrong with courts interfering with schools really has little to do with courts. The problem is with the *law* interfering, or what Arthur Wise calls the "legalization" of schools.[7] That is, the institutional differences between legislatures and courts tend to be of rather academic interest compared to the underlying policy issue of legal intervention generally. Another problem is that courts are rather flexible institutions. When confronted with a problem that is not well suited to a "traditional" court, adaptations can be made.[8] Masters, experts, and committees are common in many types of litigation, including desegregation, special education, and school finance.[9] These adaptations make the court look more like the "political" branches of the government they are supposed to be distinguished from under the institutional approach. Finally, the involvement of many branches of government in the institutional reform type of litigation (as described above) implies that one of the distinctive functions of the court as opposed to other institutions of government is that it gets other branches of government involved with its decisions (just as they do the courts).

My solution to these difficulties is very rough and commonsensical. Rather than try to identify an analytically distinct set of judicial activities, I will simply reflect on patterns and generalities in some major areas where courts have been very active and visible. One of these characteristics is that the court almost never acts alone; and many of the other characteristics are really indications of legal intervention generally rather than legal intervention exercised specifically and exclusively through courts. I tend to think, in other words, that we can learn a great deal about legal intervention in schooling from the activities of courts and relatively little, though something, about the special effects of the judiciary as such. Perhaps the only characteristic of courts which I am prepared to accept as obviously unique is that, in some situations, they are willing to do things that other branches of government would not do.[10]

What Do We Mean by "Teaching"?

The effect of courts on teaching is an important topic. As far as education goes, it is probably the most important topic. Yet it is very difficult to know anything direct about the effect of any "outside" agent of change on teaching. This is partly because of the extreme organizational "flatness" and "loose coupling" of schools as organizations. Practically everything important happens at the "lowest" level of the organization in the hands of people with a gigantic amount of discretion and absence of supervision—classroom teachers.[11] Thus, one reason we don't know much about the effects may be that there aren't many effects to know about.

But our ignorance also exists because there is an enormous blind spot in our theoretical understanding of schools. We can see certain links between changes in the environment of schools (including the actions of courts) and changes in organizational behavior. We can classify environmental pressures according to how directly and indirectly they seem to affect teaching specifically as opposed to other facets of organizational existence (like finances, for example). But we do not have anything other than the fuzziest picture of how the activity of teaching acts in response to organizational changes. Not much research has been attempted which traces external change initiatives down to the rank-and-file level of organizations.[12] In the case of teaching, such research is particularly expensive and difficult.[13] Moreover, the importance of teaching presumably lies in its relationship to learning. Hence, at some level, the central question of this paper probably has to do with the effect of courts on learning. If it is difficult to specify the links between organizational change and teaching, it is at least as difficult to specify the links between teaching and learning, so that in combination, we are dealing with a blend of the mysterious with the enigmatic.

I certainly do not propose to overcome these difficulties in this paper. The approach I take is to try to relate court-initiated changes as much as I can to teaching which produces a kind of useful though indirect illumination on the subject. Otherwise, much of what can be said concerns the effect of courts on *schools* (as organizations) rather than on teaching as such. We therefore tend to see changes in the organizational framework and dynamics within which teaching occurs rather than in teaching itself. It follows that the most obvious, incontrovertible effects "on" teaching are situations in which new teaching resources are made available, rather than situations in which the conduct of existing teaching is supposed to change.[14]

PART I. AN INVENTORY OF COURT ACTIONS AND SOME RUMINATION ABOUT THE EFFECTS ON TEACHING

In this part, various kinds of judicial activism are examined with a view toward comparing their effects on teaching. The point is not so much to establish exactly what the effects were—the impossibility of that has been conceded. Yet some interesting and not very speculative thinking can be done about the kinds of effects on teaching produced by different kinds of decrees. Also, some kinds of decrees have less to do with teaching than others.

School Finance

Superficially, the effect of school finance litigation on teaching would seem to be pervasive but rather nebulous. Litigation over interdistrict inequities aims for the redistribution of resources. That has often meant the ability to maintain a broader variety of programs in poorer districts. Should we speak of this as an effect "on" teaching? Although the effect on learning is obvious, it is an effect on teaching in the sense that it changes the available curriculum. More resources may also mean more successful competition for better teachers at the entry level, although the rigidity of salary structures is a problem in that respect.[15] A significant amount of the potential educational effect of school finance litigation was drawn off into changes in taxing behavior—slightly higher taxes in wealthier districts and tax relief in poorer districts. This was partly because state legislatures controlled the spending side by such devices as "budget caps," themselves often the focus of renewed litigation.[16]

Regarding school finance litigation as exclusively "fiscal" is a mistake, however. The New Jersey court in *Robinson v. Cahill* made a conscious choice in favor of minimum educational goals rather than strict fiscal equity. Moreover, a case like *Serrano v. Priest*, which did remain pure to the cause of fiscal equity, in effect invited the education administration and legislature to worry about substantive educational change. The legislature decided to "level up" after *Serrano*, rather than "level down," so that a great deal of new state money was made available to education. Proposals for school improvement programs responded to the concern of the legislature that some worthwhile educational plans be developed for the new money.[17]

Mention of the involvement of the state legislature raises another point. I think it is clear by now that school finance litigation reinforced the long historical trend toward centralization of education in state government. This was dramatically true in California where, after Proposition 13, only the state had any extra money; but it tends to be true everywhere. In Wisconsin, for example, a school finance type lawsuit has been filed seeking to compel compliance by districts to state-mandated educational standards.[18] Poorer districts, particularly, are out of compliance. The teachers' labor union supports the standards lawsuit and ultimately would prefer to negotiate contracts with fewer and larger districts or on a statewide basis. There are those who are skeptical about a positive relationship between bureaucratic centralization and good teaching.

The relatively rare *intra*district school finance cases present quite a different picture. When Judge Skelly Wright, in *Hobson v. Hansen*,[19] redistributed "resources" from richer to poorer schools, what happened, among other things, were some rather dramatic teacher reassignments (resource teachers to "poorer" schools, for example) and changes in pupil/teacher ratios.[20] Intradistrict litigation necessarily takes a much closer look at direct educational inputs than does interdistrict litigation, although whether all of *Hobson's* strenuous efforts in the end made any difference to learning in the district has been debated.

School Desegregation

Racial integration is not primarily designed to affect teaching, but, as we all know, its effects are profound on the total school environment.

I suppose "problems" is the first thought that springs to mind about school desegregation; yet it would be neglecting the central point not to begin with the positive educational effects. School desegregation is designed to achieve a less isolated, higher quality educational experience for minority students and a multiracial educational environment for all students in a pluralistic but racially divided society. The difficulties of achieving these goals should not let us overlook that they are aspirations for better education.[21]

It seems superfluous to summarize the effects on education of desegregation; for, among education professionals of any sort, such things are common knowledge. Racial mixing itself produces "first generation" problems of human relationships—such as the need to reduce hostility and violence. Then there are the "second generation" problems often dealt with explicitly by courts—"resegregation" through ability tracking, discriminatory use of school discipline, the need to create effective counselling services. Finally, several courts have gotten directly into qualitative issues of "what lies at the end of the bus ride." Magnet schools with innovative curricula have been used to make integration a constructive experience. In Boston, a team of experts was used to overhaul the entire system at the secondary level. As with school finance, we see in these cases the propensity of an initially "modest" judicial goal to blossom into an effort at widespread educational reform.[22]

There is also the somewhat inscrutable debate about whether urban school desegregation causes "white flight." The judicial system hardly can disclaim all responsibility for this phenomenon, if it exists; for the Supreme Court effectively ruled out the possibility of metropolitan desegregation in *Miliken v. Bradley.*[23]

Due Process (Student Rights and Discipline)

At the most superficial level, student discipline does not seem to have anything to do with teaching, as such. Discipline has to do with whether a student is causing trouble, not whether he is learning. As we all know, this rather formalistic view is completely misleading. One of the more powerful findings of research on the learning process in the classroom shows that disruption of the educational environment is one of the most harmful effects on learning, because it detracts from the primary component of learning, time on task. Moreover, frequently disciplined students probably are not learning very well.[24]

What the effects of court decisions about school discipline on the overall discipline situation might be is entirely a different matter, because the effects are hotly debated. Under one view, the procedural requirements have merely added an annoying administrative burden, because schools must do what they must do in matters of discipline and the procedural requirements merely direct their necessary mission through new bureaucratic forms.[25] A second view is that some students, at least, avoid unjust punishments (including suspensions and expulsions) and acquire a new sense of dignity from being treated fairly, having their side of the story heard, and so forth.[26] If this were true, what would the effects on teaching be? The students who are treated more fairly would seem, in some sense, to receive a better education, perhaps even more education (they avoid being dismissed from school).[27] Part of the conclusion here rests upon difficult questions such as whether "soft" values, like dignity, greater participation, and greater sensitivity to the democratic process should be considered part of the educational product of school. There are further intangibles. Does the retention of more students in school, if that is a result of new procedures, result in greater net disorder? Does the fear of court sanctions lead to "defensive teaching and discipline" (similar to defensive medicine) and rigid bureaucratization of schools antithetical to a productive atmosphere of trust between teachers and students? What is the cost of the entire disciplinary apparatus in strictly financial terms, and what educational good may have been sacrificed to discharge this cost?

The debate over school discipline unfortunately takes place in terms of two competing ideologies, "visions" of the effects of courts on schools afforded by intuition rather than in terms of evidence or experience. One vision is of an entirely benign set of effects. The proceduralization of schools is perceived as basically making them more consistent with American democracy, thereby preparing the students to be more effective citizens in a democracy. In the place of sometimes arbitrary and always unquestionable authority, courts are seen as introducing a certain degree of student participation and rational "thinking through" of educational policies. The other "world view" is completely different. It regards court intervention in the procedures of schools as a clumsy attempt by an external control agency to interfere with the organic network of relationships in an institution whose functions and purposes have almost nothing to do with procedural niceties. Under the latter view, one of the more devastating, and most intangible, effects of court intervention is a reinforcement of the decades-long delegitimization of teaching in the public's eyes and loss of morale by teachers. Some commentators sympathetic to the first view agree that a long-term trend toward delegitimization exists, but they disagree about the role of courts in the trend. They regard court intervention primarily as the *product* of loss of confidence in schools (rather than the cause of it), and legal intervention may have the somewhat clumsy net effect of restoring some of the lost legitimacy.[28]

My own position is that this entire debate, while perceptive and sophisticated, basically is unproductive, because it is a debate about ideologies emerging from preconceptions. Much more helpful to me is some of the empirical research which has emerged about school discipline. A fairly large school discipline research project was done in Wisconsin, and the results have been written up by Ellen Jane Hollingsworth, Henry Lufler, and myself.[29] The most striking finding of that research was that most school discipline problems are educational problems in disguise. I could not begin to summarize the results in this paper. One example is this however: An enormous amount of the trouble-making was done by a small percentage of students. These students were alienated from the goals of education, such as going on to college or even progressing further in school. Similarly, a great amount of the disciplinary activity was dispensed by a rather small group of teachers. These teachers tended to have very strict conceptions of proper school behavior and poor relationships with students, even to the extent of being the objects of retaliation for disciplinary actions. Moreover, one of the schools had a situation of organizationwide negative morale about school discipline, in fact, a veritable siege mentality. The morale was completely out of proportion to the actual amount of disorder in the schools, compared to other schools with better morale. The source of the problem may have been the perception of the teachers and staff that their school in particular among the schools of the region was attended by students of working-class backgrounds. (There were virtually no racial minorities at all in the population investigated by the study). The perceptions of the teachers and staff of the working-class origins of their students also were greatly exaggerated in comparison to the objective proportions of such students in all of the schools. However, this "troubled school" was the only school in the district with a slight majority of working-class students, and it lacked the concentration of upper-middle-class, college-bound students whose extremely high motivations toward the educational system served as a reward for teachers in other schools.

The significance and causes of these complex factual patterns can be elaborated and debated. The only point that I would make here I think is abundantly clear from even this sketchy presentation: the possible remedies for such patterns are not legalistic or procedural in nature. They might, for example, concern changing the relationship of certain groups of students and teachers and sometimes the relationship of the entire student body to its teachers and administrators through some kind of "organizational therapy." Compliance with constitutional decrees was spotty in these schools, at best; and there was generally poor knowledge on the part of teachers and students of even the simplest legal mandates. Assuming that such compliance as there was may have been positive in its effect rather than negative, it still seems from this research that procedural requirements, no matter how good, are simply not very relevant to the underlying sources of "the discipline problem." The primary effects on teaching which might be desired from organized intervention in school discipline probably would be reduction of disorder, restoration of mutual respect and trust, and return of many students to a positive relationship with school rather than a trouble-making one. Procedural requirements may be a good in themselves, but we should realize the limited nature of this claim.[30]

Special Education

Special education presents us with a sort of schizophrenic picture in terms of its effect on teaching. On the one hand, the entire purpose of the lawsuits in various places was to make available teaching services where none existed before or to change the nature of the experiences.[31] In that respect, there could not be much of a more direct or greater effect on teaching. On the other hand, the efforts were directed toward a very small percentage of students, even if the potential clientele of special education, using vague and expansive diagnostic categories, could reach as high as thirty percent of the student population.[32]

The bridge between the small group of directly affected students and the larger groups of unaffected students is mainstreaming.[33] Mainstreaming has the effect in many places of requiring the traditional classroom teacher, often unprepared and untrained for new specialized duties, to take on the teaching mission for special students. In that way, the atmosphere and process of many classrooms was changed, although in what direction, for educational good or ill, is once again unfortunately difficult to determine. It is clear that the capacity of regular classroom teachers was upgraded in many places by means of such devices as teacher aides and resource centers.

Special education placed an extraordinary burden on one class of school employees, school psychologists, and others of interdisciplinary teams responsible for generating the vast amounts of paperwork and procedures required by the decrees (Individual Educational Plans, etc.). If one had to guess about the effect of these administrative burdens on teaching, one would hesitatingly come down on in the same way as school discipline. The extra work probably came out of the hide of school personnel without affecting teaching very much. Some commentators are extremely enthusiastic about the effects of IEP's on the quality of education, believing that such individualized planning is the key to educational reform generally.[34] Other commentators concede the possibility of a marginal improvement but believe that the administrative effort is mostly a waste of time.

For certain students, the special education litigation definitely amounted to a revolution in the availability of teaching services. They obtained services which were completely unavailable before. The effect of the procedural entitlements, the right to parent veto, the right to a hearing and appeal, and so on, are, as with any procedural entitlement, necessarily not very clear. We can tell that parents as a class acquired more power to determine educational placements, although their power is enormously diminished compared to the theoretical appearances because of the manifold pressures to follow the advice and direction of school personnel.[35] There is an analogy here to the sense of dignity supposedly produced by the right of a hearing in school disciplinary cases. The parents, in special education matters, may have an enhanced sense of efficacy and dignity. Schools may, in effect, pay for some of that parental gain by an increased amount of botheration and paperwork. Whether the substantive placements of children ultimately are better or worse is not known. One eccentric fact is that parents frequently veto mainstreaming, preferring the shelter of more restrictive environments.[36] This is contrary to the spirit of the reforms, but is it educationally bad? The net parental contribution comes down, as in the school discipline cases, to a kind of ideological intuition. To the extent that they actually make different decisions, are parents better, on the average, at making marginal judgments about the placements of their students, or do they, on the average, detract from the professionally competent decisions of school personnel with largely emotional and uninformed perspectives? Once again, we see lurking in the background that enigmatic social fact—the feeling of trust or mistrust about the competence and good faith of school professionals.

Special education litigation also won increased resources for some school systems. As in school finance cases, the increased resources were made available as new money by state legislatures or school districts. To this extent, litigation, although technically directed against the school system, can, in the end, bring in new resources.

Bilingual Education

Bilingual education presents as complicated a picture, in terms of the effects of courts on schooling, as any of the areas. If we begin from the Supreme Court case of *Lau v. Nichols*,[37] the picture presented is one of an excluded minority of students. The large number of students in the United States who do not speak any English presents an obvious problem for the educational system; any solution makes immense demands on educational resources. *Lau v. Nichols* represents the federal judiciary telling schools (via an act of Congress),[38] or really the governments of the states, that they may not choose to ignore the problem. Some educational resources, and some educational planning, must be directed toward change. Although those kinds of requirements can seem to be an unbearable burden on an already overstrained educational budget, it is hard to resist the conclusion that a requirement to teach non-English-speaking students, rather than ignore them, is a positive influence on teaching. Moreover, here again, the education system may require some new resources from the taxpayers (or in the form of reductions in other governmental functions). The magnitude of the effects on schools in this particular area can be quite large. In some school systems a substantial fraction of students are affected by bilingual policies.

Once past this initial reasonably clear point, bilingual education becomes a classic example of how implementation of a central idea of educational reform becomes entangled in a morass of competing educational philosophies, bureaucratic and traditional politics. Bilingual education is a good example of this process, but the same generalization could have been illustrated from almost any of the other areas. Change initiated by courts eventually enters the political and administrative system and becomes subject to the tremendously multiplicitous pulling and tugging of our political system.

The educational knowledge base for coherent bilingual educational policy is not good. (At least as far as I can tell). All the basic questions of how much native language instruction, how long it should continue, what subjects it should cover, and what kind of teachers should teach it are the subjects of intense and, at the moment, rather obscure educational debate.[39] Compounding the difficulty, there is a political dimension laid on top of the educational ambiguity. On the one hand, school systems are not anxious to undertake onerous financial burdens. Moreover, the special needs of minority students clearly are assigned a low priority, to put the matter somewhat delicately, by some members of the majoritarian legislative process. Finally, there is the matter of bureaucratic politics and self-interest. There is some indication that the best bilingual teachers may be fluent native speakers who are quickly trained in the basic elements of effective teaching, after having been carefully screened to identify ability and motivation. Accept this as true for the sake of argument. It is clear that most school systems are not in a position to take advantage of a resource such as this one, because to do so would jeopardize the positions of tenured teachers who would be eligible for the bilingual teaching positions. These teachers are not necessarily or even usually incompetant. Some training in the foreign language may put them in a position to do a credible job. But if they are marginally less effective than previously uncertified native language speakers, or even greatly less effective, it is clear that the basic labor welfare interests involved would overwhelm the educational goals.[40]

Of course, political forces do not emanate unidirectionally from the government and schools alone. The non-English-speaking communities themselves are interested in the nature and extent of bilingual education from a purely political perspective. Separatist elements may perceive in native language instruction a virtue all out of proportion to educational goals less politically conceived. Likewise, the issue of jobs for native language speakers from the community has an obvious and powerful political aspect.

The recent initiative of the Reagan Administration in the decade-long educational political struggle, we can say without taking sides on the underlying liberal-conservative disagreement, is an example of how an educational issue, having become complicated and politically entangled, may eventually be resolved by purely political considerations.[41]

Church and State

The emphasis so far has been on relatively recent examples of judicial activism, generally of the civil rights variety. I thought it would be interesting to include one example of judicial impact on schools whose essential outlines were established some time ago. To some extent, church-state cases are analogous to the more recent civil rights cases, because some of the most important were brought by children and families seeking religious freedom from oppressive sectarian forces in the schools.[42] However, to some extent these cases represent quite a different kind of constitutional theory. The establishment clause of the First Amendment does not require that an identifiable individual liberty or right be identified. The federal courts become involved through taxpayers' suits in regulating the general cultural relationship of the public schools to sectarian influences.[43] The significance of these cases on teaching has largely faded into the background because the fundamental constitutional principles by now seem axiomatic. However, it can be argued that the effect of these decisions on public school teaching is profound; and I would like to sketch in the nature of that argument in this section.[44]

I do not wish to discuss here the prohibition on school prayers, religious ceremonies, or the teaching of doctrines specific to one or another faith. These are politically controversial matters, of course; but their effect on teaching is indirect, and the conclusions seem unavoidable in constitutional terms. Nor do I wish to discuss the issue of aid to private schools, including sectarian schools which, in its own way, has the most profound effects on the nature and kind of teaching which goes on aggregatively in this country. The issue which seems most directly relevant to this paper is the role of church-state doctrine in shaping and confining the approach taken by public schools in the teaching of values.

Public schools presumably may not teach moral and spiritual values to children on the basis of authoritative religious tradition.[45] They may teach courses like "values clarification" in which the moral dimensions of situations are discussed. They may teach comparative religion courses in which the approaches taken by great religious traditions to various moral problems are evaluated. But the teaching of a particular system of values, even divorced from a specific religious context, would at least be controversial in terms of the First Amendment. For one thing, it would be difficult to stake out any position on a great variety of moral and ethical issues without referring at least to the basic Judeo-Christian tradition which is the substratum of the "secular morality" of the United States. The inevitable consequence, it seems to me, is that values must be portrayed as private and subjective.[46] The school brings together information, but it does not take a position.

There are those who make a powerful virtue of this condition, of course. The subjective, experimental tradition of discovering moral values, in the tradition of John Dewey, is a time-honored one in this country, having its roots in the philosophy of American pragmatism. At the same time, it must be noted that the attractiveness of a wide variety of educational experiences offered by private schools at the present time is precisely that these schools communicate a coherent orientation toward the world of ethics and morality. We know from psychological studies that children can thrive under a system in which idealism and a sense of purpose are communicated without being subjected to the doctrinaire or coercive (some would think this a contradiction in terms, of course).[47]

In other words, the constitutional cases on church-state relations amount, as far as the schools are concerned, to a fundamental but always problematic American solution to the problem of pluralistic values. It is clear enough that, among adults, all religions and systems of values must be allowed to compete without the state taking sides. (Actually, even this apparently innocuous proposition becomes very complicated when examined closely).[48] However, there is a necessary paradox in the case of children, for children are supposed to be.imbued and socialized into the very values which they will have the political freedom to espouse as adults. The idea that the public schools should be neutral, some would even say indifferent, in this period of acquiring moral perspectives is not obviously the best educational solution. I sometimes wonder if being compelled to be a moral agnostic in times of immense ethical upheaval is not as great a strain as any put on the public school teacher.

Teacher Competency

Potentially speaking, lawsuits seeking damages for incompetent teaching could have the most profound consequences on teaching of any of the subjects we have examined so far. They concern, after all, the heart of teaching itself, the success of education for the individual student. In point of fact, however, the example is included to remind us of precisely the opposite conclusion—that the legal system can confront a situation in which it is almost totally incapable of producing any change at all.[49]

Around the edges, the legal system may have a role. A school system may slip up in such an obvious and harmful way that a court can intervene. To this extent, court suits against grossly incompetent teaching or pupil assignments may play a role in deterring gross abuses. However, if we are interested in the potential of the court for improving teaching across the board by means of lawsuits, we find that the impenetrable obscurity of the "education production function" translates directly into judicial incapacity to formulate meaningful standards. If good teaching is required, what is the standard? Do we mean average or minimally competent teaching? Do we mean the specific kinds of teaching which would benefit the individual child, or do we mean teaching in accordance with generally acceptable standards of the profession? Assuming that we can agree on a standard, how do we prove a causal relationship between the failure to meet the standard and the educational outcome for the child? (This is the genuinely impossible problem). Assuming that there was negligence and a causal relationship between the negligence and the harm, what if the child or the child's parents were also partly responsible for the educational result? Would this be contributory negligence? Finally, what about the question of damages? What is the money value of that portion of a child's educational deficiency attributable to subpar teacher performance?

Singly these questions are very difficult, involving complexity upon complexity; collectively, they are overwhelming. Yet they are nothing more than the basic elements of a simple tort lawsuit. The difficulties spring from our ignorance about the educational process. If I throw a rock through a window, the impropriety of the conduct, the causal relationship, and the damages are all easy to calculate. If I bore my students, the idea of a lawsuit for damages seems preposterous (especially to me). The event perhaps most feared by teachers, that they would be repeatedly sued for educational malpractice, is impossible because ultimately the law is realistic. If we do not know enough to tell teachers how to teach, we cannot sue them for not doing it.

Summary of Part I

The preceding discussion covered a variety of substantive areas and made a variety of points within areas. Is there anything short of repetition that can be said by way of summary? A general question which lies barely beneath the surface of the topic "courts and teaching" is whether the courts have made a big or small difference to teaching. Based on the preceding discussion, I would say that the answer is "big" and offer the following particular points as a summation:

1. Courts have acted where other agencies of government would not, especially on behalf of minority rights.
2. Courts have been involved with very large redistributions of resources, as in the cases of desegregation, school finance, and special education.
3. Courts have reached deeply into the inner workings of schools, as in the education-improvement plans which accompanied school finance reform, the "second and third generation" remedies of school desegregation, mainstreaming, bilingual education, school discipline, and church and state.

Paradoxically, it is also possible to say that the courts have not become directly involved in trying to change or improve teaching (as they would under an aggressive regime of educational malpractice or, to mention a subject not discussed, aggressive First Amendment protection of teachers' discretion[50]).

PART II. SOME GENERALIZATIONS ABOUT THE RELATIONSHIP OF JUDICIAL REFORM AND EDUCATIONAL CHANGE

This part of the paper attempts briefly to identify some useful generalizations which can be distilled from the substantive discussion of the first part of the paper and from other sources. As mentioned earlier, the emphasis here is really upon the relationship between legal directives and educational change or, as Paul Berman calls it, between legalization and reform,[51] rather than specifically between judicial decrees and educational reform. There are, however, certain respects in which the unique nature of the judicial institution becomes relevant. Some of the stress upon the necessity for exact standards, for example, is especially true of the judicial institution and less so of the legislative. My approach here will be to offer a series of four propositions, using examples for each. Each proposition is stated in the form of a "paradox." The general reason for using the paradoxical statement is to indicate both the capacities of and the limits on organizational change through law. We are speaking here, in other words, of four paradoxes of the relationship between teaching and the courts.

Proposition One: *The initial success of a judicially mandated change depends upon clear standards of compliance. That demands avoiding the educational mission; yet ultimate success depends upon involving the educational mission.*

In the field of jurisprudence, it is said that, in order for a judicial decree to be enforceable, the standards involved must be clear and manageable.[52] There is a good bit of common sense and organizational learning built into this ancient rule. If a court orders an organization to deliver a "good education," the organization probably will not do anything different than it was doing before. If a court orders a school district to transfer $200 per pupil from school Y to school X, something probably can be done after the matter of resource allocation is looked into a little more carefully. If a court tells a correctional system to give the prisoners a more humane environment, little may occur. If the habitability of the environment is expressed in terms of so many square feet of living space and so many prisoners per shower, the area of disagreement and confusion is greatly narrowed.[53]

It is a hallmark of successful school litigation that the cases have begun with clear standards. School finance operated with a notion of fiscal equity defined in terms of assessed value per pupil of taxable wealth. Desegregation plans commonly operate with numerical definitions of single-race schools. Decrees about special education specify the type of individual education plan which must be developed for each child, establish detailed procedural entitlements, and try to specify what the presumption of mainstreaming means (although in this last case, the intrinsic vagueness of the presumption may lead to meaninglessness in practice).

Nothing probably would have been accomplished had the courts tried to skip this initial phase of enunciating clear standards. Yet, without exception, lawsuits eventually gravitate toward the essential educational questions. The clear standards do not really define an educational end state which is satisfactory even to the plaintiffs. This is undoubtedly because education is essentially a personal and unstructured process. Standards which might be adequate in a correctional system, such as amount of space and number of sanitary facilities, cannot be replicated when the ultimate objective is human learning.

School finance litigation probably achieved more than any other category on the strength of its clear standards. Desperately poor districts presumably can be made much better off with the infusion of new funds. Yet the substantive educational issues were lurking in the background even in the school finance area. There was the issue already mentioned of what use to put the new money. But consider even a relatively technical issue like how much money each district should get. It has become apparent that one of the key pieces of missing information is the costliness of education from district to district. We need to know, for example, which districts have an easier and harder time attracting the most qualified teachers. In order to know this, we must develop objective definitions of better-qualified teachers. Jay Chambers, at the Institute for Finance and Governance, has been working on objective measures of the relative cost of education in different places, thereby giving us a more intelligent basis for allocating dollars among the districts.[54]

Similarly, individual education plans, mainstreaming, and procedural rights all have come under a great deal of criticism, constructive and otherwise, directed at the educational result which these clear legal rights were intended to achieve. Desegregation was a painful historical learning experience in this regard. Discovering that many schools had recapitulated segregation within their own walls might have been expected from a general knowledge of race relations, but it was a grave disappointment to early desegregation litigators. The uncertain relationship of procedural disciplinary reform to underlying educational practices has already been explored.

What emerges is a model of educational reform under which the court is a change-initiator, starting the process of change by means of a clear and orderly definition of rights and responsibilities. The educational system is too complicated and fluid for these definitions to remain exclusive for very long, however. Adaptations must be made to the underlying educational mission, if the reform is to make progress. The methods by which further progress is made have been variously referred to as adaptation, experimentation, learning, and the acquisition of knowledge.

One should not underestimate the importance of the initial court action in this system of continuous change merely because clear standards in the end prove to be incomplete. Something must get the system going, and the plaintiffs in judicial actions against the schools not infrequently are groups who have not found satisfaction through other means. School systems themselves are not infrequently captured by the inflexibility of their historically acquired attitudes and routines. However, the fact that clear judicial standards must yield in the end to educational policymaking implies what is the fact, that many other kinds of decision makers and participants must in the end become active in the process of reform in order for it to succeed.

Proposition Two: *In every instance of judicially inspired change (of the "civil rights" variety), there is a problem of recalcitrance to be overcome; yet the ultimate success of the change requires cooperation of those subject to judicial action.*

The idea of the court as an initiator of change, overcoming historical resistance or inertia, corresponds again with a demonstrable fact that in most litigation the court must initially spend some of its time and perhaps a great deal of its energy overcoming a certain amount of recalcitrance. One of the genuinely unusual things about courts is that they are well suited to represent minority groups who cannot succeed in the political process yet contain enough sheer clout to get a large and very strong political and bureaucratic system moving in the direction of solving a problem.

The coercive relationship, like the clear standards, is not constructive indefinitely or for very long, however. Because educational policy matters must soon be addressed, the cooperation of policymakers and educators must be obtained fairly quickly. Thus, there are distinct periods in the relationship of a court with school systems, a time when various techniques for overcoming recalcitrance are employed, and a later time when cooperative and experimental techniques are developed. Actually, depending upon the particular type of litigation we are talking about, there may be waves of recalcitrance and cooperation rather than distinct sequential stages.

Desegregation litigation, as described, for example, in David Kirp's article, "Judge and Company," seems to follow the two-stage sequential mode.[55] In the beginning, judges employ a variety of techniques to overcome recalcitrance. One of the more interesting aspects of desegregation litigation is the skill, intelligence, and tenacity of federal judges in overcoming these formidable problems. The judge in Milwaukee seemed to use a special master as a sort of "stalking horse," who vigorously criticized the school board, defused the political resistance, and, having served his purpose, was dismissed.[56] Another judge brought the defendants into the courtroom and said simply, "What are we going to do to solve this problem?"[57] In Boston, a more protracted period of resistance and recalcitrance was involved; but, eventually, some positive developments were obtained especially through the use of educational innovations.[58] The cooperative phase of school desegregation involves the judge's seeking advice from experts and educators about how to make the change successful. Instead of confrontation, the typical modes of interaction are mediation, negotiation, planning, troubleshooting, and so on.

The model of waves of recalcitrance and cooperation seems more apt in school finance litigation. The initial time at which the legislature is told it must equalize on a statewide basis is a dramatic moment. The financial stakes are high, and the political struggle among districts is intense. There is always doubt that the legislature will comply. In New Jersey, the Supreme Court was required to go to the ultimate extent of ordering schools to close before the legislature would act.[59] In both California and New Jersey, however, the initial moment of intense crisis was followed by a series of confrontations of court and legislature over details of the legislation. In effect, the legislature had to be coaxed through a series of constitutionally inadequate compromises to the political order toward a fully acceptable plan. As in desegregation, the political actors drawn into this process come from an immensely broad spectrum of the political order, immensely broad even by comparison to the extraordinarily wide representation of parties in the litigation itself.[60]

Proposition Three: *Judicial action in education is designed to benefit children or families; yet desired change ultimately must be executed by complex organizations such as schools, school districts, or state legislatures. This means that the rights of children and families must be judicially transformed into new organizational behaviors. This dependence of legal rights upon organizational change creates intricate, baffling, and sometimes impossible difficulties for the realization of rights.*

The central and simplest insight of the theory of implementation of legal rights in complex organizations is that any legal right must be transformed into organizational change. The rights to an effective education or to special services or to bilingual education are not like monetary judgments, capable of being reduced or liquidated into a fungible medium of exchange. Such rights must be delivered in the form of a long-term relationship between complex organizations and the grievants.

In practice, this simple fact means that the immense domain of organizational dynamics and politics almost always intervenes between plaintiffs and the obtaining of educational reform through law. The most common examples are what sociologists call "goal displacements," sometimes described colloquially as "paper compliance" and familiar to almost anyone who has ever lived in an organization. Formal compliance is the chief concern in the area of due process and student rights. It has often been pointed out that a short and informal hearing does not necessarily change the substantive result of a disciplinary initiative. Paper compliance only scratches the surface of the myriad of ways that organizational dynamics interact with legal change, however. This paper has already discussed the obstacles which the welfare interests of teachers may place in the way of rapid reform of bilingual education; but the welfare of the employees of organizations, any organization, stands generally in the way of any rapid change.[61]

Another example of organizational dynamics is this: explicitly political limits on the capacity of organizational change. It appears that the elaborate structure established by the legislature in New Jersey for the purpose of guaranteeing a thorough and efficient education was substantially impeded by the unwillingness of the Commissioner of Education to exercise the broad powers given him under the legislation to revamp and revitalize underperforming schools and school districts.[62] This is a familiar pattern. The administrative agency charged with executing a judicial decree is subject to a different blend of influences from the total political system than the blend of influences confronted by the judiciary in the litigation. Partisan plaintiffs always have more power in the litigation, for example. This pattern has resulted in lawsuits at the federal level (of the *Adams v. Richardson* variety) whose purpose it is to compel the agencies to pursue more vigorously their legislative mandate.[63] Such lawsuits are not a magic remedy, however. Often, they merely recapitulate the sticky and frustrating relationship of courts to complex bureaucracies and legislatures common in the remedial stage of many types of litigation, such as desegregation and school finance.[64]

The interaction of legal initiatives with organizational dynamics is well illustrated by some of the findings of the Kirp, Kuriloff, and Buss study of the impact of the *P.A.R.C.* decree in Pennsylvania. The *P.A.R.C.* decree seemed to produce substantial change in almost every area of its requirements (unless the requirement was one which was being met before the decree anyway). However, there were distinct patterns of greater and lesser compliance.[65]

High compliance was present under the following conditions: (a) *Clear standards and high visibility of noncompliance.* The decree required some facilities for the severely retarded and the creation of written plans for individualized instruction. Because noncompliance with these requirements is easily detected, they were strongly complied with, at least formally. (b) *Effective representation at the grassroots (implementation) level.* Provisions creating procedural entitlements for parents were complied with because noncompliance would trigger complaints from the parents. (c) *Conformity with traditional functions.* School personnel complied most readily when the decree made demands consistent with the traditional roles of the personnel. School psychologists, for example, cooperated most thoroughly with new demands for pupil *assessment*, less so with demands for mainstreaming consultation, and least with special education consultation (helping with the teaching function).

Lower compliance was present in the inverse of the high-compliance situations and when compliance would be very costly. For example, school psychologists did relatively less in the areas of program evaluation and obtaining auxiliary, remedial services. These are requirements combining low visibility, little grassroots representation, and untraditional functions.

The lowest amount of compliance was with the requirement that plans and placements be reviewed every two years (instead of every three, as was the custom). Special education advocates involved in the lawsuit regarded the two-year review as very important—not a formality but a key ingredient of effective education for special children whose needs often shift dramatically in a short period of time. Yet the requirement was honored in the breach. A combination of factors apparently was responsible: (a) The two-year requirement was the single most time-consuming and costly obligation imposed on school personnel. (b) School psychologists already were pushed to the limit of their time and capacity by other requirements having greater, practical "clout." (c) The two-year requirement was a departure from the traditional practice which school personnel were comfortable with and believed in. (d) Absence of two-year review did not occasion a grassroots outcry. Perhaps the increased willingness of the system to accommodate parents absorbed potential objections in this respect.

Proposition Four: *Although in education the evaluation of legal intervention tends to be framed in terms of the relative success of the grieving parties as compared to the direct costs imposed upon schools, many of the crucial effects are external to the primary "transaction" of litigation; and these effects are probably unknowable at the margins required to make intelligent decisions.*

Conventional analysis of the costs and benefits of legal intervention in organizational life, such as found in the Supreme Court opinion in the case of *Mathews v. Eldridge*,[66] weighs the gains made by people in the position of the plaintiffs against the cost to the institution of the particular kind of intervention. This type of analysis is particularly characteristic of the procedural due process cases. Hence, we can use school discipline as a good example.

The conventional analysis looks at the possible gains to students accused of disciplinary violations in the following ways: How serious is the effect of the particular disciplinary action on students (how significant a loss is a three-day suspension, for example)? How frequently do errors in determinations of violations occur? (How prone are disciplinarians to making erroneous snap judgments, for example? Some justices believe that, since school personnel have the best interests of the children at heart, errors are quite unlikely.) The costs of proceduralism on the institution are analyzed both in terms of "hard values," such as money and staff time, and "soft" values, such as the disruption of the traditional atmosphere of trust and cooperation in schools.

There is nothing particularly wrong with this conventional analysis, although it is extremely indeterminant. (It is full of empirical guesswork, and the court does not explain how to weigh the different costs and benefits against each other).[67] I would like to point out here, however, that important considerations exist entirely outside the conventional analysis. Since these considerations are quite important but are simultaneously troubling and extremely difficult to evaluate, the already difficult evaluative process in these matters seems to become almost impossible.

A sense for the dimensions of the difficulty can be gained by considering some of the more common considerations stated in propositional or argumentative form:

1. Legal intervention contributes to the long-run decline in the sense of legitimacy of the public schools and of public school teaching as an occupation. In this sense, it is demoralizing. However, the alternative to legal intervention might be worse, because lack of trust and legitimacy preceded the litigation; and to deny all access to change would lessen legitimacy even more.

2. Law reform efforts have a cumulative impact. In other words, it is not possible to evaluate the effect of any single legal program in isolation. Every legal initiative is the nth program to be encountered by the organization. Some critics believe that the cumulative weight of interventions is causing schools to reach the breaking point.[68] Others take an opposite, and rather startling, view. They think that, as legal interventions accumulate, organizations acquire increased capacity to deal with them.[69] Unfortunately, the capacity to deal may be limited to those districts large enough and wealthy enough to create and maintain a special administrative office.

3. Any regime of legal interventions is believed by some to be inevitably concomitant with a change in social relationships and social atmosphere in the direction of greater coerciveness, greater manipulativeness, excessive rationality, fear of sanctions, and loss of self-confidence and self-esteem.[70] At this point, we pass beyond even the cumulative impact of several programs, considered in some concrete sense, and venture into considerations of law as a kind of culture. In spite of the vagueness, however, I'm sure that most people can accept such changes as at least mildly plausible and extremely unpleasant. They are particularly disturbing to contemplate in the context of the schooling of children.

CONCLUSION

One generalization from the above which seems important, though perhaps obvious, is the validity of what is sometimes called the "law and society approach" or the "sociolegal approach" to the analysis of law. This approach denies the usefulness of analyzing the law as doctrine in the abstract (except for technical legal argumentation). Instead, the impact of law must be followed deeply down the line of causation into the affairs of affected people and organizations. The usefulness of law must be tested against the realities of actual human life. The impacts of law are tightly enmeshed in and sometimes indistinguishable from politics and the processes of organizational existence.

The second conclusion is a presumption against simplistic analysis. Change through law does not involve coercion vs. cooperation but, rather, both coercion and cooperation—under different circumstances and at different stages of the process of change. Reform is not "rights" vs. organizational change but one, painfully, by means of the other. Cost-benefit analysis of legal interventions must go beyond even the intangible values, such as human dignity, which are internal to the transaction of the litigation. Spillover, such as the effect of the compliance mentality on organic, autonomous institutions, must be recognized if not expertly weighed.

NOTES

1. *See* Cannon v. University of Chicago, 99 S. Ct. 1946 (May 14, 1979), allowing a private right of action under Title IX of the Education Amendments of 1972. Although the courts in such cases technically look for legislative intent, there is much room in the "test" for considerations of policy.
2. *See, e.g.*, Ginsberg v. Burlington Indus., Inc., 24 EPD 31, 346 (SDNY, Oct. 28, 1980), awarding back pay to a discharged salesperson under the Age Discrimination in Employment Act but declining reinstatement in view of employer's doubts about the employee's competence and bitterness.
3. *See generally*, Clune with Lindquist, *Serrano and Robinson: Studies in the Implementation of Fiscal Equity and Effective Education in State Public Law Litigation*, in *Schools and the Courts* (P. Piele, ed., 1979) (hereinafter cited as *Fiscal Equity*).
4. *See generally*, M. Timpane, *The Federal Interest in Financing Schooling* (1978).
5. A. Bickel, *The Least Dangerous Branch* (1962).
6. D. Horowitz, *The Courts and Social Policy* (1977).
7. A. Wise, *Legislated Learning* 118–85 (1979).
8. Chayes, *The Role of the Judge in Public Law Litigation*, 89 *Harv. L. Rev.* 1281 (1976).
9. *See generally*, Kirp and Babcock, *Judge and Company: Court-Appointed Masters, School Desegregation, and Institutional Reform*, 32 *Ala L. Rev.* 313 (1981).
10. On the counter-majoritarian function of federal courts, see J. Ely, *Democracy and Distrust* (1980); L. Tribe, *Am. Const'l Law* (1978) § §1–7, 3–6.
11. Glassman, *Persistence and Loose Coupling in Living Systems*, 18 *Behav. Sci.* 83 (1973); Weick, *Educational Organizations as Loosely Coupled Systems*, 21 *Ad. Sci. Q.* 1 (1976); Meyer and Rowan, *Institutional Organizations: Formal Structure as Myth and Ceremony*, 83 *Am. J. of Soc.* 340 (1900).
12. An example in education is J. Murphy, *State Education Agencies and Discretionary Funds* (1974).
13. The activity of principals supervising, or not supervising, the quality of teaching is observable as a link between external initiatives and changes in teaching. *See, e.g.*, Sproull, *Managing Educational Programs: A Micro-Behavioral Analysis* (unpublished paper, 1979).
14. The resources may come ultimately from taxpayers or noneducational governmental functions. If they come from other students, in one sense the effect on teaching is a wash; in a different sense, there is a twofold effect. "Mainstreaming" in special education presents a painfully concrete case of the zero-sum redistributive problem. One of the complaints against mainstreaming is that handicapped children disrupt regular classrooms or take in-

ordinate amounts of teacher time away from nonhandicapped students. *Harvard Note*, note 36 *infra*, at 1122–24.

15. Jay Chambers, of the Institute for Educational Finance and Governance at Stanford University, has developed the hedonic wage technique of estimating school personnel costs. Better teachers go not merely to places with higher salaries, but to places with other desirable characteristics, such as low crime rates, a low cost of living, and superior cultural attractions. Under the hedonic wage technique, what school districts consider to *be* a better teacher and what teachers consider better places, as well as how much each "betterness factor" counts relative to others, are estimated statistically from market behaviors (that is, from where teachers with different characteristics go, how much they are paid, etc). Chambers, *The Hedonic Wage Technique as a Tool for Estimating the Cost of School Personnel*, 6 *J. of Educ. Finance* (No. 3, Winter 1981); Chambers, *The Development of a Cost of Education Index*, 5 *J. of Educ. Finance* (No. 3, Winter 1980).

16. See *Fiscal Equity*, note 3 *supra*, at 80, 97.

17. Such plans were not in any way required by the *Serrano* case.

18. Kukor v. Thompson, (pending, Circuit Court, Dane County, Wisconsin).

19. 327 F. Supp. 844 (1971).

20. D. Horowitz, *The Courts and Social Policy* 146–170 (1977).

21. What goals desegregation logically may be expected to achieve is debatable. Yudof, *Equal Educational Opportunity and the Courts*, 5 *Tex. L. Rev.* 411 (1973). Historically, however, it seems clear that when black Americans sought a racially integrated education, it was because, in their view, a racially isolated education was so inferior that it outweighed the certainty of prejudice in mixed schools. D. Tyack, *The One Best System* 109–25 (1975).

22. Greenblatt and McCann, *Courts, Desegregation and Education: A Look at Boston*, 1 *Schools and The Courts* 45 (P. Piele, ed., 1979); Kirp and Babcock, note 9 *supra*, at 353–55.

23. 418 U.S. 717 (1974).

24. The importance of "academic learning time" demonstrated by research, *Time to Learn* (Denham and Lieberman, eds., 1980), supports the intuitively plausible belief that learning suffers among students who are badly distracted, frightened, causing trouble, or altogether absent from school.

25. Professor Kirp considers the tension between formalistic and nonformalistic notions of due process in *Proceduralism and Bureaucracy: Due Process in the School Setting*, 28 *Stan. L. Rev.* 841, 859–76 (1976).

26. *See* Tribe, *L. Am. Const'l Law* § 10–7, for a discussion of the "instrinsic" vs. "instrumental" aspects of due process.

27. *See* note 26 *supra*.

28. Yudof, *Law Policy and Public Schools* 25–26, review of Wise, *Legislated Learning* (unpublished paper).

29. E. Hollingsworth, H. Lufler and W. Clune, *Go to the Office! Discipline in the School Setting* (unpublished book manuscript).

30. The purpose of hearings could be narrowly defined as "whatever improvement in accuracy of determinations or sense of justice in fact occurs." The almost tautological and certainly hollow nature of such a purpose is apparent. The probable impact of due process seems slight if, as seems the case, almost all disciplinary actions already are accurate; and hearings will not reduce disorder or restore chronically bad relationships between schools and repeat offenders. The best hope for systematic change in the concept of the process is that schools are taking a significant number of erroneous, arbitrary actions which the adoption of a new procedure will eliminate. See Hollingsworth, Lufler, and Clune, *supra*, Ch. 2. Sharp declines in expulsions and suspensions have been reported following the adoption of due process regimes. It is unclear whether such declines result from elimination of erroneous disciplinary actions, change in the administrative definition of substantive offenses, or mere legal intimidation which increases the number of unpunished offences (and therefore introduces a new type of error).

31. In Pennsylvania, the outreach program ordered by the court discovered about 7,400 children who had been excluded from any educational program. Special education experts and advocates had estimated the number at least ten times as high. Kirp, Buss, and Kuriloff, *Legal Reform of Special Education: Empirical Studies and Procedural Proposals*, 62 *Calif. L. Rev.* 40, 60, 63 (1974).

32. "Handicapped children form an extraordinarily diverse group estimated to include between 8 and 35% of the entire American student population (New York Commission on the Quality, Cost and Financing of Elementary and Secondary Education, 1972)." P. Kuriloff, D. Kirp, and W. Buss, *When Handicapped Children Go to Court: Assessing the Impact of the Legal Reform of Special Education in Pennsylvania* (Final Report to the National Institute of Education, Project No. Neg.-003-0192) (hereinafter cited as *Handicapped Children*).

33. Section 612(5) (B) of PL 94–142 requires placement of handicapped children with nonhandicapped peers, to the greatest extent possible, *Developing Criteria for the Evaluation of the Least Restrictive Environment Provision* 7 (U.S. Office of Education, Bureau of Education for the Handicapped, 1978).

34. The IEP is a "procedural reform," like management by objectives and needs assessment. Whether planning procedures can produce reform without substantive guidelines is open to question. *Enforcing the Right to an "Appropriate" Education: The Education for All Handicapped Children Act of 1975*, 92 *Harv. L. Rev.* 1103, 1108–13 (hereinafter cited as *Harvard Note*). On the same debate over procedural due process in school discipline, *see* notes 27–32 *supra* and accompanying text. On PPBS in the budgetary process, *see* A. Wildavsky, *The Politics of the Budgetary Process* 181–208 (2d. ed., 1974).

35. *Harvard Note*, note 36 *supra*, 1110–11.

36. *Id.*, n. 125 and accompanying text.

37. 414 U.S. 563 (1974), codified by Congress in the Equal Educational Opportunity Act of 1974, 20 U.S.C. § 1703.

38. Section 601 of the Civil Rights Act of 1964, 42 U.S.C. § 2000d ("Title VI").

39. Mirez and Cardenas, *Cultural Democracy, Biocognitive Development and Education* (1900).

40. The importance of labor-supply factors and organized labor interference in bilingual education has been inadequately appreciated. In the Eastern United States, middle-class professionals from Cuba and Puerto Rico abounded. Such people normally speak fluent, educated Spanish, but often speak poor English. In the Southwest, finding fluent Spanish speakers qualified to teach school was the more common problem. Legal or administrative constraints on the labor market also have caused problems. The requirement that teachers have a college degree and seniority rules governing teacher assignments both screen out more qualified teachers in favor of less qualified ones. Bruce Greenlee, *Implementation of Bilingual, Bicultural Education* (student paper, 1979, on file with Professor Clune).

41. At this writing, Congress has not consolidated bilingual education into a block grant allowing the money to be spent for other purposes. However, the fiscal authorization for bilingual education has been cut more than 50%, from $175 to $85 million. Moreover, federal spending for biligual education presently is not authorized at all beyond 1983. Picking up on the more separatist themes of bilingual-biculturalism, President Reagan and his advisors apparently believe that the whole program inhibits learning English—an ironic rendition of the original *Lau* initiative, to say the least.

42. I would classify Engel v. Vitale, 370 U.S. 421 (1962), the "Regents' Prayer Case," brought by parents of schoolchildren, as a "free-exercise-type case" even though it was decided on the Establishment Clause. Application of the Free Exercise Clause was technically unclear because students were not compelled to say the short, nondenominational prayer (they could leave the classroom or stand mute). Adverse public reaction to the *Engel* case was,

and, to some extent, still is, intense. L. Manning, *The Law of Church-State Relations* 51 (West Pub. Co. "Nutshell," 1981). *See also* Abington Sch. Dist. v. Schempp, 374 U.S. 203 (1963) (Lord's Prayer and Bible reading). The best-known example of a "pure" free exercise case in the school context is the flag salute case, West Virginia State Bd. of Educ. v. Barnette, 319 U.S. 624 (1943). *Barnette* is known primarily as a free speech case, however. The somewhat eccentric Wisconsin v. Yoder, 406 U.S. 205 (1972), is, therefore, probably the technically purest case applying free exercise to education.

43. Flast v. Cohen, 392 U.S. 83 (1968). *See* L. Tribe, *Am. Const'l Law* § 14–12 (1978).

44. *See* Nowak, *The Supreme Court, the Religion Clauses and the Nationalization of Education*, 70 NW. U.L. Rev. 883 (1976).

45. The whole question of where it is legitimate for the government to "get" values is terribly confused, not just constitutionally, but philosophically and politically as well. *See* L. Tribe, *Am. Const'l Law* § § 14–12 and especially 15–10 (retracting an earlier published view that the abortion case was supportable as a religion case). Religious organizations and people are guaranteed the freedom to lobby for prohibitions of conduct on moral grounds (consider laws against murder and the 5th Commandment). As law, such prohibitions constitute "secular morality," which surely may be taught in public schools, although the underlying religious teaching may not—except as an objective political fact. Fundamentalists rightly recognize "secular humanism" as dealing with "ultimates" no less than Christianity. The confusion on this matter perhaps reached a zenith when one Wisconsin legislator introduced a bill forbidding the teaching of *any* values in public schools.

46. R. Unger, *Knowledge and Politics* (1975).

47. Hollingsworth, Lufler, and Clune, note 31 *supra*, Appendix to Ch. 2, synopsizes theories throughout history on the relationship, and tension, between children's autonomy and "order" in education.

48. *E.g.*, as in the abortion controversy. *See* Tribe, note 48 *supra*.

49. *See* Sugarman, *Accountability Through the Courts*, 82 *School Law Review* 233 (1974); Elson, *A Common Law Remedy for the Educational Harms Caused by Incompetent or Careless Teaching*, 73 NW. U.L. Rev. 641 (1978).

    Courts also become involved with teacher incompetence through judicial review of administrative actions against teachers, especially firing. Direct involvement appears to be miniscule. In the five-year period 1971–76, 57 teacher dismissals were appealed to the Pennsylvania Secretary of Education (such an appeal probably is a mandatory precondition for seeking judicial review). Of eleven cases classified as involving incompetence, closer scrutiny revealed that six involved primarily other issues (e.g., commission of a crime). Of the five remaining, two were reinstated with back pay by the Secretary. There were about 115,000 public school teachers in Pennsylvania during the period of the study. Finlayson, *Incompetence and Teacher Dismissal*, 61 *Phi Delta Kappan* 69 (September, 1979). The imponderable effect of due process decisions operating through voluntary compliance, intimidation, and "defensive discipline" may be much greater.

    See generally, in the legal literature, Gee, *Teacher Dismissal: A View from Mount Healthy*, 1980 *Brigham Young Law Review* 255 (1980); Fleming, *Teacher Dismissal for Cause, Public and Private Morality*, 7 *J. of Legal Education* 423 (1978); *Legal Issues in Teacher Evaluation* (Princeton, Educational Testing Service, 1978). In the education literature, *see* Dolgin, *Two Types of Due Process: The Role of Supervision in Teacher Dismissal Cases*, 65 *National Association of Secondary-School Principals Bulletin* 17 (1981); McDaniel and McDaniel, *How to Weed out Incompetent Teachers Without Getting Hauled into Court*, National Elementary Principals, March, 1980, at 31; Munnelly, *Dealing with Teacher Incompetence: Supervision and Evaluation in a Due Process Framework*, 50 *Contemporary Educ.* 221 (1979); Palker, *How to Deal with Incompetent Teachers*, 97 *Teacher* 42 (1980); Zirkel and Castens, *Teacher Evaluation, A Legal Memorandum* (National Association of Secondary-School Principals, December, 1978); *What Do You Know about Dismissing Incompetent Teachers?* 65 *National Association of Secondary-School Principals Bulletin* 119 (1981).

50. *See generally,* Goldstein, *The Asserted Constitutional Right of Public School Teachers to Determine What They Teach,* 124 *U. Pa. L. Rev.* 1293 (1976).

51. Unpublished paper delivered to the joint Berkeley-Stanford seminar of the Law Program of the Institute for Educational Finance and Governance.

52. See *Fiscal Equity,* note 3 *supra,* at 104–06.

53. Note, *Implementation Problems in Institutional Reform Litigation,* 91 *Harv. L. Rev.* 428, 437–38 (1977).

54. *See* Chambers, note 16 *supra.*

55. Kirp and Babcock, note 9 *supra.*

56. Kirp and Babcock, *id.* at 342–43, also entertain the possibility that the Milwaukee master's gruffness was inept.

57. *Id.* at 379–80. The quotation, or paraphrase of a quotation, is from an earlier draft of this article.

58. *See* note 24 *supra.*

59. *Fiscal Equity,* note 3 *supra,* at 95.

60. *See* generally *Fiscal Equity,* note 3 *supra.*

61. A good summary of how organization theory explains why organizations change slowly is given in Murphy, note 12 *supra,* at 13–17.

62. *Fiscal Equity,* note 3 *supra,* 102–03.

63. Adams v. Richardson, 351 F. Supp. 636 (D.C. Cir. 1972) (memorandum opinion); 356 F. Supp. 92 (D.C. Cir. 1973); *mod and aff'd per curiam,* 480 F. 2d 1159 (D.C. Cir. 1973); *suppl'd* 391 F. Supp. 269 (D.C. Cir. 1975); *suppl'd* 430 F. Supp. 118 (D.C. Cir. 1977).

    The suit continues against new secretaries, and, like the famous chicken's heart tissue, seems to have achieved perpetual life. Judicial supervision of agency discretion for failure to follow statutory mandates is, in principle, an unending task.

64. Judges often find that they must make the same kind of compromises the agency was sued for making. White, *Problems of Court Ordered Implementation of Title VI: the Adams* v. *Richardson/Califano Case* (student paper on file with Professor Clune, Fall 1979).

65. The following text is distilled from *Handicapped Children,* note 34 *supra.*

66. 424 U.S. 319 (1976); *see generally,* Buss, *Easy Cases Make Bad Law: Academic Expulsion and the Uncertain Law of Procedural Due Process,* 65 *Iowa L. Rev.* 1 (1979).

67. Mashaw, *The Supreme Court's Due Process Calculus for Administrative Adjudication in* Mathews v. Eldridge: *Three Factors in Search of a Theory of Value,* 44 *U. Chi. Rev.* 28, 46–57 (1976).

68. Wise, note 7 *supra.*

69. Galanter, *Why the Haves Come out Ahead: Speculations on the Limits of Social Change,* 9 No. 1. *Law & Soc'y Rev.* 95, 98 (Fall 1974), speculates reasonably that "repeat players" have the economic incentives to develop litigation expertise. RP's thus have low start-up costs and enjoy economies of scale. It is unclear what kind of school or school district would quality as an adjudicative or administrative "repeat player." I have heard that at least one large urban district in the Boston area involved with many federal programs found it extremely worthwhile to develop a specialized staff for processing federal grants and programs.

70. Yudof, note 30 *supra.*

CHAPTER 20

The First Real Crisis

Albert Shanker

If any term has been overused, it is "crisis in education." Every year it is dragged out to describe the failure of a school board to adopt an adequate budget or the voters' rejection of it. "Crisis" is also applied to the annual state legislative fight over state aid to education. But these are the "normal" crises in education. The outcome of each struggle in 16,000 separate school districts and 50 state legislatures will make school life somewhat better—or worse—for the next year or two. This is, of course, no small matter, but it is clearly of a different magnitude from *the* crisis which public education faces in our country today—a crisis unprecedented in our history as a nation and which will determine whether public education as we have known it will continue to exist. Let's examine some of the key elements in this crisis.

RAPID LOSS OF POWER

For many years public education enjoyed great political power simply by virtue of numbers. Throughout the 1960s and 1970s close to one-third of the American voting age population had school-age children. By 1980, the proportion of the voting age population with school-age children had declined to almost one-quarter. With continued depressed birth rates, that figure may well slip below one-quarter before the end of the decade. Between 1970 and 1979, 30 states experienced a decline in elementary school enrollment. In 12 states elementary and secondary school enrollment declined by more than 15 percent between 1970 and 1979.

When the majority of the voting population had children in school, no politician dared oppose more financial support for the schools. It was a motherhood issue. Those who wanted to be less generous in support of schools did not oppose support in and of itself but opposed money for "unnecessary frills."

But now the numbers have changed. Not only is the birth rate down (something which could change), but people are living longer (a trend likely to continue), so that the school-age population is a smaller percentage of the total.

Ideally, this shouldn't make any difference in school support. After all, we do not provide education for children in order to satisfy them or their parents. All taxpayers support schools because the contributions which educated citizens and workers will make benefit all of society—and the failure to educate some will cost all of us in the future payments of welfare benefits, food stamps, medical care for the indigent. There are, as well, the costs of combating crime, drugs, and other problems associated with the uneducated.

While we should support education whether we have our own children in school or not, the fact is that we don't. Parents with children in school, teachers, and others who work in the schools and school board members comprise a group which provides

471

active support for schools. Some other citizens do, but not in great numbers, and most who have no children in school are either neutral on the issue, or in some cases, actively hostile to spending money for a service which they see as of no direct benefit to themselves.

This loss of political power is even worse than the percentage declines would indicate, because different age groups in the population have different voting habits. Older citizens who are unlikely to have children in school are not only growing more numerous—but they have higher voting rates.

The loss of relative power need not result in dramatic losses of support. After all, in the 1960s many relatively powerless groups made major gains. But this was a period of great economic growth. Everyone was doing well, and the development of new programs for minority groups, for example, was not accomplished by taking away some benefit someone else already had. Instead, the new programs were paid for out of the increasing profits of growth. But we're in a very different economic period now.

MAJOR ECONOMIC PROBLEMS: ENERGY COSTS

There is no need to repeat the story of our energy problems, but we do have to see how the increasing cost of energy has affected and will continue to affect what is available for education. By 1980, the United States was paying about $100 billion per year to OPEC for imported oil, a price 10 times higher than it was 5 years earlier. Over a 10-year period, this amounts to $1,000 billion—a trillion dollars, a huge number but one which doesn't mean much unless it's translated in some way. Investment banker Felix Rohatyn has pointed out that the value of all the companies listed on the New York Stock Exchange is less than $1,000 billion! So, another way of looking at what we're paying for imported energy is that in 10 years we will be sending enough money to OPEC to purchase the entire productive capacity which it took us over 200 years to build!

Obviously, these increasing dollars sent to OPEC are dollars which would have been in the pockets of American citizens. Had they been able to keep them, they would have been much more generous in their willingness to finance schools and other public services than they are now.

There are and will be efforts to reduce the amount of imported oil—by developing American sources and other energy alternatives. These are important in terms of keeping money and jobs here—and energy independence is needed to prevent economic and military blackmail. But the costs of independence over the next decade or two are likely to be higher than or equal to the cost of imported oil.

ECONOMIC WOES: PRODUCTIVITY AND REINDUSTRIALIZATION

In the 1960s we financed major education and social programs out of our increased productivity. Everyone enjoyed a higher standard of living—*and* there was still enough left over for big social programs. But now our productivity is down, and major industries—automobiles, steel—are in trouble.

The productivity question is complex. There are numerous studies of the American worker and of management. There is no agreement on simple answers. But there is general agreement that a major part of the problem is that, as a nation, we have behaved very much like a car owner—or homeowner—who spends every last cent of his salary on all kinds of goodies but fails to spend anything on the usual care, maintenance, and repair of the car and the house. Eventually they are beyond repair—or the repair bill is huge. That's the way we have been behaving as a society. Our plants are old and outmoded. We don't have much of a railroad system. Half of our bridges need replacement. We are losing out to Japan and West Germany because over the years they have invested much more in research and development than we have. According to sociologist Amitai Etzioni, the United States reinvests only 10 percent of its GNP in private capital information, while West Germany and Japan reinvest 15 percent and 21 percent of theirs, respectively.

According to Etzioni, the backlog is so great (we would need over $40 billion to restore our railroads to their condition in the *1940s*) that we can't do everything we want. We can't restore our productive capacity *and* maintain decent environmental and quality of life standards *and* enjoy an increasingly higher material standard of living. We must choose. And we will choose to live on less in order to rebuild a system which, in the future, will again bring better living standards. For if we don't, we will face ever-declining standards.

ECONOMIC WOES: MILITARY COSTS

A third major increase in expenditures during the next decade or more will be in military defense costs. Both Carter and Reagan pledged this, and there is a rough national consensus on the question. Even in the midst of deep and painful budget cuts, polls show the overwhelming majority of the American people still support increased defense expenditures.

The reason may well lie in some statistics provided by Alan Baron in *The Baron Report* of August 2, 1981. "The share of the federal budget going to defense has fallen from 68 percent in 1954 to 59 percent in 1959 to 54 percent in 1964 to 51 percent in 1969 to 35 percent in 1974 to 30 percent in 1979. The share of the Gross National Product going to defense fell from 12.9 percent in 1954 to 10.1 percent in 1964 to 7.5 percent in 1974 to 6.5 percent in 1979. By 1980," says Baron, "there was simply no room for any significant further reductions in defense, even in the eyes of most liberal Democrats. The debate shifted to how much of an increase should be made."

During this period Americans may enjoy very slight increases in their living standards, or they may stand still, or they may have lower standards each year. If their living standards go down, they will have to make tough choices. They will be forced to do without some things which they once were able to afford. They will be reluctant to give up house, car, clothing, vacations, cameras, and hi-fi sets. They will still want the police to protect them and the firemen to save their lives and homes, but they may not feel so strongly about the education of the child who lives down the street. Schools will face fierce competition for scarce dollars.

DECLINE IN PUBLIC IMAGE

As if the declining political power of the schools and the scarcity of dollars were not enough, there is a third serious problem the schools face. Through much of our national history, schools and teachers were held in high regard. Most people had little education. I grew up in a working class neighborhood in New York in the 1930s. No one who lived on my block or on those nearby had ever gone to college. The few who were high school graduates were considered very well educated people—as were those who had completed elementary school. Many of my neighbors asked those with elementary school education to write letters to relatives for them—since they couldn't. In those days teachers were part of a very small educated elite—they had gone beyond high school. There was a great educational distance between the teacher and most of the members of the community and parents of children he or she taught.

That educational distance is gone forever—and with it the automatic respect which teachers were accorded. Ironically, it is the very success of our schools which has brought about this change. Teachers are no longer looked up to as having more education than those around them. More and more they live in communities in which they are surrounded by other college graduates, many with more education than the teachers. Unlike the "good old days" when parents frequently viewed the school and the teacher as the salvation of their children—the only way out of poverty or the working class—many parents now believe they could do a better job of educating their children than the teacher at school—and they would if they weren't so busy making more money at their own jobs. At any rate, an educated public, whether relatively satisfied or dissatisfied with local public schools, will be more critical and somewhat less supportive.

Since the school and teachers now lack the unquestioned support that came from a relatively uneducated public, schools must now earn support. Some of our school problems stem from the fact that many school people—school board members, administrators, teachers—do not realize that there has been a change. They act as if authority and respect automatically adhere to their positions. Or they realize they've lost it and merely bemoan the fact.

TOWARD PRIVATIZATION OF SCHOOLS: TAX CREDITS AND VOUCHERS

Any one of the problems I've outlined poses a major threat to the future of public education and could easily require a decade of painful struggle and adjustment. But at the same time, the public schools must face the possibility of tuition tax credits and/or vouchers.

Clearly, if tuition tax credits are adopted in some form, each of the problems outlined here could be further exacerbated. That is, there could be an even greater decline in the number and percentage of parents who have children in public school; the cost of tax credits could mean even more brutal competition for financial support; and if nonpublic schools, by creaming off the more achieving students, could show a better record of performance than public schools, public confidence could be further eroded.

Supporters of tuition tax credits have argued that this is not their purpose, and that their tax credit proposal will not have the effect of shifting large numbers of students from public to private schools. A mere $200, $300, or $500 tax credit, with the requirement that the family pay at least an equivalent amount, is not, they say, much of an incentive.

There is no way of telling in advance whether they are right. We do know that in everyday business small incentives can make a big difference. For some years savings banks have been offering gifts to new depositors in huge newspaper ads. The continued use of these incentives must show that they pay off.

Furthermore, it is not necessary that a huge number of students be lured out of the public schools immediately in order to forecast a dire effect. Suppose we assume that some parents, a relatively small number, will take advantage of the tax credit. Let's say that of the 90 percent who now send their children to public school, 2 percent or 3 percent would use the tax credit. (This would provide a 20–30 percent increase in nonpublic school enrollment.) Which parents would be likely to make the choice? Certainly not those from the worst conditions of poverty who could not afford the additional money. It would be those parents who could (1) afford to pay the difference between the full tuition and the tax credit and (2) get their children accepted into a private school. These are likely to be children from more affluent families who are above average in achievement.

This will not represent a mere 2 percent or 3 percent loss to the public schools; the loss would be much greater. These are the parents who are active in the PTA, who campaign for adoption of the school budget and who lobby for state and federal aid. Two or three percent of the most affluent parents provide a disproportionately large share of the parental participation and political support for public schools.

Also, the removal of those children who are achieving above average will not only lower the achievement level of the entire school; it will make the school a less attractive place for the remaining parents to keep their children. The loss of some of the "best" children the first year or two will be followed by more in each succeeding year, leaving in the public schools those who can't afford to leave, those who can't get admitted into private schools, or those who have been expelled from the nonpublic sector.

Further, the argument that several hundred dollars is not much of an incentive misses the point. What is the justification for keeping the tax credit at this amount? Once the government accepts some responsibility for paying the costs of private school, and once tuition at private schools rises as a result of this largesse, why not pay more and more of the costs? Once the door is opened, each year there will be an outcry that $300, $500, $700, $1,000 is not enough. Each year there will be more and more political pressure. At the present time, the private schools have only 10 percent of the students, yet the political influence of this single-issue constituency was strong enough to win passage of tax credits in the House and fail only narrowly in the Senate in 1978. In 1980 it succeeded in getting the Republican Party to adopt a platform plank in favor of tax credits—and it won the support of Ronald Reagan. If the 10 percent now in private schools have so much political power, what can we expect if the public school/private school balance shifts modestly from 90/10 to 80/20— doubling the private school constituency?

The argument that this several hundred dollar tax credit will not bring about a major shift in the schools misses still another point—that tax credits, once adopted by the federal government, will not stop there but will be emulated by state and local governments. Indeed, the state and local governments may actually jump the gun on Washington. In discussing whether tuition tax credits represent a threat to American public education, we should not dwell on the specifics of any one federal proposal but contemplate a future in which tax credits are offered by the states and localities as well—and the amount of the tax credit is determined each year through the same political process which now determines the amount of state aid to education and the local school board budget. It is not hard to envision the demand by nonpublic school parents that their children be funded through tax credits from all three sources— federal, state and local—in precisely the same dollar amount as are public school children. Those who support school vouchers have in fact already proposed this. So the argument that the "meagerness" of the tax credit will serve to protect the integrity of public schools simply won't hold water.

There is something disingenuous about those who argue for tax credits. If they believe that credits will have no effect, or almost none, on shifting students from public to private schools, then they are not providing parents with greater opportunities for choice. They would merely be giving billions of dollars to parents who have already made the choice and can afford it. On the other hand, if it does give many more parents the ability to choose, it will bring about a major shift away from the public schools. The argument that tuition tax credits are needed to provide choice contradicts the contention that no major threat is posed to public education.

Another frequently advanced argument for tuition tax credits is that providing parents with a choice will result in the improvement of both public and private schools through the competition that evolves. According to this view, the public schools are bureaucratic, insensitive, and ineffective because they are a government monopoly. Parents have no choice—unless they can afford to pay. Force public schools to compete for students and they will be much better—and if they can't compete, why shouldn't they disappear?

This competitive model ignores the obvious—that public schools are governed by public policy, by a body of law—and that, for the most part, private schools are not. If public schools are required to adhere to public policy and private schools are not, and if these policies are unpopular, i.e., make public schools less attractive to parents, then the competition is both unfair and unreal.

In recent years, a number of obligations have been imposed on public schools. Public schools are required to integrate students and staff. They must provide bilingual education. They must educate the handicapped, provide individualized education programs for them and integrate them into regular classrooms. Students who are disruptive or even violent cannot be suspended without due process. Even if it is determined that a given student was guilty of a crime, the student is usually returned to some public school on the ground that it's a better place than any of the alternatives. Many states, under the school finance reform movement, have ruled it unconstitutional for wealthy school districts to spend more to educate their children than districts of average wealth. Public schools must hire properly certified personnel, engage in collective bargaining, issue public reports on absenteeism, vandalism, reading, and math achievement. The list of the public schools' obligations is long indeed . . . and longer still when compared with the obligations and responsibilities of the private sector.

What meaning can competition have when the government compels schools to live with policies which are largely unpopular, exempts private schools from these same policies—and then offers tax credits to help parents take their children from schools which comply to those which do not?

If tax credits are passed, it may be that the courts will eventually decide that private schools which accept the dollars must comply with the same rules and regulations as public schools, but so far none of the tax credit supporters who argue for a system of competition has urged that this be written into the proposed laws.

TEACHING: AN IMPERILLED PROFESSION?

None of this means that *teaching* is an imperilled profession. The public schools are in jeopardy. They may cease to exist as we know them. (With tax credits or vouchers, we will still have some public schools—for there will always be those students who are too difficult or too expensive to educate. Public schools could become schools for those not accepted—or those expelled—by private schools.) But whether most children are in public or in private schools, they will still need teachers. And wherever they teach, teachers will want decent salaries, adequate working conditions, job security, and dignity—so there will be unions. What is at stake in our crisis is not jobs for teachers or the existence of their unions but whether *public* education which has served the country so well for 200 years will be dismantled.

Think of it: For most of our history as a nation, one institution has taken the diverse people who have come to our shores, educated them, and turned them into American citizens, with a common language, a shared system of political values, and with it all, a respect for the differences among us. Within a very short time as the history of nations is measured, American public schools have brought us from a country of handcrafts and vast wilderness to the most powerful, productive, scientifically advanced nation on earth, capable of exploring space. Is this uniquely American institution, with its commitment to educating all of our people, to be sacked because it has problems—or because someone has a costly political brainstorm like tuition tax credits? What will replace it? A multitude of publicly funded private schools, answerable to no one, providing no common core curriculum, teaching in a multitude of languages, accepting and rejecting students on the basis of class, of race, of religion, of ethnic background, of political ideology, dividing the people of our country instead of uniting them? Public schools provide the cement that holds nearly a quarter of a billion people together. Teachers and all other Americans have an enormous stake in seeing to it that we don't come unglued.

The odds against public education are great but not insuperable. Some of the elements of a successful struggle are clear.

1. In a period in which the numbers involved in public education are smaller, the only way to be effective is to have better political organization than in the past. Effective organization by small groups can be even more successful than merely having large numbers. But effective organization means, among other things, reducing the internal conflict within the public education community. Teachers ought to be spending all their time fighting together in behalf of public education—not fighting each other in collective bargaining battles. A merger between the National Education Association and the American Federation of Teachers would be a big plus. But a reduction of conflict among teachers, school boards, parents, and administrators is a must. The external dangers are too great—and we are in no shape to be fighting a two-front war.

Conflicts within the school community are bad for a number of reasons. First of all, they tend to turn the public off. Let's say there are protracted negotiations between a school board and the teachers' union. To win points for its side, each party puts the blame for every school problem on the other. Management says the teachers are lazy and inept, concerned only with salaries and benefits. The union says management doesn't know how to run the schools, is only interested in giving patronage jobs to its friends or in posturing before TV cameras so it can get elected next time, perhaps to a higher office. By the time it's all over—even if the negotiations are concluded without a strike—the public may well believe both sides. It may conclude that the product of this school district, education, is really bad because of the shortcomings of *both* management and labor—and it may wish a plague on both their houses. Disagreements are inevitable from time to time; sharp conflict that results in pitched battles with accusations flying back and forth has only one end: a disillusioned and disgusted public ready to turn its back on public education.

Conflicts within the school community also divert energies that are needed to win friends for public schools. Gallup polls have consistently shown that the closer a person gets to the schools, the more positively he or she regards them. People with children in the schools think most highly of them, with even those who have some physical contact with the school, such as attending a forum or concert in them at some time during the year, holding a better impression than those who have never been in a school. The message is evident: Get people into the schools, reach out, don't wait for children to register—the prospective parent or grandparent is a target audience, too.

School people must also put some time into a public relations effort for the schools. With fewer people having direct contact with the schools, most get their information from newspapers and television—and news coverage of education is dreadful, focusing only on the problems, almost never dealing with the successes. Teachers, parents, school board members, administrators have the obligation to tell their communities what their schools are doing, to get across the success of our students when measured against students in almost any industrialized country in the world. How many Americans know, for example, that our 14-year-olds read better than the same age group in Sweden, the Netherlands, and Great Britain? That our kids are doing better in science than students in Britain, Holland, and Italy? Who is going to tell them if not those most intimately involved in our schools?

2. Government policies and regulations must be reconsidered. The question of tax support for private schools will not go away, even if the proposed legislation is defeated once or twice again. It is not enough to ask whether a government regulation is "good" or "right" in and of itself—we must start asking with respect to each policy: Will it strengthen or reduce support for public schools and increase demand for tax-supported private schools? Will busing bring about integration in this district—or drive middle-class parents, black and white alike, away and into the arms of the private schools? If precise regulations to aid handicapped youngsters are so costly (and so underfunded by the federal government) that they force school districts to take money away from regular programs—will this not spur some parents of nonhandicapped children to seek other schools, thus defeating the very purpose of the legislation? Government regulation is not an evil; government regulation that is poorly conceived and has the potential for making matters worse should be subject to a lot closer scrutiny. Neither minority children nor handicapped children will benefit from public schools forced to become dumping grounds for private school rejects.

3. Parents want choice? Why not give them a choice within the public schools? Why should every child have to attend just one school for which he or she has been "zoned" as a result of living at a specific address? Why not provide a choice of a "progressive" or a "traditional" school? A school in which foreign language education is stressed? A school offering a broad science education? Music? Art? All of these schools, of course, would have to provide a mandated basic skills curriculum—and all would be teaching democratic values—but why should they be the same? And if a parent is dissatisfied with his child's school, why shouldn't that parent have the right to transfer the child to another *public* school? Why do we force public school parents out of the public schools if they want something different? In most instances, after all,

it is a very specific public school a parent is unhappy with—not the concept of public schools as such. Public education needs to be more flexible.

4. For many parents who have taken their children out of public schools—and for many who want to—the key issue is safety and order. Parents don't want their children threatened with physical violence—and they don't want their children's learning impeded by the chronically disruptive few who perforce monopolize the teacher's time and attention. Jackson Toby, professor of sociology and director of the Institute for Criminological Research at Rutgers University, has made a number of useful suggestions to deal with the problem. Among them are (a) more parental involvement to bring informal pressure on students, including the routine presence of parents in junior and senior high schools, perhaps with adult education courses scheduled during the day; (b) the expulsion of chronically violent and/or disruptive students from regular schools and the expansion of alternative facilities to help and educate them; (c) the devising of lesser punishments before expulsion is used, such as "working 14 hours every weekend at the school—painting, scrubbing, polishing—for three months," and (d) the sharing among school systems of information about remedies that work. However it is done, change is needed so that in areas where discipline is a problem, the schools regain the upper hand.

5. Next to discipline, parents are worried most about standards. It is time for the public schools to confront this question head on. First on the must-do list is to establish and maintain a quality curriculum, one with tough courses and fewer chances for students to substitute easy ones. We must see to it that more students take geometry, trigonometry, calculus, chemistry, physics, foreign language—and that Shakespeare and Dickens are not replaced by courses in "modern media." Public schools must also see to it that students really spend time on their subjects. This means improving attendance—and it also means more homework. A modicum of pressure is also crucial. Not all learning is fun—some is sheer drudgery, but it lays the foundation for more learning. Pressure comes in the form of tests and grades. The failure to apply this kind of pressure represents a loss of nerve on the part of adults—and it does our students no good at all. We should be telling parents with some frequency how their children are doing in school—perhaps with report cards more often. Students who consistently fail the tests used to measure their progress ought not to be promoted. And perhaps we ought to organize more schools on a semi-annual promotion basis, so that failing students don't have to lose a full year when they're held back.

6. We have to begin to reestablish the prestige of teachers and schools. We ought to stop trying to defend ourselves by saying that "we don't really know what makes for effective learning," or "it's all a matter of opinion," or "it's all subjective." There's much that we still don't know, as is true in many fields. But there's also much that we know.

We ought to be selecting highly qualified teachers who themselves have gone through a toughened curriculum in schools of education. This means much more emphasis on traditional disciplines—liberal arts, sciences—combined with rigorous pedagogical training, including emphasis on inquiry techniques, research on teaching, and clinical and field-based classroom experiences. The difficulty of getting through a teacher education program should match the complexity of the teaching task.

Testing should be part of the initial certification process. Entrance tests must be validated to assure they accurately reflect both the content areas and professional knowledge necessary for effective teaching. It's true that a test won't tell you who'll make a good or great teacher and who's going to be a failure in front of the class, but a test will tell you who knows how to read and write the English language, which math teachers really know math and which don't, whether the French teacher is fluent in that language. Until the test is passed, there's no sense in proceeding further.

For those who do pass, there ought to be a strong internship period of one, two, or three years, an opportunity to learn, practice and sharpen classroom skills under the watchful eye of a veteran teacher. Interns should enter the profession at a negotiated base salary and have a limited teaching load. The additional time during the school day might include: work with experienced teachers who could demonstrate various teaching techniques and curricular approaches; observation throughout K–12 to develop an awareness of continuity within education; inservice training with the support of teachers, teacher educators, and the school system; acquaintance with the roles of support personnel, such as counselors and social workers; participation in curriculum development; pursuit of research projects, and familiarization with the purpose and functions of various divisions of the school structure. An essential aspect of the internship program must be frequent consultation with and feedback from participating teacher education faculty members and cooperating classroom teachers. This internship plan is fairly easy to implement at the secondary level. In the elementary grades, we will need to experiment with various team-teaching approaches. While the initial investment in internships will exceed that of the current entry system—really, a nonsystem—the payback will be a better public school education and citizens who are better equipped to function in our complex society. We don't expect doctors to deal with patients on their own, right out of medical school—why should we entrust the minds of our children to the sole capabilities of a green novice?

And, finally, we ought to continue the mini-revolution that teacher centers have brought about in the inservice training and retraining of teachers. Instead of facing imminent demise as a result of federal defunding, teacher centers ought to exist in every school system in the United States as places which combine the expertise of the university with the on-site, practical wisdom of classroom teachers to offer every teacher a chance to solve problems, get new ideas, explore a different approach in a nonthreatening, nonevaluative setting. Tens of thousands of teachers in New York City have used teacher centers, with highly trained teacher specialists, over the last few years to improve classroom management, learn how to deal with handicapped youngsters who are mainstreamed into their classrooms and become proficient in the technique of mastery learning, which is making a huge difference in the education of children in a number of districts and schools. These are by no means the only programs that the New York City Teacher Centers have offered, but they address real problems the system faces with real solutions, teacher-tested solutions. Teacher centers also foster collaboration among educators at all levels, as well as among educators and the public. Policy boards include teachers, administrators, school board members, colleges of education, parents, and business and public representatives. Training and staff development are discussed in the context of diverse needs and perspectives. Successful centers have broken down traditional barriers between schools and teacher colleges with the result that both find they have a great deal to offer and learn from each other. Participation by business and the public in the center's planning results in greater understanding and support from these groups for the schools and their personnel. Cutting off or narrowing these lines of communication can serve only to isolate schools further in a time of great need.

The teacher union plays a vital role in tightening standards and upgrading the profession. From the AFT's perspective, these goals will be met not by unions insisting on controlling education but through cooperation among unions and education's various stakeholders. All of us hold pieces of the puzzle, but none has all the answers. Working together, we can find solutions. For example, we know the basic ingredients of a good teacher education program. We also know incorporation of these elements in the curriculum could span much more than four years. Which elements, therefore, should take priority at the undergraduate, internship, or inservice staff development levels? To what level of sophistication do we require certain types of knowledge? As a teacher union, we want to share our experience and expertise with others in determining an effective teacher preparation program, and we acknowledge the similar value of other participants' input. The same holds true in accreditation, test development and selection, certification, and internships. While we're not likely to reach consensus on all issues, should we miss the opportunity to do so when we can? Education of teachers, as well as students, should be a shared responsibility requiring partnerships among various groups.

7. If the profession is to continue to attract and retain capable people, teachers' salaries and working conditions must be improved. Both the popular and professional literature on teaching are replete with reports of fewer students entering teacher education, increasing numbers of prospective teachers being drawn from the bottom third of graduating classes, escalating stress and "burnout" in teaching, and practicing teachers leaving or desiring to leave the profession. The reasons are fairly obvious.

Teaching normally draws from a large pool of qualified candidates, many of them women and minorities traditionally denied access to other professions. As these barriers come down, teaching cannot compete with careers like business, medicine, and law, which offer higher salaries, better working conditions, a greater sense of self-worth and more immediate recognition of accomplishment. Therefore, not only are many of our best teachers leaving the profession, but too few new ones are available to replace them. Critical teacher shortages already exist in math, science, computer programming, industrial arts, vocational education, foreign languages, and some areas of special education.

We know there is a connection between the decline in teachers' earning power and the decline in teaching's prestige. But the problem does not end with salaries.

In a recent study, AFT found working conditions a major stress-producing factor in schools. Some, such as poor security, discipline problems, decaying facilities, mismanagement, and lack of supplies, related to conditions within the schools. Others like isolation from adults/peers, lack of recognition, little respect from the community and general public, and few opportunities or rewards for intellectual rigor or creativity related to the teaching act itself. Interestingly, it was not teaching itself, but obstacles to it, which caused stress. Classroom interruptions, the lack of paper, supplies, textbooks and desks, and inoperative equipment all made even routine teaching tasks difficult. Cracked windows, falling plaster, peeling paint added to depressing school conditions.

Can we really expect people to work under these conditions? Just as important, can we expect learning to take place in this environment? Unless action is taken, it's not hard to imagine both teachers and students being driven out of the schools.

It's not that we don't know how to correct these problems. But for all the attention being given to standards and teacher competence, no one has assumed responsibility for actual conditions in the schools. School authorities, city governments, and community members should cooperate in assuring safety in and around schools. Conditions of schools and grounds should be regularly monitored, with steps taken immediately to correct inadequacies. No more than we would consider letting a doctor operate without surgical tools should we tolerate teachers being without the basic supplies, resources, and equipment necessary for teaching. Yet, these shortages are all too frequent. Why don't we have better accountability in resource planning and allocation? We know that the greater time a student spends on task, the greater the achievement. But who is working to minimize classroom interruptions by administrators and parents, excessive paperwork required of teachers, and other common distractions? We all can and should be doing these things and more. Principals need better training in leadership, management, and communications skills. Boards of education and teacher unions should cooperate in establishing educator support groups to prevent potential stress-causing situations from developing and to help troubled employees overcome problems. Principals, teachers, and other education staff should be afforded opportunities for collegial interactions to enhance professional skills, share ideas, minimize isolation, and improve communications. Yes, some of these answers cost additional money, but the well-being of both the profession and students is at stake. The cost of our present neglect of these conditions is far greater than any dollar amount attached to corrective action.

The problems are great and the crisis deep, but whether Americans realize it or not, our country has never been more in need of solid education. If we are to revitalize our economy, to compete successfully with Japan, West Germany, and other industrialized countries, our people have to have *more* skills, not fewer.

In the March 1981 issue of *Scientific American*, former Columbia professor Eli Ginzberg and George Vojta, executive vice president of Citicorp/Citibank, argued strongly that it was a mistake to focus *exclusively* on reindustrialization while disinvesting in the development of human skills: "We contend that the competence of management and the skills of the work force, particularly of those engaged in producer services [accounting, legal counsel, marketing, banking, architecture, engineering, management consulting, among others], determine the ability of enterprises to obtain and utilize effectively the other essential resources, such as physical capital, materials and technology." They noted that of the huge growth in the economy from 1948 to 1973, only 15.4 percent could be traced to "more capital," while about two-thirds of the new growth could be attributed to "the increase in the number and education of the work force and the greater pool of knowledge available to the workers. Simply put," they wrote, "it is the expansion of the knowledge, skills, imagination, ideas and insights of working people that creates the margins from which the physical capital is accumulated, leading through productive investment to the further accumulation of capital." People count—and they count more when they are educated.

If more people who are well educated are crucial to the expansion of our economy in this highly technological society, the same is true of our military needs. It is and will be fruitless to have a lot of very expensive, very sophisticated hardware around that very few know how to operate, maintain and repair. There are already warnings from the military that recruits are not able to read weapons manuals and other materials conveying information to military personnel. In a recent speech to an armed services conference, Dr Stephen Joel Trachtenberg, president of the University of Hartford, called education "the ultimate weapon," warning that cutting funds for education while increasing the defense budget "sets a short-term agenda at the expense of unleashing problems which are contrary to long-term defense needs and which will come to haunt us in the future." Trachtenberg said:

> It is imperative that we avoid the illusion that our national security can be preserved only by hardware. There are many lessons to be had from our involvement in Vietnam. One has to do with the continuing central role of the soldier. Buttons don't fight wars. Buttons don't make peace. People do. People matter. We see further evidence of this in third world and developing countries. The Shah of Iran, with literally billions of dollars in state of the art armaments, could not retain his Peacock Throne. And when he was gone, and his technological infrastructure departed, the Iranians could not maintain and properly utilize the gear that had cost them so dearly. People matter.

School people and other philosophers have long argued for support of education because education is a good in its own right, making for fuller and more productive lives and the kind of citizenry upon which freedom and democracy depend. That continues to be true. But just as education was relied upon to meet urgent national priorities after the Russians launched Sputnik and when President Kennedy committed the nation to landing a man on the moon within a decade, those who care about education must make the argument today that new priorities—revitalizing our economy, bolstering our defense—also require widespread support of education from pre-school through college. They will need allies in this fight—allies beyond the traditional supporters of public education, the civil rights community, organized labor, and others who have helped us fight many battles. The military is well aware of its educational needs—and the business community knows, too, that its future health depends upon a highly educated work force. School people should be making the effort to reach out to both; I think they will be pleasantly surprised.

Not only must we make the arguments and win new friends, but we had better be successful. For I truly believe that the survival and prosperity of our country depend on a well-supported public education system committed to excellence.

CHAPTER 21

Autonomy and Obligation
The Remote Control of Teaching

Lee S. Shulman

> *"...And above all in this matter of freedom. A German cannot think of freedom without rules. For us, all freedom is no freedom. We may dispute over the rules, but not that they must be there." "...It depends, you see, on how you define the contrary of freedom. For us, it is chaos. For you..."*
>
> *"Authority?"*
>
> *He nodded. "We sacrifice some of our freedom to have order—our leaders would claim social justice, equality, all the rest. While you sacrifice some of your order to have freedom. What you call natural justice, the individual rights of man."*
>
> JOHN FOWLES, in his novel DANIEL MARTIN, pp. 557–558.

THE NIGHTMARES

As the characters in John Fowles' powerful novel discuss images of contrasting political systems, they conclude that the ideals one seeks do not direct the shaping of a society's values and practices. Rather it is the darker image of one's worst fears and anxieties. We act not to achieve our ideals but to fend off our nightmares. Thus, to understand why people behave as they do, ask not what they value most, but what they fear most.

The participants in the struggles over teaching and public policy have their collective nightmares as well. For many of the policymakers, the vision is of teachers who do not teach, or teach only what they please to those who please them; who prefer the transient kicks of frills and fads to the tougher, less rewarding regimen of achieving tangible results in the basic skills; who close their schoolhouse doors and hide their incompetence behind union-sheltered resistance to accountability and merit increases; whose low expectations for the intellectual prowess of poor children leads them to neglect their pedagogical duties toward the very groups who need instruction most desperately; or whose limited knowledge of the sciences, mathematics, and language arts results in their misteaching the most able. The nightmares are remarkably parallel for liberals and conservatives among the policymakers. Each envisions an unwilling or inept teacher resisting the implementation of policies designed thoughtfully to help children, and through the young, to benefit the greater society.

The careful reading and helpful suggestions of Jack Schwille and Chris Wheeler are gratefully acknowledged. Since my ability to respond to their thoughtful recommendations was limited both by understanding and ideology, they are naturally to be absolved of any responsibility for the errors remaining herein.

Not surprisingly, teachers harbor their own nightmares. These portray a besieged and beleaguered group of dedicated professionals, inadequately appreciated or compensated, attempting to instruct responsibly and flexibly under impossible conditions. They are subject to endless mandates and directives emanating from faceless bureaucrats pursuing patently political agendas. These policies not only dictate frequently absurd practices, they typically conflict with the policies transmitted from other agencies, from the courts, or from other levels of government. Each new policy further erodes the teacher's control over the classroom for which she is responsible: pupils are yanked out of the room willy-nilly for special instruction, disrupting the continuity of their classroom experience while repeatedly upsetting the normal flow of classroom life for everyone else; a larger number of children, or bused children, or handicapped children, or inexperienced teacher aides must be accommodated in her classroom while she also, by the way, must take on an extra hour per day of reading, a new writing initiative, more rigorous mathematics and science, sex education, bicultural education and carefully maintain the detailed individual records needed to create the bureaucrat's required audit trail.

The educational scholars have their own version of the nightmare. In it they see both policymakers and practitioners pursuing their respective chores mindlessly, or at least without benefit of the carefully collected, sifted, analyzed, and interpreted bodies of knowledge that constitute the stuff of educational scholarship. This body of work includes both the most esoteric products of basic social science research and the concrete results of systematic program evaluations and reviews; the quantitative results of large-scale surveys or teaching experiments or the rich descriptive portraits of educational ethnographers. The scholar's nightmare is of an educational system at all levels uninformed by the wisdom of research, unguided by the lessons of scholarship. Much of this scholarship is directed at understanding not only the enterprises of teaching and of policy per se but also the circumstances arising when these domains of practice collide. The present volume has been designed to examine the war of these worlds and to explore ways of thinking about the dilemmas they pose.

These portraits are certainly overdrawn. Yet nightmares are caricatures of fears. They feed on the anxieties produced by daily frustrations over failed attempts to do one's job. The policymaker sees well-crafted programs fall with an impotent thud at the threshold of a classroom door. Teachers see politicians and ideologues interfering with their responsibility to judge and implement what is best for their students, like a septic malpractice lawyer leaning over the physician's shoulder during surgery. And scholars seek their work falling stillborn from the press, ignored equally by both parties or, even more likely, employed when convenient in support of positions already taken rather than being used to inform and guide emerging choices.

The plan of this volume has been to draw together the perspectives of the various parties to this enterprise. We have presented the results of research on the effectiveness of schools and of teachers, attempting to examine that research in the context of the inquiries which produced it. Here the question has been: What is the knowledge base which scholars claim ought to inform the decisions of both policymakers and practitioners? How adequate is the base for the guidance of policy?

Another set of papers discusses the character of teaching practice and of the profession. What do we know of the lives of teachers? How do they learn to teach, both from formal and informal sources? What effects have recent developments had on the performance and morale of teachers, as well as on the ability of the profession to attract and hold talented practitioners? What roles are played by the unions, state agencies, and other sources of influence on the minds, motives, and teaching performances of teachers?

Yet another set of contributions examines the policy process itself. What form have legislative policies on teaching taken? How have judicial decisions affected classroom practice? In what ways do the policy conflicts around teaching reflect far more fundamental controversies over values?

In confronting these questions we will return once more to the topic of conversation between the characters in *Daniel Martin*. If the responsible and effective teacher must be both free and obligated, how shall we define the proper mix of those typically incompatible virtues? Do we risk tyranny from above to achieve needed order and equity? Or do we foster liberty and autonomy while thereby risking anarchy and chaos?

The problems of teaching and policy defined in this volume are not ones that can be addressed lightly, much less solved readily. Nevertheless, both the problems formulated and the solutions suggested must be taken seriously by policymakers. The problems will not disappear; they will only fester. Their habitual neglect has long since ceased being benign. To evade them is no longer possible.

In this chapter we shall address several questions that bear upon the fundamental relationships among research, pedagogical practice, and educational policy. We shall begin by discussing a concrete case of policy which flows from bodies of research discussed in this volume—the school and teacher effectiveness literatures. We shall review in some detail the maxims for practice and policy emanating from this literature and the emerging experiences in implementing the policies. We will then examine the implicit model of school change and improvement which appears to underlie most discussions of teaching and policy. We shall attempt to understand the assumptions of the model and the reasons why it so rarely seems to succeed. We will then turn to the types of knowledge, both scientific and practical, which appear to provide the rationale for changes in educational policy. Finally, we will confront the central dilemmas of this volume. Can principles and practices be mandated through policy without thereby eroding the teacher's capacity to instruct flexibly and responsively? Can the rights of powerless groups to receiving an equal and excellent education be protected without placing clear limits on the discretion of individual teachers? Can we devise a system in which teachers are both responsible and free?

THE PLANS

The dilemma should be examined concretely. A good example emerges from the literature on more effective schools. Drawing from a number of sources—studies by Rutter, Brookover, Edmonds, and others—a characterization has emerged of the features of unusually effective schools for economically disadvantaged youth. The characterizations are remarkably consistent with one another, as well as with the current interpretations of much of the teaching effectiveness literature (see the chapters by Rutter and by Good in this volume).

Effective Schools

Early in the 1970's, in spite of the waves of despair regarding the value of schooling precipitated by the Coleman Report and its reanalyses, Jencks' *Inequality*, the apparent failure of Project Headstart, and other discouraging reports, the beginnings of a new research tradition emerged. Instead of asking whether schools or teachers made any difference, scholars modified the syntax of their inquiries. They asked instead what distinguished those teachers or schools that consistently produced high achievement in their pupils from those that consistently failed to do so. Moreover, they pursued their investigations through gathering data from within the walls of school buildings and individual classrooms. Instead of following resources to the schoolhouse door and then attempting to estimate their yield in schoolwide general achievement, they made direct observations of life in classrooms. They assumed that the important features of classrooms that made a difference for student achievement were not adequately represented by the levels of resources present in a school. Their assertion was that resources had to be transformed at the school and classroom level into teacher behavior and pupil responses to render a meaningful account of school effectiveness. The chapters in this volume by Rutter and by Good summarize this body of work.

Edmonds (1982) has formulated five principles of effective schooling on the basis of these studies.

> The correlates of effective schools are (1) the leadership of the principal characterized by substantial attention to the quality of instruction, (2) a pervasive and broadly understood instructional focus, (3) an orderly, safe climate conducive to teaching and learning, (4) teacher behaviors that convey the expectation that all students are to obtain at least minimum mastery and (5) the use of measures of pupil achievement as the basis for program evaluation (Edmonds, 1982).

Edmonds is one of a number of educators who have attempted to draw prescriptions for the improvement of practice from the empirical research on effective schooling. He is careful to point out that these characteristics of effective schools have not been derived from studies of intervention programs in which schools experiencing difficulties undergo planned change. Nevertheless, in many parts of the country, districts are implementing plans based on principles similar to Edmonds' or their equivalents in an effort to improve the quality of urban public education. When leading public school officials testify to the success of these school improvement programs, they ascribe the design of the interventions to the results of educational research. The mandated changes are thus justified by their ostensible association with scientific research. Further, they claim to be validated by changes in average achievement test scores earned by pupils in the system.

Effective schools programs are established in school systems in a number of ways. They typically employ total schools as their units of implementation, and the decision to become involved is usually an administrative one. Because of the key role assigned to the building principal, she must become actively involved early. The approach is highly rationalized, with the schoolwide use of record-keeping systems tied to objectives, frequent use of both locally and nationally developed achievement tests, and a broad-based commitment to academic performance and strong classroom discipline with backing from the principal's office. Efforts are directed at the achievement of tangible results—changes in the academic achievement of pupils.

It is not surprising that such programs rapidly become controversial. Opponents argue that the research base of such programs is inadequate because too small a sample of schools was studied or that programs involving planned change cannot be based on studies in which only static systems were examined without purposeful attempts to reform a system. They further point out how limited and limiting is the criterion employed in the school-effects enterprise—changes in scores on standardized achievement tests in basic skills. There is much more to school, they argue, than is reflected in students' rushed answers to multiple-choice tests. Finally, the opponents claim that such changes in practice mandated from above are rarely successful over the long haul. Teachers understandably and justifiably resist the remote control of teaching by distant bureaucrats.

There exist equally strong arguments in support of systematic mandates for teachers. Education is a public service and a public trust. It is not sufficient to engage in all the right processes of teacher involvement in policymaking and bottom-up planning if the desired academic results are not forthcoming. The bottom line that counts is results. The consequences of poor education not only harm the immediate recipients but ultimately deprive all members of the society through rendering some citizens less capable of caring for themselves, of contributing to the economic and social well-being of the nation, of exercising their political mandate wisely, and of increasing their general well-being. We all partake in the common good. Whatever diminishes the common good diminishes each of us.

An analogy can be drawn to the policies for general inoculation against communicable diseases. It is normally mandated that all members of a population receive such inoculations, not only for their own sakes but because their refusal or ignorance endangers others as well. Therefore, physicians are mandated to provide such inoculations and schools refuse to enroll youngsters who have not received the requisite immunizations. Do physicians feel that their professionalism is compromised by the mandate to vaccinate? Does not the obligation to take responsibility for the most general public good override concerns regarding the professional's need for autonomy?

The arguments that swirl about the effective schools implementations are representative of the controversy surrounding the tension between teaching and policy. Why is the juxtaposition of "teaching" and "policy" the statement of a problem? We are wont to think of teaching as a highly clinical, artful, individual act. Since instruction is interactive, with teachers' actions predicated on pupil responses or difficulties, it appears ludicrous in principle to issue directives regarding how teachers are to perform. William James compared teaching to a war in which the pupil was the enemy. Although we make heroes of the occasional combat commander whose "Damn the torpedoes; full speed ahead!" leads to victory, we more typically remember the charge of the Light Brigade or Gettysburg to acknowledge the importance of sensitively adapting tactics to the realities of a situation. Teaching is the very prototype of the idiographic, individual, clinical enterprise. Policy connotes the remote, nomothetic, and unresponsive. Teaching is intended to promote excellence and repair difficulties. Policy is intended to ensure fairness and prevent selective oppression.

Indeed, most federally mandated policies are initiated in the interests of some pupil population—the poor, the educationally disadvantaged, the handicapped, the gifted, women—whom advocates wish to protect from miseducation. In the case of effective-schools innovations, the interests of children of the poor are most frequently represented. These programs are intended to ensure that these children receive the full benefits of active teaching by committed professionals enthusiastically employing methods with a high probability of producing satisfactory academic achievement. There is a clear explanation for why these mandates so typically emanate from the federal level. The relatively powerless groups whose interests they reflect are generally unable to marshall sufficient influence at the local level to effect policy changes. It is only as they aggregate their numbers and, hence, power, that they can wield the needed political muscle. The insistence that teachers at the local level maintain the autonomy to determine policy sounds disturbingly like a return to the status quo that made the new programs necessary in the first place—a situation composed of equal portions of good intentions and poor results.

The case of effective schools is but an instance of the larger issue to which this chapter is addressed. Having described the nightmares motivating the interested parties and a specific instance of a program which arouses such anxieties, we shall now turn to a more general question. What is the conception of policy, teaching, and research which governs our current approaches to designing and implementing policies for the improvement of teaching and learning?

THE MYTHS

There exists a generally shared perception among many school administrators and laypersons regarding the improvement of public education. Its credibility is so unquestioned that few observers of contemporary schooling even think to challenge its assumptions. The following paragraph expresses its essential message.

> From a combination of recent experience and carefully conducted research, we have now come to understand the best ways to teach and the conditions for effective schooling. These understandings can be classified under such headings as "effective schools," "direct instruction," "time on task," "teacher expectations," "teaching effectiveness" and the like. Despite this knowledge, much elementary and secondary teaching is unsatisfactory. The solution is to establish and administer general educational policies designed to ensure that teachers practice those methods of teaching likely to achieve the desired results. To monitor compliance, employ a readily acceptable common metric to indicate the degree of success; standardized achievement tests are an obvious choice. Through a combination of policy and oversight, the schools can be improved.

Whenever a solution appears so simple and straightforward, the cynical among us can expect it to fail. It has achieved the status of a self-evident truth, yet it may only be a collectively held myth. Indeed, the common wisdom is that the simple solutions have thus far not borne the anticipated fruit. While most observers would consider schools better now than they were before Title I/ESEA, Headstart, Follow Through, and many of the other programs of the Great Society, the benefits are surely not unblemished. The revolution did not occur. The millenium has not arrived.

The astute reader will now raise an important question. How can the common wisdom so blithely contradict itself, by both claiming the simplicity of the solution and explaining the impossibility of the accomplishment? How can we both know that the key to educational improvement is straightforward and also know that it is doomed to the most modest of success?

One is reminded of the story of the Rabbi of Chelm, the legendary town of fools. When confronted by two men each claiming ownership of the same benighted chicken, the rabbi heard each party out in turn. When the first had finished stating his case, the rabbi nodded sagely and muttered: "You are right, absolutely right. The chicken is certainly yours." No sooner had the second congregant presented his claim when the rabbi acclaimed with equal sagacity: "No doubt about it, you are right. That chicken belongs to you." The rabbi's wife, who had been observing the litigation from a corner of the room, could contain herself no longer. "My dear husband, it is impossible that the chicken should belong to the first one and to the second as well." The rabbi turned to his perceptive spouse and responded firmly, "You are right, too, absolutely right." So it is with conventional wisdom. Its individual propositions may be absolutely right albeit mutually incompatible. As we have seen in this volume, this dilemma defines the essential character of policy questions. (For example, see Chapter 13.)

Impediments to the Simple Solution

Why does the simple become so complex? What are the possible reasons for encountering difficulties when attempting to implement policy-based solutions to general problems of teaching and learning? We shall entertain five possibilities. The list is certainly not exhaustive, but the explanations entertained will illustrate the complexities of breeding practice from policy.

1. Inconsistencies among Mandates.   A policy becomes a plan of action when translated into specific mandates. But the specific mandates may themselves be functionally incompatible. This can occur for two reasons. The policies themselves may be designed for conflicting purposes. Thus Green argues that the teacher cannot simultaneously pursue mandates to achieve both excellence and equity. Another reason for incompatibility is the inconsistency between the mandate and its intent. That is, the manner in which a policy is implemented may carry unintended consequences that dilute the very results the mandate was designed to achieve. For example, the mandate to pull Title I pupils out of regular classrooms is clearly intended to ensure the quality and intensity of the instruction they receive. The "pull-out" itself is in large measure a tactic designed to produce a readily examined audit trail. Serious questions are now being raised over the disruption in the flow of instruction, both to the target children and their colleagues, of the continuing pattern of exodus and return to classroom work.

Even in the absence of pull-out, the mandated procedures can have unintended deleterious outcomes. In a particular Title I program, funds were made available to hire teacher aides for assisting in the classrooms of high-need youngsters. Documentation was required that the aides were employed to help the Title I children. The aides indeed devoted all their energies to that specific subgroup of pupils, but unfortunately, the regular classroom teacher then devoted most of her energies to the other youngsters in the class. Thus, in the interest of responding to a particular procedural requirement of the policy, those pupils with the greatest need for skilled instruction received much of their assistance from the adult with the lowest level of preparation.

2. Limits on Resources, Time, or Energy.   Another possible impediment occurs even where the policies are compatible. In this case, compatible mandates require an aggregate of time, energy, or other resources that is simply unavailable to the teacher or school. It has been said that the curriculum can only change in one direction—it grows. We improve schooling by adding responsibilities to the school's list, never by removing them. In recent years the additions have included mainstreaming of handicapped youth, sex education, new math and science curricula, teacher aides, among many others, often with shortened school days and larger class sizes. The state and federally funded programs typically carry the shadow of record-keeping, an audit-inspired array of forms whose completion is intended to assure the proper delivery of the desired services. Each of the prescribed program changes or augmentations is well-conceived and well-intended. Nevertheless, they are like individually benign sources of radiation or pollution which only become dangerous when they accumulate at a common locus. The teacher-in-the-classroom is ground zero, and these individually justified mandates land simultaneously on shoulders already burdened with the weight of teaching many subjects to diverse youngsters.

Although this image of overwhelming multiple burdens is certainly accurate, it is also undeniable that many skilled practitioners find ways to cope. They transform the zero-sum game into a productive synergy. Instead of feeling they must trade off teaching time among too many subjects or too diverse a range of students, they use inventive approaches to subject matter integration (e.g., combining the teaching of reading skills with the study of science, literature, or social studies content) or nontraditional teaching techniques (employing peer tutoring or cooperative learning strategies that take advantage of classroom diversity for the benefit of all pupils) to exploit the opportunities presented by the complexity. But such resolutions are by no means commonplace. They require exceptional expertise—both in teaching skills and subject-matter knowledge; adequate time and support services to do the extensive extra planning and development necessary; a supportive context provided by both the work environment and the professional peer group which encourages such special efforts; and an educational system which affords professionals so skilled and committed the self-esteem and sense of efficacy needed to sustain them in the face of frequent frustration and failure. Absence of these conditions constitutes a further impediment to school improvement.

3. Limits of Teacher Expertise.   A third impediment may rest with the intellectual, emotional, or pedagogical demands made on teachers by some new programs. Many teachers may simply be incapable of implementing certain mandates. The demise of the "new math" in the sixties and early seventies may be attributed in large measure to the failures of both teachers and parents adequately to understand its rationale and principles. The current implementation of PL 94–142 may be hampered by the absence of sufficient training for ordinary classroom teachers to know how to teach handicapped youngsters. Or they may be paralyzed by attitudes toward handicapped pupils that neither training nor supervised experience has addressed adequately.

It must be remembered that our nation's teachers, though the most highly trained in the world, enter the teaching profession with far less preparation than is afforded almost any other profession (Kerr, this volume). Compared to the typical eleven years of preparation afforded the contemporary family practitioner (four years undergraduate, four years medical school, and three years supervised internship/residency), the typical teacher's four years including only a single semester of supervised internship seems limited indeed. When we consider that only about one-sixth of the typical four-year undergraduate program in teacher education is devoted to pedagogical subjects per se, with the rest appropriately assigned to liberal arts plus major and cognate education in the subjects to be taught, the expectations we hold for our teacher work force should not be too great. What is truly amazing is the frequency with which outstanding instruction is accomplished by teachers who have been provided so little training and supervised practice before being thrust into responsibilities of a mature professional.

4. Limitations of Working Conditions.   A teacher with adequate competence who is confronted with compatible mandates may remain unable to respond because of the working conditions of the schools. Teachers are a strange sort of professional. They lack the independence of prototypical professionals—physicians, lawyers, architects—because they function within complex, hierarchically organized bureaucracies. They are responsible to building principals (occasionally to department chairs), who report to superintendents, who are themselves answerable to local school boards. Barr and Dreeben (this volume) have pointed out how the teacher's choices are severely constrained by decisions made outside the individual classroom, e.g., the assignment of pupils to schools and of pupils-within-schools to classrooms, the selection of textbook series, the selection of criteria for assessing pupil growth, and the particular tests to measure those criteria (Schwille et al., this volume). The increased emphasis on controls from above, on the remote control of teaching via policies promulgated at vast distances from the squeak of the chalk and the grinding of the pencil sharpener, attempts to create a different environment from that traditionally associated with the world of professionals in general, and the life of classrooms in particular.

5. The Self-Defeating Mandate.   The mandating process itself may be self-defeating, may be carried out in a manner that increases the likelihood that it will not be implemented as intended. There are many examples of that kind. These involve situations where the manner in which a desired end is communicated carries with it the seeds of its own failure.

During the time when this chapter was being written, the Argentine armed forces had occupied the Falkland Islands. They had informed the British that they had reclaimed the islands after a century and a half of imperialism and they would not negotiate regarding sovereignty over those islands. Ironically, the British had been trying to figure out how to divest themselves of the Falklands for years, considering them as an unnecessary burden with few benefits lying some 8000 miles from British soil. Yet the manner in which the Argentine government chose to communicate its intent to the British guaranteed a violently negative response from them—despite the consonance between the action's purposes and long-term British intentions.

Murnane (1981) has observed that the important question to ask regarding how to respond to the evidence on school effectiveness is not merely what to mandate for school policies. He asks how such policies can be mandated in a manner likely to enlist the willing decision making of the teachers as collaborating allies rather than as unwilling subordinates grudgingly conceding to their lack of power.

Assumptions of the Model

All the above discussions have emerged from the assumption that we indeed know how to improve schools and that the problems lie in the translation and implementation. However, the putative knowledge may be far less complete or adequate than is claimed. Translation from research to practical action may be more problematic than is generally considered. Thus we must examine two features of the "research-to-practice" model—its assumptions regarding the current state of knowledge and its conception of the processes of transferring research knowledge to practice.

When policymakers ask after the "lessons of research," whether to seek guidance regarding a decision over alternative policies or to lend support to a choice already made, what do they typically believe they are seeking? What image of research do they have in mind?

Certainly one type of investigation—perhaps the commonly shared prototype—is the critical experiment, unambiguous in its design, unquestionable in its implications. The examples that leap most readily to mind come from medicine—clinical trials of the Salk and Sabin vaccines, experimental field studies of fluoridation for prevention of dental caries, investigations demonstrating the effectiveness of antiseptic procedures in preventing postoperative infection, or research demonstrating the effectiveness of birth-control pills in preventing pregnancy. Other examples come from agriculture, where careful experiments can be used to demonstrate unequivocally the superiority of particular types of hybrid seed, the quality of varieties of fertilizer, or the power of specific kinds of herbicide. In cases like these the desired ends are relatively unambiguous. No polio or smallpox is surely better than annual epidemics. Few tooth caries are preferred to many. Higher yields are more desirable than famines or shortages. Moreover, the manner of measuring these outcomes is generally straightforward. There are few debates over how to measure postoperative infection rates, incidence of polio or tooth decay, or crop yields.

When we consider unintended side effects, or moral dilemmas associated with mandating the means for achieving desired ends, problems reminiscent of educational inquiries begin to emerge. An example can be drawn from the controversy that once surrounded policies regarding the fluoridation of public water supplies. The experimental evidence is unassailable. The presence of fluoride in public water supplies reduces incidence of tooth decay in the population, especially among children. Direct applications by dentists also work, but are more expensive and less certain to reach all who can benefit. How could there be any controversy over a general fluoridation policy with data so compelling?

Attacks on the policy took two forms. From the scientific perspective, opponents argued that data on side effects, usually involving the mottling of healthy teeth, had been suppressed. Fluoride was a potentially toxic material which could cause widespread harm if even slight errors in quantities of dose occurred. Moreover, the truly long-term effects of use were not yet fully understood.

From a moral/political perspective, opponents claimed that, experimental data aside, no government had the right to impose a form of medical treatment on all citizens. If fluorides could be added to a public water supply without the consent of all the affected citizens, what would prevent another government from administering birth control drugs when it decided that the population was too large? If a population was deemed too restive, would some government prescribe tranquilizers for the public water supply? Where might it end?

Although fluoridation of water supplies is no longer controversial, this brief example should help us see that the acceptability of a policy rooted in research findings is not necessarily a function of the incontrovertibility of the data supporting the intervention. Policies must not only meet the tests of social science. They must also avoid undesired side effects and jibe with generally accepted political and moral standards. In the case of educational policies, it will not be sufficient merely to argue that well-conducted studies have demonstrated the efficacy of particular forms of instruction or school organization. We will have to examine what other policies may conflict with that in question, what bathwater of unintended outcomes may accompany the baby of this remedy, and what undesirable effects may develop because of the manner in which the innovation, desirable though it may be in principle, has been imposed unilaterally on members of a profession.

On the other hand, there may be good reasons why the fluoridation battles have essentially died. How long can one pursue debates over the proper forms of process when the desired positive results are achieved so unequivocally? Those who oppose the uses of educational policy to bring about changes in classroom teaching and learning must confront their responsibility to produce the educational results justifiably demanded by those who are disenfranchised by the status quo.

Discourse on Method

At this point in our argument, we will stop and take a closer look at the kinds of research that inform educational policy. Two aspects of research will be discussed. Having observed that the stereotype of medical or agricultural research does not ordinarily fit educational inquiries, we will review some of the other kinds of investigation that frequently help policymakers understand the educational enterprise they are attempting to influence. We will also briefly consider the ways in which research activity itself, far from occurring in isolation from policy disputes, is often informed by them. That is, not only does research influence policy; the conflicts of public policy also influence research.

The kinds of experiment that produce incontrovertible data rarely exist in the social science research on which educational policy rests. For example, disagreement over the "best" methods for teaching reading, arithmetic, or writing abound among both scholars and practitioners. Particular studies can clarify (or usefully obfuscate) specific issues, but rarely is the basis for a clear general policy laid by a program of research, much less a single investigation. However, bodies of educational research will frequently cumulate over time and interact with more general ideological shifts regarding the proper goals and methods of education to form prevailing views that significantly influence educational policy and practice. Neither the research nor the ideology can be viewed as the ultimate cause of the changes. They blend together to form the grounds for change. This is reminiscent of Lindblom and Cohen's (1979) description of how social science knowledge and ordinary knowledge interact to constitute usable knowledge for policymakers.

Given that the results of research interact with ordinary knowledge and broad moral/political commitments to yield policy initiatives, it is not surprising that many types of scholarship can inform policy. These not only include the relatively rare experimental contrasts, both in the laboratory and in the field. They also include the large-scale statistical studies in which natural variations are examined rather than those induced under the experimenter's control. Most of the research reviewed by Rutter (this volume) is of this type, since schools discovered to be more or less effective per se were typically contrasted. This follows the pattern of such well-known policy-relevant studies as the Surgeon General's reports on the links between smoking and cancer or the long-term Framingham studies of the correlates of heart disease.

Another increasingly influential type of research is the case study, persuasively drawn portraits of teachers, pupils, schools, or programs. They lack the hard statistical data of the more traditional policy study, but richness of portrayal or drama of human detail often sway the beliefs of decision makers far more effectively than do tables of means and frequencies. One major virtue of a case study is its ability to evoke images of the possible. One description of a successful Headstart program in Watts can persuade a policymaker to continue funding as readily as a statistical table summarizing objective data from one thousand programs. It is often the goal of policy to pursue the possible, not only to support the probable or frequent. The well-crafted case instantiates the possible, not only documenting that it can be done but also laying out at least one detailed example of how it was organized, developed, and pursued. For the practitioner concerned with process, the operational detail of case studies can be more helpful than the more confidently generalizable virtue of a quantitative analysis of many cases.

Other types of scholarship that frequently influence policy have no necessarily direct connection with the results of empirical social science research. One of these consists of conceptual or theoretical inventions, clarifications, or criticisms. Perhaps the best example of this generation was Robert Merton's conception of the self-fulfilling prophecy. This extended metaphor helped both social scientists and policymakers understand how labels and stereotypes applied to entire groups could lead to actions that would guarantee the negative outcomes predicted for them. Thus, if certain minority groups were labelled as stupid and treated accordingly, that very treatment would ensure fulfillment of the prophecy, although it would typically be interpreted as demonstration of the validity of the prediction. Merton's work stimulated the development of research on teacher expectations in classrooms, a body of work that continues to flourish today (Good, this volume). Moreover, it forced educators to confront the consequences of their expectations and to become much more sensitive to the often deleterious effects of those expectancies.

Another significant conceptual invention was John Carroll's (1963) model of school learning. In this theoretical model, originally developed to explain second-language learning, Carroll posited that aptitude could best be understood as a function of the amount of time an individual required to achieve mastery of a given instructional task. He then elaborated on this proposition, showing how units of time could be used to define student motivation and aptitude, as well as the opportunity provided students to learn.

The Carroll model became the basis for a number of significant developments in educational research and practice. Benjamin Bloom based mastery learning in large measure on the model. The studies in which "engaged time" and "time-on-task" became bywords were motivated by the Carroll model. A whole host of technologies and policies, additional conceptual inventions, as well as subsequently fruitful applied research studies, have emerged from the Carroll model of school learning.

It is not only empirical propositions ("facts" about how pupils learn or the most productive ways to teach) and conceptual innovations that result from educational research. Another important product of educational research and development is instructional technology in the form of a system, or protocol. Such systems are exemplified by Mastery Learning (Bloom, 1976) as well as by more general procedural protocols such as "active teaching" (see Good, this volume). In essence, these forms of technology combine the results of studies of school learning, important conceptual inventions, the intuitions of master developers (Rosenshine, 1981), and ordinary knowledge (Lindblom and Cohen, 1979) to produce systematic approaches to classroom instruction. At times these are formalized into computer-controlled objectives-based materials and methods. At other times they are directed by detailed teachers' guides or manuals. When field tested, they are evaluated as total packages and teachers are expected to implement them precisely as designed. At times, the designers of such programs have striven to make them "teacher-proof," immune to the modifications teachers might make in their workings. Of late, developers have more often come to understand that teachers must be free to use their judgment to adapt such programs to prevailing classroom conditions if they are to succeed.

As we review the types of research that exist to inform the policymakers, we should be reminded that the research enterprise does not roll along in serene isolation, unaffected by the sturm und drang of private passions and public policy. Educational researchers have always been quite sensitive to the prevailing ideological and political issues of their day. This is especially the case because the school and classroom have long been conceived as representing in microcosm the ideals of the democratic society into which the young are inducted. It is no surprise therefore when the trends and emphases of the research enterprise follow the ebb and flow of ideas in the market-places of public opinion. This responsiveness of research has both positive and nega-tive consequences. It certainly helps ensure that educational research remains relevant to current concerns. On the other hand, such responsiveness can damage the continuity of the research enterprise, as the virtues of slow, cumulative growth of knowledge are sacrificed to the quest for political and social relevance.

However the research was conducted and whatever the social issues that moti-vated the inquiries, questions of translation and dissemination from research to prac-tice remain. It will be recalled that the myth has two parts. The first is the existence of clear, objective bodies of research which can be readily translated into policy. We have seen that much knowledge exists, but it is certainly not packaged in the form of readi-ly applicable sets of propositions. The second is a straightforward process of trans-lation/dissemination, modelled after the common image of dissemination in medicine or agriculture.

The lack of correspondence between dissemination in agriculture and in education has been recognized by many. In a recent paper, Murnane (1981) observed how farmers were convinced to replace their time-honored rules of thumb with a pattern of resource allocation consistent with research findings and how these changes had brought about significant increases in productivity. He then asked why education was so different. Murnane argued that in agriculture the key inputs—seed, water, fertilizer—are inanimate and hence unaffected by the farmer's state of mind or motivation. In contrast, an instructional method simply cannot be conceived in isolation from the teacher who employs it, the learning climate of the classroom and school in which it is deployed, and other factors that extend beyond the disseminated product. In educa-tion, it is rarely products we disseminate; it is principles and practices. These depend critically for their efficacy on the minds and motives of the teachers and students who jointly produce the events of classroom life.

It may seem obvious to the school reformer that any intervention is desirable that raises the standardized test scores of children. How could any teacher resist such a procedure? But what if those aspects of classroom life that enliven and enrich it are the day-to-day relationships among students and teacher, the excitement of learning new ideas and their applications, and the exchanges of insights between youngsters learning new things together? And what if the methods prescribed for raising test scores reduce the opportunities for teachers and pupils to pursue such activities? While the sup-pression of such learning certainly is not the objective of contemporary "back-to-basics" school reform (and we are raising the possibility only hypothetically), if it were found to be a side effect, would we not expect teachers to resist the reform efforts?

When public health officials in India attempted to employ agricultural dissemination models to bring birth-control principles and practices to the rural poor, they encountered frustrating failures. They found it difficult to understand, because it seemed so obvious that large families were economically and medically harmful. However, it was much more clear to farmers that it was good to produce more than it was to parents that it was preferable to reproduce less. The birth-control reformers had failed to appreciate the range of outcomes associated with large families in the Indian tradition, which brought satisfactions to parents far offsetting the disadvantages stressed by the public health officials and national planners.

At this point in our discussion we have examined the nightmares that concern teachers, policymakers, and researchers as they contemplate the problems of policy for the improvement of schools. We then described a concrete example of a current plan for school improvement and the arguments advanced both in its support and against its use. We then analyzed the underlying model of research-based change implicitly used by many policymakers. In discussing this model as myth, we looked in some detail at its assumptions and at the varieties of scholarship that are found useful to inform policy deliberations. We then briefly reviewed the concepts of dissemination implied in most approaches to educational change. In the concluding section we will confront the conceptions of teaching, teacher education, and the organization of the educational enterprise needed to forge the desired connections between policy and teaching.

THE DREAM

Teaching is impossible. If we simply add together all that is expected of a typical teacher and take note of the circumstances under which those activities are to be carried out, the sum makes greater demands than any individual can possibly fulfill. Yet, teachers teach. Moreover, despite oft-cited failures to achieve results with many types of pupils, teachers frequently elicit praise and recognition from all about them. We therefore confront two questions. What makes teaching impossible in principle? How is the impossible rendered possible in practice?

Our thesis is that precisely those characteristics that render teaching impossible also present it with the potential to transcend the apparent limitations of the job and make it professionally creative and autonomous. That is, the autonomy intrinsic to teaching is achieved as a function of its multiple competing and conflicting obligations, not in spite of them. This autonomy becomes both resolution and problem, however, if the freedom to teach is also the freedom to withhold teaching from the educationally disadvantaged and others who lack the power to exert influence at the local level. Thus our question remains, How can the impossible task of teaching be both responsible and free?

What makes teaching impossible? Within the classroom, the teacher is constantly torn among competing and incompatible pedagogical demands. Imagine a situation in which a fourth-grade teacher instructs a reading group of seven children while the remaining twenty-five pupils in the class are working individually on "seatwork" in arithmetic. Pupils are taking turns reading aloud from their basal readers. Dolores makes a reading error, and it is not immediately clear to the teacher whether the error stems primarily from ignorance of a basic phonic rule, from failure to apply a phonic rule that Dolores already knows, or from a fundamental misunderstanding of the meaning of the story being read. Each of these diagnoses would entail a somewhat different tactic of feedback and correction. However, adequately pursuing this simple error to its proper resolution would demand that time be expended immediately with Dolores while the rest of the group sits and listens. Most of the others are unlikely to have the particular reading difficulty that Dolores has just displayed. Moreover, even were Dolores her only pupil, the teacher must choose between simple correction of the child's error, careful remediation of the underlying misconception likely to have caused the error, or ignoring the error entirely if paragraph meaning has not been disturbed seriously.

We thus already find the teacher trading off among competing educational demands. Some of these occur because instruction in even a single subject area—e.g., reading—entails a coordination among several frequently inconsistent purposes. Others occur because the pupil is only one of a classroom group of individuals, all of whom have a call upon the attention and care of the same teacher simultaneously. Adequately to respond to any one child's needs can frequently require that responsiveness to the just demands of other pupils be, at least temporarily, suspended.

We can conceive of the classroom as an economic system in which a scarce resource—the teacher's attention and the pupils' opportunities to perform—must be distributed on some equitable basis (e.g., Brown and Saks, 1981). The potential for each individual's personal development must be maximized, yet not at the expense of fellow members of the class, at least not over the long haul. Because some groups come to the classroom with more power than others, it cannot be claimed that perfect competition exists. For this reason, educational policies are established that attempt to equalize opportunities thus allowing the classroom marketplace to function fairly. These externally mandated equalizers are not always viewed as benign and facilitative by the teachers even though their necessity may be understood.

Another analogy can be drawn to the medical concept of "triage," whether on the battlefield or in the emergency room. Proper attention must be distributed among a group of patients in need of medical care. All cannot receive full treatment all of the time. Care must somehow be allocated to reduce involvement with those who can profit least from it while focusing on those who, for the present time, will benefit most from the therapy. Yet every patient, in principle, deserves the chance to survive.

As if the intraindividual competition among alternative educational purposes and the interindividual competition for instructional opportunities did not pose sufficient dilemmas for teachers, we must keep in mind a parallel concept of curricular competition as well. That is, as our teacher is pondering the proper way to respond to Dolores' reading error, she must also be mindful of the other curricular obligations she must meet. She must teach not only reading but all the other mandated subjects as well. Even if an approach to reading instruction can be devised that will adequately accomplish both the individual and collective needs of the full class of pupils, it must not encroach on the time allocated to the other subjects of the curriculum. If reading is taught well at the cost of teaching science not at all, or if adequate coverage of the basic computational skills is achieved through the reduction of time available for instruction in writing, our teacher is once again caught in an "impossible" bind. The notion of a good general education implies breadth of coverage in the several curriculum areas, not only depth in a few. A semblance of equity must be achieved not only among pupils and goals but also among topics and subjects.

Finally, the classroom teacher performs her functions in the larger context of a total school and school system. That aspect of the system reflected in the sequence of grade levels demands that certain topics within subjects be covered during certain years so that teachers of subsequent grades can properly fulfill their obligations. Those functions of the school involving management and discipline oblige each individual teacher to behave consistently with the more general patterns of school rules and standards. Research on the characteristics of unusually effective schools (Rutter, this volume) typically calls attention to the ways in which all the teachers in a building come to share similar goals, expectations, standards, and even teaching procedures.

The impossibility of teaching in the best of times results from the confluence of multiple competing role demands on the teacher. She must be individual tutor, distributor of scarce resources among many pupils, curriculum completer, and school team member. She is also a publicly employed representative of a society obligated to be mindful of its own unequal distribution of power and opportunity. Therefore, from outside the school itself descend policy mandates that further exacerbate the routinely devilish complexity of pedagogical life. Such policies as school integration or mainstreaming increase the variability among pupils and thereby make the allocation of teaching resources even more problematic. Minimum competence standards are established to ensure that all children receive a decent education, or new school topics are added to make the program more relevant to the technological or social concerns of the day. As this occurs, the teacher's responsibility for covering the mandated curriculum becomes an even heavier burden. Schoolwide disciplinary procedures or homework schedules are adopted to aid in the creation of a consistent academic learning climate, but the classroom management flexibility of the individual teacher is thereby reduced. Underlying the cross fire of policies, mandates, expectations, standards, and interactive demands are fundamental tensions between values as priorities for public education (see Green; Fenstermacher and Amarel; Greenstone and Peterson; all in this volume).

How can we think about the ways in which individuals cope with complex and contradictory expectations? From the perspectives of individual teachers, how can these multiple demands be tolerated? What makes teaching possible? Sociologists refer to the condition accompanying such multiple competing expectations as "role complexity." Although we have focused on teachers in this analysis, similar examples of such role complexity can be found in many occupational and personal situations. Moreover, it can be argued that role complexity, far from being a debilitating source of decisional paralysis, constitutes instead the seedbed of individual autonomy. Rose Coser expresses this position eloquently:

> The multiplicity of expectations faced by the modern individual, incompatible or contradictory as they are, makes role articulation possible in a more self-conscious manner than if there were no such multiplicity. Rather than automatically engaging in behavior that is expected, the modern individual has choices and makes choices consciously and rationally. By this it is not meant that everybody always makes conscious and rational choices, but that there is a greater possibility for doing so than there would be in the absence of such multiple expectations (Coser, 1975, p. 239).

How does this conception of teacher autonomy fit with broader notions of policy formation and implementation? Theorists who write about the character of large organizations such as business firms or governments have grown fond in recent years of referring to them as "loosely coupled systems" (e.g., Weick, 1976). Loose coupling describes the relationships between levels of an organization through which policy directives ostensibly flow. Rational models of such organizations predict that mandates should move vertically from level to adjoining level. With proper communication, training, and oversight, a directive emanating from the highest administrative level of the bureaucracy ought to be implemented as intended "where the rubber meets the road." But both general experience and disciplined empiricism have taught that such rational models of bureaucratic decision making and action function only in theory. In practice, policy is transformed as it moves through the system, receiving its final stamp at the hands of the "street-level bureaucrat" with ultimate responsibility for taking the actions mandated by the directive.

Therein lies the problem. When powerless groups must depend on the efforts of federal governmental policy to protect their interests, talk of professional autonomy and street-level bureaucracy brings precious little solace. The street-level bureaucrat can use that autonomy to preserve the inequities of the status quo, frustrating the intents of legislation or court orders. Loose coupling therefore buffers uncaring practitioners from the moral or legal consequences of their actions.

The language of loose coupling conjures up images of a somewhat random process of recombination and distortion, much like the old party game of Telephone, where a message is transmitted seriatim through a dozen celebrants until its thoroughly reconstituted form emerges for begiggled appreciation. Another image is that of a communication line with poor connections, so that pieces of messages are lost or muddled at random. In most of these views, the loosely coupled system is problematic, a defect in the system as it ideally should work. Our earlier analysis of the impossibility of teaching, however, and the autonomy fostered by the multiplicity and complexity of the role demands of teaching, demands a quite different interpretation of loose coupling. The loosely coupled system is adaptive, not defective. It is a response to the requirement for a system that can set policy, yet mandate autonomy. Loose coupling is not a problem for policymakers to overcome. Properly understood, it is the solution to the otherwise irresolvable conflict between policy and professional practice. Yet its critics are also correct. The freedom it creates is a two-edged sword. It can be used in the interests of the greater society and its goals. Or it can merely serve to shield the practitioner's expedient exercise of providing privilege to the powerful.

In a loosely coupled bureaucracy the local-level practitioner can act autonomously without facing inevitable sanctions for insubordination. The autonomous practitioner, confronted with a welter of individually well-grounded and justified directives can behave in response to some at one time, to others in other circumstances. While the goals of any particular policy will never be pursued unilaterally at all times, the goals of policy writ large can be addressed. A set of goals will have been set out that represent significant ideals in a pluralistic democratic society. Like any set of ideals—even the Ten Commandments—they will frequently be incompatible in practice. (If my father, whom I am to honor, asks me to violate the Sabbath...) The mandated regulations and auditing requirements that accompany each policy are intended to ensure that it is taken seriously. In a tightly structured "rational" system, in which no variability of response could be tolerated, the impossibility of coping with contradictory policies would lead to paralysis or an endless series of policy changes. The only solution would be to suspend the quest for representative pluralism and to replace it with an attempt to design monolithic values and their attendant policies. In a loosely coupled system, these contradictory role demands become the seedbed of individual autonomy. Without the autonomous actor, policymaking in a democratic society becomes impossible. Without multiple competing policy demands, autonomy at the street level would be far too dangerous. The system does not result in mere anarchy because the total set of policies represents a particular subset of the universe of possible policies. The autonomy of the teacher is thus constrained and rendered responsible by the particular configuration of policies operating during a given period. Loose coupling permits the ostensibly incompatible elements of policy and autonomy to blend smoothly into the wisdom of practice.

This view of the virtues of loose coupling and teacher autonomy is certainly optimistic, perhaps even Pollyannaish. Little evidence can be marshalled to support the claim that the system in fact is working in this manner currently. Our argument is that the system ought to operate this way, given a proper combination of well-prepared professional educators and well-crafted, intelligently administered policies.

What forms should policymaking and implementation take if we come to view loose coupling as a matter of design rather than chance? How do we construe policy when judiciously managed variation of local response is understood as the necessary rule rather than as an anomaly? Coordinately, we must learn to think of the educational enterprise and of educators themselves in new ways. If professionals are to exploit the opportunities offered by autonomy in the interests of youngsters, how must they be educated, selected, supported, and supervised? What is needed on the parts of educators if they are to render intelligent and proper judgments regarding choices among competing policies, trade-offs between alternative goals or decisions regarding fruitful methods? Writers of many chapters in this volume have addressed themselves to those dual questions: how properly to reformulate the nature of educational policy and how to ensure that the talented and principled individuals needed in our teaching force are attracted, held, and nurtured in their roles.

Educational policies must be designed as a shell within which the kernel of professional judgment and decision making can function comfortably. The policymaker can no longer think of any given mandate as a directive which bears continuing correspondence to teacher actions at all times. Instead, policies represent moral and political imperatives designed with the knowledge that they must coexist and compete with other policies whose roots lie in yet other imperatives. Federal and state policies profess a prevailing view, orienting individuals and institutions toward collectively valued goals without necessarily mandating specific sets of procedures to which teachers must be accountable. The role of the teacher in such a situation is similar to that of a judge in a court of law. Laws and regulations are written to direct and control human action consistent with conceptions of individual and collective rights and obligations. But these rights and obligations often, even typically, come into conflict with one another. The rights of the accused conflict with those protecting person and property. The legitimate interests of landlords conflict with the just rights of renters. We do not expect that laws, regulations, or clear precedents cover each and every decision a judge must render. Indeed, the justification for courts and judges lies in the clear understanding that it is in the nature of any system of law that such controversies are inevitable.

In this sense, policies are very much like laws and teachers like judges. Educational systems are organized to permit the design of policies and their interaction in the court of the classroom. Teachers must understand the grounds for the competing demands on their time, energy, and commitment. They must be free to make choices that will cumulate justly in the interests of their students, the society, and humanity. Moreover, they need the opportunities to influence policy as well as respond, to initiate as well as broker.

The image of the teacher we have just drawn certainly does not correspond to the way teaching is. Papers in this volume by Lightfoot, Freedman et al., and Weinshank et al. have painted poignant portraits of the lives of teachers and their attempts to influence the system in which they work. Sykes, Kerr and Nemser have examined the problems of recruiting teachers, preparing them adequately before and after initial matriculation, and holding them for the duration of a professional career. These papers should be read together, for the conditions of teaching set severe limits on the potential for reform. The descriptions of teaching have helped us to appreciate the strains of the working teacher, the frustrations of the profession that foster burnout and the even more insidious charring that slowly eats away at a teacher in the performance of her duties. Without an improvement of those conditions, or a massive shift in the expectations that make them commonplace, talk of improvements in the teacher education process or of dramatic changes in the quality of those who opt for teaching seems pointless.

There is an agricultural analogy that may be helpful in thinking about the need for the educational system continuously to reinvest in the growth and instructional vitality of teachers. The learning teacher is as much a proper object of the system's concern as is the learning pupil. Much like the farmer's need to work with the soil so that it produces its crops yet does not lose its capacity to produce, the school must exploit the teacher's many skills yet nourish the continued fertility of the teacher as a medium for education. The society that mindlessly burns out its teachers will no more profit from their continued effectiveness than will the agricultural community that selfishly rapes its precious topsoil.

The solution requires a combination of improved human resources for the teaching profession and considerable improvement in the conditions of teaching. Sykes (this volume) and Kerr (this volume) have explored how improving the quality of personnel can be addressed. If the teacher's role is, in principle, that of a broker under siege, then the kind of person who becomes a teacher must be examined in relation to the kind of person a teacher becomes. It certainly cannot be the docile rule follower putatively sought by the regulatory policymaker. It is only the intelligent, moral, well-educated, and continually developing autonomous decision maker who can broker effectively among those legitimate, albeit competing demands. To attract and hold such people, we will have to make teaching a more satisfying, stimulating, and rewarding career, a profession rather than a form of technically sophisticated labor.

Kerchner and Mitchell (this volume) provide a particularly illuminating analysis of four contrasting ways to formulate a conception of teaching: as profession, as art, as craft, and as labor. The four conceptions emerge from consideration of two aspects of work—its degree of rationalization, i.e., how precisely the activities of the practitioner are defined a priori and the mode of oversight, i.e., how meticulously the work is supervised and monitored. The only justification for minimal job specification and little direct oversight is when the nature of the job, the very structure of the setting and the character of its problems, requires the exercise of highly flexible decision making. Even here, the particular areas over which autonomy is to be exercised must be carefully defined. This is consistent with our notion of loose coupling by design, not exclusively by chance. Should the teacher be the final arbiter of means (methods of teaching), but not of ends (objectives of instruction)? Of proximal goals (today we shall concentrate on initial consonants) but not distal purposes (motivation to read will take precedence over technical skill)? Of immediate tactical means (calling on students in order rather than randomly) but not long-term procedural protocols (we shall employ mastery learning as a system for all math teaching)? Of strategy (discovery learning) but not content (whether or not to teach a geometry unit in fourth-grade mathematics)?

The issue of degree of autonomy will not be answerable easily. We must somehow find a way to make teaching and systems of education simultaneously both responsible and free. Schwille and his co-workers (this volume) distinguish between authority over content and control of strategy. It can be inferred from their analysis that it is important for the control of content to lie beyond the individual teacher, thus ensuring the continuity and consistency needed to sustain an educational system. But teachers must maintain control over instructional strategies to be used in the teaching of that content. Through a combination of expert strategies for the teaching of consensual content, instruction will become both responsible and free.

A question which must be raised is whether this combination is consistent with the admonitions of Rutter and other school-effects scholars. Can the teacher follow the dictates of the effectiveness literature yet retain control over strategies of instruction? Or would Edmonds, Brookover, Rutter, and others mandate in the area of strategies as well? For example, mastery learning, a policy certainly within the realm of mandatable innovations, specifically limits itself to the definition of strategy, not content. It purports to be content neutral. Yet we must be prepared to raise serious questions about the usefulness of the convenient distinction between content and strategy. In many subject areas the two aspects of curriculum appear to interpenetrate inseparably.

Fenstermacher and Amarel argue strongly that the teacher must, above all, be responsible for setting the goals of instruction as she brokers between the powerful interests of the State and of the child. They argue that she must attempt to set these goals from the perspective of the interests of humanity, a perspective which has no other representative in the classroom except the teacher. Their view may appear highly idealistic at first blush. But their sense is that teachers must be imbued with a set of values that transcends those of particular policies or particular children. They cannot be merely value-free brokers, trading off among competing goods without any deep commitments of their own. Indeed, they must have commitments to a vision of educational excellence in fair and just societies, a vision that motivates their choices and lends wisdom to their exercise of professional autonomy.

Operationally, we will have to ask what is the size of the irreducible kernel of professional judgment without which teachers will not be able to respond adequately to the unpredictable complexities of life in classrooms? And what is the irreducible contour of the shell of policy if the State's obligation to ensure comprehensive and equitable education for all youngsters is to be fulfilled? These are questions that cannot be well answered abstractly and will probably have to be determined in particular contexts. In large measure, teachers will be collectively responsible for negotiating the role definition they acquire as they deliberate with school boards, administrators, and governmental policymakers regarding their future responsibilities and conditions of employment.

Finally, more intelligent use must be made of the research reported in chapters by Rutter, Good, and Barr and Dreeben (all in this volume), as well as others concerned with synthesizing the pedagogical and organizational techniques that lead to more effective teaching and learning of basic skills. We must go even further with such research. We have come to understand enough about teaching and learning to press on with the invention and deployment of systems of educational technology. These include approaches employing the hardware of computers to instruct as well as manage records. More important, this conception of technology calls for the formal deployment of systems of procedure that resemble the complex therapeutic protocols used in medicine to manage the treatment of many diseases. Examples of such protocols include Good and Grouws' approaches to mathematics teaching (Good, this volume) and Mastery Learning (Bloom, 1976). Rather than such forms of technology threatening to deprofessionalize teaching, properly deployed they become the prerequisites for professionalization. In the hands of gifted teachers empowered to use these methods rather than obligated to run alongside them, they help the teacher become a professional with powerful tools and a growing scientific base.

But the teacher must remain the key. The literature on effective schools is meaningless, debates over educational policy are moot, if the primary agents of instruction are incapable of performing their functions well. No microcomputer will replace them, no televison system will clone and distribute them, no scripted lessons will direct and control them, no voucher system will bypass them. It seems unlikely that increasing the financial rewards of teaching alone will suffice, though it is certainly necessary. The character of the work itself will have to change in order to attract and hold the more highly trained, talented, and committed teacher required for the 1980s and beyond.

REFERENCES

Block, J. H. (ed.). *Schools, society, and mastery learning*. New York: Holt, Rinehart and Winston, 1974.

Bloom, B. S. *Human characteristics and school learning*. New York: McGraw-Hill, 1976.

Brown, B. and Saks, D. The microeconomics of schooling. In D. Berliner (ed.), *Review of research in education*, 1981.

Carroll, J. A model of school learning. *Teachers College Record*, 1963, *64*, 723–733.

Coser, R., The complexity of roles as the seedbed of individual autonomy. In L. Coser (ed.), *The idea of social structure*. New York: Harcourt, Brace, Jovanovich, 1975, 237–264.

Edmonds, R. Working paper. Center for School Improvement, Michigan State University, 1982.

Lindblom, C. E. and Cohen, D. K. *Usable knowledge*. New Haven: Yale University Press, 1979.

Murnane, R. J. Interpreting the evidence of school effectiveness. *Teachers College Record*, Fall 1981, *83* (1), 19–35.

Rosenshine, B. Master teacher or master developer. Colloquium address, Institute for Research on Teaching, 1981.

Weick, J. Educational organizations as loosely coupled systems. *Administrative Science Quarterly*, March 1976, *21*, pp. 1–19.

Index